Third Edition

WORLD PROSPECTS

A CONTEMPORARY STUDY

Third Edition

WORLD PROSPECTS

A CONTEMPORARY STUDY

John Molyneux

Marilyn MacKenzie

PRENTICE HALL CANADA INC.

Canadian Cataloguing in Publication Data

Molyneux, John, date-
World prospects: a contemporary study
3rd ed.
Includes index.

ISBN 0-13-706633-3

1. Social history - 20th century. 2. Economic history - 20th century.
3. World politics - 20th century. 4. Industrialization.

I. MacKenzie, Marilyn. II. Title.

HN16.M65 1994   909.82   C93-093481-4

Prentice-Hall, Inc., Englewood Cliffs, New Jersey
Prentice-Hall International Inc., London
Prentice-Hall of Australia, Pty., Ltd., Sydney
Prentice-Hall of India Pvt., Ltd., New Delhi
Prentice-Hall of Japan, Inc., Tokyo
Prentice-Hall of Southeast Asia (PTE) Ltd., Singapore
Editora Prentice-Hall do Brasil Ltda., Rio de Janeiro
Prentice-Hall Hispanoamericana, S.A., Mexico

ISBN 0-13-706633-3

Managing Editors: Elynor Kagan and Carol Stokes
Project Editor: Rena Sutton
Production Editors: Diane Lapeña and Rena Sutton
Production Coordinator: Sharon Houston
Permissions Research: Karen Taylor
Design: Suzanne Boehler and Olena Serbyn
Cover Composition: Olena Serbyn
Page Layout: Jerry Langton
Cartography: Jim Loates Visutronx
Technical Art: Frank Zsigo and Paul Sneath
Film: Compeer

Printed and bound in Canada by Friesen Printers

1   2   3   4   5   DWF   98   97   96   95   94

CONTENTS

CHAPTER 3   RESOURCES AND DEVELOPMENT 151

CHAPTER 4   CULTURE AND POLITICS   227

CHAPTER 5   PROSPECTS AND POSSIBILITIES   291

APPENDIXES   353

PREFACE

The major themes in former editions of *World Prospects* — population growth, economic and human development, and the environment — continue as important issues facing the world's people. However, the world changes with the passage of time. Some nations grow while others fall apart; international priorities are rearranged; and traditional approaches to and ideas about the global economy and society must adapt to changing realities. This third edition of *World Prospects* has been completely rewritten to reflect these changes. Current examples and updated statistics are provided to further illustrate these points.

As in previous editions, readers are constantly encouraged to explore different opinions about issues, to seek and examine facts, to develop ideas through discussion, and to use and analyze statistical data. However, this text takes a more integrated approach. The relationships between the various topics are examined throughout the book to help readers become aware of the interconnectedness of the world.

There are also some new features in the text. Terms which may be unfamiliar to some readers are printed in boldface upon first use and defined in a glossary. Appendix 3, "Techniques of Analysis," includes information on subjects such as organizing inquiries, writing essays, holding debates, and working in small groups, in addition to statistical and graphing techniques.

Much of the statistical analysis required in the questions can be done on a computer. Nevertheless, all such questions are worded in the text so that the calculations may be shared among a number of small groups instead. Many opportunities for group and individual learning exist throughout the text.

While the world may be changing, the need to try to understand it continues. We hope that this book will be useful to you in attempting to reach this understanding.

Our thanks go to Rena Sutton for her considerable assistance throughout the time it took to write this book and to Diane Lapeña for her help in its final stages. We would also like to express our appreciation to the reviewers whose many comments helped to shape this text and to Brian Smith for organizing and analyzing these comments. Additionally, we wish to thank Lesley Boggs for sharing her knowledge of African wildlife with us, and Tasneem Khan for providing invaluable advice about women and Islam.

John Molyneux and Marilyn MacKenzie
Toronto, 1994

CHAPTER
1

ISSUES AND DIVERSITY

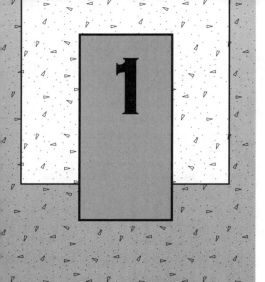

ISSUES AND DIVERSITY

The world has always been in a state of flux. In the sweep of earth history, **tectonic plates** have formed, continents have been created, and climates have varied beyond current recognition. In the time that humans have inhabited the earth, people have increased in number and have spread over most of the earth's surface. Societies have prospered and collapsed, and inventions and discoveries have set in motion forces that affect all life in many ways.

At many times during human occupancy, people — individually and in groups — have had to make decisions regarding their lives. They have had to decide whether or not to attempt to make changes. Then, if changes are desired, they have had to decide how to achieve them. Such decisions usually prompt discussion, since views often vary from person to person.

The purpose of this book is to examine some of the choices the human race faces today in matters commonly agreed to be of importance to the **quality of life** on this planet. Such matters include population numbers, hunger, and economic and human development. They also include nationalism, human rights, the global environment, the impact of technology, and individual dignity. Should changes be sought? If so, which changes? What action is needed to lead to change? Where should the sum of human effort be directed?

Consider the following readings related to the matter of population numbers, and answer the questions at the end.

DENIAL IN THE DECISIVE DECADE

Before August 1991, few people imagined that change so monumental could happen virtually overnight. In a remarkable series of events, the Soviet brand of **communism** crumbled irreparably, relegating the **cold war** to history. As striking and swift as these changes were, the remainder of this decade must give rise to transformations even more profound and pervasive if we are to hold on to realistic hopes for a better world. At issue is humanity's badly damaged relationship with its earthly home, and the urgency of repairing it before more lasting and tragic harm is done.

Sandra Postel,
State of the World 1992,
Worldwatch Institute, 1992

POPULATION AND HUMAN RESOURCES

Present rates of population growth cannot continue. They already compromise many governments' abilities to provide education, health care, and food security for people, much less their abilities to raise living standards. This gap between numbers and resources is all the more compelling because so much of the population growth is concentrated in low-income countries, **ecologically** disadvantaged regions, and poor households.

Our Common Future, The World Commission on Environment and Development (*The Brundtland Report*), 1987

THE WEST GROWS OLD

Imagine a world where schools are closed down and converted into emergency hostels for homeless old(er) people. ... Many shops and businesses have closed as well. The Western world is in the throes of a deepening economic depression as its working-age population shrinks every year.

This is what the Western world could be like by the first half of the 21st century. The growing role of women in the work place, declining **birth rates** and longer **life expectancy** mean that the average ages of populations throughout the **developed world** are on the rise. In Britain in the year 1900, for example, those over 65 years of age accounted for only 4.7 percent of the population. Today, they represent 15.1 percent of the total. By the year 2040, one out of every four persons living in the **European Community** will be over 65.

This trend to ageing populations holds great social, political and economic consequences for the years ahead.

Richard Evans, *Geographical Magazine*, 1989 4

FOREWORD

The 1990s began with dramatic changes. Many countries in Eastern Europe and elsewhere initiated ambitious reforms of their economic and political systems. Not only in Eastern Europe, but also in Africa, Asia, Latin America, and the Middle East, people are seeking escape from poverty and oppression to gain control over their own destinies and find better lives for themselves and their families.

Barber B. Conable,
World Development Report 1991,
The World Bank, 1991

GROWING NEED FOR FARMLAND ERODES GUATEMALA FOREST

GUATEMALA CITY — A dry season in the lowland forests of Guatemala's Petén region is coming to a close. Thin columns of smoke rising across the horizon and a pervasive haze give the landscape the appearance of a war zone.

For three decades now, immigrants pouring into the Petén's lush forests have made burning of trees and vegetation an annual ritual of survival for themselves, and one of unending alarm to environmentalists. As the thin soil sown with corn and beans is exhausted, the pilgrims must move on to clear new plots for *milpas* (cornfields) or face starvation. "Every new road brings colonists, and when you have colonists you have milpas, and when you have milpas you have no need for trees," says an official with the United States Agency for International Development.

Fig. 1-1 *Population pressure on land forces people to clear forested hillsides for new farmland. This is a newly cleared plot in Guatemala. What difficulties do you think these people have probably faced in setting up a home on this land? What advantages does their new home offer? What problems are they likely to face in the future?*

Forty years ago, Guatemala's population was a modest 3 million. Today, in a pattern that is all too familiar globally, three times as many people spread out from the country's crowded highlands in search of the land, fuel, and grazing areas needed to survive.

The result is that some 65 percent of the country's original forest cover has been destroyed, most in the last three decades. At current rates, the highest in Latin America, the remainder will disappear within 25 years.

Shelley Emling, *The Christian Science Monitor*, 1992 7 10-16

SOURCE: CIDA/Benoit Aquin

POPULATION: FOOD

If food was distributed equally, the world would have enough food to feed everybody. But because of unequal distribution millions of people do not have enough to eat.

As the world's population has grown, food production technology has continued to improve and in theory there is enough food to feed everybody. In practice however, the distribution of that food is incredibly uneven and millions of people are malnourished.

Most of the additional 1 billion people that the world will have to support this decade will be born in the less developed world (**developing world**). This will create tremendous problems in these countries — many of which are already struggling.

Per capita (per person) food production has been declining in 51 out of 94 developing countries. As well as this the demand for food in developing countries is actually increasing faster than population growth anyway. This is because rising incomes are allowing people to eat more food, particularly more meat and dairy products.

In many less developed countries, the populations are doubling every 25 years. This is placing an enormous strain on the countries concerned as any efforts to develop are thwarted by the growing numbers. The less developed countries will be turning to the more developed countries for food, such as the grain producers of North America. The grain producers are however already becoming nervous as they realize that the poorer countries will have difficulty paying for food to feed their future populations.

There does not appear to be any shortage of land theoretically capable of producing food, even for the high projection of 14 billion people[1]. One survey showed that the lands of developing countries alone would be capable of feeding 33 billion people. But at what expense??

Well, to begin with, every square metre of possible land would have to be used to produce a barely sufficient, mainly vegetarian diet, using large amounts of fertilizer and pesticides. As most of the potential land for this lies in the tropics, massive migrations of people would be needed to provide the necessary labour force, and staggering amounts of the rain forests would have to be cleared.

This is obviously completely undesirable and unrealistic. As well as this, a substantial proportion of the lands which are considered to be cultivable are actually **marginal** areas. For example, out of Africa's supposed 805 million hectares of land that could be farmed, 409 million hectares are marginal, providing only half the yields possible on suitable land.

Marian Storkey, *Green Teacher No. 21*, 1990 12

[1] World population projections for the future from various sources vary from a low of about 10 billion to a high of over 20 billion.

DISCUSSION AND RESEARCH

1. In groups of four or five, identify and list the concerns outlined in the previous readings. Report your group's findings to the class, justifying any differences between your group's list and the lists reported by other groups. In class, discuss which concern seems the most important at this time.

2. In groups of four or five, brainstorm (see Appendix 3) a list of concerns of global importance not mentioned in the readings. Report your list to the class. As a class, rank the importance of these concerns in relation to those mentioned in the readings.

ISSUES

Population size has long been a subject of discussion. In ancient Greece and Rome, large populations were thought to be associated with great military and economic power. At about the same era in China, Confucius argued that large populations reduced the share of the nation's wealth for each individual and increased the likelihood of conflict among the citizens.

Issues, both important and unimportant, arise out of disagreements among people. Global issues arise out of worldwide disagreements among large numbers of people about the ways they wish the future to evolve. Such views of the future determine current behaviours, and are equally affected by current beliefs, which vary widely around the world. Differences in beliefs are often caused by differences in cultural and community values, local traditions, **ethnic** and religious customs, family upbringing, and personal aspirations.

For example, whether or not the growth of the world's population should be controlled is the subject of worldwide debate. Many people favour unchecked population growth for religious reasons. Others support it out of a desire for greater national military or economic strength. On the other hand, some people oppose unregulated population growth because they believe it will lead to higher rates of poverty and hunger. Many oppose it because it places increasing pressure on the earth's natural environment. The continuing growth of the world's population is an important world issue. It arouses strong and widespread feelings about possible alternative futures. It affects current behaviours. It is affected in turn by current beliefs. The issue is examined in detail later in this chapter.

FACTS AND OPINIONS

Facts are unbiased information about reality. Opinions are judgements and views about reality. Facts are not inherently "better" than opinions. They are different. Facts are objective and unarguable, although how they are selected and presented may be arguable. Opinions are subjective and arguable.

Facts and opinions are often intertwined. The introduction of particular facts into a situation may generate certain opinions, or cause existing opinions to be changed. Conversely, the expression of particular opinions about a situation, by altering present human behaviours, may cause future facts to be different from present facts.

For example, according to the World Health Organization, at least 40 million people in the developing world are blind. One of the major causes of this is vitamin A deficiency in infancy, which can only be prevented through improved nutrition for both mother and baby. These are facts. It is in the matter of how to improve the situation that differing opinions arise. These opinions vary according to the beliefs and values of those who hold them. For instance, there are differences in opinion about the role of foreign food aid versus domestically grown food in the pursuit of better nutrition for local populations. Resources in the developing world that might be allocated to health care are also subject to competing demands from education, housing, economic development, military power, and government. How these differences are resolved may change the future fact of the extent of blindness in the developing world.

When presenting one side of an issue, people often select facts that support their opinions. There are always many other facts, since each fact is only a small part of the total reality. In order to bolster their arguments, two sides in an issue may use different facts, all equally true, but differing in their time frame or geographical perspective. For example, critics of the United States health care system may point out that the **infant mortality rate** in the United States in 1992 was 9/1000 compared with 7/1000 in Canada and 5/1000 in Japan. Defenders of the system, on the other hand, could point out that in 1970 the United States infant mortality rate was over 20/1000, and that in 1992 the United States was one of only 20 countries in the world that had infant mortality rates below 10/1000. All the facts are true, but they are used selectively in order to support the views of the different sides.

The infant mortality rate is the yearly number of babies who die before their first birthday per 1000 live births. Details for individual countries are given in column 12 of Appendix 2.

DISCUSSION AND RESEARCH

3. Consider the following reading and answer the questions at the end.

FAIRER TRADE

Ever wonder how much of the $14.95 you pay for an exotic, finely woven basket at Pier One Imports was actually shared with the person who crafted it? Chances are, the basket was made in the Philippines by a woman who received no more than $1 for the full day of work that went into collecting, preparing, and weaving the grass, rattan, and bamboo that make up the basket.

So Pier One makes a tidy $14 on the transaction? Not exactly. Pier One may have paid $3 to an exporter, and another $9 may have gone for such varied expenses as import duties, distribution, shipping, handling, and advertising. Pier One makes $2 on the basket.

According to Jacqui MacDonald, managing director of Bridgehead, a nonprofit alternative trade organization based in Ottawa, Canada, a commercially sold basket may have passed through six commercial agents, who have marked up the basket 300 percent, before it even reaches Manila, where it is then exported to North America. Upon landing, it either enters the distribution network for a big chain like Pier One, or is picked up by yet another wholesaler for further distribution.

If you buy the same basket from the mail-order catalogue of Bridgehead, says MacDonald, about $7 of your $14.95 purchase — instead of $1 — would go directly to the Filipino basket maker. Her organization is able to do that by keeping overhead (general business expenses such as rent and wages) low and buy-

ing directly from the Bohol Basket Weavers Cooperative in the Philippines.

Bridgehead is one of more than 200 alternative trade organizations that connect consumers throughout North America, Europe, Japan, and Australia to thousands of craft producers in the **Third World** through a fairer trade relationship. Most of these organizations, like Pueblo to People, Self-Help Crafts, Oxfam Trading, and Bridgehead, are nonprofit and deal in handmade crafts and gourmet foods, from Indian batik silk scarves to Kenyan musical instruments to organic coffee from Central America. Alternative traders sell these items through catalogs, gift shops, and craft fairs.

Self-Help Crafts of Akron, Pennsylvania, is North America's

largest alternative trade organization. It works with more than 30 000 producers in Asia, Africa, and Latin America, and has annual sales of $8 million. It keeps costs down by using volunteer help in its hundreds of stores across the United States. Pueblo to People, based in Houston, Texas, works with 85 cooperatives throughout South and Central America. Its colorful mail-order catalogue, offering products ranging from Salvadoran folk art jewelry to hand-blown Guatemalan mugs made of recycled Coca Cola bottles, reaches more than 600 000 Americans.

The majority of alternative trade organizations are based in Europe, where they are more established and control larger portions of the Third World "imports" market than their North American counterparts. Oxfam Trading in the United Kingdom and GEPA-Aktion Dritte Welt Handel (GEPA) in Germany are each larger than all North American alternative trade organizations combined. Oxfam Trading now operates 625 retail shops, making it the sixth largest retailer in Great Britain; GEPA has operating revenues in excess of $17 million. Yet compared to Pier One Imports, America's largest commercial retailer of Third World crafts, even these organizations are tiny. Pier One had sales of $680 million last year, compared with an estimated world total of $200 million for alternative trade organizations.

But the success of alternative trade is not measured by its sales volume or the number of Third World workers it touches. By dealing exclusively with small producer cooperatives that have demonstrated a commitment to social and economic justice within their own organizations and their towns and villages, alternative trade has reached far beyond a handful of isolated households. Alternative traders create lasting partnerships with these groups and provide them with various free services — such as instruction in packaging, shipping, or bookkeeping, or advice on product design and marketing — that traditional commercial traders have neither the interest nor the time to offer. In fact, alternative traders have helped producers take over aspects of production and marketing that are traditionally controlled by commercial traders. For instance, with help from a group of American and European alternative trade organizations, CooCafe, a cooperative of 3000 small-scale coffee farmers in Costa Rica, now roasts and packages its own coffee. Processing and packaging, which dramatically increase the profits from coffee, are usually done in the importing country.

Alternative traders also replace piece work (payment for each unit produced) with long-term contracts. Payment to the producer is made up front, up to a year in advance, not after merchandise is received.

This new trade relationship can make a world of difference for peasant farmers and artisans in the Third World who otherwise have very little bargaining power and few — if any — options for marketing their goods. Mostly uneducated and desperately poor, they are routinely exploited by local merchants and commercial traders who pay them barely enough to cover the costs of materials needed to make their products or grow their crops. In contrast, alternative trade organizations pay farmers and craftspeople what the producers themselves determine is a fair price.

"In some instances, we offer producers even more than they initially ask for," says Doug Dirks, producer relations director of Pennsylvania-based Self-Help Crafts. This happens because most craftspeople have no idea of the true value of their work after marketing their goods for decades at fixed prices. Outfits like Bridgehead or Oxfam Trading pay them four to five times as much as local traders and merchants pay. The Bohol basket weavers can earn up to ten times more than they would otherwise by selling to alternative trade organizations.

Women, especially, benefit from alternative trade. Dirks estimates that about three-quarters of Self-Help Crafts' producers are women, who typically earn 75 percent of family cash income. Alternative trade organizations also take pains to buy crafts and organic foods that reinforce the rich cultural traditions and farming practices of the people producing them.

As a replacement for the dominant commercial system, alternative trade organizations have their limitations. Many are financially dependent on the good will of volunteers at the stores and catalogue operations, and many more rely on consumers who place a higher value on hand-made or organically produced goods than the "mainstream" market might bear. But European organizations have shown that alternative traders can combine sound business sense and good intentions without compromising their commitment to social and economic justice. In fact, several of these organizations have decided to sell "fair" products via existing commercial channels to make these goods more readily available to consumers.

In the Netherlands, the Max Havelaar Foundation has established a fair trade mark to distinguish coffee grown by democratically run cooperatives of small-scale producers who receive a fair price for their coffee. Max Havelaar coffee is distributed through both alternative trade and traditional commercial networks and is now available in 90 percent of all supermarkets in the Netherlands.

Similarly, alternative traders may slowly teach businesses the value of incorporating social concerns into their strategies. There are signs that the message may be getting through. "There are hundreds of points where alternative trade can break down, but the organizations that do it have wonderful drive and vision for people...and when it works it is wonderful and very rewarding," says John Baker, a merchandising executive for Pier One.

Vicki Elkin, *World Watch*, 1992 7-8

(a) Identify (i) the facts and (ii) the opinions presented in the reading.
(b) Describe the overall point of view of the writer.
(c) List the words and phrases used by the writer to add emphasis to her general argument.
(d) Using the facts identified in part (a) of this question, develop an opposing argument.

ISSUES ANALYSIS

The essence of issues analysis rests in attempting to bring the situation and the different views about it into FOCUS:

- **F**ind the **F**acts of the situation;
- **O**btain various **O**pinions about the issue;
- **C**onsider the different **C**hoices;
- **U**nderstand the relative **U**rgency of the situation; and
- **S**ynthesize (put together) one's own **S**tand on the issue.

This book FOCUSes on some of the major issues dividing world opinion in the 1990s, such as population growth, the environment, quality of life, resource use, development, culture and politics, and future directions.

The reality of the world is that all these issues are interrelated, and interdependent. For example, population growth is related to quality of life. The issues also illustrate the relationships among the various parts of the world which are affected by them. For instance, trade decisions in one part of the world have effects elsewhere, as shown in the previous reading, "Fairer Trade." Wherever possible in this book, connections to other issues and among different parts of the world are noted when discussing individual issues, but students should constantly ask themselves about other linkages. In all cases, various viewpoints

SOURCE: Marilyn MacKenzie

Fig. 1-2 *A small group of students and teachers bring a situation into FOCUS.*

are presented, and students are asked to come to conclusions about the issues based on their own analysis of the facts and opinions.

Because of the scope and complexity of the various global issues, the readings in this text present a number of different views and understandings. Students should keep in mind that the opinions stated in the readings reflect particular points of view. For instance, they may include ethnocentric points of view. **Ethnocentricity** exists whenever the behaviour of another society or **ethnic group** is judged by the standards of one's own society or group. People's views are often influenced by the particular culture of their country, by its traditions and beliefs, and by conversations with friends. Such views may differ from those of other people in the same country, but there tends to be some similarity in a nation as a whole when compared to other parts of the world. A Canadian view of another part of the world is really a "Canadocentric" view, and is no more legitimate than, say, a Japanese view or a Filipino view. For example, many people in Canada describe the countries of the western Pacific rim as the "Far East." To the people of those lands, the region is the centre of their existence. To them, the Far East could be British Columbia. Equally, the term "Western" as applied to the nations of Europe and North America is true only from a more eastern standpoint.

One of the risks facing those who hold an ethnocentric point of view is that they may consider any other way of life but their own to be somehow abnormal. Inhabitants in the rest the world, however, consider their own way of life to be normal, notwithstanding any changes to their society that they may be seeking. An even greater risk facing people who hold an ethnocentric viewpoint is that they may believe their own culture to be superior to those of others. They may justify their view on the basis of any number of criteria, such as military power or the number of television sets per hundred people. The choice of such criteria is highly subjective; thus, these views contain no justification in fact.

The views expressed in the readings are those of individuals. While these views are often widely held by other people, there are also many who disagree. Disagreements brought about by differing points of view exist in all parts of the world.

You should also watch carefully for logical fallacies in the readings. There are several types, but two are very common. One is what is called the *Post Hoc, Ergo Propter Hoc* fallacy. This means that people will argue that if Y occurs after X, then Y is caused by X. In reality, Y may or may not have any connection to X, but it is a common fallacy to say there is a connection. Another fallacy is the false syllogism. This means that if some, even most, of X are also Y, then some people will argue that all X are also Y, and that any individual member of X must also be Y. This leads to the problem of stereotyping.

Another element to be aware of in the various readings is bias. Bias is the presentation of an issue from a single point of view. It may often be detected by examining the type of language used by the author, especially in his or her selection of verbs and adjectives. For example, a minority group presenting a written request to the government for more political independence may be described as "meekly submitting a petition" or "defiantly demanding their rights."

Bias may also occur when a single, extreme example is used to represent a complex issue in its entirety. For example, if someone wished to support the argument that poverty was rampant in a certain country, illustrating its existence solely with an example of a person

What examples of post hoc and false syllogism fallacies can you think of?

Beetle Bailey

Fig. 1-3 *The words chosen to describe a situation may reflect the bias of the speaker.*

who lives on the street would be an extreme statement. The opposite extreme, which might be used by someone wishing to refute that poverty is a problem, would be to claim that the people in that nation are generally the richest in the world, as though every citizen shared equally in the wealth.

Bias may also be evident in the selection of material used by an author to describe a situation. Supportive data are included; other data are omitted. The task of the reader is to examine the data for completeness, and to investigate what has been omitted. This often involves research.

Research is the basic tool for all analysis. Libraries provide the basic resources of card catalogues, computer searches, vertical files, and periodicals. Daily newspapers, radio reports, and television news magazines provide up-to-date information on many world issues. Weekly news magazines also contain useful information, as well as expert analysis and opinion.

Maps are another basic geographical tool. *World Prospects, Third Edition* presents much information on world maps. Because the real world is spherical, it is impossible to show both shapes and sizes of land masses accurately on maps. The shapes of large areas, such as continents or large countries, are therefore distorted, although it is possible to show the correct shape of smaller land masses.

Despite the difficulty of reflecting shapes correctly on maps, correct size may be obtained through the use of equal area maps. The art of making good equal area maps rests on achieving correct size without distorting shapes too much. All the world maps used in this text are equal area maps. Distortion of land shapes is minimized as far as possible by using an arrangement of latitude and longitude lines that divides the oceans. Look, for example, at Fig. 1-9.

Maps may also reflect a point of view. The real world is a spinning globe; to an observer its surface has no single centre, but a continuous sequence of centres. Maps, however, are static, and thus to an observer have a single centre. Different map-makers may choose different centres. Maps produced in Japan, for example, show the world centred on Japan, with the Americas on the far right across the Pacific Ocean, and Europe and Africa on the far left. To this extent, maps represent an ethnocentric view of the world. Similarly, some maps produced in the Americas show the Americas in the centre. Most maps in the world show Europe and Africa in the central position for the practical reason that such a placement produces the least shape distortion for the largest number of countries, although Alaska and northeastern Siberia are seriously distorted. The maps in the text should be regarded as a practical solution to the difficulties of map-making rather than representing a particular ethnocentric view of the world.

The maps in *World Prospects, Third Edition* show information only for those countries that have sufficient area to be mappable at this scale. All very small countries are marked with an asterisk in the data

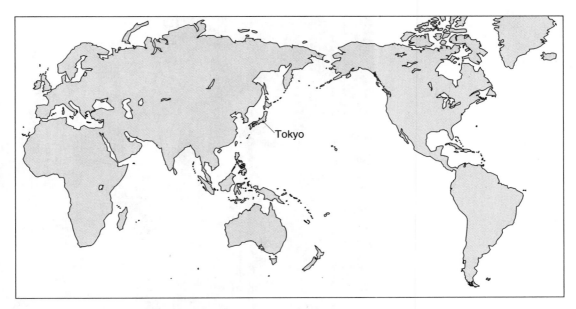

Fig. 1-4 *The world as seen from Japan. This is a widely used arrangement of the continents and oceans on maps in Japan.*

tables in Appendix 2 at the back of this book, and are not shown on the maps. Additionally, one of the mappable countries, Western Sahara (also called Minurso), does not publish data because it is claimed by Morocco, and its political status is in dispute. Its location is indicated on the maps, but no statistical data are indicated. Further, some countries such as the U.S.S.R., Yugoslavia, and Czechoslovakia no longer exist as single states, and their areas are now occupied by several independent states. Similarly, Ethiopia became two independent nations in 1993, when Eritrea was officially recognized as a separate country. So far, though, the former countries are the only source of statistics for these areas. In all cases, maps are based upon the most recently available statistics.

The main purpose of the maps in this book is to help the reader identify patterns. When identified, all patterns require explanation and critical analysis. Students should be aware that patterns do not have to be strongly evident in order to be significant. A total lack of pattern may also be significant. However, the analysis and explanation of weak or zero patterns will be different from that for strong patterns.

This book also uses statistical analysis as a tool to help clarify issues, and requires students to use a selection of the more common statistical techniques. As far as possible, the book relies upon statistics from international bodies such as the United Nations (U.N.) and its various agencies. Even so, the precision of some of the statistics may be questioned. International bodies have to rely largely on national governments to collect and release statistics, and not all

SOURCE: Unesco/Alexander Shaw

Fig. 1-5 *Government representatives ask questions for a housing survey in Kabul, Afghanistan. What does the photograph suggest about the difficulties of obtaining statistics?*

countries have equally efficient statistical departments. As well, many countries are able to collect their statistics only infrequently, so their statistics may be out of date when they are published. Other countries do not collect or publish some statistics which the United Nations regards as important and it therefore has to estimate them. Nevertheless, international bodies make every effort to ensure that their published statistics are as accurate as possible.

An additional difficulty occurs when statistics about money values are used. Since there is no single world currency, individual national currencies have to be converted into a common one so that they may be compared. Because the United States dollar (US$) is the most widely accepted currency in the world, it has become the one that all other currencies are converted into.

There are two major ways of converting any national currency into US$. One method is by using the conversion rates established on foreign exchange markets. Another method is by using the **purchasing power parity** of different currencies. This compares how much of one currency it takes to buy the same goods as it takes in US$. Both methods of conversion are used by international bodies. Both produce slightly different results. The first method, foreign exchange values, is used more widely, and is used in this text.

In either case, interpretation of money values requires care. **Inflation** changes money values over time and distorts comparisons between different years. Also, prices of government services vary from one country to another because of differences in the level and use of taxes.

Governments may also report their money figures in different ways. For example, some countries report their total annual generation of income and production on a **Gross National Product (GNP)** basis, while others report on what is called a **Gross Domestic Product (GDP)** basis. The difference between the two is based on what is included in the nation's income. For example, the GNP of country X includes the incomes of X's citizens living abroad and excludes the incomes of foreigners living in X. GNP is thus the value of all income received by the nationals of a country, even if some of it is received from work or investments in other countries. The GDP of country X excludes the incomes of X's citizens living abroad, but includes the incomes of all foreigners living in X. GDP is thus the value of all income received within the country, regardless of the citizenship of the recipients. In order to simplify international accounting, more and more countries are starting to standardize their statistics on a GDP basis.

Issues resolution can be difficult, even when preceded by analysis. Sometimes, individuals or groups on either side of an issue may not be willing to examine alternative viewpoints, nor may they be willing to cooperate with plans while in disagreement with them. In the case of some issues, resolution by political decision may end the matter, with both sides accepting the decision of the political majority. This is most likely when all parties involved have had an opportunity to express their views and have heard the arguments of others.

One means by which peaceful resolution of an issue may be secured is called force-field analysis. This technique calls for one side to identify the arguments operating for and against it, and to devise strategies and additional arguments that reinforce the arguments in its favour and minimize or even negate the opposing ones. Because of the strong opinions and beliefs held by some individuals on both sides of various global issues, though, the task of resolving these issues peacefully may seem insurmountable. However, as Winston Churchill, British Prime Minister during World War II (1939-45), said, "Jaw, jaw is better than war, war."

> Inflation is a condition of rising prices associated with the availability of increasing amounts of money in relation to the quantity of goods and services available.

DISCUSSION AND RESEARCH

4. The following two readings present different views about the issue of large dams on rivers. The first reading deals with the importance to Egypt of the Aswan High Dam (see Fig. 1-6), built between 1960 and 1970 to provide 10 billion **kilo**watt-hours (**kW.h**) of hydroelectricity annually as well as irrigation water for 400 000 hectares (ha) of farmland. The reading was written at a time of unusually low water in the reservoir (Lake Nasser). It provides insight about what life in Egypt might be like without the dam, and indicates the extent to which Egypt relies upon it. Lake Nasser filled up again a year later, and the situation returned to normal.

   The second reading deals with the problems created in northwest India by the Narmada dams (see Fig. 1-7), which are now under construction as the world's largest current dam project. They are not scheduled for completion until about 2035. After you have examined the readings, answer the questions at the end.

EGYPT IS THIRSTY

The rains that fall on Ethiopia's highlands have failed for the last eight years, depriving the Nile River of its main source of water. As a result, Africa's largest river has been steadily shrinking. For the people of Egypt, who depend on the Nile for everything — industry, agriculture, tourism — this may mean the disaster of the century.

The Nile's water keeps Egypt's fertile delta land alive, and slakes the thirst of the country's 53 million people. It is pumped...to the coastal city of Mersa Matruh and to settlers along the Cairo-Alexandria highway.... It is loaded on to tank trucks and carried to Sharm al-Sheikh, on the Red Sea at the tip of the Sinai peninsula, where the Marina Hotel recently closed its doors for two days because the trucks had broken down along the highway.

Egypt thought that after it built the giant Aswan High Dam, which holds a lake 550 km long and contains trillions of litres of water when full, the country would be insured against drought. But for

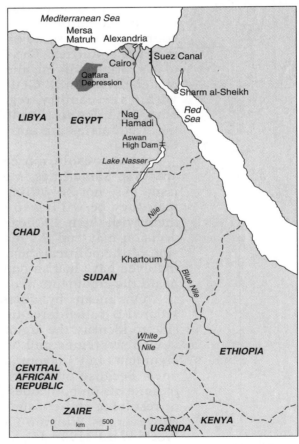

Fig. 1-6 *Location of the Aswan High Dam in the Nile valley.*

eight years now more has been taken out of the dam's lake than the river has put in. The water level behind the dam has sunk 15 metres over the last four years. The consequences are already dramatic.

The two power plants on the old and new Aswan dams, which under normal conditions provide 1750 **megawatts** — a third of the nation's supply — every year, have recently halved their output. This will mean cuts in Egypt's industrial output at a time of economic difficulty. The nation has a foreign **debt** of more than $40 billion and is already falling behind on its rescheduling (repayment) plan, signed in 1987.

To tackle the power shortages, the Minister of Energy, Mahir Abasa, wants to build 13 thermal power plants, most of them to be fueled with cheap natural gas. Egypt is also taking another look at an idea long considered dead: making use of the altitude difference between the Mediterranean and the Qattara Depression. The depression's bottom lies 150 metres below sea level, and Qattara is 15 km from the coast. A canal would bring water from the Mediterranean. Swedish experts are working on a new study of the plan. Most of all, Egypt would like to turn to nuclear power. What is lacking is money.

Meanwhile, rationing measures have been implemented. Recently people were prohibited from using drinking water to wash cars, clean streets, and water yards. Television stations plan to cut their broadcasts to three hours a day. Every part of Cairo has been affected. If the drought continues, plants such as the energy-intensive Kima fertilizer factory at Aswan, or the aluminum plant at Nag Hamadi, will have to be shut down altogether.

The worst effects of the water shortage may come in agriculture. Only 4 percent of the country's area is farmland, and it is entirely dependent on irrigation from the country's only river. The rest of Egypt's 1 000 000 square kilometres is desert. This year's main harvest has not been affected, but by this fall the situation could be critical. Various measures have already been planned: rice farming, because of its high use of water, will be cut back, and brackish (salty) water, which is readily available in the main north coast rice-producing area, will be used on many farms; sugar beets will replace the water-guzzling sugar cane; no new irrigation canals will be built; and the building of sprinkler systems, which use only a fraction of the water necessary for traditional irrigation will be encouraged....

Der Spiegel, quoted in *World Press Review*, 1988 8

INDIA BE DAMMED

...in one of the most grandiose schemes ever envisaged in human history, the river (Narmada) and its valley are to be transformed by a series of more than 3000 major and minor dams into a chain of giant pools and reservoirs. So huge is the project that it will take more than a hundred years to complete; but two of the biggest dams — the Narmada Sagar dam in Madhya Pradesh and the Sardar Sarovar dam in Gujarat — received the go-ahead last year.

Between them the two dams are expected to irrigate more than 1.5 million hectares and generate 400 megawatts of electricity; but opponents of the scheme have always argued that it will destroy more wealth than it will create. They point out that the Narmada Sagar will actually submerge more land than it will irrigate, and argue that the project cannot be justified on social, environmental, or economic grounds. They say the cost-benefit analysis on which it was approved is the result of data-manipulation and fraud, and accuse the government of playing cynical power politics with the poor. The only beneficiaries, they say, will be the landed elites of Gujarat and Madhya Pradesh...and the construction contractors who have pushed through the approval.

What is at stake is not just the desecration of a holy river. According to New Delhi's Institute of Urban Affairs, the Narmada Valley project will eventually drive more than one million people from their homes.

• • • • •

There is talk of cash for the dispossessed, of 2.5 ha of irrigated land for each ousted family. But where? Almost all cultivable land is already under the plough. The rest is

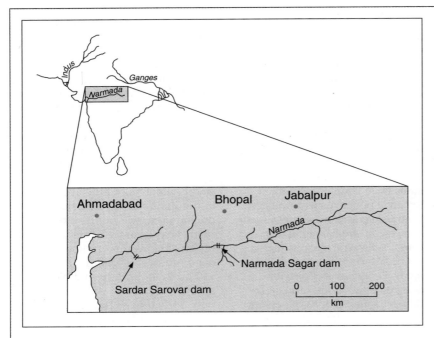

 Fig. 1-7 *Major dams in the Narmada valley.*

poor grazing land with hardly any soil cover and is quite useless for growing crops.

Those about to be forcibly resettled face a hopeless future. The majority are tribal peoples — Tadavis, Bhils, Pawara, and others. Many are forest dwellers but, since they possess no deeds and the land has been acquired by the Forest Department and therefore legally belongs to the government, they are not entitled to compensation.

Survival International, the leading international organization working to defend the rights of threatened peoples, has long urged the World Bank not to fund the Sardar Sarovar project. Dr. Marcus Colchester, Survival International's Projects Director, has spent several weeks in India visiting the local communities. "The Indian Government has still not identified land for the resettlement. There's no plan, because there is no land," he says, citing internal government documents which admit that 'big chunks of cultivable land are not available' for resettling the oustees of Sardar Sarovar.

The indigenous peoples living under the shadow of the Sardar Sarovar dam have begun to despair of their future. The endless thunder of passing trucks and the boom of blasting as the dam's foundations are carved from the rock only serve to remind them of the inevitable — that their lands are soon to be flooded and they will have to move elsewhere. "The government's commitment to the technical aspects of the project has not been matched by a concern for its impact on the tribal peoples, who have been completely isolated from all planning and decision-making," says Colchester....

For these villagers, when the waters rise, it is not only homes, fields and forests that will go under. Festivals, songs and dances, customs and traditions — the very culture and beliefs which underpin their way of life and sustain their identity are about to be submerged as the uprooted people are dispersed to fend for themselves as best they can.[1]
. . . . .

If the Narmada Sagar dam is built it will also drown at least 40 000 hectares of prime teak and sal forest. The trees will be clear-felled before the waters close over them but, in a country chronically short of animal fodder, the ripples of a disaster in the making can be clearly foreseen.

The surrounding country is already over-grazed and many villagers drive their cattle into the forests to find food. Already the fodder crisis is so acute that any delay in the **monsoon rains** spells death by starvation for thousands of animals.

According to an official estimate, nearly 200 000 cattle now depend on the doomed forest. If they are driven out they can only add to the misery of the scrawny herds in the denuded countryside.

At the same time, the rich wildlife of the forest lands is to be abandoned. There is no provision for any kind of animal rescue. When the waters rise, the animals are expected to flee to safety. But the forests are surrounded by cultivated fields and crowded villages. With no wooded corridors along which the wild animals (can) migrate to a new refuge, many will undoubtedly move out into the fields and be shot. The rest will be left to a watery grave.

A similar fate could befall the people condemned to live in the shadow of the dams. The Narmada basin with its faults and fractures is known to be vulnerable to earth tremors. In the last 200 years nearly 30 earthquakes have shaken the region. The worst, in 1936, had a magnitude of 6.3 on the **richter scale**.

It is also known that the sheer weight of a giant reservoir such as the one planned at Narmada Sagar can sometimes trigger an earthquake of high magnitude. No wonder some experts have expressed concern.

Other unpleasant side-effects are predicted. Words like **siltation**, waterlogging and salinity sound as dry as the pages of an agronomist's ledger, but they define ways in which the land is abused beyond endurance.

Siltation happens when soil conservation is neglected and precious topsoil is washed away into rivers. When a dam is built the silt builds up in the reservoir, reducing its storage capacity and shortening its useful life. Increasing deforestation and overgrazing in the Narmada basin can only swell the silt deposits trapped by the dams and cripple their economic viability.

Waterlogging is a common phenomenon with major irrigation schemes which lack efficient drainage to flush away surplus waters. Without such drainage, the build-up of trapped surface waters brings about a rise in the water table. As a result, ground waters percolate to the surface and evaporate, leaving nothing but salts. In India at least ten million hectares of land have become waterlogged and more than twice as (many) are threatened with salinity. If the Sardar Sarovar dam is built there is little doubt that vast tracts of the Narmada basin will go the same way.

As if this was not enough, the transformation of the river system will destroy profitable fisheries with a gross output valued in tens of millions of **rupees**; and to cap it all there is the inevitable likelihood of an increase in malaria, cholera and other water-related diseases.

. . . . .

Alternatives exist that would produce power and irrigation without destroying the environment and displacing huge numbers of people; but these would be numerous small-scale projects which carry very little prestige.

Brian Jackman, *Geographical Magazine*, 1989 6

[1] Many local people have organized to oppose the Narmada project. Opposition also comes from environmental groups within India and across the world.

In small groups,
- (a) Analyze the two readings to identify and list:
  - (i) the facts;
  - (ii) the opinions;
  - (iii) the different choices.
- (b) Discuss what Egypt might be like today if the Aswan Dam had not been built.
- (c) Suggest what the Narmada region might be like in the future when the project has been completed.
- (d) Record your group work, and report it to the class.

5. Not all issues are presented by words alone. Cartoons and comic strips are both used frequently to highlight an issue. Consider the comic strip by Jim Unger in

Fig. 1-8. In small groups attempt to (i) identify the issue being highlighted and (ii) analyze the argument presented.

Fig. 1-8   Herman

SOURCE: Universal Press Syndicate

A DIVERSE WORLD

There are many inequalities — or **disparities** — from one part of the world to another in the way people live. In some areas, individuals may have political **freedom**; in other areas, they may not. Inequalities also exist in such matters as human rights, gender equality, material wealth, educational provision, and health care, which are broadly measurable. When these factors are measured and individual countries compared, as in Appendix 2, they are rarely found to be equal.

Another component of world diversity relates to differences that are not measurable. These matters are largely cultural in nature. They include language, customs, religion, and ethnic heritage. There are no disparities in such matters, only differences.

People argue about whether there should be more or less diversity in the world. They argue about whether there should be uniformity, about the extent of acceptable uniformity, and about the means to be used to achieve greater uniformity. For example, should the entire world be encouraged to attain low birth rates? To forsake its nationalistic tendencies? To protect the natural environment? If so, how? In all cases, should the goals be set by local people or by an international agency? These are just some of the subjects which give rise to strongly held views. In some instances, violence may occur when individuals driven by passionate belief are not restrained by reason.

The birth rate is the number of live births in a year per thousand of existing population at the mid-year mark.

Life expectancy is the average number of years people are expected to live (see column 15 in Appendix 2). Literacy rates indicate the percentage of the population, excluding young children, able to read and write a simple sentence.

The term "temperate" refers to the areas between the polar circles and the tropics. The northern temperate area lies between the Arctic Circle and the Tropic of Cancer; the southern temperate area lies between the Antarctic Circle and the Tropic of Capricorn. The term "tropical" refers to all the areas between the Tropics of Cancer and Capricorn.

North and South became popular terms after the 1980 publication of the *Brandt Report (North-South: a Program for Survival)* by the Independent Commission on International Development Issues.

Geopolitics is broadly the study of interrelationships between geography and politics.

The term "Third World" came into use after the 1955 Bandung Conference in Indonesia which was attended by 77 African and Asian nations. These nations wanted to establish a "third force" in the world beside the two existing "East" and "West" power blocs.

The maps in Figs. 1-9 to 1-12 (birth rates, **literacy** rates, life expectancies, and Gross National Product per person per year (GNP/cap/y)) show some of the disparities among the different parts of the world. Despite the omission of small countries and the lack of data for a number of others, some fairly clear conclusions about world diversity may be drawn from examining the patterns on the maps. Look at the patterns produced, and examine the **correlations** that exist among the groups of countries. What conclusions do you arrive at?

The broad patterns shown on the four maps support the concept of a diverse world, if it is assumed that the four categories mapped reflect patterns that would be evident from mapping other categories too. Overall, the pattern shown here has been used by many people to divide the world into two groups, broadly named "North" and "South." To better reflect the countries' locations in the world, however, more appropriate names might be "Temperate" and "Tropical."

World diversity is enhanced by the fact that disparities exist in the individual countries belonging to the two broad groups identified by the four maps. Some countries are in the same group in all four maps (see Fig. 1-13), but many belong to one of the groups in fewer than four categories. For example, Venezuela is a member of the "North" group in three of the four categories while Brazil is a member in two of the categories; and Madagascar is a member of the "South" group in three of the categories, while Nicaragua is a member in two.

Identification of a core "North" and a core "South", as shown in Fig. 1-13, also produces many countries that are not clear members of either group, thus raising the question of the suitability of a simple division of the world into "North" and "South." Nevertheless, use of the terms is widespread. An advantage their use offers is that one group need not feel it is being measured against the other.

The countries of the world have also been classified using three divisions called First World, Second World, and Third World. This classification was very popular during most of the second half of the 20th century. It rested on a **geopolitical** situation — the relationship between the territory of a state and its political importance — that had the so-called Western bloc countries (**capitalist**, **free enterprise**, or **market economy**) classified as the First World and the Eastern bloc countries (communist, **state controlled**, or **command economy**) classified as the Second World. All other countries, despite the tremendous differences among them, were classified as the Third World. China, potentially a member of the Second World as a communist country, always preferred to claim membership of the Third World because of its relative lack of industrialization.

The disappearance of state-controlling communism in eastern Europe and north and central Asia at the start of the 1990s made the Second World classification virtually obsolete, with the exception of Cuba, North Korea, and Vietnam. The term "Third" became illogical

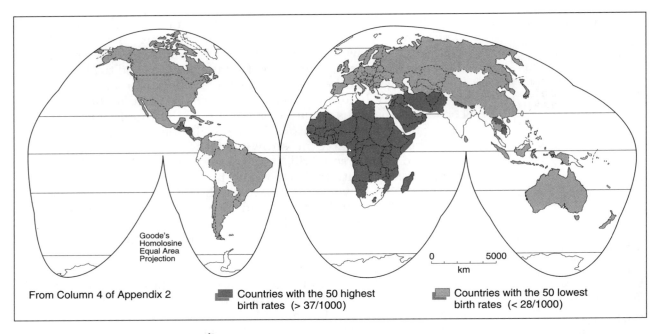

From Column 4 of Appendix 2

Countries with the 50 highest birth rates (> 37/1000)

Countries with the 50 lowest birth rates (< 28/1000)

Goode's Homolosine Equal Area Projection

Fig. 1-9 *The countries with the 50 highest and 50 lowest annual birth rates.*

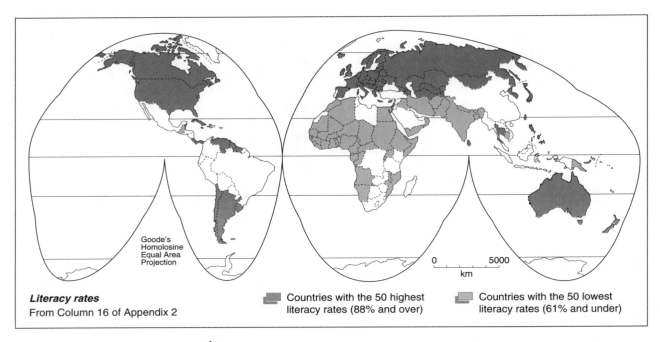

Literacy rates
From Column 16 of Appendix 2

Countries with the 50 highest literacy rates (88% and over)

Countries with the 50 lowest literacy rates (61% and under)

Goode's Homolosine Equal Area Projection

Fig. 1-10 *The countries with the 50 highest and 50 lowest literacy rates.*

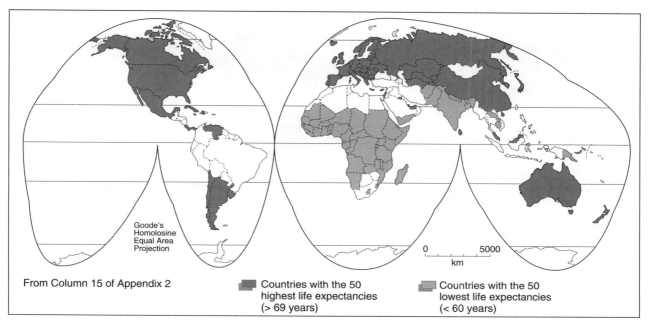

Goode's
Homolosine
Equal Area
Projection

From Column 15 of Appendix 2

Countries with the 50
highest life expectancies
(> 69 years)

Countries with the 50
lowest life expectancies
(< 60 years)

0   5000
km

Fig. 1-11 *The countries with the 50 highest and 50 lowest life expectancies, in years.*

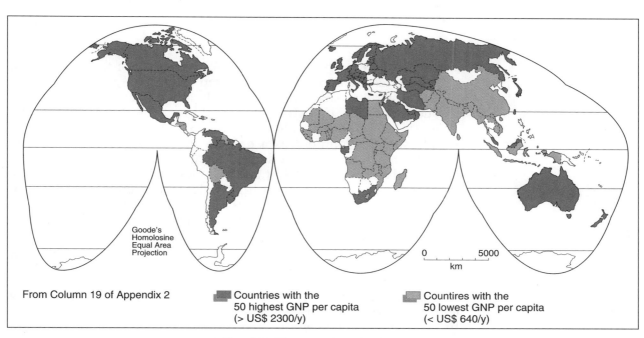

Goode's
Homolosine
Equal Area
Projection

From Column 19 of Appendix 2

Countries with the
50 highest GNP per capita
(> US$ 2300/y)

Countires with the
50 lowest GNP per capita
(< US$ 640/y)

0   5000
km

Fig. 1-12 *The countries with the 50 highest and 50 lowest GNP per capita (per person).*

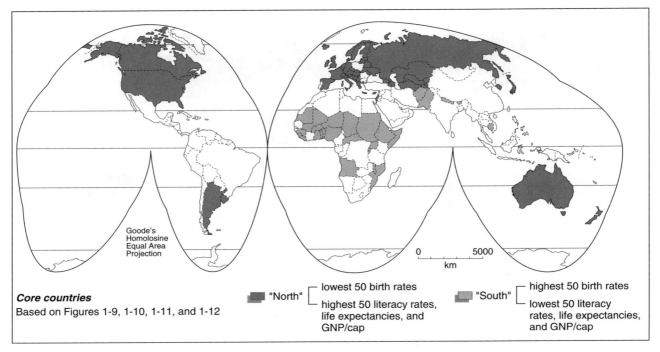

Goode's
Homolosine
Equal Area
Projection

0   5000
km

Core countries
Based on Figures 1-9, 1-10, 1-11, and 1-12

"North" ⎡ lowest 50 birth rates
       ⎣ highest 50 literacy rates,
         life expectancies, and
         GNP/cap

"South" ⎡ highest 50 birth rates
       ⎣ lowest 50 literacy
         rates, life expectancies,
         and GNP/cap

Fig. 1-13 *The "core" countries of the North and South, according to information in Figs. 1-9 through 1-12.*

when there were only two worlds. As a result, the terms First and Third Worlds are no longer widely used.

Another way that countries are classified is to divide them into the developed (or industrialized) world and the developing world. There is disagreement about the use of these terms, too. Some people see development as a process that all nations are passing through, albeit at different stages. They prefer terms such as more developed countries (MDCs) and less developed countries (LDCs). Others suggest calling them highly developed countries (HDCs), moderately developed countries (MDCs), and less developed countries (LDCs). In both cases, the least developed countries (known as LLDCs, the Least LDCs) are often identified separately. This book uses the terms developed and developing to classify the countries of the world because these two terms are now the ones most commonly used.

Diversity also exists within each developed and developing country. Although most of the world's relatively wealthy persons live in the developed world, their numbers in the developing world are growing rapidly. It is just as grave an error to think of people in developing countries as uniformly poor as it is to think of people in developed countries as uniformly rich. All countries have some rich people and some poor people. But the proportions differ from one part of the world to another. The meanings of rich and poor may also differ. This will be discussed further in Chapter Three.

Some individuals see a major advantage in classifying countries according to stage of development because of its dynamic quality. Others view this classification as a disadvantage because it compares countries according to their stage of development, as though it were a race. On the other hand, this division does not lock a country into a classification because of its unchangeable north or south location. Instead, it provides an impetus for the changes that many seek. Not all people see these changes as desirable, however, and argue that by classifying countries in this way, obtaining the characteristics of the industrialized world is portrayed as the universal goal. Indeed, many people question whether the development process should have only the single goal of becoming like the developed countries. They argue that each country should set its development goals to reflect its own culture.

An economic qualifier is sometimes added to the developed and developing classification, restricting the meaning to economically developed and economically developing. Some complain about this restriction, claiming that many countries held to be in the economically developing group have poor records in human rights or in improving the status of women, for example. They believe that to restrict the classification of countries to economic characteristics alone is unjust to many people living in those countries. Others counter that this view of the importance of human rights and improving the status of women is essentially a Western view. They believe that economically developing nations should have the right to determine their own social and political culture, and that Western standards should not be regarded as the ideal. Still other people question the entire matter of economic development, arguing that the earth lacks the resources, and the earth's environmental systems the capacity, to support continuing economic growth. They propose a process of "undevelopment" or development-denial, and a less technologically driven life for all.

These are significant concerns about economic and human development. Some people fear that economic and human development as has taken place in the developed countries threatens local cultures in the developing world. They question whether the developed countries have any right to influence the manner in which developing countries pursue their own development. Others, including some people in the developing countries, argue that global disparities should be reduced. These matters are examined in more detail in subsequent chapters.

Another argument favouring continued world diversity is that local self-sufficient economies make good ecological sense. This argument contends that such economies must rely upon local

Economics is broadly the study of how humanity organizes itself within the environment for the production of goods and services, and how those goods and services are distributed among society's members. The word has the same root — the Greek *oikos*, meaning house or home — as ecology.

resources, and that in order to survive they must develop practices that sustain the environment. This argument views the trend to globalization as a threat, because globalization links countries together, allowing countries in one part of the world to draw upon resources in another through trade without any regard to the impact on the environment of the originating country. The argument states that the strength of local communities is weakened by globalization, and that the environment is therefore exposed to greater danger.

The political and economic diversity of the world is increased by its social and cultural diversity. For example, there are major differences among world religions in beliefs and practices which are often independent of other differences. Islamic beliefs and practices exist in places as economically and politically different as Saudi Arabia and Bangladesh; Christian beliefs and practices exist in places as economically and politically different as Europe and Sub-Saharan Africa. Other forms of human diversity are broadly ethnic and cultural in type. They include language, custom, skin colour, food, music, and history. Indeed, what are the elements that humanity has in common? What are the elements that make groups distinct? There is continuing debate on all these matters, for the world is a diverse place.

SOURCE: CIDA/John Flanders

Fig. 1-14 *A class of Islamic children. What evidence do the text and the picture offer as to the country where the photograph was taken?*

DISCUSSION AND RESEARCH

6. In detail, Figs. 1-9 to 1-12 illustrate a number of points. For example, in Central America there is a fairly clear distinction between Costa Rica and Panama on the one hand and their neighbours Guatemala and Nicaragua on the other. Similarly, in southeast Asia, Thailand and Malaysia are clearly different from Laos and Cambodia.

    (a)   As a class, suggest possible reasons why such differences might exist between neighbouring countries.

    (b)   Set up an inquiry (see Appendix 3) to verify or reject suggestions relating to any pair of neighbouring but differing countries. Communicate your findings and conclusions in a two-page essay.

7. In small groups, discuss whether or not diversity in the world should be encouraged.

STATISTICAL ANALYSIS

8. Refer to columns 17 and 18 in Appendix 2 at the back of this book. They show the literacy rates for males and females in each country's population. Be aware that these data show basic literacy rates, which indicate ability to read and write a simple sentence. They do not show functional literacy, which is the ability to read and write well enough to perform satisfactorily in the local job market. Since literacy demands in jobs vary even from job to job within the same country, no one has ever been able to define acceptable levels of functional literacy for the world as a whole. There are therefore no data for functional literacy. Nevertheless, overall basic literacy (shown in column 16 of Appendix 2) may be used as a guide to the general level of development within a country. A comparison of male and female literacy rates may also act as an indicator of the level of gender equality that exists within each country.

    (a)   Divide the mappable countries (those without an asterisk) among small class groups. Calculate the percentage of female literacy to male literacy for each country assigned to your group. For example, Afghanistan's rates of 14 percent female literacy to 44 percent male literacy yield a rate of 32 percent female literacy to male literacy.

    (b)   In the manner of Figs. 1-9 to 1-12, plot the 50 countries with the highest percentages on a copy of the world map in Appendix 1. Using a different colour, plot the 50 countries with the lowest percentages. Indicate on the map those countries that do not publish data for columns 17 and 18.

(c) Describe the distribution patterns on your map, and make a comparison with the distribution patterns shown in Figs. 1-9 to 1-13.

(d) Suggest explanations for the disparities between male and female literacy rates.

(e) Select any country with a low percentage of female to male literacy and, from defining the topic to communicating your conclusions, organize an inquiry (see Appendix 3) into the reasons why this situation exists.

(f) In small group discussion, suggest ideas to raise the female literacy rates in those countries where the gap between male and female literacy rates is large.

A GLOBAL VILLAGE

The term "global village" was first coined by Marshall McLuhan in the late 1950s, in response to the growing speed with which different parts of the world could communicate with one another electronically. News could be transmitted around the world almost instantaneously. The moon landings of the late 1960s, and the accompanying photographs of the earth from space, added a further dimension of meaning to the term. It became more apparent that the earth was a finite place, and many people realized that humanity needed to learn to live in harmony with it. The term spaceship earth came to be used by some people to express the idea that we are all passengers together on the earth's journey on its orbit through space. The modern idea, or concept, of a global village encompasses topics addressed in this text such as environmental protection, equality of human development, and a decent and sustainable quality of life for all.

To what extent is the world a global village? The diversity illustrated in the previous section would indicate that it is not one at all. Communication among the different parts of the world may occur more or less instantaneously, but all that may mean is that news of events such as elections, earthquakes, scientific discoveries, and famines are broadcast faster to the rest of the world. Communication may be necessary to produce assistance to people in need, but it does not always do so. People in a position to help are sometimes unwilling or unable to provide assistance. However, communication may alter people's attitudes by opening their eyes and minds to situations of which they would otherwise remain ignorant, and because of this, many people believe that the world will eventually be a global village.

SOURCE: NASA

Fig. 1-15 *One of the first photographs of the earth from space. What does the photograph suggest about how humans can use the moon?*

Canada has signed free trade agreements with other countries, but trade barriers still exist between provinces. According to the Canadian Manufacturers Association, these barriers cost Canadians $6.5 billion each year in higher prices.

Many people who value diversity feel that the creation of a global village need not require world uniformity. Instead, it would require people to live in harmony, to be tolerant of differences, and to trade freely with one another. It would also require that everyone have a universally acceptable quality of life, care for their environment, help others in distress, and share equally in the world's governance.

Currently, many people do not live in harmony: rivalries, jealousies, and hatreds exist, as do wars, revolutions, and barbaric practices such as **genocide**. Examples are numerous, and — because feelings run deep — usually enduring. In Europe, the break-up of Yugoslavia in the early 1990s released ancient hatreds; in India, religious tensions between Hindus and Muslims create frequent hazards. Other examples may be found in today's newspapers.

Neither do people trade freely with each other: national **trade barriers** are commonplace, and trade wars and disputes are typical. At the start of 1993, for example, Japan did not permit imported rice, the United States did not permit imported sugar, and Canada did not permit imported milk. Nor do all people have an acceptable quality of life: poverty, hunger, substandard housing, inadequate medical care, and illiteracy are part of the daily lives of millions of people in all parts of the world.

The global environment is under great stress almost everywhere: while improvements are occurring in some places, in other places people continue to despoil the environmental base. The idea of helping others in distress is accepted to some extent, but the help provided has often in the past been the wrong sort (see Chapter Three for more information about foreign aid), and there is reluctance on the part of some donors to provide continual funding.

The establishment of the United Nations was a move in the direction of universal governance. However, it is plagued by a perpetual shortage of funds, ill-defined membership duties, and the nationalistic tendencies of some of its members. Even so, the United Nations has done much to bring the countries of the world together. Its very existence provides a common meeting ground where nations may interact with each other. Its numerous agencies, such as the World Health Organization (WHO) and the Food and Agriculture Organization (FAO), have been very active in spreading information and assistance, and in bringing experts from different countries together to examine problems of common concern. One example of successful international interaction under the auspices of the United Nations is the elimination of smallpox throughout the world, which has improved the quality of life for millions.

There are those who object to the idea of globalization because they fear a loss of local or national control. They believe that the more integrated a country becomes with a larger group, the more it yields power to the larger group. Many **nationalists** in all countries object to this, preferring to retain as much power as possible within their own nations. Another objection is the ecological view noted at the end of the preceding section, "A Diverse World," that many locally self-sufficient communities form a more sustainable option. Other environmentalists disagree, asserting that humanity needs to realize sooner rather than later that it occupies a single planet. The modern concept of a global village continues as an ideal for many people. However, many issues concerning this concept remain to be resolved.

DISCUSSION AND RESEARCH

9. In small groups:
   (a) Suggest and record the various social, economic, and political features that the world's nations have in common.
   (b) Explore and recommend different methods to promote the concept of a global village among the world's people.

WORLD POPULATION GROWTH: THE FACTS

For many people the most pressing world problem is the current rate of population growth. Opinions about the rate of growth conflict. Some consider it too fast, while others consider it too slow.

Figure 1-16 illustrates the rate of growth of world population since 1840. It is drawn with a logarithmic scale on the vertical axis. (The purpose of logarithmic scales is explained in Appendix 3.) The starting date of 1840 is chosen because it took all of human history until the 1840s for world population to increase by its first billion people. How long did it take for world population to increase by its last billion?

While the future rate of population growth is unknown, the graph makes it easy to suppose that world population will exceed 6 billion by the year 2000, and that it could reach 10 billion by 2020. These assumptions rest on a projection of present trends into the future. Although this may be reasonable to do over the short term, it becomes quite hazardous over the long term. For example, what would trend projections made in

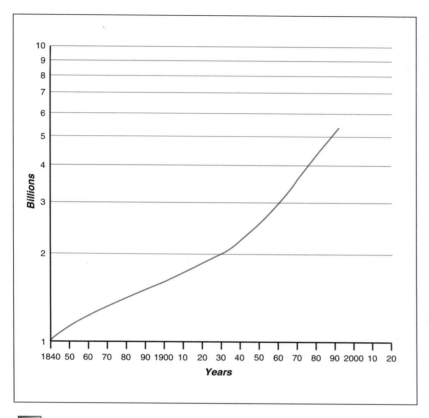

Fig. 1-16 *World population growth, 1840-1992.*

the 1920s have forecast for a total world population in 2000? In any case, circumstances in the future may differ from forecast trends because of changes in collective human behaviours. What sorts of changes do you suppose might cause world population projection trends to go up or down?

The rate of world population growth in the early 1990s was about 1.7 percent per year (1.7%/y), having declined from about 2.0%/y in the 1970s. A rate of 1.7%/y on a base of 5.5 billion means an additional 93 500 000 people per year, which is equivalent to 256 000 per day, or 10 666 per hour. This is almost 180 per minute, or three additional people in the world per second. These additional people are the excess of births over deaths, not just new births.

The annual excess of births over deaths is called the **natural increase** (N.I.), and its rate is measured, like birth and

Because birth, death, and N.I. rates are always quoted per year, the y in the rate is often omitted.

A millennium (pl., millennia) is a period of a thousand years.

death rates, as so many people per year per thousand of existing population. For example, a birth rate of 25 per thousand per year (25/1000/y) coupled with a death rate in the same country of 15/1000/y produces a natural increase rate of 10/1000/y, which translates into a population growth rate of 1.0%/y. A rate of 1.7%/y requires a gap of 17/1000 between birth and death rates, whatever the absolute values of the two rates. The essential component of rapid population growth is therefore that birth rates greatly exceed death rates.

For millennia of human existence, both birth rates and death rates were high (over 40/1000/y) and total population growth was small. At times of widespread plague or famine, total population actually decreased. For example, Europe's population was reduced by about 35 percent during the years of bubonic plague in the 14th century. Because of the general uncertainty of life during these millennia, high birth rates served to ensure human survival. Large numbers of children almost guaranteed that at least two or three would survive into adulthood. Large numbers of children also provided a domestic work force to help in hunting or farming, and they provided a promise of future security as parents grew older. In addition, the only reliable form of birth control was abstinence. For all these reasons, large families were the norm, and the role of women became closely linked to child-bearing and child-raising. Male virility and female fecundity became prized, and belief systems that extolled the value of children became common. Parts of the world where women still have large families are shown in Fig. 1-17.

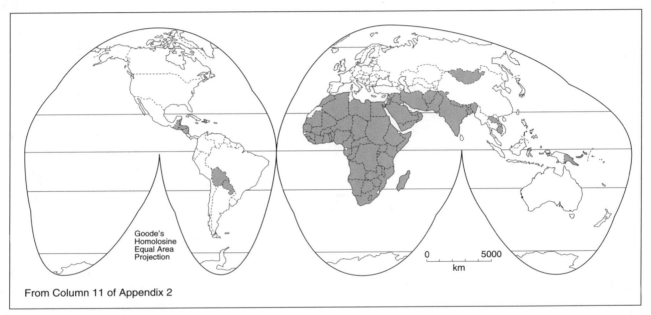

Goode's
Homolosine
Equal Area
Projection

0   5000
      km

From Column 11 of Appendix 2

Fig. 1-17 *Countries reporting a Total Fertility Rate (TFR) of 4.0 or over per woman. TFR is the total number of children that, on average, a woman is expected to have during her life.*

POPULATION GROWTH IN DEVELOPED NATIONS

In Europe in the 18th and 19th centuries prevailing high death rates began to decrease. The chief reasons for the decrease appear to have been improved food supplies, a rising **standard of living**, and medical advances, including better personal and public health facilities. Death rates decreased as more children began to survive into adulthood and fewer women died in childbirth. All in turn produced more children, not only because that was the accepted pattern of behaviour, but also because knowledge of contraception was limited. Death rates accordingly fell sooner and faster than birth rates, and the natural increase gap widened, as shown in Fig. 1-18.

Total population in Europe began to grow rapidly. People moved to newly industrializing cities for work, and nations sought areas abroad for empire-expanding settlement, forcing existing inhabitants off the more desirable lands. Europeans emigrated to various different parts of the world, adding to the populations descended from settlers of the 15th and 16th centuries.

During this period of rapid population growth in Europe, a number of individuals became concerned about population numbers, especially in relation to the ability of the world to support its inhabitants. The best known of these people was Thomas Robert Malthus, an Englishman, who developed a theory that while populations would grow geometrically, food supplies would grow only arithmetically. Thus, over successive periods of

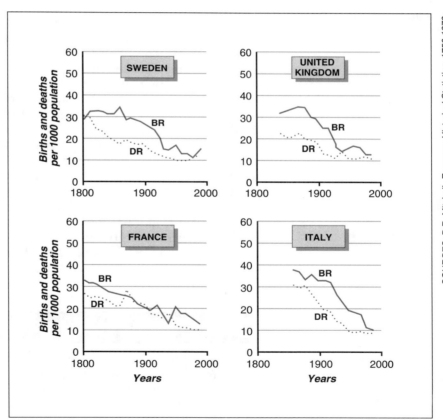

SOURCES: B.R. Mitchell, *European Historical Statistics, 1750-1970*; *World Development Reports*, 1982 and 1992

Fig. 1-18 *Birth and death rates in four European countries, 1800-1990. BR = Birth Rate, DR = Death Rate.*

time, population would grow in each period by a geometric factor of two and food supplies would increase by a factor of only one:

	Periods of time (e.g., generations)				
	A	B	C	D	E
Population (geometric)	1	2	4	8	16
Food Supplies (arithmetic)	1	2	3	4	5

According to Malthus, this situation could not continue for long. There would be no problem during periods A and B, but in period C some people would begin to go hungry. In period D far more people would go hungry, and many would die of starvation. Associated with increasing hunger would be more disease, and a greater risk of social disorder, riots, open warfare, and the overthrow of governments. These factors would increase the number of deaths, which would keep the population in check. This in turn would prevent a period E situation from occurring, and restore a period C or D situation to a period A or B situation.

The situation in the areas settled by European people did not turn out as Malthus had warned. Birth rates began to decline fairly soon after the decline in death rates commenced (see Fig. 1-18). People gradually realized that human survival — as well as their own future security — no longer depended on having large numbers of children. They also realized that machinery could replace child labour quite efficiently. Women in particular realized that their role in life need not be limited by the need to have many children. They began to enter the general work force in increasing numbers; and they began to pursue political and economic rights, as well as equal social and legal status.

As a result of declining birth rates, the gap between birth rates and death rates gradually began to narrow. The natural increase rate slowed correspondingly, and is now less than 10/1000 throughout areas of European settlement. Indeed, in Germany it is zero per thousand, while in Denmark and Hungary it is negative, at -1/1000.

> The factors associated with a relatively high death rate are widely known as the Malthusian checks on population.

DISCUSSION AND RESEARCH

10. Examine Fig. 1-18 and answer the following questions:
    (a) List the similarities and differences among the graphs.
    (b) Identify the country that appears to have the most distinctive demographic history, and research reasons for this distinctiveness.

POPULATION GROWTH IN DEVELOPING NATIONS

Since 1867, when Japan began to pursue economic development along the same lines as Europeans, its demographic characteristics have rapidly become like those of the European nations.

Numbers of indigenous peoples killed by imported European diseases are very uncertain, but estimates run into several millions in Africa and throughout the Americas.

Elsewhere in the world, except for Japan, changes in medical and techno-logical practices were slower to take hold. Medical changes generally came first, adding to, and sometimes replacing, existing practices. The changes accompanied a variety of European missionaries, colonists, traders, and imperial administrators. As they encountered new diseases, Europeans acted quickly to find cures so that they could protect them-selves. These cures were also made available to indigenous peoples because of growing guilt about the large numbers of them killed by dis-eases carried from Europe at the time of first contact. Humanitarian instincts toward those in other nations grew in Europe. The founding of the World Health Organization (WHO) under the United Nations in 1948 greatly expanded the availability of medical assistance over much of the world, and death rates began almost universally to shift downward.

Figure 1-19 shows 1990 death rates as a percentage of 1960 death rates. The map is an example of "graded shading," where the intensity of the shading reflects the intensity of the phenomenon being mapped (see Appendix 3). Countries where the percentage is less than 100 have reduced their death rates, many of them significantly. Countries in the top category (in which 1990 death rates are less than half of 1960 death rates) have made significant progress in reducing death rates. Those in

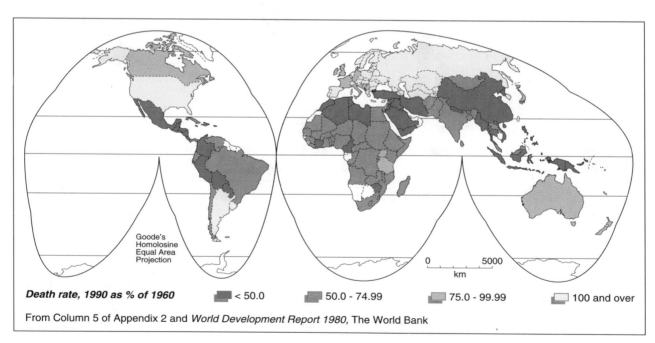

Goode's Homolosine Equal Area Projection

0   5000
km

Death rate, 1990 as % of 1960   ▰ < 50.0   ▰ 50.0 - 74.99   ▰ 75.0 - 99.99   ▱ 100 and over

From Column 5 of Appendix 2 and *World Development Report 1980*, The World Bank

 Fig. 1-19 *Death rate changes: 1990 death rates as a percentage of 1960 death rates.*

the second category (where 1990 death rates are from one-half to three-quarters of 1960 death rates) have also made good progress. Note that in several countries (those in the over 100% class), death rates increased from 1960 to 1990.

As in Europe almost two centuries earlier, and for very similar reasons, birth rates failed to decline as quickly or as soon as death rates. Indeed, in some countries birth rates remained stable or even rose between 1960 and 1990. These countries are shown in Fig. 1-20 as having 1990 birth rates that are 100% or more of 1960 birth rates. All other countries reduced their birth rates from 1960 to 1990, but in varying degrees. The smallest percentage reductions occurred generally in the Arabian peninsula and tropical Africa, whereas the largest reductions occurred in Thailand and South Korea (along with Singapore and Hong Kong, which are too small to map).

Several countries experiencing rising birth rates are in Africa; some Africans claim that one reason for this trend is the repopulation of their continent after losses caused by European diseases and slave raids.

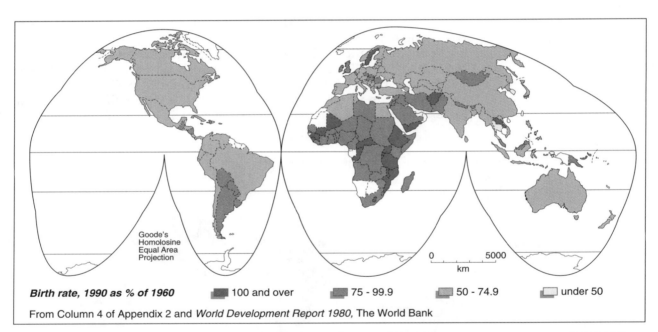

Birth rate, 1990 as % of 1960   ■ 100 and over   ■ 75 - 99.9   ■ 50 - 74.9   □ under 50

Goode's Homolosine Equal Area Projection

From Column 4 of Appendix 2 and *World Development Report 1980*, The World Bank

Fig. 1-20 *Birth rate changes: 1990 birth rates as a percentage of 1960 birth rates.*

Comparison of the rates of change between birth and death rates (see Fig. 1-21) shows that only in the economically developed world did birth rates fall faster than death rates from 1960 to 1990. Everywhere else, death rates fell faster than birth rates, generally causing a widening natural increase gap to appear. In several of these countries, such as Uganda, Afghanistan, and Laos, birth rates increased, widening the natural increase gap still further.

Accordingly, much of south and east Asia, the Arabian peninsula, Africa, and Central and South America began to experience high rates

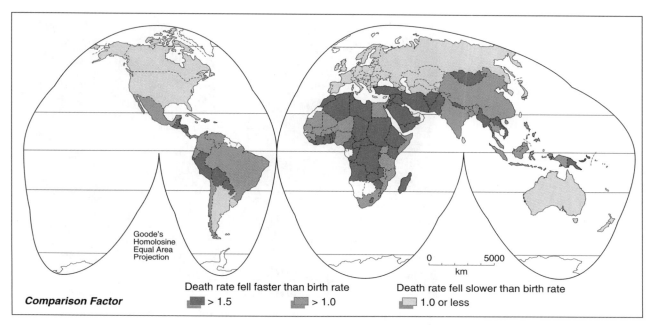

Fig. 1-21 *Comparison of birth rate changes, 1960-1990, and death rate changes, 1960-1990.*

of population growth. Because populations in countries such as China, India, Pakistan, Indonesia, and Bangladesh were already large to start with, the annual additions were also very large, and the term population explosion became commonly used to describe the world's population growth. Several countries eventually established programs to try to reduce birth rates, to speed up a process similar to what had happened in Europe more or less spontaneously a century before.

However, the overall situations were not identical. Europeans had been industrializing at the same time, providing many jobs in cities for extra workers. Europeans were also able to use their overseas empires to accommodate extra people, and to provide access to vast additional resources. As a consequence, Europeans generally had a rising material standard of living. By contrast, many countries with rapidly increasing populations in the second half of the 20th century remained largely rural and agricultural. Jobs were scarce and overseas safety valves did not exist, except as immigration was permitted by host countries. As a result, poverty for millions continued. Children were still needed for work in most of these countries because mechanization was slight. They were also needed for old age security. The conditions for a spontaneous decline in birth rates either did not exist or were coming into existence too slowly for many national governments to accept. Family planning programs aimed at limiting the total number of births therefore became widespread. China eventually instituted a "One Child" policy; India established a "Two is Enough" policy.

What other reasons can you suggest for people continuing to have many children in countries with increasing populations?

SOURCE: Saskatchewan Government Photograph

Fig. 1-22 *This photograph of a Saskatchewan wheat farm illustrates how machinery displaces the need for human labour. The land is often described as one of the world's "bread-baskets." What does this mean?*

Birth rates in Europe took many years to fall from even the 30s to the mid-teens per thousand (e.g., U.K. 35/1000 in 1870, 16/1000 in 1970; France 32/1000 in 1820, 17/1000 in 1970). Similar — and even greater — declines were achieved in the 30-year period from 1960 to 1990 by Hong Kong (35 to 13), Singapore (38 to 17), South Korea (41 to 16), and Thailand (46 to 22).

Gradually, birth rates have begun generally to fall and the natural increase gap to narrow, but the progression is uneven across a diverse world. For example, Malawi's birth rate in 1960 was 53/1000; in 1990 it was still high at 54/1000. Conversely, Bangladesh reduced its rate from 51/1000 in 1960 to 35/1000 in 1990. Over the same time period, China cut its rate from 36/1000 to 22/1000 and India reduced its rate from 43/1000 to 30/1000. Peak growth rates of over 2%/y occurred in the 1960s and early 1970s, but the rate has fallen slowly since 1974, and in 1992 was about 1.7%/y.

However, a declining growth rate does not necessarily mean fewer additions to total population each year. In 1960, world population was about 3 billion, and the annual growth rate was 2%/y. There were thus 60 000 000 additional people by 1961. Although the annual growth rate in 1992 was down to 1.7%/y, the base population had risen to 5.5 billion, so there were 93 500 000 additional people by 1993. If the growth rate in 1992 had still been 2%/y, however, there would have been 110 000 000 additional people by 1993 instead. A lower growth rate reduces population increases from what they would otherwise have been.

When one generation has exactly enough children to replace itself in the next generation, it is sometimes called a replacement level of fertility.

Only a zero rate (called zero population growth) will produce a stable population. This may be achieved when the average number of daughters a newborn girl will bear during her lifetime is 1.0, exactly sufficient to replace herself. This figure is called the Net Reproduction Rate (NRR), and it measures the extent to which a group of newborn

SOURCE: CIDA/Pat Morrow

Fig. 1-23 *China's "One Child" policy has come under criticism for many reasons, but it has often meant that the one child each couple is permitted is valued very highly. Such children are sometimes called "Little Emperors." Why are they called this?*

girls will replace themselves in the future. If the NRR rises above 1.0, the population will grow; if it falls below 1.0, the population will decline.

POPULATION GROWTH: THE FUTURE

In a number of countries, death rates have recently risen. Such countries are almost all in Europe, but also include Uruguay and South Korea. Rising death rates are chiefly a function of an ageing population. When the age structure of a population changes to one with a relatively large proportion of older people from one with a relatively large proportion of children (see Fig. 1-24), the number of people dying each year becomes an ever larger proportion of the total population, and the death rate rises correspondingly. The age structure of a population is usually shown by what is called a population pyramid, which also shows the proportions of males and females in each age group. Figure 1-25 shows two population pyramids for Canada, one as it existed in 1851 and the other in 1991.

Note that the population pyramid for Canada in 1851 is quite different in shape from the 1991 pyramid. In 1851, the base was wide, indicating a high proportion of children. Indeed, over 18% of the population was aged under 5 years, while about 45% was aged under 15 years. The Canadian birth rate in the mid-19th century was clearly high. Conversely, older people formed only a small proportion of the

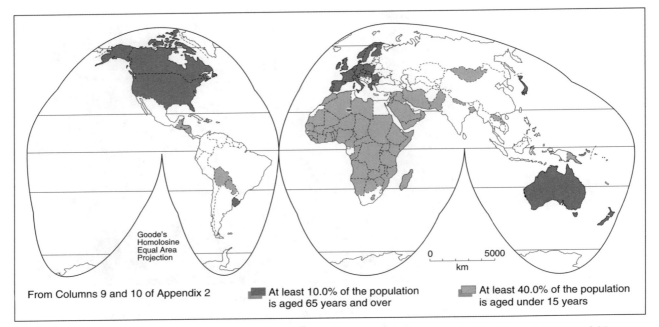

Goode's Homolosine Equal Area Projection

From Columns 9 and 10 of Appendix 2

At least 10.0% of the population is aged 65 years and over

At least 40.0% of the population is aged under 15 years

Fig. 1-24 *Countries with at least ten percent of their population aged 65 years and over and those with at least 40 percent of their population aged under 15 years.*

total population, suggesting that the death rate was relatively low. In fact, in 1851 the birth rate in Canada was about 47/1000 and the death rate was about 24/1000, figures which are not dissimilar from those of Sierra Leone in 1992 (birth rate 47/1000; death rate 22/1000). However, as a reflection of the improved medical assistance which led to world-wide death rate reductions in the second half of the 20th century, it is worth noting that no country in the world in 1992 had a death rate as high as 24/1000. Sierra Leone's death rate was the highest.

The 1991 pyramid for Canada typifies population structures throughout much of the economically developed world. In comparison with the 1851 pyramid, it shows a relatively narrow base, reflecting low birth rates, and a much larger proportion of older people, suggesting a likelihood of increasing death rates. Indeed, as was noted earlier, death rates have already begun to rise in several countries.

There has been sufficient similarity in the overall trends of birth rates and death rates in many countries to popularize use of the demographic transition model (see Fig. 1-26). Initially, in phase 1, both birth and death rates are fairly high, the natural increase gap is small, and populations grow slowly. In phase 2, death rates decline; but birth rates do not decline at the same time; the natural increase gap becomes larger, and populations grow more rapidly. Eventually,

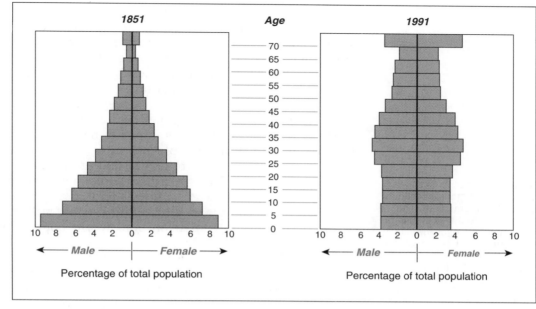

SOURCES: 1851 pyramid, Urquhart and Buckley, *Historical Statistics of Canada*; 1991 pyramid, Statistics Canada

Fig. 1-25 *Population pyramids for Canada, 1851 and 1991.*

Birth rates have not always declined; in some countries they have risen. Such countries are said to be in the "demographic trap": rapid population growth presses ever harder on resources, living standards and quality of life fall, and people never reach the stage of wanting fewer children.

birth rates also begin to decline, marking the start of phase 3. The natural increase gap starts to narrow, and population growth begins to slow. Phase 4 begins when birth rates come close to death rates again, but this time at a low level. Natural increase becomes small, and population grows slowly.

Phase 5 in Fig. 1-26 is an extension of the usual four-phase demographic transition model. It is marked by rising death rates as the population ages, to the extent that death rates exceed birth rates. The natural increase rate is inverted to a natural loss rate, and population begins to decline. Denmark and Hungary already appear to be in phase 5, with Austria, Bulgaria, Germany, Italy, and South Korea very close. These five countries all have annual natural increase rates of 1/1000 or 0/1000.

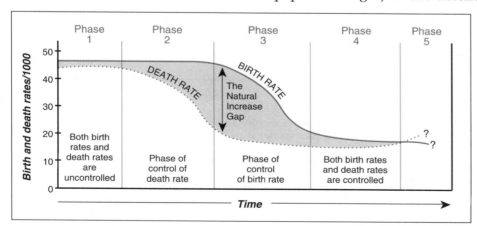

Fig. 1-26 *The demographic transition model.*

The length of time it takes for a country to pass through the demographic transition helps to determine the size of the phase 4 population relative to the phase 1 population. An extended duration of phases 2 and 3 produces a larger total population than a relatively brief duration of phases 2 and 3. A long period of time in phase 2 has the largest impact on the size of the final population. If the population in phase 1 is large to begin with, the phase 4 population will be much larger. For example, the total impact on world population of China's 15/1000 natural increase rate is over 17 million additional people per year, whereas Pakistan's much higher natural increase rate of 30/1000 produces "only" 3.5 million additional people. The world's highest natural increase rate (in Oman, 38/1000) produces as few as 55 000 additional people. Large or small, these and many other countries are still in phases 2 and 3 of the demographic transition, and world population looks set to continue growing for at least several more years.

It is impossible to say when world population will stop growing, or just how large it will be at that time. Estimates vary widely depending upon the sorts of assumptions that are made about future human behaviours. For example, the **World Bank** in its *World Development Report 1992* provides three estimates using three different sets of assumptions. These estimates of future world population size and date of stabilization vary from stabilization in 2100 at about 10 billion to stabilization at a population of 23 billion toward the end of the 22nd century. Details are shown in Fig. 1-27.

A built-in tendency for a population to grow is called population momentum. The term refers to the existence of large numbers of children in the age structure of the population. Thus, even if current birth rates fall sigtnificantly, the existing children will be having children themselves in 15-20 years time, so that the total population will increase.

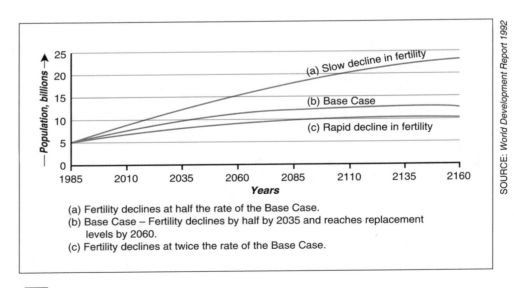

(a) Fertility declines at half the rate of the Base Case.
(b) Base Case – Fertility declines by half by 2035 and reaches replacement levels by 2060.
(c) Fertility declines at twice the rate of the Base Case.

SOURCE: *World Development Report 1992*

Fig. 1-27 *World population projections under different fertility trends, 1985-2160.*

STATISTICAL ANALYSIS

11. (a) Using the data in Fig. 1-28 and the information in the preceding section on population pyramids for Canada in 1851 and 1991, arrange the countries into order from an early stage of demographic transition to a later stage.

(b) Using the section on population pyramids in Appendix 3, construct population pyramids for the countries shown. Include with each pyramid a short written analysis of its main features.

Age in years	A Barbados Male	A Barbados Female	B Ecuador Male	B Ecuador Female	C Italy Male	C Italy Female	D Libya Male	D Libya Female	E Thailand Male	E Thailand Female	Age
70	3.4	4.9	0.9	1.2	3.6	5.8	0.6	0.7	0.9	1.3	70
65	1.3	1.8	0.7	0.8	1.9	2.4	0.5	0.5	0.7	0.8	65
60	1.4	1.9	0.9	1.0	2.6	3.0	0.7	0.7	1.1	1.2	60
55	1.5	2.0	1.1	1.2	2.9	3.1	1.0	0.9	1.4	1.5	55
50	1.6	2.0	1.4	1.5	3.0	3.2	1.3	1.2	1.7	1.8	50
45	1.8	2.1	1.7	1.8	3.2	3.3	1.6	1.5	2.0	2.0	45
40	2.3	2.6	2.2	2.2	3.2	3.2	1.9	1.8	2.4	2.4	40
35	3.3	3.4	2.8	2.8	3.4	3.4	2.4	2.2	3.1	3.1	35
30	4.2	4.3	3.4	3.3	3.4	3.4	2.8	2.6	3.9	3.9	30
25	4.9	4.9	4.0	4.0	3.9	3.8	3.4	3.2	4.6	4.5	25
20	5.1	5.2	4.8	4.7	4.3	4.2	4.1	3.9	5.4	5.2	20
15	4.8	4.8	5.4	5.3	4.1	3.9	5.5	5.3	5.6	5.4	15
10	4.4	4.4	6.0	5.9	3.7	3.5	6.8	6.6	5.7	5.5	10
5	4.1	4.1	6.9	6.6	2.9	2.7	8.1	7.9	5.8	5.7	5
0	3.9	3.8	7.9	7.6	2.6	2.4	10.3	10.0	5.8	5.6	0

SOURCE: U.N. Demographic Yearbook, 1990

Fig. 1-28 *Age and sex data for five countries. Note: All figures are percentages of total population.*

12. National birth and death rates are given in columns 4 and 5 of Appendix 2.

(a) Divide into class groups, with each group responsible for assessing the demographic phase for a certain number of countries. Share your assessments with other groups. Countries in phase 2 may be recognized by a combination of a birth rate of 40/1000 or more and a death rate below 40/1000. Countries in phase 3 have a birth rate over 20/1000 but under 40/1000, and a death rate below 40/1000.

(b) On a photocopy of the world map in Appendix 1, construct a graded shading world map to show those countries experiencing phases 2 and 3 of the demographic transition. (Refer to the section on graded shading in Appendix 3.) Use a strong bright colour for phase 2 countries, and a paler version of the same colour for phase 3 countries. Which of the previous maps printed in the text is your map most similar to? Explain why this is so.

Fig. 1-29
Populations of selected countries, 1960 and 1990.

	Population	
	1960	*1990*
Brazil	70 967 000	152 505 000
China	650 000 000	1 133 683 000
Egypt	28 721 000	54 706 000
India	439 073 000	849 746 000
Indonesia	97 085 000	190 136 000
Italy	50 464 000	57 664 000
Japan	93 419 000	123 643 000
Mexico	34 923 000	87 870 000
Nigeria	55 654 000	118 819 000
Portugal	8 889 000	10 354 000
United States	179 323 000	248 710 000
Zimbabwe	3 849 000	10 392 000

SOURCES: *Statesman's Year Book 1966; World Development Report 1992*

13. Figure 1-29 shows the populations of a number of countries in different parts of the world for 1960 and 1990.
    (a) Refer to the section on rates of change in Appendix 3, and calculate the average annual percentage growth rate for each country in Fig. 1-29 during the period 1960 to 1990.
    (b) Compare these 1960-90 average rates with the projected rates for the same countries for 1990 to 2000, shown in column 7 of Appendix 2.
    (c) Devise a method of showing for each of these countries the degree of change from its 1960-90 average rate to its projected 1990-2000 rate.
    (d) Rank the countries in order from most change to least change. Note that not all countries have changed in the same direction. What general conclusions can you draw?

14. India's population (see Fig. 1-29) grew from 439 073 000 in 1960 to 849 746 000 in 1990.
    (a) Using your answer from Question 13 about India's average annual rate of increase from 1960 to 1990, calculate, by compounding the growth from 1990 onwards, the year in which India would reach a population of one billion if it maintained the same average annual growth rate.

    (b) As shown in column 7 of Appendix 2, India's growth rate from 1990 to 2000 is projected at 1.7%/y. Given this projected growth rate, calculate the year in which India's population will reach one billion.

(c) In the year 2000, how many fewer people will India have if the 1.7%/y growth rate replaces the average 1960-90 rate?

15. The Rule of 72 is a formula for determining how many years a population will take to double its present size. The formula is $d = 72/i$, where d is the number of years for doubling to occur, 72 is the formula constant, and i is the average annual percentage rate of increase. For example, if a country maintains an average annual rate of population increase of 0.8, then the doubling time (d) is 90 years ($d = 72/0.8$).

    (a) By using the Rule of 72 and the projected population growth rates in column 7 of Appendix 2, divide into class groups and calculate the projected doubling times for the mappable countries (those without an asterisk).

    (b) Use a photocopy of the map in Appendix 1 to draw a graded shading world map. Shade most brightly those countries which are projected to double their existing populations (shown in column 2 of Appendix 2) in less than 25 years. Shade lightly those countries which are projected to double their populations within 25-50 years.

    (i) Describe the pattern on the map.

    (ii) Analyze the relationship that exists between your map and those printed previously in the text.

WORLD POPULATION GROWTH: THE OPINIONS

The following readings present a variety of different views about the topic of population growth. As you read through them, make two lists: one of the arguments and views in favour of growth; the second of the arguments and views opposed to growth.

THE SOFT UNDERBELLY OF DEVELOPMENT: DEMOGRAPHIC TRANSITION IN CONDITIONS OF LIMITED ECONOMIC CHANGE

Fertility is falling in at least some parts of all other world regions, and the question arises as to whether in some way Africa is different. Caldwell and Caldwell, in a series of works originating in the Changing African Family Project and the Nigerian Family Study, argued that Africa is different. Because religion and family economics mutually reinforced the demand for high fertility, Africa is probably the most **pronatalist** of the world's regions. Lineage structure, especially in West Africa, is represented in terms of religion by the cult of the ancestors, who intervene in this life and who favour high fertility. The usual return from children that traditional societies offer to parents is reinforced by feelings of guilt, and even fear, if filial duties are not adequately performed. One reflection of pronatalism has been the deep horror of barrenness, which led to the ill-treatment of barren women and to a dread among women of either having no children or of becoming childless through the death of all their children. Our study of all women in Ibadan City in 1973 who were completing their family size and had intentionally and successfully restricted that family to fewer than six children showed that they were subject to enormous pressures from their relatives to prevent them from acting in this way and risking becoming childless through the death of all their children. The result was that only 1.3 percent of women had taken this risk, the majority of whom had broken with their husbands and husbands' families as a result. It is of interest to note that, in fact, they had experienced unusually low mortality among their children, as apparently has been the case in one-child families in China, doubtless in both cases because of the extra care parents have shown because of their fear of **child mortality**.

This pervasive fear persists in Africa despite the fact that infant mortality has already fallen below 100 per 1000, the level reached in Northwest Europe when fertility transition had already reduced the total fertility rate to little over half

SOURCE: CIDA/Bruce Paton

Fig. 1-30 *Women working the land with hoes in Zimbabwe. What does this suggest about the roles of men and women in the economy?*

that currently found in Africa, and that of France to one-third of that currently found in Africa. The onset of the French fertility decline occurred at an infant mortality rate about 300 per 1000. The evidence is that despite the levels attained by such socioeconomic indicators as education or income, the mortality threshold for fertility decline in Sub-Saharan Africa will be well below that of other regions. Perhaps infant mortality levels of 50 to 70 per 1000 will be required, with no more than 10 percent of all births resulting in deaths by five years of age. These are levels that few countries are projected to reach before the year 2000 and that many will reach much later. The fear of barrenness also appears as a fear of wishing for barrenness after any particular age by denying wanting any more children. This explains the uniquely small proportion of women at

any parity (i.e., no matter how many children they had previously borne) in recent surveys who said they wanted no more.

There are other factors in the persistence of high fertility in the region. Land has traditionally been communal and cultivated with digging sticks and hoes so that, although investment was difficult or impossible in land or farming equipment, it was possible in farm labor, usually acquired by marriage or reproduction. The lineage implies shared responsibility for the costs of children. Indeed, massive fostering of children in West Africa means that there is little relationship between reproductive decisions and reproductive economic burdens. The willingness to foster in can be taken as evidence that there is no economic loss in having children. This is compounded in West Africa for fathers by the fact that, although men and their families of origin control fertility decision making and certainly the decision to cease childbearing, mothers bear the burden of most day-to-day costs. In a polygynous (polygamous) society there is a certain logic in each woman and her children forming a separate economic unit....

The right of the patrilineage to make fertility decisions is paid for by bride-wealth (a payment at marriage from the bridegroom's family to the bride's family). Thus men can make reproductive decisions with little extra economic burden in raising the children and with a resulting near certainty of support in old age (and earlier). This is a guaranteed recipe for high fertility. It might be expected that the position of women would be very different, but this is not so. Because of the weakness of the spousal economic bond, women become increasingly dependent on their children, and few feel safe without a considerable number. Thus, the majority of women, even with very large families, tell survey interviewers that they want more children. A deep fear of terminal barrenness — or at least of expressing a desire for it — means that very few women state that they want no more children.

John C. Caldwell, *Proceedings of the World Bank Annual Conference on Development Economics 1990*, The World Bank, 1991

'FEWER CHILDREN — FEWER BURDENS'

Officials at the United Nations estimate China may reach the frightening and virtually unmanageable population mark of 2 billion as early as the year 2030.

That news has set alarm bells ringing all over China and triggered a massive new propaganda campaign to try to limit the nation's population.

Right now, China contains 22 per cent of the world's people but occupies only 7 percent of its arable land. And population pressures are destroying that limited resource at a rate of 670 000 hectares a year.

"If we don't do something to control our population, China will become so much poorer," says He Jun, director of Chongqing's municipal Family Planning Commission.

"People in the West don't understand that," she adds. "But it's like pollution. It's not just China's problem. It affects the whole world."

In Chongqing, a major industrial city in Sichuan, China's most populous province, a baby is born every three minutes.

The strains that sort of growth places on the country are enormous, threatening Communist planners with massive food shortages, soaring demands for health care and housing, socially destabilizing unemployment, overburdened public transport and a rapidly deteriorating environment.

Population experts here estimate each new person in China will ultimately consume more than 400 kilograms of grain annually, forcing the country's already strained agricultural community to produce an extra 6 billion kilograms of grain each year.

China's staggering economy also has to create 15 million new jobs each year to cope with its swelling labour force.

Recently, the Beijing-based newspaper, *Economic Daily*, estimated 20 percent of China's annual increase in national income is being devoured by "excessive births."

"In 1987, 48.5 percent of the country's increased grain output; 45.6 percent of its increased meat output; 35 percent of its new hospital beds and 30.7 percent of its new housing space in urban areas was taken up by increased population," the newspaper said.

"If our (birth control) targets are significantly breached, there will be no hope for national modernization," the newspaper warned.

China's population pressures are so great the government already refuses to provide coal to heat the homes of people living south of the Yangtze River during the winter.

In the industrial coastal city of Tanjin, near Beijing, city officials have recently taken to holding mass burials at sea to avoid devoting any more land to graveyards.

Even more threatening to planners in Beijing, however, is the fact China's soaring birth rate is not simply the result of ignorance or mathematics. Frequently, it is an act of defiance, a deliberate rejection of Communist Party policy by increasingly assertive young people who are unwilling to accept state interference in their private lives.

Last year, nearly nine million of China's babies (one-third of the total) were born outside the restrictions of the one-child policy, which requires couples to seek permission to have a baby from their employers and party-controlled neighborhood committees a full year in advance of every birth.

Under China's family planning laws, each province and city is awarded a yearly quota for the number of births and work units; neighborhood committees decide who gets the right to reproduce.

Coercion underlies the policy; local officials rely heavily on a system of strict penalties and rewards to enforce their rationing.

• • • • •

In cases where families refuse to practise birth control, they can have their water and power supplies cut off by a neighborhood committee.

If a woman becomes pregnant out of turn, by accident or by design, she can be subjected to day and night visits by local officials and neighbors enlisted to urge her to have an abortion.

One in three pregnancies in China ends in abortion, a rate more than double that of Canada.

When a couple does give birth to an unapproved child, the family can be severely punished.

Urban workers, employed in state-run factories, can lose their jobs or be fined up to 15 percent of the couple's combined salaries for the next 14 years.

Doctors and neighborhood committees also often refuse to provide parents expecting an unauthorized child with the certificate they need to receive free medical care in a hospital.

In rural areas, parents are told unauthorized children will never be allotted farm land. Everywhere, unapproved children lose their rights to school and health care **subsidies**.

By contrast, couples who sign a contract with the state agreeing to have only one child can benefit from yearly cash bonuses equal to about one-third of an average worker's monthly pay. They can also receive tax reductions, a bigger food subsidy, longer maternity leave, more farm land and improved housing opportunities.

Despite an annual budget of $1.2 billion, a staff of 190 000 family planners and 13 million neighborhood volunteers, China's birth control program is consistently failing to meet its targets.

Enforcement of the one-child policy succeeds mainly in the cities, where party workers use household registration, food subsidies and the threat of a lost job to ration reproduction. But in the countryside, where 80 percent of China's population lives, birth rates are still climbing.

The Communist Party finds itself in a bind. If it fails to reduce China's birth rate, its plans for economic expansion will collapse. If it rigidly enforces birth control in rural areas, it risks alienating China's massive peasant population. And if it fails to bring rural birth rates down, it will fuel the resentment of urban residents who already feel farm families are being allowed "to buy" more children, while they themselves are subjected to increasingly unpopular and intrusive state control.

"We simply have to go on telling people they have to change their ideas," says He, of the Chongqing Family Planning Commission. "We must try our best to convince people that more children and big families are harmful to the quality of their life."

Peter Goodspeed, *The Toronto Star*, 1991 1 11

WORLD POPULATION: PROGRESS IN SLOWING THE INCREASE IN PEOPLE ON THE EARTH IS CRITICAL TO FINDING SOLUTIONS FOR GLOBAL PROBLEMS IN THE 21ST CENTURY

"There's no question that population growth is eventually going to come to a halt," says Stanford University demographer Paul Erlich. "The question is whether it's going to end because we manage to humanely lower birthrates or because we exceed the earth's **carrying capacity**."

The fact that most of today's 5 billion people have escaped famine is credited partly to the **green revolution** that started in the 1960s. The dramatic increases in world food production that resulted from breakthroughs in plant technology, irrigation, and farm management are a hint, say some economists, of the limitless possibilities offered by technology and human ingenuity to keep up with the needs of an expanding world population.

But as the growth in human numbers rolls relentlessly past the finite productivity of the green revolution, the future seems less promising. Since the mid-1980s, increases in food production in some regions have fallen behind population growth. In the poorer nations of Latin America, harvest deficits have been widening for a decade. In Sub-Saharan Africa, which was once self-sufficient in agriculture, food production is growing at only half the rate of population, leaving an estimated one-third of the continent undernourished.

· · · · ·

Population growth has also contributed to the worsening poverty that now affects hundreds of millions of people living in Africa, Asia, and Latin America.

Many economists and demographers warn that population growth combined with inefficient agriculture, inappropriate government policies, and outdated technologies has brought the world to critical thresholds of sustainability. Demographers point to the contribution of relentless population growth to deforestation, overgrazing, and the degradation of the very agricultural lands needed to sustain such growth.

Finding solutions to the global problems that will dominate the agenda of the 21st century will be nearly impossible without progress on the population front.

George D. Moffett III, *The Christian Science Monitor*, 1992 7 10-16

SEX, LIES AND GLOBAL SURVIVAL

"'The earth is being murdered,'" experts say. "And population growth is the culprit." Our investigator Anuradha Vittachi has her doubts. And sure enough, when she sets out in search of the truth she finds her trail blighted by lies, alibis and false accusations.

Population paranoia is rife. During the recent Earth Summit in Rio (international conference on the environment, 1992) every newspaper I opened, every television news bulletin I watched, every journal that landed on my desk, seemed to have someone's views on population and its relationship to the environment. Most blamed the South, some blamed the North, some thought each was a bit to blame. Everyone had a particular axe to grind. Awash with contradictory information, it seemed to me high time to sort out for myself some firm ground on which to stand.

It's an issue I have wanted to think out for many years. I knew myself to hold confused and contradictory responses. I couldn't help noticing my disapproving feelings when I heard of acquaintances being pregnant with their fifth or sixth child. These weren't villagers who needed to have many children for survival's sake. They were people who lived in affluent countries or were from the affluent classes of the developing world. So what was their excuse? But then, why should they need an excuse?

I also believed...in the human right of every parent to choose if and when to have children. Did I now think that population growth was such a heavyweight problem that it overrode the sanctity of this particular human right? Or was "overpopulation" not really a problem at all, but merely an excuse by people who didn't want to give up their addiction to over-consuming?

My own confusions were reflected in the conflicting views being offered to me. On April 30 this year, the UK's *Daily Mail* chose to report the UN's views on population in a front-page story under the sensationalist headline, "The Human Time Bomb." The story began:

The world is on the brink of a population catastrophe, a chilling United Nations report warned yesterday. Unless immediate action is taken to control the spiralling numbers, the very future of humanity is at risk as the planet's resources are swamped. The growth will take place almost entirely in the Third World, where poverty is already rife.

So rapid population growth stood accused — apparently with UN authority — of being the potential murderer of all humanity. And it was firmly identified with the developing world and its poverty; population growth in the industrialized world was not presented as an issue.

Writer Gore Vidal put it like this: "Think of the earth as a living organism that is being attacked by billions of bacteria whose numbers double every 40 years. Either the host dies, or the virus dies, or both die. That seems to be what we are faced with." But by no means all population experts agree. Dr Barry Commoner, U.S. environmentalist, states firmly that: "The theory that environmental degradation is largely due to population growth is not supported by the data." And Edward Goldsmith, one of the founders of the ecology movement in the U.K., told me categorically last week,

"Population is not the fundamental problem."

Other experts have it both ways: they assert a belief in the human right of a parent to decide "freely" how many children to have as long as the parent behaves "responsibly." But they don't say who has the right to decide the nature of that responsibility: the parent — or a coercive bureaucrat from a government or a birth control agency who thinks she or he knows how a parent should behave.

Why has population become such a hot issue? Now that an ecological crisis of global survival looms near, rising panic in the North is strengthening the arm of the anti-populationists — those who believe that reducing population growth as soon as possible is the solution to the world's problems. The further threat of a flood of refugees from the South is adding to that paranoia.

· · · · ·

Does it really matter whether or not population is pinpointed as the fundamental problem? Yes — because if it turns out not to be the real source of the global ecological crisis, then as long as we are distracted by it the real culprit is free to escape.

Finding the real culprit is not only a matter of practical urgency but of justice. Dr Maurice King, Professor in Public Health at the University of Leeds, recently advised against the introduction of

SOURCE: CIDA/Robert Semeniuk

Fig. 1-31 *World issues such as population growth could affect the very survival of children such as these from a Cambodian village.*

public health measures like oral rehydration therapy (ORT). This is a simple concoction of salt, sugar and water used to save small children from dying of diarrhoea — and diarrhoea is the biggest single killer of under-fives, causing the deaths of between four and five million small children each year. King's argument for denying the children this remedy was that they would "increase the man-years of misery." In other words, we shouldn't offer these humanitarian remedies to save the lives of children in poor areas, for if they survived that would create more population growth, which in turn would bring about a quicker descent into ecological catastrophe.

Should we perceive these small children, then, as the destroyers of the planet? If King's accusation turns out to be wrong, the affluent in the North will have victimized these Southern children twice over: first by contributing to the poverty they are born into and second by wrongly representing them as the source of the environmental crisis.

And what we are dealing with here is not just a theoretical change of perception but a spur to policy changes that have life-and-death implications for millions of small girls and boys.

Anuradha Vittachi, *New Internationalist*, 1992 9

POPE DECRIES FALL IN BIRTHS

FERRARA, Italy — Pope John Paul II called yesterday on Western nations to reverse their falling birth rates, a phenomenon he described as a "menace."

The Polish pontiff, visiting a north-central Italian city that has lost almost 5 percent of its population in the past quarter-century, described the declining birth rate of the industrialized West as "worrying."

John Paul called the decline in births "a menace for all of the rich West."

"Faith feeds optimism, a sentiment which is growing scarce in the Western world. Society is getting older and there are few babies being born.

"How can there be hope for a better future without children?" he said to a crowd of several thousand. "We cannot watch with indifference the worrying phenomenon of the constant fall of the population."

UPI, 1990 9 23

A DANGEROUS GAME: THE IMPACT OF POPULATION GROWTH AND INCREASING CARBON COMBUSTION ON THE ATMOSPHERE

Since the discovery of fire, carbon combustion — whether in the form of wood, coal, oil, or natural gas burning — has been the main source of energy for humanity. Up until the time of the Industrial Revolution, fuelwood was the principal source of combustion-generated energy for a global population of approximately 800 million, with coal also used to some extent. Since that time, there has been a significant shift to the use of **fossil fuels** for energy, and an enormous global increase in the amount of carbon combustion to satisfy human energy needs.

Table 1 (Fig. 1-32) shows the gaseous products of carbon combustion. Some of these gases are also generated by practices involving carbon combustion but are unrelated to energy extraction — for example, slash-and-burn farming or burning tropical forests to clear land for agriculture. Non-combustion sources are also significant: landfill sites, rice paddies, and cattle all release methane, while nitrogen-based fertilizers release nitrous oxide.

These gases remain in the atmosphere in a balance that is maintained by geological and biological processes. Through geological studies of gases trapped in ice bubbles from polar ice caps and sediments from the ocean floor, we know that the composition of the atmosphere and the average global temperature have altered over time. Some of the atmospheric gases — carbon dioxide, methane, and nitrous oxide — are heat-trapping **greenhouse gases**;...studies have determined that the average global temperature has varied directly with concentrations of these gases. In turn, the concentrations appear to vary according to the amount of sunlight that the Earth receives, and that amount fluctuates with slight cyclical changes in the Earth's orbit around the sun, over periods of 20 000 to 100 000 years.

In addition to the greenhouse gases, the oxides of nitrogen and sulphur combine with water vapour to form acids, and increase the regional acidity of precipitation. The result is damage to the fauna and flora of lakes and forests, and currently even to human constructions.

We now see changes in the composition of the atmosphere occurring in response to human activities....global population, oil consumption, and reactive atmospheric gases are all increasing. In the Canadian province of Ontario, not only are there more households, but each household is using more than six times as much electricity as in 1941. This consumption has increased arithmetically, but in Brazil — as in most developing nations — the demand for electrical power is expanding exponentially (by a fixed percentage). Increasing suburbanization of the cities and the phenomenal growth of travel and tourism are but two of the factors contributing to the use of fossil fuels for transportation. As the cities have sprawled, mass transit ridership has decreased in the United States. At the same time, the con-

TABLE 1			GASES		
Source	Carbon dioxide	Carbon monoxide	Methane	Nitrogen oxides	Sulphur oxides
Coal	yes	yes	yes	yes	yes
Oil	yes	yes		yes	yes
Natural Gas	yes	yes	yes	yes	yes
Transportation Fuels	yes	yes		yes	yes
Fuelwood	yes	yes	yes	yes	
Deforestation	yes	yes	yes	yes	
Industry	yes	yes		yes	yes

 Fig.1-32 *Gases produced by burning carbon.*

centrations of reactive gases in the atmosphere have registered a linear increase.

The Industrial Revolution marked the beginning of a period of change never before seen on our planet. Mechanization of agriculture and improved public health dispelled the threat of a Malthusian catastrophe, and human population doubled first to 2.5 billion in 1950 and then, only 37 years later, to five billion. The same period saw change in the number of humans using carbon-based energy, and also in the amount of energy each individual used. Not only have absolute population numbers greatly increased, but the intensity of energy use has risen unevenly. Those living in the developed nations consume energy at a rate far higher than residents of developing nations. On a per capita basis, Canadians rank fourth as producers of carbon dioxide, and lead the world in per capita energy consumption.

Figures (see Fig. 1-33) show the changing concentrations of three important trace atmospheric gases as measured over geological time. These are extraordinarily rapid rates of change for geological processes. They can be attributed directly to changes in the absolute numbers of human beings on the planet, and in the patterns of carbon combustion and related activities by those people.

• • • • •

There is good reason to question the sustainability of these trends. Certainly, stocks of **biomass** and fossil fuels are limited, and so the trend to increasing dependence on carbon combustion for energy cannot continue indefinitely. Can a world population of 10 to 15 billion be sustained by relying primarily on carbon-based energy sources for

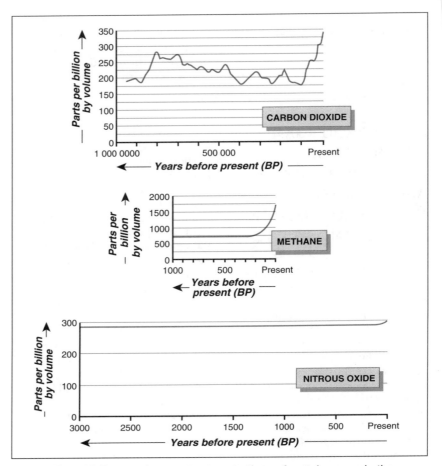

Fig.1-33 *Past and present concentrations of certain gases in the atmosphere. Note scale differences.*

the production and transportation of food, as well as for heating, cooling and light?

We do not know what will be the effect on the atmosphere of such dramatic changes to the concentrations of minor and trace gases over so short a geological time period. Wally Broecker of Columbia University has stressed the danger in continuing to increase atmospheric emissions of these gases without knowing the consequences.

Fossil fuels and biomass stocks are limited, and present

trends in consumption are not sustainable. We do not know the full magnitude of the impact of atmospheric change on the Earth's climate and overall livability, but most certainly change there will be. Efforts should begin now to develop alternative energy sources for the present generation, and for the extra five to 10 billion people the world will have by the year 2100.

Judith G. Patterson, *Ecodecision*, 1992 3

JAPAN TRIES TO RAISE BIRTHRATE. GOVERNMENT TARGETS CAREER WOMEN WHO ARE SINGLE, IN THEIR 30S

TOKYO — Rika Kawai — aged 24, single, working, and college-educated — is the type of Japanese woman who annoys her government. She has "delayed" marriage and motherhood.

"I think raising a child would be an interesting experience, but I still want to work," Ms. Kawai says. "I don't think the system is yet in place to do both."

Kawai and other women have been the target of a year-long government campaign to raise Japan's birthrate, which is the world's third-lowest, after Germany and Italy. Despite a population of 124 million, Japan is short on Japanese. Some demographers joke that if the trend continues, the Japanese **race** could be extinct in 700 years. Last year, the number of children under 14 was the lowest in postwar history.

Faced with the prospect of fewer workers to support an ageing society, Japanese leaders asked 17 agencies and ministries "to create a social environment that would enhance happiness and joy in child rearing." The unspoken official goal is to get more young people to marry and multiply. The task is ominous in a society largely built for work and economic growth.

• • • • •

This year the government improved subsidies for raising children. Parents with first-born babies now get 5000 yen ($38) a month for three years. Such bonuses, however, are small peanuts for most Japanese. "It's like they're putting women on a string and saying: 'We'll do this for you, so raise the birthrate'," says Kawai, a Tokyo television assistant producer.

Officials keep a low profile in their efforts, fearing criticism that they are reviving a pre-war campaign that urged women to "Give Birth, Build Japan." But their goals include: more maternity leave and child care; cheaper housing; more playgrounds; less pressure on kids to pass the national university exam system; higher subsidies for child support; and more counseling on child rearing.

More than 95 local governments now offer cash rewards for a birth....

Clayton Jones, *The Christian Science Monitor*, 1992 7 10-16

DECLINING BIRTH RATE BORNE BY RUSSIANS

MOSCOW — In a telling indication of the toll from Russia's economic hardships in the past several years, the country's birth rate has dropped to a postwar low and, so far this year, has been exceeded by the death rate.

The birth rate, which recent studies show has plunged 28 percent from the 1986 peak, is starting to cause alarm. The average life expectancy has dropped 0.3 percent to slightly under age 64.

In 1991 there were just 1.8 million births in Russia, whose total population is about 148 million.

"This worries us a great deal," says Alexander Kvasha, professor of demographics and director of the population research centre at Moscow State University, which conducted the studies. "Having children is an indication of hope for the future."

Mr. Kvasha said that surveys conducted by his institute found couples citing the poor standard of living as the main reason for having no children or only one child

Although couples say they would like to have two or more children they do not think they can afford more than one, Mr. Kvasha said.

...The Moscow newspaper *Komsomolskaya Pravda* recently outlined the cost of a baby, starting with birth and including the price of food, clothes and medical care.

It calculated that, in a country where the average monthly salary is 2000 **rubles**, a new baby will initially cost at least 2000 rubles and will continue to eat up 1000 rubles a month after that.

The Russian parliament has conducted hearings for the past week on the low birth rate and is examining reasons for its cause. There have been calls for the government to step in and offer more assistance to families....

The Wall Street Journal, 1992 6 3

BABY POWER

"Dua Anak Cukup" (two children is enough) proclaim signs in villages throughout Indonesia. Large families with six or more children are normal in most Asian countries, which together account for almost 60 percent of the world's population — 45 percent in China and India alone. In response, most Asian governments are — more or less effectively — implementing **anti-natalist** policies, striving to reduce fertility rates to the replacement level of two children....

It may then come as a surprise to hear Malaysia's Prime Minister Dr Mahathir Mohammed encouraging Malaysian women to "go for five" (children). This slogan is part of the New Population Policy, announced in August 1984, which aims to increase Malaysia's population from 18 million — low by Asian standards — to 70 million by 2100.

Previously, Malaysia followed an anti-natalist policy in line with most other nations in the region. Peninsular Malaysia's population growth rate of over 3 percent a year in the early 1960s was successfully reduced to 2 percent by the early 1980s following the formation of the National Family Planning Board in 1966.

• • • • •

...Malaysia's TFR is still well above replacement level, despite a steady decline since the 1960s, and the country is still relatively underpopulated. "Many people feel it could do with a bigger population base," says Chan Kok Eng, associate professor of geography at the University of Malaysia in Kuala Lumpur.

This raises the question of what constitutes being "underpopulated." Much depends on the perceptions of its leaders and the ideology of its people. A comparison with neighbouring countries may also give the impression of underpopulation. "If the population growth rate is declining, it can create the impression that the country is in some way lagging behind its neighbours, and may be dwarfed in the future," says Chan. Malaysia is relatively underpopulated by comparison with its neighbours. By mid-1987 Malaysia had an average population density of 50 people per square kilometre. This compares with 194 in the Philippines, 104 in Thailand, and 4497 in Singapore.

A small population can also be a limiting factor in economic and industrial expansion. In Malaysia, labour shortages exist in certain sectors of the economy, especially plantations, which have traditionally been provided by immigrants and the rural Malay population. Illegal immigrants from the Philippines and Indonesia now take many of these jobs and help to fill this gap.

However, Malaysia is undergoing rapid industrialization, and the Government is aware that a larger population would provide both a larger home market for industrial goods, and a larger workforce to staff the growing number of factories and businesses.

Of course, as Chan points out, a larger population does not guarantee economic success: "Social, cultural and other factors affect economic growth — not just the population base. It is no good having a large population if it is lazy and not hard working." The Government is aware of this. Mahathir said in 1984 that the 70 million population target was conditional on "good values including diligence and discipline (being) inculcated among the population, particularly the new generation." The Government will believe its policy is justified only if the population grows without a drop in the standard of living.

• • • • •

Women who want small families do not readily have more children just because politicians tell them to. The whole effectiveness of pro-natalist policies is debatable. Policies can embrace two strategies: restricting access to contraception and abortions; and the provision of incentives and facilities to encourage child-bearing....

• • • • •

But it is clear that there are other political reasons behind Malaysia's New Population Policy.... Malaysia (is a) multi-racial nation, comprising mainly Chinese (32%), Malays (58%), and Indians.... Ever since the Chinese won Malaysia's elections in 1969, which led to race riots, the Malays have been trying to increase their population.

• • • • •

The fertility rate of Malays is decreasing much more slowly than that of the Chinese owing to a number of factors: almost all Malay women get married, whereas increasing numbers of Chinese women do not, or marry comparatively late; a greater proportion of Malay women refuse to use contraception; and Malays are almost without exception Muslim, with a growing Islamic fundamentalism encouraging larger families.

The net effect in the coming century will be that the proportion of Malays in Malaysia will continue to grow, and the proportion of Chinese will drop significantly.

Charles Tyler, *Geographical Magazine*, 1992 1

EGYPT PURSUES FAMILY PLANNING

Throughout the 1400-year history of Islam, the world's second-largest faith, children have been considered one of the greatest blessings of Allah. The religion's long tradition, based on the Prophet Muhammad's injunction to "marry and have children," is one reason why large families have usually been the rule in Muslim nations.

But in the realm of Islam, as in Roman Catholic countries, old teachings are bumping up against the hard realities of population trends that have fundamentally altered daily life. Responding to new circumstances, senior Muslim clerics...are accenting a side of Islam, expounded by various Muslim scholars, that is more conducive to family planning. As governments in the Muslim world step up to the task of bringing population growth under control, religious leaders have become crucial allies.

"You can't disregard the fact that you have to get Islamic support. We couldn't have gotten started without it," says Aziza Hussein, founder and chairman of the Cairo Family Planning Association. "If Islamic leaders know the size of the population problem, they have to back family planning, because Islam says you have to do what's in the interest of the community."

For Egypt, the issue of overpopulation is no academic matter. Most of its 56 million people are squeezed into a thin strip of fertile land bordering the Nile River that is barely twice the size of the state of New Hampshire. One million more are added every eight months as the nation races toward the 100-million mark by the year 2020.

Belatedly convinced that overpopulation would overwhelm modest economic growth, Egypt launched its family-planning program in 1965. Since then, fertility rates have dropped from an average of six children per family to four, while contraceptive use has risen to more than 40 percent of couples — a success story that, with the indispensable support of religious leaders, has been approximated in some other Islamic nations.

• • • • •

In post-Khomeini Iran, high birth rates and deteriorating economic conditions have led to a massive government campaign to curb population growth. Where mullahs once claimed contraception was a plot by the toppled Shah, many now find support for family planning in the Koran.

• • • • •

In Sudan, the continent's most chronically destitute nation, different lessons are drawn from Islam. Fatima Ahmed, a Sudanese mother in her late 30s, explains:

"Sudanese people think (birth control) is shameful. The Muslim thinks that every child comes into the world with his (or her) own chances."

• • • • •

The debate within Islam is mirrored in the competing societal forces of modernization and tradition that have created dilemmas for millions of couples of reproductive age. The pressures of overcrowded cities are causing many Egyptians to question the wisdom of large families. Schools operate on a shift basis. Housing is at such a premium that families live in every available space, from garages to construction sites. Holidays find every free space from roadside curbs to thoroughfare medians crowded with families seeking a respite from their overcrowded apartments.

President Hosni Mubarak rarely misses an opportunity to remind Egyptians that the country's resources are near exhaustion because of the demands of its growing population.

But against these arguments for having smaller families are the intense pressures that are still placed on many young couples to have children early and often.

As in other more traditional societies, many Egyptian women are confined to domestic roles. For men, large families are often considered a measure of masculinity and the failure of a wife to produce children is common grounds for divorce.

Television ads sponsored by Egypt's state family-planning agency respond by advising women to stop having children so they can retain their beauty and keep their husbands from divorcing and taking other wives.

Carol Berger, *The Christian Science Monitor*, 1992 7 10-16

THE NEED FOR AN EFFECTIVE POPULATION POLICY

We are greatly concerned that the population in many countries of the South is growing at an explosive and, in the long run, unsustainable pace. The present high rates of population growth increase the burden of dependency and reduce the resources available for raising productivity to what is sufficient just to maintain subsistence levels. In several countries, the pressure of growing numbers on the limited fertile land is accelerating the degradation of land and water resources and causing excessive deforestation. Rapid population growth is also a principal factor in the uncontrolled growth of vast urban agglomerations. In many large cities of the South, islands of affluence are surrounded by sprawling slums in which the evils of poor housing, polluted air and water, bad sanitation, and widespread disease are compounded by the activities of drug peddlers, smugglers, and other undesirable elements.

In the long run the problem of overpopulation of the countries of the South can be fully resolved only through their development. But action to contain the rise of population cannot be postponed. The present trends in population, if not moderated, have frightening implications for the ability of the South to meet the twin challenges of development and environmental security in the twenty-first century.

It takes time before even well-designed policies can have a material impact on the birth rate. It

SOURCE: CIDA/Pierre St-Jacques

SOURCE: CIDA/Benoit Aquin

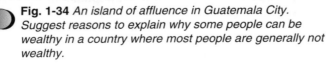
Fig. 1-34 *An island of affluence in Guatemala City. Suggest reasons to explain why some people can be wealthy in a country where most people are generally not wealthy.*

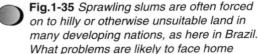
Fig.1-35 *Sprawling slums are often forced on to hilly or otherwise unsuitable land in many developing nations, as here in Brazil. What problems are likely to face home owners on hillsides in tropical countries?*

is therefore necessary that countries with high birth rates should act without delay....

Measures to raise the social, economic, and political status of women are fundamental to the success of population policies. It is equally essential to universalize access to elementary education, priority being given to the education of girls. Simultaneously, cost-effective health care measures must be put into operation, seeking in particular further reductions in infant mortality rates; this will reduce the social pressure on families to have as many children as possible as a way to insure against a high rate of child mortality. Family planning services must be made available to all at affordable cost. And all these activities have to be an integral part of policies for poverty alleviation, so that the poor do not need to pursue the type of survival strategies that consciously or unconsciously promote improvident maternity. The societies of the South must willingly accept a firm commitment to responsible parenthood and the small-family norm.

We are conscious that we are dealing with issues that touch on some of the deepest human emotions. The pronatal sentiment has strong roots in most traditional societies. Willing acceptance of the small-family norm therefore necessitates the active involvement and support of local communities and responsible guidance and encouragement from civic and religious leaders.

The task is indeed formidable, but the consequences of inaction can be disastrous. The South must summon sufficient political will to overcome the various obstacles to the pursuit of a sensible policy on population.

The Challenge to the South: The Report of the South Commission under the chairmanship of Julius K. Nyerere, 1990

MAKING BELIEVE ABOUT THE WORLD POPULATION CRISIS

World population, now 5.5 billion, is growing by about 90 million every year, and is projected to reach 12-14 billion in the next century. Nevertheless...

Let's keep on MAKING BELIEVE that a world population of that size (or even our present size) would be sustainable for the long term.

Let's keep on MAKING BELIEVE that our already over-stressed **ecosystem** could provide an adequate standard of living for such numbers.

Let's keep on MAKING BELIEVE that family planning alone, or education, or economic development, or all of these together, are capable of halting world population growth before it reaches catastrophic levels.

But...if we keep on MAKING BELIEVE, and keep on pretending that those preposterous proposi-tions are true, we are going to wind up where we are now headed: in a world of 14 billion impoverished people. Such a world would be a place where none of us would care to live, a world of almost universal poverty, with an ecosystem in ruins.

NPG (Negative Population Growth) believes that the optimum size for world population is not more than two billion, and that a substantially larger population would simply not be sustainable indefinitely. (World population was two billion about 60 years ago.)

In our view, only with a world population of that size could we hope to create a world economy that would be sustainable indefinitely, with an adequate standard of living for all, in a healthy environment. The basic reason why so many people profess to believe otherwise is probably because they do not see how world population could possibly be reduced to an optimum size.

In fact, according to the conventional wisdom, there is simply no way that world population can be halted short of 12-14 billion, so it accepts that as inevitable. Rather than face up to the grim reality that this would bring on an economic and ecological catastrophe, it prefers to MAKE BELIEVE that all will be well.

But the truth is that sustainable development for a world of 12-14 billion people, is simply an impossible dream.

Toward An Optimum World Population

Further population growth on the gigantic scale now projected is not inevitable. If we could only summon the will, we could start now on the path toward a sustainable world population of not more than two billion.

To reduce world population size, we need a negative rate of population growth. For that, we need a below replacement level of fertility, which a considerable number of developed countries have already achieved.

If almost no parent on earth had more than two children the

world's total fertility rate (average number of children per woman) would fall well below the replacement level (roughly 2.1). That is because many women choose voluntarily to have no children at all, or only one child.

A below replacement fertility rate will be tremendously difficult to achieve in the developing countries, where 90 percent of future population growth is projected to occur, and where couples commonly want from three to six children. In 1992 the fertility rate in these countries was 3.8.

In developing countries, there must be programs of real population control geared to family limitation (no more than two children) rather than to family planning alone. Family planning must be supplemented by non-coercive incentives to encourage the two-child maximum family.

In 1992 the world's total fertility rate was 3.3. According to the most recent United Nations projections, if present fertility and **mortality rates** continue, world population would grow to 109 billion in 2100 and 694 billion in 2150!!

By contrast, with a below replacement level fertility of 1.7, or about half the 1992 level, the United Nations projects that world population would peak at 7.8 billion in 2050, but then fall to 4.3 billion 100 years later. If we could only follow that path, the world would be well on its way to an optimum population of not more than two billion.

How We Can Help

· · · · ·

...we should encourage Third World countries to recognize that a replacement level fertility rate is a totally inadequate goal. That is because, even after replacement fertility is reached in those countries, the momentum of past growth would still cause their populations to roughly double.

Let's Stop Making Believe

If we could only turn from MAKING BELIEVE to realistic analysis as a basis for action, the world could achieve a negative rate of population growth that would set us on the path to an optimum population size of not over two billion.

The fate of the world, and of all future generations, hangs on our success in achieving that goal.

From an advertisement by NPG in *Foreign Affairs*, Winter 1992/93

DISCUSSION AND RESEARCH

16. Each of the readings presents at least one opinion about the issue of population growth. In small groups, analyze each reading to identify its major viewpoint. Identify the facts presented in support of that viewpoint.

17. Refer to the two lists you made as you went through the readings (arguments in favour of and arguments opposed to population growth) and classify the arguments into those that are primarily economic, those that are primarily political, those that are primarily social, and those that are primarily religious. In small groups discuss which category you believe contains the most persuasive arguments.

18. Research and prepare a two- to three-page paper which attempts to define some of the meanings of the term "overpopulation" (see the section on research papers in Appendix 3). Conclude the paper by developing and justifying your own definition.

19. Examine Figure 1-36.

Fig. 1-36 *Viewpoints.*

Photo: Roger Lemoyne

Photo: CIDA/David Barbour

What do you see? *The overwhelming problem of population growth. People made poor by too many children.*

Look at it this way: *People have large families because they are poor and need the extra hands to earn enough to survive. It has been shown that when people break out of poverty, population growth slows.*

Photo: CIDA/Roger Lemoyne

Photo: CIDA/Peter Bennett

What do you see? *A typical image of the Third World — people rendered helpless by crushing poverty. An image of despair. A miserable present. A hopeless future. A case for charity.*

Look at it this way: *The situation is not hopeless. In literacy, life expectancy, and nutrition, the Third World has achieved in 30 years what took the industrialized world 100 years to achieve. Yes, the problems are severe. But there is enormous potential for improving the lives of the poorest people and nations.*

SOURCE: Canadian Council for International Cooperation

(a) Identify the central message that is being presented in each horizontal pair of photographs and captions.

(b) Analyze to what extent each caption matches its accompanying photograph.

(c) Discuss the roles of realism and idealism in the formation of government policy.

(d) Discuss the roles of pessimism and optimism in the formation of government policy.

(e) Suggest ways in which the two photographs on the right can be achieved when for many people the two photographs on the left currently reflect their lives.

20. You work for an advertising company that has just been hired by a national government to develop an advertising campaign to persuade people to have fewer babies. The general literacy rate among the population is 63 percent, there is an average of one radio for every 214 people, and 81 percent of the population lives in rural areas. Company policy is to group its creative personnel into teams of four or five people. Outline the steps you would take in developing an advertising campaign. Describe your campaign.

21. Your provincial government is concerned about the province's declining birth rate because a smaller population could lead to a loss of provincial seats in the House of Commons. The government has hired you as a consultant to help develop measures to encourage people to have more babies.

(a) List the advice you would give the government to help form its policy;

(b) Prepare a press release explaining the government's policy on trying to raise provincial birth rates.

22. Examine Figure 1-37. It shows those countries that have either more than twice or less than half the population density of the world as a whole. Compare this map with the others in this chapter and determine which countries with a rapidly growing population appear most able to accommodate it, in terms of having enough room. Identify also those countries with a high rate of population growth where accommodating future increases of population appears difficult.

23. Select any one of the articles one page or longer from among the readings immediately preceding this block of questions, and critically analyze it to identify

(a) logical fallacy,

(b) bias, and

(c) ethnocentrism.

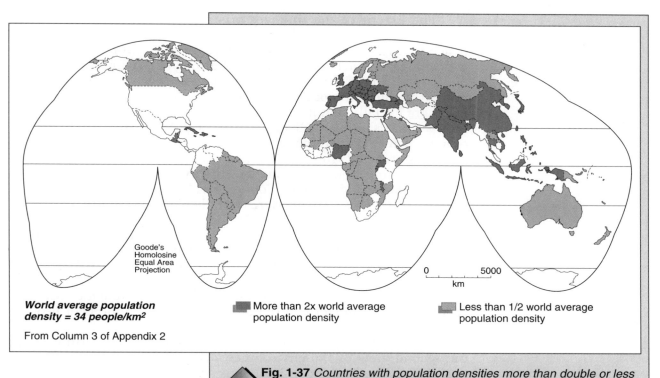

Goode's
Homolosine
Equal Area
Projection

**World average population
density = 34 people/km²**

From Column 3 of Appendix 2

0   5000
km

■ More than 2x world average
   population density

■ Less than 1/2 world average
   population density

Fig. 1-37 *Countries with population densities more than double or less
than half the world average population density.*

ENVIRONMENTAL IMPACTS

It was noted previously that issues do not stand alone. They exist
as part of a meshed web of human activity within the physical environment. It is characteristic of this meshed web that activities in
one part of the world ultimately produce reactions elsewhere. For
example, hurricane damage in Florida produces reactions elsewhere
in North America in the form of aid generation. Also, actions at a
certain point in time produce reactions at a later time. The clearing
of forest for farmland in Central America has many long-term
effects, including shortages of wood for fuel and increased soil erosion in the same area, although it also increases the amount of
farmland available.

The extent of the linkages arising from the meshed web of human and environmental activities is a measure of the interdependence that exists among the various parts of the world. Some linkages are strong, such as between the burning of coal and the increase of air pollution. Other linkages, such as between the atmospheric release of chlorofluorocarbons (CFCs) and the thinning of the ozone layer, are initially unnoticed, and even unexpected. Also, some linkages, such as sharing medical advances, appear beneficial to humans; others, such as the international illicit drug trade, are harmful.

It is probably true to say that the attitudes which people have towards various issues are related to their views about the durability of the physical environment. Some individuals believe that the environment is under severe pressure. They believe that additional population, increasing economic development, and the unchecked use of resources will further harm the environment. As a result, the quality of life for everyone on earth will inevitably deteriorate. Other people claim that, provided care is taken of the environment, the earth is quite capable of supporting more people, more economic development, and more resource use. They feel that only through continued economic development can the quality of life for billions of people actually be improved.

Regardless of the pessimism in the first and the optimism in the second view of the environment, there is common agreement that certain pressures exist, including: soil degradation, water and air pollution, global climatic change, and disappearing wilderness. Since about 1950, world economic growth has compounded at about three percent per year (3%/y). This growth rate is sufficient to double the level of world economic activity every 24-25 years. Continued growth at this rate will likely increase the pressures on the environment, unless there are changes in the nature of production. For example, fossil fuels provide about 95 percent of the commercial energy used in the world economy today, and their use is growing worldwide at the rate of about 2%/y. Combustion of these fuels constitutes the largest source of greenhouse gas emissions into the atmosphere. Greenhouse gases are those such as carbon dioxide and methane that hinder the return to space of the heat the earth receives from the sun, causing the atmosphere to retain some solar heat. If greenhouse gases did not exist, the earth would be much colder. The problem as some people see it, however, is that amounts of greenhouse gases are increasing, causing the earth to slowly become warmer. The United Nations Environ-mental Program (UNEP) and the World Meteorological Organization (WMO) have concluded that a 60 percent reduction in carbon dioxide emissions is needed to stabilize the amount of carbon dioxide in the atmosphere at current levels. Protection of the earth's climate may therefore require significant reductions in fossil fuel use even as the world economy continues to expand.

Alternatives to fossil fuels include biomass, geothermal, hydroelectric, hydrogen, nuclear, solar, tidal, and wind energy. They are described in Chapter Three, pp. 161 – 162.

There has been growing awareness for the last two or three decades of the need for the nature of production to change. Much work has gone into improving fuel efficiencies and making more economical use of resources. Work has also gone into cleaner production. For example, the Sudbury area in Ontario, one of the world's major nickel-mining centres, was once regarded as among the most devastated landscapes on earth, but is now widely hailed as a model of environmental revival. The need for production changes was first recognized at the world level at the United Nations Conference on the Human Environment in Stockholm, Sweden, in 1972. Since then there has been increasing realization that environmental issues are inseparable from those of human welfare and the process of economic development. Further, many people realize that some existing forms of development degrade the environmental resources on which human livelihoods and welfare ultimately depend.

SUSTAINABLE DEVELOPMENT

In 1987 the United Nations World Commission on Environment and Development, chaired by Gro Brundtland, who later became the Prime Minister of Norway [1990–], published *Our Common Future*, widely known as *The Brundtland Report*. On page 4 of this report, the commissioners note that "we came to see that a new development path was required, one that sustained human progress not just in a few places for a few years, but for the entire planet into the distant future. Thus "sustainable development" becomes a goal...."

The Commission defined sustainable development as a level of development which enabled humans "to meet the needs of the present without compromising the ability of future generations to meet their own needs." Limits on development were accepted, notably those imposed by the relationship between technology and environmental resources and by the capacity of the **biosphere** (the zone of all life at or near the earth's surface) to absorb the effects of human activities. Still, the Commission believed that technology could be improved "to make way for a new era of economic growth."

The Commission further stated that sustainable global development requires that those who are more affluent adopt a way of life within the planet's ecological means. It also stated that — in relation to rapid population growth — sustainable development can only be pursued if population size and growth are in harmony with the changing productive potential of the **ecosystem**. As the Commission concluded, "Painful choices have to be made. Thus, in the final analysis, sustainable development must rest on political will."

SOURCE: Weyerhaeuser

Fig. 1-38 *A worker in Oregon plants seedlings to ensure a sustainable yield from the region's forests.*

These two views are often labelled wealth creation and wealth sharing. The first view claims that all will benefit only if wealth is created; the second view alleges that all will benefit only if existing wealth is shared. What do you think?

Upon the signing of the North American Free Trade Agreement (**NAFTA**) by Canada, Mexico, and the United States in 1992, the President of Mexico hailed its chief benefit to Mexico, a developing nation, as access to developed world markets.

Reactions to the concept of sustainable development have been favourable in general but mixed as to specific applications. Some people argue that continued economic growth is desirable to relieve world poverty. They believe it is possible to make development cleaner and more efficient to prevent further environmental degradation.

Others argue that the key to future world stability rests in greater equity, not only between present and future generations but also between the affluent and the poor in today's world. They believe that such equity can be achieved only through a major redistribution of current wealth, and not through increased economic growth. Many people who argue this last point believe that sustainable development is a contradiction in terms, and that further growth cannot in fact be sustained.

Many individuals feel that in order to make a sustainable future possible, people facing daily problems of survival need to be given reason to hope. They encourage industrialized countries to become more efficient and to develop cleaner and less resource-wasteful technologies. They also encourage industrialized countries to share environmentally friendly technologies, and to open their markets to the produce of developing nations to help achieve greater global economic equity. In this respect, international negotiations have been held continually since 1948 under the sponsorship of the General Agreement on Tariffs and Trade (GATT).

Equally, a number of countries characterized by rapid population growth are attempting to make progress toward stable populations. Many of these countries realize that rapid population growth places severe strains on their resources. It undercuts economic development; and it makes difficult the universal and ongoing provision of clean water, good health care, and effective education.

The problems of rapid population growth are compounded by increasing **urbanization**. Cities provide economic hopes, but also large concentrations of wastes and pollutants. Consequently, many people believe that much development work needs to be aimed at rural areas in order to slow rural-urban migration. The question of cities is examined in more detail in the case study at the end of this chapter.

The role of women in these countries is particularly important. In many cases they are the environmental managers of the household: they grow the crops, tend the animals, raise the children, and gather the fuel and water. Yet the education and health of women are often neglected in comparison with those of men. It is generally believed that greater investment in the education and health of women can produce many benefits.

DISCUSSION AND RESEARCH

24. As a class, suggest a variety of global linkages that create interdependence between the members of your class and the rest of the world, for example, family ties and travel experiences. Once a list has been generated, analyze the items that affect you personally to determine their strength (strong-weak) and immediacy (now-later). Evaluate these linkages in terms of the benefit or harm to you personally.

25. Sustainable development is widely held to be a positive direction for the future. Examine your own anticipated future way of life, and evaluate it in terms of its sustainability. What actions will you take as a result of this evaluation?

STATISTICAL ANALYSIS

26. Fig. 1-39 is a scattergraph (see Appendix 3) showing the extent of the relationship between female literacy rates and GNP/cap/y for the 114 countries in Appendix 2 for which both sets of data are available. Individual countries may be identified by finding the appropriate values from Fig. 1-39 and scanning columns 18 and 19 of Appendix 2 to find a match.

    The overall pattern is positive. It shows that as one factor increases, so does the other. However, the pattern is also rather loose, indicating that the correlation is far from perfect. For example, the two countries in the bottom right-hand corner of the graph (Guyana and Vietnam) both have relatively low GNP/cap/y figures despite their relatively high female literacy rates. Very clearly, female literacy is not the sole determinant of the level of incomes, nor is income level alone sufficient to determine the level of female literacy. Nevertheless, the overall pattern of the graph is clear enough to indicate that some relationship exists.

    (a) Dividing the calculations among small groups, determine the mathematical extent of the correlation between female literacy rates and GNP/cap/y by using the coefficient of correlation technique explained in Appendix 3.

    (b) Suggest several reasons to explain why the correlation is less than perfect.

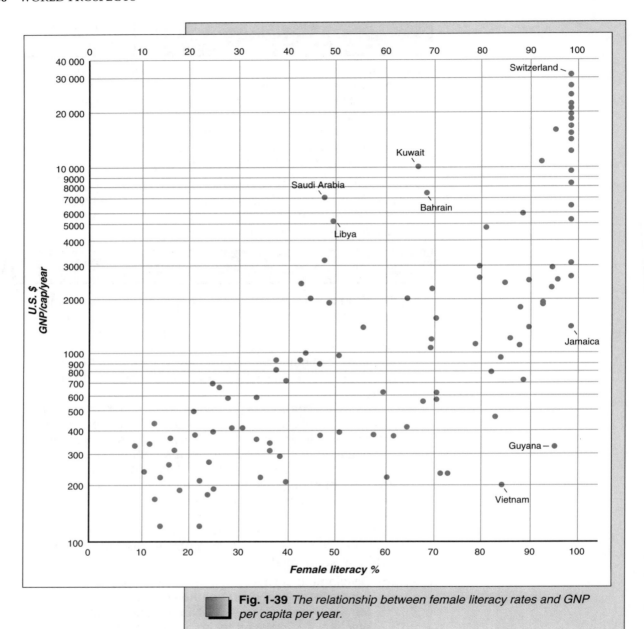

Fig. 1-39 *The relationship between female literacy rates and GNP per capita per year.*

CONCLUSION

The ideals and points of view of human beings around the world, as we have seen, are diverse. Attitudes to a variety of issues, such as population growth, reflect these differences. Is one attitude intrinsically superior to the others? Or are any number of attitudes created or permitted by different economic circumstances? Do the various attitudes simply reflect different stages along the same path of human history?

Whatever the answers, there is no doubt that world population growth is linked to many other issues. These issues include economic growth, the role of women in society, the means available for old age support, the environment, and the overall quality of life. People differ in their views about these matters, as well as in the priority they accord them. The population issue is therefore very complex.

Many people view rapid population growth as a major threat to the environment and a serious obstacle to securing an acceptable quality of life for the world's people. Other people see it as a legitimate expression of human optimism and regard the current rate of resource consumption in the industrialized countries as the main threat to the environment. The next chapter examines issues relating to the environment and quality of life in more detail.

- What are the different choices?
- How urgent is a resolution of the situation?
- Where do you stand on the issue?
- What actions can you take personally to improve the situation?

CASE STUDY

THE GROWTH OF LARGE CITIES

Although evidence of urban life can be found in the Middle East as far back as 8000 years ago, the world's population remained overwhelmingly rural and agricultural until the late 19th century. In 1850, only three cities, London, Paris, and Beijing, had more than one million inhabitants and only 110 cities had more than 100 000 inhabitants. In that year, out of a world population of between 1.2 and 1.3 billion persons, only about 6.5 percent lived in urban areas. Over the next century, 1850-1950, however, the number of large cities in the world increased from 110 to 946, and by 1950, 29 percent of the world's population lived in urban places. By 1975 the number of urban areas contain-ing at least 100 000 inhabitants had grown to 1773.

By the year 2000 the number of urban areas will double again, with the number of cities containing one million inhabitants growing to about 400. Half the world's popula-tion will live in urban areas and a fifth will live in places with more than one million inhabitants. At present, there are at least six urbanized areas with over ten million inhabi-tants (Tokyo, Sao Paulo, New York City, Mex-ico City, Shanghai, and Bombay), and the United Nations projects the emergence of at least another 24 cities of that size by the year 2000. It seems quite probable that in the near future there will be urban centres of over 30 million.

Experts disagree on an optimum size for cities, but many agree that 500 000 people is ideal, especially if full employment is a prior-ity. When a city grows beyond one or two million inhabitants, it is difficult to maintain a rea-sonable standard of living for all its citizens. These, however, are only average estimates; an ideal size that could apply to all cities in all countries is not attain-able. Cities with a moder-ate growth rate, however, are more likely to maintain high employment rates and a reasonable standard of liv-ing as they grow than those cities experiencing very rapid growth.

Although the greatest urbanization initially took place in the developed world, today the most dra-matic urbanization is tak-ing place in the developing world. Large-scale rural-urban migration began to take place in Latin America

SOURCE: CIDA/Pierre St-Jacques

Fig. 1-40 *Urban populations are growing rapidly throughout the developing world, as here in Sao Paulo, Brazil. What social and economic problems are likely to face people living in areas of very high population density? What advantages does high population density offer?*

several decades before it did in Asia and Africa. African cities, the last to experience enormous increases in population, are now growing at an annual rate of over six percent, which will double their urban population in just 12 years.

Among the various regions of the world, factors such as unfavourable conditions in the countryside and inequitable land ownership contribute to the swelling numbers moving to the cities. Large areas of land in southern Asia, Africa, and South America have been subject to such misuse that soil erosion has become a serious problem. Additionally, because of deforestation in these regions, the land no longer retains water very well during rainy periods, so flash floods are created that damage irrigation systems and wash away topsoil. Such conditions lead to massive rural-to-urban migration. For example, as many as 2000 migrants a day are drawn into each of Calcutta and Bombay, India's two largest cities. Most of these migrants are young men with no assets who come from the country's innumerable villages to start new lives.

In China, a deliberate policy of restricting urban growth by refusing residence permits and ration cards was pursued in the past. This policy no longer exists because the countryside can no longer support its own population growth. The country's interior and northern regions are so impoverished and water and fuelwood so scarce that it is predicted that tens of millions of Chinese will in the near future try to leave for the cities.

A high natural increase rate has also fueled the rapid growth of cities. This is now the main cause of growth in Latin American cities. Because of improved health standards, urban death rates, especially infant mortality rates, are generally somewhat lower than those of the same region's rural areas. At the same time, birth rates in new migrant families continue to be high, following the trend of having many children in rural areas. Thus, in Latin America, although urban migration has subsided, natural increase continues to fuel population growth.

Cities are often viewed by potential residents as places of hope, with a greater number of employment opportunities and better education facilities and health services than in rural areas. Despite these attractions, the poor form the largest single economic grouping of urban residents in the developing world where rapid growth is now the norm. Many have an income that is barely enough to survive on. One solution to this problem has been to develop small programs which provide local jobs. For example, the University of British Columbia is working with five Asian cities, Beijing, Shanghai, and Guangzhou in China, Bangkok in Thailand, and Bandung in Indonesia to provide work and improve living conditions by having local residents install basic services such as water pipes, communal toilets, and drainage ditches.

The hunger that accompanies poverty is also problematic in many cities. However, some families have managed to find a solution. In 1985, in the slum communities of Lima, Peru, a small group of women rebelling against the high cost and low quality of food available to their families decided to pool their resources, purchase in bulk, and share meal preparation. Thus the people's kitchens began. Now there are 2000 of these community centres in Lima, where lunch is prepared and served by local women for the families in their community. Some of these community centres also offer health care, day-care, and small craft workshops where women can earn some needed income.

In the developed world, as well, there are individuals who don't have enough money to buy the minimum requirements of food, shelter, and clothing to survive. Urban residents around the world face a number of problems requiring creative solutions. The most pressing issues include access to water, waste disposal, clean air, housing, and a solution to political and social violence.

WATER

In the cities of the developing world, turning on a tap for clean drinking water is a luxury because their populations have increased too rapidly for the supply of piped water to keep up with demand. For example, in Manila, the capital of the Philippines, a typical poor family must get its water from a distant standpipe, which may cost it 15 percent of its total income.

Many cities are also worried about the availability of future water sources. In Bangkok, the capital of Thailand, six million inhabitants draw their water from a natural underground storage area known as an aquifer. Although there is plenty of water for present needs, more is being removed than is being replaced by rainfall and runoff. The result is land subsidence (a downwards settling of the land) and a potential shortage of water. Cities such as Lima, Beijing, Mexico City, and Manila are also over-pumping their aquifers. In Manila, the level is dropping by four to ten metres a year and in Lima, Beijing, and Mexico City the water is retreating downward from one to three metres a year.

Because of Mexico City's location, the water shortage there has other consequences. Situated on a valley floor 900 metres above sea level, Mexico City requires vast supplies of power to pump water upwards from neighbouring valleys at lower elevations to supplement the water from its own aquifer. This limits the power that is available for other purposes, a constraint that is felt most keenly during the dry season when the city needs extra water. The additional power required puts a strain on the availability of electricity and the city becomes subject to brownouts and blackouts, which have a significant impact on industrial output. Brownouts refer to receiving a weak supply of electricity; blackouts to no supply at all.

Another problem for cities is water contamination originating from industrial or agricultural wastes as well as human excrement. In Karachi, Pakistan, only 70 percent of necessary water is provided by the city. Poor people are forced to drink from untreated supplies often contaminated with disease. As a result, the incidence of various diseases, particularly hepatitis, is elevated.

Programs to clean up water may begin with the assistance of outside organizations. For example, a Canadian organization called Watercan sponsors small clean-water projects in the developing world. One of these projects improved the water supply for 800 families in a poor neighbourhood on the outskirts of Managua, the capital of Nicaragua. So far, in total, Watercan has supported over 40 projects in 27 countries, bringing clean water to thousands of people.

WASTE DISPOSAL

Another issue in both developed and developing countries is the mounting problem of what to do with accumulating solid wastes. The following illustrates the difficulties faced by various large cities around the world and describes some solutions.

- Tokyo, at the present discard rate, will run out of dump sites by 1995. The city has been building artificial islands in Tokyo Bay to hold garbage, but cannot continue to do so without threatening both the fishing and shipping industries. One scheme that is working involves burning sewage and using it to regulate temperatures in downtown buildings.

- In Cairo, the Zableen tribe collects 1600 tonnes of trash a day, compared to the 1450 tonnes picked up by three times as many people hired by the city. The women of the tribe sort the trash, use the organic materials to feed their pigs, and sell the glass, paper, plastics, metals, and cloth. It would cost the city of Cairo more than its entire city budget to pick up the garbage without the help of the Zableens.

- In Curitiba, a city in southern Brazil, a garbage recycling program not only saves waste by encouraging the separation of domestic garbage into organic and non-organic materials, but also provides employment at the recycling plant on the outskirts of the city. A second initiative in Curitiba encourages shanty town dwellers to collect garbage in exchange for bus vouchers or food. This serves the multiple purposes of providing goods to low-income groups, promoting environmental awareness, and cleaning up hard-to-reach areas such as steep slopes and valleys.

CLEAN AIR

Air pollution is a serious problem which occurs in all the world's largest cities. Regulations to control emissions from automobiles and industry are, in general, weak or absent. In some areas of Calcutta, air pollution is regularly at a level dangerous to human health; Delhi, the capital of India, is often shrouded in dense smog. In Beijing, the World Health Organization has reported that there are, on average, only 93 days a year when breathing is not a health hazard.

In Mexico City, when the wind is still, the fumes of three million vehicles and 35 000 industrial sites become trapped by the high ring of mountains surrounding the city. One of the greatest risks automobiles present to human health is the lead in gasoline. On occasion, drivers have been banned from using their cars one day a week; in 1993 all new automobiles produced in Mexico were required to have pollution controls and use unleaded gasoline.

The city of Cubatao, located near Sao Paulo in Brazil, turned an air pollution problem into a success story. By 1985 heavy industry, including fertilizer and chemical producers, was literally poisoning the air, the land, and the residents, forcing yearly emergency evacuations. Both the state and the private sector have worked to clean up the air with the result that some chemicals have been reduced by 97 percent; water quality has so improved that after a 30-year absence, fish have returned to the Cubatao River.

HOUSING

Since the 1950s a combination of a rapidly growing low-income population and a scarci-

SOURCE: CIDA/Roger Lemoyne

Fig. 1-41 *Housing next to a contaminated stream in Bangladesh. Citing evidence from the photograph, suggest some of the problems that dwellers in these homes might experience.*

ty of government investment in construction has meant that many people living in the cities of the developing world are unable to find suitable housing. They have to buy, build, or rent housing in illegal settlements because they cannot afford to obtain these facilities legally. Virtually all of these settlements are dusty, densely populated, and lack trees, paved roads, adequate supplies of water, drains, schools, and even rudimentary health centres. These dwellings, which outside observers may call shanty towns or slums, provide a home for between one-third and two-thirds of the inhabitants of most developing world cities.

In some cases today, new shanty towns are created when a group of families targets a piece of vacant land, preferably publicly owned, such as a dump site, then takes possession by putting up shacks over night. Some governments recognize squatters on public lands as legal owners after a period of time because it is often easier to do this than to pay eviction costs. In Venezuela, for example, a plan has been adopted for granting land ownership to shanty town residents in the hope that this will give residents an incentive to upgrade their homes.

Governments in some countries have tried to build low-cost housing, with mixed results. In the developing world, this housing may still be too expensive for the poor to maintain. With thousands of newcomers moving into the cities, the value of low-cost housing often increases to the extent that it is more profitable for the poor to sell to the middle class and move back to the streets.

The development of co-operatives or community organizations that draw on participation and leadership from within these communities has helped upgrade the standard of living for their inhabitants. The World Bank, an organization affiliated with the United Nations, was founded in 1945 to help raise the standards of living in developing countries. While in the past it generally financed large-scale projects, it now increasingly supports small community-based initiatives. One such project is the Kampung Improvement Program in Jakarta, the capital of Indonesia. Its success grew out of a decision to give squatters title to plots of land. In return, the new landowners agreed to help build footpaths, improve drainage, and reduce garbage.

POLITICAL AND SOCIAL VIOLENCE

The type of human violence that plagues various cities of the world may be a symptom of social unrest or ethnic and racial disputes, or an instrument used by the government to control its citizens. This type of violence is not necessarily limited to cities in the developing world; in Los Angeles in 1992 the acquittal of four white policemen accused of beating a black motorist triggered a rampage of looting and arson. Although the criminal trial and its decision in Los Angeles sparked riots, a human rights trial involving the same four men in 1993 resulted in a conviction for two of them and there was peace in the city when the results were announced. Other examples of violence in the developed world include the ethnic and religious fighting in Belfast, Northern Ireland and Sarajevo in Bosnia-Herzegovina. The roots of the violence in Belfast and Sarajevo are based on conflicts which are centuries old.

The American situation has its roots not only in **racism** but in technological changes that are affecting the work force. The industrial revolution that created mass production (and in turn, mass education and a mass labour force), is now over. The new wave of manufacturing is based on short runs of products made in computer-driven factories. As a result, economic opportunity for many individuals, regardless of race, is not the same as it was in the past. The resulting displacement of workers and social upheaval may create tensions that can lead to violence.

Political leaders may attempt to control cities through organized violence and fear. For example, although Zaire is a country rich in natural resources, its capital, Kinshasa, is crumbling under the corruption of leader President Mobutu. The social fabric of the city has been destroyed by government troops going out on looting sprees or ferreting out opposition to Mobutu's rule. There are no efficient civic operations left in the city as a result.

The causes of such violence are often complex and intertwined. They result from issues which may have been disputed for centuries. The solutions, therefore, are not easily forthcoming.

PLANNING FOR THE FUTURE

Now, more than ever before, city governments in all parts of the world are seeing the need to plan their policies and the use of the land under their control carefully.

In the developed world most large cities have comprehensive **land use controls** involving **zoning** and tax policies. Thus, expansion can occur fairly systematically. Being able to pay for the services needed for expansion is the problem. Currently, many urban planners are suggesting that city governments encourage builders, mainly through tax incentives, to build on previously unused spaces within a city. Adequate provision for parks and a more thoughtful approach to integrating homes and workplaces can ease the problem of very high densities and have the positive reward of cutting down travelling time between jobs and home.

Cities in the developing world face a different set of problems. Few land use controls exist, so expansion often occurs in a very unorganized fashion. As well, these cities are developing at such a rapid rate that it is impossible to provide

services. Most urban planners advocate community-based development. Community groups are often successful at providing services without government help.

As these cities develop land use controls it is important that they recognize their own particular structure. Cities in the developing world are a mixture of rural and urban lifestyles. For instance, in Nairobi, one-third of all households grow crops or raise small livestock. Building standards also must recognize that most city dwellers can afford, for

SOURCE: Marilyn MacKenzie

Fig. 1-42 *A park in Bombay provides enjoyment for city children.*

example, only mud walls and pit latrines rather than brick walls and plumbing.

Chandigarh, the state capital of the Punjab in northern India, is an example of a pre-planned modern city. The ideas developed here are of use to both the developed and the developing world. In 1950 the famed Swiss-born French architect known as Le Corbusier was commissioned to draw up a master plan for a city of 500 000. He planned an urban highway network which would be linked to a secondary network which in turn would feed into more local roads with lower capacities and slower speed limits, all in the interests of ease of movement and peaceful living. Neighbourhood units were to contain housing limited to five stories high and encompass shopping centres, schools and health centres. Today, Chandigarh's inhabitants still regard it as an ordered city even though the area now houses a million people and has become a major university centre as well as a political centre.

In Curitiba growth was planned along pre-determined axes with strict zoning regulations for land use. An efficient mass transportation system along these axes was given priority over private cars. Traffic flows freely along wide, tree-shaded avenues. Outlying shanty towns are integrated into the city's structure through small innovative programs.

The process of urbanization has produced significant problems and often shocking effects around the world. However, cities are also the centre of creativity and ambition, and there is enormous determination among much of the urban poor to better their lives. It seems that a great city balances vitality and chaos. Cities like Chandigarh and Curitiba are leading the way.

FURTHER ANALYSIS

1. Research the land use policies which govern your community. Try to determine the reasons for their existence. List the procedures which exist to enforce these policies. Depending on the size of your community it may be necessary for you to limit your research to a particular category of policies in order to keep your investigation manageable.

2. (a) Over a period of two weeks collect newspaper articles which pertain to urbanization issues anywhere in the world. Organize these articles in order to develop an overall perspective of the causes and proposed solutions to these issues. Write a paper on your findings.
   (b) Investigate and report on how the perspective developed in part (a) of this question applies specifically to urbanization issues which exist in an urban area near you.

CHAPTER 2

ENVIRONMENT AND QUALITY OF LIFE

2

ENVIRONMENT AND QUALITY OF LIFE

The environment consists of those things that make up an organism's surroundings. The natural environment is the atmosphere, land, rocks, waters, and all forms of vegetable and animal life (sometimes called flora and fauna), collectively called the biosphere. More than most organisms, people have developed the ability to modify their natural environment. Such human-modified environments are called phenomenal environments. Many people think that the environment, whether natural or phenomenal, should be regarded as an ecosystem, and that humans are a part of this ecosystem.

Indeed, there has always been a very close connection between a natural environment and the quality of life of the people inhabiting that environment. From earliest times, the natural environment provided the life-supporting resources that enabled humanity to survive. The quality of life of the earliest survivors depended upon the various opportunities for hunting and gathering in their natural environment.

Farming, which evolved much later, provided more stability, but neither survival nor a satisfactory quality of life were guaranteed. Life continued to be harsh for many; thus humanity strove to improve its lot. The advent of farming, however, marked a major change in the way humans interacted with the natural environment. As the concept of farming spread from its origins in southwestern Asia, people increasingly regarded the natural environment as something that could be manipulated to their benefit. The natural environment was no longer merely a source of animals, nuts, and berries; it appeared to be a resource that could be managed and made to yield.

Humanity has grown in numbers and changed the environment for thousands of years. The accumulated effects of environmental modification along with increased numbers of people, all expecting an improved quality of life, place the natural environment under great pressure. Consider the various human-environmental interactions that are noted in the following readings. As you go through the readings, create two lists. One list will be of examples of human interactions with the environment that, in your view, enhance the overall quality of human life. The second list will be of examples where the relationship threatens the overall quality of human life.

TIGERS AND LYNX FLOURISH

Of the 37 species of wild felines, 22 are endangered to varying degrees, according to the World Wide Fund for Nature (formerly the World Wildlife Fund). Agriculture, forest exploitation and urbanization are gradually depriving them of the spacious habitats they need. With this in mind, the Indian Government and the WWF have carried out a vast joint campaign for the protection of tigers as a result of which India's tiger population has more than doubled in fourteen years. Similar results have been achieved with the lynx which, despite protests from sheep-raisers on whose flocks the lynx preys, has been reintroduced in several European countries.

Greenwatch, Reprinted from *The UNESCO Courier*, 1992 6

THE PRICE OF AMAZONIAN GOLD

Mercury in Brazilian gold mining is reaching alarming concentrations in local ecosystems, according to recent studies. After gold-bearing deposits are dredged from river-bottom sediments, mercury is alloyed with the gold and later burned away in the final recovery. In the Madeira River basin, in the southwestern corner of the Amazon watershed near the Bolivian border, officials estimate that about 100 tonnes of mercury were discharged by mining operations during a recent six-year period — 45 percent into the river and 55 percent into the air. Mercury recovered from the process usually is reused three or four times before being dumped in the river. Tests show mercury levels in some fish from nearby tributaries at five times the Brazilian safety limit for consumption. Tests on hair samples taken from local Indians and gold miners, especially those with a diet high in fish, suggest acute mercury poisoning. (However, because symptoms of mercury poisoning are similar to those of malaria, which is prevalent in the region, it is difficult to differentiate actual causes of observed symptoms.) With the Amazonian gold rush on in earnest since the late 1970s and involving more than 650 000 people today, the risk of widespread mercury pollution is a real concern for authorities charged with the already challenging task of regulating miners. Gold recovery systems that capture and recycle mercury do exist and could be promoted to ease pollution hazards.

Spectrum, *Environment*, 1990 4

AUSTRALIA CLEANS UP

Prompted by an idea that came to a solitary yachtsman appalled by the sorry state of the high seas, Australia has instituted a clean-up day for beaches, rivers and parks. On the 1991 Cleaning Up Australia Day, more than 350 000 volunteers collected some 30 000 tonnes of waste from 4452 loca-tions, twice the amount of the previous year. In all, a quarter of a million garbage bags were dis-tributed to military personnel, local authorities and associations of volunteers. All kinds of rubbish were collected, including bottles, cartons, syringes, wrecked cars, rubble, industrial waste, animal carcasses and household refuse. Plastic, glass, paper and alu-minum were recycled. Although Australia is the only country to have officially designated a spe-cial clean-up Day, volunteers on the Hawaiian island of Oahu, where Honolulu is located, gather every Saturday morning to clean up villages and remove wrecked vehicles from the roadsides.

Greenwatch, reprinted from *The UNESCO Courier*, 1992 7-8

CITES UNDER THREAT

At a meeting of CITES, the Convention on International Trade in Endangered Species of Wild Fauna and Flora, held in Kyoto (Japan) in March, Mostafa Kamal Tolba, the Egyptian-born biologist who has been head of the United Nations Environment Programme (UNEP) for the past sixteen years, said that CITES was itself endangered by North-South divergences. Zimbabwe, Namibia, Botswana and Malawi are demanding the resumption of trade in ivory, which has been banned since the Lausanne Conference in 1989. At that time the international community had voiced concern about the threatened disappearance of the African elephant. By cutting off the supply at source, it thought it could, by the same stroke, do away with demand. Yet poaching did not stop, and the profit that states could have derived from the sale of elephant tusks disappeared. "Powerful groups,

SOURCE: Lyn Boggs

Fig. 2-1 *An elephant in Zimbabwe. Which is worth more: the animal or its tusks?*

chiefly in the rich, industrialized countries, consider that the outlawing of trade in elephant products is the answer," Mr. Tolba stated, before adding that "There are also thousands of millions of people whose voices will not be heard, who use a minute part of the planet's resources and who receive a pathetic part of its revenues.... These people cannot be refused the right to use their natural heritage."

Greenwatch, Reprinted from *The UNESCO Courier*, 1992 7-8

SAVING THE PLANET IS SLOW WORK

OSLO — It's hard to believe that it's been more than eight years since the U.N. Secretary-General asked me to chair a "world commission" on how the human species could make economic progress within nature's strict laws.

• • • • •

We had intended to produce a report largely about the environment, but found that to be impossible. We realized one cannot "save the environment" without profoundly changing some basic human activities: the way people govern themselves; the way those governments cooperate; the way people trade and do business; the ways in which energy, food and timber are produced; and the rates at which our species reproduces itself.

We found many aspects of human progress ecologically and economically unsustainable. So we called for "sustainable development" — progress which meets the needs of the present while not compromising the ability of future generations to meet their needs.

We noted that prerequisites for such development included democracy and freedom of information, as people cannot change their ways without being involved in decisions over those changes. We called for a redefinition of "security" that included environmental security, and noted that there could be no sustainable development in a world that spent $1 trillion a year — and half of research and development budgets — on the military.

• • • • •

As we wrote in 1987: "Most of today's decision makers will be dead before the planet suffers the full consequences of acid rain, global warming, ozone depletion, widespread desertification and species loss. Most of today's young voters will be alive."

Gro Harlem Brundtland, *Guardian News Service*, 1992 4 22

WOMEN AND NATURE, AN ALLIANCE FOR SURVIVAL

From the very beginning of human experience, women's work has been close to, and dependent upon, Nature. In early hunter-gatherer societies, women collected seeds, nuts and roots to feed their families and communities. Survival was dependent upon an intimate knowledge of Nature and her ways. This remains true in many regions today. Women know intuitively that a society which turns its back on Nature is doomed. And many women today believe that the dominant forces of global society are, in fact, ignoring Nature's needs.

• • • • •

Women have learned that their breast milk is contaminated with dioxin, that pesticides and herbicides are present in ground water. They are told that the life-giving Sun is becoming dangerous due to a weakened ozone layer, that children everywhere are vulnerable to genetic disorders caused by contaminated environments. Women have observed these phenomena and feel alienated from a society which has lost touch with the beauty and power of Nature. They fear that future generations will be deprived of the diversity of Nature's creatures and of the music of bird song.

• • • • •

As the planet's natural resources diminish, and as a growing world population increases demands on those resources, competition for access to them will escalate. This struggle for limited resources may well result in new resource wars. Evidence of growing pressure is found in nations which depend on the Nile or the Euphrates, in Europe where the fouling of soils, rivers and air by neighbouring nations is a source of sickness and friction, and in the world's seas where competing mechanized fishing fleets of powerful nations deplete fish stocks of the poor coastal and island peoples.

Fear for the future — of a damaged and dangerous natural environment or of the violence it brings — is what unites women in today's world....

Perdita Huston, Reprinted from *The UNESCO Courier*, 1992 3

RICH VS. POOR

A major obstacle to sustainable development in many countries is a social structure that gives most of the nation's wealth to a tiny minority of its people.... What to Northern eyes seems like some of the worst environmental outrages — felling rain forests to make charcoal for sale as cooking fuel, for example — are often committed by people who have no other form of income. Yet if the barriers that keep those people poor have withstood wars of liberation and social revolutions, what are the chances that they will fall in the name of environmentalism?

The disparities that mark individual countries are mirrored in the planet as a whole. Most of its wealth is concentrated in the North. "The reality is that there are many worlds on this planet," says Chee Yokling, a Malaysian representative of Friends of the Earth, "rich worlds and poor worlds." From the South's point of view, it is the rich worlds' profligate (wasteful) consumption patterns — their big cars, refrigerators and climate-controlled shopping malls — that are the problem....

Philip Elmer-Dewitt, Reported by Andrea Dorfman/New York, Ian McCluskey/Rio de Janeiro and Anita Pratap/New Delhi, *Time*, 1992 6 1

DISCUSSION AND RESEARCH

1. Select two of the previous readings that appear to present one-sided or biased views.
   (a) Analyze the readings to identify words and expressions that lead you to believe the author is biased.
   (b) Describe the nature of the bias that you identify.

2. Assume the role of a journalist who has been assigned to write an article for your local newspaper. Your editor has instructed you to select an article that you agree with from the readings before these questions. You are to research, develop, and "publish" a counter-argument so that the two articles can be printed side by side in the newspaper.

3. In teams of two or three, prepare a press release (one to two pages of double-spaced typing) promoting international action to improve the global environment in some way that will raise the quality of life for people everywhere. First, agree upon which aspect of the environment you wish to improve and the explanation of why it should be improved. Second, suggest some actions that might be taken to promote international cooperation on the matter.

4. Interactions between two phenomena may produce gains or losses for each side in a variety of combinations: if both sides gain some benefits, the relationship may be described as a win-win situation; if one side benefits and the other side loses, the relationship is a win-lose situation; if the benefits gained by one side are equalled by the losses of the other, the situation is described as zero sum, since benefits and losses exactly cancel out; if both sides lose, the relationship is a lose-lose (or no-win) one. For example, if a polluting

factory is closed, the environment will become cleaner but people will be out of work until (and if) they find another job. The environment "wins," but the economy "loses." In small groups, examine the previous readings, and from the information provided attempt to classify the situations discussed into the following categories:

• humanity wins, environment wins;
• humanity wins, environment loses;
• humanity loses, environment wins;
• humanity loses, environment loses;
• zero sum.

When reporting the group's decisions to the class, describe difficulties encountered in finding examples for all the categories.

5. (a) As a class, brainstorm a list of ways in which the natural environment may affect the quality of human life (such as weather variations influencing the size and quality of harvests).
   (b) Break into small groups and within each group attempt to agree on a list of the five most important ways that the natural environment affects people in your community.

VIEWS ON THE HUMANITY-ENVIRONMENT RELATIONSHIP

The environment is the sum of the various conditions that influence the growth and development of all life on earth. However, there are differing views about the relationship between humanity and the environment. Reasons for such differences rest in the cultural diversity of the world, reflected in differences in values and variations in economic development.

Determinism was an early form of geographical thought which held that the physical factors of the environment, especially landscape and climate, tended to dominate, even determine, different patterns of human economic and social behaviour. For example, people who inhabited barren land next to abundant fishing grounds would fish for a living, as determined by their environment. Along the same pattern, people inhabiting fertile river basins farmed; people in game-rich forests hunted; and people in areas with known coal and iron deposits developed industries. Likewise, because of the influence their physical surroundings had on their livelihood, many peoples developed systems of beliefs based on environmental spirits. In all cases, according to the philosophy of determinism, practices and beliefs rested ultimately in human inability to control — or in any major way influence — the environment.

Environmental spirits are the spirits of air, water, fire, sun, forest, animals, and so on. A belief in such spirits is called animism.

Traditional determinism was supplanted as technology evolved. Early irrigation practices in southwest Asia and China allowed new land to be farmed. The advent of the iron plough in Europe more than a thousand years ago caused widespread deforestation of the continent's lowlands. The natural environment increasingly came to be regarded as something that could be controlled and manipulated rather than as something that controlled humanity.

The philosophy of possibilism slowly replaced that of determinism. As technology developed, the range of possibilities for improving the quality of life became ever wider. Early examples include improved food production in the Tigris-Euphrates valley using Babylonian irrigation techniques, and faster transportation of rice in eastern China using the Grand Canal. In the 18th century, improved methods of production, transportation, and food production began to flourish in Europe and North America.

Underlying possibilism in Europe and North America was the belief that humanity had the right to control and modify the environment to suit its own perceived needs. Justification for possibilism was partly biblical ("And God said...have dominion over the fish of the sea, and over the fowl of the air, and over every living thing that moveth upon the earth," Genesis, 1:28).

SOURCE: Japan National Tourist Organization

Fig. 2-2 *Many inventions have helped decrease travel times. Japanese bullet trains regularly pass Mount Fuji in their rapid passage west of Tokyo. What factors are necessary to make construction of long-distance mass transit worthwhile?*

Possibilism also reflected the rising demand for a higher standard of living throughout Europe.

The earth's resources for production and the environment's abilities to absorb waste products were known to be limited, but the knowledge was perceived to be of no practical value. In relation to the still small populations of the 19th century the earth's resources and abilities were seen by those with the new technology to be limitless. Malthus may have warned of disasters, but these disasters were not perceived by Europeans to be an immediate threat.

During the 19th and 20th centuries, many people in the pre-industrial parts of the world became aware of the technological advances made in Europe and North America. They sought access to new technology and its perceived benefits. Japan was the first nation to set out on a deliberate path of change. In 1867 the Emperor Meiji sent missions to Europe to learn about the new technology, and the transformation of Japan began.

Many of the opportunities acted upon under the possibilist philosophy have produced side effects that have changed the natural environment. These side effects are now widely regarded as either dangerous to life forms or damaging to an improved quality of life. As a result, a range of views on what humanity's proper relationship with the environment is has now developed. Fig. 2-3 illustrates these various views.

Some people still believe in possibilism, now sometimes characterized as the "economics" or "frontier" approach to the environment. They believe that human needs are more important than environmental needs, that hunger and poverty are major threats to humanity, and that economic development and prosperity should be given priority. In their view, the earth's ability to provide resources and absorb wastes is far from its limits. They argue that as the earth's limits are eventually approached, the prices of resources and waste disposal opportunities will rise because these things will become scarce. They further argue that price increases will enforce reduced use of resources and waste disposal opportunities without necessarily reducing production. Production will be maintained or even increased through greater efficiency.

Opponents of the economics approach claim that the creation of value through scarcity causes harm to people who rely upon their environment for survival. The cod fishery off Atlantic Canada is an example of a resource that appeared limitless but was gradually depleted through overfishing. The

At the start of the 19th century the earth's population was about 900 000 000, about the same as the present population of India. At the end of the 19th century it was about 1 500 000 000.

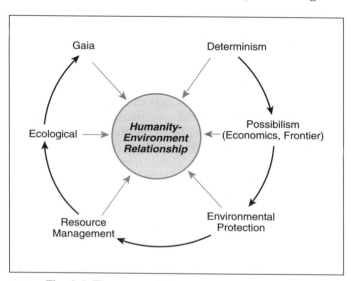

Fig. 2-3 *The range of views on the relationship between humanity and the natural environment.*

Canadian government began to close the fishery in 1992 in order to give the resource time to regenerate.

Supporters of the economics approach quote counter-examples. They state that the oil price rises of the 1970s and 1980s caused reduced consumption of oil and the construction of cars with greatly improved fuel efficiencies. In 1975, for example, world oil production was about 80 million barrels a day; by 1985 it had fallen to 70 million barrels a day. Meanwhile, the number of cars, trucks, and buses worldwide grew from 328 million in 1975 to 488 million in 1985. They also note that the increasingly expensive use of copper for telecommunication cables was replaced in the 1980s and 1990s by cheaper and more efficient glass fibre cables.

One tonne of glass fibre cable can handle 31 times as many messages as one tonne of copper cable, and requires only five percent as much energy for its manufacture.

Underlying possibilism and the economics approach to the environment is the idea of the commons. The commons are the parts of the environment that are available to anyone. Thus the atmosphere and the oceans are commons on a world scale. On a local scale, many European villagers hold grazing land in common, so that anyone may put their animals on it. The open range serves the same purpose in North America. Owners brand or colour-code their animals for recognition. Free access to commons provided an increased range of possibilities to many people.

Use of commons requires self-discipline. If all families graze one cow on a village's common land, and then someone puts on two cows, eventually more families want to put two cows on. The common land then rapidly becomes overgrazed, probably degraded, and possibly unable to support even the original number of cows. This tendency for individuals to abuse their right to free use of the commons ultimately produces common disaster called the tragedy of the commons.

Awareness of the harmful effects of commons abuse surfaced at different times in different places. Two to three thousand years ago various people in southwest Asia began to worry about the damage numerous herds of goats were doing to the grazing land; similarly in England in the 17th century, writer John Evelyn complained about the deforestation of much of England for the construction of its navy. After the start of modern industrialism in Britain in the 18th century, worries continued about the waste products of industry that fouled the lands and waters.

John Evelyn was a 17th century English writer. He was very concerned about preservation of the environment. His strong defence of forests (in his book *Sylva*, 1664) was preceded by an attack on smoke pollution in London (*Fumifugium*, 1661).

Out of these concerns for the natural environment a changing view of the humanity-environment relationship emerged; this led to the philosophy of environmental protection. The philosophy developed most strongly in Europe and North America, following the environmentally damaging excesses of early industrialization, but has since become widespread as industrialization has spread to most parts of the world. Like the economics approach, environmental protection viewed human needs as more important than environmental needs. However, the need to protect certain aspects of the environment from adverse human impact was recognized, particularly to preserve them for human enjoyment. Accordingly, various scenic areas and animal species gradually came under human protection. The first major landscape area to be protected was Yellowstone National

Park in the United States in 1872; other areas around the world became protected at later dates.

Protection of wildlife occurred more or less concurrently with protection of landscape. Bird sanctuaries and wildlife parks were established. The environmental protection approach has also urged industry to establish waste treatment operations, to reduce or disperse smoke emissions, to use resources more efficiently, and to minimize other adverse impacts.

The first bird sanctuary in Canada was established in 1887 in what is now Saskatchewan. Wildlife parks were also established, such as Wood Buffalo National Park in 1922 in northern Alberta and the adjacent Northwest Territories.

The essence of the environmental protection approach is damage control: to prevent further deterioration of the environment, and to clean up those areas already seriously damaged. Critics believe that simply protecting the environment is insufficient if the processes that the environment needs to be protected from are allowed to continue, albeit in a more restricted fashion. They claim that practices such as the setting of pollution limits is not a substitute for the total elimination of pollution.

Despite criticism, the environmental protection approach continues to have great support. Areas of scenic beauty or of irreplaceable wilderness continue to be set aside as parks; much wildlife continues to be protected; and pollution limits continue to be set.

The measurement of pollution and the setting of limits become finer as measuring techniques improve. What used to be unmeasurable at less than one part in a thousand is now measurable at one part in a billion. Similarly, polluting at levels that were formerly undetectable may now be regarded in some cases as criminal activity.

Nevertheless, there has been a growing awareness that the environment needs even better care. In response, the resource management approach to the humanity-environment relationship has developed. Rather than focusing on pollution control as environmental protectionists do, proponents of resource management focus on controlling the depletion and degradation of resources.

With the rapid growth of population in many countries, resource management beliefs are increasingly widespread across the world. Large numbers of people are finding it more and more difficult to obtain some of their basic resource needs. For example, natural woodland has been cut for fuelwood in ever-widening distances from habitation centres, causing spreading deforestation and degradation of the original soil cover. There is a growing awareness among people in many countries of the need to manage resources more effectively. In all parts of the world, many scenic areas or natural habitats have come to be off-limits for mining, forestry, and energy generation projects. With access to resources restricted to some extent, the need to improve management of available resources has grown.

Fuelwood is very difficult to carry far. Accordingly, there is a growing practice in remote wooded areas of burning wood until it turns to charcoal, which is much easier to carry. This practice is wasteful of wood, which aggravates the problem of fuelwood shortages.

The resource management approach is similar to the possibilist and environmental protection approaches to the humanity-environment relationship in that they all put the needs of humanity first. Calling something a "resource" implies that it is regarded as useful to humanity. The essence of the resource management philosophy is to manage resources better for the improvement of the human condition. Poverty and hunger are regarded, as in the other two philosophies, as threats to a decent quality of life for all people; and the growth of the economy is perceived as the chief means to raise the overall quality of life. However, supporters of resource management maintain that the operations of the economic

SOURCE: CIDA/Paul Chiasson

Fig. 2-4 *Fuelwood is often collected, bundled, and sold by merchants to villagers who regularly walk long distances to obtain it. Here in Rwanda, a woman carries home a few days' supply. What are some alternatives?*

Some theories of the development of humanity's condition regard risk as a natural challenge, and civilization as the ultimate response to that challenge. Increasingly, however, there is a trend in government legislation to reduce or eliminate risk to people.

system must not be allowed to ruin the environment so that continued improvements become impossible.

Resource management beliefs are what the *Brundtland Report*, (see p. 63) with its push for sustainable development, is based on. Two of the requirements it finds necessary for sustainable development, stable populations and reduced per capita consumption among the relatively wealthy persons on earth, have yet to be reached.

As the environmental protection and resource management philosophies have developed, analysis of risk by economists has also changed. While risk analysis has always been an entrepreneurial function (profits being the reward for successful risk taking; bankruptcy the penalty for failure), it has now gained an environmental emphasis. Degrees of risk among different possible courses of action are investigated, compared, and costed. For example, a firm or a government may ask what the risks and costs are in polluting the environment to a certain degree compared with the risks and costs of polluting to a lesser degree. The risks and costs of reducing pollution are sometimes perceived to be possible business closures and increased unemployment. Conversely, the risks and costs of continuing to pollute are increasingly to be seen in possible prison sentences and corporate fines.

A fourth approach to the humanity-environment relationship is ecological. This approach was highlighted by the publication in 1962 of *Silent Spring* by Rachel Carson, in which she drew public attention to the effects of DDT and other pesticides on the rest of the environment. The **anthropocentricism** (humanity first) of the economic, environmental protection, and resource management philosophies is replaced in ecological philosophy. Humanity is seen at best as a no-more-than-equal part of the environmental web, and at worst, by the so-called deep ecologists, as a major threat to the rest of the environment. Humans are not accorded more importance than animals or vegetation, and ecologists believe they should live without any unsettling impact upon other forms of life. Environmental harmony is the overriding principle of this philosophy, along with ideas of species equality, maintenance of species variety, and reductions in human populations. Zero or negative economic growth is also advocated, with the use of only simple or low technology, and the limiting of human influence from having a global reach to a more localized sphere of activity.

> The ecological approach sets high value on the traditional ways of life of indigenous peoples, and prizes their beliefs as representing harmony with nature. Others assert that such beliefs and lifestyles were enforced by a dominant environment.

Great value is attached within the ecological approach to pre-industrial ways of life and spiritual beliefs. To this end, the ecological view of the humanity-environment relationship would seem to favour determinism. A major difference between the ecological approach and determinism, however, is that under determinism people had little or no choice about their way of life, whereas in the ecological approach, they would have the choice but would not exercise it. For this reason the ecological approach is often criticized as reactionary and unrealistic. How valid do you think this criticism is?

The concept of Gaia is a variation of the ecological approach to the humanity-environment relationship. Gaia is the name of the ancient Greek goddess of Earth. It was reintroduced in the early 1970s by James Lovelock, a NASA scientist devising experiments to determine if life existed on Mars. He wanted the name to symbolize his view that planet Earth is itself alive, not in the sense of a thinking being, but as a tree is. He proposed that the earth is a self-regulating superorganism, and that all life-forms belonging to it are subordinate organs, with air, water, and energy flows being likened to the flows of energy, blood, and other fluids within the body. As with a single organism in the biosphere, energy or food is taken in, and wastes are excreted. Earth energy is received from the sun as solar energy; and wastes are accommodated and recycled on earth itself.

In the Gaia philosophy humanity is part of the earth's biosphere, of equal importance to all other life-forms. If humanity has an impact on other parts of the biosphere through numbers and technology, the other parts will change and adjust. Whether the changes are for good or ill does not matter under Gaia; those are moral judgments that are irrelevant to the operation of the earth system.

The Gaia concept does not assume that the current state of the environment is the optimum one; it is merely the present one. And since the earth is alive, change is inevitable: just as the present is different from the past, so the future will be different again. The earth system, through its many environmental sub-systems, will adjust. Gaia is totally non-anthropocentric. Indeed, Lovelock notes that "If we lose our habitat, the system of life and its environment on Earth, Gaia, will go on. But humankind will no longer be a part of it." (*Healing Gaia*, James Lovelock, 1991.)

All six views of the humanity-environment relationship (determinism, possibilism/economics/frontier, environmental protection, resource management, ecological, and Gaia) have proponents and opponents. Even among the increasing numbers of people expressing concern about the environment, there is no universal agreement about either the appropriate level of concern or the nature of any action that might be taken. Before you begin the following readings, set up an organizer so that you can attempt to classify the views described in the readings in terms of the six views of the humanity-environment relationship. The classification may not always be straightforward.

Other views of the humanity-environment relationship exist, particularly in many religions. Investigate some of these views to determine whether or not they correspond to any of the six views described here.

ENVIRONMENTALISM RUNS RIOT

So effectively have environmentalists greened public opinion that it takes an unashamed reactionary to question the wisdom of becoming ever greener and cleaner. Most environmental pressure-groups are convinced that the environment is so important that standards cannot be set too high, and must be met regardless of cost. When an annual public opinion poll asks Americans whether they share that view, a large majority agrees. Europeans, too, now tend to believe that anything greener must be better. Such belief will gradually come to haunt greenery's advocates. For nothing — not even cleanliness — comes free; and the costs of environmental policies are likely to rise sharply over the rest of the century. If the green enthusiasm generated over the past four years is to survive in public policy, the enthusi-asts must learn the language of priorities, and of costs and benefits.

• • • • •

Good environmental lawmaking starts by trying to pinpoint which risks really matter. For example, where new rules are intended mainly to protect health, it makes sense to ask how much they cost in preventing a single early death....

Such calculations are evidently difficult. The costs of a policy may be clear enough; the benefits hard to quantify or assess. The science, too, may be shaky. It has taken less time for governments to impose tough curbs on power stations that emit large amounts of sulphur dioxide than it has for scientists to become sceptical of the links between sulphur dioxide and the death of forests that was once attributed to acid rain. The manufacture of chlorofluorocarbons (CFCs) will be phased out before scientists really understand the relative contributions of CFCs and volcanoes to the depletion of the ozone layer. Environmentalists argue for the precautionary principle: if in doubt, clamp down on suspect practices. The flaw in such playing-it-safe is that it replaces environmental risk with risks to jobs and wealth, which environmentalists often loftily ignore.

Once governments have decided their environmental priorities, the best way to attain them is usually by looking for ways to harness the force of the market. The more companies can be given incentives to come up with technical answers to environmental problems, the more cost-effective those answers are likely to be. Broadly speaking, any given level of environmental virtue can be delivered more cheaply by using green taxes, or other measures that harness market endeavour, than by using regulation.

The Economist, 92 8 8

WORKING WITH THE WASTE PICKERS

A new philosophy...is beginning to transform solid waste management worldwide. It is grounded in "resource recognition" — the idea that most waste material can be regarded as unused resources. Environmentally sound waste management now entails the reduction of waste in production and distribution processes and the enhancement of reuse and recycling. In wealthy nations these principles are being translated into practice through government regulation, stakeholder cooperation, and citizens' initiatives. In poorer countries, however, urban solid waste management is still wedded to the conventional engineering systems and city cleansing departments tend to look to higher technology and privatization for solutions to the environmental problems of uncollected and unsafely dumped wastes.

• • • • •

The motivations of Asians who have become activists for reform of waste management systems are often more complex than those of their Canadian counterparts. While we in Canada are mostly concerned about ineffective municipal solid waste management (MSWM) for ecological reasons such as lack of landfill space and resource depletion, waste management in Asian cities is intimately linked with the lives of street dwellers and many other very disadvantaged people. In response, many Asian community action groups look beyond the ecological implications of resource recognition and consider their programmes as social action for the poor.

• • • • •

Asian cities have extensive waste economies, based on the activities of itinerant waste buyers, waste pickers, small waste shops, second-hand markets, dealers, transporters, and a range of recycling industries. How these informal systems work is affected by socio-economic change as cities grow and are better regulated. In modernizing cities the collecting and trading of clean wastes (those kept separate at the source of generation) becomes difficult because the operations of collectors are more restricted and more costly. At the same time, modern consumption by the more affluent generally renders their residual wastes more attractive both to pickers and to the municipal collection crews. Certainly the increase of recyclables in the final waste streams makes dump picking more worthwhile. But, picking (gathering recyclables from mixed wastes on streets and dumps) is also becoming more hazardous, as Asian urban refuse now contains more broken glass and cans, more toxic materials, and more biomedical waste.

During downturns in the economy more people resort to waste picking as a survival strategy. While poor and inaccessible areas are plagued by pollution from uncollected wastes, many inhabitants of these areas depend upon waste recovery and recycling to meet some of their basic needs for shelter, food and employment. They desire access to good wastes as close as possible to the sources in better-off residential and commercial areas. When cities try to increase the efficiency of waste services with more mechanization, friction between formal and informal waste systems increases.

There is no societal recognition of the importance of waste recycling to the economy, and waste pickers usually have no concept of the pivotal role their work plays in resource recovery. As a result, the social status of waste pickers is very low.

• • • • •

The history of the Waste Wise pilot project named "Garbage and Human Concern" shows how a comprehensive view of local solid waste problems can evolve from a social concern for waste pickers.

The idea grew out of the Ragpickers' Education and Development Scheme (REDS), supported by the Catholic Church in Bangalore, south India, which helped waste-picking street children. REDS' director, Anselm Rosario, was convinced that improvements for waste pickers depended upon creating a legitimate role for them in the waste management system. Waste pickers could increase their status by becoming waste collectors if households would cooperate in separating their wastes and handing them over to door-to-door collectors.

In 1990 the Waste Wise project was launched by Rosario, aided by Asha de Souza, through Mythri Trust (formed to carry on REDS). They had funding for one year from Terre Des Hommes of Switzerland. The general goal was to explore alternatives to the conventional solid waste system, based on waste reduction, separation of compostable, recyclable and other wastes, and decentralization. Socially, the goal was to improve conditions for waste pickers by lending legitimacy to informal waste work, improving earnings, and creating opportunities for upward mobility. Benefits to city authorities were to include job creation and cost reductions in collection and transportation of wastes due to waste reduction and decentralization of some waste treatment through composting. As well, the curtailment of picking from streets and dumps would limit associated health and legal problems, and mess, and partially remove the activity that most clearly symbolizes the abject poverty of many city residents.

Waste Wise carried out their pilot project in an affluent residential area, Jayanagar IV Block, which also has some offices, shops, institutions and auto repair workshops. Considerable quantities of recyclables are generated in the neighbourhood, there are a number of waste dealers' shops, and contact with existing waste workers is well established since Mythri has been working with the street pickers in the area for some time.

The Bangalore Corporation agreed to make land available in the local park for the composting and vermiculture (growing worms). The participating households use bamboo baskets to hold the dry wastes. They separate out dry and wet wastes, and leave unsanitary waste for city collection. Former waste pickers operate as a waste collecting team, picking up the separated wastes from the project households. They are equipped with handcarts and baskets, and are trained by a supervisor paid by Waste Wise. The collectors visit each house daily, take the organics to the compost site, sell the dry recyclables, and dispose of residues in communal bins. The 300 participating households pay a small fee per month for this service and since there is no municipal curbside service this saves them having to carry their wastes to street bins.

The collectors, who are 10- to 16-year-old street dwellers, are ineligible to attend school since they have no fixed address. They are paid about $14 per month from the fees collected, and receive payments for tea and food. Collectors only get the residual wastes as most recyclables are sold or bartered to itinerant buyers by householders, but they earn about $0.70 a day through the sale of recyclables to local waste shops. Between 150 and 180 kg of waste are being diverted to composting each day, with 25 to 30 kg of paper, plastics, and other dry wastes being sold for recycling.

Waste Wise is still a shoe-string organization headed by Rosario and helped by a few volunteers and one or two part-time assistants. They are frank about the problems they have encountered. Some households are not prepared to pay anything for this convenience since they consider that their property rates should cover waste services. About 70 percent of the households are, however, paying as agreed. There is a tendency of residents to be suspicious of the waste collectors, who are still perceived as street people. And there are not enough staff or volunteers to respond to a number of requests to organize this work in other areas of the city.

Christine Furedy, *Alternatives*, Vol. 19 No. 2 1993

GOLDEN STATE'S GREEN BACKLASH

The northern spotted owl, a rare bird that makes its home in old-growth redwood forests, has become the symbol of the debate over the environment versus the economy. Thousands of lumber jobs in the Pacific Northwest are threatened by logging limits imposed to protect the owl's habitat.

Yet the spotted owl is only one example of how conservation rules can be at odds with the community. The livelihoods of West Coast commercial fishermen are now at stake as the state this month moved to limit fishing hauls all along the coast to protect the future of a dwindling salmon species.

• • • • •

Endangered species are only part of the problem. Critics charge that environmental regulations designed to reduce California air pollution are wrapping businesses in red tape. Executives claim that the cost of complying with some of the rules set by the Los Angeles South Coast Air Quality Management District far outweigh environmental benefits.

For example, large employers in the region are required to persuade employees to use car pools or to find alternative non-polluting transport....

...Last year, for example, McDonnell Douglas lent new bicycles to employees willing to ride to work. Although the company provided more than 200 bikes, all but about 50 participants in the program reverted to driving. The program cost US$100 000.

But small businesses are the most vociferous critics of air quality regulators. Dry cleaners, furniture manufacturers, car painters, restaurants and other businesses must meet strict environmental codes in California.

There is also growing disillusionment in California with recycling. Although sorting waste, in the office and the home, into paper, glass, plastic and aluminium "recyclables" has become habitual in many parts of the state, there is mounting evidence that this does little to protect the environment.

Recycling programs have produced a huge supply of paper, glass and plastic waste but there are few plants that can turn this rubbish into something useful. Aluminum is the only recyclable that pays its way because it is cheaper to produce new cans

SOURCE: Weyerhaeuser

Fig. 2-5 *In the North American Pacific northwest many jobs and communities depend on the lumber industry, now curtailed by concerns over wildlife and old-growth forest. What does the future hold for these communities?*

from old than to make them from scratch.

If that is not enough to dent the enthusiasm of would-be environmentalists, then last summer's call to ease air pollution by not lighting backyard barbecues — a staple of the California diet — certainly was. Marin County's talk of banning perfumes in public places also raised more publicity than action.

Louise Kehoe, *Financial Times of London*, 1992 4 23

FATHER SUN AND MOTHER EARTH

"There are four orders in creation. First is the physical world; second, the plant world; third, the animal; last, the human world. All four parts are so intertwined that they make up life and one whole existence. With less than the four orders, life and being are incomplete and unintelligible. No one portion is self-sufficient or complete, rather each derives its meaning from and fulfils its function and purpose within the context of the whole creation.

From last to first, each order must abide by the laws that govern the universe and the world. Man (humanity)[1] is constrained by this law to live by and learn from the animals and the plants, as the animals are dependent upon plants which draw their sustenance and existence from the earth and the sun. All of them depend ultimately on the physical world. The place, sphere, and existence of each order is predetermined by great physical laws for harmony. It is only by the relationships of the four orders that the world has sense and meaning. Without animals and plants man would have no meaning; nor would he have much more meaning if he were not governed by some immutable (unchangeable) law. For the well being of all there must be harmony in the world to be obtained by the observance of this law.

"While there is a natural predilection and instinct for conformity to the great law of balance in the world of plants and animals, mankind is not so endowed by nature. But man possesses understanding by which he can know and abide by the law and so establish his place in the world order. Man must seek guidance outside himself. Before he can abide by the law, mankind must understand the framework of the ordinances. In this way, man will honour the order as was intended

by Kitche Manitou (The Great Spirit).

. . . . .

The Anishnabeg predicated (affirmed) fatherhood of the sun. In the same way they proclaimed motherhood in the earth. Both sun and earth were mutually necessary and interdependent in the generation of life. But of the two pristine elements, Mother Earth was the most immediate and cherished and honoured.

. . . . .

Men and women owe their lives and the quality of living and existence to Mother Earth. As

dutiful and loving children, they are to honour Mother Earth. The most suitable and fitting way of expressing this affection is by rendering in song and prayer the feeling of the heart. Because they love her, they avoid harming or injuring the earth. The debt of life must be acknowledged from the heart and mind.

from *Ojibway Heritage*, Basil Johnston, 1976

[1] Any subsequent usage of man, mankind, he, himself and his refers to humanity in general.

RIVALS DIFFER WILDLY ON HOW TO PRESERVE THE PLANET

NORTH BAY, ONT. — Residents of this Northern Ontario city can be forgiven if they are confused about their two sometimes-bickering environmental groups.

The offices of Northcare and Northwatch are only a few storefronts apart on Main Street West.... But when it comes to practical politics, the gulf between them is as wide as nearby Lake Nipissing.

Northcare spokeswoman Judy Skidmore insists that her group is the most committed to aiding the environment. She sniffs that the members of Northwatch "represent a different lifestyle — the sandals and the long hair and that kind of thing."

But Lloyd Greenspoon, a Northwatch activist, accuses the rival group of being a front for business that is colouring itself green. He says Northcare takes

environmental jargon, such as the term "sustainable development," and twists its meaning like a pretzel. "You can either focus on the adjective or the noun. We focus on the adjective. They focus on the noun. They want to sustain development."

Its (Northcare's) pamphlets fret that other environmentalists worry too much about birds, moose and even tourists, but ignore jobs in the timber industry. It courts business and does not shy away from asking big forest and mining companies for money to further its work, a fund-raising tactic that is anathema to most of Canada's ecology movement.

. . . . .

...Northwatch, which does not receive money from big companies, has a budget a quarter the size of its rival's.

Predictably, the two groups have totally different approaches to the biggest environmental undertakings now under way in Ontario: provincial hearings into

the effects of the timber industry on Crown lands, and the expansion plans of Ontario Hydro. Northwatch has argued for conservation, Northcare for development.

. . . . .

The squabbles rocking the environmental movement in North Bay are far from isolated curiosities. Groups elsewhere, often with ties to business and inspired by similar organizations in the United States, have emerged recently as both a challenge and a backlash to the traditional environmental movement.

In British Columbia, for instance, about 20 so-called "share" groups have sprouted up since the late 1980s. The organizations say they represent a middle ground in environmental disputes. They oppose traditional ecology groups and lobby for multiple uses of natural resources on Crown land.

Among them are Share the Stein, which is concerned with preservation battles in the Stein

River watershed (basin), and Share our Resources, based in Port Alberni.

. . . . .

In the United States, similar groups describe themselves as being part of the "wise-use movement" of "neo-environmentalism." The movement dates itself from an August, 1988 conference in Reno sponsored by the Centre for the Defence of Free Enterprise, based in Bellevue, Wash.

A book from the centre about the meeting said neo-environmentalists refuse "to accept the defeatist notion that man will inevitably destroy his own home," and they argue that human beings can respect the earth "while using it efficiently."

The emergence of such groups has caused unease among traditional B.C. environmentalists, who say there is growing tension between those arguing for wilderness preservation and workers fearful of job losses in resource industries.

"It (neo-environmentalism) blames the environmentalists for the real problems (in the forest industry), which are mismanagement and automation. They're making us the scapegoats for their mismanagement, said Colleen McCrory, head of the Valhalla Wilderness Society in New Denver, B.C.

John Hummel, an environmentalist in Tofino, B.C., worries that the tensions between the two movements could lead to

open clashes in the province, where environmental passions run higher than in other areas of Canada. The share groups, he said, view ecologists as "hippie environmentalist tree huggers on welfare."

. . . . .

In North Bay, Northcare and Northwatch have learned to live with each other. Mr. Greenspoon of Northwatch even says he likes to have the other group around. "We're an interesting foil for each other," he said. "It's good that they're around because it sets up the other point of view. It gives people a clear choice to examine."

Martin Mittelstaedt, *The Globe and Mail*, 1991 6 10

GREENPEACE SETS SIGHTS ON FOSSIL FUELS

Oil, coal and natural gas are endangering the environment, group says
LONDON — Greenpeace, no stranger to controversy, is sure to stir up troubled waters with its latest goal — phasing out the global use of oil.

"We're now talking about an oil-free future as opposed to just raising the issue of global warming," said Australian Paul Gilding, the new executive director of Greenpeace International.

"Nuclear testing was the issue for the first 20 years of Greenpeace and I think oil will be for the next 20."

For more than a decade, the international environmental

group protested nuclear testing in the Pacific. France finally changed its policy after admitting it had blown up the Greenpeace flagship, Rainbow Warrior, in 1985.

The group also helped to achieve an international agreement in 1991 to ban mining in Antarctica for a minimum of 50 years.

Gilding readily admits phasing out oil won't be easy.

"We won't take second-best for a solution. We set our sights high and have proven that it could be very successful. No one ever believed that the French would stop nuclear testing."

Greenpeace says phasing out oil and other fossil fuels, such as coal and natural gas, is necessary because they contribute to global warming and acid rain and because of the

environmental damage from oil spills.

A study commissioned by Greenpeace, called *Energy without Oil*, says other energy options are already available and that such a transition would not bankrupt economies.

"It is technically and economically feasible to halve current global use of oil within 40 years," the report said, adding oil and other fossil fuels could be phased out entirely over the next century.

It calls for replacing oil with bio-fuels derived from agricultural sources — such as plants and hydrogen — and with electricity-generating sources such as solar and wind power.

Among the report's recommendations are government support for public transport, tough new fuel-efficiency standards for vehicles and pollution taxes on oil and other fossil fuels to reflect the costs of oil spills and pollution damage.

"If the public want to see a halt to the continuing tragedy of oil spills...and also prevent climate catastrophe, the choices are now clearly available," added the Greenpeace report.

Greenpeace has been monitoring oil spills, exploration and drilling sites for many years. It is developing a long-term concept, focusing on car-free cities and oil-free cars and trying to persuade oil companies to change their policies and diversify.

Gilding and Uta Bellion, the newly appointed chairperson of the Greenpeace International board, say an oil-free future is not only viable but essential.

"The oil industry is a sunset industry," said Gilding. "It is pretty straightforward that we can't afford to keep pumping CO_2 (carbon dioxide) into the air."

Patricia Reaney, *Reuter*, 1993 4 10

POWER, AUTHORITY, AND MYSTERY: ECOFEMINISM AND EARTH-BASED SPIRITUALITY

Earth-based spirituality is rooted in three basic concepts that I call immanence, interconnection, and community. The first — immanence — names our primary understanding that the Earth is alive, part of a living cosmos. What that means is that spirit, sacred, Goddess, God — whatever you want to call it — is not found outside the world somewhere — it's in the world: it is the world, and it is us. Our goal is not to get off the wheel of birth nor to be saved from something. Our deepest experiences are experiences of connection with the Earth and with the world.

When you understand the universe as a living being, then the split between religion and science disappears because religion no longer becomes a set of dogmas and beliefs we have to accept...and science is no longer restricted to a type of analysis that picks the world apart. Science becomes our way of looking more deeply into this living being that we're all in, understanding it more deeply and clearly. This itself has a poetic dimension. I want to explore what it means when we really accept that this Earth is alive and that we are part of her being. Right now we are at a point where that living being is nearly terminally diseased. We need to reverse that, to turn that around. We really need to find a way to reclaim our power so that we can reverse the destruction of the Earth.

When we understand that the Earth itself embodies spirit and that the cosmos is alive, then we also understand that everything is interconnected. Just as in our bodies: what happens to a finger affects what happens to a toe. The brain doesn't work without the heart. In the same way, what happens in South Africa affects us here: what we do to the Amazon rain forest affects the air that we breathe here. All these things are interconnected, and interconnection is the second principle of Earth-based spirituality.

Finally, when we understand these interconnections, we know that we are all part of a living community, the Earth. The kind of spirituality and the kind of politics we're called upon to practise are rooted in community. Again, the goal is not individual salvation or enlightenment, or even individual self-improvement, though these may be things and are things that happen along the way. The goal is the creation of a community that becomes a place in which we can be empowered and in which we can be connected to the Earth and take action together to heal the Earth.

Starhawk, from *Reweaving The World: The Emergence of Ecofeminism*, Irene Diamond and Gloria Feman Orenstein, 1990

ENVIRONMENTAL PRESSURES

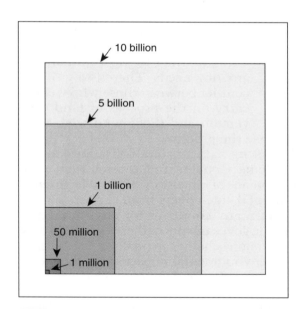

Fig. 2-6 *Comparative sizes of millions and billions.*

Humanity is commonly regarded as the chief pressure on the environment. This is partly a result of humanity's sheer size and overall rapid growth, and partly a result of economic activities, whether undertaken for basic survival or for a rising material standard of living. The case against humanity's numbers is summed up strongly by James Lovelock in *Healing Gaia* (1991): "None of the environmental agonies now confronting us...would be a perceptible problem at a global population of 50 millions...But at our present numbers — more than five billion — and present way of living, they are insupportable...If unchecked, they will kill a great many of us and other species, and change the planet irreversibly...The human species is now so numerous as to constitute a serious planetary malady. Gaia is suffering from...a plague of people."

The environmental pressures created by people fall roughly into two groups: those related to production, either for a higher material standard of living or for simple survival; and those related to the wastes yielded by both production and consumption. Figure 2-7 summarizes these environmental pressures.

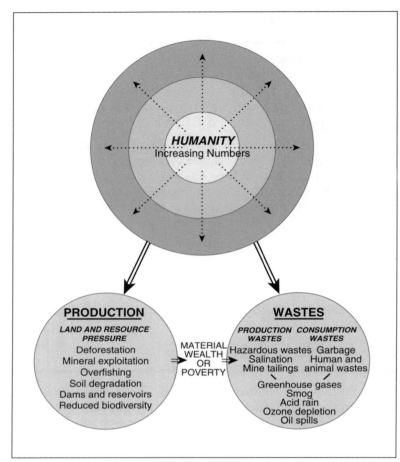

Fig. 2-7 *Environmental pressures resulting from increased production and consumption by an expanding population.*

PRODUCTION PRESSURES

Production pressures on the environment are caused for the most part by human demand for land and other resources, which has transformed large areas of the earth's surface. Human activity has included ploughing grassland, draining swamps, and building cities. However, extensive areas of purely natural environment still remain; about 25-30 percent of the earth's land area is classed as wilderness by the World Resources Institute.

As the process of conversion continues, it raises fears among some people that the natural surface environment is in grave danger of extinction. These individuals argue that conversion of the natural environment should cease and that protection or even restoration of the natural environment should take place instead. Others argue that a managed human environment is not dangerous, and that the process of conversion should continue in order to meet humanity's growing needs. There is a growing conflict between those who wish to carry on the process of land conversion and those who wish variously to slow down, end, or reverse the process.

Past conversion of land from its natural state to its human use state has not been without problems. Conversion has often been careless and neglectful, or done in ignorance of long-term effects. Heightened awareness of possible environmental side-effects from conversion has produced the current demand in many countries for environmental impact studies. Without studies, the governments of these countries may refuse permission for major conversion schemes to proceed. Permission may be refused if the results of an environmental impact study show that the environmental costs of going ahead with development exceed the advantages it would provide. The Narmada Valley dam project in India, described on page 17 of Chapter One, is an example of such a judgment call. Environmental impact studies have been done for the project, but

SOURCE: Inco

Fig. 2-8 *Open-pit mining, as here in Thompson, Manitoba, has scooped out deep holes in the earth's crust. Why are the sides of the hole made up of slanting terraces?*

without yielding consensus: some regard the environmental costs as too high for the project to proceed; others regard the ultimate human benefits as too valuable for the project to be abandoned. Where do you think the proponents and opponents of the Narmada Project stand in relation to the different humanity-environment relationship philosophies?

STATISTICAL ANALYSIS

9. (a) Sharing the work among small groups, use columns 1 and 22 of Appendix 2 to calculate the percentage of wilderness in each country's total area. Wilderness data are from satellite images analyzed by the World Resources Institute. They represent areas of land in 4000 km^2 blocks showing no signs of human activity such as settlements, roads, buildings, airports, railways, pipelines, power lines, reservoirs, or agricultural and logging activities.

(b) Classify the countries for which you have calculated wilderness percentages into five groups: those with two or more times the world wilderness average; those with one to two times the world average; those with one-half to one times the world average; those with at least some but less than half the world average; and those with none.

(c) Using four shades of green for the first four classes, and red for the fifth class, draw a graded shading map (see Appendix 3) to illustrate variations across the world in national wilderness percentages.

(d) Suggest reasons for the wilderness proportions of the countries or country groups in the highest and lowest classes (more than twice world average, and none).

DEFORESTATION

Deforestation is the oldest form of land conversion undertaken by humanity. Demands for farmland, fuelwood, furniture, construction timber, and ships have led over time to removal of increasing quantities of natural forest in parts of southwest, south and east Asia, Europe, and most recently, North America. Currently, forests are less in demand for shipbuilding timber, but more in demand for pulpwood and lumber for building houses. Despite these pressures, there has always been an element of forest protection throughout history. In early times, areas of forest were protected by the rich for hunting. They were also avoided by people who regarded them as dark and dangerous places.

Concern about deforestation at the present time centres on the remaining areas of forest throughout the tropical and temperate areas. There is also worldwide concern over areas already deforested, as in central India or parts of the interior United States. These areas are increasingly the object of reforestation projects. Ideas about forest protection, along with forest restoration and individual tree-planting, are increasingly widespread across the globe. These ideas contend with deforestation activities in other areas, notably the new logging regions of South America, Africa, and south and southeast Asia, and the older logging regions of North America and Europe.

This conflict of ideas and practices is perceived by many in the tropical developing countries to be a clash over national **sovereignty** between the economically developed world and the developing world, and has given rise to charges of **neocolonialism**. For example, when members of the developed world complain that countries with tropical rain forest permit annual deforestation at a rate of just under 170 000 km^2/y, people in those countries respond that the remaining area of tropical rain forest is more than 17 000 000 km^2 (data from *World Resources 1992-93*). Those in the developing world also state that land is needed for farming and to

The word forest comes from the Latin *foris*, meaning outside. Forest was land outside of regular human use and outside of the regular law, sought frequently as a refuge by people who were themselves outside the law.

Colonialism is the political control of one nation by another ruling foreign country. Interference by one country, usually developed, in the affairs of another, usually developing, may lead to the charge of neocolonialism.

build housing for their growing populations, and that sales of tropical timber produce valuable income and jobs. They feel that what they do with their forests is their own business, and that developed countries should reduce their own wasteful lifestyles or reforest some of their own land that was deforested long ago. As Brazil's foreign minister in 1989, Roberto Costa de Abreu Sodré, said in Veja, a Sao Paulo newsmagazine, "Brazil will not see itself turned into a nature reserve for the rest of humanity. Our most important goal is economic development."

At the United Nations Conference on Environment and Development in Rio de Janeiro in 1992, proposals by the developed nations to restrict tropical deforestation were furiously resisted by 77 tropical nations, led by Malaysia and India. A Dutch forestry expert working in Indonesia in 1990 stated that, "It is difficult for Indonesians when people from Europe and North America who cut down all their trees centuries ago come here and say this country must preserve the rain forest for the rest of the world" ("Trees or people," Ben Tierney, *Southam News*, 90 7 22).

Despite complaints about neocolonialism and interference with national sovereignty from tropical developing countries, why do so many people in the developed countries express major concern over tropical forests? There are several different but interconnected reasons.

One reason is that the tropical forests are widely perceived to act as the "lungs of the planet," absorbing carbon dioxide from the atmosphere and releasing oxygen. They certainly do this, but others believe that the little-understood phytoplankton of the oceans may be even more important in this regard (see Fig. 2-9). Possible global warming is a related concern: if tropical forests are smaller, they will absorb less carbon dioxide, and more of it is likely to accumulate in the earth's atmosphere, increasing the chances of global warming.

Another reason why many people are concerned is because of the possibility that the tropical rain forest will not regenerate once deforestation has occurred. The climate that first supported the forest may change to one of increasing drought if the forest no longer exists. The forest needs plenty of rain, and many people believe that the forest itself supplies most of the moisture for rain in a self-supporting cycle. Indeed, about 80 percent of the moisture taken in by tropical rain forest trees during rainfall is released back to the atmosphere. However, much of the initial rainfall is not absorbed by trees; it runs off to the oceans as rivers. In addition, large quantities of atmospheric moisture are constantly brought to the tropical rain forest areas by the planetary trade winds as they are drawn towards the equatorial regions.

Nevertheless, deforestation does interfere with the natural water cycle of the regions. Forests, with their network of roots and ground litter (fallen leaves, twigs, etc.), act as huge sponges, retarding the flow of water into the rivers after rainfall and supplying water to the rivers during dry spells. If the forests are removed, rainwater flows more

The greenhouse effect occurs because incoming solar radiation can penetrate the atmosphere easily, while outgoing radiation from the earth cannot. The atmosphere near the earth's surface is thus warmed. Increased atmospheric carbon dioxide further hinders outgoing radiation, which tends to increase the temperature of the atmosphere. These factors are believed to lead to global warming.

The water cycle is one of several cycles in the biosphere. Basically, it is the movement of water by evaporation from the ocean into the atmosphere, from the atmosphere back to the earth's surface as precipitation, and — if it falls on land — back to the oceans as rivers. The water cycle has many sub-cycles, but the basic pattern is constant.

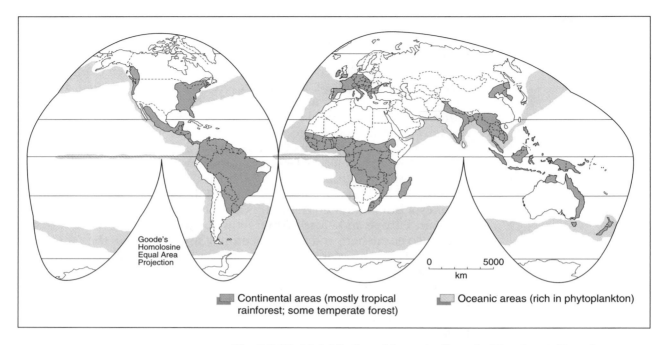

Goode's Homolosine Equal Area Projection

0   5000
km

Continental areas (mostly tropical rainforest; some temperate forest)

Oceanic areas (rich in phytoplankton)

Fig. 2-9 *World distribution of the major "lungs" of the planet. (Based on a composite photo of 31 000 images made by the Nimbus-7 satellite; composite photo prepared by C.J. Tucker, NASA, Goddard Space Flight Center.)*

Biodiversity is the short form of biological diversity, which means the number of different life-forms that inhabit an area. It is also sometimes used to refer to the amount of gene diversity in an area.

quickly into the rivers, often taking topsoil with it. As a result, floods become more frequent, and hillsides may be stripped of soil. During dry spells, conversely, river levels fall more than they did before deforestation, since the forest sponge no longer maintains a supply of water. The impact of more widely varying water levels may be felt in river navigation, fishing, village water supply, bridge construction, and ford operation. The soil eroded from slopes may cause increased siltation of river beds, further hindering navigation, and siltation of lakes, reservoirs, irrigation channels, harbours, and even offshore waters.

A further concern about tropical deforestation is the possibility of reduced **biodiversity**. Tropical forests house a great variety of animal and plant life, which deforestation jeopardizes. Because scientists argue about what constitutes a species, let alone how many there are in the rain forest, many figures are quoted about the number of species of plants and animals in rain forests and their annual rate of extinction through deforestation. However, there is wide agreement that deforestation decreases biodiversity; it is the extent of this loss that is disputed.

Drugs in tropical rain forests are not necessarily used beneficially by humans. Despite some medicinal uses, cocaine from the Amazon, for example, has harmed millions of people through abuse.

An issue of concern that is connected to reduced biodiversity is the possible loss of plants that may offer benefits to humans. Certain tropical plants contain chemicals that have been found to have medical value, and have been so used by indigenous peoples for many years. Many pharmaceutical companies in the developed world buy such products from developing countries, providing an income to the developing countries of about $25 billion per year. Approximately one in four pharmaceutical products today derives from materials originally found in tropical plants. While some pharmaceutical products are still obtained from this source, the rain forest materials are more often synthesized artificially from petrochemicals, which appear to be more effective in cures and have fewer harmful side-effects. Even so, drug companies know that in the future tropical plants may yield materials that are not yet known, and they thus generally support some preservation of the rain forest. In 1992, for example, the pharmaceutical giant Merck Sharp & Dohme signed a deal with Costa Rica to pay for the preservation of 25 percent of Costa Rica's rain forest in exchange for the right to examine plants for potential medical use. If any drugs are developed through this process, Merck has promised to share its royalties with an organization of conservation scientists in Costa Rica.

A further reason for concern about tropical deforestation is the destruction of the habitat of indigenous peoples. Tropical rain forests have been the home of people for millennia. Invasions of their territory, chiefly by Europeans in the 19th and 20th centuries, produced social disruption; increased deaths from imported diseases; and a reduction of traditional land-use areas. Areas of tropical forest where indigenous peoples live in traditional ways are diminishing in number. Government attempts to preserve land for them against forestry and mining interests have seldom been successful, because, by the nature of the territory, supervision and law enforcement are difficult. Accordingly, even land protected by law has had little protection in reality.

The remaining 10 000 or so Yanomami of the northwestern Amazon provide the best known example. Brazilian government efforts to preserve their traditional land area are under constant — and often successful — pressure by miners, ranchers, and homesteaders. While Don Aldo Mongiano, Catholic Bishop of the state of Roraima, says, "it would be an unpardonable historical sin if all the Yanomami died," Jose Altino, past president of the Union of Gold Miners, says, "handing over an area the size of Hungary to 10 000 Indians while most Brazilians are landless, jobless, and poor is ridiculous" (*The Toronto Sun*, 92 1 19). In the developed world, there are those who favour providing the Yanomami and other indigenous peoples with the opportunity to pursue traditional lifestyles. Other individuals argue that this is an attempt to keep indigenous peoples in a sort of living museum. Still others question support for ways of life that require the use of large areas of land when the world's population is increasing so rapidly.

DISCUSSION AND RESEARCH

10. In small groups, discuss the ethics of preserving large areas of land for relatively few people who live by hunting and gathering.

11. Select and research a First Nations peoples' land claim made in an area near you. In class, role play the parts of (a) the First Nations peoples' representative, and (b) the Canadian government's representative.

STATISTICAL ANALYSIS

12. Column 23 of Appendix 2 shows percentage changes in forested area from 1980 to 1990. Note that the percentage changes are for the decade; they are not annual rates. A geographical pattern may be identified if the data are mapped.
    (a) Draw the data on a world map photocopied from Appendix 1. Use a strong green for those countries with a percentage change of at least +10.0, and a weak green for those with a percentage change from +0.1 to +10.0. Use a strong red for countries with percentage changes of more than -10.0, and a weak red for those with changes from -0.1 to -10.0. Leave the countries with no changes blank.
    (b) Describe the pattern produced, and determine which of the maps in Chapter One your forestry percentage change map most resembles.
    (c) Analyze how close the resemblance is.
    (d) List some possible reasons for the resemblance.

13. One of the most commonly given reasons for deforestation is that land is needed to support growing populations. An indication of the extent to which this is so may be obtained by calculating the correlation coefficient of the full data sets in columns 6 and 23 of Appendix 2 (see Appendix 3 for information about how to perform the calculations and interpret the result). Calculate and interpret the coefficient of correlation between the annual natural increase rate and the percentage rate of deforestation for the decade 1980-90. Either use a computer for your calculations or divide the work among small groups.

OTHER PRODUCTION PRESSURES

Mining

As shown in Fig. 2-7 (p. 96), another source of production pressure on the earth is mining. Mineral exploitation by humans has always taken place, from the first search for the right sort of stone for tools and arrowheads to the development of continental shelf mining for oil and gas, and the

The earth's crust varies in thickness. In the continents, crustal thicknesses range from about 35-40 km in lowland areas to 60-70 km in mountain areas. Under the oceans, where the crust is much newer and thinner, thicknesses average only about 6 km. The world's deepest mine is Western Deep Levels Gold Mine at Carletonville in South Africa, at 3.84 km.

prospecting of ocean depths for nickel and manganese nodules. Along the way, humanity has drilled and tunnelled inside the upper parts of the crust and scooped out sections of the surface in quarries and open-pit mines. Much of this activity has produced visually unattractive results. As well, open-pit mining has destroyed original vegetation and soils, and often interfered with original drainage patterns.

Around the world, new laws are being put in place to ensure that land is restored after surface mining is completed. These laws require that the rock originally removed, called overburden, is put back, soil is replaced, and appropriate vegetation is replanted. However, there are many places, such as the gold mines of the Amazon, where existing laws are not enforced.

Apart from the environmental concerns related directly to obtaining minerals, there are concerns about the finite nature of this resource: the quantity already exists and cannot be increased. Minerals do not grow like forests, and are not renewable. They may be created, but necessary geological time-spans are extraordinarily long. Some people argue that because mineral resources are limited, they should be used sparingly and conserved for future generations. Others dislike use of the word limited, since it carries overtones of scarcity, and few think that minerals are scarce. In fact, mineral producing countries may wish that minerals were less plentiful so that they would earn more money from selling them. Several factors operate in this situation.

Recycling of mineral products adds to supply and thus depresses resource prices. Recycled quantities are large: in North America, for instance, virtually all the metal in cars is recycled, putting downward pressure on prices for iron ore and steel.

The chief factor is a constantly changing technology in the use of minerals. For example, thousands of years ago, bronze (an alloy of copper and tin) gave way to iron, so concerns about the depletion of copper and tin gave way to concerns about the depletion of iron. More recently, copper has given way to glass-fibre in communications equipment, and copper prices have fallen significantly. Changes in technology usually mean that to fulfil certain purposes, less of a particular mineral is required, or a particular mineral is replaced altogether by some other material. As technology develops, therefore, demand for minerals changes.

Additionally, technology makes it easier to obtain minerals, so that minerals may be deemed worth mining in ever smaller concentrations. For example, in Germany in the Middle Ages, copper was not considered worth mining unless it occurred in concentrations of over 25 percent in the rock; recent copper mining concentrations have been well below 1 percent. At the present time in gold mining the introduction of bio-leaching, using bacteria to extract gold from low grade ore, means that mining can be extended below the current gold concentration limit of 0.0002 percent to below 0.0001 percent. New technology has made it possible to extend the life of existing mines and to renew work in mines that were once regarded as worked out. "Finite limits" change as technology changes.

Because mining possibilities change constantly, it is impossible to produce a catalogue of the world's mineral resources.

However, technological changes rarely occur in isolation. They may be spurred by international rivalry, but they are always sought when scarcities loom and prices rise. Rising prices stimulate exploration for new sources of supply and the search for possible substitute mate-

SOURCE: *World Development Report 1992*, The World Bank

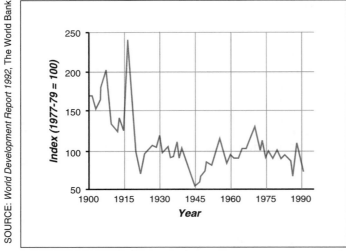

Fig. 2-10 *Index of world prices for non-ferrous metals (all metals other than iron), 1900-1991.*

The world's first oil well was drilled at Oil Springs in southwest Ontario in 1858. Production by the 1990s was very low and many people thought the area exhausted of oil. But in late 1992 a fresh, large supply was discovered east of Windsor, with a flow rate exceeding that of most wells in Alberta.

rials. Technological advances make it easier to obtain minerals, tending to make supplies more readily available. At the same time, technological advances allow smaller quantities to be used to yield the same results. The combined effect of increased supply and reduced demand is to push prices downward. Price patterns for minerals tend accordingly to be cyclic in nature (see Fig. 2-10).

The fluctuating price levels for minerals has a direct effect on the quantities of these minerals deemed to be "known reserves." Known reserves are not the amounts of a mineral known to exist, because no one knows how much of any mineral exists. They are instead the amounts that can be profitably mined at current prices. Generally, mining companies do sufficient exploration each year to maintain enough known reserves for, at most, 30 to 40 years work. If prices rise, the amounts that can be profitably mined increase accordingly, so known reserves become larger without any extra exploration. Improved extraction systems produce the same effect, since they make it possible to mine profitably those sources previously too expensive to mine. For example, world known oil reserves increased by about 50 percent from 1980 to 1990, largely because of the increasingly widespread use of enhanced oil recovery techniques. Such techniques involve forcing oil out of its underground rock pores through the use of special fluids pumped down into low pressure oil fields, many of them used and abandoned long ago.

The ever-present possibilities of technological improvement and expansion of known reserves work together constantly to keep prices of minerals from rising rapidly. For example, it is as much the existence of the Athabasca Oil Sands in Alberta and the Oil Shales in Colorado (both largely too expensive to mine at current prices and so only minutely "known") as the increased efficiency of motor engines that keeps oil prices from rising sharply today. What is more pressing than worries about the finite quantities of mineral resources, however, is concern over their waste products, examined later in this chapter (p. 115).

Fishing

Fishing is another area where production stresses are a concern. Overfishing of such areas as the northwest Atlantic, northeast Atlantic, Mediterranean, Baltic, southeast Indian Ocean, and northwest, northeast, and southeast Pacific has been growing rapidly for the last 30 to 40 years. Lack of ownership of the commons of the

SOURCE: John Molyneux

Fig. 2-11 *The use of deep-sea trawlers, as here in St. John's, Newfoundland, has led to overfishing in the northwest Atlantic and the closure of the Canadian cod fishery. What does the design of the boats tell you about the way fish were caught?*

A nautical mile is 1/60th of a degree of latitude, which in turn is 1/360th of the polar circumference of the earth. All degrees of latitude measure 69.06 land miles or 111.12 km, yielding nautical miles of 1.151 land miles or 1.852 km. Two hundred nautical miles is thus equivalent to 230 land miles or 370 km.

oceans led initially to massive plunder by all nations that had the technology for successful deep-sea fishing. The former Soviet Union, with Japan, Peru, and some European countries, led the way. Fish provided a relatively cheap protein-rich food source to the people of these countries, and the bounty of the oceans seemed limitless. Canada joined the group when it acquired deep-sea technology in the mid-1970s.

By this time, however, there were growing concerns about the plunder of the ocean commons. From 1967 to 1982 the United Nations sponsored a series of conferences on the Law of the Sea, concluding in 1982 with the U.N. Convention of the Law of the Sea (UNCLOS). This convention awarded rights of economic management for 200 nautical miles out to sea to countries bordering oceans, but it did not stop overfishing.

By the early 1990s, many fisheries had been so badly depleted that catches were reduced and ships idled. In 1991, the Food and Agriculture Organization of the United Nations (FAO) reported that catches in the Mediterranean, northwest and southeast Pacific, and southeast Indian Ocean were at levels that exceeded their maximum sustainable yield. Elsewhere, catches of the most valuable commercial species were in decline, and fishers were turning to less desirable species to maintain production. In 1990 a special task force in the New England states of the United States (Maine, New Hampshire, Vermont, Connecticut, and Massachu-

Americans used to use drift nets to catch tuna, but they also inadvertently trapped many dolphins that swam along with the tuna. Under public pressure, this practice has ceased in the United States.

setts) noted that catches of the most valuable fish were at their lowest reported levels, causing the loss of 14 000 jobs. In 1992 Canada closed its northern cod fishery off eastern Newfoundland for at least two years. In 1993, most of its remaining Atlantic cod fishery was closed. On Georges Bank off eastern Canada and New England, the composition of the fishery resource changed through the 1970s and 1980s, so that valuable cod and flounder were largely replaced by less valuable skate and dogfish. The FAO warns that overfishing of desired species may permanently shift species dominance in an area toward smaller and less desired fish, inhibiting prospects of recovery.

Deep-sea trawling is not the only means of overfishing. The use of large drift nets is another cause of overfishing, with side effects that kill thousands of other surface fish too. They have been commonly used by fishers from Japan, Korea, Taiwan, France, and Britain. Up to 50 km long, large drift nets catch not only targeted fish but also all other creatures swimming into them. In one study of a small part of Japan's drift net fishery in the northwest Pacific in 1990, the International North Pacific Fisheries Commission reported that along with the targeted squid, the driftnets caught 1758 whales and dolphins, 30 464 seabirds, 81 956 sharks, 253 288 tuna, and more than 3 000 000 pomfret. International pressure caused Japan and Korea to restrict large driftnet fishing in some areas in 1992, but the practice continues in the north Pacific and southeast Indian Ocean. The chief countries favouring a total ban on large drift net fishing are the United States, Canada, Australia, and New Zealand.

Soil degradation

Soil degradation is the deterioration of the natural quality of the soil. Production stresses on soil occur for many reasons, and take many forms. According to a 1990 study by the International Soil Reference and Information Centre of the Netherlands, degraded soil accounts for about 11 percent of all soil across the world (see Fig. 2-12). The chief causes of soil degradation across the world are poor agricultural practices (28 percent of all soil degradation), deforestation (30 percent), and overgrazing (35 percent).

There are many poor agricultural practices. They include using too little or too much fertilizer, failing to cover the land during fallow periods, and using heavy machinery or oxen that compact the soil. Other poor agricultural practices include providing inadequate drainage, ploughing up and down slopes rather than across them, and growing the same crop year after year in the same soil (a practice called monoculture). These practices provide conditions for a wide variety of types of soil degradation. Worldwide, erosion by water, from whatever cause, is the chief form of degradation, accounting for 56 percent of all forms of soil degradation. Erosion by wind is the second most common form of degradation (28 percent), followed by chemical degradation (12 percent), and physical degradation, such as compacting and waterlogging (4 percent).

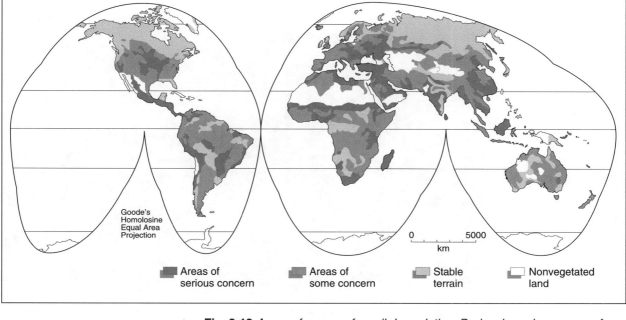

SOURCE: International Soil Reference and Information Centre, unpublished map (Wageningen, the Netherlands, 1990)

Fig. 2-12 *Areas of concern for soil degradation. Dark coloured areas are of serious concern because of localized severe or extreme soil degradation or widespread moderate degradation. Light coloured areas are of some concern because of localized moderate or severe degradation or widespread light degradation.*

Overgrazing has been a concern for thousands of years. As populations have grown dramatically during this century, population and animal densities have increased in already settled areas and many people have had to move with their animals into areas previously regarded as too dry for grazing. Under patterns of nomadic herding, natural vegetation had opportunities to recover after being eaten by livestock, since the animals moved elsewhere. But with reduced nomadism because of increased competition for land, the animals continuously trample the soil in the same areas over which they graze. They compact the soil and reduce its ability to either absorb moisture or germinate new plants. The deterioration of grazing land forms the classic example of the tragedy of the commons. The problem is most severe in Australia (where overgrazing accounts for 80 percent of all degraded land), Africa (49 percent), and North America (30 percent).

Desertification is a particular form of soil degradation that takes place in land bordering existing deserts. Here, soil fertility is lost through overgrazing, overcropping, or deforestation. Traditional patterns of human

SOURCE: U.S. Department of Agriculture

Fig. 2-13 *Good soil conservation practice in Mississippi state, shown by land ploughed across the slopes rather than up-and-down. This practice is often called contour ploughing, and it restricts water run-off, thus helping to keep soil on the fields.*

Soil generally contains particles of broken rock of many different sizes, ranging from fine clays to coarse sands. Because sandy soils cannot retain moisture as well as clay soils, and because plants obtain nutrition only from soil moisture, sandy soils are less fertile than clay soils.

occupance of these regions rested largely in nomadic herding and agriculture, but pressure on space brought about by rising populations has caused all farming to become less nomadic. The sparse woodlands of these regions have also been cut for fuel much more often in recent years than in the past. Instead of spending many hours obtaining fuelwood, people have turned increasingly to the use of animal dung as fuel. As a result, dung is not available as fertilizer for the soil. Once fertility is reduced to a point where vegetation can survive only in discontinuous patches, the soil dries out and the finer clay particles are blown away by the wind or washed out by rainfall, leaving coarser sand particles behind.

The process is slow, difficult to measure, and not necessarily irreversible. From 1980 to 1990, satellite imagery of the Sahel region along the southern edges of the Sahara Desert showed that vegetation advanced and retreated by up to 200 km between wet and dry years, without displaying any underlying trend. Attempts are now being made to counter desertification by trying to revive on a limited scale the old practices of nomadism. Securing more regular water supplies for settled occupance by means of dams or wells is also being attempted. By the first method, traditional nomadic ways of life may be supported, albeit on a reduced scale, while the second method causes nomadism to be replaced by settled farming.

Dams and reservoirs

The concept of diverting water from areas of supply to areas of need is an old one, practised by many civilizations thousands of years ago. Indeed, the remains of these projects, such as the aqueducts of the Roman Empire or the Grand Canal of China, are still evident in some areas.

Water is the most abundant resource on earth. The total volume is about 1.41 billion cubic kilometres. It covers about 71 percent of the earth's surface, and if spread evenly would form a layer almost three km deep. But about 98 percent of this quantity is too salty for human, plant, or animal use. Of the remainder, almost 90 percent is locked in ice caps and glaciers, or deep underground. The tiny remaining portion of usable water exists in rivers, lakes, and the upper portions of the ground in its passage through the biosphere's water cycle.

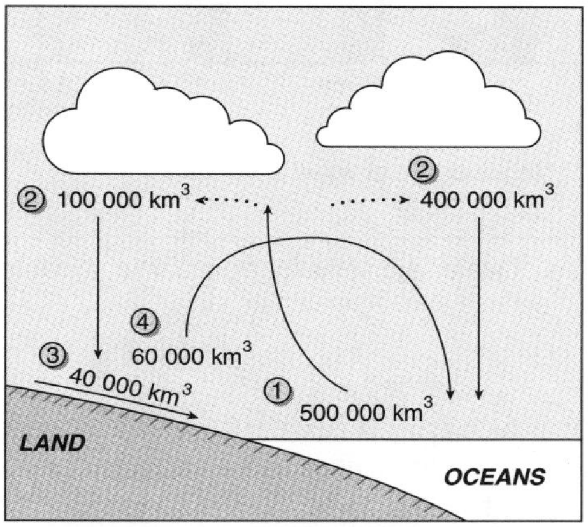

Although the amount of water in the water cycle is small, it is constantly being recycled. As shown in Fig. 2-14, evaporation removes about 500 000 cubic kilometres of water each year from the oceans, subsequently releasing it as desalinated precipitation. At any one time about 2000 cubic kilometres of freshwater are flowing in the world's rivers, 50 percent of it in South America's rivers and 25 percent of it in Asia's rivers. Constant recycling replaces river water about every 18-20 days. This means that during a year about 40 000 cubic kilometres of freshwater are available.

The purpose of dams and reservoirs is to add to the amount of freshwater available by trapping some of the return flow in rivers before it reaches the oceans. Effectively this turns a portion of oceanic salt water into useful freshwater since atmospheric evaporation from the oceans is more or less an annual constant. Dams and reservoirs also provide the advantage to humanity of water flow control. The amount of additional freshwater that has been trapped by dams (and that continues to exist each year as withdrawals are balanced by inflow) is estimated by the World Resources Institute to be about 3000 cubic kilometres.

Out of the approximately 43 000 cubic kilometres of freshwater annually available worldwide from all sources, humanity uses about 3250 cubic kilometres, mostly from dams. World distribution of water use is shown in Fig. 2-15.

As world population increases, and the pressures from rising living standards mount, it appears that pressure on water resources will also increase. The growth of industry and its subsequent demand for secure quantities of clean domestic water mean that use proportions may change, but overall demand for controlled supplies of freshwater will increase. It is likely that pressure for new dam construction will escalate. Dams also provide control of flow against low water and flood risks as well as offering potential for hydroelectricity production.

The Grand Canal was built to link Beijing with the mouth of the Yangtse River in order to facilitate the transportation of rice northward. It took almost 2000 years to construct, from about 2600 BP to 600 BP (BP stands for Before the Present).

① Evaporation from oceans (500 000 km³)
② Condensation and precipitation
  – over land (100 000 km³)
  – over oceans (400 000 km³)
③ Land run-off to oceans (40 000 km³)
④ Evaporation of land precipitation, eventual return to oceans (60 000 km³)

Fig. 2-14 *Annual water quantities in the various parts of the water cycle.*

The U.N. estimates that as many as 1.5 billion people in developing countries lack access to safe drinking water. Progress has been made, especially for city dwellers, but much remains to be done for rural populations. In Congo, for example, over 90% of city dwellers have access to safe drinking water, but only 2% of rural dwellers do.

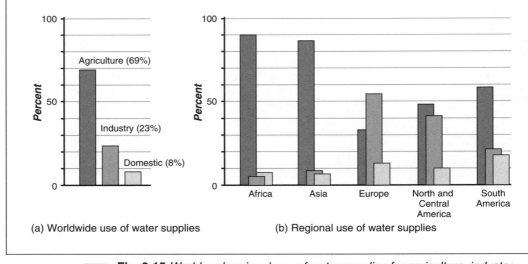

SOURCE: *World Resources 1992-93*, World Resources Institute, 1992

Fig. 2-15 *World and regional use of water supplies for agriculture, industry, and domestic needs.*

Dams and reservoirs also provoke much hostility, as evidenced by the reading in Chapter One on the Narmada project in western India. Dams are criticized for hindering fish migrations up and down rivers, for "taming" wild rivers, and for reducing freshwater flow into coastal areas (thus allowing salt water to seep into coastal lowlands). They are also criticized for trapping sediments that might otherwise form fertile silts in downstream flood plains. Dams further create reservoirs that displace existing inhabitants, kill vegetation, nurture disease-bearing insects such as mosquitoes, assist the spread of diseases such as bilharzia along irrigation channels, and leach toxic elements from the ground. Dams and reservoirs are beneficial in many ways, but the costs involved may be high.

Biodiversity
As described on p. 100, biodiversity commonly refers to the diversity of different species that exist in an area, or in the world at large, but it may also refer to genetic and ecosytem diversity. Technically, a species is a group of organisms with common characteristics, chiefly the ability to produce fertile offsprings by breeding among themselves but not with organisms from other groups.

No one knows exactly how many species exist on earth, nor in some cases exactly whether two closely similar organisms are the same species or two different species. For example, scientists have argued whether the plains and wood bison are members of the same or different species. The great unknowns are among insects and microorganisms, which account for the vast bulk of all species by any system of counting. *World Resources 1992-93* notes that "The total number of species is not

Bilharzia is technically called schistosomiasis. It is a killing and disabling disease of the liver carried by water-inhabiting snails.

Horses and donkeys can interbreed, but do not produce fertile offspring. A female horse mated with a male donkey produces a mule, which is infertile. A male horse and a female donkey produce an infertile hinny.

known. Biologists estimate that there are between 5 million and 30 million species, with a best estimate of about 10 million. Most of them are inconspicuous organisms such as microbes, insects, and tiny sea creatures. Only 1.4 million species have ever been identified and named...."

When facts are scarce, and arguments backed by figures are unsupportable, there is clearly much room for differences of opinion. Conflict may arise, because the seriousness of the issue rests in the perceived extent of the problem. Attempts to define and identify species are now assuming legal as well as scientific importance because of the efforts of many governments around the world to enact legislation for the protection of endangered species.

Biodiversity is not uniform around the world. Some habitats have greater variety than others. In general, biodiversity decreases from tropics to poles, but populations of any single species increase. This means that tropical areas tend to have a great variety of life-forms, but relatively small numbers of each form, whereas temperate areas have fewer forms but relatively large populations of each form. Accordingly, life-forms in tropical areas tend to have fairly localized habitats, whereas temperate life-forms can usually find support over very large areas. As it is easier for humans to put small areas under pressure than large areas, it is also easier to put tropical species under extinction pressure than temperate species.

Latitude, through climate, is only one of many factors affecting the number of species in an area, but it is important. For example, going from a higher latitude to a lower one, British Columbia has about 2500 plant species, California 5000, and Ecuador over 20 000.

SOURCE: Novosti Press Agency

Fig. 2-16 *Temperate life-forms tend to be fewer in variety but larger in individual numbers than tropical life-forms. This is a herd of reindeer in Siberia.*

Samples of various different plants are collected and studied in many parts of the world, but Dr. Melaku Worede, director of Ethiopia's national gene bank, one of the world's largest, has stated that there are "gaps in the types of crops collected. Crops of...socioeconomic importance to developing countries are not adequately studied...."

Fossil evidence shows nine periods when species diversity has been reduced. In the past, the Great Die-Offs have reduced species diversity by as much as 96%, followed by periods of renewed growth. Fossil evidence shows that current diversity is near an all-time high, but many ecologists claim that another Great Die-Off is now in progress.

Throughout human history, all activity that has resulted in land conversion from its natural (or "wild") state has put pressure on existing levels of biodiversity. This pressure has not always been to reduce existing levels. In many cases, humanity has changed the particular complex of biodiversity in a region by adding plants, animals, and other organisms from other areas. This process of change still occurs, witnessed by such current (accidental) introductions as zebra mussels and African bees to the Americas.

In most cases, however, human activity has reduced biodiversity. Sometimes these reductions have been deliberate, as with cultivated food plants. Today humanity derives about 95 percent of all its nutritional needs from about 30 species of plants, often with limited genetic variety.

As humans have converted land to their own use, natural breeding areas for many species have become more and more confined, fragmented, and degraded, and in certain places eliminated altogether. One of the earliest examples of the elimination (unknowingly) of a local breeding area was the drainage by the ancient Romans of the Pontine Marsh. They had thought that the bad air (mal-aria) of the swamp caused disease, so they drained the swamp. In the process they eliminated the local breeding ground for mosquitoes, which were the true carriers of the disease.

The reduction in existing biodiversity caused by the expanding demands of one of its species, humanity, generates strong arguments about the humanity-environment relationship. Some people argue that maintaining existing levels of biodiversity is important because it reflects the state of environmental health of the planet as a whole. Others add that existing biodiversity is a valuable natural gene pool, representing a bank of potentially useful life-forms that may enable humanity to live better, such as special plants that resist particular types of crop disease, or organisms that fight various human diseases. They believe that species extinction is irreversible, and that preservation of existing biodiversity keeps options open for the future. Others emphasize the beauty of many forms of wildlife, which provide wonder and joy to many human beings. Still others argue that all life-forms have an equal right to exist, and that humanity has no moral right to assume dominance among species.

There are also arguments against the maintenance of existing levels of biodiversity. Some people assert that many species are harmful to humanity, and should be eliminated by any means possible. While there is some agreement among people who think that undesirable species should be eliminated, there is also some disagreement about which species are undesirable. Worldwide, most would agree that the AIDS virus poses horrendous problems, and by general consent the list of undesirable species includes all those supporting the world's other major diseases. Others would include flies, and a wide variety of insects and reptiles, arguing that any particular niche in an ecosystem filled by a particularly unpleasant organism would be better filled by a more pleasing substitute. Yet others argue that wildlife (such as bears and wolves) that is dangerous to humans and domesticated animals should also be eliminated. The question then arises — and may not be answerable — as to how many species, and which ones, are really necessary to support humanity in good health on earth. Some people would assert that this question should not even be asked, since it represents an anthropocentric view of the biosphere.

SOURCE: David Boggs

Fig. 2-17 *Different species commonly intermingle in biologically diverse warmer regions, as here in Zimbabwe. How many different species can you identify in the photograph?*

Biodiversity preservation arguments have been successful enough to persuade many people to take action to safeguard biodiversity, and for governments to enact environmental protection legislation. Gene banks for plants and animals have been started; zoos and herbaria have been built and stocked. Land has been set aside as wildlife habitats, with degrees of wildness varying from parks to wilderness areas. Offshore marine parks have also been established, especially to protect the biodiversity of coral reefs. The world's largest marine park is the Great Barrier Reef, stretching 2000 km along the northeast coast of Australia. In 1992 over 150 nations signed an agreement to work toward protection of the world's biodiversity.

The case study at the end of this chapter provides a closer look at some of the issues in wildlife management.

DISCUSSION AND RESEARCH

14. Refer to Fig. 2-12 (p. 107). The problem of soil degradation is widespread, confined neither by level of national income nor type of economic activity taking place. Research the major causes of soil degradation in different parts of the world, and write a three- to four-page report of the situation in an area of your choice. Pay particular attention to the solutions or remedies that are being carried out.

15. Select a past or current dam and reservoir project in Canada and research the arguments both for and against its construction. Prepare a reasoned analysis of whether a past project should or should not have been completed. For a current project, analyze the situation and state whether you would recommend continuation or cessation of the project. State the reasons for your conclusion.

16. *Either*

    Consider the role of living non-human organisms in relation to humanity, and hold a class debate (see Appendix 3) on the following motion: Humanity should make major efforts to eliminate those organisms that are harmful to humanity's quality of life;

    Or

    Identify an organism that many people think should be eliminated. Two class members, after research, should role play

    (a) the part of the organism defending its existence, and
    (b) the part of the exterminator.

17. Identify the closest mining operation to your community. Research and report on the practices that the mine has followed to minimize damage to the natural environment.

18. People in many coastal communities depend on fishing for their livelihood. If the fishery is stressed by overfishing, identify in small group discussion some alternative livelihoods that the people may be able to pursue.

STATISTICAL ANALYSIS

19. (a) Examine the mapping and graphing techniques explained in Appendix 3, and select a different method than that used in Fig. 2-15 to represent the same data.
    (b) Construct a chart of the data, using the technique you selected.
    (c) Explain in a written statement your reasons for choosing that particular technique.

WASTE PRESSURES

All life-forms in the biosphere produce wastes or excretions, and these are customarily recycled by other life-forms. For example, human beings excrete carbon dioxide when they exhale, and this is recycled by green plants, which in turn excrete oxygen. Dead and decaying organisms are also recycled by smaller organisms called **decomposers**, so that decayed vegetation may be converted into soil nutrients. For thousands of years, recycling of wastes was sufficient to keep the overall environment in general good health. In fact, the creation of wastes was a vital part of the overall life cycle in the biosphere. Throughout the 19th and 20th centuries, natural recycling systems have come under increasing pressure from overload and from non-natural wastes.

Many people, including ecologists supporting Gaia, regard some wastes as normal, but define wastes beyond the treatment capacity of natural recycling systems as pollutants. Others press for zero wastes, and regard any wastes as pollutants. Either way, today there are many types of pollutants from many different sources, all putting great pressure on the natural environment.

The atmosphere and the oceans in their capacity as global commons have been most widely affected by the increase in wastes. Even **point sources** of pollutants have global impact if the pollutants are released either directly into the atmosphere or oceans or indirectly by way of rivers into the oceans. Planetary wind systems and ocean currents carry pollutants around the world; even Antarctic penguins are affected.

Securing international cooperation in atmospheric and ocean pollution control is difficult because individual nations — fearing loss of sovereignty — often put their national interests ahead of those of humanity in general. People talk of the need for action, but for many nations the pressing need for survival frequently means that little is done. For example, China has huge deposits of coal and most of its electricity is derived from coal-burning power stations; as a result, its cities have some of the dirtiest air in the world, and it produces more solid carbon dioxide waste emissions than any other country (22 percent of the world total). The Chinese are aware of the problems, but improvements are likely to be slow because of cost.

As summarized in Fig. 2-7, (p. 96) there are numerous types of atmospheric and ocean pollution arising from waste disposal from both production and consumption processes, but only a few will be dealt with here. As examples of production wastes, hazardous wastes and salination are examined in the next section. Following that, garbage disposal is examined as an example of a consumption waste issue.

World Resources 1992-93 lists the countries with the highest solid carbon dioxide waste emissions as:

China	1 964 032 000 t
U.S.	1 826 149 000 t
India	461 803 000 t
Poland	370 005 000 t
Japan	303 995 000 t

PRODUCTION WASTE PRESSURES

Hazardous wastes

Hazardous wastes are those of a toxic or radioactive nature that are generated by the manufacture of certain products. For example, the manufacture of paper has traditionally produced a variety of wastes that have

Chlorine, one of the waste products of paper manufacturing, has been much criticized as a pollutant, but it is used extensively for many cleaning and purifying purposes because of its toxicity to many life-forms. Almost all urban sewage is chlorinated; so are domestic water supplies and swimming pools.

proved damaging to downstream fish, although there is considerable disagreement about which wastes have caused the damage. Similarly the production of electricity in nuclear plants (2.2 percent of total world manufactured energy from all sources) yields radioactive wastes. Some people worry about the possible future hazards of stored nuclear waste. Industry is only partly responsible for the release of hazardous and toxic wastes, however. Farming is also a major contributor, with fertilizers and pesticides generally draining from the land into rivers or subsurface water supplies.

The problem of hazardous wastes has been addressed largely by policies of containment. Governments have legislated maximum quantities allowed for production or disposal, forcing producers to develop pollution control technologies and install treatment plants and settling tanks (water tanks where solid pollutants can settle to the bottom and be removed before the water is released back into rivers). The United States Environmental Protection Agency estimates that the cost of such containment measures accounts for about 2 percent of GNP in the United States. The measures have had some success in reducing pollution, as shown in Fig. 2-18.

While containment policies have had partial success, many environmentalists feel that preventing pollution in the first place is a better idea. They prefer to change production processes to minimize hazardous waste that cannot be entirely eliminated; then technologies to reuse or recycle these wastes should be employed. Only after these approaches have been used would these environmentalists consider waste treatment and containment.

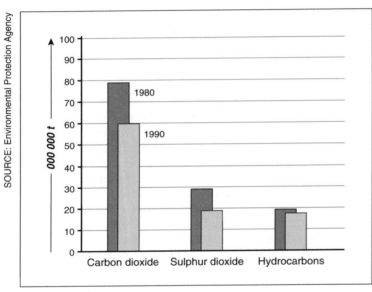

Fig. 2-18 *Pollution reductions in the United States, 1980-1990.*

The United States Office of Technology Assessment estimates that many industries could eliminate 50 percent of their hazardous wastes by using available technologies. The possibility of progress is shown by the 3M office-supplies plant in Perth, Ontario. In 1988 it sent almost 3000 t of waste a year to local landfill sites; in 1992 this had been reduced to less than 100 t. The key to this reduction has been recycling. One of their waste products, polypropylene, is now converted by another firm into plastic pellets, then sold to other firms for manufacture into coat hangers, flower pots, and toys. In a different way, Inco of Sudbury, Ontario, has changed its production technology by installing new oxygen flash furnaces, which not only cut sulphur dioxide emissions by about 65 percent, but also use 30 percent less energy. Similarly, Northern Telecom of Mississauga, Ontario, found new ways to clean circuit boards without using chloro-

Philip Environmental Inc. of Hamilton, Ontario, has even discovered a way to use dust. Waste dust produced in modern steel making is now turned into a product used by cement makers.

fluorocarbons (CFCs). In India, the burning of animal dung as domestic fuel has always caused a smoke-polluted home atmosphere, with toxicity equivalent to several packs of cigarettes a day. This hazard can now be avoided by employing biogas units that are cleaner and more efficient users of dung. As Nagamma, a mother of three in the village of Ramnagaram in southern India said, "There's no smoke, no danger...it's absolutely clean."

SOURCE: CIDA/Dilip Mehta

Fig. 2-19 *The increasing use of biogas units for cooking in India has resulted in cleaner air indoors. What other environmental, social, and economic changes are likely as use of biogas units spreads?*

Another waste issue has been the transportation of hazardous and toxic wastes from developed countries to developing countries. For years, some African countries, notably Guinea, Benin, Nigeria, and Zimbabwe, were paid to accept shipments of toxic wastes from Europe and North America. Transporting the waste was cheaper than pollution control and disposal in the developed world. The matter became so serious that in 1989 the European Community and the countries of Africa signed the Lomé Convention agreeing to end the trade in waste. This agreement was supplemented in 1991 by the Bamako Convention whereby members of the Organization of African Unity (OAU) agreed to stop all importation of hazardous wastes.

At this point, the waste trade switched to South America. The multinational environmental activist organization Greenpeace estimated in 1992 that hundreds of thousands of tonnes of hazardous waste were being shipped to South America each year. South Americans now object as strongly as Africans once did. They hope that the Basel Convention, which was signed by most South American countries, will reduce the trade effectively. The Basel Convention, which came into effect in 1992, forbids export of hazardous wastes without the prior permission of the receiving government. Many people would like to see the trade banned altogether.

Salination

Salination is another major pressure on the environment caused by production wastes. When large-scale irrigation projects were first built it was not expected that the water itself would be a source of problems. The creation of additional farmland to feed growing populations was sufficient reason for proceding, with no awareness of possible problems many years in the future. In many areas, irrigation waters were freely over-applied, with two different but equally damaging results. In some cases, irrigation water evaporated while still on the surface, leaving behind a slowly thickening crust of salt deposits from salt in the irrigation water. In other cases, irrigation water soaked into the ground, gradually raising the level of the underground water table. As the water table rose, underground salts were dissolved and brought closer to the surface, eventually reaching it and forming a salt crust as the water evaporated upon reaching the surface. Either way, heavily irrigated soil slowly supported lower and lower crop yields until eventually it became unfit for continued cultivation.

All the continents have experienced soil degradation through salination, although to unequal degrees. Total world cropland (excluding all ranch and grazing land) is about 1 478 190 000 ha. Of this, about 76 300 000 ha (5.2 percent) suffer from varying degrees of salination. Details of continental variations are shown in Fig. 2-20.

The problem is particularly severe in Asia, where the saline-degraded land exists chiefly in Pakistan and northern India, with some

SOURCE: *World Resources 1992-93*, World Resources Institute

	Total cropland (ha)	Salinized cropland (ha)	Percentage salinized
Africa	186 995 000	14 800 000	7.91
North and Central America*	273 834 000	2 300 000	0.84
South America	142 134 000	2 100 000	1.48
Asia	454 115 000	52 700 000	11.60
Europe (includes former U.S.S.R.)	370 495 000	3 800 000	1.03
Oceania	50 617 000	900 000	1.78
World	1 478 190 000	76 300 000	5.16

* Total cropland: North America   235 875 000 ha;
                     Central America   37 959 000 ha.

Fig. 2-20 *Total cropland and proportion salinized, by continent.*

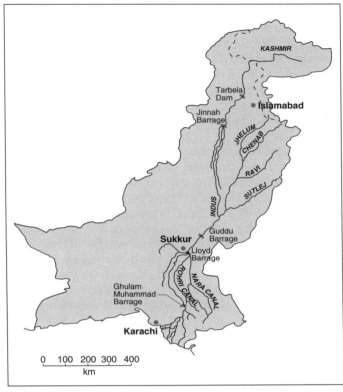

Fig. 2-21 *Indus valley dams and major irrigation canals.*

degraded land also in northwest China and the republics of central Asia. A 1990 study in northern India found that 87 percent of farmers complained that salinity and/or water-logging had forced about 30 percent of their land out of cultivation, and that rice yields on the remainder were down about 50 percent from a few years earlier.

For 5000 years, irrigation along the Indus River used small channels. The first large-scale irrigation projects in what is now Pakistan were built on the Indus River in the 1850s by the British, when the area was part of India. Local traditions and practices supported the introduction of large scale irrigation. The system has now grown to be the largest single continuous irrigation network in the world, with some 5000 major canals whose total length is about 75 000 km. Water is provided to more than 14 000 000 ha of Pakistan's cropland, producing 90 percent of total farm output (see Fig. 2-21).

Part of Pakistan's current problem with its irrigation system is that it is big and old. The combination of seepage losses from unlined channels and ground soaking from whole-field flooding has caused Pakistan's underground water table to rise closer to the surface. Altogether, about 20 percent of the irrigated area is suffering from waterlogged soils, which — since the water is also saline — inhibit root growth, rot crops and seeds, and reduce yields severely. Arable land turns slowly into salt marsh, and in parts of the lower Indus valley levels of salt are very close to those of seawater. Additionally, the evaporation of surface water leaves extensive salt crusts. For several years, farmers have seen land go out of production at a rate of about 40 000 ha/y, and overall crop yields fall well below the Asian average. Pakistan's average cereal crop yield in 1990 was 1745 kg/ha, up 14 percent from 1980, compared with Asia's average of 2713 kg/ha, up 32 percent from 1980.

Despite these difficulties, the problem may be reversible to some extent. Almost 50 Salinity Control and Reclamation Projects (SCARPs) have been established in Pakistan, each one showing agricultural gains. In the first SCARP area set up in the Indus valley in the 1960s, yields rose significantly within ten years: sugar cane by 70 percent and rice by 60 percent.

The chief method of solving the salinity problem is to lower the water table. This can be done partly with the use of pumps, which has the disadvantage of competing for scarce energy with Pakistan's growing industries. It is also being done by a procedure known as subsurface gravity-driven tile drainage, which is in increasing demand. Much of Pakistan's tile drainage is supplied and installed by Champlain Drainage of Quebec and Dillingham Construction of British Columbia. Once the water table has been suitably lowered, the salts in the soil must be flushed out by large quantities of fresh water before the soil can be used again. Reclamation costs are now significantly higher than initial irrigation costs, but steady progress is being made. Gains of restored land are beginning to exceed the still-continuing losses.

Pakistan's farmers, along with irrigation farmers worldwide, face other changes. Almost everywhere, irrigation water is heavily subsidized by governments, and farmers pay very little for its use. Relatively low costs tend to lead to wastefulness, but rising demand and higher prices for water in dry areas are placing more and more pressure on existing users to become more efficient. Sprinkler, drip, or microspray irrigation methods, all of which use water sparingly and directly on the plants, will become more common. They are more expensive than simple channels and surface flooding, and this, too, will cause changes. Low-yield crops (such as wheat) may be replaced by high-yield crops (such as corn); less valuable crops (such as cotton) may be replaced by more valuable crops (such as fruit).

CONSUMPTION WASTE PRESSURES

Garbage disposal

Disposal of garbage from homes and businesses used to be easy. All municipalities had dumps and other garbage disposal facilities, and most people regarded garbage as a necessary by-product of living. With mounting quantities of domestic and business waste, however, a growing awareness of the risks connected to garbage disposal has developed, especially in relation to human health and the preservation of a decent quality of life.

As landfill sites become filled to capacity, there is increasing worldwide opposition to the creation of new ones. Reasons for the opposition include potential destruction of farmland or pleasing scenery, and worries about harmful liquids seeping into ground water sources or harmful gases escaping into the atmosphere. Incineration, used widely, and now far less polluting of the atmosphere than formerly, is also becoming increasingly unpopular with the general population as opposition to all forms of pollution grows.

The issue of garbage disposal poses two separate problems: one lies in how to reduce the amount generated, the other lies in how to dispose of what actually is generated. In Europe, Germany has passed laws requiring that by 1995 all wrapping and containers sold in the country be recycled via retailers back to the original producers. This approach insists that garbage is the responsibility of the original producer and must therefore be returned to its point of origin. While Germany aims to become a "trashless society", its trading partners have complained loudly that such measures make it extremely difficult for them to sell goods to Germany,

Microsprayer irrigation was developed by the Israelis to provide a series of very fine sprays to a row of plants. It uses slightly more water than drip irrigation, which provides water only at the plants themselves, but it gives plant root systems access to a wider watered area and thereby promotes healthier and higher yielding growth.

Garbage dumps are not kept in reserve by municipalities. Once a dump is opened, it is filled over time, and then closed. Prior to closure, a replacement site is sought. This process is continual. Closed dumps are covered with earth, and the land is put to other uses, as with Centennial Park in Etobicoke, Ontario.

partly because of the need for secure packaging in international trade and transportation and partly because of difficulties in handling returning garbage. They argue that Germany's actions are essentially a "restraint of trade," but Germany presses on anyway.

The European Community (EC) has its own proposals, but they are looser than Germany's. Each year the European Community produces over 50 000 000 tonnes of garbage from packaging alone, and recycles less than 10 000 000 tonnes. The EC wants to increase significantly the amount recycled by having all packaging identified for either reuse or recycling, leaving member governments to develop practices that would recycle 60 percent of all packaging. Greenpeace regards this figure as too low, and has called the proposals "environmentally regressive."

Another measure that has been tried by several governments in attempts to reduce garbage has been to raise landfill dumping fees. The effect of this measure so far has largely been to cause garbage to be dumped elsewhere where fees are lower. In 1990, Toronto's municipal government arranged to dispose of garbage in an abandoned mine in Kirkland Lake, Ontario. This action was vetoed by the Ontario government, which required dumps for Toronto to be within the Toronto area. The provincial government argued that every area must be responsible for its own garbage. However, some of Toronto's garbage is now shipped to dumps in American midwestern states, where disposal fees are lower. In Europe, some of Germany's garbage is shipped for dumping in Britain, where fees are generally less than 10 percent of those in Germany.

Ontario also has a ban on approving new incinerators. There are two chief arguments against modern incineration. The first argument is that it pollutes the air — which it does, although relatively slightly compared to older forms of incineration. The second arguement is that it might cause people to think that the generation of garbage is not a major problem, and in turn cause them to reduce, reuse, and recycle less. In 1992 Ontario was the only jurisdiction in the world with such a ban; most other jurisdictions are planning to build more incinerators. Many people support incineration of garbage because it drastically reduces the quantities to small amounts of ash and can produce electricity or steam for district heating as well. However, incinerating one tonne of garbage has an energy equivalent of only one barrel of crude oil. Energy from waste (EFW) plants exist in Quebec City, Montreal, Charlottetown, and Hamilton. (The Hamilton EFW plant has been specially allowed by the Ontario government to keep operating.) Many more EFW plants exist elsewhere in the world. For example, Denmark has 38 EFW facilities scattered across the country, and disposes of more than 80 percent of its garbage in this way, chiefly because landfill space is extremely scarce. The United States, Germany, and Japan also consistently use incineration. Britain plans to build four new incinerators just outside London by 1998. For all EFW plants, however, the prime purpose is the incineration of garbage, not the production of energy.

Not all garbage in Toronto is collected by municipal trucks, which have to use local dumps. Much commercial and construction waste is collected by private firms, which can use any dumps they wish. Because of lower fees, many of these private garbage disposal firms ship waste to the United States.

DISCUSSION AND RESEARCH

20. In small groups, identify, describe, and discuss the advantages and disadvantages of the two philosophies of waste management symbolized by the different approaches of Germany and Ontario.

21. (a) In groups, research the amount and types of waste produced at your school each week and the methods of its disposal.
    (b) Make recommendations to your class about reducing, reusing, or recycling the waste. If your class agrees with you, or suggests acceptable alternatives, discuss possible courses of action in class.

22. Set up an organizer with two wide columns, one headed *How to Reduce the Garbage I Produce*, and the other headed *How to Dispose of the Garbage I Produce.* Down the left side, list your daily activities and major hobbies or interests. Complete the organizer by filling in the two columns.

QUALITY OF LIFE

DEFINING QUALITY OF LIFE

Quality of life is a rather imprecise concept. It is generally defined as the degree of well-being felt by a person or a group of persons. It is a wider measure than standard of living because it includes environmental, social, and political factors as well as personal incomes. Quality of life is therefore concerned with such matters as the environment and human rights as well as the consumption of goods and services. There is a psychological aspect to the quality of life, because it represents how people feel about their lives. There are no universally accepted objective measures of quality of life, and the best that can be done is to assume there are certain things that most people need or want, and then use the degree to which people have gained these things as an indication of the quality of their lives.

Needs and wants may appear to be much the same thing, but they are conceptually different. Needs are what must be met if people are to survive; they are the essentials of life. Basic needs have been identified by many international organizations as those needs that are related to food, health, education, shelter, water supply, and sanitation.

In developed and developing countries alike, basic needs have not yet been met for all citizens. Some people in all societies are hungry, have poor health, are illiterate, lack shelter, and have little or no access to clean water and hygenic sanitation. In developed countries the num-

SOURCE: CIDA/Michel Dompierre

Fig. 2-22 *A family in the Sahel region of Africa takes some leisure time after their evening meal. Notice the vegetation, their accommodation, and the dying fire. As this region is experiencing desertification, where will food and fuel for their next meal come from? Do similar situations of poverty exist in Canada?*

bers of such people are proportionately quite small, and in developing countries quite large, but to all people whose basic needs are not met the problems are real and personal. Why do these problems exist?

To some extent the problems of hunger, disease, and so on, are functions of existence. Reliable supplies of good food do not occur naturally in most places on earth; disease viruses are widespread in the natural environment; illiteracy exists without effort; and water is easily contaminated by careless and unsanitary practices. Overcoming these natural problems of survival — meeting basic needs — requires, at the very least, organized human effort in the effective use of the natural environment.

Some early societies, chiefly in southwest and southeast Asia, the Mediterranean basin, and Central and South America, became organized sufficiently to meet their populations' food needs thousands of years ago, but only some of these societies were able to provide clean water and satisfactory shelter. Some were able also to provide literacy, but only to their elite members. All failed to provide reliably good health to either the rich or the poor. Only in the last 200 years or so have societies begun to resolve their survival problems on a mass basis. In all societies, however, it is the poor who experience the greatest survival

Society's elites in early days were usually religious and military leaders. Frequently, literacy was the special preserve of religious leaders.

In any given year, there will almost certainly be some place in the world where people are fighting and losing their lives in pursuit of political freedom. This does not make political freedom a need rather than a want, for there are many others in the world who accept loss of freedom in return for peace, security, and an adequate food supply.

problems, and it is therefore the eradication of poverty that is the goal of most current development efforts, as examined in Chapter Three.

Beyond these needs lies the larger — and no less important — realm of wants. Wants are what drive people to try to secure improvements to their lives, once basic needs have been met. Because needs are essential to life, there is sometimes a tendency to regard wants as significantly less important, perhaps even frivolous. However, the desire for satisfaction of certain wants, such as political freedom, may lead people at times to risk or even sacrifice their lives. Wants may thus sometimes be more important than needs, and they should not be relegated to an inferior position in relation to needs.

There is much evidence, both statistical and anecdotal, to suggest that many people in all parts of the world are not fully satisfied with their lives; they demand more. Their needs and wants include an assured supply of clean water; regular food; acceptable accommodation; decent clothing; political freedom; greater social, religious, and ethnic tolerance; more consumer goods; better-paying jobs; and a host of other things. Although some of these, such as more consumer goods, place demands upon the natural environment; others, such as political freedom, generally do not. The environmentally undemanding needs and wants of people — the issues of human rights and human dignity — are examined in Chapter Four; this chapter is concerned with those material needs and wants that are environmentally demanding.

The extent to which society is able to meet the varied material and non-material needs and wants of its members largely determines the quality of life of that society. For example, if most people want political freedom, then the degree to which they have gained it may be used as one indication of the quality of their lives.

Such judgements are highly subjective. They are often also highly ethnocentric, that is, they are based on what our ethnic group values. There are dangers in making assumptions such as these, because the world contains many different values, some of which may conflict with one another. For example, many Canadians value the principle of equality for men and women, and push strongly for women's rights. However, many Canadians also support the right of ethnic groups to maintain their own traditional values, which, in some cases, subordinate the role of women. Which value takes precedence? The problem is even more difficult when Canadians have to deal with the values of other countries. If Canadians value political freedom, for instance, how much right does that give Canadians to judge other countries where political freedom barely exists? Are human rights universal, applying to everyone? Or are they subject to differences in cultural values?

Chapter Four examines human rights and different cultural values in more detail. For now, certain assumptions are made that the vast majority of the world's people have certain common material needs, chiefly food and good health. The success of the methods used by local societies to meet such material needs, and the way in which the methods interact with the natural environment, have great impact on the quality of life.

FOOD

A quantity may rise absolutely, yet fall relatively. If 550 million out of 5.5 billion live in hunger, the absolute number is 550 million and the relative number is 10%. If the number in hunger rises to 570 million while population rises to 6 billion, the absolute number rises to 570 million and the relative number falls to 9.5%.

The world produces enough food to feed every human being well, with enough left over to feed millions more. Yet estimates of the number of hungry people in the world range upwards from 500 million. And the number is growing, even though the proportion of hungry people out of the total population is falling. While some industrialized countries, chiefly in the European Community, produce more food than they can use, sell, or give away, people in other parts of the world rely on relief shipments and handouts. It is also true that although most people in the developed countries are generally well fed, some to the extent of being overfed, there are others in the same countries who rely on food banks.

Over the last two or three decades, world food production has risen at a faster rate than population. Accordingly, from 1965 to 1990, the index for the amount of food available to each person in the world rose from 100 to 114. But it did not rise equally in every country. National variations are given in column 14 of Appendix 2, and broad groupings are mapped in Fig. 2-23. What information can you derive from the map?

While there has been widespread progress in improving per capita food availability during the last two or three decades, there has also been

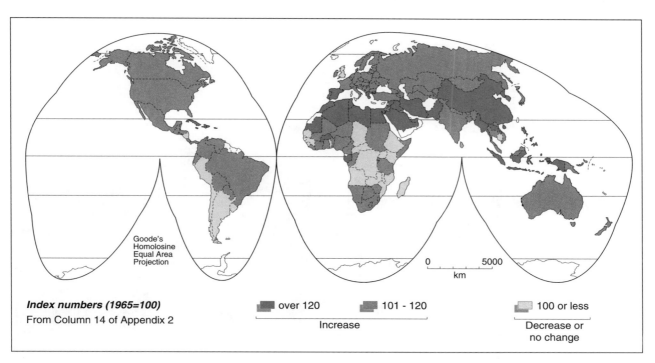

Index numbers (1965=100)
From Column 14 of Appendix 2

Goode's Homolosine Equal Area Projection

0   5000
km

over 120   101 - 120   100 or less

Increase   Decrease or no change

 Fig. 2-23 *Changes in food availability per person, 1965-1990.*

some failure. Countries shown in the lowest category in Fig. 2-23 have either made no improvement or experienced a decrease. For some countries, such as Britain and Argentina, this has not posed a problem; they were well fed in both 1965 and 1990. For some others, however, particularly in tropical Africa, decreases in per capita food availability have caused serious hardship to many people, chiefly in the form of widespread and severe hunger. Hunger alone would be bad enough, but the situation has often been aggravated in many countries of tropical Africa by the unreliable availability of even minimum quantities of food. Drought and civil war have severely disrupted farming and transportation activities in many places.

Lack of sufficient food may occur occasionally or continuously. Occasional occurrences, if severe, can lead to famine, which is defined as acute (severe but temporary) starvation associated with increased mortality. Continuous shortfalls are more likely to lead to chronic (long-lasting) hunger, but not necessarily to increased mortality. Because of its association with increased mortality, famine is easier to recognize. It is also easier to deal with, since emergency food aid can be supplied by food-surplus countries on a humanitarian basis. Chronic hunger is less easy to recognize, however, and also less easy to deal with.

Fig. 2-24 *Several parts of the world rely for food on relief shipments from other countries. Here the Canadian Forces deliver sacks of grain for use in the Sahel region of Africa.*

Hunger is difficult to recognize because there is no international agreement about standards of nutritional adequacy. It is impossible to measure the nutritional value of food consumed by large numbers of people over any length of time. Attempts have been made to measure nutritional adequacy levels by using either income levels, which relate hunger to poverty, or national per capita food availability.

Both approaches present problems. The income level approach ignores food consumption that does not arise from trade. In many countries, farmers and fishers eat the food they produce without the food having a monetary cost; the people may have very low incomes, but they may eat adequately. The food availability approach ignores income levels within a country, so that while average per capita food availability may be adequate, some people cannot afford a sufficient share.

A third approach has been tried, but with little success. This approach has involved taking physical measurements of people to assess their degree of malnutrition. Undernourishment usually results, for example, in smaller stature and lighter weight; but such physical characteristics also tend to reduce the amount of food a person needs. Accordingly, physical measurements may be of more use in assessing past rather than present undernourishment.

The most commonly accepted measure of hunger relates to national average food availability, expressed in kilojoules per person per day (kJ/cap/day). It used to be thought that people in tropical countries needed lower average food availability amounts than people in higher latitudes. Average body sizes tended to be smaller, and less food energy was thought to be expended in keeping warm. The FAO calculated appropriate amounts for each country, ranging from 9072 kJ/cap/day in Indonesia, Myanmar (formerly called Burma), and Vietnam, to 11 382 kJ/cap/day in Finland. However, recent studies suggest that smaller average body sizes in the tropics are themselves the product of former malnourishment, and that people worldwide have a more standard need for adequate nutrition. The most widely accepted standard today is one first developed in the 1950s by the British geographer, Lord Stamp. He called it the **Standard Nutrition Unit (SNU)**, and recommended a figure for national average food availability of about 10 350 kJ/cap/day. Column 24 of Appendix 2 shows how individual countries matched up to this standard at the start of the 1990s.

The amount of energy contained in food used to be — and often still is — measured in Calories (large-C Calories are 1000 times larger than small-c calories). The metric unit for energy is the joule, with kilojoules (kJ) being the units for food energy. There are 4.186 kJ in 1 Calorie.

STATISTICAL ANALYSIS

23. (a) Sharing the work in groups, calculate each country's average daily food availability (column 24 of Appendix 2) as a percentage of the Standard Nutrition Unit. For example, Canada's average daily food availability is shown in column 24 as 14 576 kJ/cap/day,

which is 140.83 percent of the SNU amount of 10 350 kJ/cap/day.

(b) Using a photocopy of the map in Appendix 1, construct a positive-negative graded shading map of the calculated percentages. Using a bright colour for all countries with percentages over 100, shade strongly all countries with percentages over 115 and shade lightly all countries with percentages between 100 and 115. Using a contrasting colour for all countries with percentages below 100, shade strongly those countries with percentages below 85, and shade lightly those countries with percentages between 85 and 100. There are no countries with exact percentages of 85, 100, or 115.

(c) Compare your map with Fig. 2-23. Make a list of those countries that appear to be having great difficulty with their food supplies in terms of being characterized by both (i) no increase or an actual decrease in food availability per person between 1965 and 1990, and (ii) average daily per person food availability below the level of the Standard Nutrition Unit. Make a second list of those countries that are not meeting the SNU standard, but are making progress toward it.

(d) Plot the countries on the two lists on a separate world map: use one colour for the first list and a contrasting colour for the second list.

(e) Examine the distribution pattern which emerges. What do you suppose may be the most likely explanations for a country to be on the first list? What would be the least likely explanations among those you perhaps first thought of?

24. Life expectancy is often regarded as an indicator of the level of basic needs development reached by a country. Life expectancies for Canada from 1871 to 1991 are shown in Fig. 2-25. Also listed

Fig. 2-25 *Life expectancy in Canada, 1871-1991, and a list of other countries.*

SOURCES FOR (a): *Historical Statistics of Canada,* Urquhart and Buckley; *The Canadian World Almanac 1991; World Resources 1992-93,* World Resources Institute

(a) Life expectancy in Canada, 1871-1991		(b) Other countries	
1871	53.5	Afghanistan	Iraq
1881	54.5	Algeria	Japan
1891	55.5	Bangladesh	Niger
1901	56.5	Botswana	Pakistan
1911	57.5	Cambodia	Sri Lanka
1921	59.0	China	Tanzania
1931	61.0	Colombia	Uganda
1941	64.5	Costa Rica	United States
1951	68.5	Guinea-Bissau	Uruguay
1961	71.5	Haiti	Zimbabwe
1971	73.0	India	
1981	75.5		
1991	77.0		

are the names of a variety of other countries. Draw a normal arithmetic line graph to illustrate the changes in Canada's life expectancy figures from 1871 to 1991; leave a two to three cm space down the right-hand side of the graph. From column 15 of Appendix 2, ascertain the 1991 life expectancy figures for the other countries listed in Fig. 2-25. In the two or three cm space provided, write in the countries' names. Plot these countries as a column of dots for 1991. Write your conclusions in a one-page report.

Food production issues

The world appears to have made good progress toward feeding its growing population over the last two or three decades, but there are also side-effects on the natural environment from increased food production.

In the matter of attempting to raise average food availability, both success and failure have environmental costs. Success has frequently been achieved by more intensive cropping, higher fertilizer and pesticide use, greater monoculture, and increased irrigation. Failure has resulted in some cases in farming marginal lands where sustained use is impossible, and where soil erosion has now become a serious problem. In other areas, land shortages have led to extensive deforestation. Land degradation caused by unsustainable agricultural practices, including overgrazing, accounts for almost two-thirds of the damage done to soils, mostly in Asia and Africa.

Some people view all such damage as the price of human existence; others assert that production can be maintained, or increased, without such damage. Various alternative farming techniques are under review and trial, and may yet provide the solution of high yields and little or no environmental damage. Examples of such alternative farming techniques include elimination of many chemicals; regular use of crop rotation, along with legume crops and animal manures, to maintain fertility; and zero or minimum tillage to protect the soil. More farm labour is required under these alternative farming techniques than under conventional practices, but other **input** costs (energy, chemicals, and so on) are lower. Alternative farming still uses some chemicals, unlike organic farming, and there is regular reliance on modern equipment, special seeds, and other technological advances.

Food subsidies form another issue in world food production. The developed countries of North America, Europe, Japan, and Australasia have come into serious conflict with one another over provision of government subsidies to farmers. The effect of these subsidies is to encourage the production of large quantities of food. In Europe, for example, the Common Agricultural Policy (CAP) of the EC sets farm product prices that are high enough to keep relatively inefficient small farmers in business. More efficient farmers, who can produce more cheaply, supply far more

Fertilizer use varies. For example, *World Resources 1992-93* notes that Singapore uses 6000 kilograms of fertilizer per hectare of cropland, Netherlands 662, Egypt 384, China 255, U.S. 95, and Canada 47.

Governments prefer to keep surplus food off the markets to avoid gluts and depressed prices. However, governments may fight trade wars by marketing surplus food precisely to depress prices and increase market share. Canadian wheat farmers have been caught in such a trade war between Europe and the U.S. for several years.

than markets can accommodate. The surplus food, guaranteed to be bought by the governments, is placed in storage, or destroyed if it is perishable. Some is sent as emergency food aid, or sold on world markets.

The countries that use food production subsidies argue among themselves because they have lost access to each other's markets. There is no longer a market in Europe for Canada's wheat, for instance, so Canada must pay support money out of general taxation to its Prairie wheat farmers, or face increased depopulation of the Prairies. The problem is aggravated by the availability of cheap surplus European wheat, which makes it more difficult for Canada to sell its own surplus wheat elsewhere. In a similar way, Canadian **marketing boards** make it virtually impossible for other countries to sell food such as chicken in Canada, even if it is cheaper.

The developed countries generally produce food in large quantities for their own highly protected markets. Food from elsewhere is rarely imported, unless the developed countries cannot produce it at all. Developing countries complain strongly about the protective aspect of developed countries' food production practices because they suffer potential loss of exports to the developed countries. Conversely, they complain about their own markets being flooded with cheap surplus food from the developed world, which often undercuts their own farming efforts.

In the developing world, farming is not usually protected by governments because the emphasis for national development has generally been on urban and industrial growth. In order to support people in the cities, governments in the developing world usually keep food prices low; in the past, attempts to raise food prices have sometimes caused riots. Because of low food prices, local farmers have little incentive to invest in methods to increase production, thus food production increases in these countries come slowly if at all. Food may be cheap, but it is not plentiful. And many farmers quit, leaving the rural areas for the possibility of jobs in the cities.

Surplus European beef is widely sold in the coastal regions of West African countries at far lower prices than traditional cattle herders in the northern parts of these countries can meet. Traditional cattle herders cannot compete, and thus have little incentive to improve efficiency.

There are some countries in the developing world, however, that have made significant efforts to support increased food production. For example, because of government price support, corn production has increased in Zimbabwe, coffee production has increased in Guinea, and peanut production has increased in The Gambia. In addition to price support, governments have also provided technical and planning assistance to farmers, along with easier access to credit, better transportation to market, and cheaper supplies of fertilizer and pesticide. Land holding has been reformed in many places, so that farmers have acquired a permanent stake in the land they farm, creating the climate for long-range productive investment.

Research into more efficient methods of farming, and into new strains of crops and animals that will resist diseases and yield more, has been supported by many governments. Such research centres are usually international in scope, and are also supported by many developed countries. Examples include the International Rice Research Institute (IRRI) in the Philippines, where rice for the Green Revolution was developed; the International Maize and Wheat Improvement Centre (CIMMYT) in Mexico, where Green Revolution wheat was developed; the International Centre for the Potato (CIP) in Peru; the International Institute of Tropical Agriculture (IITA) in Nigeria; the International Crop Research Institute for the Semi-Arid Tropics (ICRISAT) in India; and many others. The entire research program is coordinated by the Consultative Group on International Agricultural Research (CGIAR). Additionally, several of the larger devel-

SOURCE: Shell Photographic Service

Fig. 2-26 *Much research is done around the world to assist farmers in growing food more reliably. Here, a farmer in Brunei stands in a field of high-yielding rice.*

oping nations, such as Brazil, India, Indonesia, and Mexico have established their own research centres.

The story of Botswana's food security program shows what one developing country has achieved. Botswana is a drought-prone country in southern Africa, but because of good management it has less chronic hunger and acute starvation than any other drought-prone country. The reason for this is the nation's food security program, started in the early 1980s. Despite the repeated droughts of the 1980s and early 1990s, and accompanying harvest losses, severe malnutrition has all but been eliminated. The program relies on a number of related government initiatives. Food is distributed to all elementary schools and health clinics regularly. When there is no drought, all young children and pregnant or nursing women are fed daily; when there is a drought, food is provided to additional groups in need through the same channels. Food from regular aid sources is held in government stores for emergency use. Drinkable water is also provided to every community.

To provide income for food purchases during times of drought in Botswana, various projects are sponsored by the government in all rural areas. These projects, such as road and bridge building, or well drilling, are undertaken to improve the country's infrastructure. The government also loans animals to farmers who need draft power at ploughing time, and provides veterinary services. It even buys old animals from farmers to ease the environmental pressure on local grazing land.

DISCUSSION AND RESEARCH

25. The countries of the developed world produce enough surplus food to feed those in need in other countries. As a result, the issue is seen by some people as a problem of distribution rather than of production: in other words, the developed world should provide food for the developing world. In small groups,
    (a) Suggest different methods in which the developed world could provide food to the developing world, and discuss the relative advantages and disadvantages of each method. Summarize the findings in a written report.
    (b) Discuss the idea that developing countries should rely for some of their food on the developed countries rather than producing it themselves.

26. As a class, develop a list of possible causes of inadequate food production in developing countries, noting, where possible, how some factors are linked to others.

27. Research the arguments for and against food production subsidies, and present a reasoned analysis of the arguments in a four- to five-page essay.

28. In small groups, attempt to ascertain the extent to which the predictions of Malthus (described on p. 33 of this text) are coming true.

29. Some animals in the developed world, such as pets, racehorses, zoo animals, and farm animals, are better fed than some people in the developing world. As a class, discuss your reactions to this situation.

30. Write a "Letter to the Editor" explaining to a previous correspondent the meaning of the African saying, "Land feeds people, people eat land."

31. Prepare a research paper (see Appendix 3) on the Green Revolution. (See p. 48 in Chapter One.)

HEALTH

The World Health Organization (WHO) defines good health as physical, mental, and social well-being. Mental and social well-being are connected to human rights and cultural values, and are examined in Chapter Four. The use of the word health in this section is restricted to physical health.

Like adequate food, good health is a fundamental requirement for a decent quality of life. It has also been difficult for humanity to secure. Throughout human history, ill health has been a common phenomenon; in fact, plague was just as much one of Malthus's checks on population growth as famine. Humanity's search for better health started to become noticeably more successful at the same time that improvements to farming technology and industry were made in 18th and 19th century Europe. Subsequently, scientific medical knowledge spread over the globe, and the impact of diseases began to diminish.

Almost all diseases have roots in the environment. Many are associated with certain types of climatic/vegetative environments, and are usually transmitted to human beings by intermediary carrier (or vector) organisms, such as flies, snails, and mosquitoes. Other diseases are associated more closely with human environments, and may be acquired directly by human beings through the dusty air they breathe and the unclean water they drink, or through the pursuit of certain potentially hazardous activities such as smoking. Disease-producing bacteria exist in a wide variety in both natural and human environments, and many different measures are required to control or eliminate them.

Vector-borne diseases include such threats to human life as malaria, bilharzia (schistosomiasis), river blindness (onchocerciasis), sleeping sickness (trypanosomiasis), and yellow fever. To a large extent, these are diseases of tropical areas, reflecting the high levels of biodiversity in such regions and the still limited success of modern medicine in eradicating them. In temperate areas, vector-borne diseases are more limited, reflecting lower biodiversity levels, and earlier analysis and treatment. Bubonic plague was one of the great temperate zone vector-borne diseases, but it has been almost entirely eradicated.

Diseases associated with human environments include tuberculosis, cholera, typhoid, poliomyelitis, AIDS, and various parasitic worm infections. Such diseases may occur in any part of the world, and are transmitted from one area to another by humans themselves.

Treatment of vector-borne diseases requires a dual approach. Both suffering people and vector-supporting environments need treatment, and in many cases such treatment needs to be continuous. Costs are very high in financial and — sometimes — environmental terms, and success rates relatively low.

In the following discussion, malaria is examined as an example of a vector-borne disease, and AIDS is examined as an example of a human-environment disease.

The first edition of the *International Classification of Diseases* in 1892 listed fewer than 200 diseases. The 1992 edition listed more than 6000. Medical knowledge continues to increase; methods of diagnosis improve; and cures become more effective.

Malaria

Malaria is the most widespread and dangerous of the vector-borne diseases (see Fig. 2-27). The WHO estimates that over 250 000 000 people are infected each year, and that up to 2 000 000 die. In Africa alone, where malaria is most virulent, the disease mainly kills children under five since older children and adults have generally acquired some immunity. There are several different kinds of mosquitoes that transmit the disease by acting as carriers from infected persons to non-infected persons.

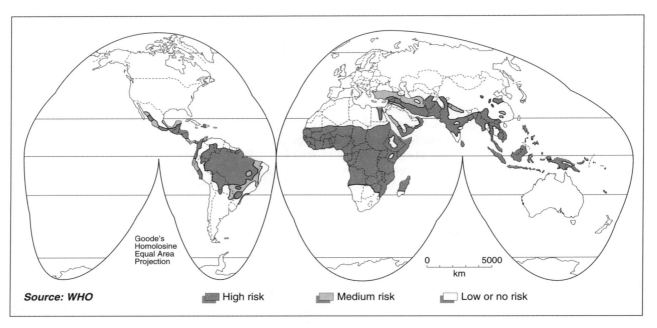

Goode's
Homolosine
Equal Area
Projection

0   5000
        km

Source: WHO   High risk   Medium risk   Low or no risk

Fig. 2-27 *Worldwide malaria risk.*

The measure of the rate at which the disease spreads is called the basic case reproduction rate (BCRR). The BCRR is the average number of new cases of malaria related to one existing case. If the average number of new cases is five for each existing case, the BCRR is five. Any BCRR over one indicates that the disease is spreading; under one, it is contracting. In many parts of south and southeast Asia, BCRR values of three to five are common, but in much of Sub-Saharan Africa, the BCRR is as high as 1000.

Such a high figure indicates that malaria is extremely difficult to control in Africa. Since malaria vectors are so common in Africa, most people are bitten and infected at an early age. Many die as young children; survivors acquire a measure of immunity, at least to death from malaria, but they suffer from the fevers and other disabilities associated with malaria. Acquired immunity is greatest in those environments, mostly the rain forests and neighbouring wet grasslands, where mosquitoes are numerous all year long. In these areas there are no malaria epidemics; almost everyone has non-fatal malaria all the time.

Malaria epidemics are most dangerous in those areas of Africa at the margins of year-round mosquito activity, because people in these environments (dry grasslands and higher altitudes) have little acquired immunity. One of the worst malaria epidemics on record occurred in the central highlands of Madagascar in 1988, killing at least 100 000 people out of a regional population of three million.

In the 1950s and 1960s, the WHO enthusiastically campaigned for the eradication of malaria, and by the end of the 1960s they had almost succeeded. However, control measures relied extensively on the use of DDT, an insecticide fatal to malaria-carrying mosquitoes. DDT also proved damaging to other life-forms in the environment, and its use was eventually banned. Additionally, the environments that supported mosquito breeding were being expanded, chiefly through the construction of new reservoirs and irrigation canals. People under pressure for land moved into many untreated regions, where cycles of infection started again. By the 1970s the WHO came to realize that eradication was an unrealistic goal. Containment through BCRR reduction by means of widespread primary health care facilities offered more long-term hope.

Mosquitoes breed on wet surfaces. Reservoirs and irrigation canals form excellent breeding grounds, but even water lying for a few hours in a hoofprint will suffice.

SOURCE: Capital Press

Fig. 2-28 *Mosquitoes thrive in conditions such as these in rural Tanzania near Dar-es-Salaam. Can you identify three different types of breeding conditions shown in the photograph?*

So far, incidences of malaria are increasing. The WHO describes the disease as a major public health problem and a continuing obstacle to human development. Part of the reason for the worsening situation is the immunity some mosquitoes have acquired to anti-malaria medicines. In some cases, people have taken doses that are too small to be effective, allowing mosquitoes to survive and acquire immunity. In other cases, people have taken doses that are too large, and those mosquitoes that survived developed very strong resistances to normal doses. In Tanzania, for example, people during the 1980s regularly took an average of 25 tablets of the chief anti-malaria drug chloroquine each year, compared with an average of 4.6 tablets in Zimbabwe and 4.4 in Ethiopia. Malaria became a major problem in Tanzania, infecting over 70 percent of the population.

Measures are currently being employed to reduce the scale of the problem. The spraying of breeding grounds, such as drains, latrines, rice paddies, ponds, swamps, and so on, now involves the use of new chemicals called pyrethroids that are less damaging to the natural environment than DDT. The same chemicals are also used to spray areas connected with human occupation, such as streets, garbage dumps, and the insides and outsides of houses.

Meanwhile, new drugs to combat malaria are sought constantly. Chloroquine is no longer as effective as it used to be, because many varieties of mosquito have developed immunity to it. In southeast Asia, UN peacekeeping forces use doxycycline, which — with other measures restricting mosquito access to skin — appears effective to date. Chinese scientists are testing a drug called arteether, which they have developed from a Chinese remedial plant used from ancient times called qinghao.

Africans who have acquired immunity to malaria usually have an increased risk of developing another disease called sickle-cell anemia.

There is another school of thought, first expressed at the Kampala African Malaria Conference in 1950, that looks at the acquired immunity of most African adults in the rain forest and wet grassland environments, and asserts that humanity should not interfere with the development of a natural equilibrium in their cohabitation of the earth with mosquitoes. Which of the six views of the humanity-environment relationship described earlier in this chapter (p. 83) do you think this view represents?

AIDS

AIDS (Acquired Immune Deficiency Syndrome) is an example of a disease with roots in human environments that can occur anywhere in the world. It is caused by a virus called the Human Immunodeficiency Virus (HIV). It emerged in the early 1980's and has since been traced to origins in Africa. By the early 1990s it had assumed the status of a worldwide threat to life, since no cure was known.

Once the HIV infects a person, it gradually takes over the body's normal immunity system. The infected person thus gradually loses (becomes deficient in) immunity to numerous infectious diseases as well as malignancies. The HIV uses cells of the immune system to reproduce and, in the process, destroys those cells.

AIDS represents a collection of symptoms which occur when the immune system has been weakened by HIV. Common opportunistic diseases include tuberculosis, meningitis, candidiasis (yeast infection), and cancers such as Kaposi's sarcoma. Infected persons ultimately die from opportunistic disease.

The cause of HIV infection is transmission from an already infected person through blood transfusion, reuse of hypodermic needles, sexual intercourse, contact between open cuts or sores, or from mother to child through placenta or during delivery. There is no evidence that the HIV is spread by casual contact such as a handshake, or by insects. Infected persons may remain apparently well for years. No one really knows how long, because AIDS is a relatively new disease. Experience so far indicates that up to 30 percent of HIV-infected people develop AIDS within five years, with the other 70 percent developing it later.

It is difficult to know the number of AIDS victims throughout the world. One reason is that clear diagnosis rests on blood tests, which are not easy to perform in some developing countries because laboratory facilities are scarce. Blood tests are also expensive. Another reason is that AIDS symptoms are the same as those of the opportunistic diseases. In several developing countries in the tropics, where there are many opportunistic diseases, it is often difficult to distinguish AIDS as a separate disease. Nevertheless, sufferers characteristically lose weight, and in many African countries AIDS is called the Slim Disease or the Skinny Disease. Yet another reason, now diminishing because of the seriousness of AIDS, has been the wish of some countries to withhold figures so as not to scare away tourists. Related to this has been the wish of some countries to avoid the moral stigma that is attached by some people to AIDS.

Despite the problems in identifying and reporting AIDS, the WHO estimated that in the early 1990s there were 12-14 million people worldwide infected with the HIV, all of whom were likely to develop AIDS at some time. Almost two-thirds of these people were in Africa (see Fig. 2-29), but the disease was spreading rapidly elsewhere, especially in south and southeast Asia and Latin America. The WHO estimates as many as 30 million cases by the year 2000, with about half in Africa, although India and Thailand are expected to have very large numbers also. Initially, North America seemed to be the next place after Africa in store for a major epidemic of AIDS, but early diagnosis combined with effective public education and widespread implementation of safety practices apparently caused the spread of the disease to peak in the late 1980s, although the number of deaths is still increasing.

The spread of AIDS is more difficult to prevent in the developing world because widespread illiteracy makes public education about AIDS less effective. Custom and cost also limit the use of safety practices. In Asia, the two chief areas at risk of major epidemics are India and Thailand. In both cases, as in Africa, the chief pattern of distribution has tended to be through migrant male labour associating with prostitutes, who then

The Worldwatch Institute reported at the end of 1991 that AIDS, despite having peaked in the late 1980s and being far more prevalent among men, was the leading cause of death among women aged 25-40 in New York City.

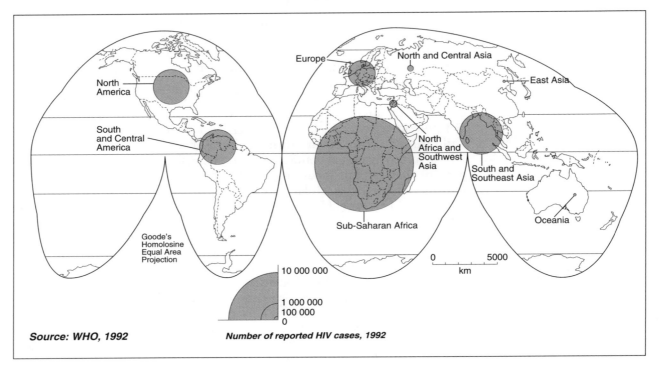

Fig. 2-29 *World distribution of reported HIV cases.*

pass the disease to local clients, who spread it further. The situation has been aggravated in many parts of Africa by civil war and the creation of numerous international refugees.

A further difference in the incidence of the disease in the developed and developing worlds is that in the developing world the disease affects men and women almost equally, whereas in the developed world the majority of HIV carriers have been infected through homosexual relations and/or needle reuse. This difference means that since many women in the developing world are infected, so are many children. In many parts of Africa, up to 25 percent of pregnant women have the HIV, and the pattern is for about 25 percent of their babies to be born already infected by the HIV. Of these babies, 80 percent die before their fifth birthday.

The impact of such high infant mortality on future population growth is considerable. Estimates suggest that increasing AIDS-related mortality may not be sufficient to cause overall populations to decrease, but the rate of growth will be slowed. For example, in *Disease and Mortality in Sub-Saharan Africa (1991)* edited by Feacham and Jamison, an estimate for an unnamed central African country gives a 33.6 percent increase in population from 1987 to 1997 without AIDS, but a 31.4 percent increase with AIDS. The estimate notes that almost all the slowing of the rate of growth will occur in cities, where AIDS is most prevalent. But the estimate adds, "Beyond the 1990s, if HIV infections continue to increase…a negative population growth rate might be possible…. The long-term demographic impact of AIDS cannot be projected with any assurance…."

One additionally damaging aspect of AIDS mortality in the developing world is certain, however: most deaths occur among adults aged 20-50. Such deaths have already orphaned many children, and they have removed potentially productive people from the workforce. Caring for all the people approaching death has placed great strains on health-care facilities, and has dangerously shifted the emphasis in many places from preventive/primary health care to chronic terminal care. Up to 80 percent of hospital beds in parts of Africa are taken by AIDS patients. AIDS is a difficult and increasing burden.

Primary health care is the goal of all developing countries. It involves a network of small clinics staffed by nurses and paramedics, along with sources of clean water. The aim is to provide simple medication and remediation at the first sign of health problems, and to educate local populations to seek help as soon as possible.

DISCUSSION AND RESEARCH

32. (a) As a class, brainstorm ways in which health care might be improved for large numbers of people in the developing world.
    (b) In small groups, critically analyze the suggestions and develop a priority list of the three or four that seem to be most practical and effective to implement.
    (c) Explain your group's reasons for selecting these priorities to the class.

STATISTICAL ANALYSIS

33. (a) Construct a scattergraph (see Appendix 3) of the values for infant mortality rate and people per physician in columns 12 and 13 respectively of Appendix 2. Use three-cycle full log (log-log) graph paper (see Appendix 3).
    (b) In a one-page report, describe the pattern shown on your graph, and the problems of providing health care that it illustrates.

34. It is a common hypothesis that rich people tend to live longer than poor people and that the populations of rich nations live longer on average than those of poor nations. Select an appropriate technique from Appendix 3 to use the data in columns 15 and 19 of Appendix 2 to test the accuracy of this hypothesis. Describe the reasons for your selection, and the results of your test.

SOURCE: *U.N. Statistical Yearbook, 1971;* Columns 2 and 15 of Appendix 2

	Start 1960s		Start 1990s	
	Population	*LE*	*Population*	*LE*
Australia	10 950 000	71	16 293 478	77
Barbados	237 000	65	262 688	75
Botswana	537 000	41	1 224 527	67
Canada	18 925 000	73	26 538 229	77
Denmark	4 684 000	73	5 131 217	75
India	463 726 000	41	849 746 001	59
Uruguay	2 648 000	69	3 036 660	73

Note: LE = Life expectancy at birth

Fig. 2-30 *Population and life expectancy data for selected countries, representing each continent.*

35. Fig. 2-30 contains information about population size and life expectancy for a selection of countries from each continent for the early 1960s and the early 1990s.

(a) Referring to the section on Averages in Appendix 3, calculate the average life expectancy of this group of countries in the 1960s and in the 1990s.

(b) Next, referring to the section on Index Numbers in Appendix 3, calculate index numbers for the countries and the group average to show the different rates at which this group of countries improved its life expectancy figures.

(c) Write down your conclusions about the index numbers in a half-page summary.

CONCLUSION

Both environment and quality of life mean different things to different people. The natural environment is regarded by some as merely the backdrop of human action, but it is seen by others as an all-encompassing web of which humans form only one part. Quality of life may be seen to rest in the degree of satisfaction of basic needs, or in the extent to which people enjoy a variety of non-material things.

In all discussion of environment and quality of life, definitions are difficult to make, and often highly personal. But it is the differences and conflicts that arise from highly personal views that create such a large number of world issues. Not only are opinions argued, but courses of action are proposed and fought over. Different priorities are determined; different justifications used. The case study examines the issue of managing wildlife in the natural environment. It looks at various responses to the problem that arise from differing circumstances.

This chapter has examined some of the prevalent concerns about the environment and quality of human life, but the themes that have emerged recur in all the chapters in the text. Views on the environment and quality of life influence almost all other human activity, and give rise to issues in almost all spheres of life. The next chapter examines how resources and development are connected to these topics.

- What are the different choices?
- How urgent is the situation?
- Where do you stand?
- What can you do personally to improve the situation?

CASE STUDY

WILDLIFE MANAGEMENT

Why is there worldwide concern about the need to preserve and manage the planet's wildlife? After all, wildlife implies a life out of reach and beyond management. Today, though, wildlife is no longer out of reach. The human population has increased to such an extent that contact between humans and wildlife is common, and the amount of available unpopulated land is dwindling.

The last great concentrations of wildlife are located in Africa, particularly in the eastern and southern regions of the continent. The countries in these areas are among the last in the world to enter phases two and three of the demographic transition model (see p. 41) and thus are experiencing a human population explosion. The resulting environmental pressure has caused a massive reduction in wildlife numbers. Although there were thought to be between 5 and 10 million elephants roaming Africa in 1930, this number had been reduced to about 1.3 million by 1979, and then to about 600 000 by 1990. Similar reductions have occurred among most species of wild animals the world over as the human population has increased. By 1992, only 320 mountain gorillas existed in the world, all of them living precariously in the Virunga Mountains of Rwanda, Zaire, and Uganda (see Fig. 2-31). Unprecedented numbers of mammals, birds,

reptiles, and amphibians are facing extinction. More than a thousand species and subspecies are presently considered threatened and hundreds more are under enough pressure that they need considerable protection.

The arguments both for and against biodiversity are discussed on pp. 110-113 of Chapter Two. This case study examines the difficulties of preserving many species. Wildlife management seems to be the least costly means available to preserve biodiversity since zoos and other captive breeding facilities cannot meet most biological conservation needs.

Essentially the dilemma is this: how to preserve a natural heritage in the midst of a rapidly growing and demanding human pop-

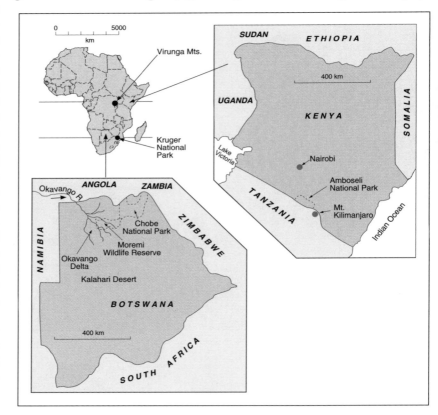

 Fig. 2-31 *Amboseli National Park and the Okavango Delta.*

ulation. Reserves and national parks are created, but, where people are starving, parks are infiltrated and animals are killed for the meat they can provide. As well, parkland provides grazing lands needed for domesticated herds. Overgrazing, logging, and the need for fuel and fodder can soon destroy the habitat of wildlife species. In addition, profitable poaching has become a temptation for people who lack the resources to meet their basic needs.

Also, wild animals, at times, kill people and their domesticated animals. For instance, the tiger, which used to protect the land of many Indians, now kills their cattle, sheep, and goats because the forest is too small to provide the food tigers require. There are also hundreds of examples where lions have mauled humans. North America has not been immune. Bears are a constant concern in the Canadian Rockies and every summer there are tragedies as well as stories to tell of near catastrophes. The potential for these interactions to rise in number as the human population increases is enormous.

A number of attempts have been made to manage wildlife in order to maintain a satisfactory animal population without creating animosity in neighbouring populations. The most compelling strategy for saving wildlife, many conservationalists now argue, is to ensure that such protection is economically beneficial to the people who must co-exist with it. For example, poaching of elephants for ivory tusks in the parks of Kenya was widespread in the 1970s and 1980s. In the 1980s ivory sold for $150 a pound. As a result the population of elephants was reduced from 140 000 in 1970 to about 16 000 by 1989. The situation was becoming desperate: poachers were being killed and other poachers were retaliating by shooting tourists. As a solution, a world ban on the trading of ivory instituted by the Convention on International Trade in Endangered Species of Wild Fauna and Flora (CITES) in 1989 reduced the price of ivory to $5.00 a pound on the black market by 1993. In addition, the new director of Kenya's Wildlife Services stepped up the campaign against poachers by hiring more game wardens, buying more vehicles, and distributing automatic rifles to the wardens.

However, anti-poaching teams can be successful only if poachers can survive without the income from poaching. Also, if the health and wealth of the local citizens is improved then there is more chance that they will become interested in maintaining their environment, including wildlife habitats. Tourism can provide that income, as well as local employment, and therefore reduce the perceived need to poach. Kenya now derives about $50 million a year from tourism and its parks have become extremely popular attractions to Europeans and North Americans. A revenue-sharing program that designates 25 percent of entrance fees collected in the game parks for nearby inhabitants has provided health clinics, water wells and scholarships for local Kenyans.

The ban on ivory created difficulties in other African countries. In Zimbabwe, Botswana, and South Africa, elephant poaching was not as widespread as in Kenya and the legal sale of ivory helped support the wildlife parks and the conservation of their elephants. Supporting animals, especially elephants, is expensive. It is estimated that it costs $200 a square kilometre per year to provide for the elephants' protection, and that each elephant needs about half a square kilometre of good grazing land to survive. Elephants forage 18-24 hours a day during which time they consume from between 150 to 250 kilograms of vegetation and 100 to 200 litres of water each. Because of these expenses, the herds need to be kept to manageable numbers. Zimbabwe, supported by Botswana, South Africa, Namibia, Zambia, and Malawi has been requesting the ban on the ivory trade be raised for them and by mid-1993 an agreement had been reached with CITES to raise the ban on the ivory trade for legally culled tusks; soon, these tusks will be marked in a way that will be difficult for illegal traders and poachers to copy. In the meantime, in order to keep the size of herds manageable in Kruger National Park in South Africa, elephants are regularly culled. The meat is cut, cooked, and canned in the park's abattoir and then sold in South Africa. The ivory tusks are put in storage.

As a result of the worldwide ban, ivory carvers, principally from Hong Kong and Japan, who have spent their lives carving figurines, jewelery, and piano keys from ivory, have had to look for alternatives. Although plastic is sometimes used as an ivory substitute, trade in ancient mammoth tusks from Russia has begun to thrive. These mammals became extinct about 10 000 years ago and it is estimated that ten million mammoth carcasses lie buried in Siberia.

In some areas reforestation projects have been undertaken outside the parks in order to provide a sustainable supply of fuel and fodder for those living in the vicinity. This prevents the local people from raiding the parks for fuel and destroying the wildlife habitat which, in turn, will threaten the animals.

Four locations in the world currently struggling with the issues of wildlife management are Nagarahole National Park in India, Amboseli National Park in Kenya, the Okavango Delta in Botswana, and grizzly bear territory in North America, particularly Alberta.

The area from the list above where there is the most contact between humans and wildlife is Nagarahole National Park, located in the southern Indian state of Karnataka on the western side of the Western Ghats mountains (see Fig. 2-32). In February of 1992 it was possible to spend an evening there and see a vast array of creatures including a variety of deer, wild boar, elephants, and gaur, the largest of the world's wild cattle. It was thought that Nagarahole may have contained the highest density of hoofed prey species in Asia. Although the park's neighbours were hostile to the park, there was very little poaching; this was largely due to the dedication of the park warden. The goal for the warden and his staff was the elimination of grazing, tree cutting, and poaching in the park. Fortunately, a number of large coffee plantations bordered the park and this reduced the number of herdsmen and land-hungry farmers who infiltrated its borders.

In March, 1992, however, a young man carrying a shotgun and apparently bent on poaching was shot to death in the forest. Though he was not killed by a park guard's gun, nearby residents blamed the park warden and his staff. The following day some 300 men appeared at park headquarters carrying the corpse and demanding that the park warden be turned over to them. When this was not done, they set buildings and a vehicle on fire and attacked several guards. They then set a fire in the forest that burned for four days and destroyed 35 square kilometres. The park warden, fearing for the life of his fami-

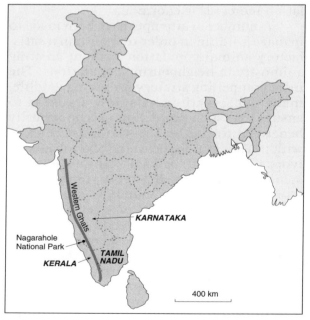

Fig. 2-32 *Location of Nagarahole National Park in India.*

ly, asked for a transfer out of the park. Other staff left as well. Markets in the neighbourhood were soon offering wild animal meat for sale. The future for Nagarahole is uncertain. The government tolerates intrusions for fuel, fodder, and meat because there is no alternative. Although only three percent of India's land has been set aside for parks and animals, the population growth is such that even this area is severely threatened.

Amboseli National Park in Kenya is located at the foot of Mt. Kilimanjaro (see Fig. 2-31). Although it consists of a flat dry landscape where trucks and animals alike create clouds of dust, it is the most popular game park of its size in Africa. It provides Kenya with much needed income from tourism. There are herds of elephants, zebras, wildebeests, giraffes, rhinoceroses, hundreds of flamingos and many other species of wildlife to be seen. Hunting is prohibited. This is the land of the Masai, who in 1973 gave up 400 square kilometres of traditional grazing lands in order to create a safe haven for the wildlife of the area. In return, the Masai ranchers were promised a series of watering holes built by the government for their cattle.

However, this arrangement did not satisfy many of the Masai. The water system broke down soon after it was built and was never repaired. The Masai began driving their cattle into the park when they needed water and forage. During the wet season some of Amboseli's large mammal species migrated outside park boundaries and trampled crops grown by the Masai. This competition for forage created friction between the Masai and the park authorities.

To demonstrate their displeasure the Masai deliberately speared wildlife, particularly the endangered black rhinoceros. Eventually, some changes were made to improve cooperation between the Masai and park authorities. Park boundaries were slightly redrawn to allow the Masai more access to prime watering areas, and additional watering areas outside the park were developed. The broken wells were repaired; an annual compensation fee of approximately $30 000 was granted to cover the grazing opportunities that had been lost in accommodating the park's migratory

SOURCE: Lyn Boggs

Fig. 2-33 *Wild giraffes at a waterhole. Why are waterholes dangerous places for many animals?*

wildlife; and a tourist campsite was relocated onto Masai lands to provide additional revenue. All firewood and road gravel used in the park was to be purchased from the Masai. These actions reduced the hostility of the Masai and they are now becoming more involved in the tourist industry. The interests and needs of the local people are continuing to be considered and this contributes to the success of the park.

In fact, the park is so popular that the wildlife now have to be protected from too much contact with tourists. As a result, tourists are allowed into the park only at set times in the morning and evening. Although this is not the natural home of all the animals in the park, they seem to be thriving. It is felt that there has been a certain degree of success in the venture but as the animal and human population changes, flexibility is required to keep all participants in this venture happy.

The Okavango Delta (see Fig. 2-31) is located in the northwest corner of Botswana on the edge of the Kalahari Desert. The Okavango River originates in the highlands of Angola and crosses into Botswana from Namibia where it spreads out to form the world's largest inland delta. This unique freshwater system sustains a multitude of wildlife and is often said to be the last remaining area of Old Africa where wildlife roamed freely, unmanaged by humans, and one of the best preserved corners of wilderness left in the world. Largely unsettled, it is a mixture of wetlands and rivers, woodlands, and savannas covering an area of about 20 000 square kilometres. Within it live some of Africa's last great free-roaming herds of Cape buffalo, zebras, antelope, and an estimated 60 000 elephants. In the wetter areas live crocodile and hippopotamuses. Since gaining independence from Britain in 1966, discovering diamonds in 1967, and developing a thriving cattle industry, Botswana has become a stable, progressive, and conservation-minded country with a sufficient wealth base to put its ideas on wildlife management into practice.

Only about 100 000 of Botswana's 1.3 million citizens live in its northern regions; however, with a birth rate of 35 per thousand, many look to the Okavango as a resource. As a result, the government faces the challenge of balancing the needs of an expanding population with the opportunity to preserve a wild inheritance as a

SOURCE: Marilyn MacKenzie

Fig. 2-34 *Tourists at Amboseli set out at dawn for a two- to three-hour safari drive. Each van holds five or six tourists, and is driven by a government-licenced guide. The vans take separate routes once on safari.*

renewable resource. Botswana has set aside 17 percent of its land as national parks or game reserves, one of the highest percentages of any nation. Within the Delta, the only protected area is the Moremi Game Reserve.

As in the other wilderness areas, the Okavango has also seen problems. In the 1980s the government built fences to the west of the Delta to prevent intermingling of cattle and wildlife in order to control foot and mouth disease. Some of these fences

SOURCE: Lyn Boggs

Fig. 2-35 *Selling these carvings to tourists is one of the ways Batswana benefit from tourism.*

restricted wildlife migration to and from traditional water sources in the Delta and as a result many animals died. Since the 1980s changes have been made to maintain migration routes.

Even in Botswana, where wildlife is still plentiful, issues of poaching, the pros and cons of culling large herds, and concern for crops damaged by marauding wildlife exist. There is also the fear that international poachers who have depleted sources elsewhere will start looking toward Botswana, particularly for valuable elephant tusks (even though trade is officially banned) and rhino horns.

Many Batswana (as citizens of Botswana are called) feel indifferent or hostile toward both conservation and wildlife-oriented tourism. Traditional meat hunting is considered by many to be a citizen's right. There is also some pressure to open up more land to cattle grazing as many people see the parks and the Delta, at present, as a benefit to only those from outside Botswana. Botswana's wildlife programs have

been traditionally underfunded but a recent boost in funding has occurred with Botswana's chance to participate in a multimillion-dollar United States Agency for International Development project directed at bringing villagers direct rewards from tourism and wildlife harvesting. It is the hope of many that the Okavango Delta can remain an example of Old Africa forever.

In North America, the grizzly bear, which once roamed over the whole of the western half of the continent, is now considered an endangered species by both Canada and the United States. An endangered species is one which is threatened with extinction through all or a large portion of its range.

Killing bears, particularly grizzlies, was traditionally done for sport and to provide meat, oil, and fur. However, with the establishment of settled human populations in North America, bears became a major threat to livestock and humans. They were then attacked even more fiercely. Only when the

SOURCE: Marilyn MacKenzie

Fig. 2-36 *A male grizzly. Grizzlies usually travel alone, except in the case of a female rearing cubs.*

numbers of grizzlies were reduced to low levels did both Americans and Canadians begin searching for ways to save them.

The grizzly bear is yellowish-brown to black in colour, often with white-tipped hairs, giving it a grizzled appearance. Its most distinguishing features, making it different from the black bear (which is not always black), are the distinctive hump between its shoulders and its very long claws. Its average weight is 250 to 300 kilograms. It has a low, clumsy walk, in which it swings its head back and forth, but when necessary it can run as fast as a horse. A person cannot outrun a grizzly if the bear is determined. The grizzly bear has always instilled fear in people, and its scientific name, Ursus arctos horriblis, makes reference to its size and ferocity. Its natural habitat extends from Alaska, through British Columbia and western Alberta into isolated areas and national parks of the states of Washington, Idaho, Montana, and Yellowstone National Park in Wyoming.

Grizzly numbers appear to be dangerously low. Although some believe the species will survive as long as wild areas are available to it, others project that the grizzly has a survival time of 20 to 30 years. The areas where grizzlies are the most likely to disappear from next are Alberta and the American states south of Canada. There are probably between 500 and 850 grizzlies in Alberta and fewer than 900 south of Canada. The grizzly bear is difficult to count accurately because it tends to live a solitary existence, roaming over a wide territory that is as far away from humans as possible. Thus, disagreements exist as to how much protection is needed in order to preserve it.

The grizzly is disappearing because of the encroachment of humans upon its habitat. Forestry, the construction of roads, mines, pipelines, and hunting play a role in endangering the survival of the grizzly. An American study shows that even one new road in an area substantially reduces grizzly habitat effectiveness, which is the ability of an area to provide bears with the security and necessary elements to reproduce successfully. A female grizzly does not begin to bear cubs until she is six years old. Then, it is likely that she will mate only every three or four years after her cubs, from a previous mating, are on their own. There is a fairly high mortality rate for cubs, so a female may only reproduce herself once in the first ten years of her life. Since the average life-span of a grizzly in the wild is only 25 years, this has led to a very low reproduction rate.

In the United States the *Endangered Species Act* makes it illegal to kill a grizzly except in one small area of northwestern Montana where the numbers that can be killed each year are strictly controlled. Federal and state funds to the amount of two million dollars a year are currently available for grizzly research and management.

Even before grizzlies became an endangered species they were given protection in Yellowstone National Park because they were a great attraction to human visitors. Bears charmed the tourists who then influenced their local members of congress to provide funds for the park. The early park administrators brought the bears within easy view of the visitors by offering them food. Too late it was learned that when bears lose their fear of humans they become more dangerous. Today, ongoing studies indicate that grizzlies are less dangerous in areas where they are still hunted because they retain a natural wariness of people and will generally back off rather than approach at the sign of humans nearby. Visitors are now discouraged from feeding bears, and park officials often close off parts of the park in order to help preserve their wild habitat.

In Canada, although the grizzly is on the endangered species list, there are no specific protections in place and no federal laws or funding are available. Government protection is, however, available at the provincial level. Alberta, for example, allows only two percent of the grizzly population to be legally shot each year. The will allow the grizzly population to grow to 1000 bears by the year 2000, at which point culling four percent of the population will be considered in order to stabilize the population. As an argument for this level of protection, and as evidence of an increasing grizzly population, the Alberta Wildlife Service cites the fact that in the last ten years there has been a 700 percent increase in the number of people who have reported seeing a grizzly.

The president of a Canadian environmentalist group called Speak Up For Wildlife feels that grizzly numbers are at such a critical stage in Alberta that all hunting should be stopped in southern Alberta and probably in northern Alberta as well. He claims that more grizzly sightings could just mean more grizzly watchers, and that in the United States where hunting has been stopped and the habitat is protected the population has stabilized but not increased. In Alberta, bears still face hunting and habitat destruction. For example, each year in Alberta 50 000 kilometres of road are built, and even though there is a limit on the number of grizzlies that can be legally hunted, there are a substantial number killed illegally. A grizzly population study would help to decide how serious the situation is but at the cost of one million dollars, it has not become a priority for the Alberta government.

Thus, in Canada and the world, as human population encroaches upon wildlife environments, there are a number of courses of action that can be taken to save them. Creative solutions will allow the preservation of this heritage into the 21st century.

FURTHER ANALYSIS

1. In groups of three or four, list the characteristics which the four examples of wildlife management problems have in common. Role playing a government official responsible for wildlife management, suggest how you would manage a wildlife population under these circumstances.

2. The World Wildlife Fund Canada is regarded as the authority on the status of endangered wildlife in Canada. The grizzly bear is one of 230 species on their endangered species list. Pick another one of the species on this list and research the background, the issues involved, and the future conservation plans of the WWF Canada for that species.

3. One third of the world's rain forests are in Brazil. As mentioned on p. 99, they help prevent global warming by absorbing carbon dioxide from the atmosphere. They are also home to thousands of different wildlife species.

However, Brazil is struggling to provide jobs and food for its large and mostly economically poor population. The land available from deforestation of the rain forest and hydroelectric power provided from harnessing the Amazon are seen by some to be a potential source of significant economic benefits.

Using your library's vertical files and any other information you can collect, list the arguments for saving the rainforest and its associated wildlife as well as arguments for using the land to assist the people of Brazil. Suggest some possible solutions to the conflict.

CHAPTER 3

RESOURCES AND DEVELOPMENT

3

RESOURCES AND DEVELOPMENT

Resources may be defined as everything people use, including their own physical and mental powers, to enable them to live satisfying lives. Development is the combination of processes people put into effect to help them achieve this end. The types of resources and processes used vary according to the characteristics of individual societies and the times.

There is much disagreement among individuals about the nature and use of resources, just as there is a lack of consensus about what constitutes a satisfying standard of living. Equally, there is argument about the characteristics and purposes of various development processes.

Some people view resources as the total variety of non-human organic and inorganic material available on or near the

Hagar the Horrible

SOURCE: King Features Syndicate, 92/11/18

Fig. 3-1

earth's surface for human use, and define resources solely in terms of their usefulness to humanity. If an item has no known use, it is not a resource. Others include humanity in this resource mix, claiming that large populations and/or human intelligence are also resources that are available for humanity's use. Many indigenous peoples around the world, on the other hand, do not classify their surroundings into resources as such, but see their environment as a oneness or circle or life. The reading "Father Sun and Mother Earth" on p. 91 of Chapter Two provides an example of one indigenous people's view.

The difference between the first and second views of resources is to some extent reflected in opinions and practices either favouring or opposing continued population growth. In the first view, humanity is the user of resources, and — because many resources are finite in quantity — population growth tends to be generally opposed. In the second view, humanity is a resource, and to encourage its expansion, population growth tends to be favoured. Several of the readings on pages 45-58 in Chapter One examine these antinatalist and pronatalist views from a resource standpoint.

Disagreement about what constitutes a satisfactory standard of living centres largely on the issue of consumption. Some people claim that consumption, particularly by people in the developed countries, is too high, and that overly high levels of consumption use too many of the earth's resources both absolutely and relatively. They believe that in an absolute sense, the heritage of resources for future generations is being depleted wastefully, while in a relative sense, people in the developed world use a disproportionately high share of the world's resources compared with people in the developing world.

Individuals who claim that consumption levels are too high urge a return to ways of life that place less demand on resources. Others say that too many of the world's people still do not have access to the wealth that can be produced, and that it is more important to help those in need than it is to reduce current levels of consumption in much of the developed world. They believe that the standards of living experienced by millions of people in the developing world are inadequate, even intolerable, and should be improved by the increased production of all items that are in demonstrated demand.

The developed world first stated its intentions of assisting the developing world at the end of World War II, and allocated prime responsibility to the Economic and Social Council (ECOSOC) of the United Nations. Ever since then, fierce arguments have taken place about the most effective way to provide development assistance and even whether it should be provided at all.

Arguments about the effectiveness of the development process usually concern scale and direction. Should development projects be large-scale or small-scale? Should development assistance be directed to the political and economic power groups in each country or to the needy people themselves?

Complaints about high levels of consumption are not new. Two thousand years ago, in ancient Rome, Marcus Aurelius spoke in favour of a simpler life; more recently, in 1899, U.S. economist Thorstein Veblen wrote critically of "conspicuous consumption" in his book *The Theory of the Leisure Class.*

SOURCE: CIDA/David Barbour

Fig. 3-2 *Emergency grain supplies are received in Ethiopia. In what ways can such shipments affect the independence of the people receiving help?*

The South Commission is made up of individuals from the developing world. Its report, *The Challenge to the South*, states that, "underlying all the Report's recommendations is our recognition, and clear statement, that responsibility for the development of the South lies in the South, and in the hands of the peoples of the South."

Arguments about the very existence of development assistance focus on the issue of dependence. In both the developed and developing worlds, some people argue that development assistance breeds a sense of dependence in those being assisted, and reduces local pride and initiative. They also argue that development assistance is often a form of neocolonialism, and that it weakens the political freedoms that many former colonies gained upon achieving independence.

Conversely, some people in both the developed and developing worlds argue that development assistance is morally just since the world family cannot stand by and allow some of its members to live less well than the rest. They argue also that development assistance further serves moral justice and human rights by making up for the exploitation of developing countries by developed countries in colonial times. Supporters of development assistance point additionally to the prospects of greater world harmony if all people lead more satisfying lives.

All the questions that people have about the nature of resources, about defining satisfying standards of living, and about the existence and direction of the development process are compounded in importance by the ongoing growth of the world's population, as outlined in Chapter One. The following readings provide a number of views about these issues. As you go through them, imagine that each reading is the answer to a particular question. Write down what you think the question might be for each reading. Use the issues noted in this introduction as a guide to developing the questions.

OVERVIEW

The achievement of sustained and equitable development remains the greatest challenge facing the human race. Despite good progress over the past generation, more than 1 billion people still live in acute poverty and suffer grossly inadequate access to the resources — education, health services, infrastructure, land, and credit — required to give them a chance for a better life. The essential task of development is to provide opportunities so that these people, and the hundreds of millions not much better off, can reach their potential.

But although the desirability of development is universally recognized, recent years have witnessed rising concern about whether environmental constraints will limit development and whether development will cause serious environmental damage — in turn impairing the quality of life of this and future generations. This concern is overdue. A number of environmental problems are already very serious and require urgent attention. Humanity's stake in environmental protection is enormous, and environmental values have been neglected too often in the past.

World Development Report 1992, The World Bank

A GEOGRAPHY OF WELL-BEING

...it is the task of geographers to demonstrate to governments, decision-makers and other influential groups the existence of these inequalities in well-being and their diverse manifestations, whether it be malnutrition, illiteracy or inadequate housing. But does the geographer's responsibility end there? Nowadays, most geographers agree that this responsibility should extend to include at least researching the causes of the inequalities and possibly identifying the costs of their consequences. But what about applying the fruits of that research to the design of policies and programmes of action aimed at eliminating or reducing the causes? And beyond that, what about the implementation of those policies? The causes of the inequalities stem intrinsically from malfunctions within the world's political, economic and social systems. These defects inhibit the crucial factors of distribution, access and opportunity. The critical question is, therefore, whether or not modern geographers should become much more "political" by assuming the mantle of activist rather than leaving others to pursue the necessary reforms. Should not geographers themselves be leading the campaign to replace today's two geographies of hunger and plenty (deprivation and advantage), by a single geography of social justice and equitable well-being?

Michael Witherick, *Geographical Magazine*, 1989 11

STORY BY GILBERT OSKABOOSE, SERPENT RIVER FIRST NATION

"White people came here a long time ago. Took all the furs. Trapped all the beaver out; and the otter and the mink; things like that. And they gathered all these things up. They went away and they left us with the bush and the rocks. It wasn't too much later they came back again. They call that logging. Cut down all the trees: white pine, red pine, cut it all down. And they left us on the bare rocks. Then they discovered uranium here...."

Quoted in Uranium Mining, Irene Kock, *Earthkeeper*, 1992 5-6

DRAWING POOR AND ILLITERATE WOMEN INTO THE MARKET ECONOMY

BARTANDI, NAWALPARASI DIS-TRICT, NEPAL — Mrs. Tamang and her husband were pioneer settlers in this hillside village when it was established about 160 kilometres south-west of Kathmandu 18 years ago. The Government provided them with a small parcel of unirrigated land. The land was too poor to support them, however, and they both worked as agricultural labourers during the peak season.

When they arrived in Bartandi, the Tamangs owned four cows and two goats and clothed themselves by borrowing from a local money-lender at 25 per cent annual interest. They soon fell behind, however, and as the family grew their children were often hungry.

In 1986, Mrs. Tamang joined a group of six other people and approached the Production Credit for Rural Women Programme for a loan. The Rastriya Banijya Bank accepted the group as reliable co-guarantors, and Mrs. Tamang was able to secure 2500 rupees (about C$100) — a significant sum considering that the family income the previous year had been just 800 rupees. The loan enabled Mrs. Tamang to buy seven goats. The animals multiplied and by the end of 1988 she was able to sell six full grown males for 6000 rupees and keep eight goats for herself. She paid off her debts with

Fig. 3-3 *What does the photograph suggest about the way of life for these inhabitants of rural Nepal?*

interest, and bought a buffalo.

The experience encouraged Mrs. Tamang to take out a new loan of 4000 rupees and buy more livestock, giving her family a total of four cows, one ox, one buffalo and fifteen goats — a source of livelihood which continues to expand. The family income has grown fourfold in the past four years and Mrs. Tamang has continued to reinvest in livestock and to use the remaining profits to pay for her children's school fees, clothing and medicines. The Tamang family has also been able to gain access to another small but irrigated plot of land and take a half share of the rice and vegetable harvests.

The Tamangs have five children today, and their increasing livestock production has given the family a strong sense of security and has become a substantial asset. Continued interventions by the credit programme in their community have yielded other benefits as well. A safe drinking water supply in the village has reduced the time spent fetching water from two hours a day to about 15 minutes. The creation of community woodlots has reduced the collection of fodder from two hours to 30 minutes a day, and a child-care facility has expanded Mrs. Tamang's free time for other activities. She is only semi-literate but has used this time to join training programmes. By attending literacy classes, she has also learned to sign her name, read and count.

UNICEF Canada Fact Sheet, 1992

SOURCE: John Molyneux

EDITORIAL: BUILDING FOOD SECURITY LOCALLY AND GLOBALLY

...food security means more than simply the absence of hunger at any given moment. By definition, food security means that all people, at all times, have both physical and economic access to enough food for an active, healthy life. Inherent to this concept is that the ability to acquire food is assured, that the food itself is nutritionally adequate and personally acceptable, and that this food be obtained in a manner that upholds basic human dignity.

Of course, food security is dependent upon the world's ability to harvest enough food for our entire population. While population growth and unsustainable practices threaten the world's future ability to feed itself, the amazing thing is that today, the Earth produces more than enough food to meet the nutritional needs of everyone. Yet worldwide, hundreds of millions of people go hungry. Why?

The answer to that is simple and universal. They are poor. There is enough food, but hundreds of millions of people don't have enough money to buy that food, or enough land to grow their own. That's where aid, trade and debt come in. With the stated intention of helping them develop and become self-reliant, rich countries like Canada give aid to underdeveloped nations in the Third World. However, as we give money with one hand, we take away more with the other. Trade policies that discriminate against their exports cost developing countries far more money every year than they receive in aid. On top of that, no matter how desperately they need the money, we demand that poor countries pay interest on their debts — in amounts that far exceed what we give them in aid and new loans combined.

Even in Canada, one of the richest countries in the world thousands (perhaps millions) of people cannot claim food security.... Though food banks have prevented the kind of severe undernutrition experienced in many developing countries, they fall short of building food security.

Gary Bellamy, *World Food Update 1992*, The World Food Day Association, 1992 10

DISCUSSION AND RESEARCH

1. In small groups:
   (a) compare the questions for each reading that you wrote down with those of the members of your group;
   (b) discuss the questions to find out if your own analysis matches that of the other group members;
   (c) attempt to reach a consensus about the most appropriate question for each reading; and
   (d) as a group, develop a possible alternative answer to any one of the questions that you select. Report this answer in writing.

2. The reading "A Geography of Well-Being" on p. 155 calls for geographers to develop an action plan once inequalities have been identified and researched. Organize a research project to examine the inequalities in your province. Identify the appropriate "government, decision-makers, or other influential groups" that could deal with the issue, and prepare an action plan to submit to them.

RESOURCES

The widest view of resources includes humanity itself. In this context, resources may be classified into two broad groups, each subdivided as follows:

Non-human resources:
- Finite, non-renewable, inorganic, or stock resources
- Infinite, renewable, organic, or flow resources

Human resources:
- Physical, related to numbers and muscle power
- Mental, related to intelligence and creativity.

It should be remembered that the use of the terms finite and infinite to subdivide non-human resources is relative. Infinity is an open-ended concept that does not apply in absolute terms to earth history. Although some resources may be deemed infinite, and are infinite in relation to the span of human existence, in absolute astronomical terms they are finite. As the sun gradually uses up its energy over the next few billion years, the earth will steadily receive diminishing amounts of solar energy and eventually become lifeless.

NON-HUMAN RESOURCES
FINITE, NON-RENEWABLE RESOURCES

Finite, non-renewable, inorganic, or stock resources are those such as minerals and quarry products, which are depletable. Normal geological processes continue to create rocks and other minerals, but so slowly in human terms that for all purposes the quantities that exist may be regarded as finite. A quantity exists, and diminishes if used. As noted in Chapter Two (p.103), however, the concept of depletion, which defines non-renewable resources, is subject to qualification. The chief qualifications are those of technological change. For example, use of a resource may cease altogether if superior substitutes are discovered; or use may diminish as greater efficiencies of production are developed. Also, recycling of the already used resource may significantly slow the depletion rate. About half of all steel now made in the world depends upon recycled scrap, and about one-third of all aluminum. There is indeed general agreement among most people that non-renewable resources are in plentiful supply. As the *Gaia Atlas of Planet Management* notes, "No essential mineral resource will run out…."

Petroleum, for example, is currently in plentiful supply, and likely to remain that way for a long time because of the virtually untouched — but expensive to obtain — supplies still locked in the Colorado Oil Shales and the Athabasca Tar Sands. In addition, there are possibly other supplies that have yet to be discovered. However, oil is a hydrocarbon fuel that releases carbon dioxide when burned, and will likely in time be substituted by cleaner fuels such as hydrogen. It is possible that petroleum will be sub-

The energy of the sun — like all energy — is never lost. This is the first law of thermodynamics. However, the second law of thermodynamics states that every time energy is converted from one form to another (as by the burning of fuel) it becomes less concentrated. The earth receives only a microscopic portion of all energy radiated by the sun.

Some people consider it unnecessary for the present generation to avoid using resources in order to preserve them, as future generations may need entirely different resources. They believe this situation can be likened to stone age people refraining from making too many flint axes and arrowheads so that the present generation could have some.

Fig. 3-4
Sources of commercial energy production, by continent and major producing nation.

SOURCE: Calculated from data in *World Resources 1992-93* and *The Universal Almanac 1993*

	Coal	Oil	Gas	Hydro	Nuclear	Other[1]	Total
AFRICA	4.8	14.6	2.6	0.2	•••	0.0	22.2
Algeria	0.0	2.8	1.7	0.0	0.0	0.0	4.5
Egypt	0.0	2.2	0.3	0.1	0.0	0.0	2.6
Libya	0.0	2.7	0.3	0.0	0.0	0.0	3.0
Nigeria	0.0	4.2	0.2	•••	0.0	0.0	4.4
South Africa	4.5	0.0	0.0	0.0	•••	0.0	4.5
ASIA	34.9	53.1	9.0	1.7	1.1	0.0	99.8
China	25.5	6.7	0.7	0.5	0.0	0.0	33.4
India	5.8	1.7	0.4	0.3	0.1	0.0	8.3
Indonesia	0.2	3.1	1.4	•••	0.0	0.0	4.7
Iran	0.0	7.0	1.0	•••	0.0	0.0	8.0
Iraq	0.0	6.8	0.2	•••	0.0	0.0	7.0
Japan	0.3	•••	•••	0.4	0.8	•••	1.5
Korea, N.	1.7	0.0	0.0	0.1	0.0	0.0	1.8
Korea, S.	0.5	0.0	0.0	•••	0.2	0.0	0.7
Kuwait	0.0	3.8	0.2	0.0	0.0	0.0	4.0
Malaysia	0.0	1.4	0.7	•••	0.0	0.0	2.1
Oman	0.0	1.6	0.1	0.0	0.0	0.0	1.7
Qatar	0.0	1.0	0.3	0.0	0.0	0.0	1.3
Saudi Arabia	0.0	13.1	1.2	0.0	0.0	0.0	14.3
United Arab Emirates	0.0	4.6	0.9	0.0	0.0	0.0	5.5
EUROPE	21.2	10.5	9.9	2.0	3.3	•••	46.9
former Czechoslovakia	2.0	•••	•••	•••	0.1	0.0	2.2
France	0.5	0.2	0.1	0.2	1.3	0.0	2.3
Germany	6.7	0.2	0.7	•••	0.7	0.0	8.3
Italy	•••	0.2	0.7	0.2	0.0	•••	1.1
Netherlands	0.0	0.2	2.7	0.0	•••	0.0	2.9
Norway	•••	3.7	1.5	0.5	0.0	0.0	5.7
Poland	5.6	•••	0.2	•••	0.0	0.0	5.8
Romania	0.9	0.5	1.3	•••	•••	0.0	2.7
U.K.	2.8	4.5	2.0	•••	0.3	0.0	9.6
former Yugoslavia	0.8	0.2	0.1	0.1	•••	•••	1.2
CENTRAL AMERICA	0.3	7.5	1.3	0.1	0.0	•••	9.2
Mexico	0.3	7.1	1.2	0.1	0.0	•••	8.7
NORTH AMERICA	27.6	25.8	24.8	2.3	2.6	0.1	83.2
Canada	2.0	4.4	4.7	1.2	0.4	0.0	12.7
U.S.A.	25.6	21.4	20.1	1.1	2.2	0.1	70.5
OCEANIA	4.7	1.3	0.9	0.2	0.0	•••	7.1
Australia	4.6	1.2	0.7	0.1	0.0	0.0	6.6
SOUTH AMERICA	0.9	10.0	2.4	1.4	•••	0.0	14.8
Argentina	•••	1.2	0.9	0.1	•••	0.0	2.2
Brazil	0.1	1.5	0.2	0.9	•••	0.0	2.7
Colombia	0.6	1.0	0.2	0.1	0.0	0.0	1.9
Venezuela	•••	5.1	1.0	0.1	0.0	0.0	6.2
former U.S.S.R.	17.7	29.8	31.6	1.0	0.9	0.0	80.9
WORLD TOTALS	112.1	152.6	82.5	8.8	7.9	0.2	364.1

[1]Geothermal (from the earth's heat) and wind energy.

••• Some production, but less than 0.05 EJ

All figures in exajoules (EJ): 1.0 EJ = 10^{15} kJ, or 10^{18} joules, equivalent to 163 400 000 barrels of oil or 34 140 000 tonnes coal.

stituted as a specific fuel by another cleaner fuel long before petroleum supplies are physically depleted. In the meantime, technological change has improved the efficiency with which petroleum is used, so that more is achieved with relatively less, and harmful emissions have been reduced per unit of fuel used.

For most non-renewable resources, pressures on production exist more for health and amenity reasons than for fears of physical depletion. All hydrocarbon fuels — fossil fuels such as coal, oil, and gas — are under pressure because they release harmful gases and solid particles when burned. The dirtiest hydrocarbon fuel is coal, particularly those types that have a high sulphur content, while gas is cleanest. However, coal is plentiful, widely available in many countries, and cheap. Worldwide, the use of coal ranks second to the use of petroleum (see Fig. 3-4). But while the use of coal in developed countries rises slowly at about 1%/y, use in the developing world is rising quickly at about 3%/y. In many developed countries, gas is being increasingly substituted for coal, although conversion is costly and therefore slow.

Since most countries in the developing world produce very small quantities of commercial energy from their own resources, they import much of what they use. There is considerable world trade in energy products (see Fig. 3-5), although the vast bulk of it is in oil shipments from the oil-producing regions of southwest Asia, Latin America, and the North Sea to industrial areas in North America, Europe, and Japan. Smaller quanti-

> Very roughly, since qualities vary, oil is 1.5 times dirtier than natural gas, while coal is twice as dirty.

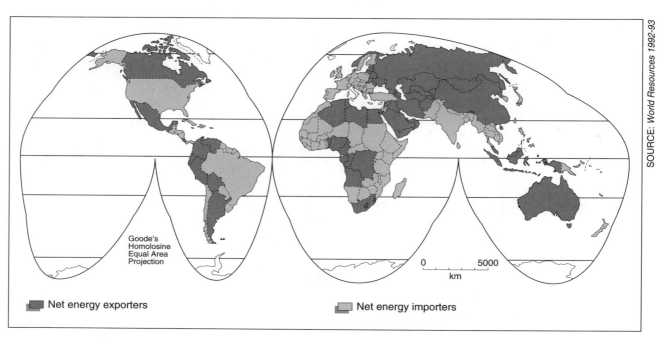

SOURCE: *World Resources 1992-93*

Goode's Homolosine Equal Area Projection

0   5000
km

■ Net energy exporters

□ Net energy importers

Fig. 3-5 *Net energy exporting and importing nations.*

Apart from oil and gas in the north and coal in the south, Africa has few fossil fuels. But it has a huge potential for hydro-electricity production, so far only about five percent realized. Meanwhile, Africa generally remains short of both industrial and domestic energy.

ties of coal and oil are imported by the developing nations. Even so, there are large areas of Africa and Latin America that have little access to coal or oil. People in these regions rely instead on traditional fuels such as animal dung and fuelwood, although these are increasingly scarce in some parts of the world.

Small amounts of energy — in world terms — also come from finite, but plentiful, supplies of uranium. Nuclear energy is widely regarded as the least polluting of finite energy sources, but many people are fearful of both nuclear energy generation and nuclear waste disposal. In some countries, such as Canada, construction of nuclear power stations is almost at a standstill, but in others, such as Japan and China, construction proceeds.

Renewable energy is any source that exists in one of the environment's regular short-term cycles, such as the water cycle, the ebb and flow of tides, the growth of biomass, the daily radiance of the sun, and the circulation of the atmosphere.

In addition to energy from finite resources, supplies are also available from a variety of renewable resources. Hydroelectricity is the most important. It is relatively non-polluting, but its production is often criticized for other reasons. Reservoirs occupy large areas, and their creation has often caused relocation of people and disruption of existing ways of life. The reading on the Narmada project in Chapter One, p. 17, outlines typical criticisms.

Other renewable sources of energy are the winds, tides, and waves of the biosphere, and the internal heat of the earth (called geothermal energy). Some energy is also derived from incoming solar radiation (solar energy). All these sources are in fairly regular use in several parts of the world, but there are problems involved in their use. The major problem is that the quantities of energy they generate are small and variable in rela-

SOURCE: CIDA/Paul Chiasson

Fig. 3-6 *Wind energy is used here for drawing water in Kenya.*

tion to their cost compared with fossil fuels or hydroelectricity. For example, winds seldom blow strongly and regularly enough to produce electricity steadily; tides differ every day in height and timing; and waves vary in direction and intensity. Also, geothermal "hot-spots" are not widely distributed; the sun does not always shine, either because it's night-time or days are cloudy; and the areas of land needed to support sufficient numbers of solar panels or wind turbines are huge compared to the quantities of energy generated. All these systems work, but the cost required to produce large quantities of energy is an obstacle.

Research is taking place into various means of converting solar energy more efficiently into large quantities of electricity, but progress is slow. Meanwhile, many scientists are experimenting with the possibility of obtaining energy directly from water. The process involves splitting a water molecule into its component atoms (two hydrogen, one oxygen), and separating the hydrogen for use as a fuel. Oxygen would be the waste product of this process. In use, the hydrogen would burn by combining with atmospheric oxygen, and yield water as the waste product. The concept is straightforward, and the environmental benefits considerable. The problem at the moment lies in developing the energy needed to split the water molecules in the first place, especially on the scale that would be needed to maintain or increase existing world economic activity. An allied problem lies in ensuring that the energy available from the splitting of water molecules is greater than that required to split them (see Fig. 3-7).

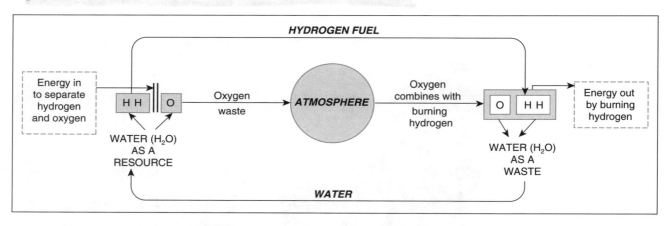

Fig. 3-7 *Water may be used as a raw material to produce hydrogen energy.*

The following three readings outline some of the issues connected with finite resources and renewable energy.

MINING THE EARTH

Human welfare and mineral supplies have been linked for so long that scholars demarcate the ages of human history by reference to minerals: Stone, Bronze, and Iron. Cheap and abundant minerals provided the physical foundation for industrial civilizations. Societies' overall prosperity still correlates closely with per capita use of mineral products.

Industrial nations' abiding preoccupation with minerals is thus not surprising. In the United States, for example, periodic waves of concern over future mineral supplies have led to the appointment of at least a half-dozen blue-ribbon panels on the subject since the twenties. In 1978, a U.S. congressional committee requested a study whose title expressed the central question of virtually all these inquiries: Are we running out?

Recent trends in price and availability of minerals suggest that the answer is "not yet." Regular improvements in exploitive technology have allowed the production of growing amounts at declining prices, despite the exhaustion of many of the world's richest ores. For many minerals, much of the world has yet to be thoroughly explored.

The question of scarcity, however, may never have been the most important one. Far more urgent is, Can the world afford the human and ecological price of satisfying its voracious appetite for minerals? Today's low mineral prices reflect only the immediate economics of extraction: purchases of equipment and fuel, wages, transportation, financing, and so on. They fail to consider the full costs of devastated landscapes, dammed or polluted rivers, the squalor of mining camps, and the uprooting or decimation of indigenous peoples unlucky enough to live atop mineral deposits.

Although minerals remain essential for human survival, the negative effects of today's unprecedented extraction rates threaten to outweigh the benefits. Where mining is regulated to protect the environment, it still causes substantial damage; where regulated poorly or not at all, it creates environmental disaster areas. Around the world, mining and mineral processing play an important role in such environmental problems as deforestation, soil erosion, and air and water pollution. Globally, the mineral sector is one of the largest users of energy, thus contributing to air pollution and global warming.

The environmental impacts of mineral extraction are particularly severe in developing countries, which produce a large portion of the world's mineral supplies but use a relatively small share. Responsibility for the majority of the damage ultimately lies with those who use the most minerals — the fifth of humanity who live in industrial nations, enjoying material comforts others only dream of.

Reducing the mineral intake of rich nations is thus a top priority. Hope for success lies in the economic maturity of these countries: a certain amount of minerals is required for the infrastructures of prosperous societies, such as housing, office buildings, schools, hospitals, and transportation systems. Beyond these basics, the quantity of materials used need not determine the quality of life. After a certain point, people's welfare may depend more on the caliber of a relatively small number of silicon microchips than on the quantities of copper, steel, or aluminum they use.

The sooner the whole world reaches such a point, the better. At the end of the minerals- and energy-intensive development path taken by today's industrial nations lies ecological ruin. Mining enough to supply a world that has twice as many people, all using minerals at rates that now prevail only in rich countries, would have staggering environmental consequences. To avert such a fate, a new development strategy is needed — one that focuses on the improvement of human welfare while minimizing the need for new supplies of minerals.

John E. Young, *State of the World 1992*, Worldwatch Institute

QUENCHING THE TIGERS' THIRST

In 1991 Asian countries (including Australia and New Zealand) consumed 23% of the world's energy, the equivalent of 35m barrels of oil per day (b/d). A decade earlier, the figure had been closer to 18%, or 21m b/d. Compare this with Europe and North America, where energy consumption hardly increased at all.

Coal, meeting 48% of demand, is Asia's favourite fuel, mainly because India and China use their abundant domestic supplies. The richer countries care more about oil, which provided 37% of all energy consumed in Asia last year. Nearly half of Asia's oil needs are met by imports from outside the region — and, as prospering Asians buy more cars, the proportion could climb to two-thirds by the year 2000. Japan, for one, bought 76% of its oil from the Middle East in the first quarter of this year, against 72% over the same period last year.

Asia's indigenous oil producers are unlikely to lessen the dependence on imports. China alone pumps up nearly half of Asia's oil, and has impressive reserves, but the Chinese are scarcely able to keep up with their own demand. Reserves in Indonesia, the region's second-largest producer, are dwindling: at current rates of extraction, proved reserves will last barely a dozen years. With its booming economy, Indonesia faces the prospect of becoming a net importer early in the next century unless it finds new reserves or improves the extraction rates from its present fields. In Australia, proved reserves could be exhausted by the end of the decade.

Fig. 3-8 *Motor traffic in the cities of the developing world has grown enormously in recent years.*

SOURCE: CIDA/David Barbour

Although Asia has plenty of untapped reserves, these tend to be a long way from potential consumers. The ex-Soviet republics of Central Asia are thought to be sitting on substantial quantities of oil and gas (Kazakhstan recently signed an agreement with Chevron to develop the Tengiz oilfield, holding an estimated 3 billion-5 billion barrels of recoverable reserves) but their existing pipelines point in the wrong direction, towards Russia. China's most promising oilfields, in Xinjiang's Tarim basin, suffer from the same remoteness.

That leaves the pauperized countries of Indochina to narrow Asia's petroleum gap. They cannot do so by much. Although Vietnam quadrupled its oil production between 1989 and 1991, to some 72 000 barrels a day, it remains a midget among oil producers. Meanwhile, power cuts already curse many of Asia's cities and much of its industry. The tempting cure in India and China will be to rely still more on coal, a home-produced commodity but a dirty one. Nuclear power — the obvious clean alternative for richer countries — remains difficult to sell to increasingly assertive voters.

A clean and politically palatable answer would be natural gas: here, at least, production has kept pace with demand, most of it from Japan, Taiwan and South Korea. Indonesia, the region's largest producer, accounts for nearly 40% of world exports of liquefied natural gas (LNG); Malaysia also has substantial gas reserves, followed by Australia, Pakistan, India, China, Brunei and others.

Yet the incentives for investment in export facilities (such as pipelines and liquefaction plants) are as yet limited by low gas prices on the world market. For LNG to become more attractive, oil prices will have to go up. The snag is that LNG facilities are always developed jointly by producer and consumer. No consumer likes higher prices.

The Economist, 1992 8 15

SOLAR ENERGY UTILIZATION IN CHINA

Like many other developing countries, China has a large population, scarce natural resources and an environment under stress — problems that seriously threaten social progress. China is home to some 23 percent of humanity, or 1.16 billion people, but to feed them it has only seven percent of the world's arable land. Its primary energy production currently equals 1016 million tonnes of coal equivalent per year, making it the world's third biggest energy producer; but energy supply falls short of demand by some 50 million tonnes of coal equivalent a year, even though per capita energy consumption remains low — 860 kilograms of coal equivalent in 1989, or one third the world average.

Coal is the main energy resource in China, providing as much as 76 percent of the energy supply in 1991. Because of widespread use of this fuel as well as primitive combustion techniques, China faces high atmospheric levels of suspended particulates and sulphur dioxide. Many cities often experience smog, and acid rain affects the southern, southwestern and eastern areas of China. Nevertheless, for the foreseeable future, coal will have to remain the country's main energy resource.

In the countryside — where 80 percent of China's people live — there is an enormous demand for energy for use in homes, agricultural production and industry. However, the rural energy supply is limited, and will continue to be so for some time. In rural households, 75 percent of the energy used still comes from biomass —

in particular, firewood. Some 230 megatonnes of biomass are burned every year, seriously depleting this energy resource and causing increasing rural environmental deterioration. The past half-century has seen extensive soil erosion, desertification and grasslands degradation.

On the other hand, China is rich in various kinds of natural energy resources. Two thirds of its territory receives annual solar radiation equivalent to 0.6 megajoules per square centimetre, and exploitable wind power amounts to 160 **giga**watts. Solar and wind power thus offer environmentally sustainable solutions to the rural energy shortage.

The search for such solutions is a high priority in China. A policy has been formulated for the development of new and renewable sources of energy. In the short and medium term, this policy focuses on eliminating the energy shortage in rural and remote areas, and developing small-scale, decentralized, renewable energy technologies for practical use. The Chinese government has allocated 28 billion yuan (C$6 billion) for implementing this policy, and has established a State Environment Protection Commission. These measures will go far toward achieving the United Nations' Nairobi Programme of Action for Development of New and Renewable Sources of Energy.

China's approach to solar energy emphasizes low-temperature solar thermal utilization and small-scale, decentralized solar photovoltaic (electricity from light) systems for domestic use in rural and remote areas, as well as some other specialized uses.

More than 100 small factories are manufacturing solar water

heaters for a booming domestic market. China has imported advanced production technology and equipment, greatly improving the quality of Chinese-made solar collectors. Each year, the use of solar water heaters could save fuel amounting to approximately 200 000 tonnes of coal equivalent.

Passive solar heating techniques are also being explored for buildings in rural areas. Computer-assisted design (CAD) technology is being used to achieve optimal thermal design for passive solar buildings. Depending on the climate, these require as much as 60 to 80 percent less energy for heating than conventional buildings, thereby saving an average of 66 kilograms of coal per square metre each year. However, a period of two to eight years is needed to recover the initial investment, which is considerable.

Solar cookers with parabolic dish reflectors are popular with Chinese farm-dwellers. The materials used are simple: aluminum, plastic and pig iron. Equally simple is operation: the devices are manually adjusted to track the sun. Solar cookers have an important role to play in improving the ecological balance in rural areas.

Three types of solar drying system are common in China: greenhouses, solar collectors and drying cabinets. These are used to dry such items as agricultural byproducts, fruit, cut wood and unfinished industrial goods. They require from 50 to 75 percent less energy than conventional systems, and their low and uniform temperatures yield a higher quality of dried products. The initial investment can be recovered within two to five years.

China has built 12 solar pho-tovoltaic (PV) factories with a capacity totalling 4.5 megawatts. The efficiency of commercialized solar PV modules currently ranges from 5.6 to 12 percent.

Initially, the high cost of PV units limited their use to special applications, such as navigation beacons, railway signals, electric fences and power for satellites. As technology has improved, howev-er, costs have been lowered. Further, the capacity of installed systems is increasing: the largest PV system now is 10-kW, and a 20-kW system will be built in 1992. In addition, market prospects seem bright for small-capacity PV kits of 20 to 50 watts' capacity;

these are particularly popular in isolated or remote areas.

The experience of the past decade shows that solar energy can and must play an important role in easing energy shortages in remote rural areas in the short term. It also has a longer-term role in improving the regional and glob-al environment. Finally, the use of solar power can promote the worldwide transition to sustainable forms of energy generation.

Technological progress is bound to improve the cost-effec-tiveness of renewable energy con-version products. However, for developing countries, the technol-ogy must be adapted to their own social and economic conditions.

At the global level, we need international co-operation — both North-South as well as South-South — in the fields of information exchange, education and training, joint research and development, technology transfer, joint demon-strations and joint ventures to pro-mote the use of solar power. Concerted efforts are essential for introducing worldwide changes in energy generation.

With that co-operation, we will be able to implement the Nairobi Programme of Action, and make the switch to renewable sources of energy.

Hu Chengchun and Lu Weide, *Ecodecision*, 1992 3

DISCUSSION AND RESEARCH

3. On p. 163, the reading "Mining the Earth" from the Worldwatch Institute states that developing countries "produce a large por-tion of the world's mineral supplies...." Examine the truth of this common assumption by identifying ten major minerals, and researching the amounts of each produced annually. For each mineral, list the chief producers, with amounts produced, and estimate the proportions of world production that are produced by developing nations.

4. From the three preceding readings, select any unsupported statement other than the one in question 3, and research the facts which may justify or negate the statement.

5. The previous readings suggest several linkages between mining and other subjects.
   (a) Consider the nature, extent, and interrelatedness of these linkages, and
   (b) Construct a web diagram (like a spider's web) showing all the linkages involving mining you can think of.

6. Many people talk of the costs involved in degrading the natural environment through the obtaining of finite resources.

(a) Select any finite resource that is being obtained in or near your local area.

(b) In small group discussion, identify and list the environmental costs of obtaining the resource identified.

(c) Suggest ways in which these costs could be given a monetary value.

STATISTICAL ANALYSIS

7. Your company is preparing a presentation to an international commission on world energy supplies. Your task is to prepare the visuals. Refer to Fig. 3-4, and consult the graphing and mapping sections in Appendix 3.

(a) List the various graphing and mapping techniques that could be used to illustrate the data in Fig. 3-4.

(b) Note briefly the relative advantages and disadvantages of each of the techniques listed for showing the information in Fig. 3-4.

(c) Prepare the visuals.

INFINITE, RENEWABLE RESOURCES

Views about soil as a resource range from describing it as absolutely essential for the support of life to characterizing it as something needed to prevent plants from falling over.

Infinite, renewable, organic, or flow resources are those such as forests, crops, livestock, soil, and water that can be renewed if used. Renewable resources can be damaged and wasted, however, so care is needed in use. Undoubtedly the two most important renewable resources are food items and water. Life would cease without them.

There are many different food items. Those that form the basis of the diet for millions of people are known as food staples, and on a world level include rice, wheat, corn, and potatoes. On a local level, they may also include meat, as for the Masai in Kenya, and fish, as for the Japanese. Other food staples occur only in certain regions, such as yams in Sub-Saharan Africa. World food staples are mostly grains because, compared with other foodstuffs, grains grow relatively easily and plentifully, and yield relatively high levels of nutrition per unit of land and labour. More people can thus be supported per unit area.

The food staple for most people is rice, especially in the developing countries of south, southeast, and east Asia. This area is often collectively called monsoon Asia (see Fig. 3-9) because of its reliance on water supplies provided by the annual summer monsoon rains. As it is important as a food staple for a large proportion of the earth's population, rice

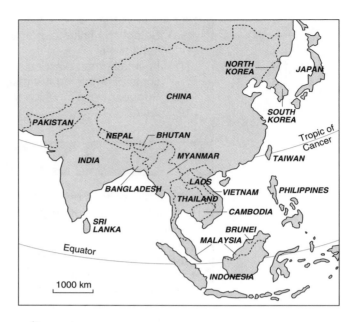

Fig. 3-9 *The countries of Monsoon Asia.*

The pruning of flower plants achieves a similar effect. Cutting off stems and foliage leads the plants to use their converted solar energy in flower production instead.

has been the object of much intensive recent research. In the mid-1960s a well-known college text on economic geography said, "…it is worth noting that even though [rice] meets the…food requirements of about half the world's population, less is known scientifically about it than about any other major crop." Since then the situation has altered considerably.

Research work was pioneered in the mid-1960s by the International Rice Research Institute (IRRI) in the Philippines. Its first successful experiment in producing higher yielding rice came at the eighth attempt, and the high yielding variety (HYV) was called IR8. It was a dwarf rice in height because the focus of the experiments was to have the plant convert more solar energy into grain production and less into foliage and stem production. A heavier grain head would require a sturdy stem, which — if the plant were also tall — would consume a lot of solar energy at the expense of grain production. IR8 was first grown by farmers in 1966 in the Philippines and soon spread to Indonesia, Sri Lanka, and Vietnam. By the early 1970s, dwarf rice was being widely grown throughout monsoon Asia.

IR8 rice soon ran into problems, however. Its higher yields came at a price. For one thing, the new rice was a **hybrid**, and new seeds had to be purchased each year. Water was needed more regularly than before, requiring the construction of expensive irrigation systems. Pumping the extra water made additional demands upon power generation. More fertilizers and pesticides were needed, and more trucks and storage facilities were required to handle farm surpluses to market, replacing a common pattern of local subsistence. Additional input and handling costs for IR8 rice production caused many smaller debt-laden farmers to sell their plots to more profitable farmers; average farm sizes thus increased, and dispossessed farmers left to seek work in cities. Also, the new HYV proved unable to defend itself against mutating pests.

Scientists at IRRI are constantly seeking improvements, and much of the work is focused on developing pest resistance because of the environmental need (often legally enforced) to reduce world use of agricultural chemicals. Since the mid-1960s, IR8 has been replaced successively by IR20, IR26, IR36, IR56, and IR64.

Despite the problems associated with rice HYVs, their use has become highly popular over the last 25 to 30 years. From zero use in 1965, HYV rice spread by 1990 to almost 1 500 000 km² throughout monsoon Asia. In the process, rice yields increased greatly. Depending upon input factors such as fertilizer and irrigation water that varied from place to place, yields per hectare increased by at least 10 percent and as much as 150 percent. Total rice production approximately doubled, more than keeping pace with the overall increase in population, which almost doubled. Crop reliability also improved, and famine was virtually driven from monsoon Asia.

SOURCE: CIDA/Bruce Paton

Fig. 3-10 *Use of HYV rice has spread from Monsoon Asia to other lands, as here in Nigeria.*

Like all money, the value of the $US is determined by what it will buy, that is, its purchasing power, spread over many items.
Individual items may rise or fall in dollar value (i.e., price) within this overall framework, and the entire valuing system ($US) may rise or fall in value as well, just as the $US fell by an average 5%/y.

People also benefited from lower rice prices, because increased production more than offset higher input costs. In 1965 the price of a tonne of rice was over $300; by 1990 the price was down to about $250. In **real terms**, allowing for inflation, price reductions were even greater. International commodity prices are normally quoted in United States dollars (US$), and from 1965 to 1990 the US$ suffered an average annual rate of inflation of about 5 percent. Such an average annual rate meant a total drop over 25 years of over 70 percent in the value of the US$. In turn, this meant that a price of $250/t in 1990 was equivalent to $75 in terms of 1965 values.

The following reading deals with aspects of another major renewable resource, meat.

DEVELOPING AFRICA

The traditional cattle trade of the Sahel has always moved from north to south. The markets of Lagos and Port Harcourt feed on meat which has walked slowly down from the Hausa lands (see Fig. 3-11). Abidjan and Accra receive their meat on the hoof from the extensive pastures of Timbuctoo. The meat is sometimes a bit tough: there isn't much fat left on a steer which has just walked 1500 kilometres. But if it is tough, at least it is local. In recent years Sahel meat has become less tough, as more of the cattle travelled by truck. But business is bad. Sahelian herders have been losing coastal markets to meat coming in by sea.

Some of this meat comes from Argentina. Faced with European (and especially British) import bans due to war,[1] or to various disease scares aimed at diminishing Argentine imports to the European Community, what did the Argentinian traders do? They cut prices and redirected their ships to Africa. On the whole, the Argentinian trade is

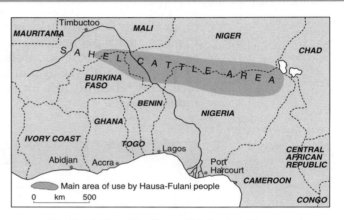

Fig. 3-11 *Coastal cities and inland cattle areas in West Africa.*

fair, since they produce more cheaply than we do in the Sahel and they can carry huge quantities by sea at a reasonable cost. But the other source of competition is in the European Community. What a sick irony: the commission spends millions of Ecus (European currency units) on "development," while it sabotages that same development with unfair trading practices. Because the meat you buy in a Dakar supermarket is subsidized meat from the EC. Probably it has been three times subsidized. The first European subsidy is cheap inputs

(including tax-reduced gasoline)...the resulting over-production is then purchased by the Commission at prices negotiated above the market rate by the powerful farmers' unions...the produce is then stored for free and transported to flood the African market and ruin the Fulani cattle herders.

I was therefore interested to visit the periurban (near a city) fattening cooperative, which provides meat to the burgeoning meat-eating population of our capital city. Here is a commercial activity in full development, harnessing private enterprise, putting **value-added** on to the nation's primary raw materials. The majority of the owners are merchants or civil servants, who are running a second business-cum-hobby on the side. They are in competition with the traditional Fulani cattle herders, of course. But while they may be taking trade away from the nomads, they are also showing the traditional herders how to make a profit.

Nomad herders are notorious for keeping large "uneconomic" herds. In fact their rationality is no different to that of the West. Profit and prestige. In nomad society, social status lies in a big herd and a fine old bull....

Planners dislike nomads for all sorts of reasons. For a start, you cannot easily count moving herds...and therefore you cannot easily tax them either. Smaller nomad herds might reduce the annual conflicts with sedentary farmers. The environmentalists have a justifiable complaint: the more animals there are, the more they eat, which is bad for the ecology (although nomads also produce wealth from lands which would otherwise remain unproductive). Veterinarians argue that if there were fewer, fatter animals, meat would be better, health would be better, and disease more easily controlled; while vaccinations and other treatments would be fewer and cheaper and easier to handle. And a new "economic" attitude among meat-producers would mean cleaner sales yielding more sales tax. In fact everybody would be happier with smaller, better herds.

All this cogent reasoning is put at nought by a cycle of drought: when the nomad's key objective becomes survival.... If you have no more animals, you have no more security (more animals to sell to buy millet, and more to eat, and more chance to survive in a catastrophe). For nomadic herders, survival (more animals) is allied to status (larger herds...). No one can change the logic of survival, so maybe we can change the perception. If nomads were admired more for the quality of their livestock than for simple numbers, they would come to see an advantage in reducing their herd size.

We need prizes for the best herd and the best bull. We need to create in Africa the same breeding pride which was developed in Europe and U.S.A. through a thousand agricultural shows. We need to replace quantity with quality. We need to change perception of prestige so that the highest accolades go to the herder who has the best fatted calf (and gets the best price), rather than fifty scraggy beasts which cannot supply a single decent rump-steak between the lot of them.

[At a cattle fattening station in Nigeria, a Fulani herder from the Sahel learns] new ideas about commercial farming.... This is the first time he has worked with 20 fat animals.... He will have learned about marketing milk and meat in the city. He will know about intensive feeding for suburban cattle, so different from the nomads' extensive grazing. He will know about protein feed supplements like cotton seed and groundnut cake.

The new knowledge and approach may or may not change his ideas about the prestige value of having lots of mangy animals, rather than a smaller number of handsome cattle: but his approach to herding is bound to be slightly different from his father's, after exposure to these new methods and standards of judgment.

I have no illusions about the difficulties of changing age-old perceptions and values. Not all young Fulani herders are able to adapt to the money-profit objectives of periurban fattening units. My neighbour "Old Brother" is also into the fattening business, and recently he found himself in conflict with his Fulani cowman.

It was round Christmas, and the rains were a distant memory. We were watching the herd of 45 cattle come up from watering in the river, after a day's grazing in the dusty hills. Cotton seed was in short supply, and no other convenient forage is available.

"The end of the grass has come," said Old Brother. "I want you to select 20 head for the slaughter house, and we'll keep a nucleus of 25 through the dry season."

The (herder) was outraged! "What? Sell your stock? Reduce your herd from 45 to 25? Slaughter 20 animals? But that is completely impossible! Never will we commit such a sacrilege while I am in charge of your cattle!"

So Old Brother had to get rid of him, and find a Fulani cowman with more modern ideas.

Robert Lacville, *Guardian Weekly*, 1992 8 9 and 16

[1]In 1982, Britain fought a war with Argentina over ownership of the Falkland Islands.

DISCUSSION AND RESEARCH

8. Various groups of people are opposed to the idea of obtaining food from cattle. Through research and small group discussion, develop a list of reasons for holding such views. Also develop a list of counter-arguments in favour of cattle farming. Report both lists to the class.

9. Set up a formal class debate on the following motion: The countries of West Africa should cease buying meat from abroad.

10. Through research,
    (a) Make two lists: one of the renewable resources used in your school, and one of the non-renewable resources.
    (b) Examine ways in which your school might switch from use of some non-renewable resources to use of renewable resources, without increasing the cost.
    (c) Write a report on your findings, complete with recommendations for any changes you may find desirable, and present your report to the school authorities.

11. Korean writer Ch'oe Nam-son (1890-1957) wrote

> The sea — a soaring mountain —
> Lashes and crushes mighty cliffs of rock
> These flimsy things, what are they to me?
> "Know ye my power?" The sea lashes
> Threateningly, it breaks, it crushes.
> No fear assaults, no terror
> Masters me. Earth's power and pride
> Are tedious toys to me. All that the earth
> Imagines mighty is to me no more
> Than a mere feather floating by.

In an interview reported in *The UNESCO Courier* of 91/11, Jacques Cousteau (1910-) said

> I first really started to learn about water when I
> was ten years old. I was in a holiday camp near a
> lake in the United States. We had to collect
> garbage from under the children's diving platform,
> and to do that I learned how to dive and swim under
> water. I had no goggles or any other special
> equipment and bringing the garbage to the surface was

quite a job. I spent two or three weeks diving into that lake and eventually I learned how to hold my breath under water.

In small groups, analyze the possible messages contained in the quotes of Ch'oe Nam-son and Jacques Cousteau. Report your group's conclusions to the class.

STATISTICAL ANALYSIS

	1975	1980	1985	1986	1987	1988	1989	1992
Purchasing power of US$ (1975 = $1.00)	1.00	0.654	0.508	0.492	0.475	0.456	0.436	0.388
Prices in $US								
Cocoa (kg)	1.29	2.60	3.03	2.43	2.24	1.70	1.41	0.97
Cotton (kg)	1.20	2.05	1.77	1.24	1.85	1.50	1.91	1.12
Lead (t)	431.60	906.00	526.32	476.14	667.92	705.00	768.00	740.00
Petroleum (bbl)*	10.86	29.40	37.80	16.09	19.18	14.73	18.60	21.27
Tin (t)	6926.40	16 437.00	15 521.28	7225.89	7480.98	7617.61	9736.50	7740.00
Wheat (t)	187.66	190.80	233.10	188.33	149.30	192.68	229.50	215.90
Wool (kg)	2.84	4.60	4.79	3.88	5.05	6.22	6.10	4.62

* bbl = barrel

SOURCE: Calculated from data in World Resources 1992-93

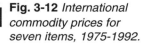

Fig. 3-12 *International commodity prices for seven items, 1975-1992.*

12. Refer to Fig. 3-12. It shows that the value of the United States dollar dropped steadily between 1975 and 1992, and that the actual prices of different natural resources varied considerably during the same period. But given the falling value of the dollar, higher prices did not necessarily buy more for the people selling their resources. In order to make a real comparison, therefore, the value of the dollar must be held constant to its 1975 value, just as all other units of measurement, such as tonnes and kilograms, are standardized. When the money value is standardized, the results are said to be in constant dollars. In this case, the 1975 value is the standard, and values for other years are said to be in constant 1975 dollars.

(a) In order to bring all the actual (or current) prices into constant 1975 dollars, convert the actual prices shown to the value they would have had if the dollar had remained constant at its 1975 value. See the section on constant dollar calculations in Appendix 3 for details of the conversion technique. Complete the calculations for all the commodities for all years shown.

(b) All prices are now shown on a constant scale of value measurement, but a comparison is still not possible because the commodities themselves have different units of measurement (tonnes, kilograms, and barrels). Complete the comparison by converting all constant 1975 dollar prices into index numbers (see Appendix 3), using 1975 as the base year (1975 = 100).

(c) From among the different graphing techniques described in Appendix 3, select the one that you think most suitable for showing the change in the index numbers from 1975 to 1992. When the graph has been drawn, answer the following questions:

 (i) Describe the overall pattern from 1975 to 1985 in comparison with the pattern from 1985 to 1992.

 (ii) Record the commodity which brought its producers the greatest overall net gain from 1975 to 1992.

 (iii) Record the commodity which showed the most persistent decline in 1975 constant dollars from 1975 to 1992.

 (iv) Analyze the graph to determine which major group of commodities generally performed best from 1975 to 1992. Which major group performed worst?

 (v) What does the graph suggest about investment and aid needs in developing countries?

HUMAN RESOURCES

Physical human resources are found in people who can perform work requiring dexterity or muscle power. For thousands of years, societies throughout the world relied extensively on this resource in order to survive and grow. The great civilizations of the past, whether in China, India, southwest Asia, the Mediterranean Basin, the Nile Valley, or Central and South America, used the physical labour of large numbers of people to construct their irrigation works, transportation canals, roads, temples, fortifications, and other massive structures. In more recent times, physical labour, assisted by machinery, has been used to develop basic industrial strength, as in 19th century Europe or 20th century Japan and Hong Kong. Large numbers of people have also been encouraged to migrate to lands already — but sparsely — occupied to spread national power, as in Sumatra and the Amazon region in the second half of the 20th century.

Starting in 1969, Indonesia planned to move millions of people from Java and Bali into sparsely settled lands in Sumatra, Kalimantan, and Irian Jaya. By 1992, about 2 500 000 people had been moved, with mixed success. The program continues.

Fig. 3-13 *Physical labour, assisted by machines, has been used to develop industry. This is a factory in Kyrgyzstan which produces over a million light bulbs a day.*

In 1928, in an episode known as the *Persons Case* the Supreme Court of Canada decided that women were not "persons" for the purpose of holding office as senators. Since Canada was at that time not fully independent of Britain, it took the British Privy Council to overturn the ruling in 1929.

For most of human history, physical human labour has been the basis of survival and growth. Hunters and gatherers, and subsequently farmers, used their own labour to provide for their needs. Others were forced by more powerful members of society into various forms of slavery, or coerced labour. Such coerced labour may have been quite sophisticated, as under medieval European feudalism: powerful landowners arranged for people with little or no wealth to use their land for survival in return for required and regular service. In many places, though, slavery was much simpler: the economically weaker members of society were permanently owned as chattels by the economically powerful members, to do their bidding at all times. The use of Africans in the plantations of the Americas from the 16th to 19th centuries is just one example. The chattel position of women in most societies was similar to slavery in many ways until the 20th century. In a number of countries today, women are still regarded as chattels. Indeed, coerced labour still exists in the world, as shown in the case study about child labour at the end of this chapter.

Mental human resources are, however, gaining in importance over physical human resources. The world economy is slowly shifting from a physical labour emphasis to a mental emphasis, first in the world's cities, then elsewhere. The shift has been occurring throughout the 20th century in the developed world, and is now spreading to the developing world. It is highlighted by Alvin Toffler in his book *The Third Wave*.

Fig. 3-14 *Average earnings in Canada, by age and education.*

Age	Secondary	Certificate/diploma	University
20-24	$13 841	$13 677	$13 978
25-34	$22 682	$24 626	$29 214
35-44	$25 125	$30 253	$43 404
45-54	$28 567	$30 600	$51 202
55-64	$26 971	$27 869	$47 822

SOURCE: Statistics Canada, *Survey of Consumer Finances*, unpublished data

The mentally-based approach to production is increasingly called the New Economy, to distinguish it from the Old Economy of factory production lines reliant on physical labour.

The shift, brought about by technological changes, means that jobs and economic survival increasingly depend on mental rather than physical skills. In the past, it was widely considered enough for survival if people could physically labour to produce sufficient food for themselves. Mental skills were not as important. But, increasingly, mental skills are the key to survival and physical human resources are not as crucial. The following reading illustrates the situation.

BRAIN POWER HOLDS THE KEY TO THE FUTURE

The total of all knowledge gained throughout history to 1991 is just one percent of the information that will be available in the year 2050!

Most Canadians are not prepared for the kind of information economy this fact implies. Even today, when we have a million unemployed, we have up to 600 000 jobs that cannot be filled because no one can be found who qualifies.

And yet, there is a 30 per cent decline in enrolment in computer and engineering courses! Fifteen per cent of high school students are functionally illiterate!

The valuable commodities in this Information Age are knowledge and brain-skills. We must shift from processing raw materials into areas where knowledge adds value to work.

Our workers can't just assemble widgets and go home and forget about the job. We are entering an era that requires engaging our employees' minds and tapping their enthusiasm.

The new knowledge-based work force has to be prepared for lifetime learning. Today's graduates likely face more than ten job changes in their careers. All will involve new knowledge. Ability to absorb new information will be essential.

Business leaders must tell society these truths. We must help people prepare for the Information Age. Together, we can create the "change awareness" and "information awareness" we need to succeed.

Janice Moyer, President, *Information Technology Association of Canada*, 1992 1 21

The shift in importance to a mental resource base from a labour resource base has political and economic impacts too. It is mirrored, for example, in the growth and collapse of the Communist Party of the Soviet Union (CPSU), although this shift cannot be considered the only cause of its collapse. During the 19th and early 20th centuries, communism developed as a major political and economic philosophy supporting the importance of physical labour, as shown by the use of the hammer and sickle as its rallying symbols. As much of the world economy began to change to an emphasis on mental skills, communism gradually waned as a major philosophy. It has virtually disappeared as a political and economic operating system from many areas where it was once dominant.

The following reading provides some further details on human resource issues.

THIRD WORLD LOSSES

LONDON — The world's poorer nations are subsidizing rich ones with an export worth billions of dollars: brainpower, two British scientists say.

That is the benefit Third World scientists and engineers bring when they move to industrialized countries, a study released yesterday says.

The study says skilled people in essence are part of a country's capital, and when they leave, in a "brain drain," they take that capital with them.

Adding the money that it takes to educate a scientist or engineer and their average productivity, the two professors estimated that India transferred $51-billion (U.S.) in human capital to the United States between 1967 and 1985.

"Although the international mobility of scientists is an important way of exchanging expertise, under the present setup the underdeveloped nations are currently the net losers in this exchange," Professor Alan Smithers of the University of Manchester told a Royal Society of Chemistry conference.

Prof. Smithers and Professor John Pratt of the University of Surrey said in their study that industrialized nations, most notably

SOURCE: John Molyneux

Fig. 3-15 *Developing countries can ill afford to lose skilled people like this pharmacist now in Canada, but skilled people can often find higher-paying jobs elsewhere.*

the United States, encourage an influx of scientists to meet a growing demand.

The study found that between 1974 and 1988 the number of immigrant scientists and engineers in the United States almost doubled, to 10.5 percent of the total from 5.8 percent, and the five leading sources of this talent were India, Britain, Taiwan, Poland and China.

Those numbers are sure to go up in the future, they said. Forty percent of the country's PhD students in engineering and mathematics are foreign, and past history

has shown that those who study in the United States tend to remain.

In 1970, the UN Conference on Trade and Development found that some developing countries lose between 20 and 70 percent of their annual output of doctors.

UNCTAD calculated that the value of imported scientists, engineers and doctors to the United States in that year was $3.7 billion, compared with U.S. development assistance to the Third World of $3.1 billion.

Reuters News Agency, 1991 4 8

DISCUSSION AND RESEARCH

13. Hold a formal class debate on the motion: Developed countries should not accept highly educated immigrants from developing countries.

14. Along with three other people, you are a member of a conference planning committee. Every year, your committee stages a one-day conference with an invited keynote speaker, a lunch-time speaker, and eight to ten workshop leaders. Total attendance is normally about 250-300 people. Your conference this year will be on world resources. The conference planning committee has to decide on the most interesting and worthwhile topics for the keynote speaker, the lunch-time speaker, and the eight to ten workshops. Brainstorm some suggested topics, then allocate selected topics among the speakers and workshops. Remember that the keynote speaker should set the overall tone for the conference.

STATISTICAL ANALYSIS

15. Refer to Fig. 3-16. Use three-cycle semilog graph paper (see Appendix 3) to construct a scattergraph of the countries shown, and answer the following questions:
    (a) Describe the relationship which exists between GNP/cap and the percentage of GNP that a country spends on education.
    (b) To what extent can it be claimed that a country has high average personal incomes because it spends a lot on education?
    (c) To what extent can it be claimed that a country must have a high average income level before it can afford to spend much on education?
    (d) Identify five to ten countries that appear to be preparing their people for a shift in economic activity from physical labour to mental skills.
    (e) If you were the investment manager for a group of Canadian manufacturers wishing to invest in a new factory in Argentina, what sorts of industrial activity would you recommend?
    (f) List the types of developmental aid you would suggest for Haiti.

SOURCE: From Column 19 of Appendix 2 and *Human Development Report 1992*, United Nations

Country	GNP/cap US$	Education spending as percentage of GNP
Argentina	2370	1.5
Barbados	6540	6.9
Bolivia	630	2.3
Brazil	2680	3.7
Canada	20 470	7.2
Chile	1940	3.6
Colombia	1260	2.9
Costa Rica	1900	4.4
Cuba	2000	6.6
Dominican Republic	830	1.5
Ecuador	980	2.6
El Salvador	1110	2.0
Guatemala	900	1.8
Guyana	330	8.8
Haiti	370	1.8
Honduras	590	4.9
Jamaica	1500	6.6
Mexico	2490	3.8
Nicaragua	610	3.9
Panama	1830	6.2
Paraguay	1110	1.5
Peru	1160	3.5
Suriname	3050	9.5
Trinidad and Tobago	3610	4.9
United States	21 970	6.8
Uruguay	2560	3.1
Venezuela	2560	4.2

- can economies support it?

Fig. 3-16 *GNP and education spending for 27 countries in the Americas.*

STANDARDS OF LIVING

Almost all societies have tried to raise the average standard of living — the supply of food and other material goods — for their members from the level of survival needs to the realm of wants. The nations of the developed world have so far done this for most of their populations. The nations of the developing world — starting later — still have much to do.

The entire matter of standards of living has become an issue. It has become an issue because some people think that the developed nations consume too large a portion of the earth's resources in trying to satisfy their populations' wants. These individuals believe that if developing nations succeed in achieving similar levels of material wealth then the earth's life-support systems will be overloaded, leading to disaster. But many people in developing nations view increased material wealth as a sign of progress, and they want more of it, above and beyond basic needs. The chief barrier to increased material wealth in developing countries is lack of income. World income distribution is shown in Fig. 3-17.

The readings which follow Fig. 3-17 illustrate these two points of view.

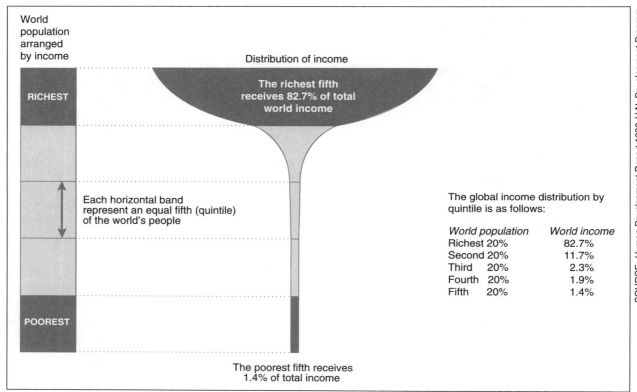

World population arranged by income

Distribution of income

The richest fifth receives 82.7% of total world income

RICHEST

Each horizontal band represent an equal fifth (quintile) of the world's people

The global income distribution by quintile is as follows:

World population	World income
Richest 20%	82.7%
Second 20%	11.7%
Third 20%	2.3%
Fourth 20%	1.9%
Fifth 20%	1.4%

POOREST

The poorest fifth receives 1.4% of total income

SOURCE: *Human Development Report 1992*, U.N. Development Program

Fig. 3-17 *World income distribution by quintile.*

DIMENSIONS OF SUSTAINABLE DEVELOPMENT

The world faces a wide variety of critical environmental threats: degradation of soil, water, and marine resources essential to increased food production; widespread, health-threatening pollution; stratospheric ozone depletion; global climate change; and loss of biodiversity. At the same time, it faces enormous human problems in the form of widespread, persistent poverty and human misery — despite growing affluence for many — and a pattern of economic growth that is worsening rather than remedying such disparities.

Such problems are troubling enough. But if human societies in decades to come are to inhabit a world that is environmentally secure, economically prosperous, and characterized by growing peace, freedom, and human welfare, then current generations must also come to grips with underlying trends that threaten to make these problems far worse. One of the most basic trends is that world population has doubled since 1950 and is expected to roughly double again by the middle of the next century. Similarly, as people everywhere have struggled to improve their standards of living, world economic activity has grown at about three percent per year since 1950; if this rate continues in the decades ahead, then the world economy will be five times larger in the year 2050 than it is today.

Such growth in population and economic activity has the potential to increase dramatically the pressure on natural resources and natural systems — from farmland to fisheries to the global atmosphere — which are already suffering serious levels of degradation. Consider just two examples:

• Well over one billion people in the world are malnourished. To provide an adequate level of nutrition as the population doubles will require more than doubling current food production. Under the best conditions, that would require making very productive use of the world's stock of arable land. Yet according to new estimates by the world's leading soil scientists, more than 1.2 billion hectares of vegetated land — an area as large as India and China put together — have been significantly degraded since World War II. If such degradation continues or accelerates, expansion of food production on the scale required will be extremely difficult, if not impossible, and greatly worsened human misery will be increasingly likely....

• Fossil fuels provide about 95 percent of the commercial energy used in the world economy, and their use is growing worldwide at the rate of about 20 percent per decade. Combustion of those fuels constitutes the largest source of emissions of climate-altering greenhouse gases to the atmosphere. Scientists convened by the Intergovernmental Panel of Climate Change under the auspices of the United Nations Environmental Programme and the World Meteorological Organization concluded that a 60 percent reduction in carbon dioxide emissions would be necessary to stabilize carbon dioxide concentrations in the atmosphere at current levels. Protecting the Earth's climate therefore may require significant reductions in global fossil fuel use, even as the world economy expands; alternately, continued expansion of fossil fuel use at current rates will double atmospheric levels well before the middle of the next century and thus increase the risk of significant climate change.

As these examples illustrate, the world is not now headed toward a sustainable future, but rather toward a variety of potential human and environmental disasters....

World Resources 1992-93, The World Resources Institute

A WORLD DIVIDED

Three and a half billion people, three quarters of all humanity, live in the developing countries. By the year 2000, the proportion will probably have risen to four fifths....

. . . . .

The countries of the South vary greatly in size, in natural resource endowment, in the structure of their economies, in the level of economic, social, and technological development. They also differ in their cultures, in their political systems, and in the ideologies they profess. Their economic and technological diversity has become more marked in recent years, making the South of today even less homogeneous than the South of yesterday.

Yet in this diversity there is a basic unity. What the countries of the South have in common transcends their differences; it gives them a shared identity and a reason to work together for common objectives. And their economic diversity offers opportunities for co-operation that can benefit them all.

The primary bond that links the countries and peoples of the South is their desire to escape from poverty and underdevelopment and secure a better life for their citizens. This shared aspiration is a foundation for their solidarity, expressed through such organizations as the Group of 77 — of which all countries of the South except China are members — and the Non-Aligned

Movement, with a large and growing membership from all continents in the South.

The decision-making processes that govern the international flows of trade, capital, and technology are controlled by the major developed countries of the North and by the international institutions they dominate. The countries of the South are unfavourably placed in the world economic system; they are individually powerless to influence these processes and institutions and, hence, the global economic environment which vitally affects their development. For this reason they have made a collective demand for the reform of the international economic system so as to make it more equitable and responsive to the needs of the vast majority of humanity — the people of the South. The struggle for a fairer international system has consolidated their cohesion and strengthened their resolve to pursue united action.

Were all humanity a single nation-state, the present North-South divide would make it an unviable, semi-feudal entity, split by internal conflicts. Its small part is advanced, prosperous, powerful; its much bigger part is underdeveloped, poor, powerless. A nation so divided within itself would be recognized as unstable. A world so divided should likewise be recognized as inherently unstable....

The Challenge to the South, The South Commission, Tanzania, 1990

SOURCE: CIDA/David Barbour

 Fig. 3-18 *Many people in the developing world wish to escape from economic poverty, as depicted in this scene from Egypt.*

DISCUSSION AND RESEARCH

16. Using local area topographic maps, and your own knowledge and observations of the local area, identify the boundaries of the area you consider to be your own community. Use Statistics Canada census data to assist you if it is available in sufficient detail.
    (a) In groups of about three to five, research the different standards of living within your own community.
    (b) Analyze why some people appear to live more comfortably than others. This may require you to interview people about what they consider important.
    (c) Prepare a four- to five-page report outlining the reasons for the differences in standard of living. Prepare an accompanying local map defining the area of your local community and showing the areas within it where the differences occur.

17. Brainstorm in class the advantages and disadvantages of having different standards of living within the same community.

18. In the reading "A World Divided" on p. 181, the South Commission makes a plea for a one-world view of the differences that exist between the developed and developing countries. Examine your own values in the matter, and suggest ways in which your possible future actions can help to contribute to the development of a one-world view.

19. If you have to reduce your own standard of living in the future to ease pressure on world resources, list the things which you could do without or use less of. Determine which world resources would benefit from your self-denial. What impact do you think your actions would have on the people of the developing world?

20. Discussion of the actual characteristics of different standards of living often leads to discussion of the possible characteristics of an ideal standard of living. In small groups, discuss and agree upon the characteristics of an ideal standard of living. Determine also the characteristics that are not agreed upon. Decide as a group whether life would be acceptable without agreement about these qualities.

STATISTICAL ANALYSIS

21. Refer to Fig. 3-19 on the following page. It shows income distribution within 21 nations around the world according to the percentage received by each quintile. A quintile is one-fifth or 20 percent of the population. Refer also to Lorenz curves in Appendix 3.
    (a) Select any two apparently contrasting countries and construct two Lorenz curves on a single graph to illustrate their different income distribution patterns.
    (b) Attempt through research to explain the different patterns illustrated by the Lorenz curves for the two countries selected.
    (c) Examine the data for all 21 countries listed and develop a justified generalization about income distribution in nations.
    (d) Calculate for each country the multiple by which the highest quintile is larger than the lowest quintile. For Bangladesh, for instance, the multiple is 3.72. List the countries in descending order so that the country with the largest multiple is at the top of the list. Write a paragraph about your conclusions regarding the order of countries on the list.

Country	Percentage share of income by quintile groups				
	Lowest quintile	Second quintile	Third quintile	Fourth quintile	Highest quintile
Bangladesh	10.0	13.7	17.2	21.9	37.2
Botswana	2.5	6.5	11.8	20.2	59.0
Brazil	2.4	5.7	10.7	18.6	62.6
Canada	5.7	11.8	17.7	24.6	40.2
Ghana	7.1	11.5	15.9	21.8	43.7
Guatemala	5.5	8.6	12.2	18.7	55.0
Hong Kong	5.4	10.8	15.2	21.6	47.0
India	8.1	12.3	16.3	22.0	41.4
Indonesia	8.8	12.4	16.0	21.5	41.3
Ivory Coast	5.0	8.0	13.1	21.3	52.7
Jamaica	5.4	9.9	14.4	21.2	49.2
Japan	8.7	13.2	17.5	23.1	37.5
Morocco	9.8	13.0	16.4	21.4	39.4
Pakistan	7.8	11.2	15.0	20.6	45.6
Peru	4.4	8.5	13.7	21.5	51.9
Philippines	5.5	9.7	14.8	22.0	48.0
Poland	9.7	14.2	18.0	22.9	35.2
Sweden	8.0	13.2	17.4	24.5	36.9
Switzerland	5.2	11.7	16.4	22.1	44.6
United States	4.7	11.0	17.4	25.0	41.9
Venezuela	4.7	9.2	14.0	21.5	50.6

SOURCE: *World Development Report 1992*, The World Bank

 Fig. 3-19 *Income distribution in 21 countries.*

(e) Describe the process you would use to identify the country that most closely approximates to the average for the 21 countries listed. Identify this country.

(f) For all countries, suggest ways in which the lowest quintile of population could gain a larger percentage of income.

(g) Develop and write a rationale to justify income inequality.

22. Good health is one of the universally accepted basic needs for a decent standard of living. However, the need is not universally met. For example, the immediate causes of the deaths of women in childbirth are numerous, often related to individual health, transmittability of diseases, availability and quality of health care, standards of nutrition, and frequency of previous births. Column 25 of Appendix 2 provides data showing the number of maternal deaths per 100 000 live births. The figures vary greatly, and provide an indication of the variations in standards of living among the different countries of the world.

On a photocopy of the world map in Appendix 1, shade all the countries that have maternity death rates of 100/100 000 and more. Compare your map with other maps that are printed anywhere in this text, and that you have constructed yourself in answering questions. In a two-page essay, write your conclusions, paying particular attention both to the general pattern and to the exceptions.

23. Good nutrition is one of the universally accepted basic needs for a decent standard of living. It is not universally met. There is disagreement too about appropriate types of food. Meat eating is regarded by some people as a waste of resources insofar as livestock consume grain that might be used instead to feed far more people directly. Several countries use 50 percent or more of their grain supplies to feed livestock, and it is these countries in particular that receive the heaviest criticism for wasteful consumption. Column 27 of Appendix 3 shows the percentages of grain supplies fed to livestock in each country.
    (a) On a world map, colour those countries that use at least 50 percent of their grain supplies in this way.
    (b) There are some anomalies (countries that do not fit the general pattern) in the distribution shown on the map. Select any two of these anomalies, and through research attempt to explain why relatively large amounts of grain are fed to livestock in these two countries.
    (c) Research reasons for meat's wide acceptance as a food.

24. Energy consumption is one of the items usually targeted by people who think the developed world should consume less. Column 29 of Appendix 2 contains data about annual energy use per capita in gigajoules (1 GJ = 1 billion joules, or a million kilojoules, equivalent to about 0.1634 barrel oil or 0.03414 tonne coal). Column 30 shows the percentages that traditional fuels (fuelwood, charcoal, crop wastes) form of total fuel use. Construct a scattergraph of the two data sets on full log (log-log) graph paper, using three cycles for Energy Consumption in GJ/capita on the vertical axis and two cycles for Traditional Fuels as % of Total Fuel Consumed on the horizontal axis.
    (a) Describe the overall appearance of the graph and the nature of the correlation between the two sets of data.
    (b) Explain why so many countries are bunched in the lower right portion of the graph.
    (c) Several countries are plotted in the lower left portion of the graph, including some along the lower portion of the left vertical axis. Compare the energy situation in these countries with that existing in the countries of the lower right portion of the graph.

(d) From an identification of the countries in the upper left portion of the graph, analyze how (i) easy and (ii) useful the reduction of energy consumption by the developed world might be to achieve. Attempt also to determine whether it is advisable to recommend a universal cap on average energy consumption per person. If so, recommend what the cap should be and how it might be achieved.

DEVELOPMENT

DEVELOPMENT TO THE PRESENT

Development, the process whereby humanity organizes its relationship with its natural environment to better satisfy its needs and wants, has been a continual part of human history for many thousands of years. There have so far been three periods in human history when great changes in the relationship with the natural environment have occurred, permitting on each occasion a major increase in human population (see Fig. 3-20).

The first occasion of change was the discovery that certain natural items such as stone, wood, bone, and antler horn, could be used as tools to assist production. The change to tool-making did not occur simultaneously throughout the world, but began perhaps half a million to a million years ago (usually written as 500 000-1 000 000 BP) in the river valleys of south, east, and southeast Asia, and the grasslands of East Africa, slowly spreading, or being **diffused**, from these "hearth regions" to the rest of the world. This huge period of time is called the old stone age, or Paleolithic period. It exist-ed in some remote islands and forests well into the present century, but generally it lasted only until sometime between 5000 BP and 10 000 BP. By the end of the period 5000-10 000 BP, world population may have been five to ten million, and human beings had occupied the earth for as much as 99 percent of the total time from their origins to the present day. Only in the last one percent of their existence to date have humans made any other major changes to their relationship with the natural environment.

The second occasion of change about 5000-10 000 BP started when some of the hunter-gatherers of the Paleo-

where it developed
1st

The idea that humans appeared on earth roughly 500 000 years ago is being challenged by the new *Out of Africa* theory, which maintains that our first ancestors appeared about 100 000 years ago, and that skeletal remains that predate this are not those of our ancestors. Researchers are split over the issue.

The sizes of large numbers are hard to imagine. While one million seconds pass in about 11.5 days, it takes nearly 32 years for one billion seconds to pass.

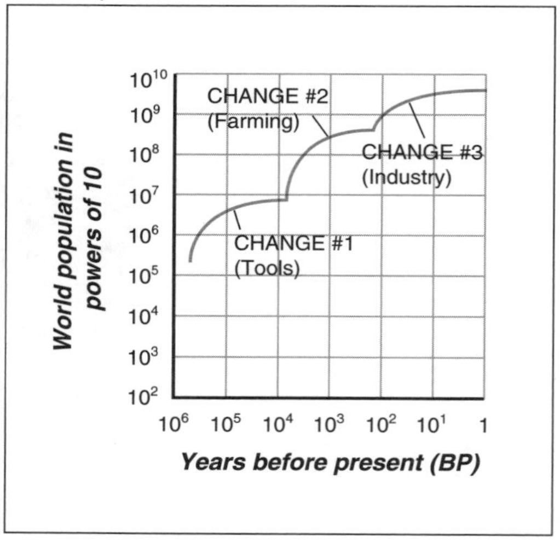

Fig. 3-20 *The growth of world population as it relates to technological change, shown on a full-log graph.*

lithic period discovered that certain plants could be cultivated and certain animals domesticated. Again the change did not occur simultaneously throughout the world. It happened first among the peoples occupying the river valleys of southwest Asia and south Asia, probably in the period 6000-8000 BP, then subsequently in China and southeast Asia (5000 BP) and on the plateaus of Central and South America (3000-4000 BP), and eventually elsewhere.

The period at the start of the second change is called the new stone age, or Neolithic period. Tools became more complex, the manufacture of pottery and woven cloth started, construction of dwellings rather than use of caves became commonplace, and storage of surplus grain in lined pits commenced. All staple crops in use today, including wheat, rice, corn, millet, and yams, were first used in the Neolithic period. Other developments included bread-making, beer-making, and the growth of cities and inter-community trade. Human numbers increased rapidly. By the end of the farm-based second change during the 18th and 19th centuries, when the vast majority of the world's population had come to depend on farming for its food supplies, world population was approximately 400-500 million.

The third occasion of change — to industrialization — had its seeds in new attitudes which arose during the Renaissance and the Age of Discovery in the 15th and 16th centuries in Europe. It accelerated during the Industrial Revolution of the 18th and 19th centuries, and continues with vigour in many parts of the world today. Yet again, the change did not occur simultaneously in all parts of the world. It began in Europe, moved quickly to North America and Japan, and is now spreading elsewhere.

Like the first two periods of change, the third change permitted a rapid increase in human numbers, and assumed a significantly more effective, and potentially damaging, role in the humanity-environment relationship. Competition for land use has intensified, and farmers, once ousters of hunters, now feel increasingly threatened by industrialism. Each change that has taken place has enabled humanity to use land with greater efficiency, but has also wrought more damage to the environment than the previous use. Hunting and gathering need the largest areas to support the smallest populations; farming can support more people on a smaller area; industry supports the most people and uses the least land area of all. Additionally, industry has also made it possible for reduced numbers of farmers to increase food supplies from given areas of land through the use of machinery, fertilizers, pesticides, seed selection, livestock breeding, and so on.

A number of other changes have resulted along with the huge increases in production brought about by the third great change. Rapid large-scale urbanization is one of these, along with the growth of so-called tertiary, or service, activities. In parts of the world where the process of industrialization has already occurred, most people are no longer employed in farming or industry but in various sorts of service activity. Some people regard this change as a process of de-industrialization, but this is true only with

The earliest traces of beer — more than 5000 years old — have been found on clay jars unearthed at Godin Tepe, a Sumerian city in what is now Iran. It is thought that beer-making was the easiest way of preserving barley, since grain was susceptible to spoilage by insects, rats, and rot.

Human economic activities are classified into three groups: **primary**, **secondary**, and **tertiary**. See p. 325 in Chapter Five for a discussion of these terms.

SOURCE: CIDA

Fig. 3-21 *Industrial techniques provide farmers with the ability to produce more food from given areas of land, such as by livestock breeding here in Vietnam.*

Just as people in North America and Europe in the late 19th century had to adjust to the loss of farm jobs and the growth of factory jobs, people need to adjust in the late 20th century to the loss of factory jobs and the growth of service jobs.

regard to employment. Industrial output has in fact increased in these societies, but chiefly through the use of computers and automated techniques which require ever fewer industrial workers. This is the industrial parallel to increased food production requiring fewer farmers.

As with the other two great changes in human history, the third change has also produced a great — and still continuing — increase in human numbers. Employment therefore becomes a critical issue, since additional people are in diminishing demand for agricultural and industrial output. And it is precisely in this context that issues of world development occur.

DEVELOPMENT ISSUES FOR THE FUTURE

The major development issues for the future are:

- How to provide the various primary benefits of industrialization uniformly throughout the world without damaging the environment. These benefits include a reliable supply of good quality food, satisfactory health care, adequate sanitation, improved shelter, and increased material wealth. This is the issue of sustainable development (see Chapter One).

- How to provide additional benefits uniformly throughout the world including increased literacy, greater human freedom and choice, and improved human rights, without coercion of some nations by others. Broadly, this is the issue of equity, human rights, and individual self-fulfilment, examined in more detail in Chapter Four.

- How to provide employment to people while meeting the first two goals and without creating widespread dependency and frustration. This is the issue of employment, examined in more detail in Chapter Five.

The key to the first two aspects of development may be the third, for without employment there is likely to be poverty. With poverty there is likely to be little food, frequent ill-health, and restricted choice.

It should be noted that some countries believe that development assistance threatens local values and they therefore oppose it, fearing an invasion of foreign values. As well, developed countries themselves increasingly take the view that their assistance to developing countries should be related to the cultural values, including human rights values, of the developing countries. Where local cultures or governments foster values that are deemed by aid donors to be unacceptable in terms of universal human rights, as in Haiti in the early 1990s, aid may be reduced or eliminated. Development may therefore be slowed.

DEVELOPMENT AND THE REDUCTION OF POVERTY

It is commonly asked why so many societies are economically poor. Others ask why some are economically wealthy. Which question makes more sense in today's world?

Attempts to reduce or eliminate poverty around the world have been varied in type and mixed in effect. For centuries of human existence, some poverty among members of society was regarded as normal. Many societies had charitable institutions or social practices which assisted the poor.

During the second half of the 20th century there have been much more intensive efforts to reduce poverty. The first moves were international in scope, with rich nations attempting to remedy the poverty of poorer nations. Initial strategies included working towards large-scale industrialization (such as building steel mills, power dams, and national airlines), since these seemed to be necessary attributes of more developed societies. Such strategies generally failed, partly because they were introduced in ways that did not address the basic needs of the populations in the countries that received the assistance, and partly because necessary **infrastructure** was usually lacking.

Strategies in the 1970s and 1980s had more emphasis on meeting basic needs. Many of these programs also failed because individuals in some of the aid-receiving countries found little accompanying growth in economic opportunity from this type of aid.

Current thinking in the world's development community is, for the most part, that the alleviation and ultimate eradication of poverty needs a two-pronged approach: economic opportunities must be increased and basic needs must be met at the same time. It is also felt that the existence

SOURCE: CIDA/Patricio Baeza

Fig. 3-22 *Increased economic opportunity does not always accompany otherwise successful development assistance. Jobs are not guaranteed for these trainee surveyors in Bolivia.*

By the early 1990s, China, North Korea, Vietnam, and Cuba were the only remaining communist controlled nations. China and Vietnam, however, had decided that their economic growth should take place under market conditions, leaving Cuba and North Korea with the only **centrally planned** economies.

of active, competitive markets is the best mechanism for securing increased economic opportunity. In addition, government-regulated, but not necessarily government-run, health, education, and welfare programs are thought to be the best mechanisms for ensuring the provision of basic needs.

One reason for this thinking is the failure over the last 50 years or so of certain government-directed economies to provide sustained improvements in economic well-being, especially in eastern and central Europe (e.g., Poland), parts of Africa (e.g., Zambia), southeast Asia (e.g., Cambodia), and Central and South America (e.g., Argentina). Another reason is the demonstrated government corruption of some aid-receiving countries (e.g., Nigeria, Philippines), where benefits intended for the many have been siphoned off by the powerful few. As the South Commission states, "…governments must bear a large part of the responsibility for corruption in the South…they have not regarded its eradication as a priority…."

CAUSES OF POVERTY

The reduction of poverty is a worldwide need, but its root causes vary greatly from region to region. Three broad types of regions may be identified: the developing world, the former communist countries of eastern and central Europe, and the developed world.

There are many causes of poverty in the developing world, and arguments rage over their relative importance. Some people claim that former colonial exploitation by European imperial powers (as of land for sugar plantations in the Caribbean islands) is largely to blame. Many of these people also see **multinational companies** as agents of today's neo-colonialism and a cause of local poverty.

Multinationals (sometimes also called **transnationals**) are firms with headquarters in one country and operations in several other countries. Restrained only by the laws of the different countries in which they operate, multinationals tend to act as if all their operations took place in a world without borders. They are seen as powerful agents in the globalization of production. These companies may invest in one country and reduce operations in another country to help them achieve their goal of producing goods for the lowest competitive prices and highest profits.

Accused of ignoring local interests in their decision-making, multinationals are also criticized for providing uniform consumer goods to a culturally diverse world. Others criticize them for doing most of their research and development work (R & D) in their home country, and creating branch-plant economies elsewhere. For these reasons, several countries allow entry to multinationals only on a shared basis: for example, Peru requires at least 51 percent local ownership of any company operated by a multinational.

On the other hand, multinationals are welcomed by many countries, where they are viewed as a source of jobs and income, and a provider of technology and training. They are perceived to bring new ideas and new methods of production into the host country. As a link to the global

SOURCE: CIDA

Fig. 3-23 *Women in an Indian village. What does the photograph suggest about their standard of living?*

economy, they are praised for producing exports that earn valuable foreign currency. For these reasons, several countries, such as Indonesia, advertise in international journals to attract investment from multinationals.

Rapid population growth is also held by some people to be a chief cause of poverty in the developing world. Among them, some people claim that the former imperialists are responsible for this growth because they introduced improved medical care without ensuring that local economies were prepared for the upswing in population. Others believe incidents of local mismanagement and corruption in many developing countries have been important in maintaining poverty. Many individuals note that wealth creation is a slow process at best, and that developing countries merely started later; they plead for patience and assign no blame.

In the former communist countries of eastern and central Europe, reasons for poverty are held to be rooted in the apparent lack of opportunity for **personal initiative**, as central governments exercised total control. Also, the emphasis on heavy industry and military production effectively restricted the production of consumer items.

Poverty in the developed world is less easy to explain. By comparison with all other existing countries and all former preindustrial societies, the countries of the developed world are immensely wealthy, but there are millions of economically poor people within them. Frequent investi-

SOURCE: Marko Shark

Fig. 3-24 *Volunteers work in a food bank in Canada. The existence of food banks has been a point of controversy in Canada. Why might this be so?*

gations into causes have revealed little other than general characteristics of poverty, such as low educational attainments (see Fig. 3-14), lack of access to society's power structures (such as government), and little property ownership. The most common debate about poverty is between those who believe that it is caused largely by the way society is structured and those who believe it is caused largely by lack of individual effort on the part of the poor. Others believe there may be some truth in both views.

POVERTY REDUCTION IN THE DEVELOPING WORLD

The need for poverty reduction is most pressing in the developing world. The problem is most severe here partly because of the already existing large scale of poverty, and partly because it is in these countries that population growth is most rapid and the future need for jobs is highest. Indeed, it is likely that in the next 25 to 30 years, 95 percent of all new entrants to the world's labour force will be in the developing countries. The present pattern of economic development in these countries is very uneven, depending on whether past development emphasis has been placed on economic growth or basic needs, or spread evenly between both.

Compare, for example, the development patterns of Brazil and Sri Lanka. Brazil has placed emphasis on economic growth, Sri Lanka on basic needs services. For six criteria selected from Appendix 2 (columns 12, 14, 15, 16, 19, and 24), compare the data for Brazil and Sri Lanka. Development has occurred differently in both countries. Now — for the same categories — compare both Brazil and Sri Lanka with South Korea, which has placed shared emphasis on economic growth and basic needs services.

Governments in developing countries have been important to the process of development, but it has been a challenge for many governments to play a balanced role. Over the last 40 to 50 years interventionist governments (as in Argentina), which have established quotas, erected tariffs, set prices, offered tax incentives, and decided levels of foreign ownership, have generally fallen behind in economic growth relative to countries where governments have tended to let market forces and open competition be the vehicles for growth. Some interventionist governments, such as in South Korea, however, have been more successful, chiefly through policies promoting industrial efficiency and access to export markets. Too little government intervention has also been unhelpful in some cases. Governments, such as in Brazil, have failed to become readily involved in matters including establishing fair rules for market operations; establishing fair tax systems; providing for environmental protection; or providing for the development of infrastructure, particularly in transportation, education, and health care. They have seen economic growth benefit their militarily or economically powerful citizens, with other citizens remaining poor and often surviving in a highly degraded environment.

In recent years the governments of a number of developing countries have reduced their intervention in the economy in attempts to encourage faster growth. Examples include China, Ghana, India, Indonesia, Mexico, Morocco, and Turkey. The result has been accelerated economic growth in these countries, with China showing growth rates of over ten percent per year. Despite the success of these policies, many economists feel that some non-interventionist governments, such as in Brazil and Pakistan, may need to become more involved in basic needs provision, since their basic needs indicators (Appendix 2) are relatively poor. Even where the actual provision of basic needs services is by regulated private interests, as of education in Kenya, Philippines, and Zimbabwe, or of health care in Rwanda and Zambia, the statistics suggest to many people that governments should maintain — and in some cases increase — their involvement in providing for basic needs. The statistics also suggest to many observers that governments should start or continue to reduce their involvement in the production-oriented economy. They believe governments need only to establish fair rules for trading, investment, employment, property rights, and financing to create a climate favourable to economic growth under market conditions.

Even where the development focus of a government is on basic needs, choices must be made about how funds and programs can be used to the greatest benefit. For example, in Nigeria, the economic interests of rural populations could be emphasized over those of urban populations. In Brazil, cheaper preventive health care could be emphasized instead of

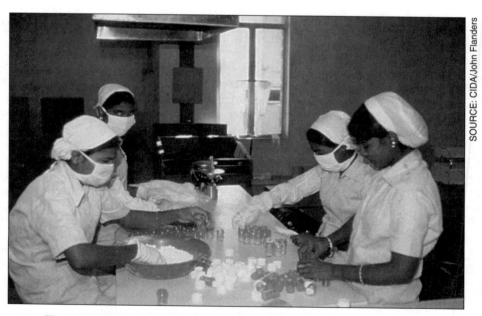

SOURCE: CIDA/John Flanders

Fig. 3-25 *Health professionals preparing medicines in Bangladesh as part of the drive for primary health care.*

expensive curative health care. Examples of successful basic needs programs are widely held to include primary school enrolment in Peru and rural health care in the state of Kerala in India.

Where governments have not fostered local enterprise and competition, but established non-competitive protected environments instead, economies have generally not worked well. Successes gained by Indonesia and Mexico after opening their economies to competition have been repeated elsewhere (in China, for example), and are now widely regarded as models to follow. Governments that have attempted to integrate their nations' economies with the world economy by trying to encourage exports and imports and international flows of technology and investment have also generally met with success. Foreign competition has been shown to have positive effects on the efficiency and productivity of successful domestic producers in countries such as Chile and Turkey when their domestic markets were opened to foreign competition in the late 1980s. The same reasoning motivated Mexico in 1991 to seek a free trade agreement with Canada and The United States.

However, it should be noted that competition produces some economic casualties. Many traditional producers cannot compete with cheaper imports, and are forced out of business. Unemployment and migration to cities increase, and there is added pressure on social support mechanisms provided by governments and families. Each country that opens its markets faces these costs, and weighs them against expected benefits.

Opening their markets to competition from developed countries may force producers in developing countries to be efficient, but it offers little overall advantage if they are not allowed the same access to developed world markets. The developed countries are indeed often unwilling to ease restrictions on imports from developing countries. Arguments by developed countries for protectionism include the following: jobs will be lost for developed countries' workers; developed countries' firms may be forced out of business; low-wage labour in developing countries is unfair competition; and developing countries do not have satisfactory environmental regulations. Such arguments are common among people in North America opposed to a free trade agreement with Mexico.

A number of significant questions about the issue of development therefore arise:

- Can development in developing countries occur without the developed world paying a price?
- Can the developing world become more fully part of the **global community** unless the developed world pays a price?
- What will happen in developing countries if the developed world does not pay a price?
- What will happen in the developed world if it does not pay a price?
- Should individuals in the developed world be concerned about development in developing countries?

Developing countries have long sought "Trade, not Aid" as their preferred means of development, but developed countries have set up hundreds of trade restrictions, not only against products from developing countries but also against each other.

Average wage rates in the developed world in the early 1990s were about $15 per hour; in the former communist countries of eastern and central Europe about $5/h; and in the developing countries from less than $1/h to about $3/h.

- Should the developed world be able to influence development in developing countries?

- Is the price expected from developed countries fair to their citizens?

- What will be the impact of development on local cultures in the developing world ?

- Are there long-term benefits to global economic integration for people in both developed and developing countries that make the price worthwhile?

Development economists feel that governments in many developing countries need to provide stable financial management. Some have borrowed too much in the past from willing developed world lenders, and have been unable to meet debt repayments. Some of these loans have been forgiven by developed world governments and banks, and others have been rescheduled for easier repayment. The debt crisis of the 1980s, where some developing countries defaulted on their loan repayments, is now therefore past; but the amount of money repaid by a number of developing countries each year is still larger than the amount sent to them as foreign assistance by the developed countries. These countries are shown in Fig. 3-26.

Country	Official development assistance (ODA)[1]	Total foreign debt	Net[2] repayments of principal and interest
Algeria	227	26 806	-2578
Argentina	172	61 144	-1665
Brazil	164	116 173	-3186
Colombia	87	17 241	-1991
Ecuador	154	12 105	-241
Korea, South	52	34 014	-2214
Nigeria	234	36 068	-1653
Oman	69	2484	-825
Panama	92	6676	-98
Trinidad & Tobago	10	2307	-331
Uruguay	47	3707	-325
Venezuela	79	33 305	-1630
former Yugoslavia	48	20 690	-1972

[1] ODA is the money value of all assistance provided to developing countries by governments of developed countries. It does not include assistance provided by non-government organizations (NGOs).

[2] International investment money and interest payments move in and out of all countries. The net figure represents the inflow minus the outflow. The minus figure indicates that more moves out than in.

Note: all figures are in millions of US$.

SOURCE: Based on data in *World Development Report 1992*

 Fig. 3-26 *The countries that receive less official development assistance than they pay out in principal and interest payments.*

Apart from inability to repay, problems with overborrowing may lead to inflation, overpricing of the domestic currency on foreign exchange markets, and loss of export competitiveness. Overborrowing may also lead to reduced investment, since developed world owners of money may feel there is less risk in lending than in investing. Countries that have run into serious problems with overly high international debts and its effects include Bolivia, Brazil, Ivory Coast, and Zaire, whereas Botswana, Chile, Colombia, and Thailand, among others, seem to have managed better.

The countries of the developed world also attempt to maintain a supply of investment capital for use by developing countries, partly for reasons of possible profit and partly for humanitarian reasons, but, like reducing trade barriers, this policy has its obstacles. Developed countries like Canada, Italy, and the United States are heavily in debt themselves, and the two other major sources of investment funds, Germany and Japan, both have pressing domestic problems. Since 1990, Germany has been occupied with the costs of reunifying the former separate countries of West Germany and East Germany. Japan is overburdened with internal debt. In such circumstances, international institutions like the World Bank assume crucial importance.

The World Bank is an agency of the United Nations. Its official name is the International Bank for Reconstruction and Development (IBRD). It started operations in 1946 with the purpose of facilitating international investment to increase production, raise living standards, and assist in the growth of world trade.

The World Bank is one means by which funds may be allocated among countries. It acts as a channel for money from a variety of sources (governments, corporations, individuals) to be fed into investment in the developing world. Bank projects are extremely diverse, and are now much more environmentally sensitive than they used to be. Recent examples of Bank activities include reforestation in Madagascar, family planning in Kenya, irrigation in Turkey, garment production in Mauritius, and protection of parrots in Chile.

SOURCE: CIDA/Patricio Baeza

Fig. 3-27 *Development assistance is directed toward many different projects. Here a woman builds houses on a construction site in Bolivia.*

OECD members: Australia, Austria, Belgium, Canada, Denmark, Finland, France, Germany, Greece, Iceland, Ireland, Italy, Japan, Luxembourg, Netherlands, New Zealand, Norway, Portugal, Spain, Sweden, Switzerland, Turkey, U.K., U.S. Mexico's application for membership was approved in 1993.

OPEC members: Algeria, Gabon, Indonesia, Iran, Iraq, Kuwait, Libya, Nigeria, Qatar, Saudi Arabia, United Arab Emirates, Venezuela. Ecuador withdrew from membership in 1993.

Individual governments may also provide funds to developing countries. Such funds, called official development assistance (ODA), come from members of the Organization for Economic Cooperation and Development (OECD) and members of the Organization of Petroleum Exporting Countries (OPEC). OECD members provide about 90 percent of all ODA; OPEC members about 10 percent. The chief contributors in absolute terms are shown in Fig. 3-28. The countries that give the largest amounts relative to their own GNP are shown in Fig. 3-29. The agreed goal for all donor countries is 0.7 percent of GNP, but few countries achieve this and the average is about 0.35 percent. The world's three largest economies, the United States, Japan, and Germany, give about 0.21, 0.31, and 0.42 percent of their GNP respectively each year.

In addition, a variety of non-governmental organizations (NGOs) provide or receive funds and other forms of assistance such as personnel and equipment. Examples of donor NGOs include the International Red Cross, the Canadian Foodgrains Bank, Oxfam, and CARE (Committee for American Relief Everywhere). Examples of recipient NGOs include Disabled Peoples' International, World Council of Indigenous Peoples, Pan-African Institute for Development, and International Council for Adult Education.

SOURCE: World Development Report 1992

Country	US$ millions	Percent of total ODA
United States	11 394	18.39
France	9380	15.14
Japan	9069	14.63
Germany	6320	10.20
Saudi Arabia	3692	5.96
Italy	3395	5.48
United Kingdom	2638	4.26
Netherlands	2592	4.18
Canada	2470	3.99
Sweden	2012	3.25
WORLD TOTAL ODA	61 973	

Fig. 3-28 The ten chief contributors of official development assistance (ODA).

SOURCE: World Development Report 1992

Country	Percent of GNP
Saudi Arabia	3.90
United Arab Emirates	2.65
Norway	1.17
Netherlands	0.94
Denmark	0.93
Sweden	0.90
France	0.79
Finland	0.64
Belgium	0.45
Canada	0.44

Fig. 3-29 The ten countries that give the highest percentages of their GNP in ODA.

The amounts of development assistance given are small in comparison with the effort needed to produce both economic and basic needs improvements in developing countries, partly because donor nations have financial problems themselves. The South Commission, consisting of representatives of several developing countries, notes that the developing world "cannot count on a significant improvement in the international economic environment for its development in the 1990s." (*Report of the South Commission, 1990*). It notes that the development of the South will need to be financed largely out of its own resources, using a self-reliant and people-centred approach.

The Commission accepts that the overall quality of life must be improved both by attention to basic needs and by rapid economic growth. It asserts that priority should be given to "the modernization of peasant agriculture and the strengthening of the pace of industrialization while also improving its employment creating effects, competitiveness, and trade performance." The Commission also wants greater social justice and a fairer distribution of income and productive assets like land. The aim is to achieve, by the year 2000, universal primary health care and elementary education, and a substantial increase in vocational and technical training, along with a slowing down of population growth. The Commission further claims that development strategies should not aim to produce ways of life that imitate the consumption patterns of "affluent industrial societies" since this would be possible for only a small minority of the population and intensify existing environmental strains.

Spiritual values are also given as a reason for not proceeding with western-style economic growth. As the Prime Minister of Malaysia said in 1986, "The ideology and logic of materialism have all too easily influenced human society...."

In addition, the Commission states that "a people-oriented development strategy will have to take much greater note of the role of women; a nation cannot genuinely develop so long as half its population is marginalized and suffers discrimination. ...Yet, in almost all countries of the South, (women) play a vital role in productive activities and in maintaining their families and households. Thus, on the grounds of both equity and growth, development programs must give due prominence to the specific con-

SOURCE: CIDA/Pierre St-Jacques

Fig. 3-30 *"Women play a vital role in productive activities and in maintaining their families and households," as in this village in Mali.*

cerns of women and ensure that ample resources are marshalled to satisfy their needs and aspirations."

POVERTY REDUCTION IN THE FORMER COMMUNIST WORLD

The former communist countries of eastern and central Europe face some similar problems in development, especially in securing more widespread access to material wealth and creating a cleaner environment, but in other ways their problems are radically different. Population growth is minimal, and the need for economic growth to provide future jobs appears to be much less pressing than in the developing world. Additionally, there appears to be a high degree of basic needs provision: health and literacy are generally high by world standards, shelter is for the most part adequate, and food supplies are potentially ample. The problems seem instead to be largely those of economic organization, especially in relation to maintaining and enhancing material standards of living. The role of government was paramount for over 70 years, and is only slowly being replaced by effective market mechanisms for production and distribution.

In this manner, the demands of eastern and central Europe and the developing countries are similar, and both regions require vast amounts of investment. In both cases, internal resources are likely to be the chief source, since the developed countries have their own pressing financial problems. It is noteworthy that in 1993 Canada announced that it was reducing its overall foreign aid donations because of its own high international debt burden. Canada also announced that some of the aid that had previously gone to developing countries would be redirected towards the former communist countries of eastern and central Europe. Also in 1993, in Vancouver, Russian President Boris Yeltsin met with the American President Bill Clinton to seek increased development assistance from the United States.

Reasons for the collapse of central planning, practised throughout eastern and central Europe under communism, are varied. Most observers blame the rapid deterioration of production from the 1970s to the end of the 1980s. This was caused largely by unsustainable levels of military spending and the lack of incentive for individual workers to increase — or even maintain — production. Reduced production, and lack of availability of consumer goods, caused increasing dissatisfaction among the various national populations. For example, from 1970 to 1989, Romania's output declined steadily from an annual +9.3% to -10.2%; Poland's from +5.4% to -14.0%; Hungary's from +4.5% to -6.5%. All these countries are now committed to the development of market economies similar to those in western Europe.

Many economists agree that the switch to a market economy for the former communist countries involves four major and interacting changes:

The former Soviet Union used to provide aid to a number of developing countries, but this has now ceased as the countries of the former Soviet Union seek aid themselves.

Financial stability is an unrealized goal for almost all countries. Switzerland perhaps comes closest to stability, with Germany and Japan not far behind. North American currencies have regularly lost value against Swiss, German and Japanese currencies; but they are still among the most stable currencies in the world.

First, financial stability must be secured. Related to this change, currencies must be exchangeable with other world currencies; a banking system geared to consumer use and productive investments must be created; and some form of stock ownership and exchange must be implemented.

Second, competitive markets must be created for labour and capital as well as consumer items. Related to this change, prices must be allowed to be determined by the interaction of supply and demand instead of by government edict; and imports and exports must be encouraged.

Third, existing production units for both farm and industrial goods must be privatized. Enterprise should be fostered; and private ownership of property must be allowed.

Fourth, the role of government must be reduced to one where it regulates economic activity instead of commanding it and where basic services and infrastructure become its chief concerns.

Although the process of change has begun, progress is uneven among the former communist countries. Up to 1993, Poland and Hungary had gone farthest in making the four major changes, although the fourth change was not being implemented as quickly as the other three. Russia was close behind these countries, but arguing internally about the pace of the transition. Bulgaria and Romania were late starters. East Germany's reunification with West Germany, brought about heavy investment demands. It is expected that full implementation of the necessary reforms will take several years, but the goal is clear and the desire appears strong. An added problem, however, is the numerous ethnic rivalries that appear to have been unleashed by the collapse of centralized communism, causing some societies to place national priorities on independence rather than development. Nationalism is examined in more detail in Chapters Four and Five.

POVERTY REDUCTION IN THE DEVELOPED WORLD

The economic and social development problems of the developed countries relate for the most part to improving the standard of living of their own economically poor populations. There are economically poor people and regions in all the developed countries. Poverty here is difficult to define, partly because absolute poverty — an inability to secure even the most basic necessities of survival — is rare. Instead, poverty is relative, defined in relation to society's norms.

In Canada, for example, the Canadian Council on Social Development defines a family as poor if its annual income is less than 50 percent of average Canadian family income for families of similar size. Based on this measurement, approximately 25 percent of Canadians will always be classed as poor, whatever their absolute levels of income.

Statistics Canada uses a slightly different approach, adding 20 percent to the average spent by all families on food, clothing, and shelter, and classifying all who spend more than this proportion of their incomes (average plus 20 percent) on these needs as poor. By this means, about 12 to 13 percent of Canadians are defined as poor. Again, since average amounts of spending form the basis of classification, there will always be some Canadians classed as poor, unless the range of variation around the average is less than 20 percent. This is a function of the distribution of incomes throughout society, examined earlier in this chapter. Some degree of income inequality is the norm.

Measures to alleviate poverty in the developed countries rest partly in the government's ability and willingness to transfer income from high earners to low or zero earners through taxation and subsequent redistribution. Figure 3-19 shows that some countries manage to do this better than others, even among developing nations. There is a widespread feeling in many countries that the best way to decrease relative poverty in developed nations is to encourage the low or zero earners to become more economically productive. Not all these people have the capability, because signigicant proportions are elderly, seriously handicapped, or single parents without easy access to child care. Nevertheless, many agree that the most promising means of reducing the proportion of economically poor people are to introduce appropriate education and job training programs.

This situation is likely to become more difficult to resolve as developed world economies shift increasingly to knowledge-based output. People who have worked in jobs that required little formal education will require extensive retraining. By the early 1990s, for example, there were already more people in North America making computers than making cars. The major growth areas for the 1990s and onward are expected to be in similar high-technology areas such as software development, electronic instrumentation, medical research, and telecommunications. The shift of less skilled jobs to the labour-rich developing countries to support their own development adds yet another obstacle to the alleviation of developed world poverty.

The following readings present some views about development and poverty reduction. As you go through them, make two lists: one of examples of ways in which poverty is reduced; another of examples of ways which fail to reduce poverty.

According to an economics research group (Nuala Beck & Associates), Canada's electronics industry in 1992 was bigger than its pulp and paper industry; and communications and telecommunications were larger than mining and petroleum combined.

Developing countries are short of skilled job opportunities, and accordingly lose many of their skilled personnel to higher paying opportunities in the developed world. In the early 1990s, for instance, about 10 000 skilled Nigerians were living in the United States.

GHANA'S TRAGIC HYDRO-ELECTRIC PROJECT

LONDON — Future historians will look back on the 20th century as a moment without precedent in human existence. We have catapulted from agrarian, even hunter-gatherer societies into a world of petrochemicals, computers, space travel and global telecommunications and economics.

As we careen towards a new millennium, provincial and national governments alike point to science and technology as the means of carving out a niche in the international economy.

Yet as the potential of science and technology is trumpeted (and it is truly awesome), little attention is paid to history that provides the only real experience with which to compare the impact of new technologies against the claims, promises and predictions.

The BBC-TV series *Pandora's Box* makes the comparison powerfully. It looks at the history of innovations such as DDT and nuclear energy, the use of scientific methods to manage society and economics as a predictive discipline.

In each case, the great promise of the enterprise becomes grotesquely distorted and sidetracked by the demands of economics and politics. And above all, each reveals our egregious (conspicuous) ignorance about human behaviour and the world around us.

Today, hydro-electric megaprojects from Brazil's Plan 2010 to China's Three Gorges Dam, India's Narmada Dam and Quebec's James Bay project, are predicated on a belief that huge hydro-electric projects are the key to industrial and economic growth.

"Black Power," one of the programs on *Pandora's Box*, looked at a case study of a project based on that very assumption.

In 1951, a British colony, then known as Gold Coast, became the first African nation whose citizens voted for independence. A charismatic leader, Kwame Nkrumah, was swept into power as head of what would become Ghana.

The country seemed to be a model for the rest of Africa — rich in natural resources, with its own universities, doctors and lawyers, and led by a man with vision.

SOURCE: United Nations

Fig. 3-31 *The Akosombo dam on the Volta river in Ghana, designed to produce electricity for the manufacture of aluminum. It was Kwame Nkrumah's dream to provide the power necessary for economic development.*

Nkrumah wanted to transform Ghana into a modern industrial state within a generation and believed it could be achieved through hydro power.

. . . . .

Cheap electricity, Nkrumah reasoned, would light up Ghanaian homes and attract foreign industrial investment. Britain encouraged this vision with promises of technical and financial help for the project in return for cheap aluminum.

However, history deflected these plans in 1956 when Britain invaded Egypt to protect its interests in the Suez Canal. This costly venture forced Britain to back out of the Volta River project. But when Ghana became independent in 1957, the Volta River project had become a central element of Nkrumah's political future and vision for his nation's destiny.

Nkrumah turned to the U.S. and was encouraged by then-president Dwight Eisenhower to con-

tact Edgar Kaiser, who needed power for his aluminum company. Kaiser promised to build a plant in Ghana and this allowed Nkrumah to secure the largest loan ever given by the World Bank at that time to build the Volta River dam.

But Ghana's bauxite deposits could create a fully integrated industry, from mining the ore to processing it and manufacturing finished products. Fearful that a profitable aluminum industry in Ghana would be nationalized, Kaiser forced Nkrumah to agree to process American bauxite.

And once the World Bank loan was assured, Kaiser demanded electricity at the lowest rate paid by his global competitors. In essence, Ghana would be subsidizing an American company to process American bauxite to provide aluminum ingots to American manufacturers. But by then, too much was riding on the project for Nkrumah to pull out.

By the time the dam was completed early in 1966, Ghana was deeply in debt, its foreign reserves depleted. Ghana was also caught up as a pawn in the Cold War and two months later, a coup that some claim was engineered by the CIA, overthrew Nkrumah. He fled to Guinea, where he died in 1972.

By the end of the 1970s, Ghana had endured seven coups.

The World Bank loan was repaid and the aluminum company profited, but the country failed to realize its bright promise. Instead, Ghana and Nkrumah seemed to fulfil all of the negative expectations of the industrialized world, even though their fate had largely been caused by exploitation by the rich countries.

The BBC program barely hints at the considerable environmental and social consequences of the Volta River project. But as Canadians debate the ecological and economic costs of large dams, the tragic story of Ghana resonates. As we chart our way into the future, we cannot afford to ignore the painful lessons already provided by the history of others.

David Suzuki, *The Toronto Star*, 1992 8 15

BLOOMING BUSINESS A GROWTH INDUSTRY

Deep in the Rift Valley, on the placid north shore of Lake Naivasha, Peter Kiragu Mwangi thinks he has seen Africa's future, and it's coming up roses. Literally.

On his 93-hectare hillside farm, where hippos once ran amok, Mr. Mwangi grows 25 million stems of flowers a year — mostly delphinium, statice and confetti — for export to Europe. Not satisfied with his modest success, the 45-year-old farmer wants to expand to roses. "The profits," he said, "are much higher."

More important, the shy former banker, who took up farming in 1985, wants to show Kenyans that private enterprise is the country's best, if not only, hope for economic growth. "There are many ways to help build your country," he said, walking between lavender-coloured rows of statice. "This is my way."

Once vilified by African governments, private operators such as Mr. Mwangi are now seen as economic saviours. To woo them, many African countries have traded usurious (high) tax rates and complicated regulations for tax holidays, training credits and foreign-exchange allowances. The aim: to make Africa competitive.

In the 1980s, while global trade surged ahead, African exports sputtered. Their growth rate was a paltry 0.2 percent a year. And that was despite massive currency devaluations. With a stronger private sector in agriculture and manufacturing, many Africans think they can change that.

They first need investment. While the poorest African countries — the likes of Mali, Niger and Guinea — are not likely to attract even the most modest amounts of private investment, others such as Uganda, Nigeria and Cameroon already are. In those countries, where a business infrastructure exists, a race has begun to attract "footloose" industries — garments, leather, horticulture — that can draw investment and create jobs and exports almost overnight.

In the floriculture business, Kenya has increased its exports fourfold since 1986 to about $50-million (U.S.) in 1991, thanks to an inflow of investment. Two other standouts, Botswana and Mauritius, have surged ahead to East Asian rates of growth on the backs of cattle-ranching and garment-making, respectively.

With almost no prior knowledge of flower-growing, Mr. Mwangi has in seven years created 900 jobs on his farm and about $1-million (U.S.) worth of exports for Kenya. …Mr. Mwangi admits in his good-humoured manner that he is not the typical African farmer. When he is not driving around his flower farm in a Land-Rover, he often sits in his modest farmhouse reading *Fortune* magazine and listening to market reports on the BBC World Service.

While working as a commercial banker in 1980, Mr. Mwangi spent four weeks touring Canada.

"I saw what small business can do," he said.

Five years after he returned to Kenya, he quit his job, mortgaged his house and bought a farm, along with half a dozen trucks, an irrigation system and an electrified fence to keep Lake Naivasha's hippos at bay.

"It was hard to give up a secure job, but the freedom is wonderful," he said. "I put my ideas to the test every day, and if they fail I have no one to blame but myself."

Unlike the officials at many government-run enterprises, Mr. Mwangi quickly developed a keen marketing sense. He had to. When his first batch of flowers fetched a low price in Europe, he nearly lost his farm, and with it his life savings. "I almost lost everything, my house, everything," he said. "I didn't understand what the buyers in Europe wanted."

So he…started to phone buyers directly to hear their demands. This fall, he plans to install a computer and fax machine on his farm (he has had to wait for improved public telephone lines). If profits improve, he plans to build a cold-storage unit at Nairobi International

Airport, two hours away by road.

Mr. Mwangi has also learned to plan his crop around peak selling days such as Christmas, Easter and Mother's Day....

"I find a niche and make sure the quality is superior. That way, I can double my prices," he said.

For most of Africa, where the pace of economic reforms is well behind those in East Asia and Latin America, the hope for a foreign-investment boom has faded, leaving local entrepreneurs such as Mr. Mwangi to fill the void.

"I don't blame the foreigners. I wouldn't invest in most of these countries either," said Michael Chege, a Kenyan program officer with the Ford Foundation in Harare. "We have to rely on local capital first. Foreign capital will follow suit, not the other way around."

Mr. Chege argued that Africa faces few shortages of talent or capital; they just have not been used properly. "If you give ordinary people in Africa a chance, you'd be surprised how attuned they are to market economics," he said.

Even now, most African entrepreneurs operate in the informal sector, where they are free from the grip of regulation and taxation. In West Africa, informal trade may be as much as four times the level of official trade.

To draw that informal economy into the open, some countries have tried to cut business taxes and regulation. But in much of Africa, budding entrepreneurs still wilt in the shade of government bureaucracy. Mr. Mwangi only recently won the right to import European fertilizer for his flowers.

Larger industries often face greater barricades. Parts of Zambia's mining industry still use technology from the 1930s because the country lacks the foreign exchange to pay for newer equipment.

The same is often true in neighbouring Zimbabwe, where the government continues to keep a tight rein on foreign exchange, which it needs for debt payments, military purchases and food imports.

For those industries that dearly need the scarce funds, Peter Thomson, owner of one of Zimbabwe's largest construction companies, sounds a frequent lament: "We've done our part to be competitive, now the government has to live up to its side of the bargain."

There is not much support for new enterprises, either. In the late 1980s, an International Labour Organization study found that few African countries could offer small-scale credit schemes for business start-ups.

In Harare, Ann Sabau Chitsamba, 30, has watched her profitable decorating business decline for lack of financing. She needs $500 to buy imported dyes, but the local banks do not offer commercial loans of less than $12 000.

"Where else can I get the money to expand?" she said in exasperation.

Until recently, loans of any size were rare commodities. Where governments set interest rates, they often were so low compared to inflation that people refused to save money. And scarce savings were too often consumed by government **deficits**.

John Stackhouse, *The Globe and Mail*, 1992 10 20

 Fig. 3-32

Today's "Invisible Hand"

GROWING, GROWING...

Malaysians dream of the three Cs — cars, condos and credit cards — and many are seeing those dreams come true. Annual car sales in Malaysia doubled between 1985 and 1991, from 56 810 to 121 600. Housing developments are springing up where rubber and oil palm trees once grew. The icon of the consumer society, the credit card, has become ubiquitous (is everywhere): in 1990 Malaysians racked up $4.3 billion in credit-card transactions, a 75 percent increase over the year before.

Steve Norris, an Asia-Pacific marketing executive for Visa International, anticipates nothing will slow the growth: "We could see 30 million to 50 million Visa cards in this area in ten years." In Indonesia chains of locally owned restaurants are multiplying to meet burgeoning demand, and everyone is flocking to new shopping malls.

As living standards rise, local businesses are developing goods and services to satisfy needs that did not exist a few years ago. The travel industry is one example. According to the Hong Kong Tourist Association, since 1987 the number of visitor arrivals has grown about 66 percent, to more than four million. And Southeast Asian tourists now spend more each day per capita ($206) in Hong Kong than West European visitors ($195). Says Douglas J. King, the Tourist Association's general manager: "Ten years ago, there was only a middle class in Hong Kong and Singapore. That's not the case anymore, and these people think part of being advanced is to see the world."

George M. Taber, *Time*, 1992 9 14

MCDONALD'S OPENS SECOND MOSCOW STORE

George Cohon launched phase two of McDonald's Restaurants of Canada Ltd.'s Russian invasion yesterday, with the opening of the fast-food giant's second Moscow restaurant and 12-storey office building in the shadow of Red Square.

As senior chairman of Toronto-based McDonald's, Cohon spearheaded the move into the former Soviet Union during the glasnost era, opening its first restaurant three years ago.

"I feel a tremendous sense of pride as a Canadian," Cohon said yesterday, adding, "President Boris Yeltsin is stopping by (Wednesday) for a burger."

The Moscow prototype, which seats 700 patrons, is the busiest McDonald's outlet in the world, serving an average of 40 000 people a day. "We've served the entire population of Canada twice — with just one location," Cohon said.

Both the original store and the second, which seats only 30, are joint partnerships with the Moscow city council, which holds a 51 percent stake in the restaurants. Cohon said McDonald's is negotiating to take a controlling stake in future locations. A third store is slated to open in July.

McDonald's plans to open as many as 20 stores in Moscow which has a population of ten million. It is also scouting locations in St. Petersburg.

The new Moscow store, located one block from the Kremlin, occupies the first floor of the McDonald's Building, a $15-million glass office tower that is already home base to "a who's who of business around the world," Cohon said.

Tenants include Coca-Cola Co., Motorola Inc., Munich Re-Insurance Co. of Germany and ABB Asea Brown Boveri Ltd. of Switzerland.

Paul Brent, *The Financial Post*, 1993 6 2

CHINA'S ECONOMY THRIVING: MARKET-STYLE REFORMS CITED FOR RAPID INDUSTRIAL GROWTH

BEIJING — China's economy is running at full speed, with figures showing sharp rises in trade, investment and industrial output.

The value of industrial output jumped 21.8 percent in July from the same month last year, pushing the increase for the first seven months to 19 percent, according to state statistics bureau figures.

State investment in fixed assets (buildings, roads, machines, etc.) surged 42.2 percent, totalling 35.5 billion yuan ($6.6 billion U.S.).

. . . . .

Chinese economists often point to the increased role of market forces to justify optimism that the high rates of growth will not lead to the kind of inflation that slammed the brakes on a previous spurt in the late 1980s.

They argue that market-style reform being pushed by paramount leader Deng Xiaoping is making state industry more efficient and promoting better use of scarce raw materials.

The value of industrial sales increased 24.3 percent during July, with 96.4 percent of industrial output sold. Stimulated by a construction boom, production of cement and rolled steel was up 30.3 percent and 18.2 percent respectively.

The growth of imports outpaced that of exports by 6.5 percent in July, reflecting increased demand for imported equipment to build new plants.

Imports in the first seven months totalled $39.32 billion, up 22.6 percent, and exports hit $42.75 billion up 16.4 percent, for a difference of $3.43 billion.

. . . . .

The main fear is that rapid growth will hit a brick wall of industrial inefficiency. Western economists see little prospect that state factories can reform themselves quickly enough to stop that happening.

Large state enterprises employ 70 million workers in strategic industries such as energy, transport and defence. They are forced to sell their output at low prices, and keep surplus workers on their books under the "iron rice bowl" (equal shares for all) system that has crippled their operations.

Reuters News Agency, 1992 8 19

WHAT PERU NEEDS NOW

This spring's coup in Peru is the fourth I've experienced. It was not a surprise. We will have to live with it. It has not been a classic bloody coup, but I'm afraid more dramatic moments will come.

Why did it happen? What does it reveal about the current economic, political, and social situation under President Alberto Fujimori? And what should we expect in the near future?

From the point of view of the Peruvian people, the most important issue is the economic

crisis. In the next three decades Peru's labor force will grow by a greater absolute number than all of Europe, West and East together....

. . . . .

Indeed, one of my strongest hypotheses about the causes of the coup is that the government is trying to divert attention from the economic crisis. In justifying his action, Fujimori has presented the issues in inverse order of relative importance. He knows that his medium-term popularity depends much more on how the economy is doing and how people expect it will do in the future than on his capacity to (1) change the institutions of the political

system, (2) fight it out with the **Maoist** guerillas of the Shining Path, or (3) reduce corruption.

In any case, government policy has itself been a factor in recent Shining Path growth. It was a common view, even within the very highest levels of the constitutional government's executive branch — and also in the community of retired military and civilian experts — that there was no clear and unified strategy against the Shining Path. Much less a good one.

It would have been part of a good strategy to help autonomous organizations of women in charge of food programs in the pueblos jovenes, or shanty towns. But, while the Shining Path was killing unarmed women like María Elena Moyano and others, the government was starving them. There has not been any social emergency program during the harsh period of "stabilization" under Fujimori's drastic austerity program and transition to a free market. These courageously unarmed women are currently very afraid, terribly demoralized.

There has been a practical lack of legal means to defend basic food, shelter, and other needs. Fujimori's message has been very clear: Strikes, marches, etc. are to be absolutely ineffective in all that affects the budget.

. . . . .

In my view, the economic stabilization program has to be changed, even at the risk of helping this government remain in power longer than expected. The current program is not efficient since it neither reduces inflation to the required level nor is linked to a growth project that creates hopes and opens opportunities. The best short-term bridge to a new economic situation would be strong measures against tax evaders and a renegotiation of the foreign debt that also helps to balance the budget. A huge and democratically managed social emergency program is also urgently needed. Institutional reforms and privatization in the economy will not help Peru move ahead if they concentrate property in fewer hands and do not open investment, employment, and participation opportunities for youth.

. . . . .

A truly participatory democracy is essential, because as

SOURCE: John Molyneux

Fig. 3-33 *Peru's government spends relatively little on services such as paving roads and installing drainage, especially in rural areas.*

pride grows — as it is growing in Peru in spite of our long crisis — the feeling of being a stranger in your own country is quite rightly subversive. Democracy, openness, *glasnost* if you like, is needed to make that still common feeling of alienation constructive, productive, jointly binding — a source of strength and not of inferiority complex.

Education, entrepreneurship, women's political participation, the widespread rejection of servile status, the mutual knowledge through mass media, and many other more powerful realities than the recent coup — these show Peruvian society is moving ahead. Today's armed violence impedes it. The remaining racism — indigenous peoples vs. upper-class people of European descent — and segregation make progress dangerous and costly.

. . . . .

The alternative to the current situation is not just eco-

nomic growth but also distribution. As important, if not more so, is true equality of status. That is, I am sure, the most powerful productive force Peru has today. The conquest of Peru by the Peruvians, as has been said a thousand times, is an ongoing, indestructible process.

Javier María Iguíñiz-Echeverría, *World Monitor*, 1992, 6

Javier María Iguíñiz-Echeverría has written many books on economics published in his home city of Lima, Peru, where he has been a professor at the Pontificia Universidad Católica del Peru since 1973. He has also taught in England (Oxford) and the U.S. (Notre Dame). This spring (1992) he was a visiting scholar at Massachusetts Institute of Technology, department of economics. This article is adapted from a lecture he delivered at the Fletcher School of Law and Diplomacy.

A THIRD-WORLD LESSON

Microenterprise, an idea borrowed from the third world, is giving some Americans a dramatically different point of view toward our own social policy.

Microenterprises are small, simple businesses owned and run mainly by poor people. Organizations like Shorebank in Chicago and the Good Faith Fund in Arkansas have successfully nurtured hundreds of new businesses run by poor people without training or prior business experience, many of them former welfare recipients.

...A new organization, the Association for Economic Opportunity, is helping to turn the efforts of more than 100 local microenterprise programs into a national movement.

Microenterprise is good social policy. It costs the government little or nothing. The enterprises provide income that sustains families and helps finance investment in education and business growth. At the same time, microenterprises develop the skills of their owners and workers. Most importantly, as they build a business, microentrepreneurs build pride in their own accomplishments. This sense of confidence can spread through their communities.

The idea of assisting microenterprises developed in the third world during the 1980s. Some dramatic successes there, notably the Grameen Bank's outreach to one million very poor women in Bangladesh, prompted United States organizations to take up the idea.

But like most borrowed notions, it had to be reshaped to fit the American context. This has not always been easy. America's social safety net discourages poor people from starting a business, both at a direct, practical level, and

at a much deeper, almost philosophical level.

Welfare regulations generally prohibit people from accumulating assets while remaining eligible for benefits, even assets used only in a business. The simple equipment and inventory needed to start a catering or seamstress business often exceeds the asset limit. Potential microentrepreneurs must choose: your business or your benefits. That choice generally confronts them before their business is generating a reasonable income.

At the request of domestic microenterprise programs, several U.S. congressmen have introduced legislation to amend these regulations. Microenterprise is becoming a small weapon in the battle over welfare reform.

...the concept of microenterprise challenges the very foundation of the social safety net. It reveals a fundamental difference in the way poverty is approached in the third world and in the U.S. While America has been trying to perfect and expand its social safety net, developing countries have to create strategies that work without one.

In developing countries, poor people find their own ways of coping with poverty. Starting a tiny enterprise is one of the most important ways — involving as much as one-third of the workforce in many countries — but it is not the only way. If there are no banks, people create savings and credit clubs. Such clubs — called *tontines* in West Africa, *stokvels* in South Africa, *arisans* in Indonesia — flourish on every continent. They help people build assets and protect themselves from risk.

If they cannot afford a mortgage, they build their own houses. In the famous Pueblos Nuevos in Peru, as in many other countries, people begin with minimal dwellings and

continually invest in home improvement, provided the government assures them of a right to stay and provides basic utilities.

Similarly, transport systems run by and for the poor outcompete public transportation systems in offering convenient routes, frequency, and low price, while acting as a major employer and keeping profits in the communities.

Most important, poor people in developing countries rely on their families. Family members are the main source of care for children, the sick, and the aged. Families also provide financial resources for emergencies, education, and investment.

These coping strategies are healthy, constructive, and creative solutions, which flourish despite the absolute level of poverty found in the third world.

The developing-world approach to poverty recognizes that poor people themselves are the most effective and most readily available resource for combating poverty. The American model, based primarily on income redistribution, assumes that the greatest resource for combating poverty is the federal budget.

Microenterprise and the third-world approach to poverty offer a stunning challenge to the U.S. They tell us that we need to do a much better job of harnessing the energies of the poor. Not only are their energies a tremendous and underutilized resource, but an approach based on those energies is socially healthy.

The question facing us at this time is, can we develop social policies that release those energies without abandoning the basic protection offered to the genuinely needy by the social safety net?

Elisabeth Rhyne, *The Christian Science Monitor*, 1992

ENVIRONMENTAL ASPECTS OF DEVELOPMENT

It is widely believed that all development, whether in developing countries, former communist countries, or developed countries, leads to the challenge of resolving existing environmental damage and preventing further harm. Great damage has been done to the natural environment in many parts of the world while reaching present levels of development.

In the developing countries, rapid population growth has forced many members of society to seek food and fuelwood on marginal lands. As noted in Chapter Two, the cost to the environment includes soil erosion, reduced soil fertility, desertification, deforestation, depleted fish stocks, reduced biodiversity, and pollution of rivers. Such degradation aggravates existing poverty for both present and future generations. Women are particularly affected by this process. Because they must spend more time obtaining fuel and water than previously, they have less time to devote to food production and education. In many instances women are also the sole head of household because their spouses have left to seek work — often unsuccessfully — in the growing cities.

Additional environmental problems in the developing world relate to industrialization and the widespread use of coal, especially in China and India. Pollution control technologies are rarely available locally, and imported technologies are expensive to install.

SOURCE: United Nations

Fig. 3-34 *These heavily polluting factories are in Albania. Should they be shut down?*

Among the hundreds of individual places with environmental degradation in central Europe, the most seriously devastated zone is the Silesian Coal Belt which stretches through eastern Germany, the northern part of the Czech Republic, and southern Poland.

In the former communist countries of eastern and central Europe, little consideration was given to the environment in the drive to achieve output. Economic emphasis was placed on heavy industry and low energy prices, resulting in widespread use of coal, much of it low-quality and highly polluting. Waste products were routinely discharged into rivers and atmosphere. Because of the emphasis on output and jobs, state enterprises had no reason to treat natural resources as a valuable asset. Resources were often wasted through inefficiency, and there was little incentive to find substitutes or improve technology. Most countries had environmental regulations, but enterprises that disobeyed them merely paid the fines and recovered the costs out of the state's budget. Citizen protests about the deteriorating environment were inhibited by the nature of the political regime.

Not until the recognition of the Solidarity Party in Poland in 1980 did conditions begin to change. In this year the first independent environmental movement — the Polish Ecological Club — was founded and a major emitter of toxic fluorides, the Skawina aluminum works southwest of Krakow, was closed. There are now environmental parties in all the former communist countries of eastern and central Europe.

The developed countries — in the eyes of many critics — have caused a great deal of damage to the environment in their quest for economic growth. Their use of several world resources is disproportionately

	Canada	France	Germany	Italy	Japan	U.K.	U.S.A.	Total G7[1]
Population	0.5	1.1	1.5	1.1	2.3	1.1	4.7	12.3
Cropland area	3.1	1.3	0.8	0.8	0.3	0.5	12.9	19.7
Cattle numbers	1.0	1.7	1.6	0.7	0.4	0.9	7.8	14.1
Fossil fuel use	2.5	1.9	4.5	2.2	4.8	2.9	24.8	43.6
Coal use	1.2	0.8	6.0	0.6	3.4	2.8	20.6	35.4
Oil use	2.9	2.9	3.9	3.4	7.1	2.8	27.1	50.1
Gas use	3.7	1.6	3.2	2.2	2.7	3.0	26.8	43.2
Steel use	1.8	2.2	5.6	3.5	11.7	2.2	12.9	39.9
Aluminum use	2.3	4.0	7.7	3.6	13.5	2.5	24.2	57.8
Nickel use	1.4	5.3	11.1	3.2	18.9	3.9	14.8	58.6
Lumber use	5.1	1.1	1.3	0.4	2.4	0.2	14.7	25.2
Paper use	2.7	3.6	6.2	2.9	11.9	4.2	33.1	64.6
Fertilizer use	1.5	4.3	3.2	1.3	1.4	1.6	13.1	26.4
Cement use	0.6	2.2	4.2	4.1	7.0	1.5	8.2	27.8
CO_2 emissions	2.1	1.6	4.5	1.8	4.7	2.6	22.1	39.4

[1] The Group of Seven: the seven largest economies in the Organization for Economic Cooperation and Development (OECD).

SOURCE: *World Resources 1992-93*

Fig. 3-35 *The G7 countries' percentage shares of world population and world resource use.*

high compared with their populations, as shown in Fig. 3-35. The sorts of environmental stresses produced by the OECD's drive for economic growth are numerous. Some are examined in Chapter Two. It is the opinion of the World Resources Institute that such high levels of resource use and pollution production "do not yet meet" the criteria for sustainable development.

Some improvements have been made, and pollution technology is a rapidly growing field of endeavour. But pollution of air and water, and disposal of wastes, remain serious problems. There are continuing needs for more sparing use of resources and use of more efficient, minimal waste (some would say zero waste) production techniques. Technological innovation in both these areas is considered a high priority in sustaining economic growth and equalizing living standards around the world.

The following readings provide two different opinions about issues surrounding development and environment. After you have read them, answer the questions that follow.

POLLUTING THE WATERS AND OCEANS

Assuring an adequate supply is not the only water problem facing many countries throughout the world: they also need to worry about water quality. The first global assessment of freshwater quality, recently carried out, found that contamination of water resources continues to increase in much of the world.

Throughout the world, water quality is impaired — often severely — by pollution and misuse of water, land and even air. Damage is done by domestic waste water, industrial discharges and land-use runoff, while leaching from mine tailings and solid waste dumps, and acid rain are growing concerns. Contamination by organic pesticides, PCBs and other synthetic organics is widespread and locally serious in both high-income and low-income countries.

Most rivers in the industrialized world have seen some reduction of the levels of certain types of pollutants since the 1970s. Such progress came as a result of clean water legislation, and the treatment of domestic wastes.

But despite progress in some areas, there are clearly grounds for growing concern. Nitrate levels in some European rivers are 45 times higher than those in the natural background. Heavy metals are severe problems in Scandinavian rivers and the Rhine, and are locally severe elsewhere in Europe and North America. Countries in Eastern Europe and the Commonwealth of Independent States (former Soviet Union) are also experiencing extremely high levels of pollution from all sources — domestic, industrial, agricultural — with industrial pollutants the most obvious and serious problem.

In most industrializing countries, both organic and

industrial river pollution are on the increase, as annual per capita income and population rise. Over the past few decades, industrialization was seen as more important than concerns about pollution. As a result, in some regions, notably East Asia, degradation of water resources is now considered the most serious environmental problem.

In less developed countries, where the population is growing rapidly and where domestic sewage treatment is limited, water pollution by organic wastes is widespread, especially in large cities. Excessive organic pollution levels have been found in many streams and rivers in Central and South America, as well as in South and Southeast Asia. In India, close to 70 percent of the surface water is polluted. China's rivers also seem to be suffering from increasing pollution loads. In Malaysia, some 40 major rivers are so polluted that they can no longer support fish or other aquatic life. Runoff from the increasing and uncontrolled use of fertilizers and pesticides represents an additional threat.

Overall, the quality of water in the developing world is so bad that, as a result, millions of children die each year from water-related diseases, such as

diarrhea, that can be prevented by proper water and sanitation facilities.

Development, CIDA, Spring 1992

SAVING THE PLANET IS JUST A PASSING FAD

"The world," physicist Harold Lewis told me when I called him in Santa Barbara, "has gone bonkers over the subject of risk. Is "bonkers" a word you're familiar with ...?"

Is it ever! ...Bonkers is the word for all those people rushing around proclaiming that the sky's melting, the drinking water's poisoned, and bonkers is precisely the word for us consumers snapping up any old supermarket product just so long as it has a green label.

You can always be sure of one thing with this funny old human race: If something is worth doing, we always do it to excess. Right now we're making terrible fools of ourselves in the name of saving the planet.

The environment has become a fad. On the radio this week I even heard an environmental Santa preaching to kids in heavy-handed fashion about the need to recycle their toys.

Heaven knows, there's nothing wrong with recycling, nothing wrong with conserving, and I, too, have a passing interest in saving the planet.

The problem arises when people go overboard, when they become obsessed with the environment. Because you know if they're that intense about it today, they'll have forgotten it tomorrow in favor of some new enthusiasm.

SOURCE: John Molyneux

Fig. 3-36 *Coal mining in Nova Scotia helps to supply many electricity generating stations. What are the hazards associated with coal mining?*

And the other thing that happens is that people get so worried and upset about the risks of day-to-day living that they become prey to every sort of irrational thinking. You know what I mean — what's going to get us first: the greenhouse effect, ozone depletion or AIDS?

That's what concerns Lewis, a University of California scientist who has just written a book, *Technological Risk*, pointing out how skewed our notions are on the subject of risk. "The field has been taken over by demagogues," he told me.

North America, he said, was thrown into a panic last year over insignificant amounts of pesti-

cide in apples. In his book, he quotes the work of a biochemist who points out that we consume 10 000 times as much natural pesticides — developed by plants over millions of years to protect themselves from insects — as we do man-made ones.

So what are the real dangers that could put you or me in the way of providing business for the local funeral home? "Smoking," said Lewis without hesitation....

But nearly everything carries a risk and it's important to measure the benefit against the risk. "I run," said Lewis, "although I read about joggers having heart attacks."

Probably the issue people are most confused about is nuclear power. There is a risk in nuclear power, said Lewis, "but there happens to be more risk in coal-fired power stations and I understand you have a special concern about acid rain (to which coal-fired power stations contribute) in Canada." Burning coal, in addition to killing lakes, damages the ozone layer, causes cancer and kills coal miners.

. . . . .

I'm all in favor of conserving but, as Lewis says, one person's waste is another person's necessity. People without cars, for example, think other people shouldn't have cars. Hydro is putting its main hopes in persuading business to be more saving and in promoting energy-efficient homes and appliances.

Good luck to them, but when it comes to getting people

to change their lifestyles and do without air-conditioning, clothes drying and all the other luxuries that have become necessities for most, in the long run they haven't a chance.

Because by then, believe me, conservation will be just yesterday's fad.

Frank Jones, *The Toronto Star*, 1990 11 29

DISCUSSION AND RESEARCH

25. Through research,
    (a) Identify a water resource in your neighbourhood that is experiencing degradation caused by some form of economic development;
    (b) Describe the major causes and sources of pollution of this resource; and
    (c) Prepare the script for a short video production to outline the problem to the community with the purpose of moving community leaders to act.

26. In small groups, develop and present to the class two lists. One list should contain reasons why you think people should make concern about the natural environment their top priority. The other list should contain reasons why you think concern for the natural environment should not be humanity's top priority.

27. There is an ancient European battlefield approach to deal with casualties called triage. Casualties are examined and divided into three groups: those who will likely survive, with or without treatment; those who will likely survive only with treatment; and those who will likely die even with treatment. Because battlefield medical resources are normally too scarce to be provided equally to everyone in need, effort is traditionally concentrated on those in the second group. Investigate as a class, in small groups, or individually,
    (a) who gains and who loses from the use of triage, and
    (b) whether the triage approach has any value as a means of allocating development assistance to the people of the developing world.

28. A common problem in many developing countries is unstable military government. Several of these countries experience widespread fighting and civil unrest. Such fighting is frequently a cause of famine, because it removes the settled conditions needed by farmers. Famine also imposes a serious need to end the fighting. However, government and rebels alike often ignore starving citizens, assuming that foreign emergency food aid will be provided to them. Some aid workers in war-torn famine zones may ask, "Should we save 500 000 people this year and allow five more years of fighting, where every year there will be another disaster? Or should we let the people starve in hopes of ending the war? Which is better in the long term?"

As a development consultant, counsel these aid workers about how to resolve their questions.

29. Examine the cartoon in Fig. 3-32, and in small groups research the meaning of the symbols — the title of the suitcase, the title at the top, and each of the two figures. Analyze the message of the whole drawing, and suggest what the artist might believe about the issue of development assistance. Report your conclusions in a written statement of one page or less.

30. Select any issue connected with resources and development, and draw a cartoon of your own to illustrate a point related to the issue you have selected.

31. Set up a research project to investigate and report on the causes of poverty in your local area.

32. One of the basic beliefs about development held by many developing countries is that their products should have ready access to the markets of the developed countries. Such access may put workers in developed countries out of work. Developed countries protect themselves against this by placing high tariffs on imported products. Hold a class brainstorming session to list the appropriate courses of action for governments of developed countries.

33. Elisabeth Rhyne, in "A Third-World Lesson," makes the point that the existence of a social welfare safety net (income support for people without much money) inhibits the poor in rich nations from making the same effort to escape poverty as those in poor nations. In small groups, discuss this notion, and make a justified recommendation either to maintain or to abandon the safety net approach.

34. Organize an inquiry into a multinational company of your choice. Your inquiry should investigate:

(a) the extent and nature of the company's global operations;

(b) the nature and strength of any welcoming or critical statements or actions in the various foreign countries the company operates in.

35. The opening of McDonald's restaurants in Russia may have far-reaching effects on the way the Russian economy develops. In small groups, suggest ways in which McDonald's may have an impact on the Russian economy. Report your suggestions to the class.

STATISTICAL ANALYSIS

36. Column 31 of Appendix 2 shows the amounts of carbon dioxide emitted by industrial processes in the various countries of the world. The world total is over 20 billion tonnes, and over 85 percent of this is produced by just 20 countries.

(a) Identify the 20 countries that produce the largest amounts of industrial carbon dioxide emissions.

(b) Using the procedure explained in the section on proportional circles in Appendix 3, on a photocopy of the world map in Appendix 1, draw located proportional circles representing the industrial carbon dioxide emissions from the 20 chief countries.

(c) Describe the distribution plotted on the map, and your conclusions, in writing. Make special note of any relationship you see between industrial carbon dioxide emissions and the development process.

37. Carbon dioxide is released into the atmosphere by the burning of forest and grassland in land clearance schemes for extra farmland. Data are not available for all countries, but those that are available are shown in column 32 of Appendix 2. The total for the countries shown is over 6 billion tonnes, and— as with industrial carbon dioxide emissions — over 85 percent is produced by just 20 countries.

(a) Identify the 20 countries that produce the largest amounts of carbon dioxide emissions from land use, and draw a world map showing located proportional circles for these 20 countries. (See Appendix 3 for guidance on drawing proportional circles and Appendix 1 for a world map which can be photocopied for your use.)

(b) Make a written comparison of the distribution shown on this map with the distribution shown on the map drawn for assignment 36. Suggest reasons for the differences.

38. In columns 31 and 32 of Appendix 2, 73 countries are shown with data for carbon dioxide emissions from both industry and deforestation.
    (a) Dividing the work into groups, calculate for each of the 73 countries the ratio of carbon dioxide produced from deforestation to that produced from industry. For example, Guinea produces 37 000 000 tonnes from deforestation and 1 000 000 tonnes from industry, giving a ratio of 37:1. The ratios differ enormously from country to country.
    (b) Select the 20 countries with the highest ratios; they are all more than 20:1.
    (c) In small groups, discuss what these high ratios might mean.

39. The 30 countries with the highest total carbon dioxide emissions per capita are listed below. (From columns 2, 31, and 32 of Appendix 2 and *World Resources, 1992-93*, World Resources Institute.)
    (a) Calculate the total carbon dioxide emissions per capita for

Australia	Bahrain	Belgium
Bulgaria	Canada	Colombia
former Czechoslovakia	Ecuador	Finland
Gabon	Guinea-Bissau	Ivory Coast
Kuwait	Laos	Liberia
Luxembourg	Madagascar	Malaysia
Nicaragua	Norway	Paraguay
Poland	Qatar	Saudi Arabia
Singapore	Trinidad & Tobago	U.K.
United Arab Emirates	U.S.A.	former U.S.S.R.

    each of these countries by adding the data in columns 31 and 32. Note that the data are in thousands of tonnes, so multiply each total by 1000 to obtain the correct figure for each country.
    (b) Divide these totals by the population of each country (column 2 in Appendix 2) to obtain the total carbon dioxide emissions per capita.
    (c) Arrange the results in rank order, with the highest at the top.
    (d) Write one to two pages explaining your conclusions about the size and ranking of the calculated values for the different countries.

40. Refer to Fig. 3-35. In almost all cases the percentage use of world resources is greater than the percentage of world population.

(a) In order to standardize the data to facilitate comparisons, calculate ratios as follows: divide all the percentages for each country (and G7 total) by the population percentage for that country (and G7 total), omitting the percentages for the line labelled fossil fuel use (to avoid double counting). For example, the ratio of Canada's cropland percentage (3.1) to its population percentage (0.5) is 6.2 to 1. Since the ratios will all be based on each country's population being 1, only 6.2 needs to be entered for Canada's cropland ratio.

(b) Enter the ratios in a table similar to that in Fig. 3-35, excluding population and fossil fuel use.

(c) Circle the country ratios that are higher than the G7 average ratios. Which country has most ratios above the G7 average? Which country has least?

(d) For each G7 country, calculate the average of the 13 individual ratios. Use these averages, as well as the individual ratios, to write a short essay on the environmental impacts of each G7 country's resource use.

CONCLUSION

It is realistic to state that a billion people or more still exist in dire poverty, and the vast majority of the remainder do not have all they want. But while development is both a need and a want, there is a growing awareness that it cannot continue to take place without serious attention to improving its relationship with the natural environment. The essential tasks of development are therefore to provide and upgrade opportunities for all people to reach their human and economic potential while at the same time creating a relationship with the natural environment that is sustainable into the future. These are difficult tasks for all countries individually, but are more complicated when certain differences exist among countries.

Rapid population growth continues to be a worldwide development concern, with increasing numbers of people often forced to take a diminishing share of any increases in total output. In addition, heavily protected domestic markets restrict the opportunities available to other countries for trade and growth. Free trade opens markets and allows for international growth, but causes concern over domestic jobs. People do not agree with each other about it, anywhere.

Beyond these concerns lie others, relating to basic needs, equity, human rights, international (including inter-ethnic) cooperation, and human dignity. None of the concerns of development will be met, however, unless some human priorities change and others are reinforced.

- What are the different choices?
- How urgent is a resolution of the situation?
- Where do you stand on these issues?
- What can you do personally to improve the situation?

The next chapter examines some of the root causes of human priorities, and looks at the major issues arising from them.

CASE STUDY
CHILD LABOUR

As many as a quarter of all children between the ages of ten and 14 in some regions of the world may be working, according to a report issued in 1992 by the Geneva-based International Labour Organization. Children are defined as people under 14 years of age. Many are employed illegally, and work in hazardous conditions. Most are illiterate. While some of these children work for wages, others would be classified as slaves. Still others are classified as street children, who do not have a formal job, but nevertheless must provide for themselves.

There is much evidence that slavery is still entrenched, especially in Asia, Africa, and Latin America. The 1956 United Nations Supplementary Convention on Slavery defines slaves as those individuals unable to withdraw their labour voluntarily. Exploited children who can be cut off from their families to work long hours for little or no income fall into this category. So do those individuals, including children, who are still considered chattels or the property of a master. Although this latter type of slavery is illegal everywhere in the world it still exists in the Arabian peninsula and across North Africa and examples can also be found in Amazonia where Indians are enslaved by ranchers or miners.

Chattel slavery was officially abolished in the 1960s and 70s in much of the Arab world, yet because of the isolation of many desert communities some slaves do not know that they have been freed. Recently, in Mauritania, a ten-year-old girl was sold to another master for four camels and was immediately dispatched to her new master's home many kilometres away from her parents across the desert. Although she attempted to run away she was caught and returned to her new owner. It is unlikely that she will ever see her parents again.

In Sudan, chattel slavery is on the increase as a result of the civil war between the Arab, Muslim north and the black animist southerners. Arab militias raid the villages in the south and sell the children they capture as slaves for about $15 each in the north.

Children are openly sold at auctions in Bangkok, Thailand and it is common practice for the children working in the carpet belt in the Indian state of Uttar Pradesh to have been bought by the loom owners from their parents for about $20 each. These boys, some as young as six and seven, knot New Zealand wool for 12 hours a day six or seven days a week for as little as 50 cents a week. In total there are approximately 55 000 looms at which about 100 000 boys labour. They are often locked into the huts where they work, are fed only two meals a day of rice and onions, sleep in the same room where they work, and get very little fresh air or exercise. Some of their carpets are sold in Canada.

Two South African newspapers have exposed the existence of slave trafficking involving young Mozambicans who, in an attempt to escape war and famine in their own country, cross the border into South Africa and are trapped. Once sold, the often unpaid boys and girls find it difficult to escape. Some end up as labourers, while others are sold for sexual exploitation.

The number of children sold as chattels is actually small compared to those in the world categorized as **bonded** children. These children become captive employees of someone because they are in debt to that person. A debt accumulates because their salary doesn't cover their expenses and they must borrow money. Usually the interest on the loan, frequently as high as 200 percent annually, coupled with a low rate of pay ensure that the loan cannot be repaid in a person's lifetime. Debts of $100 can take more than a generation to repay. At least 25 million bonded children exist in India, Pakistan, Bangladesh, Nepal, and Sri Lanka. Another seven million live in

Brazil. There, whole families may be employed in one location, then transported to another where they are told they must pay for their fares, their tools, and their food out of a salary that doesn't cover these expenses. The result is that they are immediately in debt and have no one to turn to as they are now hundreds of kilometres from home.

In India most bonded children are employed in rural areas, either in agriculture or road building. Others work in brick kilns or stone quarries. Although illegal in India since 1978, bonded labour is deeply rooted in the Hindu culture. Hindu society has traditionally been divided into what originally were occupational categories and ordered according to a sense of religious purity. The lowest group, formerly called the untouchables, handled the most menial and unclean tasks. Most bonded labourers come from this bottom rung of the Hindu caste hierarchy. Otherwise they are tribal peoples, who are outside the caste system altogether. Much of the bondage is inherited, with debts passed on down through the families. Children are expected to take on their parents' debts.

The Dominican Republic's sugar plantations illustrate another example of bonded labour. The contributions of Haitian workers, many who are underpaid and abused have become essential to the economy of the Dominican Republic. Workers of all ages are recruited by agents in Haiti who promise them satisfactory employment. Dominican soldiers at the border then pay a few dollars a head to the agents and transport the workers to the sugar plantations. Though workers may earn $3 a day they quickly fall into debt because they have to pay for rent, food and tools. Some workers are even denied food if they do not cut enough cane during the day. In addition, they may be prevented from returning to Haiti.

Then, there are those born into a job for life. Big agricultural estates including, for example, the tea plantations in India and Bangladesh, are sometimes staffed with large numbers of such families. They live, work, eat, and sleep on the plantation and due to their poverty and lack of education know very little of the outside world. The same sort of conditions exist for workers on rubber and oil-palm plantations in Malaysia.

Statistics on child labour also

SOURCE: UNICEF/John Isaac

Fig. 3-37 *Boys prepare mud to make bricks baked in kilns in Lahore, Pakistan.*

include the children who work for wages to help support their families with whom they live. Conditions are often only slightly better. For example, street vendors are popular attractions for tourists in Lisbon, Portugal. Many of the vendors are children who live with their parents but do not attend school. They work the streets often as late as 4:30 in the morning selling snacks to the nightclub crowd. These are just a few of the estimated 200 000 Portuguese children who work. The majority are found in the industrial north. There, shoes and textile factories produce inexpensive goods with the help of children who work for far less than the minimum wage. An average child's salary is about $90 a month. As one of the poorest countries in Western Europe, Portugal finds it difficult to compete with the rest of the continent. Child labour makes it possible.

Across the Mediterranean in Morocco, the carpet-making industry relies mainly on the labour of young girls. If they are apprentices they are not paid. More experienced workers receive a daily wage equivalent to the local price of a loaf of bread. But, unlike the boys in Uttar Pradesh, these girls have the opportunity of returning to their families at night.

Italy is believed to employ at least 500 000 children in various industries. For example, in the shoe-making belt around the city of Naples, school-age girls are employed sticking soles to uppers, often in unventilated basements. Environmental safeguards do not exist. As a result, a high incidence of an illness which affects the nervous system and can cause paralysis has been recorded among these girls.

Street children are classed as a sub-category of child labour. These children live by begging, stealing, or selling whatever they can, including their bodies. It is difficult to put a figure on the number of street children in the world but it is known that they exist in almost every large city, both in industrialized and developing countries. As the populations of cities in the developing world swell, the number of street children grow, particularly in Latin America where the problem is most acute. Homeless children literally live on the streets. They have no access to education, basic services, or family affection and support. For example, an estimated 200 000 youths live on the streets in the big cities of Brazil. Most of them are African Brazilians, and they lead a life of crime and drugs. Brazil has a very protective child statute which says that children under the age of 18 may not be arrested unless caught red-handed. To the drug gangs who rule the favelas, or slums, the children's freedom from punishment makes them ideal workers, thieves, and couriers.

Recently, a new phenomenon, that of killing these young people, has added a different dimension to the problem. Brazilian police statistics show that more than 6000 youths under the age of 18 have been murdered in the early 1990s. Some have been killed by the police, but others have been killed by death squads hired by local merchants to combat stealing and by the drug gangs who kill the children when they learn too much or outlive their usefulness.

In Kathmandu, the capital of Nepal, children as young as eight who have gravitated there from poor villages often end up sleeping in the streets and under bridges. By day they sift through piles of garbage to find pieces of rags, paper, metal, and plastics to sell. Recently, the organization Child Workers in Nepal (CWIN) estimated that there were about 500 children living on the streets of Kathmandu. There are also the sewer children of Bogota, Colombia. During the day they hide out in the filth of underground tunnels. At night they emerge to beg, steal, and buy food and drugs. Some of these children are born in these conditions. Although they often live with severe health problems and drug addictions, they are extremely skilled at stealing and can swiftly remove a windshield wiper or a tire. The vast majority of street children are boys. Girls turn to prostitution at an earlier age than boys and more frequently take jobs in domestic service. There they still may be exploited and abused, but they are not on the streets.

Why is child labour so prevalent today? The principal reasons lie in the extreme poverty found in parts of the developing world, which has forced children into the workplace to help support their family. In many places parents offer their children's services as the only hope of immediate survival. They cannot be concerned that children in the labour force now can lead to a future of unhealthy and ill-educated adults. There are those who argue that cheap labour provided by children helps economic development, even though the use of child labour may also mean fewer adults in the work force.

Children have always worked, but the sophistication of the world's economy today delegates child labour to the lowest category of unskilled labour. It has also become a negative factor in attempts to raise the education level of all the world's children. In Africa, a combination of civil wars, political turmoil, and natural disasters has led to massive population transfers and the breakup of families, forcing more children to support themselves. In southern Asia, millions more children are bonded or committed to work by their parents in repayment of family debts.

In many developing countries financially strapped governments have cut spending on education to such an extent that school fees are too expensive for parents to pay. With no chance to go to school, children end up in the work force. Street children typically come from homes where they have been abused or neglected, while abandoned children are the offspring of poverty. Most developing countries do not have the means to protect the children in their midst. Although many of the world's working children are employed in agriculture, they no longer work on a family farm. The industrialization of agriculture is changing the structure of production, so that more and more landless peasants work for others, and children work as hard as their parents in order to ensure their family survives. In some places adults are only employed on condition that their children help as well.

However, it is in the cities of the developing world that child labour is

SOURCE: UNICEF/Sean Sprague

Fig. 3-38 *These children look in a garbage dump in Mexico City for items they can sell.*

increasing at the fastest rate. The mechanization of agriculture has meant a gigantic shift of rural population to the cities. For many countries this influx of people to urban areas has overwhelmed both the government's ability to deliver services and the economy's ability to create jobs. As a result, huge slum settlements have sprung up around the cities. Under these conditions, the streets seem to offer more hope to some children than the despair and abuse they experience with their families.

What effect does this exploitation have on these children and what hazards do they face? Exploited children are usually underfed, suffer from poor hygiene, and have little access to education. Most grow up illiterate. Working in windowless rooms with little exercise, their limbs may become atrophied and some end up blind. Other health hazards are faced by youngsters who are forced to work in mines, brick yards, glassworks, or tanning factories. They are often beaten and tortured. When young boys and girls are forced into prostitution they are so traumatized that even if they are rescued it is usually difficult to help them resume a life where they are not victimized. Street children often survive on one meal a day; others get by on scraps from restaurants. In South America, children will use drugs to suppress their hunger. The young are particularly vulnerable to sexually transmitted diseases, especially AIDS, about which they know very little. Children and young people on the streets are exposed to a whole range of negative influences which usually cause a disturbed adult life.

What is available to help these young people? There are a number of organizations that attempt to study the exploitation of children and create opportunities for them to escape to a better life, although there are limitations. In Rio de Janiero, there are more than 600 private groups which tend to the needs of Rio's street children. To succeed off the streets it is necessary to avoid drugs and return to school; many of these children have suffered for so long they no longer have the initiative needed to make the change. In Bogota there is also help available for the sewer children, but many of these children are addicted to drugs and prefer to stay where they are free to take them. These children also find it difficult to be reintegrated into family life. They want to be respected and live a healthy life but because of the abuse they need far more support than is generally available.

The Bonded Liberation Front organization in India and Pakistan is one of the organizations trying to help bonded labourers, especially children. The law states that all bonded labourers who go to court and ask to be freed, will be. However, few labourers know how to proceed. The Bonded Liberation Front attempts to provide that help. Sometimes, because the labourers are so accustomed to being dominated, they fall back into bondage after being released. These workers have feelings of inferiority which lead them to continue submitting to a master. As one slave, Mbarek, of Mauritania, said recently, "A master is a master and a slave is a slave."

Governments have also passed laws restricting child labour and have made rules as to who is employable, but it is often difficult to enforce these laws in developing countries due to a lack of funds. The industrialized countries have suggested **boycotts** of products produced by children, but the developing world is critical of such measures. A more realistic goal, they often say, is to work towards making the lives of child labourers happier and healthier by insisting on more humane working conditions, fewer hours of employment, and some access to educational opportunities and leisure time.

However, there have been some successes in helping these children. For example, the United Nations Children's Fund (UNICEF) reported recently that 80 percent of the world's children have been immunized; only

10 percent had been immunized by the late 1970s. UNICEF also helps by providing clean water, sanitation, adequate nutrition, health care, and education to as many children born into poverty as its funds allow.

In Bogota, Jaime Jaramillo, a wealthy petroleum engineer, runs a series of shelters which provide a home for some of the city's former street and sewer children. He has gone into the sewers to rescue the children himself, and often provides food to those he has not yet succeeded in tempting to leave. More than 300 children are now in the care of his foundation. His greatest successes have been in obtaining jobs in the petroleum industry for some of these former lost children.

In Canada, a charitable organization called Street Kids International (SKI) has a number of projects, mainly in the developing world, but also in Canada, to assist children who live on the streets. For example, in Bangalore, India and Khartoum, Sudan, SKI operates a courier service employing street children. They deliver parcels, documents, and newspapers by bicycle each day after they have had an hour and a half of schooling. SKI also operates a shoe-shine cooperative in Santo Domingo, Dominican Republic, that employs street children. In Lusaka, Zambia, and Dar-

es-Salaam, Tanzania, SKI has opened drop-in centres for street youth. These centres are designed to provide a safe place for children to wash their clothes, have a shower, eat a

SOURCE: Street Kids International

Fig. 3-39 *These eight boys were the first group of recruits for the Bangalore SKI Courier Service. They are very proud of their achievements.*

hot meal, and receive basic health care. In Canada, SKI supports a program for Toronto inner-city youth focussing on adventure and skill-building in an outdoor setting.

Through such efforts, both locally and internationally, some children are being offered a chance for a better life. It is clear, though, that much remains to be done.

FURTHER ANALYSIS

1. Refer to your library's vertical files or computer search program to find other success stories where children who work are being helped towards a better life.

2. In groups of three or four suggest how the future of the world's peoples would be different from what they are now if every child learned to read. Report your ideas to the whole class for further discussion.

3. A number of Canadian companies refuse to do business with foreign companies that employ child labour on their production lines. List the possible consequences, both domestically and internationally, if Canadians did not allow such products into Canada.

CHAPTER
4

CULTURE AND POLITICS

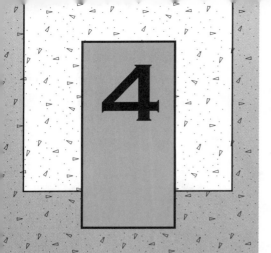

CULTURE AND POLITICS

When different groups of people interact, issues arise. People become members of some groups at birth. In size, such groups range from the immediate family to the major world religions. In type, they also include ethnic groups and national groups.

Fig. 4-1 *A group of Canadian high school students stage a demonstration for their rights at the Board of Education offices. What rights do you think students should have?*

People may also belong to other groups out of choice. These groups include political parties which reflect different social and economic belief systems. Political parties may be formal, seeking election, such as (alphabetically) the Liberal, New Democratic, Progressive Conservative, and Reform parties in Canada. They may also be informal, seeking to influence elected representatives to particular courses of action, in which case they are often called lobby groups. An example of a lobby group is the National Action Committee on the Status of Women. If their chosen attempts at influence are violent in nature, they may also be called terrorist groups, freedom fighters, secret police, or the military, depending upon one's point of view.

Other groups people may choose to join include religions — provided religious conversion is accepted by the potential receiving religion — and nations — provided immigrants are accepted as citizens by the potential receiving nation. Nations vary in their acceptance of immigrants; they vary even more in their granting of citizenship to immigrants. Germany, for example, accepts many immigrants. In the 1960s it searched for immigrants to act largely as factory and municipal workers but it granted citizenship to none of them, unless they could prove a Germanic ethnic heritage. Few could, so that Germany today has millions of immigrants who are denied citizenship.

Below the level of these large groups lies a further set of groups, mostly reflecting combinations of people with similar, generally peaceful, interests, such as athletes, hobbyists, musicians, and members of such organizations as the International Red Cross and Red Cresent.

Groups of people, however they originate, tend to develop strong **group cultures**. The reasons are rooted in whatever cultural qualities the individuals in the groups have in common with other members: bloodties, heritage, language, religion, beliefs, history, traditions, or interests. The more numerous the factors, or the more important they are, the stronger the group bonds tend to be. In some cases, the strength of group bonds is illustrated by the willingness of people to risk death for their group.

Strong group cultures may have great effects upon the quality of life experienced by individuals. People whose values correspond closely with those of their group culture may feel a strong sense of personal fulfilment, and experience a satisfying quality of life regardless of their actual standard of living. It is therefore the aim of many community leaders in materially poor areas to foster a strong sense of group culture to enhance satisfaction with the quality of life. Religion frequently plays a large part in these efforts, so that, for example, religious leaders in materially poor areas are usually also important community leaders. Equally, people whose values largely conflict with those of the dominant group culture may feel out of place and alienated. Such people are likely to experience an unsatisfactory quality of life, also regardless of actual standard of living. Are there any current examples?

For example, there is almost unanimous agreement among nations that release of chlorofluorocarbons (CFCs) damages the upper atmospheric ozone layer, but there is much disagreement about the pace of elimination of CFCs.

Interaction between groups may be peaceful or confrontational. There are many examples of peaceful cooperation between groups, which rarely generates issues except when people disagree about the extent, nature, or pace of cooperation. Examples of cooperation at the level of national governments include the work of the United Nations and numerous international treaties and trade agreements. There are also many examples of international cooperation by non-government organizations (NGOs), such as Human Rights Watch and Amnesty International.

When interaction between groups is confrontational, human rights are sometimes an issue. For example, the human rights of members of one group may be attacked both collectively and individually. Such attacks may be approved by the government, as in the case of China, where political opponents may be held in prison without trial. In 1993, the world's largest clothing manufacturer, Levi Strauss Inc., announced that it would make no investments in China, and terminate all existing contracts with Chinese firms, because of what the company called "pervasive violations of basic human rights" by the Chinese. Attacks may also occur without government approval, as in Germany, where a number of Turkish immigrants were killed by German extremists in the 1990s.

Each year, the United Nations Commission on Human Rights receives about 400 000 complaints of human rights violations from individual victims, their families, and groups such as Amnesty International who act on behalf of others. The complaints involve cases of abductions, arbitrary killings, detention, torture, religious intolerance, and the sale of children for pornography and prostitution. The Commission appeals to accused governments regularly, and sends investigative teams that often fail to achieve government cooperation. Human rights abuses continue.

The Universal Declaration of Human Rights was adopted by the United Nations in 1948. The declaration was strengthened in 1968 by the Proclamation of Teheran, which stated that the declaration had the status of international law and was binding on all nations. There are 29 points in the declaration, starting with the declaration that "all human beings are born free and equal in dignity and rights." The declaration further notes that everyone is entitled to all the rights and freedoms set out in the declaration, "without distinction of any kind, such as race, colour, sex, language, religion, political or other opinion, national or social origin, property, birth, or other status."

Among the rights to which all human beings are entitled, the declaration lists a variety of civil and political rights such as life, liberty, freedom from torture, equality before the law, freedom of movement (including emigration), ownership of property, and freedom of opinion and expression. The declaration also lists a variety of economic, social, and cultural rights, including free choice of employment, equal pay for equal work, unhindered trade union membership, a standard of living suitable for health and well-being, social security, economic development, and free participation in the cultural life of the community.

In 1993, the United Nations organized the World Conference on Human Rights, held in Vienna, in order to reaffirm the major thrust of the declaration: that human rights are universal and indivisible. Many countries reject some of these rights, arguing that they are contrary to the beliefs and practices of their traditional local culture. For example, Malaysia has argued that certain democratic freedoms, such as equality before the law, are un-Islamic (Islamic law treats men and women differently, for instance). Other countries take the view that human rights are universal, and that local cultural traditions must be secondary.

There is deep disagreement about this issue. At the World Conference on Human Rights, several countries, led by China and Iran, argued that their national circumstances were their own affair, and that other nations should not interfere. The Secretary General of the United Nations, Boutros Boutros-Ghali, supported by the United States, argued in rebuttal that arguments for non-interference were made to hide human rights violations, and that "sovereignty by authoritarian regimes in order to conceal their abuse of men, women, and children…is already condemned by history."

Further, because of the importance of human rights in the overall quality of life of any nation, such cultural disagreements among nations produce corresponding disagreements over the quality of life. If, by common consent, people in any country place traditional cultural values ahead of universal human rights, who shall say they experience a lower quality of life? Indeed, such group cohesion around its traditional values may be felt by the members of the group to yield a higher quality of life. This topic is also examined in Chapter Five.

This chapter examines some examples of both peaceful and confrontational interaction arising among ethnic, religious, economic, and political groups. As you go through the following readings, classify each topic as an example of either peaceful or confrontational interaction. Some may be difficult to classify. Note the nature of the groups involved in the interaction in each reading, and write down an analysis of the forces that appear to motivate the groups.

NATIVE STRANGER

Women fought side by side with men to liberate Eritrea. Now they are in a new struggle to make sure women's rights remain a vital part of the Eritrean revolution. Elsa Gebreyesus went to do her part.

The high-pitched ululation (wailing) splits the quiet morning air at Asmara airport. As we cross the tarmac, the woman in front of me pauses to express her joy at returning home to Eritrea after who knows how many years of exile. For me, an Eritrean by heritage, it is the first time on my native soil. Tears trickle down my face and I join her ululations.

I was not born in Eritrea, but instead grew up moving from country to country, eventually settling in Canada. But my primary identity was always Eritrean, even if I only saw my homeland in pictures or on maps. Most of the people I know back in North America have no idea what it feels like to learn another culture, language and way of life while trying to keep one's own precious culture and customs alive. But now I have come to see with my own eyes the birth pangs of my people as together we take the first steps towards becoming an independent nation.

Asmara, the capital of Eritrea, is our largest city with

some 350 000 people, but it has more the feel of a big neighbourhood. Those who live there behave like members of an extended family giving life a lightness and a warm sense of security. For me this contrasts sharply with the West where there is little empathy and strangers are ghosts or apparitions that happen to occupy the same time and space.

I had expected that years of famine and military rule would leave people obsessed by how much death and devastation had been visited upon this one small place. Or perhaps recent violence would not loosen its grip, leaving people volatile and likely to strike out at any time. To my surprise I saw nothing but patience in people's eyes, heard nothing but gentleness in their voices and hope in their words.

I had promised myself that when I returned I would work with the women of Eritrea. How do Eritrean women live in a strict patriarchal culture where traditions are lead weights on their minds, bodies and souls? Was there something in me that came from them — perhaps this was a source of the strength I had used in overcoming my own barriers.

I knew that the women of Eritrea had an equal claim with men to self-determination. They earned that status in the liberation struggle. So I contacted the foreign office of the National Union of Eritrean Women (NUEW) and offered my services.

Freedom did not come easily to Eritrea. This I know when I see the hundreds of fighters wounded in the war, or the massive destruction of some of our cities. The price of our freedom is counted in lives lost — not least the lives of women. The level of women's participation in the

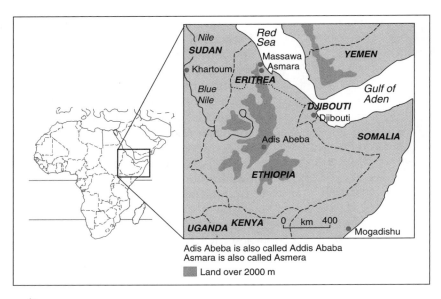

Fig. 4-2 *Eritrea and Ethiopia.*

Eritrean liberation war was unique. Women overcame deeply rooted patriarchal traditions to stand with men on the...front or join in the attack on Massawa.

Women's participation increased as the Eritrean People's Liberation Front (EPLF) replaced the more religious-based Eritrean Liberation Front in the forefront of the war. By 1979 women were 13 percent of the fighters and 30 percent of the EPLF as a whole. These women were no mere support group for men. They were trained to use different types of arms and worked as mechanics, drivers and doctors.

This took a lot of work on everyone's part. Both men and women had to leap a number of cultural and social barriers. Men simply did not believe that women had the emotional and physical strength to fight. Many women were themselves unsure.

I believe that the femininity of women fighters was strengthened by their ability to endure

hardship. All soldiers lived with death staring them in the face and with few in the outside world knowing or caring about the horror of their war. But in one way the women were better off than men.

For men, to let out their emotions, admit their fears and cry was a sign of weakness. They had to hide these feelings. Women, on the other hand, did cry. Despite all their training as soldiers, they were never afraid to weep after overcoming difficult situations, and so were stronger to move on.

The first thing a woman did on arriving at the front was to cut off her hair — culturally a sign of beauty. This eliminated any outward sign of physical attractiveness and was not only a practical step but a symbolic action, severing ties to past social beliefs and strengthening present commitments.

A new form of gender-neutral greeting also evolved in the

field. In Eritrean culture women kiss three times on the cheek and men shake hands — unless they know each other well, in which case they also kiss. But in the field the new form of greeting became the shoulder kiss whereby people rub and bump shoulders while shaking hands. This genderless greeting is beautiful to watch and has eliminated the social uncertainty of whom to kiss and whom not to.

Innovations were also made in religious practices to eliminate divisions but still keep ceremonies sacred. Everyone who joined the EPLF, whether Christian or Muslim, had to distinguish their loyalty to liberation from personal loyalties. So it was decided that at all sacred ceremonies which involved fighters the space formerly occupied by prayer would be occupied by silence. This respected everyone's point of view, while creating a binding ritual for those who believed in liberation.

In many Third World countries...women participated in the liberation struggle but found their rights placed on the back burner once independence had been achieved. It is only natural to ask what precautions Eritrean women are taking to avoid this fate.

They are up against a deeply rooted patriarchal culture which traditionally gives them little chance to be independent. From early childhood young girls are taught their "inherent" roles as respectable daughters, wives, mothers and homemakers. Their families are expected to come first. And often an individual woman is identified as her father's daughter, which erases her individuality. These paternal strings affect a woman's future marriage or inheritance and her respectability, and women are forever on their guard not to do or say anything that might be considered unfitting. So they evolve a double personality — one that knows what to say when dealing

with the outside world, and one with opinions and dreams hidden deep inside.

Organizations like the National Union of Eritrean Women (NUEW) are well aware of the issues women will have to face. At present they are establishing themselves as an independent grassroots organization able to lead the fight. The Union is not wealthy but is supported by a loyal and growing membership.

I have faith in a positive future for women in Eritrea. The tradition of women's resistance has forged a new identity for them that can never be erased. Now (that) they have begun the long journey towards self-empowerment and liberation, my hope is that they will never be stopped.

Elsa Gebreyesus, *New Internationalist*, 1992 12

Elsa Gebreyesus works as a project officer with the National Union of Eritrean Women in Asmara.

RECESSION SEEN AS FUELLING FIRES OF INTOLERANCE

Sometimes it's blatant: a burning cross in the darkness outside Provost (Alberta), or slurs sprayed on the sides of homes, stores and places of worship.

Other times it's subtle: a joke some people find uncomfortable; cabs passed on because of the driver's colour....

• • • • •

"Calgary presents this pretty face, but there's definitely a lot of racism out there," says Isobel Rainey, president of the Citizens Against Racial and Religious Discrimination.

"People won't come out and identify themselves as being racist, of course. Nobody speaks freely about it."

Violet Marin does not consider herself one.

"It's not right to be racist of any kind," says Marin, 64. "But I feel that the immigrants should take a few knocks before they get the privileges that our children do not have."

Federal immigration policies offering newly arrived Canadians housing incentives and subsidized courses create an unlevel playing field — one penalizing young males like her son Vincent in their quest for jobs.

"I don't care who you are — black, white, green or purple — I

still want the same chance as you do," Marin says. "Racism is alive and well, and it'll get worse in this country if we don't get our young people back to work."

That's the catch: according to University of Calgary psychology professor Michael Boyes, **xenophobia** — or the morbid dislike of foreigners — is generally heightened during periods of recession and high unemployment.

Xenophobia has spread rapidly throughout Europe — now home to millions of Third World refugees — and many feel with unemployment hovering around 12 percent and the economy sputtering, Canada won't be far behind.

Ottawa is already under renewed pressure to limit immigration, and although racial tension is far from explosive, there's still concern we're headed towards ghettoized neighborhoods and an increase in racially motivated violence.

"People need scapegoats — someone to blame because you don't seem to be able to make things work the way you used to," Boyes explains. "It's an us-against-them mentality."

A 1991 survey conducted by pollster Angus Reid for Multiculturalism and Citizenship Canada found Canadians less comfortable with people from the following groups: Indo-Pakistanis, Sikhs, West Indian Blacks, Arabs and Muslims.

The same study found 32 percent of Canadians felt it was best if immigrants forgot their cultural backgrounds as soon as possible. That compared with 28 percent in 1974.

Assuming current immigration policies and demographic trends continue, by the year 2030 about one in four Albertans is likely to be a first-generation immigrant.

Real-estate agents are already noticing a "colour barrier." ...

"Customers won't come right out and say a choice is racially motivated." says a senior manager with a local real-estate company, who doesn't want his name used. "But you know that's what they're thinking."

He says people know the "colour" of an area, and may request to live in certain parts of the city because they are perceived as having white schools and services. The requests, he adds, are increasing geometrically throughout the city.

People also request white drivers when they call a cab company. That happens often enough that the Human Rights Commission did a study three years ago of potential racial and ethnic discrimination in Alberta's taxi industry.

It focused on Edmonton, and ultimately cleared the industry of racism even though 60 percent of the drivers interviewed thought discrimination was being practised.

There was almost no evidence of customers calling to request white-only drivers, but the drivers said racism is regularly evident at taxi stands when minority drivers are passed over for white ones.

Studies suggest that racial intolerance is passed from parents to children the same way bad driving habits are passed, or poor table manners.

• • • • •

Boyes points out that kids pick up cues from their parents at an early stage. There are also studies to suggest that children lose their racial tolerance as they progress from elementary school to junior high and on to high school, but the jury is out whether that has more to do with racism at home or values acquired through peers and the community.

Karen Lazaruk, an 18-year-old high-school graduate, never sensed any serious racism at her school. "I never heard any name-calling or stuff."

But she did notice adults consistently seemed more preoccupied with immigrants and minorities than their kids.

Gail Kingwell, who supervises multicultural programs with the public school board's department of curriculum, says racism in the school system appears to be declining.

Reginald Bibby, a University of Lethbridge sociology professor, says...there's been a decline in prejudice nationwide since the mid-1970s adding about ten percent of the population are bigots.

If the prevalence seems greater than that, he says, it's because the media is largely to blame for giving racism larger-than-life coverage.

Chris Dawson, *Calgary Herald Writer*, The *Edmonton Journal*, 1993 4 4

A CELEBRATION OF BLACK HISTORY

It is Boxing Day, with turkey leftovers in the refrigerator, scraps of wrapping paper strewn everywhere and an odd feeling of emptiness.

But for millions of people of African descent around the world, this is a day to begin a new celebration that owes nothing at all to Santa Claus. While you're saying "Pass the Pepto-Bismol," they are exchanging greetings in Swahili: *Habari gani.*

Kwanzaa is a seven-day holiday, beginning today, initiated by black Americans and now marked by an estimated 18 million people in the United States, Canada, Britain, and African countries such as Kenya and Zimbabwe.

Maulana Karenga was a young doctoral student when he looked around at the destruction caused by the 1965 riots in the Watts district of Los Angeles and began his search for something to unify blacks.

Mr. Karenga was deeply involved in the 1960s black-power movement and consciously reached back into African history and fashioned a synthesis of various agricultural festivals. He called it Kwanzaa after the Swahili word for "first fruits."

"The question was 'What could we borrow from the past to give more meaning and fullness to our lives on which to build our future?'" Mr. Karenga, now chairperson of the black-studies department at California State University at Long Beach, said in an interview.

Unlike Christmas and Chanukah, Kwanzaa is not a religious holiday, so ethnic Africans of all faiths can and do celebrate it.

The purpose of the holiday, as Dr. Karenga saw it, was the "re-Africanization" of blacks. From the beginning, the celebration of "family, community and culture" had a political meaning in the deepest sense of the word.

"I believe culture is a fundamental part of struggle and that until you break the monopoly the oppressor has on our mind, liberation is not only impossible but unthinkable," Mr. Karenga said.

The seven days of the celebration highlight the seven principles of Kwanzaa. Each day, a candle is lit and placed in a seven-cup candelabrum called a *kinara* that sits on a straw mat adorned with fruit and vegetables.

The participants discuss the principles or *Nguzo Saba* of Kwanzaa: unity, self-determination, collective responsibility, cooperative economics, purpose, creativity and faith. On the final night of the holiday, friends and relatives gather for a feast known as *Karamu*.

Gift-giving is not a fundamental part of Kwanzaa, although books and symbols of African heritage are often exchanged.

"What we're doing," Mr. Karenga said, "is giving community values as opposed to the vulgar individualism of the dominant society."

In recent years, as it gained popularity, Kwanzaa has picked up the label of "the black Christmas." But Mr. Karenga bristles at the characterization. "This is a cultural holiday, not a religious holiday."

Indeed, the celebration was placed between Christmas and New Year's partly to honour African harvest festivals but also to avoid the pre-Christmas commercialism and to provide an alternative to Christmas.

The celebration caught on quickly among black nationalists looking for an alternative to the European-inspired events that dominated in the United States. In recent years it has similarly attracted the interest of more moderate blacks looking for a return to root values.

In Washington, D.C., churches hold nightly observances and the Smithsonian has added a program of Kwanzaa activities to its Christmas and Chanukah celebrations. In New York there have been poetry readings and music performances at the American Museum of Natural History, and in Toronto the red, green and black colours of Kwanzaa have become familiar to some students.

Yolanda Anderson, assistant principal at Crenshaw High School in a predominantly black area of Los Angeles, said she has noticed a surge in interest among her students in the past few years.

"As they become more aware of the ties to Africa," she said, "they will be more appreciative and more involved."

Several books about the celebration have been published, including Mr. Karenga's own authoritative guide and a compendium of recipes that can be used during the week. Greeting cards are being mar-

keted and there are reports that Christmas-style gift-giving is becoming fashionable.

Indeed, there seems to be a relentless attempt in some quarters to commercialize the celebration, a pressure symbolized by the creation by one author of an African wise man, Nia Umoja, who is portrayed as "an African answer to Santa Claus."

Mr. Karenga is having none of this. He advises, for example, that the best kinara are those made at home from driftwood, and he suggests that children should become versed in the seven principles and not be reduced to "mere recipients of gifts."

Despite Kwanzaa's roots in the Watts disturbances, Mr. Karenga dismisses a suggestion that the civil unrest last spring in Los Angeles ought to have made Kwanzaa more relevant to a new generation of young blacks.

For a start, he said, the 1992 events were different from those a generation earlier because they were not specifically grounded in the culture of the black-power movement.

"You have a different kind of revolt in 1992," he said. "It's shorter and there's less willingness (on the part) of the participants to bear the burden of struggle."

But beyond that, he argued that Kwanzaa must be seen as something positive that transcends violence or the social problems that afflict some portions of the black community.

"Kwanzaa has an independent relevance," he said. "It's a cultural celebration. It's the glue that holds us together. It's not something that responds to episodic events."

Murray Campbell, California Bureau, *The Globe and Mail*, 1992 12 26

BEING BLACK DOESN'T MEAN BEING AFRICAN

...I cannot help feeling that the recent shift toward Afro-centrism among blacks in the United States and Canada is a step away from the light of realism to the shadow areas of racism. The only difference this time is that it is a few blacks, and not whites, who are asking people to accept simplistic solutions.

Proponents of Afro-centrism claim Africa as their own, and in doing this they do a double disservice: to the people of Africa and to the hard-earned heritage of blacks in North America.

Africa is a continent of 800 million people, speaking thousands of languages and dialects. Each area, each region, each province and country has a distinct culture and history.

This is why I cringe when I see black North Americans wearing Kente cloth caps and celebrating pseudo holidays like Kwanzaa.

The Kente pattern that is used to make caps, scarves and other badges of Africanness is from Ghana. Kwanzaa is taken from Swahili — a language of Eastern Africa.

By borrowing freely and from opposite ends of the continent, proponents of Afro-centrism show the same attitude toward Africa as the colonial powers did in the past. While the colonialists drew political boundaries without regard for indigenous cultures, proponents of the motherland are asking people to disregard existing distinctions among the peoples of Africa.

• • • • •

Expressing a connection to one's heritage is necessary and good, but blind imitation and

SOURCE: Canada Wide

Fig. 4-3 *Rosemary Brown has contributed to Canadian society as a women's rights activist and in 1993 was appointed Commissioner of the Ontario Human Rights Commission.*

neglect of the present is untenable.

If one celebrates culture from Africa, then the immediate question must be which culture? Which language does one speak? Mandingo, Arabic, Ibo, Yoruba, Swahili or Amharic? Do you practise Islam, animism, ancestor worship or Christianity?

Eddy Harris, a travel writer and a black American, journeyed north to south through Africa. In his book *Native Stranger*, he writes that he went to Africa to discover the "line" which connects him to the continent.

Mr. Harris found, as have others who have travelled to Africa to "find themselves," that the colour of one's skin means little in Africa, "that something as subtle as culture (means) infinitely more than something as overt and obvious (as) the colour of (a person's) skin."

Mr. Harris's journey ends at the southern tip of the continent,

where he concludes: "My skin is black. My culture is not."

• • • • •

The greater problem posed by Afro-centrists in their blind embrace of African cultures is the eclipse of the considerable contributions made by blacks on this continent....By romanticizing Africa, Afro-centrists neglect the scientific and artistic contributions of blacks.

In Canada, black history stretches back an incredible three and a half centuries to 1629. I am willing to bet that this important fact has barely caused a blip on Afro-centrist screens.

People like William Hall, the first Canadian to receive the Victoria Cross; Dr. Charles Drew, American founder of the first blood bank; jazzman John Coltrane, anti-apartheid crusader Randy Robinson, women's-rights activist Rosemary Brown, and many, many more, have all contributed immensely to Canadian and U.S. society. Many other countless, anonymous and unnoticed black lives have gone into the building of North America. By focusing exclusively on Africa, Afro-centrists are attempting to give away ownership of the only heritage blacks truly own.

Blacks must claim their rightful place in Canadian and American society. This does not mean anyone should forget the very real connection to Africa that exists. But, as Gerald Early recently wrote in Harper's, "It must always be remembered that our blood is here, our names are here, our fate is here, in a land we helped to invent."

Zahir Paryani, *The Globe and Mail*, 1993 3 16

THE SINISTER IDEOLOGY OF "ETHNIC CLEANSING"

BELGRADE — A chilling new term, spawned in Yugoslavia, recently entered the international political vocabulary: "ethnic cleansing." The Serbs use it in public only to describe the practices of their enemies. Equally, Croats and Muslims employ the term when denouncing the murders, internment of civilians, expulsions and seizures of property suffered by members of their communities in Serbian-controlled areas.

According to the Belgrade-based historian Andrej Mitrovic, the notion of "ethnic cleansing" and its resultant policy first appeared in the region during World War II under the Nazi puppet regime of Ante Pavelic in Croatia. He adds, however, that the notion has always been "naturally" inherent in the ideologies of major national movements in the Balkans, whether in the Greece of 1830 or more recently in Serbia, Montenegro, and Bulgaria.

In such cases, Mitrovic argues, it was a "normal" policy designed to restore ethnic structures after various invasions and was implemented "painlessly." It was only just before the last war that the policy took a more violent turn under the influence of 19th-century racist ideas resuscitated by Hitler.

Mitrovic admits that once it had been used by Croatian extremists like Pavelic and Branko Jelic the doctrine probably held attractions for Serbs thirsting for revenge after the terrible atrocities carried out against them by Croats between 1941 and 1945.

When the pro-Nazi Ustache Party took power in Zagreb in April 1941 and proclaimed an independent state of Croatia, its leader Pavelic was the first to resort to "ethnic cleansing," hounding Jews, gypsies, and, above all, Serbs, whom he accused of being members of the orthodox church of Constantinople.

The policy was an official one: it was quite openly proclaimed that, of the 600 000 Serbs then living in Croatia, "a third would have to convert, a third expatriate themselves, and a third die." The Muslims of Bosnia-Herzegovina (then part of Croatia) were regarded by Pavelic as Muslim Croats and thus escaped genocide.

At about the same time the Serbs were also attracted by the doctrine of "ethnic cleansing." In their book *The Genocide of the Muslims*, two historians, the Croat Antun Miletic and the Serb Vladimir Dedjer, describe the "Stevan Moljevic plan" of June 1941. This plan for a "homogeneous (uniform) Serbia" called for the restoration, when the war was over, of a Greater Serbia "in all ethnic territories in which Serbs live," and advocated "the expulsion and permutation (rearrangement) of inhabitants, mainly Croats from Serbian territories and Serbs from Croatian territories."

The plan was complemented in September 1941 by the programme of the Serbian Chetnik movement led by Draza Mihajlovic. It suggested that there should be a "de facto (real, but without legal authority) demarcation of the frontiers of Serbian territory," within which the population would consist solely of Serbs, and that "the cities should be radically cleansed and filled with fresh Serb elements."

Three months later Mihajlovic instructed the commanders of his forces "to create an ethnically pure Greater Serbia within the frontiers of Serbia, Montenegro, Bosnia-Herzegovina, Srem, Backa, and Banat..., to purge the state, territory of all national minorities and all non-Serbian elements..., and to carry out a purge of the Muslim inhabitants of Serbia and the Muslim and Croatian inhabitants of Bosnia."

As for the demarcation of the frontier with the Croats, the leader of the Chetniks ordered that "as soon as the opportunity arises all territories marked on the map should be taken and cleansed before the enemy has a chance to react."

Mihajlovic, who rebelled against the Croats but also fell out with the Communists, was defeated by Tito's partisans (Tito was the leader of the Yugoslav Communist Party from 1937 to 1980) and eventually shot in 1946. Despite the Chetniks' exactions (oppressive acts), particularly against Muslims in eastern Bosnia, Georges Castellan, a French expert on the Balkans, is of the opinion that they cannot be accused of genocide.

Today, the repression which Bosnian Muslims and the non-Serb inhabitants of Serbian-occupied Croatia are desperately seeking to escape goes once again under the name of "ethnic cleansing." It would seem that the people responsible for dredging up that sinister ideology were 16 members of the Belgrade Academy of Sciences and Arts, in a memorandum they wrote and circulated secretly in 1986.

The text was largely conceived by Dobrica Cosic, the nationalist writer who last May became president of the "new Yugoslavia" (Serbia and Montenegro) and is regarded as the spiritual father of the Serbian leader, Slobodan Milosevic.

The memorandum never got beyond the draft stage, because it was exposed in September 1986 by Alexandar Djukanovic, a journalist on the Belgrade daily *Vecernje Novosti*. He described the document, extracts of which were published by his paper, as "anti-Communist and nationalist," and saw it as a "further appeal for a fratricidal war and yet another bloodbath."

The memorandum, which attacked four decades of Communist rule and listed all the

SOURCE: Marilyn MacKenzie

Fig. 4-4 *This is Mostar in southeastern Bosnia. It was the scene of heavy fighting in the 1990s. The bridge, built in the 16th century, was destroyed in November, 1993. What evidence does the photograph provide that the city contained many Muslims?*

frustrations of the Serbs, advocated "the defence of the Serbian people" against the threat of "discrimination" by the Croat Tito and the Slovene Edvard Kardelj, who, through the 1974 constitution, executed their plan to confederate the Yugoslav state by restoring full sovereignty to the country's six republics and two autonomous provinces.

According to Cosic, now the most influential member of the Belgrade regime, the 1974 constitution resulted in the dismemberment of Yugoslavia and placed Serbia and the Serbs in a position of downright inequality.

In his view, not all the nations in the Yugoslav Federation had been treated equally: the Serb nation had not obtained its own state. On top of that, members of the Serb population who lived in other republics enjoyed no rights and suffered from ethnic discrimination.

Such arguments are not new. The academicians responsible for the 1986 memorandum pointed out that Serbs living in Croatia, whose numbers had already sharply decreased as a result of genocide during the last war, accounted for a decreasing percentage of the population of Croatia (11.5 percent in 1981, as against 14.5 percent in 1948). They also stressed that the regions where Serbs were in the majority (Lika, Kordun, and Banja) were the least developed parts of Croatia. The economic backwardness of those areas had "encouraged Serbs to emigrate to Serbia or to parts of Croatia where they were in a minority, treated like an inferior social group and forced to assimilate."

The academicians also noted that, "apart from the period when the independent state of Croatia existed, Croatian Serbs have never been under such threat as they are today. The settlement of their national status is therefore a political priority." They warned that "unless a solution is found, there will be disastrous consequences not only for Croatia but for the whole of Yugoslavia."

So from 1986 on, Belgrade launched into a new crusade to arouse the Serbian national conscience — a crusade which was soon joined by the young Communist leader Milosevic, and which eventually led to the barbaric upsurge of Serbian nationalism at the beginning of the 90s.

At that time there was talk not of "ethnic cleansing" but of restoring to the Serbs all their "historical, national, and democratic rights to live in a single state." Cosic argued along precisely those lines in a text on "Yugoslavia and the Serbian question" published in January 1991. Such a state could be a "democratic and federative Yugoslavia," but only if all the peoples living in it wanted it to be.

The Serbs, he went on, had no reason to stop the Croats or the Slovenes seceding from Yugoslavia and creating their own autonomous states if they so desired. "But they will be able to create them only on their ethnic territories. If they also do so by annexing Serbian ethnic territories they will be invaders and warmongers." The present president of the new Yugoslavia wrote those words over a year and a half ago. The rest of the story is familiar.

Cosic's policy entails a de facto displacement of populations or, to put it another way, a change in the ethnic structure of those territories to which the Serbs lay claim but in which they are no longer in the majority. Hence the need to "cleanse" the so-called "Serbian lands" in both Bosnia, Croatia, and Vojvodina, the multinational autonomous province in northern Serbia, which was once part of the Austro-Hungarian Empire, then annexed to Serbia just before the creation of the first Yugoslavia.

Even if the architects of Serbian nationalist policy like Cosic have not specifically called for "ethnically pure" territories, that ambition has become one of their unavowed policies. From the start of the conflict, the Serbs have banked on the principle of the fait accompli. It so happens that "ethnic cleansing" has the "advan-

tage" of being a process that is difficult to reverse.

However, it is an ideology that can backfire by reviving the thirst for revenge on the part of the communities subjected to "cleansing." About half of Zagreb's 100 000 Serbs, fearing Croatian resentment, have made themselves very scarce. They are thought to have sought refuge in Belgrade.

In western Slavonia, the Croats have gone in for out-and-out "cleansing" — destroying Serbs' homes. The fighting in Bosnia makes assessment of the situation there difficult. But the independent Belgrade newspaper *Borba* reported on August 22 (1992) that Serbian civilians living in the centre of Sarajevo had been expelled from their homes and murdered.

The paper noted that, even in a situation where Serbs were themselves besieged and had shown solidarity with the other inhabitants of Sarajevo, they eventually fell victim to hostility and reprisals.

Florence Hartmann, *Le Monde*, Paris, France, 1992 8 30-31

LONELY CRIES OF DISTRUST

· · · · ·

Across the country, in court battles, in land-claims negotiations and at the constitutional table, First Nations peoples are asserting their right to substantial swaths of resource-rich land — and their inherent right to govern that land. The First Nations peoples' claims draw their authority from the past, stretching from their millennia-long occupancy of the land to 19th-century treaties, once-forgotten colonial laws and the Supreme Court of Canada's emerging definition of existing aboriginal and treaty rights. Politicians can no longer ignore those claims: in June, 1990, Cree legislator Elijah Harper effectively killed the Meech Lake constitutional accord when he blocked its introduction in the Manitoba legislature because it failed to address First Nations peo-

ples' demands. Harper argued that the accord recognized Quebec's place in Canada, but that it ignored First Nations peoples' rights and contributions. Partly as a result, many Canadians began to take another hard look at their nation's troubled history. Says University of Saskatchewan law professor Donna Greschner: "Non-aboriginal Canadians cannot pretend that the past does not exist. If non-aboriginal Canadians truly believe in justice for aboriginal peoples, we must face up to our responsibility for the profoundly racist policies of the past — and for their continuing legacy."

...Initial encounters between the two groups were usually respectful: from the 16th to the 18th century, First Nations peoples were valued trading partners and skilled military allies. But that relationship degenerated after the War of 1812 as the immigrant population swelled and the number of external threats to Canadian sovereignty dwindled. As a minority in their own lands, First Nations peoples rapidly lost power. Governments set out to minimize their land base and to force their assimilation....

• • • • •

In many cases, the government's repressive approach clearly worked against its own goal of assimilation. Under the terms of the first Indian Act, which took effect in 1876, Indians lost their status if they became doctors, lawyers or ministers; the price of education was the loss of traditional identity. In 1894, western Indians were compelled to enrol their children in schools run by missionaries, the price of basic learning was a childhood away from their families in an often abusive and disease-ridden environment. Finally, because the Royal Proclamation of 1763 stipulated that Indians could cede title to their lands only to the Crown, Indians could not mortgage their reserve lands to obtain capital for economic projects. For many, the price of community living was often poverty.

• • • • •

First Nations peoples in Canada received little benefit from Confederation. The Constitution Act of 1867 observed that "Indians and lands reserved for the Indians" were under the exclusive jurisdiction of the federal government. With that power, through 11 so-called numbered treaties between 1871 and 1921, Ottawa negotiated title to vast swaths of the West in exchange for reserves, gifts such as medicine chests, and annual payments to First Nations peoples. Still, land-cession treaties did not cover the Maritimes, northern Quebec, most of British Columbia and the Arctic. The reasons for that neglect were varied, ranging from lack of funds to carelessness to the simple assumption that legislatures had unilaterally taken title to the long-settled parts of the country....

Without power or land, riven by disease and poverty, First Nations peoples in Canada were slow to rediscover their pride. The modern First Nations peoples' movement emerged in 1969, when the Liberal government of Pierre Trudeau unveiled proposals to abrogate the treaties, repeal the Indian Act and transfer responsibility for Indian programs to the provinces. The government's proposals also dismissed the concept of "aboriginal rights," countering that continuing Indian claims to the land were "so general and undefined that it is not realistic to think of them as specific claims capable of remedy." First Nations peoples reacted with fury. Their fledgling national organizations united in a powerful lobby group. As Donald Purich, the director of the University of Saskatchewan's Native Law Centre, observed in his 1986 book, Our Land, "National and provincial Indian organizations suddenly gained a new life. They had gained a cause — their very existence as Indians." In June, 1970, a chastened Trudeau dropped the proposals.

Still, it took a convoluted court battle to shift the balance of power between Ottawa and First Nations peoples. In 1973, the Nishgas of British Columbia argued before a seven-member panel of the Supreme Court of Canada that they still held title to their land — because they had never signed a treaty surrendering it. In an extraordinary decision, three justices agreed with the Nishgas; another three justices conceded that aboriginal title once existed — but they ruled that the British Columbia government had extinguished the Nishgas' title; a seventh judge rejected the case on a technicality. Although the Nishgas lost their case, they scored an important legal point: mere recognition of the existence of "aboriginal title" raised concern among federal politicians because it implied that the increasingly activist First Nations peoples in Canada clearly possessed undefined rights as aboriginals.

• • • • •

Two decades after the Nishgas case, the concept of aboriginal rights remains the focus of fierce constitutional debate, in the courts and in land-claims negotiations. Until Ottawa and the provinces amended the Constitution in 1982, Indian treaties were accorded the status of contracts by the courts. As a result, Parliament had the right to pass laws that regulated or extinguished treaty rights — but federal law shielded those rights from provincial interference. On nontreaty territory, the courts have recognized that aboriginal rights — such as the right to hunt and fish — could still exist. But the courts have also ruled that, before 1982, Parliament was legally empowered to extinguish those rights — and provincial legislatures could, at the very least, regulate them.

In 1982, after a massive aboriginal pressure campaign, Canada entrenched the recognition of "existing aboriginal and treaty rights" in the Constitution. During the latest round of constitutional talks, First Nations peoples have argued that those entitlements include the inherent right to self-government — and they have demanded its explicit entrenchment in the Constitution. Meanwhile, the courts have tentatively entered that complicated maze. In 1990, in the so-called Sparrow case, the Supreme Court ruled that the Musqueam Nation of British Columbia retained an aboriginal right to fish because governments had never extinguished that right. The court added that any attempt to extinguish rights must be "clear and plain." Observed University of Toronto law professor Patrick Macklem: "In the Sparrow case, the Supreme Court stated that aboriginal rights include those rights that protect activity that is essential to an aboriginal community's self-definition. Does that include self-government? Does that include aboriginal jurisdiction over areas such as criminal justice or child welfare? And what constitutes 'clear and plain' extinguishment of those rights?"

• • • • •

Mary Janigan, *Maclean's*, 1992 3 16

DISCUSSION AND RESEARCH

1. (a) As a class, brainstorm a list of examples of bias or prejudice found in each of the previous readings. Distinguish between bias described by the writers and bias held by the writers.
    (b) Analyze the suggested examples as a class and discuss the bias or prejudice in each reading identified in (a).
    (c) Individually, select one of the readings and rewrite it to retain its meaning, but without any bias or prejudice in either the content of the reading or your rewritten presentation of it.

2. In small groups, select one of the previous readings that illustrates conflict, and develop a possible solution scenario. Use the force-field approach described in Chapter One (p. 15).

3. Examine the written analysis of motives that you made as you went through the readings. In small groups,
    (a) Attempt to reach a consensus as to which group overall appears to have the strongest motive for its actions, and
    (b) List the criteria you used to identify the group that appeared to have the strongest motives.

4. In small groups, discuss whether human rights should be universally recognized or qualified according to local cultural values. Report your conclusion, and the reasons for it, to the class.

5. As an investigative reporter, write an article for your local newspaper about the role of group cultures in helping to determine the quality of life.

6. Hold a class debate on the motion that the average quality of life in Canada should be the goal of the developing world.

7. Write an essay critically examining the proposition that all groups should determine what their own ideal quality of life is.

HUMAN ASPIRATIONS

All fields of human group endeavour tend to be interlinked. Religious activities may mirror ethnic activities, which may reflect socioeconomic practices. Political activities will in turn be affected because of linkages to these other activities. All are mainsprings for human group action; all are inseparable from one another, although not necessarily equally important.

For example, the ongoing conflict in Northern Ireland has a variety of linked causes: English colonialism, religious differences, inequities in economic opportunity, disparities of socioeconomic class, and nationalist aspirations for independence. On one side are the descendants of settlers "planted" in Northern Ireland by the English conquerors in the 17th and 18th centuries. Members of this group tend to be Protestant in religion, better off in job opportunities, land ownership, and income, and English in political loyalties. The cultural, political, religious, social, and economic aspects of their lives are intertwined and inseparable. It is the same for the other side, who tend to be Roman Catholic in religion, worse off in job opportunities, land ownership, and income, and Irish in political loyalties. It is therefore difficult to classify the issue in Northern Ireland as purely a religious issue, a political issue, a social issue, or an economic issue. It is all of these.

English involvement in Ireland dates back to the 12th century, when Henry II claimed overlordship. In the 17th century, "plantations" of English and Scottish landholders were established in Northern Ireland on land seized from the Irish.

While interlinked, the issues are not necessarily equally important. A case could be made that the issue is primarily political, since independence from — or dependence on — England seems to be the main focus of the struggle. The lines are also clearly drawn between the two main religions, although less clearly in socioeconomic matters. The decisive question is: What is it that the two sides most wish to achieve? Is it to convert the other side to a different religion; is it to create a different socioeconomic balance; or is it to gain a political goal?

Interlinked human aspirations that are producing major forces for action and reaction among different groups in the world of the 1990s include:

- national sovereignty,
- ethnic recognition and independence, and
- religion.

Varied in origin, human aspirations are no less complex in expression. A desire to find and rejoice in one's heritage, for example, may cause people to search through ancient graveyards, to travel to other lands, to read old literature, to collect ancient artifacts, or — as in the example of one of the readings in the introduction to this chapter — organize modern festivals. It may also lead people into war.

PEACE AND WAR

Wars have been described as the continuation of diplomacy by other means. They are a means by which a group of people tries to achieve its most important goals, usually resorted to only after other means have failed.

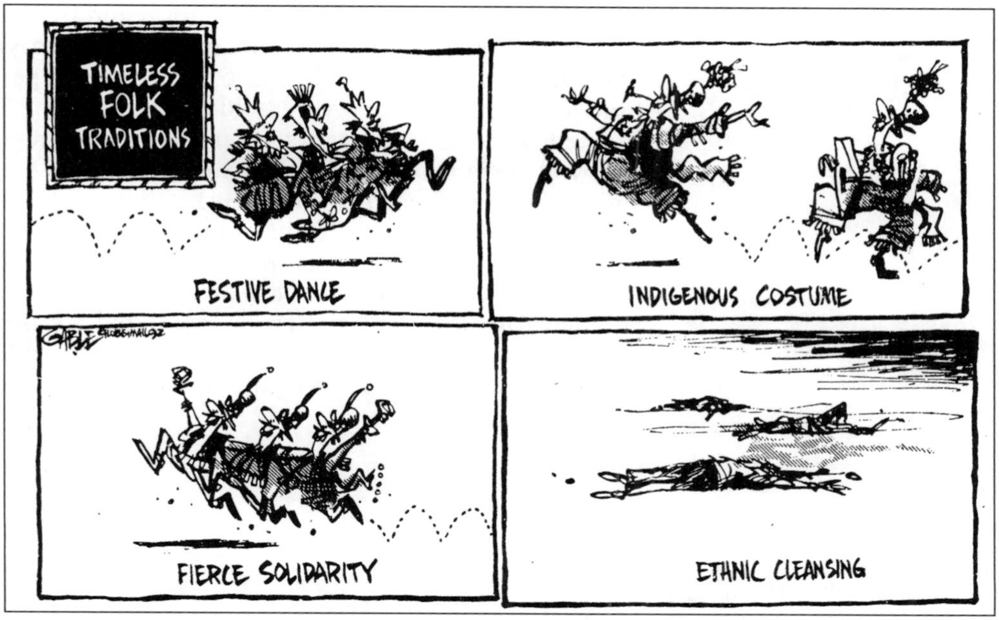

SOURCE: *The Globe and Mail*, 92/08/12

Panels: TIMELESS FOLK TRADITIONS / FESTIVE DANCE / INDIGENOUS COSTUME / FIERCE SOLIDARITY / ETHNIC CLEANSING

Fig. 4-5 *What strategies can you suggest to prevent this sequence of events from taking place?*

Military force may be the way in which one group tries to dominate another group, in order to acquire the other group's land, resources, or people (as slaves or forced labour). Examples of such wars in the past are those that were caused by expansionary groups backed by military force, such as the Romans of 2000 years ago in Europe and north Africa, the 16th century Spaniards in the Americas, the 19th century British in Africa, and the Chinese of the 1960s in Tibet. Wars may also be the way in which one group tries to reject domination by another group, as the Swedes fought for independence from Denmark in the 16th century, and the people of Western Sahara fight for independence from Morocco in the 1990s.

Some wars may be international, between nations; others may be internal (known as civil wars), between different groups within a nation. International wars, when one nation sought to control another, were more common in the past. Thus nations that perceived themselves at risk sought alliances with other nations for common protection. Some of these alliances still exist. The North Atlantic Treaty Organization (NATO) was founded at the end of World War II (1939-1945) largely by the nations of Western Europe and North America to counter the perceived threat from the former Soviet Union. Since the Soviet Union no longer exists, the defensive alliance is seeking a new role for itself. The counterbalancing Warsaw Pact, designed as a defensive alliance by the Soviet Union and its satellite nations in eastern Europe against the perceived threat from NATO, no longer exists.

NATO members in 1993 were Belgium, Canada, Denmark, France, Germany, Greece, Iceland, Italy, Luxembourg, Netherlands, Norway, Portugal, Spain, Turkey, the United Kingdom, and the United States.

The era in which the Soviet Union and the United States ranked as the world's superpowers, each capable of destroying the other, is now over. Instead, the world has one remaining superpower — the United States. The part of the world held together by the Soviet Union has fragmented. In 1990, 15 different nations (see Fig. 4-6) replaced the former Union of Soviet Socialist Republics (U.S.S.R.), while in 1992 the former Yugoslavia split into several parts (Bosnia-Herzegovina, Croatia, Macedonia, Serbia, and Slovenia), not peacefully, and not all parts recognized internationally. In 1993 the former Czechoslovakia separated into the Czech Republic and Slovakia. In many cases the break-up of the former countries provided opportunities for ethnic groups who had felt oppressed to seek political independence, even from some of the newly independent nations. The following reading presents a part of the picture in Russia.

Fig. 4-6 *New countries formed from the break-up of the former U.S.S.R.*

AN ETHNIC NIGHTMARE IN THE CAUCASUS

The villages have been scorched into a wasteland of burned houses and deserted lanes. Nervous Russian soldiers patrol the empty streets, wondering whether the heavily armed residents will open fire. In Vladikavkaz, the capital of the semi-autonomous (semi-independent) North Ossetian republic, the young soldiers listen helplessly to machine guns rat-tat-tatting through the night. A month after (Russian President) Boris Yeltsin sent troops to the region, the

 Fig. 4-7 *The Caucasus region.*

heaviest fighting has stopped and a curfew keeps most citizens at home, but there is no real peace. "Snipers are everywhere," says Fatima Khablova, a local government employee. "There's shooting all over the place."

For Yeltsin, North Ossetia is a nightmare come true. The Russian president has struggled for months to contain ethnic unrest in the former Soviet republics. But it now has spread into Russia for the first time since the Soviet Union broke up. In October, locals say, an Ossetian tank accidentally ran over and killed a boy from the Ingush ethnic minority. Ingush civilians retaliated, and the resulting violence has already left 261 dead and 584 wounded. Ossetian nationalists have mortared and burned Ingush houses by the hundreds; some 33 000 Ingush have fled. Both sides display mutilated bodies to prove that atrocities are being committed by the enemy. Yeltsin has

imposed emergency rule and sent some 3000 soldiers to restore peace; last week the local government asked him to extend the state of emergency by two months. "This is the first test case for us, in the Caucasus," Sergei Stankevich, a top Yeltsin adviser, told *Newsweek*. "We should have reacted earlier, in a more organized way."

The Caucasus region, home to dozens of independence-minded nationalities that the czars forcibly corralled in the last century, has been boiling ever since the onset of *perestroika* (restructuring). Ethnic conflicts have erupted among as many as ten Caucasian nationalities beyond Russia's borders. In an effort to head off trouble at home, Yeltsin last spring brokered a federation treaty among Russia's semi-autonomous regions. But in North Ossetia, that agreement proved no match for an old grudge. In 1944, Stalin (General Secretary of the Communist Party of the Soviet Union from

1922 to 1953) deported thousands of Ingush as alleged Nazi collaborators. Most returned after Stalin's death (in 1953). But now the Ingush, less than ten percent of North Ossetia's population of 650 000, want to recover the land they lost....

Yeltsin's stake in the dispute is immense. If he looks weak, his ultranationalist critics will accuse him of squandering the czarist patrimony (inheritance) of a strong and unified Russia. By committing troops, he hoped to pre-empt such an attack. But other regions could step up their independence claims. Such republics as Tatarstan and Bashkortostan (from the Kazakhstan border half-way to Moscow) are increasingly restive. Entire regions of Siberia have claimed ownership of their raw materials. A provincial tax revolt already is draining Moscow's coffers.

The burden will worsen dramatically if the North Caucasus becomes a military quagmire. Stankevich says the problem has been "localized." But when the troops moved through North Ossetia to the border of nearby Chechnya, the Chechens threatened to declare war on Moscow. Recently Ingush fighters attacked Russian troops and seized several Russian armored personnel carriers. Local fighters have taken Russian soldiers hostage. "The task is to make a man forget his memories," says Sergei Shoigu,

Yeltsin's deputy administrator in Vladikavkaz. But as long as the traces of the Russian Empire remain, the past will continue to haunt Moscow and its unhappy republics — and Yeltsin's ethnic troubles are likely only to get worse.

Dorinda Elliott in Moscow and Steve LeVine in Vladikavkaz; *Newsweek*, 1992 12 7

THE UNITED NATIONS

The disappearance from the world scene of one of its two opposed superpowers has opened the way for the United Nations to play an increasingly important political role. During the so-called Cold War, the two superpowers dominated world geopolitics, and the United Nations concentrated on humanitarian rather than political activities. Nevertheless the United Nations approved armed support for South Korea when it was invaded by North Korea in 1950, and it consistently sponsored a large variety of peacekeeping missions around the world with soldiers supplied by member states, chiefly Canada.

Since the disappearance of the Soviet Union, however, the United Nations appears to be taking a more proactive stance towards the world's many trouble spots. In 1991, at Kuwait's request, it sponsored armed intervention by a multinational army (led by the United States) to oust the Iraqi army from Kuwait. Starting in 1992 it took the initiative in organizing armed support (chiefly from the United States) for famine relief operations in Somalia. Its involvement in other areas such as Angola, Lebanon, Mozambique, and the countries arising from former Yugoslavia, however, has stretched United Nations resources fairly thin.

The term Cold War was applied to the stand-off between the so-called West (NATO) and East (Warsaw Pact).

Canada, with about 0.5 percent of the world's population, has supplied about ten percent of all U.N. peacekeeping personnel, more than any other nation.

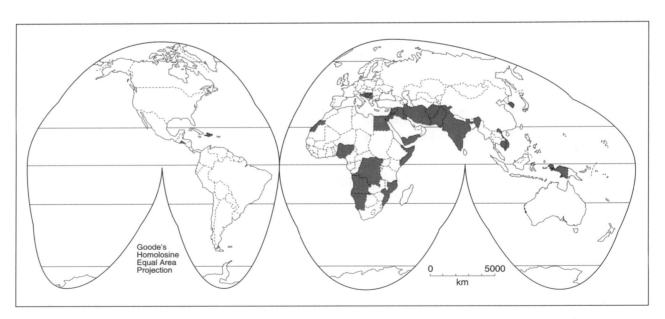

Fig. 4-8 *Areas where Canadian peacekeeping forces have worked, 1947-1993.*

There has been criticism that in some regions, such as Angola, the number of United Nations forces has been inadequate for the task. Critics point to the growing ethnic and religious unrest in the world that is creating a demand for United Nations peacekeeping. They state that this demand cannot be met by the voluntary contributions of armed forces from governments that often have other priorities. For example, there is increasing international pressure for Canada to supply more peacekeepers, while many people within Canada are pressuring the government to reduce spending on armed forces.

Peacekeeping requires that a cease-fire exists, allowing U.N. peacekeeping forces to move in between the two combatants.

The role of peace*making* as opposed to peace*keeping* is new for the United Nations in the 1990s, and it raises some concerns. One of the charter principles of the United Nations is that it will not interfere in the internal affairs of a member nation, unless requested. It is possible that peacemaking may not be requested by any government in the area. In fact, the area may not even have a recognized government. Peacemaking is a step toward the concept of a world police force, which — as with a local police force — would not wait to be called in if it saw a disturbance of the peace or other harm taking place.

The Secretary-General of the U.N. in 1991, Javier Perez de Cuellar, suggested that governments could no longer regard national sovereignty as a protective barrier behind which human rights could be "massively...violated."

The creation of a world police force sponsored by the United Nations would be a challenge to national sovereignty. Nations might not feel as free to oppress minorities or otherwise act in a manner contrary to international standards of human rights behaviour if they believed they would be subject to invasion by a United Nations police force. The idea of such a body entering a country to right perceived wrongs, by armed force if necessary, is difficult for supporters of national sovereignty to accept. For many people the idea is made even more difficult to accept because the world now really has only one major source of armed power — the United States. Many nationalists would regard loss of sovereignty to a world police force as, in effect, a transfer of power to the United States. At the same time, others believe the onus is on the United Nations to take action against violence wherever it occurs. The following reading, written in 1992 by Boutros Boutros-Ghali, then Secretary General of the United Nations, makes a plea for a more active role for the United Nations.

EMPOWERING THE UNITED NATIONS

A new chapter in the history of the United Nations has begun. With newfound appeal the world organization is being utilized with greater frequency and growing urgency. The machinery of the United Nations, which had often been rendered inoperative by the dynamics of the Cold War, is suddenly at the centre of international efforts to deal with unresolved problems of the past decades as well as an emerging array of present and future issues.

The new era has brought new credibility to the United Nations. Along with it have come rising expectations that the United Nations will take on larger responsibilities and a greater role in overcoming pervasive and interrelated obstacles to peace and development. Together the international community and the U.N. Secretariat need to seize this extraordinary opportunity to expand, adapt and reinvigorate the work of the United Nations so that the lofty goals as originally envisioned by the charter can begin to be realized.

Peacekeeping is the most prominent U.N. activity. The "blue helmets" on the front lines of conflict on four continents are a symbol of the United Nations' commitment to international peace and security. They come from some 65 countries, representing more than 35 percent of the membership.

Peacekeeping is a U.N. invention. It was not specifically defined in the charter but evolved as a noncoercive instrument of conflict control at a time when Cold War constraints prevented the Security Council from taking the more forceful steps permitted by the charter. Thirteen peacekeeping operations were established between 1948 and 1978. Five of them remain in existence, and are between 14 and 44 years old. Peacekeeping has sometimes proved easier than the complementary function of peacemaking. This shows that peacekeeping, by itself, cannot provide the permanent solution to a conflict. Only political negotiation can do that.

During the Cold War years the basic principles of peacekeeping were gradually established and gained acceptance: the consent of the parties; troops provided by member states serving under the command of the secretary general; minimum use of force; collective financing. It was also learned, often the hard way, that peacekeeping success requires the cooperation of the parties, a clear and practicable mandate, the continuing support of the Security Council and adequate financial arrangements.

The end of the Cold War has led to a dramatic expansion in demand for the United Nations' peacekeeping services. Since

SOURCE: DND Photo

Fig. 4-9 *Canadian United Nations peacekeepers working to keep Sarajevo airport open for relief flights to Bosnia in 1992.*

1988 14 new operations have been established, five of which have already completed their mandates and been disbanded. In the first half of 1992 the number of U.N. soldiers and police officers increased fourfold; by the end of the year they will exceed 50 000.

Some of these new operations have been of the traditional, largely military type, deployed to control unresolved conflicts between states. Examples are the military observers who monitored the ceasefire between Iran and Iraq from 1988 to 1991 and those who currently patrol the demilitarized zone between Iraq and Kuwait.

But most of the new operations have been set up to help implement negotiated settlements of long-standing conflicts, as in Namibia, Angola, Cambodia, El Salvador and Mozambique.

Namibia was a colonial situation but each of the other four has been an internal conflict, albeit with significant external dimensions, within a sovereign member state of the United Nations.

There is another aspect to the end of the Cold War. The thawing of its frozen political geography has led to the eruption of savage conflicts in, and sometimes between, newly emerging independent states. The former Yugoslavia has become the United Nations' largest peacekeeping commitment ever. Ethnic conflict across political borders and the brutal killing of civilians there are reminiscent of the ordeal that U.N. peacekeeping forces faced in the 1960s in the then Congo. U.N. forces again are taking an unacceptable level of casualties. It is difficult to avoid wondering whether the conditions yet exist for successful peacekeeping in what was Yugoslavia.

The 1990s have given peacekeeping another new task: the protection of the delivery of humanitarian supplies to civilians caught up in a continuing conflict. This is currently underway in Bosnia-Herzegovina and Somalia, member states whose institutions have been largely destroyed in a confused and cruel web of civil conflicts. This task tests the established practices of peacekeeping, especially the circumstances in which U.N. soldiers may open fire. Existing rules of engagement allow them to do so if armed persons attempt by force to prevent them from carrying out their orders. This licence, used sparingly in the past, may be resorted to more frequently if the United Nations is to assert the Security Council's authority over those who, for personal gain or war objectives, try to rob or destroy humanitarian supplies destined for suffering civilian populations.

All these new modes of peacekeeping have had far-reaching implications for the way in which U.N. operations are organized and conducted.

In internal conflicts, or indeed in interstate conflicts where one or other of the governments is not in a position to exercise full authority over territory nominally under its control, not all the parties are governments. As a result the peacekeepers have had to learn how to deal with a multiplicity of "authorities." The leaders of such groups are often inaccessible and their identity even unknown; chains of command are shadowy; armed persons who offend against agreements signed by their supposed leaders are disowned; discipline is nonexistent or brutal. And everywhere there is

an evil and uncontrolled proliferation of arms.

Peacekeeping operations still invariably include military personnel. But now the civilian elements often have an even more important role. This is especially true when the task is to help implement comprehensive and complex settlements, as was or is the case in Namibia, El Salvador, Cambodia and Mozambique. Political action is required to resolve disputes between the parties and persuade them to implement the agreed arrangements. Information programs must explain the United Nations' role and advise the people of the opportunities the settlement gives them. Refugees must be brought home and resettled. Elections must be observed and verified or even, in Cambodia, organized and conducted by the United Nations. Local police must be monitored to ensure that they carry out their duties in the spirit of the new order and not the old. Respect for human rights must be verified, an especially important task in El Salvador and Cambodia. In the latter country the United Nations also has responsibility for controlling the key parts of the existing administrative structures.

All of these tasks, some of them very intrusive, must be carried out with complete impartiality by civilian peacekeepers. Staff members of the U.N. system, with policy and election observers made available by member states, have risen to these new civilian challenges.

The involvement of such a variety of civilian personnel, alongside their military colleagues, creates a need for tight coordination of all aspects of an operation. As a result it has become normal for the overall

direction of a multifaceted peacekeeping operation to be entrusted to a senior civilian official as special representative of the secretary general, to whom the force commander, the police commissioner, the director of elections and other directors report.

One of the lessons learned during the recent headlong expansion of U.N. peacekeeping is the need to accelerate the deployment of new operations. Under current procedures three or four months can elapse between the Security Council's authorization of a mission and its becoming operational in the field. Action is required on three fronts: finance, personnel and equipment.

On finance, the member states should provide the secretary general with a working capital fund for the start-up of new operations, so that cash is immediately available. They should also revise existing financial procedures so that the secretary general has authority to spend that cash, within reasonable limits, as soon as the new operation is authorized.

The question of personnel is more complicated. Procedures for the transfer of U.N. staff to new operations in the field are being simplified for more rapid reaction. But most peacekeeping personnel (troops, police, election observers) are made available by governments. The answer is not to create a U.N. standing force, which would be impractical and inappropriate, but to extend and make more systematic standby arrangements by which governments commit themselves to hold ready, at an agreed period of notice, specially trained units for peacekeeping service.

A handful of governments already do this. A recent invitation to all member states to volunteer information about what personnel and equipment they would in principle be ready to contribute, if asked, produced disappointing results. I have now decided to take the initiative and put specific proposals to governments, in order to identify with reasonable certainty sources of military and police personnel and equipment that governments would undertake to make available at very short notice. These commitments would constitute building blocks that could be used, when the moment came, to construct peacekeeping operations in various sizes and configurations, ranging from a small group of military observers to a full division, as required.

Allied with this effort will be the provision of more extensive guidance to governments on training troops and police who they may contribute to the United Nations for peacekeeping duties.

Equipment can cause even greater bottlenecks than personnel. There are two complementary ways in which this problem can be eased. First, member states should make it possible for the United Nations to establish a reserve stock of basic items (vehicles, radios, generators, prefabricated buildings) that are always required for a new peacekeeping operation. Second, member states could agree to hold ready, at various locations around the world, reserves of such equipment. These would remain their property but could be made immediately available to the United Nations when the need arose.

An even more radical development can now be envisaged. It happens all too often that the parties to a conflict sign a ceasefire agreement but then fail to respect it. In such situations it is felt that the United Nations should "do something." This is a reasonable expectation if the United Nations is to be an effective system of collective security. The purpose of peace enforcement units (perhaps they should be called "ceasefire enforcement units") would be to enable the United Nations to deploy troops quickly to enforce a ceasefire by taking coercive action against either party, or both, if they violate it.

This concept retains many of the features of peacekeeping: the operation would be authorized by the Security Council; the troops would be provided voluntarily by member states; they would be under the command of the secretary general; and they would be impartial between the two sides, taking action only if one or other of them violated the agreed cease-fire. But the concept goes beyond peacekeeping to the extent that the operation would be deployed without the express consent of the two parties (though its basis would be a ceasefire agreement previously reached between them). U.N. troops would be authorized to use force to ensure respect for the ceasefire. They would be trained, armed and equipped accordingly; a very rapid response would be essential.

This is a novel idea that involves some obvious difficulties. But it should be carefully considered by the international community as the next step in the development of the United Nations' capability to take effective action on the ground to maintain international peace and security.

• • • • •

Boutros Boutros-Ghali, *Foreign Affairs,* Winter 1992/93

DISARMAMENT

At the same time as pressures mount for armed intervention to create and keep peace, contrary pressures to attain peace through disarmament also exist. Many groups argue that arms and the international arms trade are major causes of warfare, and that money spent on military equipment would be better spent on human and economic development. Such groups note, for example, that in the early 1990s, 15 children in the world died every minute for want of essential food and inexpensive vaccines while — also every minute — the world's total military expenditures amounted to about $1 750 000. Military spending in real terms rose regularly after World War II (see Fig. 4-10). It appears to have peaked in the late 1980s, and has declined slightly into the early 1990s. The map in Fig. 4-11 shows the annual amount of military spending per person.

Dismantling nuclear weapons safely is time-consuming and costly.

There have been numerous arms control and disarmament agreements over the last 25 to 30 years, mostly related to preventing the spread of nuclear weapons, or limiting their testing and deployment. One of the earliest treaties was the Nuclear Test Ban Treaty of 1963 (signed by 114 nations), which banned nuclear weapons testing in the atmosphere, oceans, and outer space, and any underground explosions that caused radioactive fall-out beyond the nation's borders. In 1968 the Non-Proliferation Treaty was signed by 141 nations. It banned the transfer of nuclear weapons or weapons technology to nations without nuclear weapons. More recently, the Strategic Arms Lim-

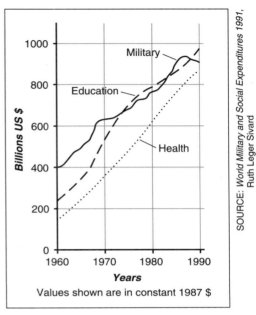

SOURCE: *World Military and Social Expenditures 1991*, Ruth Leger Sivard

Values shown are in constant 1987 $

Fig. 4-10 *World military, education, and health spending, 1960-1990.*

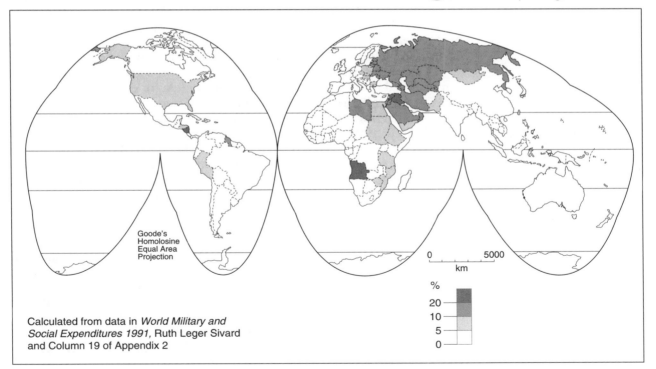

Goode's Homolosine Equal Area Projection

Calculated from data in *World Military and Social Expenditures 1991*, Ruth Leger Sivard and Column 19 of Appendix 2

%
20
10
5
0

Fig. 4-11 *Military spending, US$ per person. How many different patterns of expenditure can you identify on the map? How can you explain the patterns?*

itation Treaties of 1972 and 1979 (SALT I and SALT II) signed by the United States and the former Soviet Union have been followed by the Strategic Arms Reduction Treaties of 1991 and 1993 between the United States and Russia (START I and START II). The total nuclear strategic (intercontinental) warhead strength of the two countries will have been reduced to about 6000 by the year 2003 from a peak of about 24 000 in 1989 (1989 data from *World Military and Social Expenditures 1989*, Ruth Leger Sivard).

The redirection of military spending to human and economic development is widely called the peace dividend. The peace dividend was expected to be large after the end of the Cold War in 1990, but subsequent events have somewhat frustrated these high expectations. While the two major nuclear powers have agreed to reduce their stockpiles, other nuclear countries have not so far agreed to do the same. The nuclear arsenal of the former Soviet Union was inherited by some of the new nations besides Russia (notably Belarus, Kazakhstan, and Ukraine), although by late 1993 they had agreed in principle to return the weapons to Russia for dismantling. The other nuclear nations of China, France, Israel, and the United Kingdom had by the same time made no moves to reduce their nuclear weaponry. Further, some countries, such as India, Iraq, Pakistan, and South Africa, have been engaged in secret development of nuclear weapons, and may already have the capability of producing them. In 1993, South Africa admitted as much, but claimed to have destroyed its capability. There is also the strong possibility that some of the former Soviet Union's nuclear warheads that are officially listed as "missing" have been secretly acquired by other countries, such as Iran.

Apart from nuclear weaponry, there is still a growing and entirely unregulated international trade in non-nuclear (or conventional) arms. Data are unreliable, because much of the trade involves secrecy and deception. However, the chief manufacturing and selling countries from 1970 to 1990, according to *World Military and Social Expenditures 1991* by Ruth Leger Savard, appear to have been Russia/U.S.S.R. (about 40 percent of the world arms trade), the United States (25 percent), France (seven percent), United Kingdom (four percent), Germany (three percent), and China (three percent). Weapons manufacturing is no longer solely concentrated in the countries of the developed world, as China is now a leading producer. Other developing countries emerging as weapons producers are Brazil, India, and Iraq.

The developing countries are the main market for the international arms trade, accounting for almost 80 percent of world total arms imports, and supporting over 60 percent of the world's armed forces. In the 30 years after 1960, the developing world increased its military expenditures in constant dollar terms more than 500 percent (see Fig. 4-12), while GNP/cap rose less than 200 percent. The map in Fig. 4-13 shows military expenditures per person as a percentage of GNP per person, and gives an indication of the differing ability of countries to support arms expenditures.

In 1992 the Russian Air Force reduced its orders for new military hardware by over 60 percent. Russian arms makers thus turned to export markets. They justified these tactics by the need to earn money so that they could eventually convert to peaceful products.

The World Bank announced in 1992 that it would look at the amount of money spent on arms by 85 developing countries receiving aid when deciding how much to lend them for development assistance.

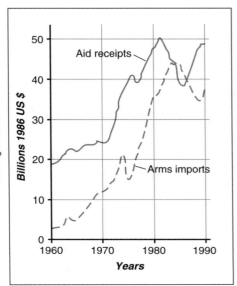

SOURCE: World Military and Social Expenditures 1991, Ruth Leger Sivard

Fig. 4-12 *Values of foreign aid received and money spent on arms imports by developing countries, 1960-1990.*

Additional limitations to the expected peace dividend arise from the continuation of warfare in many countries of the world. Indeed, many people fear an increase of warfare throughout the world as centralized authority weakens. While the world existed in a Cold War, the possibility of mutually assured destruction (MAD) by the two superpowers was enough to maintain a high level of world peace. Wars still occurred, but they were remote from the core areas of the superpowers. The wars may have been triggered by either of the superpowers in attempts to destabilize or distract the other by creating political instability. Afghanistan and Nicaragua are examples of countries that experienced superpower involvement in their affairs during the 1980s. Although both were fairly remote from the superpower core, they were close enough to create risk.

The collapse of the Soviet Union did more than end the Cold War and change the existing power structure. It left a power vacuum in its own former area of influence, and removed some sense of purpose about world involvement in the NATO countries. It also removed opportunities for many governments in the developing world to play one superpower off against the other for their own gain. The ability of the former

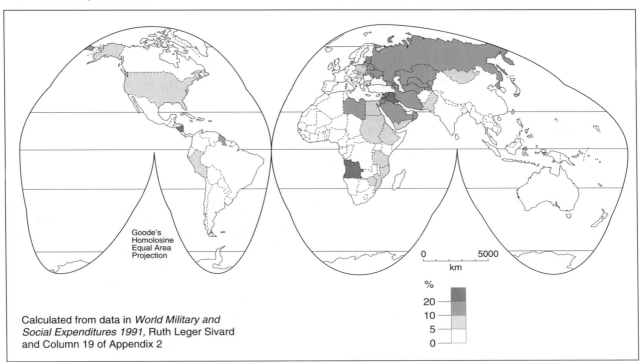

Calculated from data in *World Military and Social Expenditures 1991*, Ruth Leger Sivard and Column 19 of Appendix 2

Fig. 4-13 *Military expenditures per person as a percentage of GNP per person. Which countries appear to be most burdened by arms expenditures?*

Soviet Union, and the political need for NATO countries, to provide development assistance to the developing countries was now greatly lessened. The world of the 1990s therefore became much less structured and much less controlled than the world of the Cold War period. National roles became more confused.

The situation was seriously aggravated by the huge debts many countries had built up during the Cold War. Debts were incurred to provide for military spending and for the extension of each country's social security net. The two countries, Germany and Japan, that suffered defeat in World War II, and that were constitutionally forbidden to operate armies, became major sources of money for borrowing. Their economies were not burdened by large military expenditures, their defence was provided for by NATO, and their populations were economically productive, so they prospered. They had money to lend. However, in the 1990s, Germany faced huge costs in integrating the former West and East German economies, while Japan faced huge internal debt loads because of borrowing to finance economic expansion. Meanwhile, the countries that had borrowed to raise their quality of life found that increasingly high taxes could not meet annual interest payments and maintain a high level of social services at the same time. Many countries therefore tended to withdraw from global involvement. International commitments began to assume a secondary priority.

Reductions in foreign aid to developing countries, along with pressure in developed countries for more highly protected markets, placed constraints on many developing nations. Annual increases in wealth, already slight in many developing countries, diminished. In several countries, under the threat of increasing poverty, old hatreds were rekindled. Religious and ethnic rivalries surfaced. Governments faced pressure to survive, and were overthrown in some countries, such as Haiti. They resorted to oppression of human rights in other countries, such as Algeria. Central authority weakened, as in Zaire, or disappeared, as in Angola and Somalia. The world faced an increasingly turbulent future, and to many people the anticipated peace dividend increasingly appeared to be a mirage.

DISCUSSION AND RESEARCH

8. Using at least two different news sources, research the causes of any single example of armed conflict that is taking place at the present time. Report your findings in a written paper, complete with a sketchmap (see Appendix 3) of the main area and the causes and nature of the conflict. Use atlas maps and maps accompanying journal or newspaper articles as the basis for your sketchmap.

Include in your written report any recommendations which might lead to a more peaceful resolution of the issue.

9. As the inner cabinet in a developed country's government, your small group is faced with two situations:
   (a) A developing country has a government which is under sustained attack from rebels. The rebels believe the government should be greatly speeding up the process of breaking large farm estates into small holdings for local farmers.
   (b) A long-established government is under sustained attack from rebels who believe the government should be adopting religious values in its daily conduct of affairs.

   Your group has to recommend to the Prime Minister which one of the two situations the government should become involved in, and which side should be supported by military action if necessary or other, more peaceful, means. Make and justify such recommendations.

10. Research Canada's peacekeeping role in the world. Then in pairs role play two parts. One person is to advise the federal government to increase its spending on the armed forces. The other person is to recommend a reduction in Canada's military spending.

11. In small groups, discuss the idea that the United Nations should establish a global "police force," and design a plan that might produce such international cooperation without affecting the sovereignty of individual nations.

STATISTICAL ANALYSIS

12. Examine the data in columns 33 and 34 of Appendix 2.
    (a) In small groups, calculate for each country its military expenditures as a percentage of its education and health expenditures.
    (b) On a world map, shade in one colour those countries where military spending is more than 100 percent of education and health spending. Shade in a contrasting colour all the countries where military spending is less than 50 percent of education and health spending.
    (c) Describe and comment on the pattern produced.

NATIONAL SOVEREIGNTY

Many nations have a constitution which provides legal authority for the existence of government. In some nations, such as Jordan and Saudi Arabia, ultimate authority rests in the Monarchy, which is guided by law. In other nations, military governments rule their nations through use of force.

A sovereign nation is one with a national government that is able to control what happens within its borders, unrestricted by the policies and actions of other nations. National sovereignty, in essence, is a legal concept, with ultimate national authority resting in either its constitution or its government. Recognition by other sovereign nations of this national authority gives international validity to any nation claiming sovereignty. If such international recognition is lacking, as it is for, say, Transkei or Kurdistan, then national sovereignty is at best questionable.

International law recognizes nations in much the same way individuals are recognized. Disputes between nations may be brought to the International Court of Justice at The Hague in the Netherlands. The Court is part of the United Nations. Disputes are resolved by judges delivering verdicts after weighing arguments from each nation's lawyers. Nations that participate in the process usually abide by the rule of law, and accept even unfavourable verdicts, as Canada did in 1984 when the Court ruled partly against Canada's claim for sovereignty over the fishing grounds of Georges Bank in the western Atlantic. While some nations settle their disputes at the Court, others prefer more violent means, as indicated in the previous section, "Peace and War."

Indeed, acceptance of the rule of law is not yet universal. Even within countries such as Canada that — as nations — abide by the rule of law, there are some citizens who do not. All nations therefore maintain mili-

SOURCE: CIDA/David Barbour

Fig. 4-14 *All countries except Costa Rica and Iceland maintain both military forces and police forces for the maintenance of law and order and the defence of the state. Costa Rica abolished its army in 1948, but maintains a paramilitary civil guard; Iceland has no army at all. Both countries maintain police forces.*

tary and/or police forces for security purposes. In several nations, military forces actually form the government. The maintenance of military and police forces is needed to combat criminality in all nations, although never with complete success. Even in generally law-abiding countries such as Canada, murders and other criminal acts sometimes remain unsolved, and riots occur, as in Montreal after the 1986 and 1993 Stanley Cup victories. But in some countries the existence of military and police forces has been used by governments to oppress sections of the population. The oppressed sections are usually ethnic or religious minorities, but may also include political or socioeconomic groups opposed to government policy. Examples of oppression are numerous, and include such Canadian cases as attempts in the 19th and 20th centuries to eliminate First Nations peoples' culture and religion, and imprisonment of Japanese-Canadians in World War II. In some cases, such as Ukraine in the 1920s and 1930s, Germany in the 1930s and 1940s, and East Timor (eastern Indonesia) and Bosnia in the 1990s, oppression of minorities occurred on a massive scale, resulting in millions of deaths.

In other cases, people with dissenting political views have been oppressed. They have been killed, put in prison, tortured, and generally subdued, as in the former Soviet Union from about 1920 to 1980, and in Cambodia in the 1970s.

International organizations such as Amnesty International and Freedom House monitor and report on cases of oppression around the world. At the start of 1992, Freedom House reported that only 25 percent of the world's population lived in conditions of political freedom, a decline from nearly 40 percent at the end of 1990 (see Fig. 4-15).

Because of widespread lack of concern over their situations, several minority groups in 1991 founded the Unrepresented Nations and Peoples' Organization (with the official-sounding acronym UNPO), with headquarters at The Hague in the Netherlands. Within two years, membership had grown to about 40, with many more groups organizing to join. Officials of UNPO claim that they represent more than 100 million people, including groups as varied as Abkhazians, Albanian Greeks, Assyrians, Australian Aborigines, Kurds, Mohawks, Russian Crimeans, and Tibetans. As Julie Berriault, director of UNPO's San Francisco office, says, "These conflicts around the

Millions of Ukrainians and other minorities were starved to death by Soviet leader Stalin's policies in the 1920s and 1930s; in the 1940s millions of Jews and other minorities were killed during the Holocaust as a result of Hitler's policies in Germany.

Brutal suppression of political opponents, often called dissidents by the government, is characteristic of what is called a police state.

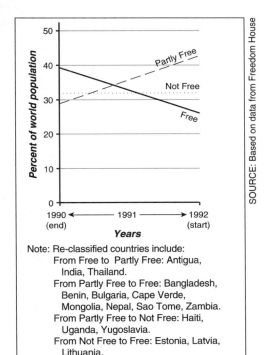

SOURCE: Based on data from Freedom House

Note: Re-classified countries include:
From Free to Partly Free: Antigua, India, Thailand.
From Partly Free to Free: Bangladesh, Benin, Bulgaria, Cape Verde, Mongolia, Nepal, Sao Tome, Zambia.
From Partly Free to Not Free: Haiti, Uganda, Yugoslavia.
From Not Free to Free: Estonia, Latvia, Lithuania.

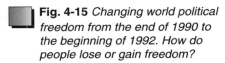

Fig. 4-15 *Changing world political freedom from the end of 1990 to the beginning of 1992. How do people lose or gain freedom?*

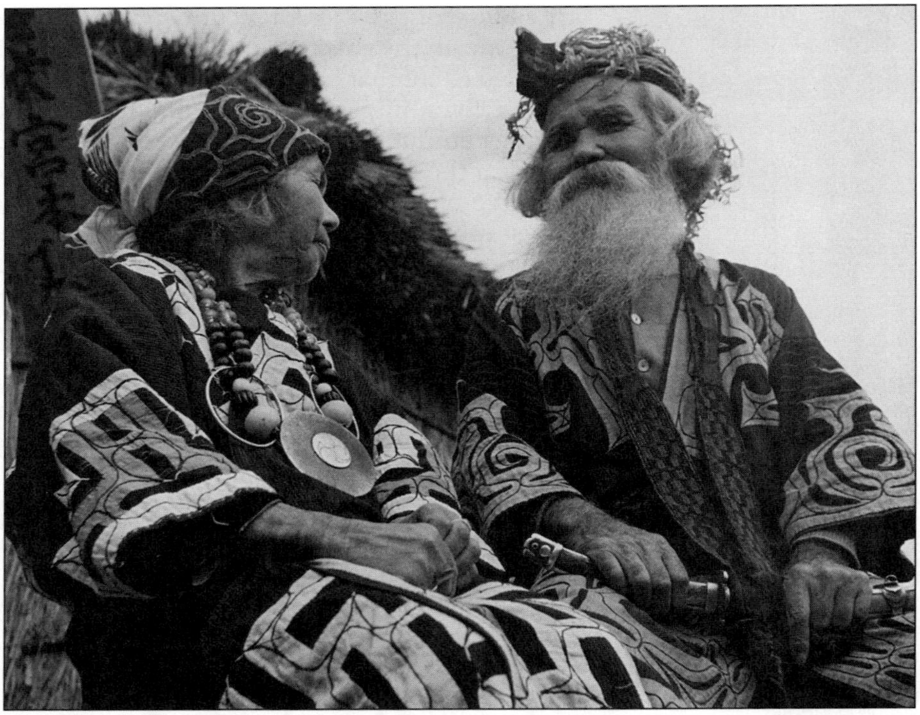

SOURCE: Japan National Tourist Organization

Fig. 4-16 *Japan is one of the very few nations with almost complete ethnic homogeneity. Its few minorities, such as these Ainu of Hokkaido in the north of Japan, are small in number, and often have difficulty retaining their distinctness.*

world, these issues of nations and peoples reaching out for what they think is rightfully theirs, are going to exist, whether we like it or not. The international community has a choice as to whether these people reach out for these aspirations in a violent or a non-violent way."

The United Nations is concerned about UNPO, warning that the international community may feel threatened by rampant "micro-nationalism." The U.N. argues instead that nations and peoples should band together in the interests of peace.

Sovereignty also contains possibilities for good. A nation may develop strong educational or medical programs for its people; it may encourage a sustainable economy; it may establish environmental protection priorities; and it may sponsor a distinct national culture. It is for these and similar reasons that some people are highly protective of the concept of sovereignty, and unwilling to see it diminished.

Nevertheless, several forces are at work diminishing national sovereignty (and, conversely, encouraging the growth of the global village). As mentioned in the previous section, "Peace and War," the idea of a global police force is a threat to national sovereignty. Sovereignty is also weakened by the increasing ease with which ideas and images flow across national borders by means of the electronic media. Countries have tried jamming radio and TV broadcasts from other nations in the past, but signals still get through. Borders, especially now that communication satellites exist, are open to electronic signals from around the world. Chapter Five examines this situation in more detail.

The growth of world trade also weakens national sovereignty. The increasing international movement of travellers, goods, and money, the three main components of international trade, lessens the significance of national frontiers. It is physically easier to control travellers and goods, through passports and customs offices, than it is to control money flows. In the past, flows of money were easy to control, because gold was the main form of internationally accepted money, and it was difficult to transport securely. Now, virtually all international money flows occur electronically through computers and satellite links to the international banking system, and are as difficult to control as the flow of ideas.

Given the ease with which money can be moved, and the increasing demand for the freer movement of people and goods, many countries have begun to dismantle their border controls on trade. Major impetus to this end was given initially by six of the countries of Europe when they agreed to form the European Common Market (now the European Community) in the 1950s. Many other countries have since joined the European Community. In other parts of the world, similar arrangements to dismantle trade barriers have occurred among groups of neighbouring countries. The North American Free Trade Agreement (NAFTA) designed to link Canada, Mexico, and the United States was signed in 1992, to take effect in 1994. Despite opposition in the United States and Canada, NAFTA was eventually ratified in late 1993. As in Europe, other countries may join

Billions of dollars are moved internationally every day through computer links. Trade payments are one reason, but other reasons relate to travel, investment, loans, and currency speculation. On average, the total amount of money entering and leaving Canada electronically every minute of every day is over $1 billion.

The original six members of the European Common Market in 1957 were Belgium, France, Italy, Luxembourg, Netherlands, and West Germany.

SOURCE: John Molyneux

Fig. 4-17 *Travellers and goods commonly reach Nepal by air, keeping links open to the rest of the world. This is an Air Nepal plane at Kathmandu airport.*

Argentina, Brazil, Paraguay, and Uruguay are members of Mercosur.

Members of ASEAN are Brunei, Indonesia, Malaysia, Philippines, Singapore, and Thailand.

By early 1993 the European Community had grown to 12 full members, with five more in the European Economic Area, and ten more from central Europe and the Baltic region with Association and Cooperation Agreements.

Sanctions are imposed by governments, and boycotts by large numbers of people acting unofficially but collectively. In the 1980s, Canada's fur trade was virtually destroyed by a largely European boycott of imported Canadian furs. Was Canada's sovereignty diminished by this action?

this group (if approved), and Chile is widely expected to be the first to do so. Meanwhile, the Mercosur Trade Agreement links several countries in South America. In 1993, the Association of South East Asian Nations (ASEAN) announced that its members intended to form a free trade bloc.

Moves to form trade blocs are not universally supported. Within the blocs, there are many who complain about the inevitable reductions of sovereignty and loss of national character. Outside the blocs, there are others who see reduced opportunities for trade, since they expect the members of a bloc to trade more among themselves than with outsiders.

On the other hand, experience since the start of the European Common Market in the 1950s shows that trade blocs are usually open to new members. Those who wish to remain outside the bloc, as Switzerland chose to do, are free to apply at a later date. Further, many people argue that the growing world trend to free trade blocs in certain regions is a giant step along the way to an eventually fully integrated world. Larger bodies (trade blocs) replace smaller bodies (nations), and the world becomes less fragmented.

During the 20th century, the rapid growth in number and size of a variety of international organizations has also worked to diminish national sovereignty. The United Nations, along with its many agencies, is only one example, but its impact on sovereignty is not limited to peacemaking. One United Nations agency, the International Monetary Fund (IMF), for example, has been involved in managing the economic affairs of several countries. Other international organizations that have the potential to weaken sovereignty are those such as Freedom House that monitor and report on the activities in different nations, thereby holding nations to international account. All international environmental groups, such as Greenpeace, form a similar category. Boycotts and **sanctions**, designed to produce change in another country's internal behaviour, have a parallel effect.

Other international organizations that weaken sovereignty are the various large businesses that operate globally. Known as multinationals — or occasionally as transnationals — companies such as Sony, Shell, and Seagram can move money and productive capacity to wherever they are welcome. Equally, they can sell into almost any market. In all countries they are subject to local laws, but if the laws become unwelcoming, the firms can go elsewhere. Because of their access to international money, and their general willingness to bring international skills to areas that might otherwise lack them, multinational companies are often welcome investors in many countries of the world. As they are global companies, they are often accused of lacking national identity or national loyalty. They are accordingly criticized by those who believe strongly in national sovereignty for not being sufficiently "national." Chapter Three deals with multinationals in more detail (see p. 191).

A further pressure on national sovereignty is the growing realization that some of the world's problems cannot be solved by individual nations acting alone. International cooperation is necessary to deal with such issues as a thinning ozone layer or global warming. All such aspects of cooperation require the ceding of some sovereignty in order to meet international obligations.

Pressure on national sovereignty also arises from migrants and refugees, examined in a later section of this chapter.

ETHNIC RECOGNITION AND INDEPENDENCE

The right of an ethnic group to political independence if it so wishes — the right to self-determination — has long been accepted in principle, but often ignored in practice. Hundreds of ethnic groups around the world have sought, but been denied, recognition and independence. Examples exist in all continents. First Nations peoples in North America, Québecois in Canada, Scots and Welsh in Great Britain, Basques in Spain, Kurds in southwest Asia, Tamils in Sri Lanka, Blacks in South Africa, Palestinians in Israel, Dinka in Sudan, and Eritreans in Ethiopia, to list but a few, have all engaged in struggles for recognition and independence. In almost all cases their efforts have been resisted by the existing governments, because their success would most commonly mean the break-up of the existing nations.

One of the most serious problems with the concept of ethnic independence is that in practice few ethnic groups have sole habitation of an area of land.

SOURCE: Lyn Boggs

Fig. 4-18 *A youth in a yard in Soweto, South Africa, displays a sign of globalization — a Los Angeles Lakers' jersey — as he waits for the outcome of political policies in South Africa.*

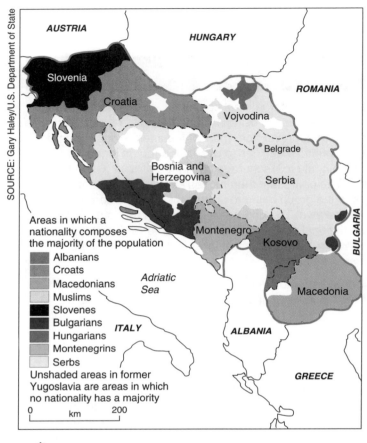

Areas in which a
nationality composes
the majority of the population

Albanians
Croats
Macedonians
Muslims
Slovenes
Bulgarians
Hungarians
Montenegrins
Serbs

Unshaded areas in former
Yugoslavia are areas in which
no nationality has a majority

0   km   200

Fig. 4-19 *Major ethnic areas in the former Yugoslavia.*

What are the various factors
that cause you personally to be
proud of Canada?

Members of other ethnic groups usually share the territory, often in a very jumbled manner. Conversion of an ethnic minority within an existing nation to an ethnic majority in its own smaller territory would usually create other ethnic minorities within the new territory. The dangers of this situation became apparent in the early 1990s in Bosnia, when ethnic Serbs fought and killed thousands of ethnic Croats and Bosnian Muslims in an exercise they called ethnic cleansing. The purpose of the military action was to create an all-Serbian area, with no competing minorities. Croats and Bosnian Muslims responded with similar policies of their own, so that fighting developed among all three groups (see also the earlier reading, "The Sinister Ideology of "Ethnic Cleansing"" on p. 237). Further, in 1992, Kumar Rupesinghe, Secretary-General of the Standing International Forum on Ethnic Conflict, Genocide, and Human Rights, predicted that by the year 2000 there would be 46 civil wars and 100 million refugees in the world.

Another problem with the concept of ethnic independence is that its realization would produce literally hundreds of small new nations. The United Nations estimates that the world could contain about 400 independent nations, giving rise to the possibility of an increased number of international disputes at a time when much of the world appears to be moving toward closer cooperation and the existence of fewer — but larger — groups on the way to a global village. United Nations Secretary-General Boutros Boutros-Ghali commented in 1992 that a hypothetical example of a worst-case scenario would be in Africa, already split into 50 countries. "There are 5000 tribes," he said, "Suppose each tribe would say it has the right to self-determination; you will have a kind of new micro-nationalism with small states of 50 000 or 100 000 people."

A further problem with ethnic independence is that many individual people in the world are not members of any single ethnic group. They have ancestors in a variety of ethnic groups, and feel that any national loyalties they have are less determined by ethnicity than by other factors such as shared aspirations, common culture, political ideology, or religion.

While the national aspirations of many members of ethnic minorities are powerful, often sufficient for them to risk death, there are also many members of ethnic minority groups who want to be left to live in peace,

SOURCE: *Africa, Its peoples and their Culture History*, G. P. Murdock

Fig. 4-20 *Major tribal areas in Africa. Note the large number in relation to the number of countries in the continent. What reasons can you suggest to explain why most of the tribal areas across the northern and southern parts, and in the Horn of Africa in the east, are much larger than those in West Africa and throughout the central regions?*

as the Turks in Germany. Sometimes it is the ethnic majority that disrupts the lives of the minorities. The majority may dislike having a minority in their midst: they may claim that the minority will not adjust to the majority culture; they may be disdainful of the minority's traditions and customs; and they may think that minority members are taking jobs away from majority members. Such views raise questions about the rights of

Xenophobia exists in all parts of Europe, characterized by physical and verbal attacks on "foreigners." In Germany, several refugees and guest-workers were killed in the early 1990s and hostels and homes were fire-bombed. At the same time in France, parliamentary leader Jacques Chirac spoke about "noisy, smelly immigrants."

minorities, and about human rights in general. They also bring up the intertwined matter of quality of life, since a social atmosphere of oppression and disruption has an adverse impact on everyone.

Whatever the reasons, there have been many instances of oppression of minorities. The minorities are regarded as foreigners, even in their land of birth, and may be extensively persecuted. Hatred of foreigners — called xenophobia — is a recurring problem in many parts of the world. In some cases the oppressed minority is also racially different from the majority, and racism may then accompany xenophobia. In 1992 there were many examples in Europe, quite apart from Bosnia, where these hostile feelings produced serious civil unrest, including murder. The incidents were well documented, reported on international television, and extensively analyzed in various magazines and newspapers.

Sometimes, situations may not always be so clear. The following reading about Sudan shows how confusing ethnic issues can be.

SUDANESE ETHNIC GROUPS FORCED FROM HOMELANDS

NAIROBI, KENYA — One of Africa's most traditional peoples, the Nuba of Sudan, is being forced off its ancestral lands by the government, according to human rights groups.

A large-scale relocation of Nubas, a composite of ethnic groups marked by a rich culture of traditional music and dance, is under way. Tens of thousands are being trucked by the Sudanese government from the low Nuba mountains of central Sudan to large camps in the Northern Kordofan Province.

No one denies the relocation is taking place, but there are sharply contrasting explanations for it.

The Sudanese government says it is a humanitarian move to help the Nubas escape a civil-war zone.

But in a Sept. 9 report, Africa Watch, a Washington-based human rights group, claims the relocation is forced — part of an attempt to "eradicate" the cultural identity of a pre-

dominantly non-Muslim people who have never cooperated with Sudan's Islam-oriented governments.

It amounts to "ethnic cleansing," according to both Africa Watch and a United Nations official, using the term now applied to the Serbian pressure to force Muslims out of their home areas in Yugoslavia.

The Nuba mountains lie in the Southern Kordofan Province in central Sudan. The range provides fertile ground for Nuba farmers and ranchers.

It is also the northern-most battle area between the Islamic Khartoum government and the mostly Christian and animist Sudan People's Liberation Army (SPLA) of southern Sudan, whose members seek greater autonomy and an end to state-imposed Islamic law.

Both the government and the SPLA have committed abuses in the area, including assassinations of civilians, according to Africa Watch. More than 40 000 Nubas have already been trucked out of Southern Kordofan to camps in Northern Kordofan, the Africa Watch report says.

According to a recent report of the United States State Department, most Nubas in the camps are "sick and malnourished," and receive "inadequate" relief from Sudanese government and Islamic organizations.

A Sudanese official says the relocation became necessary after more than 150 000 Nubas fled their mountain homes in the past two months. The refugees crowded into and around Kadugli, the provincial capital, where lack of shelter made the ongoing relocation necessary, he says.

"Nobody's forcing them" to move, the official contends.

Africa Watch disputes this explanation. The report charges that many Nuba villagers had no choice but to flee their homes. Their villages were destroyed either in fighting between the SPLA and the government, or "purely for the purposes of relocating the population."

"This appears to amount to a systematic attempt to eradicate the identity of the Nuba," the report states.

Africa Watch Associate Director Alex de Waal, who wrote the

study, told *The Monitor* there are "mixed motives" behind the relocation. One aim, he says, is to move Nuba civilians out of a war zone.

But there is a commercial motive as well, Mr. De Waal contends. "A lot of farms will be built on the land vacated," and Muslims are the likely new owners. He expresses concern that the relocated Nubas are likely to end up working on large commercial farms as labourers.

An international relief official who has been to the Nuba mountains says the relocation puts the Nuba people into "slavery...." The official says the villagers will get very low wages working on the new farms.

A Christian church worker in Sudan, who requested not to be identified, says the government is "taking strong men to cultivate farms. The women are taken for domestic slavery."

Africa Watch speculates that women and children eventually will be sent to stay with families in Northern Kordofan while the men are likely to end up working on farms owned by "wealthy merchants."

Historically, the Nuba people have been a target of Arab slave traders and Sudanese Muslims seeking to convert them. De Waal says the relocation puts many Nubas under government control, where pressure will be applied to convert them to Islam.

Another analyst, an American anthropologist with years of experience in Africa, says: "Islamization of the Nuba is a high priority for the fundamentalist Muslims" in Sudan.

Relocated Nubas who are Muslims or convert to Islam are given preference in food allocation in the new camps, according

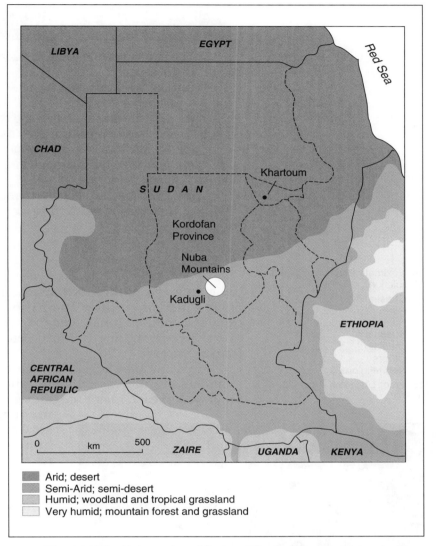

Fig. 4-21 *The Nuba region of Sudan. Note the great expanse of arid and semi-arid land, and the location of the desert in relation to the Nuba Mountains.*

to several Sudanese Christian church workers in Sudan.

The Sudanese official claimed that the US relief organization CARE had helped in the relocation, and that the UN is fully aware of the operation.

But officials at the CARE headquarters in New York had no

details on the effort, and UNICEF official Angela Raven-Roberts says as far as she knows, international agencies have not been allowed into the camps.

• • • • •

Robert M. Press, *The Christian Science Monitor*, 1992 9 14-20

DISCUSSION AND RESEARCH

15. The reading on the Nuba in Sudan presents two different versions of the situation.
    (a) List any evidence which the report contains to justify the truth of either version.
    (b) List any reasons which the report suggests may account for the lack or presence of evidence.
    (c) Suggest ways in which more evidence could be obtained.
    (d) Analyze what the report tells you about the value of information.
    (e) Describe the criteria you would use to assess the validity of information received through the print or electronic media.

Approximate Percent of World Population

Christianity	33
Islam	17
Hinduism	14
Buddhism	6
Judaism	1
Others	8
Non-religious	21

(Source: *Universal Almanac* 1993)

SOURCE: John Molyneux

Fig. 4-22 *A Shinto shrine at Ise in Japan. Shinto developed in the 8th century from the nature-worship typical of Japanese folk religions. The religion is for the most part confined to Japan, and still has a large measure of nature-worship within it.*

RELIGION

Religion is one of the world's great international forces. It links people of different cultures and nationalities, just as it divides people from one another. It has been the source of some of humanity's greatest achievements, just as it has been the excuse for some of its gravest transgressions.

Problems arise largely because there is often intolerance between members of different religions, and between members of different sects within each major religious group. By common accord, the five major religious groups in order of size are Christianity, Islam, Hinduism, Buddhism, and Judaism. There are many other religions. Some have mainly local membership, such as Shintoism in Japan, Jainism in India, and Confucianism in China. Others have widely dispersed representation, such as Sikhism and Baha'ism. Additionally, many religions are divided again according to how the faith is interpreted, just as Christianity is split by different Roman Catholic, Orthodox, and Protestant beliefs. In turn, there may be differences in belief within sub-groups, in the manner, for example, of Anglican, Baptist, Presbyterian, and United under the Protestant umbrella.

Christianity and Islam have been the most active religions in seeking to increase their numbers of believers. The other religions have been either much less aggressive

The act of seeking converts is called proselytizing.

(e.g., Buddhism) or do not actively seek adherents other than by birth (e.g., Hinduism and Judaism). Christianity and Islam have thus been the major sources of inter-group friction. Practitioners of other religions have at times been involved in hostilities, often as the target, as for Jews, but sometimes on their own initiative, as Sikhs in India.

In the past, Christians and Muslims (as believers in Islam are called) have been militant from time to time. Both have succeeded in spreading their faith to others, so that from a common area of origin in southwestern Asia they now have members in all continents, and — between them — account for the religion of about half of the world's people. Such growth has not been achieved without much turmoil and bloodshed.

The phases of growth for Christianity and Islam have tended to be part of comprehensive cultural, commercial, military, and colonizing expansions. The reasons behind such periodic expansions are complex, and may at times have been related to migrations caused by excessive population growth, characterized by many young people with little or no access to

land, as is the case today in much of the Islamic world. In such circumstances, a religious belief can provide a high-level motive and a powerful organizing force. Within one hundred years of the death of Muhammad in 632, for example, Islamic forces had created an empire that stretched from France to India, through Spain, North Africa, and southwest Asia. Almost a thousand years later, another major expansion brought Islamic forces from Turkey through southeastern and central Europe to the gates of Vienna in Austria. This expansion formed the Ottoman Empire, and was halted at Vienna in 1683. At the same time, Islamic forces also moved from south-central Asia into India to start the Mogul empire, which endured from 1526 to the late 18th century.

Islam was founded in the seventh century by Muhammad in what today is Saudi Arabia.

Islamic forces swept across North Africa, into Spain (where they were called Moors) and north into France. They were turned back at the Battle of Tours in 732, but continued to occupy parts of Spain until 1492.

SOURCE: Marilyn MacKenzie

Fig. 4-23 *Evidence of former Muslim conquest is widespread throughout northern India. This is the main entrance to one of the most famous Muslim buildings, the Taj Mahal. It was built at Agra in the 17th century as a tomb for Mumtaz Mahal, wife of one of the Mogul Emperors, Shah Jahan.*

Archbishop Tutu of South Africa once commented that when the Europeans came to Africa, "they had bibles and we had the land. They said 'let us pray' and when we opened our eyes, they had the land and we had the bibles."

Upon independence in 1947, India was partitioned. The Hindu areas formed India; the Muslim areas Pakistan (which subsequently split into Pakistan and Bangladesh). Hindus and Muslims did not occupy entirely separate areas, so there was massive relocation and much fighting. However, there are still as many Muslims in India as there are in Pakistan or Bangladesh.

Similar surges have also characterized Christianity's growth. The first surge was through the western Mediterranean basin, initially encompassing the Roman Empire in the 300s, and reaching across Europe from Ireland to Poland between 400 and 900. During the 15th and 16th centuries, Christian missionaries accompanied the ships, traders, colonizers, and armies that spread European influence to the Americas. More Christian missionaries accompanied traders, colonizers, and armies in the 19th and early 20th centuries, as European influence was pushed further into Africa, southeast and east Asia, Australasia, and North America.

In almost all cases, intrusions by Christian and Islamic forces have produced long-lasting hostility, quite apart from any benefits that either side may perceive to exist. For example, the Islamic Turkish penetration of the Balkans from the 14th through the 19th centuries caused many local Slavic people to convert to Islam. Their descendants include the Muslims of Bosnia, now victimized by Serbs who are descendants of those who resisted conversion to Islam (see "The Sinister Ideology of "Ethnic Cleansing"" on p. 237). Similarly, the Islamic Mogul penetration of India from the 16th through the 18th centuries brought about the building of many Muslim forts, mosques, and tombs. One of the lesser mosques — the Babri mosque — was built at Ayodhya in northern India upon a site claimed by Hindus to be the birthplace of one of the most sacred Hindu deities, Lord Ram (also called Rama). In 1992 the mosque was destroyed by rampaging Hindus, sparking religious riots that resulted in thousands of deaths within weeks. Despite the benefits introduced by the expansion of Islam, the violence in both Bosnia and India is in part a reaction to the former expansion of Islam. The following reading explores the situation in India in more detail.

INDIA SEEKS HARMONY AMID DIVERSITY

It is ironic that the worst Hindu-Muslim violence in recent times should have taken place in Ayodhya, literally meaning the land of no fight. Even more ironic is that proponents of Hinduism, a religio-social way of living that preaches nonviolence, have become demagogues. In a stroke, one of the world's oldest cultural systems seemed to lose its poise and dignity as fanaticism surfaced in its practitioners.

On Dec. 6, 1992, a frenzied crowd of more than 200 000 Hindus stormed the territory of a disputed mosque in Ayodhya, northern India and leveled the 16th century structure. In the aftermath of the crime, more than 1800 people, mostly Muslims, have died. To understand the recent events in India, one must revisit the foundations of the Muslim and Hindu conflict in the context of present-day India.

Picture a multi-storied apartment house in which a different family has lived in each apartment for generations. Each has a different cultural orientation, speaks a different language, and eats different food. A visit to any one apartment reveals a different form of art, entertainment, and music. To this add different religions and, at times, their conflicting practices. The ultimate *masala* (mixture) obtained is a potpourri of cultures called India.

The nation suffers from (a) serious social and economic malaise. There is hunger, poverty, bureaucracy, and corruption. While slowly moving toward extinction, the rigid caste and dowry systems prevail. The pressure of a population still growing at about two percent a year has pushed millions of Indians into wretched living conditions. Even within this intractable framework, the Indian economy, often compared to a lethargic elephant, has lurched ahead. The success of the Green Revolution seemed to herald a new era in agriculture. India's space program and peaceful nuclear program place it among the top industrial countries. Only 18 months ago, Prime Minister P. V. Narasimha Rao began a drive to unshackle the economy. Despite having to live on a per capita income of less than $400 a year, Indians have maintained a functioning secular democracy.

The goal of remaining secular has often been hampered by the diversity of languages, people, and religions. For example, there are more than 15 major languages, nearly 24 other languages, each spoken by a million people or more representing different broad ethnic groups.

Historically, relations between the Hindus and Muslims have not always been placid. But despite the difference between the two religions and their practices, they have lived for decades in relative harmony. During the struggle for independence (from England), Muslims and Hindus worked shoulder to shoulder for an India free from colonial domination. The discontent between Hindus and Muslims can probably be traced to a few legal actions by the colonial masters in the early part of this century.

In an attempt to officially recognize the large Muslim population in India, the English government passed bills that designated Muslims as a voting block separate from the Hindus and other Indians. The law mandated that Muslims could vote only for their Muslim leaders. By accident or design the separatist sentiment of being a "Hindu" or a "Muslim" was reinforced every time Indians went to the polls.

As the image of majority rule by Hindus in free India loomed, greater efforts were made by Muslims to build the Muslim League, led by Jinnah, into a strong national party. The Indian National Congress remained a secular party of Hindus and Muslims. The League, however, had one major difference in that it was a party of Muslims only and had one agenda — the creation of a separate Muslim state to safeguard the interests of its members.

The transition to an independent state was anything but

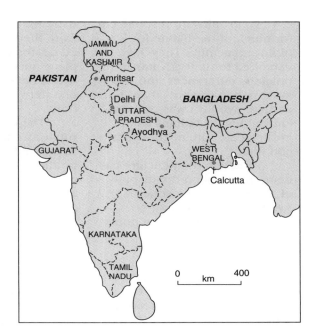

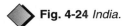

Fig. 4-24 *India.*

easy. The national betrayal and trauma associated with the cruel dissection of India engendered widespread animosity. More than half a million Indians were slaughtered and more than six million people were displaced on either side of the new border. The creation of Muslim Pakistan in 1947 did not solve the problem of communal strife.

The dastardly act in Ayodhya wiped the slate clean of India's achievements since independence. Around the world, people rightly scorned the incident as the nation's shame and ridiculed the Indian government. What had gone wrong? More importantly, is India, with its religious diversity, another time bomb in the world's stockpile of ethnic and religious explosives?

Politicians are responsible for much of the blame for India's quagmire. They have exploited to their advantage the religious differences, the caste system, and the poverty of the people. Ayodhya was perhaps known best to Indians as the birthplace of the mythological god Ram.

Although the judiciary has been debating on the dispute of *Babri Masjid* (mosque) in Ayodhya for more than 40 years, it had remained a nonissue until the mid-1980s.

It is not a mere co-incidence that the Hindu Bhartiya Janata Party (BJP), which in 1984 had only two seats in the *Lok Sabha* (Lower House), won a strong 119 seats in the 1991 election. Undoubtedly, it has done so largely by campaigning to retain the territory of the disputed mosque to "safeguard" the interest of Hindus.

During the struggle for independence India's leaders had vision and a vibrant intellectual capacity to debate "what ought to be" as opposed to "what is." Today, many politicians, having grown up in an ideological vacuum and with a distorted world view, find themselves bankrupt of ideas to solve India's problems.

It is a mistake to take the act of 200 000 Hindus as representative of the feelings of 710 million Hindus in India. This minority calling for a Hindu state has been systematically brainwashed by extreme right-wing politicians. Even the violence and reported deaths that have taken place have occurred in areas which have a strong presence of a network of Hindu organizations.

The extent to which runaway emotions can be harnessed will largely depend on the actions the government of India takes. In the aftermath of the crime, the government banned the Hindu BJP and Rashtriya Swayamsewak Sang (RSS), arrested their leaders, and dismissed some of the state governments. These are token measures to keep the Muslim sentiments in check and will solve nothing.

Many leaders in the banned parties are well versed in the techniques of noncooperation and civil disobedience launched by Mahatma Gandhi. They will not hesitate in using them to further their cause.

Among the alternatives reported are challenging the banning of the Hindu parties by initiating thousands of legal appeals, organizing massive rallies to fill jails, and generally harassing the Indian people.

Observers who believe that banning parties in India will mitigate fanatical party allegiance are mistaken. The RSS is the same disciplined party that played a major role as an underground resistance force during India's fight for freedom. Moreover, arresting the party chiefs may only transform them into heroes and boost party membership.

The ruling Congress party must seize the political moment and quell the growing communalism. But it first must address internal divisiveness. It is a national party with proven access to the common person. It should use this power to counter vested, albeit minority, interests' messages of hatred. Bringing the warring factions to the negotiating table can still pay dividends, as can striking a balance between economic reform and the needs dictated by socio-political conditions.

The fires of fanaticism will take time to cool. The debates on the unity of, and **secularism** in, India have only begun. Many questions remain. How differently is secularism practiced in India compared to its practice elsewhere? In a society as diverse as India, can secularism be synonymous with complete religious freedom? Or should secularism be guided by the freedom to practice what the state judges, within restrictions imposed by diversity?

India has survived many crises, and once again it seems to be at a crossroads. Whether it emerges from the present crisis a better, stronger, and a more united country will depend on the collective commitment to secularism and democracy.

Rajeev Malik, *The Christian Science Monitor*, 1993 2 5-11

Christian expansion into the Americas provoked a rather different reaction among the indigenous peoples. The nature of the European forces arrayed against them was more overwhelming than was the case with Islamic forces in either Europe or India. In Central and South America, Christianity was more adopted and adapted than accepted, and there are still some practices in Latin American Christianity that have a pre-Christian origin. In North America, however, there has been an enduring hostility among many First Nations peoples toward Christianity. Christianity was perceived by the First Nations peoples to be one of the instruments of European power aimed at eliminating aboriginal culture and lifestyles.

Since the 1960s, there has been a resurgence in interest in First Nations peoples' spirituality, especially on the part of many other North Americans. One of the reasons for this change, where Christianity has a diminished emphasis, is that many people view First Nations peoples' spirituality as offering an environmentally sustainable philosophy, as outlined in the reading "Father Sun and Mother Earth" in Chapter Two (p. 91). First Nations peoples' beliefs are seen as a counter to the materialism of much of modern life.

Currently, Christianity appears to be in the throes of resolving various human rights issues. For example, should women be ordained as ministers? Some branches of Christianity say no; other branches have already done it. Should the churches support political and economic change, even revolution, or should they remain purely religious in purpose? Both views — and many in between — are held by different groups of people. The differences appear to rest largely in the degree of what is often

To many environmentalists, Christian beliefs favour treating the environment as subservient to people, and — through the "work ethic" — tend to foster economic growth.

SOURCE: John Molyneux

Fig. 4-25 *An aboriginal memorial ground on the coast of British Columbia. What does the photograph suggest about the religious beliefs held by First Nations peoples?*

called fundamentalism — the interpretation of the basic and traditional beliefs and practices of the religion. Generally, the more fundamental, or orthodox, the beliefs, the less support there is for equality of status for women or for political and economic activities that might change the existing patterns.

In both Christianity and Islam there have always been people with fundamentalist views, opposed to those with more "liberal" views, and at various times they have predominated. The Inquisition — the activities of the Roman Catholic Church in seeking and countering people called heretics who denied its basic beliefs — is perhaps the best-known example. The Inquisition was established in the 13th century and lasted into the 19th century, but it was most active from the 14th to 16th centuries in Spain. However, while fundamentalism exists in Christianity, its impact is not currently widespread.

Fundamentalism in Islam in the late 20th century has diverse impacts. Perhaps the most significant impact results from attempts by Orthodox Muslims to change the nations where they form a majority from states not governed by religion (**secular states**) to states governed by religion (religious states). The process is ongoing, and often violent. States that have already changed to religious rule, with the Islamic code of law (called *sharia*), include Iran, Pakistan, Saudi Arabia, and Sudan. Other nations with Muslim majorities have experienced strong pressure from Orthodox Muslims and militant extremists to become religious states. In consequence, Afghanistan and Lebanon are in turmoil; Iraq has religious rebels in its southern parts (in addition to ethnic Kurdish rebels in its northern and western parts); Turkey and Egypt — as states that are determinedly secular — face periodic attacks from religious militants; and from Morocco to Libya strong civil and military authorities have jailed many fundamentalist leaders. In Syria, many Islamic fundamentalists have been massacred, as by the Syrian army at Hama in 1982.

In Algeria, the army cancelled elections and banned the Islamic Salvation Front in 1992 when it appeared certain that fundamentalists would form the next government. The new military government opened four detention centres in southern Algeria for Islamic dissidents. Later in 1992, the new President was assassinated. Representatives of the Islamic Salvation Front warned that the country was on the verge of civil war. More peacefully, in Bangladesh, the Nationalist Party, which promotes creation of an Islamic state, won 138 of 330 parliamentary seats in the elections in 1991.

Meanwhile, across south-central Asia in the nations created by the disappearance of the Soviet Union, there is much disagreement about the future direction of the new states. Both Iran and Saudi Arabia would like to see Islamic states established across south-central Asia, but they are competing with each other because Islam itself is split into two major sects: Sunni (over 90 percent, including Saudi Arabia) and Shia (under ten percent, mostly in Iran). At the same time, Turkey also competes for influence in south-central Asia, wanting to restore its ancient

Orthodox Muslims believe that human life should be organized the tenets of the Koran (sometimes written as Qu'ran), which contains guidance for all aspects of living including the organization of the state.

In attempts to overthrow the secular government in Egypt by cutting off one of the main sources of income, fundamentalists murdered several foreign tourists in 1992.

Saudi Arabia is governed by a royal family (the Saud family) which belongs to a strict sect of Sunni Muslims called the Wahhabi.

importance in the region (many of the inhabitants are of Turkic origin) and persuade the new states that secular government is preferable.

The conversion of a nation from a secular state to an Islamic state reinforces many traditional Islamic cultural values. It often has a profound effect on the role of women in society. Implementation of sharia law could, among other things, segregate men and women in public places and require a dress code for men and women. It could also reduce the already limited legal rights of women and deprive women of access to many jobs outside the home. Secular states such as Turkey and Egypt regard these possibilities as undemocratic. However, fundamentalist philosopher Abdel Salam Faraj from Egypt says, "In the Islamic countries, the enemy is at home; indeed it is he who is in command." What do you think he means? The status of women in Islamic states and elsewhere is examined in more detail in the case study at the end of this chapter.

DISCUSSION AND RESEARCH

16. The preceding section discussed several countries in which Islamic fundamentalism, or orthodoxy, was causing political difficulties.
    (a) Research the world distribution of Islam,
    (b) Draw a world map to show the distribution of Islam, and
    (c) Devise a way of showing on the map the areas referred to in this section according to the nature of the political difficulties.

17. After examining the following reading, develop — in small groups — an appropriate policy for the Chinese government to pursue that might satisfy the wishes of the Muslims in Xinjiang while retaining them as part of China.

CHINA COURTS ETHNIC UNITY IN XINJIANG

"Allahu Akbar" — "God is great" — sounds the refrain. ...men with...decades of experience etched on their faces attend Friday prayers in their local mosque.

The nearby bazaar bustles with commerce. From deep in the cavernous interior wafts the aroma of mutton kebabs, which can be bought by the skewer hot off the coals. Rug merchants preside proudly over their carpets, offering tea and flat bread to facilitate the process of the deal....

Not an unusual sight in any Muslim country. But this is China, a definitely non-Muslim country. Out of its billion-plus people only 16 million are Muslims. But half of them are concentrated here in Xinjiang Uighur Autonomous Region,... with the country's richest lode of strategic minerals....

• • • • •

Chinese geologists claim the region may contain more than 5.8 billion barrels of oil. And Xinjiang's Tarim Basin is "very likely to become the country's major oil and natural gas production center," reported the China Daily, the official English-language newspaper.

Xinjiang also has rich deposits of gold, platinum, iron ore, and copper, according to the Chinese government, and one-third of China's total coal reserves.

The Taklimakan Desert...is home to the Lop Nur nuclear missile test site — the largest in the world, according to the Natural Resources Defense Council, an environmental research organization. Above-ground testing continued here until 1980, 17 years after the U.S. and Soviet Union discontinued it, and underground tests are still occurring. The most recent one was August 1990, the NRDC reported.

Strategically, Xinjiang is probably the most sensitive of China's autonomous regions — bordering (the former) Soviet Central Asia to the north, Mongolia to the east, Afghanistan and Pakistan to the west, and Tibet to the south.

There are 120 000 troops deployed in the Lanzhou military region, of which Xinjiang is a part.

But that troop presence is not only for what lies beyond China's borders. A military presence of that size underlines Beijing's concerns about (its) population in Xinjiang....

Forty of China's 55 minority groups live in Xinjiang. The largest of these is the (Muslim) Uighurs — the oldest known Turkic-speaking people, accounting for more than 40 percent of Xinjiang's 15 million inhabitants. Other Muslims include the Kazakhs, the Kirghiz, and the Uzbeks, all of Turkic origin. With their Caucasian features, hazel eyes, and brown hair, most of Xinjiang's minorities, or *shao shu minzu* in Chinese, bear little resemblance to the more than a bil-

lion Han people of China. Most have more in common with their ethnic brethren in neighboring...Central Asia — including language.

· · · · ·

The area around Kashgar, the fabled oasis along the ancient Silk Road, was officially made off-limits to foreigners a year ago, after a reported Muslim revolt in Baren, 22 miles (35 km) south of Kashgar. Details are few, but Beijing's denial of permission to build a mosque was followed by a riot in which 22 (by official count) and as many as 60 (unofficially) died as a result of action by the security police. It was only late last summer that foreigners were once again allowed into the area.

As a result of the uprising, the government last fall announced the purging of some local Communist Party and government officials in Baren, because of their "implication in the rebellion." New religious restrictions have been introduced, including the banning of Koranic schools and the advocating of "holy war" by clerics, who are also forbidden to meet foreigners.

The region is no stranger to communal tension. Xinjiang's history has been punctuated by episodes of resistance to Han rule. The great Muslim rebellions of the 19th century were crushed one by one, just as opposition has been in the last decade.

· · · · ·

Since the Cultural Revolution (1966-76), Beijing seems to have treated Muslim unrest more discreetly. Then, mosques were razed and Muslim elders were made to parade in the streets with pigs' heads strung around their necks.[1] But the last decade has seen a veiled approach by central authorities. Minorities have been allowed to marry younger, have been permitted limited religious freedoms, and, until last year, were exempted from the one-child-per-family policy aimed at limiting population growth.

In recent years hundreds of Xinjiang Muslims have been permitted to make the pilgrimage to Mecca. But this loosening of the reins has also engendered nationalist feelings, precisely what the government had hoped to avoid.

· · · · ·

...In centuries past it (Xinjiang) was beyond China. It was here that the Silk Road entered Central Asia. Rulers of Imperial China realized the strategic and economic advantages of the area and conquered it three times in all, most recently in the 18th century — during the Ching Dynasty, when China was ruled by the Manchus. It was they who gave this region the name Xinjiang, which means "New Dominion."

But consolidation of Han power here did not come until the Communists' victory in 1949 ended the existence of the short-lived East Turkestan Republic, which had declared itself independent during the chaos of China's warlord period. Like other minority areas, such as Tibet and Inner Mongolia, Xinjiang was granted the status of autonomous region in 1955. But its autonomy exists in name alone.

Fearful of unrest after the elimination of the (East) Turkestan Republic, Beijing began relocating millions of Han to Xinjiang during the early days of Communist China. In the 1950s less than six percent of the population was Han; today the figure is more than 40 percent (20 percent in the city of Kashgar), and the area has the uneasy feel of a family gathering coping with the intrusion of unwelcome guests. Four decades have done little to lessen the animosity between the Han and the Uighur.

· · · · ·

Just as during the height of the Cultural Revolution, the government has once again resorted to sloganeering to stress its message of ethnic unity. Such tactics are a measure of its concern. Billboard campaigns with neat little slogans sum up the importance of the minorities issue.

"Splittism is the prime danger to the unity of the Motherland," read one.

"The minorities can't be parted from the Han and the Han can't be parted from the minorities," claimed another.

There is a deceptive calm in Xinjiang. Local residents are wary of talking to foreigners, as they fear they may be watched. Just as with the 1989 Beijing demonstrators, the government likes to blame outside agitators, and journalists were barred until late last summer. Now they are

welcomed only when accompanied by government officials.

But, upon gaining people's confidence, we found a sense of nationalism and resentment toward the Han.

"The Uighurs, the Kazakhs, and the Kirghiz are the real owners of Xinjiang," said a defiant young Uighur. "Being part of China means we are in the minority. That has been a disaster for development. It is better for us to be independent. Then we will be in the majority."

· · · · ·

Madhulika Sikka and James A. Millward, *World Monitor*, 1991 4

[1] The Koran generally forbids the consumption of pigs by Muslims, but they are a common part of the Chinese diet. What was the real meaning of making Muslim elders wear pigs' heads strung around their necks?

18. List various examples of the ways in which major religions may either reinforce or weaken national sovereignty.

19. Write an essay examining the interrelationships between religion and ethnic groupings.

20. In small group discussion, examine and report on factors that support the spirit of "my nation" among people.

21. Some individuals have commented that people of many religions believe that they should accept their earthly lot, and that their rewards will be in the next life.
    (a) Discuss the possible effects of such beliefs on overall human and economic development.
    (b) Discuss the possible effects of the opposite belief — that people should not accept their earthly lot, but strive to gain their rewards in this life — on overall human and economic development.

22. Figure 4-26 is a list of some of the minority situations in the world identified by a British organization called The Minority Rights Group. Select any one of the situations.

Organize an inquiry (see Appendix 3) to find out more about it, and report your findings in writing.

AFRICA
Asians in East and Central Africa
Namibians
San of the Kalahari
Victims of genocide in Burundi
Victims of inequalities in Zimbabwe
Western Saharans
Peoples in Uganda
Peoples in Sudan
Asians in East Africa
Nomads of the Sahel
Falashas

THE AMERICAS
Blacks in Brazil and Cuba
East Indians in Trindad and Guyana
Indigenous peoples of South America
Indigenous peoples of Central America
Indigenous peoples of the United States
First Nations peoples of Canada
Mexican Americans
French Canadians
Haitian refugees in the United States
Puerto Ricans
Inuit of Canada

ASIA
Minorities in Japan
Chinese in southeast Asia
Adivasis and Biharis of Bangladesh
Nagas in India
Minorities in Central Vietnam
Tamils of Sri Lanka
Untouchables of India
Baluchis and Pathans
Tibetans
Sikhs
Lumad and Moro of Mindinao

EUROPE
People in conflict in Ireland
Crimean Tatars and
    Volga Germans
Basques and Catalans
European Gypsies
Migrant workers
Peoples of Cyprus
Hungarians of Romania
Flemings and Walloons
Saami of Lapland
Rastafarians

Indigenous peoples of the Russian
    Far North

SOUTHWEST ASIA
The Bedouin of the Negev
Oriental immigrants and Druzes of Israel
Palestinians
Armenians
Baha'is of Iran
Kurds

OTHERS
Maori of New Zealand
Peoples of East Timor and West Irian
Peoples of New Caledonia
Peoples of Fiji
Australian aborigines
Palau in Micronesia
Women in Arabic countries
Women in Asia
Women in Sub-Saharan Africa
Women in Latin America
Children
Disabled people

Fig. 4-26 *List of some of the world's minority situations identified by The Minority Rights Group of the United Kingdom.*

MIGRANTS AND REFUGEES

Migrants generally choose to move voluntarily, while refugees are generally forced to move in order to survive. Refugees are defined by the United Nations as people who leave their homeland because they have well-founded fears of persecution based on race, ethnic origin, political opinion, or membership in a particular social group. The United Nations estimates that there are about 18 million refugees in the world, up from two million in 1951 when the U.N. first counted them. Migrations are caused largely by the desire for a better life. Most seek a materially richer life, but others migrate for greater political or religious freedom.

Migrants are easier for a government to control than refugees, because they normally have to apply for admission and are accepted ahead of their arrival in the host country. They can also be rejected at the government's discretion. Refugees, on the other hand, often arrive unannounced in large numbers. They usually bring few possessions with them and they may be hungry and in ill-health. As a result, they require a significant amount of assistance. Yet due to political and human rights considerations, they are difficult for a country to reject.

Acceptance of migrants may offer several benefits to both receiving and sending countries, apart from any benefits gained by individual migrants. Receiving countries may gain needed additional population and new skills; a more varied culture; wealth, if migrants bring money with them; and a gain in international human contact. There is an intermingling which may break down purely nationalist feelings. Sending countries may gain from release of population pressure on relatively scarce housing or employment situations; wealth, if migrants send some of their new earnings back to relatives in their former countries; and access to new skills and trading opportunities.

There may also be problems for both receiving and sending countries. Receiving countries may experience difficulties in developing agreement on whether or not to try to assimilate people from different cultures. They may experience social unrest, especially where cultural values clash. Traditional lifestyle differences may provoke misunderstandings. They may suffer financial loss as migrants remit part of their earnings to their relatives. Some in the receiving nation may feel that immigration

American folk singer Joan Baez, although a tourist, was refused admission to a German night club in 1993 because, as she was told, "there are too many foreigners here already."

SOURCE: Novosti Press Agency

Fig. 4-27 *During the life of the Soviet Union (1922-1991), many ethnic Russians from the lands west of the Urals were encouraged to settle in Siberia and other non-Russian areas in interior Asia, where they now form ethnic minorities. These are apartments for Russian immigrants to Igarka on the banks of the Yenisei River in Siberia.*

threatens the ethnic stability of their nation, increases competition for jobs, and dependency upon welfare or other claims. Sending countries may experience the loss of their most educated or enterprising people, especially if suitable home job opportunities are scarce. They may also suffer financially as relatively wealthy migrants take their money with them.

Refugees tend to increase the globalization of world activity in much the same ways as migrants, but they sometimes do so less permanently. Because refugees have been forced (rather than chosen) to move, they are more likely than migrants to return to their homelands if conditions there change. For example, many Vietnamese who left as so-called boat people in the late 1970s are returning there in the 1990s because conditions in Vietnam have changed. Further, host countries do not always wish to retain the refugees they accepted during a crisis, and so send them back. Hong Kong cannot accommodate all the Vietnamese who landed there in the 1970s, and is gradually returning them to Vietnam whether the Vietnamese refugees want to return or not. In much the same way, the United States has intercepted boatloads of Haitian refugees in the 1990s and returned them to Haiti.

The term "boat people" may be used to describe any group of refugees fleeing from an area by boat. In 1993 the boat people were Haitians fleeing to Florida.

One of the fears underpinning resistance to unannounced refugee arrivals lies in the difference in relative rates of population growth in the developing and developed worlds. As examined in Chapter One, population growth rates are much higher throughout the developing world than they are in the developed world. Standards of living are also generally lower in the developing world. Many people in the developed world fear that their countries and cultures may be under increasing risk of irreversible change if refugees are accepted in ever larger numbers. The situation may be aggravated by the growing belief in the developed world that large numbers of arrivals claiming refugee status are really economic migrants. As the *Third World Guide 93/94* says, "Even states which had traditionally been welcoming to political or economic refugees of various regions have gradually modified their policy towards foreigners. In Europe the process has been accompanied by a rise in nationalistic feelings which have often become expressed in xenophobic or racist movements."

Source regions for refugees shift as situations around the world change. In the past, there have been major refugee movements from many countries that now appear to have stabilized. For example, many Hungarians and Czechs left their homelands in the 1960s, and some have since returned. In the 1980s, many Afghans fled, and they too are now returning to their homeland.

The troubled areas that have developed during the 1990s include many of the newly independent states of the former Soviet Union, as well as the former Yugoslavia. Several other areas continue to be troublespots, since the causes of fear remain. Such continuing areas of fear include several countries in Africa, notably Angola, Somalia, Sudan, and Zaire. Elsewhere, people are fleeing oppression in Haiti and East Timor.

The world's refugee situation is fluid, and new source regions may appear on the world scene without much warning. Additionally, environmental degradation in certain parts of the world may create new sources of refugees without any of the usual political or social pressures that might otherwise cause people to seek refuge. Environmental refugees form a new type of refugee, so far not recognized at an international level. The following reading examines the phenomenon of environmental refugees.

THE ENVIRONMENTAL REFUGEE: A NEW APPROACH

Since the mid-1980s, the concept of the environmental refugee has gained currency. This has been defined in very broad terms as someone fleeing from environmental decline.

The problem with this definition is that it is so wide as to render the concept virtually meaningless. Reports have spoken of tens of millions of individuals who fall, or soon will fall, into this category of people displaced by floods, deforestation, rising sea levels, nuclear accidents and other phenomena of natural or human origin.

Uncritical definitions and inflated numbers lead to inappropriate solutions and compassion fatigue. We should not, however, reject outright the concept of environmental refugees. Instead we should formulate a definition that is more narrow but more precise.

One way to narrow the definition is by applying the familiar distinction between refugee and migrant. The latter moves by choice from an area, while a refugee is compelled to flee. This classic distinction seems appropriate to those displaced because of environmental changes. This is an obvious difference between the flooding of a habitat as a result of dam building, and the slow but steady erosion of farming topsoil. In both

cases populations will be displaced; but there the similarity ends.

Accordingly, we have not one but two categories. The first is the environmental migrant. Such a person makes a voluntary, rational decision to leave a region as the situation gradually worsens there. In that decision, environmental deterioration may be only one factor among others.

In fact, environmental degradation has a usually long-term, cumulative impact closely akin to the effects of long-term economic change — itself the major impetus for migration of agricultural populations in the developing world. The environmental factor swells the stream of migrants, but those driven by that factor are not thereby distinguishable from other migrants.

They can, however, be distinguished from environmental refugees. These are people or social groups displaced as a result of sudden, drastic environmental change that cannot be reversed. The degradation compromises or removes a group's basic conditions for existence, and it does so within a very short time.

Residents of the area thus have little opportunity to respond to the problem, and little choice but to leave. They are more vulnerable than environmental migrants, and need more assistance to adjust to their altered circumstances.

Often that help is not forthcoming from the governments concerned. The displaced persons are

therefore true refugees, being unable to turn for support to their own governments.

The separation is not absolute between the categories of environmental migrant and refugee. Instead, there may be a shading between the two.

In an area that is gradually being degraded, for example, residents with more resources decide at an early stage to move elsewhere. The last to leave are those with least resources, least know-how on how to migrate, and fewest contacts to help them along the way.

These people typically wait until a crisis arrives. Then, in desperation, they are forced off their land. Their migration is the result entirely of "push," not "pull." And they are most likely not to succeed in re-establishing themselves elsewhere in reasonable comfort.

It is for these people that the term "environmental refugees" should be reserved. They tend to be the most marginal, powerless and therefore vulnerable groups in their society.

It is possible to trace these two types of displacement, and the shift from one to the other, in response to various forms of environmental deterioration.

Uphill reforestation, for example, causes soil erosion and more frequent downstream flooding. Over time affected farmers along the riverbank will experience more frequent loss of the harvest, lower productivity and lower output. A common response would be for one or more family members to migrate on a seasonal or permanent basis, typically as a result of "pull" and "push."

Deforestation, however, also creates refugees — notably tribal force inhabitants who lose their habitat as it is logged or cleared for farming. Such people are clearly displaced against their will.

The rise in sea levels is a gradual process which has a severe impact on coastal areas or low-lying island countries. In the case of severe floods, displaced people will turn to national or international relief agencies for help until the waters subside, and will then return to their homes. In the longer term, they will migrate to other regions or countries. In the end, as the low-lying areas disappear, a no-choice situation will develop, and the displaced in effect become refugees.

Drought or desertification is another cumulative process that tends to displace people. Affected peasants or pastoralists may move to new grazing land, to farmlands or to towns. As the situation approaches a crisis, herds are killed and seed grain is consumed for food. The populace migrates to relief camps in what is clearly a refugee-type situation.

Like any population displacement, the movement of environmental migrants or refugees could have a positive impact on the host area, introducing valuable new labour and skills. But it could also lead to conflict, either within or between nations.

Conflict, however, is not the only nor the most important undesirable result of environmental degradation. More likely outcomes are acute exploitation, social tension and suffering. No less than actual conflict, these compromise security and need to be addressed.

The most basic way of dealing with the syndrome presented here is by re-examining policy. It is necessary to reconsider the development strategies that are often the underlying causes of environmental degradation — for example, inappropriate **cash cropping**, the uncritical extraction of natural resources such as timber or minerals, large-scale irrigation, and other strategies associated with export-oriented growth. And it is necessary to assess the political and economic forces that prompt the adoption of such strategies.

Changing those strategies, however, is not easy. They are usually part of an overall policy. And they are often supported by foreign capital.

If the root causes are intractable, it may be possible at least to mitigate the problem through a "technical fix" — any of a number of technical solutions that minimize the harmful effects. These may be such practical measures as building terraces to prevent soil erosion in deforested upland areas, raising embankments to protect against flooding, or improving irrigation to avoid land degradation.

More ambitious than these are remedial policies such as reforestation, or zoning land for multiple uses to prevent displacement of marginal groups. Such measures implement the principles of sustainable development.

At times, not even remedial action is possible, or a crisis has been reached. All that can be done then is to offer relief assistance to those who are displaced — for example, tribal people pushed out of the forest. Such people very likely have no other means of sustaining themselves, and could end up being severely exploited.

Action is needed at all three levels. This will help the people who have been forced from their land, and mitigate or eventually end the practices that led to their displacement.

Astri Suhrke and Annamaria Visentin, *Ecodecision*, 1991 9

DISCUSSION AND RESEARCH

23. Select an example of a current refugee situation.
    (a) Research its causes, and
    (b) Develop recommendations that would help to resolve the issue.

24. The United Nations estimates that only about 20 percent of the world's 80 000 000 migrants are legally registered in their adopted

countries. The remainder are illegal immigrants, mostly in North America and Australia. Lack of appropriate documents deprives illegal immigrants of many human rights, such as rights to a fair wage or to social security. Discuss the advantages people seek by migrating illegally, and the disadvantages they may face in their adopted countries.

CONCLUSION

Interaction among different groups of people may be either cooperative or confrontational. Cooperative interaction exists in government organizations such as the World Health Organization, and non-government organizations (NGOs) such as the International Olympic Committee. It exists also across almost all fields of human endeavour, such as trade, health, development assistance, environmental protection, the arts, sport, and international communications. This growing globalization of activity is seen by many observers as a positive step towards creating the groundwork for a world in harmony with itself and its natural environment. Others criticize the trend to globalization because they say it reduces national sovereignty and places their own national cultures and standards of living at risk. They say also that globalization permits economically or militarily powerful nations to dominate weaker nations, placing the economies and cultures of less powerful nations at risk too.

While much interaction is cooperative, there is still a great deal of confrontation. Differences arise among groups over a wide variety of issues, related in a large part to ethnicity, religion, social and economic equity, and the nature of past interactions. In many cases, the roots of current conflict stretch deeply into history. Such roots are strong and may not easily be broken. Unless conditions change and the roots of conflict wither, it is likely that inter-group confrontations will continue.

How can such conditions be changed? As in all conflicts, effort must be put into promoting attitudes of at least tolerance, if not goodwill. Acceptance of differences, protection of individual and collective human rights, clear ideas of the importance of both rights and responsibilities, willingness to abide by the rule of law, and the development of a sense of world citizenship are goals that many people seek to achieve. They hope at the same time to diminish selfishness, overbearing pride, and anger. Can they succeed?

The next chapter examines some of the major trends in the world, and looks at some possibilities for the future.

- What are the different choices?
- How urgent is the situation?
- Where do you stand?
- What can you do personally to help?

CASE STUDY

WOMEN IN TODAY'S WORLD

Over the past 40 years, the United Nations has gradually changed its priorities with regard to women. During the 1950s and 1960s women's issues were discussed mainly within the context of human rights. During the 1970s the perspective changed; women were recognized as part of the development process and their contributions were sought out. As a result, it was recognized that it was necessary to improve the status, nutrition, health, and education of women. It wasn't until the 1980s that United Nations organizations began to promote the idea that women should be treated as equals. At the World Conference for Women in Nairobi in 1985 women were specifically recognized as intellectuals, policy-makers, planners, and contributors.

In spite of this change, a Washington-based population agency, gathering statistics from the United Nations and the World Bank as well as various countries' census data, recently announced that there is no country in the world where women enjoy full equality with men. Their study showed that in spite of a rise in consciousness about the status of women, females are slipping below the poverty line with greater frequency than males in most countries. The survey showed that the earlier women marry and bear children, the less chance they have of education, a subsistence wage, or a healthy life. In Bangladesh, where women's status is the poorest, three-quarters of women are married by 18, and most have children soon afterwards. In Sweden, highest in the ranking, only one percent of women marry by 19. A third of all developing countries don't have sufficient school facilities to educate their children, and girls are the last to obtain an education. In every part of the world women are in employment ghettos where pay scales, fringe benefits, working conditions, and mobility are poor.

Women almost everywhere have the right to vote, yet they play a very minor role in high-level political and economic decision-making in most countries. Nevertheless, progress is being made. On the same day in 1993, citizens of both Turkey and Canada chose women to lead the parties in power in their respective countries. They joined ten other women in the twentieth century world-wide who have headed governments.

WOMEN'S ROLES IN VARIOUS SOCIETIES

A woman's position in her particular society is defined by a great range of influences, including religion and culture. Most women belong to a religious group which encompasses a set of traditions, practices, and beliefs about their position within that society. Each religious group interprets today's women's movement within the context of long-held traditions. A look at the Islamic world illustrates one religion's way of reconciling the ideas of today with tradition.

The Koran is generally accepted to advocate a tolerant system of social justice, including rights for women. It states, however, that although men and women are created equal, they have different responsibilities within a marriage. Females have the primary responsibility for nurturing their children, while males are primarily responsible for providing for and protecting the family. However, women have equal rights within the marriage, can remain economically independent if they so wish, and can maintain their maiden name. Married women can work as long as their careers as a wife and mother are not compromised. All professions are permissible as long as work does not place a woman in an environment where her dignity is undermined.

Koranic teaching also requires that both men and women dress modestly. The dress code for women is designed to give them freedom from exploitation. Nurjehen Mawani, the head of Canada's Immigration and Refugee Board, and a Muslim woman of Indian descent, says "I have never found any inconsistency between women's rights, gender equality, and my understanding of Islam. Islam is a very egalitarian religion."

In today's Islamic world there are different interpretations made of the Koran and Muhammad's teachings, and some followers of Islam have chosen to revive laws developed in the 7th and 8th centuries by Islamic legal experts of the time. Cultural traditions also play a role in the way society is organized in different Islamic countries. As discussed on p. 272 of Chapter Four, the Islamic world today is experiencing the growth of political parties or groups who wish to adopt what is referred to as an orthodox view of life within Islam. The term "fundamentalist" is commonly used for these groups. There is considerable anti-Western sentiment within most of these parties, and by interpreting Islam strictly, it allows a society to separate itself from Western influences. As much of Western society embraces feminism and equality for women at home and in the workplace, Islamic society has experienced an upsurge of interest in what to many appear to be limitations to the freedom of women. The degree of orthodoxy and how it affects women differs greatly from one Islamic country to another.

In three of these countries, Iran, Afghanistan, and Sudan, the extremist groups are the dominant political power and this has had considerable influence on the restrictions women within these countries face. For example, in Iran, with the ascendancy of the Ayatollah Khomeini in 1979 and the establishment of Iran as an Islamic Republic, the requirement for modest dress was strictly interpreted. Women were required to wear head-to-toe robes covering all but their face and hands. Make-up and jeans were not permitted, and hair was not to show around the face. If women failed to obey they were arrested. Some Iranian women considered the chador or long black

SOURCE: Marilyn MacKenzie

Fig. 4-28 *A woman dressed in a chador followed by her small child on a Moroccan street.*

robe a liberating step because it meant they were judged on their abilities rather than their physical appearance. Other Iranian women could not accept these rules and objected to their lack of choice.

In Khomeini's Iran, many occupations were closed to women because it was deemed not seemly for women to be involved in them. Since Khomeini's death in 1989 the rules have not been enforced as strictly, and the position of women is changing slowly. Large numbers of women are entering university and women are pushing to enter professions which were formerly closed to them, such as law and engineering. Support is growing to allow women to study alone outside the country and the government is now operating family planning clinics in most major cities.

Other examples of Islamic fundamentalism are found in Saudi Arabia and Dagestan. In Saudi Arabia, the Wahhabiyah sect, founded in the 18th century and supported by the current ruling family, dictates that women must cover themselves in public, should be barred from many kinds of work, may travel only if accompanied by a husband or a male blood relative, and are not allowed to drive. In 1990, when Saudi Arabian women demonstrated for the right to drive cars, the government responded by banning all public dissent.

In Dagestan, one of the autonomous republics in the Commonwealth of Independent States, the former U.S.S.R., the citizens are also turning towards a path of Islamic orthodoxy. Women are being raised in a more traditional manner. More often, they are required to remain at home rather than go away to university, to get married earlier, and to dress conservatively.

There are groups attempting to influence their governments by pushing for more extreme policies in several other Islamic countries. For example, in Algeria, the Islamic Salvation Front, which almost formed the government in 1991, is pushing to forbid women to work outside the home.

In 1988, Benazir Bhutto of Pakistan became the first woman to serve as head of government of a predominantly Islamic country. One of her first moves as prime minister was to release all female prisoners charged with crimes other than murder. Many of these women had been imprisoned under laws which gives a man's testimony twice as much weight as a woman's. In general, though, she adhered to traditional beliefs. In 1990, the president of Pakistan dissolved her government, charging her administration with corruption. In the elections that followed, the new prime minister, Nawaz Sharif, rose to power with the support of Islamic extremists. Consequently, limitations on the activities of women are in existence, although actual punishments for non-obedience are infrequently carried out. Nevertheless, the state requires all women appearing on television to wear a scarf over their head and shoulders. New elections occurred in 1993 and Benazir Bhutto was returned as prime minister. Again, the oppor-

tunity exists for her to further influence women's lives in Pakistan.

In India, a woman's place in the community is dependent upon the culture of her region and her social class, as well as religion. Women's rights are enshrined in the constitution, but many live relatively isolated and uneducated lives in thousands of small villagesd. An active women's movement is attempting to reach out to these women in order to ensure that the constitution is upheld. Nevertheless, it is still a common custom for parents to arrange their children's marriages. Even when a marriage has not been arranged it is often expected that a bride will bring a dowry or gift of goods and money to her husband's family on the occasion of her marriage. As a result, in a society where millions of families are impoverished, female infants may be seen as a financial burden. If they are not the firstborn or do not follow the birth of a son, their parents may kill them.

Srinivasa Prasad, writing for Associated Press, states that two social service groups conducting surveys in the southern Indian state of Tamil Nadu recently determined that female infanticide touches one out of every two families there. Publication of these findings resulted in local officials not only being more vigilant about arresting parents who kill infants, but also offering a solution to couples who do not want their baby girls. Cradles have been installed outside 116 hospitals and clinics so parents can leave unwanted babies there. Eighteen girls were left to be brought up in a government orphanage over a recent two-month span.

Middle class Indian families with moderate incomes and more education have sought other means to prevent the birth of too many daughters. Private prenatal clinics offer ultrasound and amniocentesis tests to determine whether the mother will give birth to a male or female. If the parents are told to expect a girl, an abortion often follows. The practice has become so widespread that the Indian government is proposing legislation to curb such abortions by banning testing solely for the purpose of determining sex.

In marriage, likewise, Indian women are not always treated well. It is illegal for a family to demand a dowry either before or after a marriage, but cases have surfaced where a new wife has been mistreated and abused because her family did not yield to increased dowry demands. Indian women traditionally go to live with their husbands' families and become answerable to their mothers-in-law when they marry. Thus, they can easily be set up as hostages and threatened with harm unless new demands are met by their own families. In New Delhi, women's organizations and social workers agree that if dowry demands are not met, some young married women die as a result of fires set by their husbands or their husbands' families. These deaths are declared suicides and the husbands are then free to marry again. Despite concern about this system — originally meant to give brides some financial security — actual protests against it are rare.

Culture plays a significant part in defining the role of women in other parts of the developing world, such as in Latin America. There, many females are subjected to the male cult of machismo, characterized by an exaggerated assertion of masculinity, an emphasis on a man's virility, and the domination of women. Although this cult emphasizes the importance of a man becoming a father, it does not obligate him to fulfill parenting responsibilities. As a result, there is a high percentage of female-headed households in Latin America.

Economic status also plays a part in defining the role of women in Latin America. Much of the rural Latin America economy is based on subsistence agriculture, and most people are poor and illiterate. Women looking for improvement in their lives generally gravitate to the cities where they are employed as domestics or street vendors, or they work on assembly lines in the clothing, textiles, and electronic industries. For women, the move to an urban area offers the opportunity for educational advancement. Women there have made significant gains in the past few decades in health, education, and economic participation. Statistics show that literacy rates among women are higher in the cities and that birth rates are lower. On the other hand, men looking for jobs often migrate to mining and oil field locations. This type of employment does not offer the same educational opportunities, and isolates men from their families, further accounting for the high percentage of female-headed households.

Membership in a community group seems to work well in enabling migrant women to adapt to urban life. In one poor community on the outskirts of Cuzco, Peru, the women have

SOURCE: CIDA/Pierre St-Jacques

Fig. 4-29 *Women in Brazil upgrading their literacy skills.*

formed a club to pool their resources in order to buy food for themselves. Despite their poverty they have been able to install water taps for community use and to begin work on a sewage system. They have helped set up a day-care centre, a primary school, a cooperative fuel store, and a soup kitchen.

The former communist world is one group of countries where women had considerable power because communist doctrine upholds equality between the sexes. In the former U.S.S.R., 33 percent of the representatives in the Soviet parliament were women. Large numbers of doctors, engineers, chemists, architects, scientists, and educators were also women. Ninety percent of women of working age either worked or studied. They were also entitled to free day care for their children, paid maternity leave, and many educational opportunities.

However, there were other aspects of life for women in the former Soviet Union which continued to create inequalities. Women were responsible for raising children, shopping, and preparing meals for their families. Shopping in the cities meant lining up for food for as long as two hours a day. Housekeeping, laundry, and cooking were done in many cases without modern appliances.

Although communism is being replaced by a market economy in the former U.S.S.R., improvements to women's lives have yet to materialize. The new system has created considerable instability and many plants and firms are struggling to survive. More women than men occupy a greater proportion of the lowest rungs of the employment ladder. It is these groups who are the first to lose their jobs. Recent figures show that 70 percent of the unemployed are women. Women have also lost their position in parliament. In the new Russia only six percent of the elected representatives are women. In some parts of the country, self-help women's committees have sprung up, but for most women long term political equality is not the issue. They are seeking support and relief from the stress of maintaining two jobs, one in the home and one outside the home.

WOMEN'S EDUCATION

In 1992, a vice-president of the World Bank stated that improving girls' education would not only reduce fertility rates but also reduce child deaths, improve nutrition in the family, help prevent the spread of AIDS, and help save the environment. The overall cost of educating as many girls as boys in the developing countries would be $3.2 billion, less than one percent of the total investment in new capital goods by governments in the developing world. In Africa and the countries of southwest and southern Asia where birth rates are the highest in the world, women are much more poorly educated than men. Not only are girls sent to school less often, but they are often fed less and when ill they are less likely to be treated. This creates weak generations of women less able to learn when the opportunity arises.

Much has been written about the developing world's educational gender gap; the 1990 World Conference on Education for All at Jomtien, Thailand, focused on this issue. However, the case made for educating girls almost always concerns their future as mothers: educated women give birth to fewer and healthier children. Their rights and opportunities as girls and women in a non-mothering context are usually not considered.

Nevertheless, in the developing countries, the gender gap in primary education has decreased by half in the past 20 to 30 years. Substantial progress is being made in Latin America, the Caribbean, and most of Asia; less progress is being made in southern Asia and Sub-Saharan Africa. According to United Nations estimates, the extensive boost in primary education in the past few decades has increased literacy rates, although there are still serious deficiencies. The most serious is in rural Africa, where 75 percent of women aged 15 to 24 are illiterate. In India, many girls must still watch as their brothers go off to school at the age of six, while they look after the younger children in the family and are taught how to clean house and cook.

The primary school drop-out rate for girls in developing countries is much higher than that for boys. The United Nations Human Development Report 1992 states that out of 100 million children not in primary school, two-thirds are girls. An Indian national committee set up to formulate long-term plans for women's advancement has suggested that nursery facilities should be provided in schools so that girls may bring along the siblings they have to care for.

In Bangladesh, one grassroots group, the Bangladesh Rural Advancement Committee, (BRAC), is trying to bring education to the country's villages by building 6000 non-formal village schools exclusively for pupils who have never started school and those who have had to drop out. Following affirmative action precepts, one of the conditions to maintaining such a school is that at least two-thirds of the students must be female. In practice, three-quarters of the 180 000 pupils are girls. Many of them have had to persuade their fathers to allow them to attend, but the two-and-a-half hour daily session is scheduled to fit around seasonal work and religious obligations. BRAC has had remarkable success in keeping the drop-out rate to a minimum.

Another example of success in educating girls has occurred in Accra, the capital city of Ghana. No Ghanaian girl was admitted to a secondary technical school before 1987. Now several hundred girls are enrolled in welding, carpentry, masonry, and technical drawing courses. These subjects were first introduced to the girls in elementary school. The main challenge for educators in Ghana is to see that girls get into elementary school in the first place. This is particularly difficult in northern Ghana, where poverty and distance from

schools means that only two in every 20 make it through the full six primary years. Scholarships are now offered to needy girls and this has helped to boost enrolment.

Canada's public school system has always been overwhelmingly co-educational. In higher education, although enrolment is about equal among the sexes, women are nevertheless deterred by various discriminatory practices and attitudes from participating in many subject areas. Female university teachers hold lower academic ranks and receive lower pay, and women are underrepresented in science and mathematics, dentistry, engineering, architecture, and business. Although the patterns are changing somewhat, this situation contributes directly to the maintenance of a sexually segregated work world.

WOMEN'S EMPLOYMENT

The United Nations Convention on the Elimination of All Forms of Discrimination against Women has been signed or ratified by two-thirds of the world's countries. It commits governments to ensuring equal employment opportunities for both genders. These include opportunities for promotion and the right to maternity leave. Ensuring access to financial credit is also part of the convention.

In the 1970s, research indicated that women did 65 percent of the world's work, but earned only ten percent of the world's income and owned less than one percent of the world's assets. At conferences and meetings about women's concerns, women from around the world were making it clear that the ability to obtain credit was what they needed most, ahead of better education, housing, and health care. Once they could obtain credit, they said, they could use it to generate the funds required to satisfy all their other needs. In 1980, a group of women from various parts of the world fortified with a $250 000 grant from the United Nations, as well as some of their own money, began the Women's World Banking (WWB) organization. Currently, this organization is helping thousands of women from developing nations start up and manage their own businesses. Existing banks in the clients' home countries make the loans after the organization guarantees them. The WWB then provides the training and support services to help the borrowers pay the loans back. In some developing countries there are also groups who have followed the Women's World Banking lead and have set up alternative lending institutions.

Two examples of Women's World Banking success stories can be found in India and Rwanda. In a small town in India a woman made enough money to feed her children by selling papier-maché toys she had made from waste paper her children had collected on the streets. With a loan of about $75 from WWB she began to buy paper from print shops and to use better dyes. Her products are now selling so well that she no longer needs loans; she uses advances from the merchants ordering her products to pay for her raw materials.

In Rwanda, a group of Muslim women, who traditionally lived in isolation in their homes, used a loan to establish and operate their own slaughterhouse, butcher shop, general store, and primary school. Their children are benefitting from better nutrition and education and the women are enjoying more social and economic freedom.

Another example of successful female entrepreneurship is found in Togo, a small country located on the Gulf of Guinea in West Africa. Female cloth merchants, referred to as Nanas, buy and sell batik cloth to most of the rest of the countries of West Africa. Many men and women of West Africa wear colourful patterned cotton robes, dresses, and head coverings. The cloth is imported from Holland, England, China, and Java by large, long-established European import-export houses. The Nanas act as agents between the importers and their clients in West Africa. As well, the Nanas choose the fabrics from European designer samples. Part of their strength is their ability to predict fashion styles months ahead since the fabrics may arrive up to eight months later.

The Nanas handle enormous sums of money and have become very wealthy. Their money is invested mainly in real estate and jewellery, and their children are all sent to university. Female children, greatly desired, study economics and management so they can be prepared to inherit their mother's business. Although these women live in a patriarchal and polygamous society they have created a powerful niche for themselves. Similar entrepreneurial skills are typical of neighbouring women in Benin, Nigeria, and Ghana.

The right to maternity leave is another area where progress has been made in the work-

SOURCE: CIDA/Peter Bennett

Fig. 4-30 *This organization operates similarly to Women's World Banking by providing credit to business women in Uganda.*

ing world. The International Labour Organization recommends 14 weeks total time away from a job before and after childbirth, full or partial replacement of wages, and a guarantee that mothers will have a job when they re-enter the workforce. More than 100 of the world's countries mandate maternity leave and follow at least some of the provisions listed above. Most of the countries of northern and eastern Europe offer four months of leave and pay at least 90 percent of wages for the duration of the leave. Sweden and Austria offer one year maternity leave with full wages; the Soviet Union, before the break-up, paid full wages for 18 months of leave. Canada offers 60 percent wage replacement for 25 weeks of leave with additional rights to leave varying from province to province. The United States in 1993 approved 12 weeks unpaid leave for parents in specific employment situations. In Africa, nine countries in West Africa and Tunisia pay 90 percent wages over 14 weeks. In Latin America, Cuba, Costa Rica, Panama, Brazil, and Chile mandate 14 weeks of leave and provide at least 90 percent wage replacement.

Other problems exist in the developed world in the fight to provide equality for women in the workplace. In the United States and Britain, women hold about two percent of seats on the boards of large corporations. Why are there so few women in senior positions today? One reason is that managing paid employment and being primary caregiver for a family is difficult. When the demands become too great, women who have alternate sources of income may choose to remain at home. Added to this, some companies fear that women who have children to care for will be less committed to their work than men.

SOURCE: Marilyn MacKenzie

Fig. 4-31 *A Canadian woman who has sought promotion is seen carrying out her job as the project officer in an innovative educational program.*

Other reasons have been suggested for the low number of senior businesswomen. If people who work in large organizations have a tendency to hire and promote those who resemble themselves, and if most are men, then men will be hired and promoted in larger numbers than women. However, women's employment is often seen as something good for the company's image. For example, bidders for American government contracts are often vetted for the number of women they employ.

As the numbers of the population in the 30- to 40-year-old age group declines, and the smaller post-**baby boom** population reaches these ages, companies will either have to hire more women or accept men who are less well qualified. In the 1950s, when there was a shortage of personnel, employment opportunities for women improved greatly.

Business opportunities are also difficult to obtain for women in Japan. In 1985 an Equal Opportunity Law was passed which forbade companies from discriminating on the basis of sex in their hiring, assignment, and promotional practices. Despite this law, in 1992, in three of Japan's largest companies, 12 women and 538 men were hired into career-track positions. In the government, in 1990, women occupied fewer than one percent of management-level positions. Many Japanese women feel that the law is a step forward, but in order for it to be effective, the government must have the power to punish employers who do not obey. Many women are applying for such jobs, but they believe they are still being questioned and judged according to their appearance, their demeanor, and their family background rather than on their abilities.

Some women in Japan refrain from applying for managerial positions because they do not wish to copy the work ethic of Japanese men, which often involves long hours away from home. Being a homemaker, say many who have married, is preferable to working outside the home, because they have the time needed to run the household, oversee their children's education, and pursue their own interests. As few Japanese men do any housework, outside employment becomes an extra burden for women.

At the same time, in Canada, like other countries in the western world, a women's movement has emerged which has as its goal the creation of social justice for all women. Officially, women enjoy equal rights under Canada's constitution and much has been achieved in the areas of education, labour, and the law. Changes to labour laws initially focused on equal pay for equal or the same work, whereas new legislation emphasizes equal pay for work of equal value. However, creating social justice for women involves a restructuring of society and of the way people think and experience the world. Creating a just society for women means the elimination of sexism, particularly in the legal system, in the organization of society, and in the perception and treatment of women in the arts, education, and the mass media.

FURTHER ANALYSIS

1. This case study illustrates examples of changes that have positively affected women's lives as well as examples where changes have yet to come. List in separate columns the examples of each situation. Comment on the results when you have finished.

2. Machismo is an influential force in Latin culture. Research its cultural origins and analyze the effect it might have on the women's movement in Latin America. Discuss different ways that women can deal with its impact.

3. a) Using the information in the case study construct a charter of rights and freedoms for women. Draw up an action plan showing how this charter could be used to improve conditions for women around the world.
   b) Obtain a copy of the Convention on the Elimination of All Forms of Discrimination Against Women, the United Nations international bill of rights for women, and compare it to your own charter.
   c) Suggest changes to one or both documents if you think that improvements can be made.

4. Research and report on recent actions that have been taken towards improving conditions for women in India.

5. Research and report on the conditions for women in a country not examined in this case study, such as China. Include examples of actions being taken to improve the situation of women in this country.

CHAPTER 5

PROSPECTS AND POSSIBILITIES

5

PROSPECTS AND POSSIBILITIES

Prospects are views of what is and what might be. *World Prospects, Third Edition* describes the current world situation and its future outlook.

The situation the world is in today is the result of past developments and events, many of which were unpredictable in outcome. Over time, the world's history becomes longer, and the unwinding of past events becomes more complex. The present — today — moves constantly through time as humanity invades the future. Change is thus an inevitable process. This chapter examines the forces that bring about change, and looks at some views of the future.

People have long sought clues about what the future holds. They look at past patterns and trends, and predict that these will continue for some time into the near future. In addition, omens and prophecies have a powerful place in the beliefs of many of the world's people. Religions have grown to provide guidance to people about how they should behave in the present and to give them a sense of purpose about the future. Political ideologies have developed to put forward particular views about what the future should be like. Much effort is devoted to trying to arrange the future to suit particular wishes.

In other cases, where people think they cannot change what will happen, energy is devoted to trying to find out what the future may be like, and making plans to deal with it appropriately. Weather forecasting is an example. A great deal of time and energy is put into trying to produce the most accurate (or least inaccurate) predictions possible. All sorts of human activities are influenced by weather conditions, from airline flights and crop harvesting to baseball games and boating.

Some idea of at least the near future may be gained from identifying existing trends (in weather, population growth, etc.) and projecting (sometimes called extrapolating) them into the future. Attempts to shape the future are called plans.

Predicting the future is very uncertain, although some aspects of it are easier to predict than others. It seems certain, for example, that the world's population will double before 50 more years have passed. On the other hand, it seems highly uncertain that all of humanity will be well fed, in good health, and living in peace by this time. It is difficult to predict to what degree these conditions will exist.

Various factors contribute to the differing degrees of uncertainty about many aspects of the future. Many people regard human nature as relatively unchanging, perhaps even unchangeable. They regard the outcomes of situations that depend largely upon human nature as highly predictable. These people may make claims, for example, that "history repeats itself." The laws of economics fall

Fig. 5-1 *Religions provide guidance to millions of people. This is a Hindu temple in Delhi, India.*

into this category. For example, the law of demand states that people tend to buy more of something if its price falls, and less of it if its price rises. This law is based on observation of large-scale human behaviour. It is expected to hold true most — but not necessarily all — of the time. Some theories about the behaviour of birth rates fall into the same category, especially those that claim birth rates are likely to decline as people become more secure economically. These theories equate a reduction in population pressures with economic growth.

Others regard human nature as more flexible and capable of change. Following the maxim "those who do not learn from history are condemned to repeat it," they allow that the human race can adapt and learn. Those who do not believe that human nature can change point to commonly repeated situations such as wars arising from ancient ethnic hatreds. Conversely, believers in the possibility of changing human nature point to widespread examples of cooperation and humanitarianism such as many cases of international peacekeeping. They also point out that if changes to human nature can be made in some areas of activity and for some people, then it cannot be argued that human nature is unchangeable. The questions then become *How can changes be made?* and *What sorts of changes should be made?*

While human nature may or may not be changeable, there are other factors that affect the future. These include unpredictable matters such as developments in technology. Will a cure for AIDS or cancer be found? Will a safe and non-polluting source of energy be discovered in the quantities needed? They also include relatively predictable — and potentially controllable — matters such as changes in the natural environment: how can we deal with global warming, or with deforestation?

Whether future changes are planned or occur unexpectedly, they all have the potential to be beneficial or harmful to people. Most people in the present try to minimize the risks of future harm and maximize possible benefits. The world's insurance industry is built on the concept that their clients want to minimize possible future harm. Conversely, the world's investment industry is based on the idea of maximizing future benefits. In both cases there are risks if the future turns out differently than expected. For example, the extension of life expectancies throughout most parts of the world is placing insurers who operate retirement incomes and pension funds under considerable financial pressure. Should the insurance companies have foreseen this, and started to raise their rates 40 or 50 years ago to accommodate it? Similarly, the enormous popularity of various types of personal computers for business use has meant that investments in large computer ("mainframe") production — once thought of as the wave of the future — have lost much of their value. Should the mainframe producers have foreseen this change, and adjusted their own production in time?

The following readings provide a number of views about the forces of change. Some of them look at changes that have already occurred; others look at changes that might occur. Before you go through the readings, divide a blank page into four quarters by drawing one line across the middle of the page and another down the centre. Each quarter represents a different combination of the types of change. Enter the headings for each quarter as follows:

Upper left quarter: planned, beneficial change;

Upper right quarter: unplanned, beneficial change;

Lower left quarter: planned, harmful change;

Lower right quarter: unplanned, harmful change.

Looking back and saying that a particular decision should obviously have been made is called hindsight.

Herman

SOURCE: Jim Unger/Universal Press Syndicate, 91/12/13

"The next six months will be mainly sunny or cloudy, with dry and rainy spells. Winds will be from most directions."

 Fig. 5-2

As you read, list examples of each type of change in the appropriate quarter of the page. Note that the changes described in some readings may belong in more than one category.

REVOLUTION: A FABLE

It all began when Shanti was late again for school. The rain was to blame. It had churned up the mud so much that she had had to drag her lame leg way beyond the usual river crossing to find a safer spot. Crossing the river was harder than she'd expected. She reached school, exhausted, muddy, wet — and pleased with her success. But the teacher, Mr. Pahad, had shouted at her. "You silly child! You should stay at home when it rains."

He was in a bad mood today — not helped by the fact that he knew he would probably feel compelled to help Shanti get home after school. That would mean getting mud on his suit — and tonight he was going to a banquet to receive an award for his contribution to the welfare of the disabled children at his school.

A thought came to him. What if all disabled people, children, adults and older people, were sent to a special village where everything was designed to meet their special needs? There would be special schools, special sport, special employment and special housing.

Whenever he had a spare moment during the rest of that day Mr. Pahad re-wrote his speech for the banquet. Then he had another brainwave. He would take Shanti with him. She looked so sweet and shy with her muddy dress and twisted foot. He would explain her plight and ask for

donations to build a disabled village for all the disabled people of the district.

So a dazed Shanti found herself at the banquet, being waited upon by servants in spotless uniforms. She felt embarrassed by the mud on her dress and wanted to use the washroom but Mr. Pahad insisted, "No, no. I want everyone to see you the way you are." Mr. Pahad made his speech and, indicating Shanti, explained his proposal for the disabled village. People liked the idea. They clapped and cheered. Later they arranged committees for fundraising. It was decided that the village would be built on the other side of the river and that it would be a village for wheelchair users. If it worked other villages would be built for the blind, deaf and people with learning difficulties.

By the end of the evening Shanti had been generously patted and kissed but never actually spoken to. In the weeks that followed her picture appeared on a large fundraising poster all around the district. The poster read "Shanti and others like her need your help. Give generously for the disabled village."

On the day the village was opened flags flew, there was food for all. The disabled people were lined up to meet famous guests. Speeches were made and more awards given to Mr. Pahad. When the festivities were over the able-bodied caregivers and professionals established a convenient (for them) routine to get the resi-

dents out of bed in the morning and back into bed in the evening. During the day the villagers had occupational therapy.

At first the villagers hated being taken away from their homes. But as time passed they found that being together had certain advantages: they could meet more easily and share ideas and feelings. Shanti liked being in a place where everything was arranged for people who lived in wheelchairs. You could do all sorts of things which you were prevented from doing "beyond the river" as the able-bodied world was now called. You could even do your own shopping. This made the residents think: if they could do their own shopping why should they not work in the shops themselves too? They suggested this to Mr. Pahad. But he said it was "unrealistic." So were most of the other suggestions residents made. Relations between staff and residents got worse and worse as one suggestion after another was trashed by the able-bodied authorities.

The villagers got together to discuss the situation. They debated for several hours. Some felt that with the force of argument they could change the attitudes of Mr. Pahad and his helpers. Others felt there was no point — that able-bodied people didn't begin to understand the experience of disability. The villagers finally formed a committee and began plotting revolution.

A few days later, when most of the helpers had gone over the river for their regular monthly staff meeting with Mr. Pahad, the disabled residents took direct action. They barred the village gates, closed off all entrances and exits and flooded pathways leading to the village.

Shanti, being the smallest and lightest, was lifted onto a wall where she could watch for the returning helpers while disabled villagers prepared to do battle. "They're coming, they're coming." Shanti screamed with excitement. From where she sat she could see everything.

First the helpers were surprised. They never expected disabled people to do anything without their assistance. Then they got angry as their feet got wet and muddy in the pathways and they found all the entrances closed. When they realized that their jobs were on the line the helpers became all the more convinced that "the disabled" urgently needed their help. They broke down the gate and rushed in — only to bash their heads and fall flat on their backs. A low ceiling of poles had been tied into place with just enough room for wheelchair users to move freely underneath but too low for the "walkers"!

Then a row of villagers moved forward, pushing the dazed caregivers out of the village with scoops that had been fitted to the front of each wheelchair. Eventually the helpers gave up and left the village.

There were many changes after the Revolution. Roads and paths were dug up and replaced with wheelways. Doorways and ceilings were lowered to a more reasonable height for wheelchair users. The shops, the school, and places of employment were all altered. Fashion became

more interesting as the village shoe shop began selling multi-colour designer tires for wheelchairs.

As Shanti grew up the memories of the able-bodied soon faded and the villagers forgot that they were supposed to be disabled. In this village they were the "normal." Life went on peacefully for several years until one day the villagers were once again brought face to face with the able-bodied from across the river.

It happened during a particularly heavy rainy season when the river burst its banks and flooded the able-bodied village. Those who escaped made their way to the nearest high ground — which just happened to be the disabled village.

Shanti was busy making a pot when she spotted the first flood survivor on the main wheelway. Then another, and another. A whole stream of able-bodied people poured into the village, getting their feet stuck in the wheelway tracks, and knocking themselves out on the doorways as they stumbled into houses, looking for shelter. Soon the village doctors had their hands full. Other villagers prepared food for the victims — who had to eat off the floor because the disabled villagers had long dispensed with tables. Their own wheelchair attachments were suited to all uses.

The disabled villagers felt sorry for the able-bodied. They seemed so clumsy, helpless. Many of them couldn't even get out of the old community centre building that had become their residential home without damaging their feet in the wheelway tracks. Special transport was devised so that a little trolley for

the able-bodied could be attached to a wheelchair.

But who was going to look after the able-bodied? They could not work as everything was designed for people in wheelchairs. Soon able-bodied cripples in ill-fitting clothing made for wheelchair users were to be found on wheelway corners begging for food and money. More fortunate able-bodied refugees were taken from their residential home to the day centre where they could do some basket work and other useful occupational therapy.

The biggest problem for the medical profession was the chronic bruising of heads. The village doctors diagnosed this as "cerebral indigene" and recommended either a harness to keep the able-bodied bent double at wheelchair height or padded guards which were strapped to the forehead.

Shanti was becoming increasingly concerned about the welfare of able-bodied cripples. She was asked to organize a public appeal for money to provide the able-bodied with "care in the community." Then someone suggested that instead of care the money might be used to set up a special place where the able-bodied could live. This reminded Shanti of Mr. Pahad's original scheme for the disabled village — and she was opposed to it.

"Disability," she protested as she addressed a public meeting on the subject, "isn't something that you have. It is something that happens when one group of people create barriers by designing the world only for their style of living."

And she went on: "We will not make any progress by keeping disabled people on one side of the river and non-disabled people on the other, with each side creating barriers. What we need is to build up the banks so that the river does not flood and

to build bridges across the river so that we can meet, exchange experiences and create an environment where we can celebrate human difference." She had

become quite an idealist, had Shanti.

Vic Finkelstein, *New Internationalist*, 92 7

INDIAN LAND USES ARE PUT ON THE MAP

TEGUCIGALPA, HONDURAS — For centuries, Sinito Waylan's family has lived with and in the forest. Generations of the Miskito Indians of Honduras have built their homes and dugout canoes from its wood, used its medicinal plants, and made ceremonial clothes from its tree bark. Their food has come from hunting wild animals, fishing in the ocean and rivers, small-scale cultivation, and gathering wild herbs and fruit.

But 500 years after Columbus's arrival in his land, Mr. Waylan is unsure if his son will be able to continue this traditional lifestyle.

"If just the next generation could live as I have, that would mean eternal happiness for me," he says in Miskito, his first language.

Waylan is one of 22 indigenous representatives who gathered information that was used to create a land-use map like no other in Latin America. The map could be the key to obtaining legal rights to their land.

More than 35 000 Indians live in the Mosquitea, a land of

tropical forest and savannah made known by the book and movie *The Mosquito Coast*. They are placing their hopes on a four-year-old program administered by MOPAWI, a non-profit agency that is helping Indians organize and petition the government for land titles in the face of encroaching colonists who clear the forest for cattle and crops.

...the program recently sponsored the First Congress on Indigenous Lands of the Mosquitea, at which the Indians impressed the Honduran vice-president, land authorities, government ministers, military officials, and others with the presentation of the unique land-use map. The information on the map will serve as a reference for government authorities in charge of land titles, development, and resource management.

"We hope the congress has provided base-line information that will orient land-tenancy thinking and economic-development policies," Mr. Leake (the program coordinator) says. "It's a historic event. And it's interesting (to see) the factors that

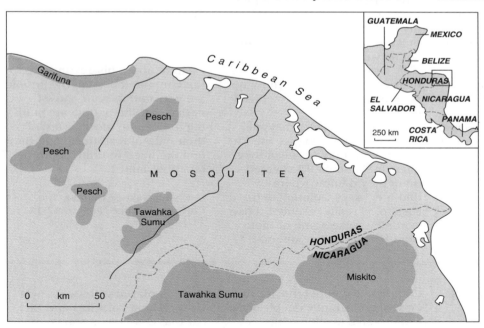

Fig. 5-3 *The Mosquitea region of Honduras and Nicaragua, showing main locations of indigenous peoples.*

have come together to make it possible — the Indians, the agency, the donor, and the academic."

The donor is Cultural Survival, an organization based in Cambridge, Mass., that works with indigenous peoples and financed the land-legalization program, including the map and the congress.

"In most countries in Central America, there is no history of legislation (dealing with) Indian lands which are communal lands, and the map and congress focus attention on this," says Mac Chapin of Cultural Survival. "The whole process of the congress gets a lot of the Indians thinking about what kind of development they want. We're going to try to do this throughout Central America."

The academic is Peter Herlihy, a cultural geographer and professor at Southeastern Louisiana University in Hammond, La., who has lived in the Mosquitea and drew up the map.

"Indigenous areas throughout Central America are the least-known areas, and we're putting the Indians on the map," Professor Herlihy says. "If you're talking about natural-resource conservation in protected areas, you have to talk about indigenous populations and their social use of the land. For example, there are 240 protected areas in Central America,

and indigenous populations live in or have access to resources within 85 percent of those areas."

Information for the land-use map was collected by representatives of 22 regions of the Mosquitea, including four indigenous groups: Miskitos, Garifunas, Tawakhas, and Pesch. They met with 200 communities to ask their residents where they cultivate, hunt, fish, pan for gold, gather materials for house and boat construction, and collect medicinal plants. They traveled in dugout canoes, with and without outboard motors, by horse, motorcycle, bicycle, and on foot, sometimes in heavy storms in isolated areas.

"The weather was terrible," recounts Olegario Lopez, a member of the Garifuna ethnic group, who visited eight communities. There was so much mud that it came up to the chest of my horse, so I had to get off and pull him out. My questionnaires got all wet."

Others were stung by mosquitoes and nearly bitten by poisonous snakes. Some received death threats.

"In one village, they told me that they would give me information only because they knew me, and so if I cheated them they'd know where to find me," says Quintin Castro, a Miskito. "I really resented those words because some of them were friends and neighbours."

Almost all the 22 surveyors encountered villagers fearful of saying too much, such as where they find hardwood trees and pan for gold, and information government officials or a private company could use for personal economic interests.... Also, rumors have circulated that the government plans to relocate inhabitants from a reserve in the Mosquitea, making people suspicious of questions about land use.

After filling out their questionnaires with the communities, the surveyors met in Puerto Lempira, where they shared the information with Herlihy. He spent some 100 hours looking up more than 5000 points on maps. The result was a land-use map of each of the 22 regions, which the surveyors took back to the communities to be reviewed and corrected. Herlihy then made one single map of the entire Mosquitea.

"The map caused a sensation," says Tomas Rivas, another Miskito, about his second trip to the communities. "All the people are very enthusiastic. Now I notice that the people are starting to become more aware of their natural resources, and they feel the need to unite and protect their land."

Lisa Swenarski de Herrera, *The Christian Science Monitor*, 92 12 11-17

MACHINES WITH VISION

In a typical working day, Alan Mackworth, a professor in the University of British

Columbia's computer science department, thinks deeply about ways to give machines the ability to see. He also gets to play with toy electric cars. The

game is played with two six-inch-long Porsches and the car that can nose a squash ball past the other is the winner. It may sound frivolous, but the underlying purpose of the game is utterly serious: it is part of a thrust among scientists to develop robots with senses and intelligence. In Mackworth's experiments, an overhead television camera acts as a vision system for the cars, with a computer providing information on what the camera sees. Analyzing the data, the cars shift from defensive to offensive modes of operation as they steer around the tabletop playing field. Similar experiments are under way in robotics laboratories across Canada, as scientists in a wide range of disciplines explore ways of endowing machines with human capabilities.

The explosion of robotics research in Canada has developed in the past ten years to the point where more than $60 million is currently being spent on programs in university laboratories. The purpose of it all: to develop a distinctive high-technology sector that will help Canada to survive in the post-industrial global economy.

To a remarkable degree, that plan, backed by Canadian governments and private industry, appears to be working. A shining example is Spar Aerospace Ltd. At the headquarters of Spar's advanced technology systems group just outside of Toronto, officials heaved a collective sigh of relief last week after the U.S. House of Representatives voted 220 to 196 to fund a scaled-down version of the space station Freedom. When it begins operating in space in 2001, Freedom will carry a 57-foot-long remote manipulator arm and a smaller device called a dextrous manip-

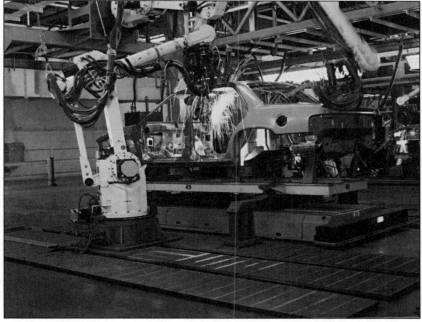

SOURCE: General Motors Canada/Tom Hurlbert

Fig. 5-4 *Much work involving repetitive movement is already done by simple robots, as here on a car assembly line. The platform holding the car body is another robot, which moves automatically to its next station when ready, guided electronically by wires embedded in the floor. Robots that can perform more complex tasks, including analyzing a situation to determine appropriate action, are under constant development.*

ulator. The two robotic units, built by Spar and a consortium of Canadian firms, will help the station to function in space. Says Karl Doetsch, director general of the space station program at the Canadian Space Agency: "Canada has a real international lead in this area."

While Canadian expertise in robotics and the closely related field of artificial intelligence has been building steadily through the past two decades, researchers got a badly needed boost in 1983 with the establishment of the Toronto-based Canadian Institute for Advanced Research, which channels fund-

ing from government and private industry to researchers across the country. The institute, in turn, spawned PRECARN Associates Inc., a not-for-profit corporation backed by major Canadian industrial firms that is dedicated to research into robotics and intelligent systems — jargon for advanced computer-based operations. Currently, PRECARN is channelling $40 million into research in the field over a five-year period that ends in 1996. As well, PRECARN manages one of the programs launched in 1990 under the federal Network of Centres of Excellence initiative and is distributing $23.8 million over a four-year period for research into robotics and intelligent systems.

• • • • •

The surge of activity in Canadian laboratories ranges from work on computer-controlled systems designed to cope with emergencies in nuclear power plants to research into ways of using robotics to help physically handicapped children. Much of the work centres on robot vision. Allan Jepson, a University of Toronto professor of computer science, is working with other scientists to develop a vision system that would enable a robot to enter and work in areas where there are high radiation levels or other hazardous conditions. The robot is being designed for the publicly owned power utility Ontario Hydro, which operates a network of nuclear reactors. The prototype is a squat, three-wheeled machine with a video camera mounted on top to act as the robot's eyes.

• • • • •

As well as vision, Canadian robot scientists are also tackling such areas as balance and touch. At the University of British Columbia, Dinesh Pai, an Indian-born computer scientist, is developing an unusual robot shaped like a tetrahedron, a solid form with four triangular surfaces. With a leg at each of the tetrahedron's four points, the robot is designed to operate on uneven terrain; even if it took a tumble, the robot would always land with three feet on the ground. At Queen's University in Kingston, Ont., experimental psychologist Susan Lederman is helping engineers in an attempt to design a robot with a sense of touch.

• • • • •

Canada's push to develop superior expertise in robotics and intelligent systems has begun to pay off economically. At Spar Aerospace, technology developed for the U.S. space program has been used in such earth-bound applications as remote handling systems for servicing nuclear reactors. As well, university robotics programs have helped to spawn companies that put esoteric technology to practical use. According to (Martin) Levine, (director of McGill's Research Centre for Intelligent Machines), McGill's robotics program has played a part in the establishment of at least five local companies, including Mayan Automation Inc., which manufactures vision systems for industrial use.

Still, some scientists say that corporations are often slow to recognize the value of advanced robotics. Peter Lawrence, a professor of electrical engineering at the University of British Columbia, completed development last year of a device that allows operators to manipulate the working parts of heavy construction or logging equipment through a single hand control. The patented device, called a Co-ordinated Control System, would replace the clumsy controls currently used on excavators and give the operator a more direct "feel" for the equipment he is using. So far, says Lawrence, heavy equipment companies have not shown much interest in his device, perhaps because of the costs involved.

That could change. Experts say that there is usually a lag time of five years or more before new technology makes its way into the marketplace. Given that, it may not be long before Lawrence's ingenious control, Alan Mackworth's experiments with computer vision for toy cars and other Canadian developments begin finding applications in a world where robotics seems certain to play an ever-increasing role.

Mark Nichols, *Maclean's*, 1993 7 12

NATIONALISM IS NOT NECESSARILY THE PATH TO A DEMOCRATIC WORLD

Across much of the contemporary world, we are witnessing a supposedly welcome revival of nationalism. Nationalism, it is said, is the driving force behind the...political movements in (Central and) Eastern Europe, responsible for the unification of Germany as well as for the...breakup of the U.S.S.R. Flags, languages, cultures long suppressed (or supposedly forgotten) have now been revived.

There are two welcome aspects of this phenomenon. First, what we are seeing in (Central and) Eastern Europe...is the development of democracy, increased freedom for peoples who have long been denied it. Because nationalism asserts the rights of distinct peoples to independence, it plays an important role in democratic politics.

The changes in (Central and) Eastern Europe are also reasserting a cultural diversity — in language, writing, music — that draws on the richness of traditions among these peoples.

Insofar as "internationalism," as imposed by the U.S.S.R., denied these two things, the world is well rid of it. But to welcome greater democracy and self-determination, and the extension of cultural diversity, is not to welcome nationalism itself. Nationalism may well incorporate such positive forces, but it is not identical with them and is itself beset with myths and dangers.

For all the emphasis that nationalism in its various forms places on uniqueness and special character of a country, nationalism in different countries is in many respects all the same, and it rests on three recurrent ideas, each of which is unfounded.

The first is that nations have existed for a long time. Peoples, cultures, communities — with varying degrees of continuity and homogeneity — have existed for centuries and more. But nations, in the sense of communities practicing the right to self-rule, are all less than 200 years old....

The second myth of nationalism is that in some way nations correspond to something real — to a history, a tradition, a common race, language, territory, fate, and, in some cases, a divine order. All this is nonsense. Counting newly independent Namibia, there are now 170 sovereign entities in the world that we dignify with the term nation-state. But there is nothing "given," by history, God, or anything else, that makes our contemporary political map correspond with the diversity of peoples in the world. Language, the first try of anyone trying to define a nation, defines very few

— not just in the Third World, but in many parts of Europe too, not least Switzerland and Belgium. There are more than 4000 languages in the world. Perhaps there should be 4000 states?

Race, the other most common criteria for what constitutes a nation, is a dangerous concept at best. Even if it were not, it would not get very far with most of the nations in the world. None of the societies created since the year 1500 make much sense in terms of race. The United States, Australia, Brazil, and dozens of others actually represent a vigorous mingling of races. Even in more settled continents, the dividing lines of the contemporary international system fell haphazardly, with little respect for existing communities and peoples.

The third myth of the nation is that in some way we all belong to one. But many people in the world have more than one national identity....

In many nation-states of the world, the official nationalism is that of one dominant group using its supposed legitimacy to enforce the subordination of others. It is conventional to say that this is true of Third World states, but it is equally true of the United Kingdom, a multinational state forged by conquest and long maintained by force.

But even for people who qualify, the idea of belonging is equally bogus. For what is the entity to which they are supposed to belong? How is its identity defined? Here the ready answers of nationalism draw upon tradition in one form or another, as if what constitutes the nation is handed down by

earlier generations. This is an absurdity. Tradition is an artifact, a selective collection of myths and inventions made for contemporary purposes; and what constitutes tradition is defined by those with power.

It is these myths that underlie all nationalism. In themselves these myths might be seen as innocuous, necessary for identity and a sense of security in the modern age. Yet once accepted they provide a basis for oppressing those within the community who dissent, and they provide an excuse for arrogance (or worse) toward those seen as foreign or alien.

The dangers of nationalism are not confined to oppressor states. Other peoples, including those currently or recently oppressed on national and ethnic grounds, may well reply in kind, and often against other oppressed peoples. The current upheavals in...Eastern Europe have already unleashed their own crop of ethnic and communal conflicts in Bulgaria, Romania, Armenia, and Azerbaijan as well as the rise of anti-Semitism in Russia and Poland.

In recent years many political activists around the world have abandoned the idealistic notion of internationalism. I believe that internationalism is still relevant in the contemporary world, particularly in two respects: the rejection of nationalist myths (whether these be the myths of "others" or of one's "own" people) and support for democratic forms of international cooperation in the face of international trends that are neither.

Yet true internationalists must question the terms on

which the world is being internationalized today. A question arises: On whose terms is this internationalization taking place? In the media, for instance, we can see a growing concentration of power at the international level. The same thing is happening in many other sectors of our world economy.... The questions that arise with regard to both nationalism and internationalism are the same: How far do they lead to greater or lesser democracy, and how far do they promote or preclude cultural diversity? On their own, both can be instruments of control by social classes, states, genders, or dominant ethnic groups.

Fred Halliday, *New Statesman and Society*, 90 3 30

NEW VICTORIES IN AN OLD WAR

An estimated two million people die of malaria each year. More than 300 million suffer the excruciating cycle of fever, chills, and sweating that comes from being infected by one of the four kinds of malaria-causing Plasmodium parasites, which make their way from the saliva of an infected mosquito into the red blood cells of a human. Since the 1960s the situation has gotten worse rather than better, as the Plasmodium parasites have become increasingly resistant to quinine and related drugs. But now at last there is reason for hope: in recent months researchers have announced the successful testing of a new class of drugs for treating malaria and of a promising new vaccine for preventing it. Both developments have their origin in the Third World, which is for the most part where malaria kills.

The new drugs are actually new only to the West. The Chinese have been using the original source of the drugs, a medicinal herb called qinghao, for thousands of years — first as a cure for hemorrhoids; later as a way to break a fever, including a malarial one. For 20 years now Chinese scientists have known that the antimalarial ingredient in qinghao is an extract they call qinghaosu.

Here in America the plant is called sweet wormwood, or *Artemisia annua*; it belongs to the same genus as common wormwood, the source of the reputedly poisonous flavoring in absinthe. The antimalarial extract of sweet wormwood is called artemisinin, and it appears to be poisonous only to *Plasmodium* and a few other microbes.

Although Chinese doctors have administered artemisinin to more than a million people, the extract has yet to gain widespread acceptance as a malaria treatment outside China. This is partly because scientific exchange between China and the rest of the world has been almost nonexistent, and partly because of economics. "You need several grams of artemisinin to cure a human being, and the plant doesn't yield a heck of a lot," explains chemist Gary Posner of Johns Hopkins (University). It would not be economical, says Posner, to farm enough wormwood to make enough artemisinin to solve the world's malaria problem.

Artemisinin was synthesized in the lab in 1983, but that achievement too had little medical impact. "The synthesis requires at least 15 chemical steps," says Posner. "That's too time consuming, too costly, and too labour intensive. It's not viable for large-scale production." So chemists and physicians have been racing to develop a simpler chemical, one that's equally effective against malaria but easier to make than artemisinin. Posner has now found several promising candidates. "We stripped down the chemical structure of the Chinese drug to its bare bones, and in so doing we simplified it so its synthesis takes only six or seven steps," says Posner.

• • • • •

After a few more years of animal testing, the new drugs should be ready for safety testing in humans. But how long it will be before Posner's compounds or any other artemisinin derivatives (other research groups are following strategies similar to his) reach the world's malaria victims may depend on business and politics as well as science. "This is not a disease that affects U.S. citizens very much," says Posner. "It's a Third World disease and therefore U.S. industry is not very interested in funding the research."

Indeed, the new vaccine against malaria was developed by researchers in Colombia (although they did build on work originally done in the United States and Europe). The leader of the Colombian group is Manuel Elkin Patarroyo, a doctor at the Immunology Institute of the Hospital San Juan de Dios in Bogota.

• • • • •

Patarroyo's strategy apparently works. He and his colleagues recently announced the results of a clinical trial in which they administered their vaccine to 738 volunteers from La Tola, on the southern Pacific coast of Colombia. When all the data were in, Patarroyo found there were nearly 39 percent fewer cases of falciparum malaria among the vaccine recipients than among a control group. Two groups fared particularly well: there were 77 percent fewer cases of malaria in children between one and four, and 67 percent fewer cases in volunteers over 45 years old.

More recently Patarroyo has completed a second trial on 468 volunteers in Ecuador, with even better results, showing 68 percent fewer cases of malaria among all vaccine recipients. Later this year the Walter Reed Institute expects to begin testing the vaccine in Thailand; another trial, sponsored by the World Health Organization, began last January in Tanzania. Since 90 percent of all falciparum malaria deaths (and nearly 90 percent of malaria deaths of any type) occur in Sub-Saharan Africa, some researchers regard the Tanzanian trial as the acid test of Patarroyo's vaccine.

Patarroyo, however, believes he already has all the test results he needs. He thinks it is time to stop the trials and start giving the vaccine to whoever needs it. Although a 39 percent protection rate is not extraordinary for a vaccine, 39 percent of two million malaria deaths a year is nearly 800 000 lives a year that might be saved if Patarroyo's vaccine were universally available — and if it works as well as it appeared to in the trials.

Lori Oliwenstein, *Discover*, 1993 6

A CALL FOR A NEW KING SOLOMON

As unemployment remains a problem...around the world, politicians in Canada, the United States and elsewhere call for more retraining programs to shift workers from nongrowth sectors to those with bright prospects. The problem is, where is the King Solomon out there in the education or political realm who can tell our society which skills in which sector and in what numbers will be needed? Politicians and educators are probably the least capable of distinguishing "winning" from "losing" industries, mostly because, as servants in the public sector, they are totally removed from the commercial world. Even entrepreneurs and company presidents cannot be counted on to find niches that will guarantee success in the future. Witness how the corporate landscape is littered with the corpses of those who guessed wrong.

That is why politicians and so-called industrial strategies are not the way to help Canada make the transition to whatever the future holds. The best way is to give Canadians, who are basically entrepreneurial, the tools to help forge their own opportunities.

After all, not everyone can, or wants to, become an electronics engineer or software designer. Although those professions will be in demand for years to come, economies will need far more people who can start new dry-cleaning establishments, restaurants, doughnut shops and boutiques, or who...specialize in packaging products from abroad or who can sell anything from advice to autos. And the rewards for such undertakings, not to mention the sense of satisfaction,

SOURCE: Marilyn MacKenzie

Fig. 5-5 *Many small business are owned and operated by families, as here in Spirit River, Alberta.*

can be great for those who work hard, and work smart. That is why, out of necessity and choice, increasing numbers of people throughout the industrialized world are going into business on their own.

Between 1979 and 1990, self-employment jumped to 37 million workers or ten percent of the total employment in all 24 nations that belong to the Organization for Economic Cooperation and Development (OECD). Of the new entrants, more than half have opted to be self-employed by leaving an existing job, according to the OECD's 1992 Employment Outlook. Only about 20 percent came from the ranks of the unemployed.

Self-employment varies greatly from country to country surveyed. In Canada, the self-employed represent 7.4 percent of our entire workforce, compared to 6.7 percent in 1979. Italy has 22.3 percent self-employed, Spain 17.1, Australia 12.4, Britain 11.6, Japan 11.5, France 10.3, Germany 7.7, the United States 7.6 and Sweden seven. In most OECD countries, the rate of self-employment growth outpaced total employment growth.

That is why the most enlightened retraining policy a government can deliver is to give the unemployed, or anyone else, the generic skills to enable them to be self-employed. It's not a complicated curriculum: how to keep a set of books, deal with regulations, tax collectors, employees, suppliers, bankers, landlords and lawyers. Would-be proprietors should also take a basic training course on how to sell; how to read financial statements, the business press and **macroeconomic** indicators; how to prepare loan requests, budgets and mini-strategic plans; how to find investors or lenders, manage cash flow and analyze a business's or product's prospects. I would also throw in an afternoon on the ten most common reasons for business failure plus another on famous swindles, or how to smell a business rat.

In short, more people should be taught the basics of entrepreneurship. Critics would say those skills aren't worth a damn because the ability to spot opportunities or live with risk are not traits that can be taught in a classroom. That is true, but many a risk-taker has failed merely because he (or she) had never mastered, nor been told that he (or she) should, the basic skills that are required to run one's own affairs successfully.

• • • • •

Supporting the unemployed forever or embarking on costly retraining programs that may be outdated or inappropriate is financially impossible, as is the task of choosing winners and losers. That is why the best curriculum around to train Canadians how to cope with the future is to teach them how to be their own boss.

Diane Francis, *Maclean's*, 93 1 11

DISCUSSION AND RESEARCH

1. Examine the chart you made as you went through the readings. In small groups, (a) discuss the classifications in order to reach a consensus, and (b) report your findings to the class.

2. Select two of the previous readings. Make lists of the material in the readings that is relevant to the argument being developed and that which is irrelevant.

3. From among the previous readings, select the one that appears to be the weakest or least acceptable in its content and argument. In writing, examine the reasons for your selection, and attempt to develop an opposing position.

4. Each of the readings examines an aspect of change, and provides indications of the reasons for change and the means — the change agent(s) — whereby change is brought about.

> (a) In a class discussion, analyze each reading to identify and list the chief reasons for the change and the nature of the change agent.
> (b) In writing, develop a list of general factors that produce pressure for change.

PEOPLE AND CHANGE

Change may be sought and welcome, as when people choose to migrate from their homelands for greater economic opportunity elsewhere. Change may also be feared and unwelcome, as when people are forced to migrate as refugees from war and persecution in their homelands.

Most of the reasons for seeking or resisting change are connected in some way with different qualities in human nature. For example, people may be angry, or they may be pacific; they may be envious or content; selfish or cooperative. Such qualities produce different responses to situations. However, there is an underlying desire among most people to live a better life, although people define better in many different ways.

The factors that different people claim lead to a better life include improved health and education, greater international cooperation, zero economic development, and greater national independence. They also include more trade, sustainable development, more children, more religion, reduced birth rates, more secularism, and greater national self-sufficiency. Many of these factors contradict one another.

The often contradictory forces for change are examined in the following sections: "Global Unity or Diversity"; "Equality or Inequality"; "Technology and Restructuring"; and "Ecological Balance."

GLOBAL UNITY OR DIVERSITY

The cooperative forces for global unity include such political, humanitarian, and economic organizations as the United Nations, with all its agencies (see Fig. 5-6), the International Telecommunication Satellite Organization (INTELSAT), the International Red Cross, and the International Criminal Police Organization (INTERPOL). These organizations have almost all the nations in the world as members. They do not represent particular regions or particular interests, as some other international organizations do (such as the Commonwealth, the Organization of African Unity, the League of Arab States, the Organization of American States, and the Roman Catholic Church).

The forces for global unity also include a number of political, social, and economic practices, such as:

- world conferences;
- summit meetings;

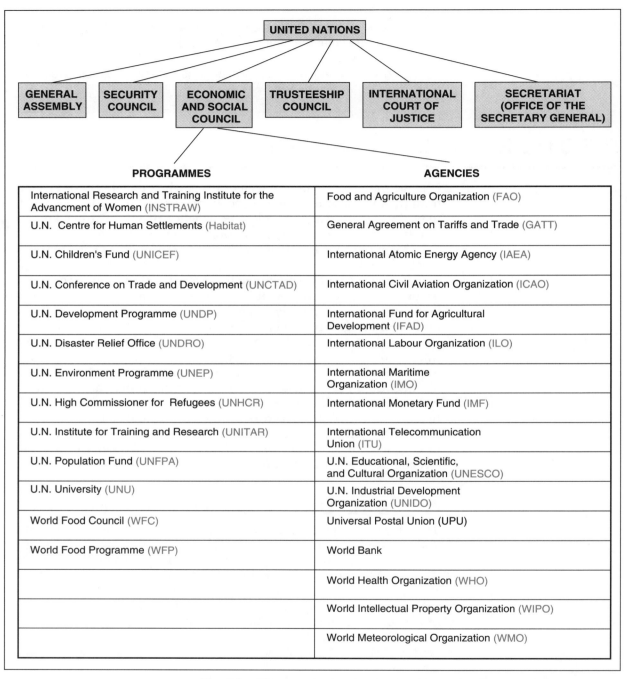

Fig. 5-6 *The organizational structure of the United Nations. Nations belong to agencies on an individual basis.*

- international trade;
- international tourism;
- radio and television communication;
- provision of asylum for refugees;
- global production by multinational companies;
- trade sanctions and boycotts;
- international agreements or treaties; and
- international sports (including the Olympic Games).

The forces for global diversity include such political, economic, and social organizations as national governments, national economic policies, national social policies, and a host of other governmental and nongovernmental bodies. Membership in these bodies may be international, as in most major religions, or confined to only parts of nations, as it is for hundreds of separatist groups across the world. The case study at the end of the chapter considers the situation of the Kurds in southwest Asia.

The forces for global diversity also include such political, economic, and social practices as:

- local, national, and international conferences for people with particular interests (e.g., Scottish clan reunions);
- trade barriers;
- **foreign exchange controls;**

SOURCE: Cliff Trowell, Canadian Hunger Foundation

Fig. 5-7 *Solar-powered radio enables this person in a remote area of Kenya to stay in touch with the rest of the world.*

- barriers to immigrants;
- national industrial strategies;
- avoidance of international treaties and other international obligations;
- jamming of foreign radio and TV broadcasts;
- banning of foreign newspapers and magazines; and
- non-participation in international sports.

The forces for both unity and diversity are persistent and strong. It is likely that all nations will continue to be pulled between nationalism and internationalism. The situation in Canada forms a useful example. Some recent events suggest that Canada might be moving toward a stronger internationalist approach. Other events suggest a strong nationalist tendency. The following is a list of some Canadian events, organizations, and practices. Decide whether each one represents a nationalist or internationalist approach, or if it is even relevant to this issue. If you are uncertain about the details of some of the items, research them in the vertical files in your library.

- Canadian ratification in 1993 of the free trade agreement with the United States and Mexico (NAFTA);
- the foundation of the National Party;
- the general expansion of immigrant and refugee numbers;
- the requirement for a certain number of hours of Canadian content on Canadian-owned television;
- the existence of the Assembly of First Nations;
- the expansion of peacekeeping operations to Somalia and Bosnia;
- the existence of marketing boards for several types of food produce;
- the decision by some provinces to participate, and by others not to participate, in international mathematics and science tests for students;
- the debate about the expansion of the Canadian Football League into the United States; and
- the call by many people in Quebec for recognition as a distinct society.

The pull between nationalism and internationalism is not confined to Canada, as the following readings indicate. As you read the articles dealing with issues or areas outside Canada, list any Canadian parallels that you can think of.

HOW TELEVISION IS RESHAPING WORLD'S CULTURE

Historians looking at the 20th century from the next millennium will likely pinpoint 1945 as the most pivotal year since the voyage of Columbus.

Two nuclear bombs exploded over Japanese cities, providing a glimpse of the apocalypse. And an obscure British radar officer named Arthur C. Clarke (theorized that it would be) possible to relay pictures around the world almost instantly by bouncing radio signals off a few satellites orbiting high above the Equator.

Both developments changed the course of humankind.

Asked once what had caused the stunning collapse of

communism in eastern Europe, Polish leader Lech Walesa pointed to a nearby TV set. "It all came from there."

If it has helped topple totalitarian governments and promote democracy, television has also, for better or for worse, led a modern Crusade, spreading pop culture over the Earth as medieval knights once spread Christendom.

In fact, nearly 30 years after Canadian philosopher Marshall McLuhan coined the phrase "global village" to describe how the electronics revolution was shrinking the world and shortening the time between thought and action, the Media Millennium is at hand.

TV sets are more common in Japanese homes than flush toilets. Virtually every Mexican household has a TV, but only half have phones.

More than half of North Americans alive today may not remember a time without TV in their home. They're surprised if someone doesn't have 25 or 30 channels to choose from. But for much of the globe, television is still relatively new, and changing fast. Today, there is hardly any spot on Earth untrammeled by a satellite "footprint" — the area, sometimes spanning whole continents, within reach of signals from its parabolic antennas.

The rapid inroads of satellite-based "borderless television" are changing the way the world works, the way it plays, even the way it goes to war and makes peace. Even countries that have long limited what their citizens can watch on nationalized TV are slowly being forced to relax their vice-like grip.

• • • • •

Spurred by technological advance and the worldwide trend toward privatization, a global TV

SOURCE: John Molyneux

Fig. 5-8 *One of the earliest transatlantic communication satellite dishes in Cornwall, England. Built in the early 1960s, it was designed to receive transmissions from the American Telstar satellite.*

economy is growing at a blistering rate. Consider:

• More than one billion TV sets now populate the globe, a 50 percent jump over the last five years. The number is expected to continue growing by five percent annually, and by more than double that in Asia, where half the world's population lives.

• Worldwide spending for television programming is now about $65 billion, and the tab is growing by ten percent per year, according to Neal Weinstock, media project director for the New York research firm Frost & Sullivan Inc. TV programs are a major U.S. export now worth about $2.3 billion annually.

• The number of satellite-delivered TV services around the world is more than 300 and climbing rapidly, says Mark Long, publisher of the World Satellite Almanac. Truly global "super channels" such as MTV reach hundreds of millions of house-

holds, while CNN is seen in 137 countries.

• Scores of new communications satellites are planned for launch in just the next five years, which will mean a huge jump in the number of space-borne TV channels.

The cultural, political and economic effects of this global television revolution are enormous.

Whether in the situation room at the White House or in living rooms at home, it is clear to viewers that television is no longer simply a limp witness to history.

Television is how most people now experience history, as happened when viewers watched live satellite pictures of U.S. troops landing on the beach at Mogadishu.[1] Conversely, history is now shaped by television, a reality eloquently symbolized by East German youths when they hoisted MTV flags over the Berlin Wall as it was torn down.

Oxford political scientist Timothy Garton Ash dubs television "the third superpower" whose influence will only grow as satellites and cable revolutionize its content.

A complex set of problems and issues arise from that power.

Ash warns that borderless TV threatens to make even more painfully obvious the economic gulf between rich and poor nations. Diplomats in Libya contend that television is undermining Moammar Gadhafi by tempting the country's relatively poor and otherwise largely sheltered population with the consumer delights seen in Italian commercials.

Even more alarming to some is the prospect of a world full of couch potatoes. The French now spend more time watching TV than working. Spanish schoolchildren are heavier viewers than their American counterparts. In Canada, the Vancouver-based Media Foundation, which publishes a magazine called Adbusters, has launched a frontal assault on TV's incessant buy-buy message by producing and attempting to air "anti-consumption" commercials.

Some worry that TV watching will make the rest of the world lose its appetite for reading, as has already happened to two generations of North Americans.

With satellites beaming down literally hundreds of TV channels over whole continents and oceans, countries lose control over the information crossing their borders — an unstoppable migration of ideas, images and culture that raises basic questions about the meaning of national sovereignty in the modern world.

"The nation-state is less and less able to control what goes in and out of it," said Everrete E. Dennis, a media scholar and executive director of the Freedom Forum Media Studies Centre. "It really makes customs and other nuances from the past kind of irrelevant."

What is happening around the world is the outcome of nearly two decades of global deregulation, spreading capitalism and advances in technology that are making electronic communications perhaps the world's pre-eminent growth industry.

"Technology has made it possible to add a number of channels in a variety of ways," said Eli Noam, an expert in global television at Columbia University in New York. "And the old state-run broadcasting systems are running out of steam."

Many of the new channels are being financed by advertising generated from an increasingly industrialized world looking for new outlets for its consumer and manufactured goods.

In Europe, TV advertising is expected to more than double to $36 billion by the turn of the century. The Pacific Rim's nascent TV ad market, just emerging from years of heavy-handed government regulation, has already reached $14 billion. With worldwide satellite networks, the Holy Grail of marketing — global advertising — is finally a reality.

"In another five years, there will be a direct broadcast satellite all over the Arab world," said Abdallah Schleifer, professor of television journalism at American University in Cairo. "And whether (people) want it or not, everyone is going to have access."

Historically, empowered elites have sought to suppress the wider distribution of ideas, wealth, rights and, most of all, knowledge.

This is as true today as it was 536 years ago, when the German printer Gutenberg invented movable type to print the Bible. For two centuries afterward, government tightly controlled what people could read through the widespread exercise of "prior restraint."

Some governments still go to great lengths to make the news fit their purposes.

The Chinese government doctored videotape of the 1989 Tiananmen massacre, reversing the order of events to make it appear the killings were a justified reaction to mob violence.

If you can't lick 'em, some governments apparently feel, you may as well join 'em. There are presently more than 40 established or planned government-run satellite TV channels, many with the same propagandistic purpose as their terrestrial predecessors.

Egypt's Space Channel, for example, originally launched to entertain homesick Egyptian troops in the Saudi desert during the gulf war, is seen as a response to Middle Eastern Broadcasting's Pan-Arabic news channel, owned by Saudis with royal connections.

Like ambitious states that want to join the nuclear club, a country today barely ranks as a world-class power unless it lofts a satellite bearing its own acronym: Asiasat, Aussat, Turksat, Thaicom, Arabsat, Insat, Indonesia's Palapa and Spain's Hispasat, to name a few.

"It's frequently a question of political sovereignty, not just economic rationality," said Meherro Jussawalla, a research economist with the East-West Center in Honolulu. "Each country wants to control its own satellite system for domestic purposes."

Even more than on politics, however, the greatest influence of satellite television is on culture. Whereas it used to take decades or centuries for one culture to seep into another, television today can spread lasting images in a matter of seconds.

"Foolish programs coming in foreign languages to our cable television stations are as much a danger to us as some attacks on our frontier," threatening Israel's culture, heritage and language, Foreign Minister Shimon Peres said not long ago.

Ironically, Peres shares this concern with Islamic fundamen-

talists in Algeria who now call satellite receiving dishes — *les antennes paraboliques* in French — *les antennes diaboliques.*

But neither quotas nor religious edicts are likely to slow the onslaught of borderless television. Rather than homogenizing the world, it is possible that the revolution will instead lead to a greater diversity in programming, especially as developing states

become more sophisticated in the use of the medium.

The global village won't be called "Dallas."

John Lippman, *Los Angeles Times*, 1992 12 21

[1]Mogadishu is the capital of Somalia where U.N. troops, led by the U.S., invaded in 1993 in an attempt to make peace among warring Somali factions.

TELEVISION NEWS

For years, scholars of the subject have complained that too much of the world's news flows from north to south, and from the first world to the third. The West, it is said, sets the agenda because it owns the news services, and thus spreads its own ideals at the expense of local ones. Is this really so? A new study, published on January 31st by the International Institute of Communications (IIC), a London-based think-tank, shows that far from turning into cultural colonies of America, most places are interested only in themselves.

The imperialists have a point. Except for Tass (now cozily renamed RITA, for Russian Information Telegraph Agency), the world's big wire services are all western-owned. So, too, are the three big television news-clip providers — VisNews, World Television News and CBS News International. These firms make money selling on newsfilm to stations that cannot afford their own on-the-scene camera crews. Unsurprisingly, their output tilts homewards. In a 1980 study Anthony Smith, an Oxford don (professor), showed that 40% of Reuters's and AFP's stories

covered European events, and 70% of UPI's American or Canadian ones.

The same imbalance does not seep abroad, however. The IIC study surveys the news broadcast on one evening, November 19th 1991, by 87 television channels in 55 countries. Four big events dominated the day: fighting in Yugoslavia, the release of hostages Thomas Sutherland and Terry Waite the day before, a massacre in Indonesia, and the reappointment of Edward Shevardnadze as (former) Soviet foreign minister.

The survey's most striking discovery is not that countries covered these stories in a similar way, but that most hardly covered them at all. Outside Europe, the Yugoslavian fighting was almost ignored. Outside Asia, the Indonesian massacre hardly got a mention except on a Portuguese channel, where footballers were seen to observe a minute's silence. On the vast majority of channels, domestic stories came top of the news. Sao Paulo's Channel 5 told viewers about a traffic jam in Rio; Bangkok's station railed at the cost of eggs; Delhi led with the anniversary of Indira Gandhi's birthday, with women's hockey not far behind.

True to form, Japan emerged as peculiarly isolated. NHK, the state-owned broadcaster, led with sumo wrestling. Tokyo Broadcasting's only foreign story was about the release in America of a raunchy Michael Jackson video. In turn, the world ignored Japan. A mild earthquake, which halted Tokyo traffic for 20 minutes, failed to cause tremors anywhere overseas.

Americans are obsessed with health stories; Australians love sport. Places with royal families give them lots of space. Britain's Sky News, Spain's TVE-1 and Thailand's Channel 3 all ran stories about local royalty. A Paris station, typically, found a story in the royal house of Monaco, and seven out of ten of Kuwait's lead items featured the doings of the ruling sheikh.

So the world's news is not all alike. But is it becoming more so? Graham Chapman, the geography professor who compiled the study, points out that although developing countries cover domestic news for themselves, and give it lots of prominence, they tend to buy in coverage of foreign events from western agencies. The survey produced few direct reports by journalists of one third-world country about events in another. So although developing countries' views of themselves are their own, their perspectives on the rest of the world are at least partly the West's.

Second, since broadcasters are state-controlled in most places, television news often reflects less what viewers want to watch than what governments think they should. African channels eagerly report worthy symposiums on birth control and crop-breeding; Eastern Europe is still heavily "cultural." If they could get uncensored commercial television, both the first world and the third might turn out to be far more interested in foreign news than they seem today.

The Economist, 1992 2 8

SHARE THE WEALTH OR GET READY FOR TROUBLE

The world's poor and war-shattered people have hit the road in record numbers in the past decade, striking genuine fear into the hearts of the wealthy nations that are their destination.

In response, those nations have tried to bar the door, as though this were the Middle Ages and they could simply raise the drawbridge around their comfortable castle to keep out the hordes.

The poor nations, for their part, are using the spectre of mass migration in a kind of North-South extortion. Mexican President Carlos Salinas Gortari is particularly good at this. His message, put more or less this bluntly, is "give us the jobs or we'll send you the unemployed." By the millions.

It is a typical standoff, the kind that has characterized relations between the rich and the poor nations of the world for decades.

What makes it different this time is that it is beginning to dawn on some world leaders that the developing countries finally have the upper hand — not by the justice of their position (although it has some justice), or because they have played their cards well in this game of international poker (they haven't), but by the sheer depth and extent of their misery.

The current recession in the industrialized world has produced measurable discomfort in the rich nations: high levels of unemployment, the exacerbation of homelessness and hunger among the poor, a pervasive pessimism and a sense that many of these countries have simply lost their way.

Painful though that is, it doesn't hold a candle to the suffering in the developing world.

The United Nations Fund for Population Activities reported recently that "between 1950 and today, per capita income in the rich countries has almost tripled, while in the poor countries there has been no improvement."

How you view that situation depends on which side of the ideological divide you occupy.

Economic conservatives argue that poor countries brought their problems on themselves through political and economic mismanagement. They made their beds, and now they must lie in them.

Liberals tend to believe the major culprits are international trade practices skewed toward the wealthy countries, and debt burdens on the Third World that amount to international usury.

There's a good case to be made for both arguments, but where has it got us to hammer away at those positions? Governments are in stalemate. Their only idea is to tighten immigration laws and hope (fruitlessly) that the worst is over.

A clear sign of their bankruptcy is the message coming privately out of the U.N. that governments won't take a global view unless citizens force them to. One U.N. diplomat suggests that something on the order of the ban-the-bomb movement, involving millions of citizens in First World countries over a period of years, might do the trick.

Good thought, but those citizens are the ones who will have to take a real hit in their standard of living if global solutions are to work.

Mass migration won't abate — as experts have repeated until they're blue in the face — until economic and social conditions in the Third World improve enough that staying home is as attractive an option as leaving.

But that would mean sharing the wealth; it would mean that 23 percent of the world's people could no longer consume 85 percent of its resources, as they (we) now do.

Those are not comfortable thoughts, and there is no sign that First World leaders are prepared to think them. In fact, aid budgets are actually declining, and they are increasingly targetted not at improving the lot of the world's poor but at improving the trade of the world's rich.

If that doesn't change, the 23 percent at the top of the economic heap are on a collision course with the 77 percent below them. And that's not a very comfortable thought either.

Linda Hossie, *The Globe and Mail*, 1993 6 25

DISCUSSION AND RESEARCH

5. In small groups or as a full class, devise a 25- to 30-question questionnaire that could be answered by the rest of the school or the local community to determine its opinion on the nationalism-globalism issue.

6. Whatever your personal views on the national-global issue, some people will disagree with you. List the various points you could make to try to persuade them to change their minds.

7. Develop two different one- to two-page scenarios for the future as it might exist in 20 to 25 years, for presentation as a short simulated radio or television broadcast to the class. One scenario should describe what the world might be like if the forces of nationalism become dominant; the other should outline what the world might be like if the forces of globalism become dominant. If a third scenario were to develop, describe what it might be like.

EQUALITY OR INEQUALITY

Many people say "we are all equal." What do you think they mean? Do you agree?

The countries of the world are not equal in any measurable way. Some countries may be similar to others in some ways, enabling them to be treated as a group, but there are no measurable characteristics shared to the same degree by all. Examination of any column in Appendix 2 will confirm that inequality is the norm. Will it remain so, or will the countries of the world move toward greater equality?

Global inequality is not limited to differences between countries. Inequality also exists within individual nations. As a result, different approaches emerge. For example, some people in Canada say that Canada's first efforts to lessen inequality should be made within Canada itself. Others say that Canada has a more pressing duty to humanity — as a matter of fairness, or equity — to try to lessen worldwide economic inequality. The government must thus determine how available resources should be allocated between national social welfare needs and international aid.

Human rights inequalities also exist among and within countries. In the matter of human rights, however, it is possible that concepts of equity and justice are more important than the concept of equality. There is much overlap among the concepts, but equity and equality also have sig-

SOURCE: Marilyn MacKenzie

Fig. 5-9   *A school in Fort St. John, British Columbia. Compare it to the school shown in Fig. 5-10.*

SOURCE: Marilyn MacKenzie

Fig. 5-10   *A school in Quito, Ecuador, built with financial help from the Netherlands and Israel. Where should the Canadian government concentrate its efforts and resources? On Canadian citizens or on humanity in general?*

nificant differences. Ideas of equity and justice suggest respect for fairness. Ideas of equality suggest parity or sameness. What situations can you suggest in which equality would also be equitable and just? What situations can you suggest in which equality might be inequitable and unjust?

Inequalities (inequities?) in the areas of gender rights and political rights are examined in the case studies at the end of Chapter Four (Women in Today's World) and Chapter Five (The Future of the Kurdish People). The following section examines economic inequality.

ECONOMIC INEQUALITY

There are two major sets of forces working to *lessen* economic inequality across the world, both within and among nations. One is the complex of factors that act together to cause economically poor people to seek greater economic opportunity. The second is the combination of motives that cause economically rich people to live materially simpler lives.

Conversely, there are two major sets of forces operating to *increase* inequality. First are the forces working to cause economically poor people to disregard economic growth and to seek satisfaction in the non-material aspects of life. Second are the forces causing economically rich people to seek to acquire even more material wealth.

Forces working to lessen economic inequality

The forces causing economically poor people to seek economic advancement are rooted in a desire for a materially richer life. People without running water want running water; people without radios want radios; and so on. Similar desires have spurred technological invention and economic growth throughout human history. For centuries the rewards of such

SOURCE: United Nations

Fig. 5-11 *Many people throughout the world seek a materially richer life. On a farm cooperative in Vietnam, workers pool their resources to develop better ways of feeding more livestock.*

Examples of empires that were wealthy in relation to neighbouring peoples are the former empires of Zimbabwe and China, and the Incan, Mayan, and Aztec empires.

growth have spread gradually throughout human society. Within individual nations, the earliest rewards usually went to society's powerful elites, with subsequent rewards **trickling down** through successively lower socioeconomic levels. The same system also holds true for nations, so that at any time in human history — and in all parts of the world — powerful and rich nations have existed with weak and poor nations, with the latter often being exploited by, and benefiting from, the former.

The extent of exploitation and benefit is a matter of argument in each case. For example, in Britain's former control of Canada, did the exploitation exceed the benefit to Canada? Was the exploitation greater than the benefit at one time, and the benefit greater than the exploitation at another? These and similar questions are very difficult to answer, partly because exploitation and benefit are impossible to measure, and partly because a comparison is being sought between what actually was and what never was but might have been.

The forces acting to cause economically rich people to seek to reduce their wealth arise partly from asceticism — a philosophy of self-denial — and partly from a growing concern about the health of the natural environment. Ideas about asceticism date back thousands of years, but they have generally never appealed to more than a small segment of any given society. At the time of the ancient Greeks over 2000 years ago, for example, the Stoics believed strongly that people should not get what they want in order to attain peace, but should want what they get. Today, there are people who regularly fast as a way of practising another aspect of asceticism. Concern for the natural environment is a further force acting to cause some economically rich people to consume less. The first tenet of the environmental movement is, in fact, Reduce.

In an article entitled "My Decision to Live More Simply Is Not Easily Understood" in *Compass* magazine (91/1), Susan Lussier wrote that she and her husband had deliberately chosen to live more simply. "The reason has certainly not been to protect a way of life in which we consume and waste thousands of times our share of the earth's resources, while millions haven't enough to meet even their basic needs. ...Rather, we have made these choices to challenge such a way of life." She described how their furniture and appliances had been "previously owned," how their television was a ten-inch black and white model, how the family made its own birthday cards, how the laundry and dishes were hand-washed, and how food was bought at a "food co-op" which was a forty-minute bus ride away. She continued, "...We have also tried to live in an "environmentally-friendly" way, believing that if we take good care of the Earth's resources now there will be more to go around in the future."

She concludes, "I keep wanting to tell people that there is no need to feel sorry for us — that despite the inconveniences and even though we do without certain things, our lifestyle is freely and happily chosen. One of the things we very gladly do without is the stress that can accompany a frantic consumer lifestyle.

We do buy a certain number of things, of course. There will always be items we need. I suppose that's the million-dollar question. Do we really need it? Will this purchase affirm or devalue personhood (my own, my family's, a Third World factory worker's)? Who will benefit and who will suffer by the choice we make? Even though such deliberations are often very subjective and grey areas abound, I feel it is still vital to ask the questions and struggle with answering them as honestly and as prayerfully as possible."

The two sets of forces that are working to lessen global inequalities are joined by another product of existing inequality, migrant and refugee flows. Migrants and refugees both seek to move from areas that seem to offer less to areas that seem to offer more. They thus "vote with their feet" in attempting to address personally the issues of inequality and inequity, although the areas they leave may become more impoverished. More detail about migrants and refugees may be found in Chapter Four.

These forces may eventually produce a more materially equal world, especially if the mass movement of people speeds up the process. However, there are other forces working in the opposite directions.

Forces working to increase economic inequality

Individuals in some parts of the world refuse to join the widespread efforts to increase material wealth, asserting instead, like the ancient Stoics, that self-fulfilment does not rest in material possessions. Such views are particularly common among some (but not all) Buddhists and Hindus, although other religions also have members who have taken vows of poverty. Ascetic views may also be adopted by others, who —

The ultimate form of asceticism rests on the view that holiness may be achieved only by withdrawing oneself from all worldly goods beyond the minimum needed to sustain life, and that these must be donated by others rather than produced by oneself.

SOURCE: Marilyn MacKenzie

Fig. 5-12   *Consumerism in North America: to what extent are shopping malls a defining characteristic of North American culture?*

in certain regions of the world, such as Iran and Iraq — may also claim that material wealth is a "western" idea that degrades their own way of life.

The belief that "western" materialism degrades other values was shown by Jacinta Goveas, a writer from Pakistan, who wrote an article for *Compass* magazine (91/1) after migrating to Canada. Goveas was raised in a middle-class urban family, and had then been employed as a community development worker/ teacher in a Pakistani village over 1500 km from her family home. She wrote that the villagers were "economically very poor. ...But what they did have, and were rich in, was their deep sense of what was right and what was important. They always had time for their families and for the children. ...Relationships there were real. ...There was no pressure to rush around trying to meet mortgage payments or beat credit card debts, and so there was time to be present for people in a very deep way." She therefore asked, "...are we not losing sight of something very basic in this rush for collecting material wealth?"

Meanwhile, there are many people in all parts of the world who are determined to increase their wealth still further. They want, and often command the resources to acquire, new cars, bigger houses, more clothes, increased travel, and so on. The world's largest commercial firms exist to organize production to meet these wants. If they fail to meet the wants to the satisfaction of the buyers, they either change or go bankrupt. This entire sector of the world's economy is regularly accused by people opposed to it of consuming too large a proportion of the world's resources, of persuading people through advertising to buy against their best interests, and of creating a great deal of pollution.

In response, the firms continuously attempt to improve their efficiency (as well as viability and profits) by reducing inputs per unit of output, and — under much government pressure — to lessen their adverse impact on the natural environment through the use of increasingly refined pollution controls.

Another aspect of the continued drive for greater production in the materially rich parts of the world is that jobs and tax revenues depend on

In 1993, for example, Domtar announced that it had developed a new process for making fine paper out of recycled cardboard boxes without the production of any of the usual sludge wastes. Its mill at Cornwall, Ont., was being fitted with the new technology.

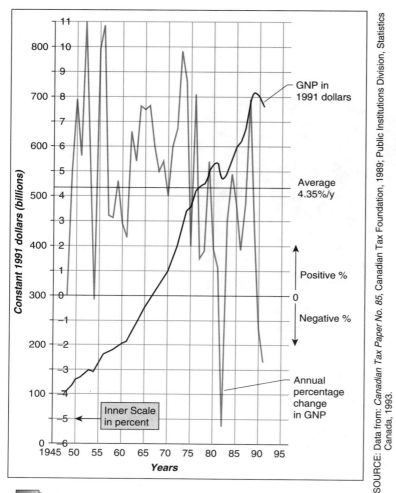

SOURCE: Data from: *Canadian Tax Paper No. 85*, Canadian Tax Foundation, 1989; Public Institutions Division, Statistics Canada, 1993.

Fig. 5-13 *Canada's economic growth, 1947–1991.*

In the U.K., for instance, the 1921 recession produced an unemployment rate of 9.6 percent (in Canada, 5.8 percent); whereas the Great Depression of the 1930s produced an unemployment rate of 13.1 percent (in Canada, 19.3 percent).

it. Any slowdown is termed a recession, or, in severe cases, a depression, and people are forced into unemployment as firms go bankrupt. Governments lose tax revenues because the total income and sales base is smaller, so they have to borrow to finance continued and increasing benefits. Government cannot borrow for ever, since lenders do not have unlimited funds, so there is much pressure from many sources to "improve the economy."

Reasons for recession or depression are difficult to identify. To a large extent they are regarded as a normal part of the business cycle, which has alternating phases of growth and recession (see Fig. 5-13). Business cycles have characterized economic production for a long time, being first noticed in 18th century Europe. Early theories of causation varied. Malthus, for example, thought that recessions resulted from underconsumption, itself caused by either too much saving by people or by low wages caused by a rapidly growing population. Other theories attributed recessions to overproduction, technological innovation, and political uncertainty. As the production process became more complex through the end of the 19th century and into the 20th century, business cycles became more severe. Increasing severity was most noticeable in the unemployment figures of the materially rich countries.

It was during the Great Depression of the 1930s that economist John Maynard Keynes produced his ideas about the role of government in the business cycle. Briefly, Keynes advocated that governments should stimulate employment and purchasing power during a recession by setting up a series of public works (building roads, and so on). This approach came to be called Keynesianism. Keynes also advocated that governments should try to reduce employment and income pressures during boom times by cutting back on public works. His basic idea was that during times of recession governments should run a financial deficit — spend more money than they take in from taxes — by bor-

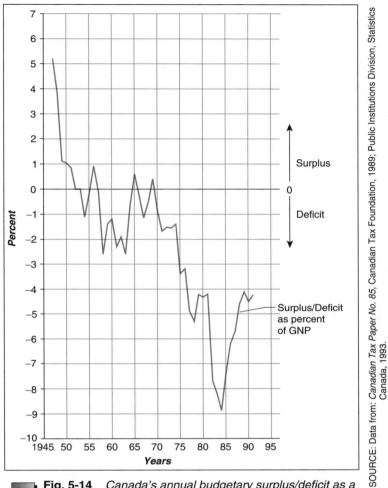

SOURCE: Data from: *Canadian Tax Paper No. 85*, Canadian Tax Foundation, 1989; Public Institutions Division, Statistics Canada, 1993.

Fig. 5-14 *Canada's annual budgetary surplus/deficit as a percentage of GNP, 1947-1991.*

rowing money, and pay off the debt by running a financial surplus during boom times. In this way, Keynes thought that the swings of the business cycle could be moderated.

Many governments have adopted Keynesian ideas during times of recession, but have neglected his prescription for boom times. Governments throughout much of the materially rich world have continued to run deficits through all phases of the business cycle (see Fig. 5-14). Since each year's deficit adds to existing total national debt, many countries have accumulated large and growing debt burdens. In doing this, governments have financed the growth of a large variety of public works, including armed forces, hospitals and medical care, pensions, social security, educational facilities, subsidized production, and so on. Citizens came to expect this rising level of services, and politicians promised delivery if elected.

There are really only two ways in which governments can finance these services: through taxation or through borrowing. Some governments tried a third way — printing more money — but this set up a range of other problems, chief of which was inflation. If the money supply is increased relative to the quantity of goods and services available in a society, prices tend to rise. Such price rises are called inflation.

Inflation has been a problem anyway, because borrowing also increases the supply of money relative to the quantity of goods and services available. Thus, increasing the national debt also increases inflation. When inflation exists, the purchasing power of money falls, because a given quantity of money buys less. The declining purchasing power of the Canadian dollar from 1947 to 1991 is shown in Fig. 5-15. Only between 1952 and 1955 did the value of the dollar remain virtually stable. In every other year the dollar lost value.

Politicians generally prefer borrowing to taxation because borrowing is less noticed by the public. Thus all governments in the materially rich

If countries are to borrow, others have to lend. For most of the time from, roughly, the 1960s to the 1990s the chief sources of funds were Germany, Japan, and Saudi Arabia.

Canada's national debt was $5 114 000 000 in 1939 and $18 443 000 000 in 1945, almost all owed to its own citizens. The value of the dollar fell during the same time by 15.7 percent, so that the debt in 1945 was worth about $15 547 000 000 in 1939 constant dollars, still a large increase.

Each year, the amount that Canadian governments have to pay in interest on the debt takes about 35 percent of all money raised in taxes. These are called debt service costs, and they form the biggest component of government expenditures. Debt service costs are payments for benefits previously received.

world have gone increasingly into debt. At first the debt was owed to their own citizens (as it is in Canada when people buy Canada Savings Bonds), but because public demand for expanded services was insatiable, governments turned increasingly to international borrowing. Meanwhile, they raised taxes, usually where they could do so without political harm. Thus to the present day, taxation levels have risen and debt loads have grown throughout the materially rich world.

For many of these years, the most-quoted example of a country coping well with a high level of government-provided services and a high level of taxation was Sweden. Calculations by the U.N. Development Programme (UNDP) show that if a **Human Development Index** (HDI) had been produced in 1970, Sweden would have ranked first. The UNDP used data relating to life expectancy, educational attainment, and GDP per capita. However, in the early 1990s, Sweden faced a serious currency crisis and found it could no longer sustain its high level of services. It began a program of reduction. *The Human Development Report* of 1993 ranked Sweden fifth, with Canada second (Canada would have been seventh in 1970).

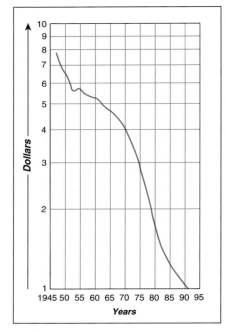

Fig. 5-15 *Purchasing power of the Canadian dollar in 1991 dollars, 1947-1991.*

Canada's experience illustrates how demand for economic growth interacts with government activity. Provision of government funding began early in Canada's history. In 1867, Canada's **national debt** was $94 000 000. Among early examples of government spending were the subsidies to the Canadian Pacific Railway to build a transcontinental line. However, government spending was generally moderate for many years. It began to increase slightly during the Great Depression, and then rapidly during World War II to finance the war effort. Attempts to reduce the federal debt after the war brought it down to $17 305 000 000 by 1950 (from a high of $18 442 900 000 in 1945), but it has grown since. Fig. 5-16 shows the growth of Canada's federal debt from 1961 to 1992.

During the period shown in Fig. 5-16, federal and provincial governments in Canada increased their overall taxation level from about 25 percent of incomes to about 50 percent. These rising taxation levels were inadequate, however, to finance increases in government spending levels. Governments, both federal and provincial, therefore increased their borrowing in international financial markets. Canada's federal debt (mostly in the form of Treasury Bills, Savings Bonds, and Treasury Bonds) is now owed about half to Canadians and half to foreigners. Because of its reliance

SOURCE: Data from: *Canadian Tax Paper No. 85*, Canadian Tax Foundation, 1989; Public Institutions Division, Statistics Canada, 1993.

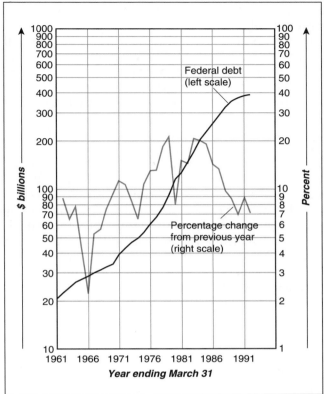

Fig. 5-16 *Canada's federal debt, 1961-1992.*

on foreign lenders, Canada's overall national debt has the largest component of international debt of all industrialized nations. Canada's national debt grows each year that taxation revenues fail to meet spending levels. The annual deficit through most of the 1980s into the 1990s has been about $30 billion, meaning that each year the total debt grows by that same amount. The only way to reduce the debt is to eliminate the deficit and start running a surplus. Deficit reduction, rather than deficit elimination, merely slows the rate at which the debt increases.

Repeated annual deficits and a constantly growing level of international debt cause many problems for Canadians. Taxes remain relatively high to help pay for expenditures; interest rates remain relatively high to attract money from foreign lenders; and governments constantly examine ways to reduce their expenditures. The total effect is generally negative for economic growth and employment, which tend to flourish best when taxes and interest rates are relatively low.

The only way in which taxes and interest rates can be lowered is to reduce levels of government spending in proportion to the total amount of wealth created in the country by the production of goods and services. In practice, this can be achieved by emphasizing either wealth creation or spending cuts or by a combination of both. There is sincere disagreement in Canada — as in several other countries — about the best policy to pursue.

Some people believe that the best way to reduce government debt is to encourage wealth creation through increased government spending. They believe that this will stimulate the economy in a Keynesian fashion, and that the economy will then grow faster than the debt. Many of these people believe also that if this happens then taxes should not be decreased, but new government programs should be put into place instead. Others say that a Keynesian approach is impossible given the high level of international debt, and that attempts to increase the debt by more than its existing rate will lead to dangerous loss of confidence by foreign lenders. They argue further that if Canada is not seen by the international community to be bringing its debt problems under control, then Canada faces the risk of losing sovereignty in the matter, since lenders may call in the International Monetary Fund (IMF) to provide financial direction to Canada. During the 1980s, the IMF was called in to help many nations in the developing world, along with Australia,

New Zealand, and the United Kingdom, so that they might be better able to handle their international debts.

Whatever the future direction — and it depends largely on political decisions — there is a strong relationship between economic growth and employment on the one hand and the level of government services on the other. Many people in the materially rich countries seek economic growth to help reduce taxes and debt levels, yet maintain or increase the level of government services.

The forces that increase global economic inequality are really the same as those operating to lessen it, but they have a different outcome on world equality depending on the group of people putting them into motion. For example, asceticism practised by both economically wealthy people and economically poor people will lower consumption levels. Among the economically wealthy, such practices tend to lessen global inequalities by bringing people closer to the global average, but among the economically poor they tend to increase global inequalities by taking them farther from the global average. The net effect of the forces may be seen in any changes that occur in annual GNP per person rates of growth or decline.

Column 35 of Appendix 2 shows average rates of change in GNP per person from 1965 to 1990. The range is from an average growth of 8.4 per-

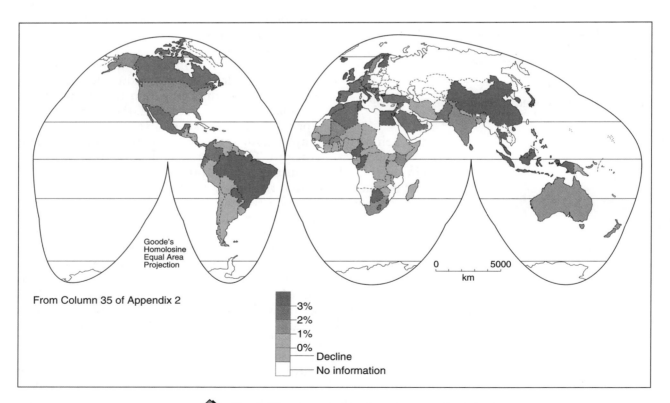

Goode's
Homolosine
Equal Area
Projection

From Column 35 of Appendix 2

0   5000
km

3%
2%
1%
0%
Decline
No information

Fig. 5-17   *Annual percentage growth rates, GNP per capita, 1965-1991.*

cent per year in Botswana to an average decline of 3.3 percent per year in Nicaragua. The countries that have experienced decline have also experienced civil war (as in Ethiopia and Nicaragua), internal terrorism (Argentina, Peru), or dictatorial mismanagement (Uganda, Zambia). Zaire has experienced these things too, but Zaire is also the only country to have announced (in 1972) that it had no intention of seeking economic growth. Elsewhere, annual per capita GNP increased at different rates in different countries, as illustrated in Fig. 5-17.

DISCUSSION AND RESEARCH

8. In its *Human Development Report 1993*, the UNDP rated Canada second in the world in human development behind Japan. In 1993, it gave Canada a Human Development Index (HDI) of 0.982 out of a maximum of 1.000. Japan was first with 0.983. The lowest country ranked was Guinea, in 173rd place, with an HDI of 0.045. In small groups, discuss the criteria that you would select for assessing human development, and attempt to achieve consensus within your group. Report your group findings to the class.

9. As an international investment analyst, organize an inquiry so that you may explain to your clients why they should invest their funds in Botswana.

10. Organize a formal class debate on the following motion: Global inequality is unacceptable.

11. List the names of class members on small separate pieces of paper and put them all in a basket or other container. Shake them up. List the following topics on small separate pieces of paper, put them in another container, and shake them up too. As your name is drawn, give a two- to three-minute talk to the class about the topic that is also drawn for you.

- Keynesianism
- Sharing
- Difficulties faced by migrants
- Economic growth
- Human rights
- Government spending
- Foreign aid
- Globalization
- Pessimism
- Predicting the future
- Motivation
- Income equality

- National debt
- Reasons for migrating
- Free Trade
- Sustainable development
- Taxation levels
- Minority rights
- Nationalism
- Optimism
- Gender equality
- Wealth creation
- Change agents
- Human diversity

Add other topics as needed.

12. Organize an inquiry to find out the nature of Canada's inequality-lessening resources.

STATISTICAL ANALYSIS

13. The data in column 35 of Appendix 2 show percentage changes in average GNP per person from 1965 to 1990. Column 19 gives the current GNP per person. Assume that a GNP per person of $10 000 provides a decent standard of living, although all developed countries except Ireland have a higher average income than this.
    (a) List all the countries with an average GNP per person of less than $10 000 (except the countries with declining or zero growth average GNP figures in column 35) and apportion them among class groups. Use the formula in the section on rates of change in Appendix 3 to calculate the number of years it will take for each country to reach an average income of $10 000. Assume that the rates of change will remain the same as those in column 35.
    (b) Consider the alternatives available in Appendix 3 for showing the results in map, chart, or graph form, and select the method you think is most appropriate.
    (c) Use your chosen method to show the results in a map, chart, or graph, and in a written statement explain why you chose that method over the others available.
    (d) What do the results suggest to you about
        (i)   the future of the equality-inequality issue?
        (ii) the capacity for economic growth in many developing countries?

14. Refer to Fig. 5-13.
    (a) Canada's economic growth since 1947, as shown by the line representing annual percentage change in GNP, has been erratic, with many minor ups and downs. Identify and list major periods of
        (i)   relatively rapid growth, and
        (ii) relatively slower growth or actual decline.
    (b) Relate the periods identified in (a) to the idea of the business cycle described on p. 316.

15. Refer to Fig. 5-14.
    (a) In which year did Canada last run a budgetary surplus?
    (b) In which 10 to 15 year period did the deficit appear to be out of control?
    (c) Make a tracing of Fig. 5-14 and lay it over Fig. 5-13. Compare the line in Fig. 5-14 with the line for annual percentage change of GNP in Fig. 5-13. Write an analysis of the two lines in relation to Keynesian ideas about moderating the business cycle.

TECHNOLOGY AND RESTRUCTURING

Technology is the application of scientific principles to production. Fundamental scientific principles such as those related to levers and pulleys have been known and applied for thousands of years. Modern technology employs these traditional principles, along with a wide range of others that have been discovered over the years. As scientific knowledge continues to expand, technology constantly has growing frontiers to develop. For example, the science of genetic engineering (sometimes called biotechnology), whereby specially selected genetic characteristics may be artificially bred into another organism, is still being expanded. When it becomes established, it could lead to breeding such produce as tomatoes that can be stored frozen, vegetables that ward off pests, and wheat that will grow in salty soil.

Advances in other forms of technology are also occurring. Developments in electronics are accompanied by developments in telecommunications; progress in metallurgy is accompanied by progress in engineering; advances in medicine are accompanied by advances in life expectancy; and so on.

The results of the use of new technologies are almost as diverse as humanity's varied activities, but the net result is most often intended to be an improvement in the quality of life and standard of living (although some technologies are used initially for destruction, as in war). Food production usually gains in reliability; transportation generally becomes easier; communication is frequently enhanced; and resources are often used less wastefully. In addition, industrial output usually becomes more efficient; and people generally become healthier.

As use of technology has increased over the years, humanity's survival mechanisms have changed also, as examined in the section "Development to the Present" on p. 186 in Chapter Three.

The three major steps in the changing sequence of jobs that has so far affected a growing part of humanity are called primary, secondary, and tertiary economic activities. Some people now add a fourth step, regarding the information aspect of tertiary activity as a separate stage which they call **quaternary economic activity**.

Primary economic activity is concerned with production directly from the natural environment. Farming is the most widespread primary economic activity, but also included are fishing, hunting, gathering, trapping, forestry, and mining. Information about the percentage of each nation's labour force engaged in primary economic activity is given in column 36 of Appendix 2. The fifty countries with the highest percentages are shown in Fig. 5-19.

The first genetically engineered tomatoes (called FlavrSavr tomatoes) were available in North American markets in 1993. The tomatoes were engineered to retain their freshness over a three- to four-week "shelf life."

SOURCE: Cliff Trowell, Canadian Hunger Foundation

Fig. 5-18 *A woman in Kenya learns about a new plant variety.*

Secondary economic activity includes the vast range of jobs associated with processing the products of primary economic activity. Food

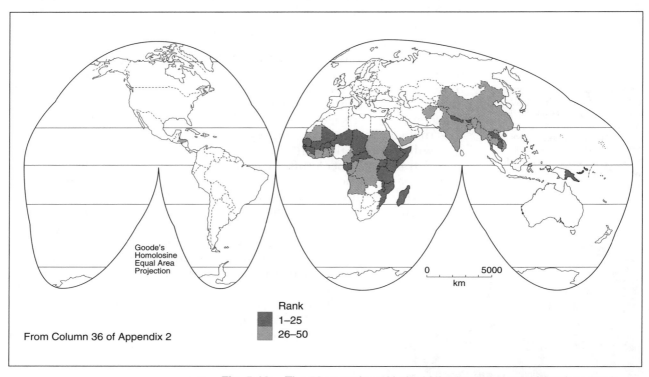

Goode's
Homolosine
Equal Area
Projection

0   5000
km

From Column 36 of Appendix 2

Rank
1–25
26–50

Fig. 5-19 *The 50 countries with the highest percentage of employment in primary economic activities.*

processing, paper making, car assembly, satellite building, and computer manufacturing are all parts of secondary economic activity. Most secondary economic activity takes place in factories, employing large numbers of people, who work to buy food and other goods. Individual manufacturers (called **artisans**) similarly trade their products for other goods. Using the information in column 37 of Appendix 2, the map in Fig. 5-20 shows the fifty countries with the highest percentage of their labour force employed in secondary economic activity.

Tertiary economic activity is the provision of all types of services to people. It includes road construction, banking, flight control, mail delivery, surgical operations, information management, hotel operation, legal help, fast-food sales, university lectures, child care, and thousands of other jobs. In many countries, services now provide people with more jobs than either farming or industry. People employed in service jobs do not generally work in farming or industry at the same time, and yet they still consume the products of farms and factories. In countries where large numbers of people are employed in services, and relatively few in farming

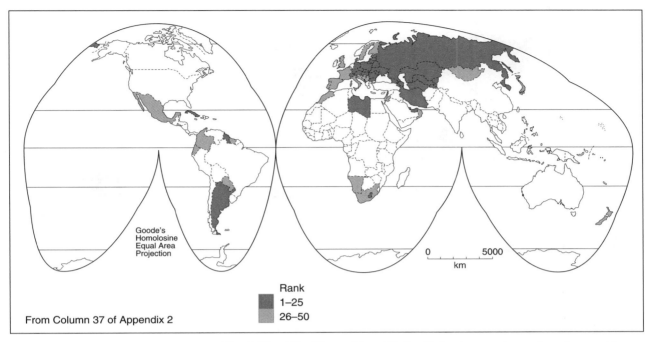

Goode's
Homolosine
Equal Area
Projection

0   5000
km

From Column 37 of Appendix 2

Rank
■ 1–25
■ 26–50

Fig. 5-20   *The 50 countries with the highest percentage of employment in secondary economic activities.*

It is equally true that increased technological efficiency in the production of food and factory goods means that fewer workers are needed. This increases the number of people available to work in the service sector.

Restructuring was also used to refer to the process whereby the IMF in the 1980s helped organize the economies of some nations to enable them to make debt payments.

and industry, the production of food and factory products has been forced to become highly efficient in terms of output per worker. Fig. 5-21 shows the fifty countries with the highest percentage of their labour force employed in tertiary economic activity, based on data in column 38 of Appendix 2. Data for quaternary activity do not exist separately because all official figures include it in the tertiary sector.

A process of major change within an economy is often called restructuring. For many people, it is a difficult process. In those areas that have experienced the changes brought about by technology, the first restructuring from hunting and gathering to settled farming caused much conflict over the use of territory. The second restructuring from farming to industry caused great social distress to people who were often crowded into cities in unhealthy conditions. The third restructuring from industry to services seems in the past to have caused relatively little damage to anyone. However, some people believe that there is a fourth restructuring now under way in some parts of the developed world.

The fourth restructuring may be defined as the shift in industrial production from workers to robots, from people to computer-controlled machines. However, it should be noted that this shift affects the manner of production, not the nature of the product. It is therefore not a restructuring in the same sense as the other three. The shift is occurring as industrialized nations meet competition from newly industrializing countries (NICs) in the developing world. Manufacturers in the developing world

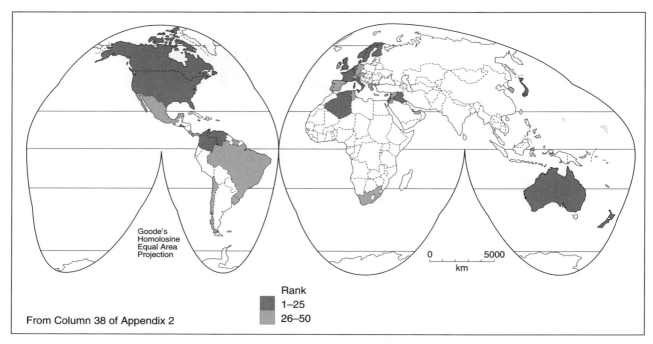

Rank
1–25
26–50

Goode's
Homolosine
Equal Area
Projection

From Column 38 of Appendix 2

0   5000
km

Fig. 5-21   *The 50 countries with the highest percentage of employment in tertiary economic activities.*

have access to a large — and increasing — supply of relatively low-wage workers. Some comparative wage rates are shown in Fig. 5-22.

Production that relies on a large supply of factory workers is therefore tending to locate in developing countries. Some of it relies on jobs — but not people — transferred from developed countries. Most of it consists of new jobs, created by producers opening factories in developing countries rather than in developed countries. Workers in developed countries are thus displaced, and often angry. They pressure their national governments to place trade barriers on cheaper imports from developing countries. At

Much thought is being given in the 1990s as to how to provide employment for people who have diminishing access to factory work. Many people stress the need for education or training for different types of jobs. They also stress the need for people to realize that they may have several different jobs during their working life.

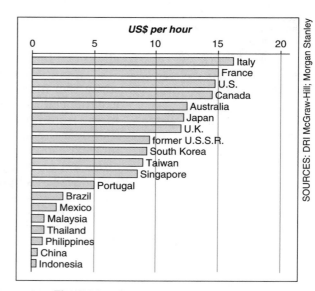

SOURCES: DRI McGraw-Hill; Morgan Stanley

Fig. 5-22   *Average wage costs in manufacturing for a sample of countries at the start of the 1990s.*

the same time, they meet opposition from developing nations who want access to richer markets for their products in order to earn money for economic and human development. Workers in developed countries also meet opposition from many of their fellow citizens who want access to cheaper imports.

An indication of the extent of the changes still to unfold in the restructuring process caused by new technologies, assuming they continue, is given by the maps in Figs. 5-19, 5-20, and 5-21. The countries where the greatest future changes are likely to occur are those currently with the largest percentages of employment in the primary and secondary sectors. More widespread use of technology causes urban jobs to develop and farming to become more productive per farmer. People thus move out of the primary sector. The countries that would seem to face the greatest degree of restructuring are shown in Fig. 5-23. This map indicates the fifty countries that have the highest ratios of primary to tertiary activity. What conclusions may be drawn from the map?

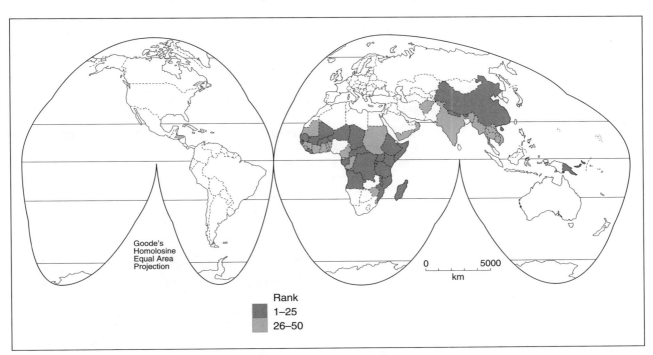

Fig. 5-23   *The 50 countries with the highest ratios of primary employment to tertiary employment.*

DISCUSSION AND RESEARCH

16. Compare the map drawn in answer to question 23 in Chapter Two with Fig. 5-19.

(a) Suggest reasons to explain why the countries with the highest proportions of farmers seem to produce the least food for their citizens.

(b) Suggest possible methods for improving the situation.

17. Technology has produced many changes throughout human history. In small groups, discuss the concepts of good and evil as applied to technologically driven change. Identify 10 to12 examples of good results and bad results of technological change, and report these to the class.

18. Some environmentalists believe that technology has often been used without proper care, and is largely to blame for the degraded state of much of the natural environment. They would generally like to see technology used less in the future. Use your imagination to develop two different scenarios: one of life in 30 to 40 years in which the use of technology is diminished, and the other of life at the same time in which technology is more developed than it is now. Write these scenarios down in a one- to two-page report.

19. Given that economic restructuring may continue regardless of whether people want it or not:
(a) Obtain information from local sources (library, trade directories, local newspapers, and so on) about the nature of the economy of your community;
(b) Examine how the restructuring process is likely to affect your community;
(c) Develop an action plan for your community to follow in order to gain the most — or lose the least — from restructuring;
(d) Present your plan to a classmate to obtain a second opinion about whether it is reasonable and practicable; and
(e) Devise a means of presenting your plan to the local community and follow through with it.

STATISTICAL ANALYSIS

20. There are three large components of any economy: primary, secondary, and tertiary activities, which differ among countries.
(a) Use the information on triangular graphs (see Appendix 3) and the data in columns 36, 37, and 38 of Appendix 2 to construct a triangular graph to show the different economic character of the following 50 countries from all parts of the world:

Argentina	Bangladesh	Barbados	Bhutan
Botswana	Brazil	Cambodia	Canada
China	Cuba	Egypt	Ethiopia
Fiji	France	Germany	Guinea-Bissau

Hungary	India	Indonesia	Iran
Iraq	Ireland	Ivory Coast	Japan
Laos	Madagascar	Malaysia	Mauritania
Mexico	Morocco	Namibia	Nepal
New Zealand	Niger	Nigeria	North Korea
Pakistan	Peru	Philippines	Poland
Romania	Saudi Arabia	Singapore	South Korea
Sweden	Syria	Turkey	Uganda
United States	Zimbabwe		

(b) Describe the pattern made by the graph.
(c) Suggest reasons that might explain the pattern.
(d) What does the distribution of dots tell you about the nature of economic development?

ECOLOGICAL BALANCE

Ecological balance is sometimes called the balance of nature. The term refers to the relatively stable adjustment of all the parts of an ecosystem to one another. A stable ecosystem is often described as being in **equilibrium**.

Research into ecosystems suggests that stability is more likely if it contains great species diversity, or biodiversity. The variety provides a cushioning effect (called resilience) to disturbances, so that negative disturbances may be compensated by positive changes elsewhere within the system to maintain the overall balance.

Stable ecosystems develop over long periods of time through a process known as **ecological succession**. This means that faced by new land to colonize, plants and organisms develop in a particular sequence. For example, lichens develop on bare rock, creating tiny amounts of soil in which mosses can subsequently grow. The mosses force out the lichens to create a new and different ecosystem. In turn, mosses create more soil, allowing small shrubs to grow and predominate. Small shrubs are eventually replaced by small trees, which compete successfully for available light, water, and soil. Through time, small trees are replaced by larger trees, and the ecosystem gradually develops to its final — or **climax** — stage of equilibrium. All stages of the succession have their own associations of plants and other organisms. The climax ecosystem has the greatest biodiversity, and is therefore relatively stable.

However, climax communities are not immune to change. External forces may induce change. Natural external forces may be slow-acting, such as the movement of the continents or changes in the global climate. Fossil evidence in the rocks of the Canadian Arctic, for example, points to their origin in tropical conditions. Extensive evidence can also be seen over much of Canada of glacial conditions which existed about 10 000 to 15 000 years ago. There is considerable evidence around Canada's shores of former changes in sea level, some still occurring. All such slow-acting changes

Land areas like Canada that were covered by ice were depressed over 1000 m into the earth's crust. They are still rising back up, as shown by the presence of sea fossils which were once submerged below sea level now at heights of up to 300 m above sea level around the shores of Hudson Bay.

disturb existing ecosystems and create different conditions for new ecosystems. Natural external forces may also be fast-acting, such as fires, earthquakes, hurricanes, and floods, which bring dramatic changes to stable ecosystems.

However, changes induced by human activity are more widespread. Ecosystems are under human pressure to change largely because of the following factors:

Population growth (see Chapter One)

The carrying capacity of the earth — the maximum number of people it can support — is unknown. Estimates vary according to the standard of living and quality of life assumed to exist. The graph in Fig. 1-27 gives some idea of future possibilities, but — like all projections — it is based on assumptions about future human behaviours that may or may not happen. Nevertheless, it seems likely that human numbers will at least double, increasing pressure on the existing ecological balance.

Demands for food (see Chapter Two)

An increased population means that more food must be produced. At present, millions do not get enough to eat. Will the problem become worse? Already, the human population consumes about 40 percent of world plant growth each year. If population doubles, and consumes 80 percent of world plant growth, what will other animal species do to survive? Will farmers be able to increase food production faster than population growth to permit more people to eat better? Some people see an answer in biotechnology; others in reducing or eliminating meat consumption, since livestock consume grain that could feed more people. Is it true, as Mahatma Gandhi said, that the rich must live more simply so that the poor may simply live?

Exploitation of natural resources (see Chapter Three)

Growing numbers of people are also likely to increase world demand for natural resources. Soil for food production is already under serious pressure from degradation in many parts of the world. Will there be sufficient soil for the large amounts of food that must be grown to feed a population double the present size? Or will farming develop more "controlled-environment" agricultural units, as a few experimental farms in the United States are beginning to do? These controlled-environment units are really food factories, using artificial soil and electric light. They are capable of producing food year round. A single factory can now produce as much food as can be grown on 100 ha of farmland over the course of a year. They rely on large quantities of energy.

World energy supplies are not scarce, but they pollute. The search for clean energy continues, but it is difficult to generate it in easily usable forms and in sufficient quantities. In 1993, China announced that it would begin development of a large-scale nuclear energy program, since coal — its chief source of energy at present — produces serious emission problems. Such a program will take many years to implement, and it is unlikely that

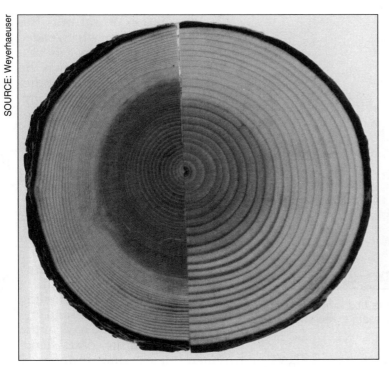

SOURCE: Weyerhaeuser

Fig. 5-24   *Comparison of a 24-year-old supertree on the right with a 75-year-old regular tree on the left.*

nuclear energy will soon displace coal as China's chief fuel. Not everyone welcomes nuclear energy, however, because of perceived radiation and waste disposal hazards. Alternative energy sources such as solar power have limitations at present. What will future energy sources be like? Will the world have sufficient clean energy to provide for a decent life for all?

Other major natural resources already under the pressure of human demand are the world's forests and waters. How can supplies be made available for future generations perhaps double the size of the present population? How will the world manage to increase supplies of wood products and water when these are already under pressure? Some people see the chief answers in supertrees that grow faster and thicker, and can yield more forest products per hectare than present trees; others prefer to see reduction of use and recycling of wood products as a more useful first option. Some people regard the extra and reliable supplies of water from reservoirs as sufficient reason to continue constructing dams; others regard dams as disruptive of existing ecosystems and lifestyles.

Waste disposal (see Chapter Three)
Wastes from current production and consumption are already at high levels. Some types of waste pose serious problems of disposal. Will more people in the future produce more wastes, perhaps overloading natural and human waste disposal systems? Most people see solutions in the reduction or prohibition of wastes, so that waste production occurs — if at all — on a manageable scale. Effort and discussion go into the problem, since it is commonly agreed that solutions are needed. Some solutions, as for atmospheric and oceanic pollution, require global cooperation. Various steps in the direction of cooperation have already been taken, such as the Montreal Protocol of 1987, an international agreement relating to the protection of the stratospheric ozone layer.

Global warming is a concern for many people. Many individuals believe it is caused chiefly by wastes that enter the atmosphere from the combustion of fossil fuels. Others regard global temperature variations as the product chiefly of natural cycles, claiming that geological evidence points to many changes in temperature throughout earth history. They say that it is quite possible that any warming trend is largely the gradual

Fig. 5-25   *Over the centuries the Dutch have built a network of dikes to protect themselves from the sea and to help them to reclaim land previously submerged.*

restoration of warmth after the last ice age, which ended about 10 000 years ago. Fossil fuel use may only be slightly speeding up something that would happen anyway. Whatever the causes of global warming, it is likely to cause a rise in world sea levels, as existing ice in Antarctica and Greenland continues to melt. Certainly, there is much evidence now that the initial melting of the continental glaciers in North America, Europe, and Asia 10 000 years ago caused sea levels to rise rapidly around the world, flooding many coastal areas, and creating islands and bays in the process. Future coastal flooding will, however, have a significant human impact, since millions of people live in the world's coastal lowlands. Can anything be done to halt global warming, or should people in coastal lowlands be prepared to follow the Dutch in building a network of protective dikes?

Migration (see Chapter Four)
The combination of rising population with any loss of land caused by global warming is likely to put added pressure on livable space. Some countries are already relatively crowded (see Fig. 1-37). Many people expect that as pressures on livable space grow, people in increasingly crowded — and maybe environmentally degraded — areas will seek to move to areas that are less crowded. Mass human migrations have occurred in the past; they are occurring now; they may become larger in the future. If the ecological balance is seriously disrupted by these human pressures, migrants may become refugees. What actions can be taken to prevent such a potential disaster? What actions can be taken to accommodate the situation peacefully if nothing can be done to prevent it?

Technology (see previous section in this chapter)
Technology may hold the answer to many of these questions, but it too is often a pressure on nature. Ecologically sustainable technologies are still not widely used throughout the world. The changeover from exploitive polluting technology to sustainable clean technology is expensive. So far, relatively few countries have decided to allocate their scarce resources to the new technologies, although all agree that sooner or later they will have to do this.

21. It has been suggested that national governments are too big to deal with small problems and too small to deal with big problems. In small groups, identify two problems of each type connected with ecological balance, and suggest what level of government would be appropriate to deal with the problems.

22. Many human activities directly or indirectly exert pressure for change on ecosystems. For the biosphere, the largest ecosystem, develop and write down two scenarios for the future:
    (a) Optimistic;
    (b) Pessimistic.

23. In class, discuss the justice of Mahatma Gandhi's view that the rich should live more simply in order that the poor may simply live.

VIEWS OF THE FUTURE

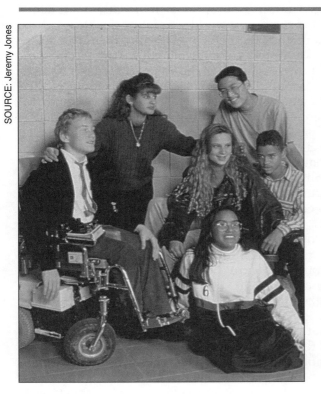

SOURCE: Jeremy Jones

Fig. 5-26 *Young people face the future. What will it hold for them?*

As the pressures for change expand throughout the world, they make it likely that the future will be significantly different from the present in many ways. It is difficult enough to project the future of a single factor such as world population. It is much more difficult to project what the future may be like when the interaction of several factors is taken into account.

There are two main methods of "futures analysis." The first method relies upon analysis of past and present trends and conditions, and how they may develop in the future. The second method relies upon setting targets for the future and then investigating how to get there. Both methods have advantages and disadvantages.

Supporters of the first method — analyzing past and present trends and conditions — claim that it is rooted in reality, and therefore likely to provide a good guide to the future. They also point out that if trends change, the projections based on them can also be changed very easily. However, supporters of this method admit that identification of the significant trends is difficult, especially in relation to the many factors that can influence a trend. What are all the different factors that influence population growth, for instance, and which ones are likely to be significant?

Supporters of the second method — setting future targets — claim that it is based on idealism, and therefore likely to produce the sort of future that is desired. They also point out that targets provide a recognizable goal to work towards. However, those who support setting future targets admit that many present realities may hinder such goal-oriented work. Another problem with this method is that future goals may not always be agreed upon.

In detail, the first method may be achieved through a variety of individual techniques, such as brainstorming, contextual mapping, and the Delphi technique.

In the brainstorming technique, members of a group initially make suggestions on a particular topic without passing judgment about each other's suggestions. Once the list has been made, discussion about each suggestion occurs until consensus is more or less reached.

In contextual mapping, graphs are made based on statistical trends for factors related to a particular topic. This technique also includes extrapolation. Extrapolation is the process of calculating a future situation based on knowledge of past and present situations. The projections of world population shown in Fig. 1-27 are an example of extrapolation. The extrapolated projections in contextual mapping are calculated for a number of related factors. Certain assumptions are usually made about the interaction of the factors (such as: if world population doubles, garbage will also double). The graph lines are then projected into the future to see what happens given the assumptions of interrelatedness for the different factors. One of the best-known examples of the contextual mapping technique was the computer-based study called *The Limits to Growth* prepared for a group of individuals who called themselves The Club of Rome.

In the Delphi technique (named after the oracle at Delphi in ancient Greece), 30 to 50 specialists on a particular topic are individually asked their views about the likely future of the topic. The organizer eliminates extreme minority views, and presents the more commonly held views back to the individual specialists for their reactions. The specialists again respond, and the organizer again eliminates minority views. Rounds of questions and responses continue to be held until consensus is more or less reached.

Within the first group of techniques of futures analysis, brainstorming and the Delphi technique offer possibilities for more insightful or imaginative conclusions. Contextual mapping and extrapolation are more mathematical or mechanical in approach.

The second method of futures analysis has fewer subcategories than the first. The chief technique is to establish certain goals for the future, examine the contrast that exists between such a future and the present (called gap analysis), and then identify what needs to be done to reach the targeted future. The establishment of future goals may be done through discussion and consensus, or it may be imposed by political or military force. The governments of many countries have engaged in this type of futures projection, which is often also called normative forecasting or plan-

The Club of Rome was an unofficial association founded in 1968. It had 100 members, who were interested in promoting new solutions to many of the world's problems.

Delphi, located almost 200 km west of Athens, was the sanctuary of Apollo in ancient Greece. Oracles were the responses of the resident priestess (called Pythia) to questions from inquirers about the future. The oracles of Delphi were sought for guidance in many matters for several centuries.

ning. Identification of what needs to be done to reach the targeted future is sometimes called backcasting. The implementation process is a task where force-field analysis (see Chapter One, p. 15) may be appropriately used.

Examine the following readings, which present some views of the future in different areas of concern. Identify for each reading the particular technique of futures analysis that seems to have been used by the writer. As you work through the readings, identify and list any underlying trends that lead to the statements made, and note also any statements that do not seem to be supported by current trends.

ASIAN NATIONS TO DOMINATE WORLD ECONOMY, GROUP PREDICTS

PARIS — Forget Europe's obsession with its single market and North America's fanfare for its free trade area.

If the Organization for Economic Co-operation and Development (OECD) is right, the centre of global economic activity is shifting inexorably to the Asia-Pacific region.

The Paris-based think tank predicts the Asia-Pacific region will account for one-third of world production by 2010, compared with roughly one-quarter in 1990.

By 2040 half of the globe's output could be "Made in Asia."

As growth in the region roars ahead by five to six percent a year, North America limps behind at just 2.5 percent, handicapped by weak productivity in the United States, low investment and fewer new workers joining the labor market.

Europe can look forward to growth in the three to four percent range, thanks to the dynamism imparted by the accomplishment of the European Community's single market. But high unemployment persists and related social problems remain a source of concern.

In *Long-term Prospects for the World Economy*, the OECD is not making forecasts but rather trying to pinpoint the main developments that policy-makers need to anticipate.

The OECD does not think there is much chance of Asia forming a trading bloc because of what it calls the extraordinary diversity of the region's countries.

"In particular, any attempt by Japan to become an hegemonic (leading) power may be strongly resisted by other Asian countries, which will try to balance the Japanese influence by seeking stronger ties with the United States or Europe," the study says.

Japan's population trend will have a profound impact on the world economy. As its work force shrinks after 2000 and savings decline, its capital exports will shrivel.

Simultaneously, Tokyo may have to let in more immigrants, and Japanese firms will step up their foreign expansion.

By 2010, the OECD reckons, 20 percent of Japan's production will be overseas — a similar level to Germany's — compared with the current level of about six percent.

Demographic trends will be a major force for the United States, too. As labor becomes relatively scarcer, real wages will rise, boosting incentives to replace workers with machines.

• • • • •

Other worries foreseen by the study include worsening poverty in Africa; a widening gap between rich and poor nations; a tripling of Asia's urban population to 2.3 billion between 1990 and 2000, exacerbating environmental problems; and possible rises in interest rates as sources of surplus capital dry up.

• • • • •

Reuter, 1992 8 10

THIRD WORLD WAR

Violence plagued India's 1983 parliamentary elections but no one expected the savage turn the campaign took on February 18 in the northeastern state of Assam. In a five-hour rampage in the town of Nellie, a group of local farmers wielding knives, machetes and spears hacked to death more than 1500 migrants from neighbouring Bangladesh. The slashed and battered corpses of men, women and children were scattered for miles, *The New York Times* reported; *The Economist* called it a "horrific massacre." Government officials attributed the killings to a dispute over Assam's fertile farmland. Assamese farmers believed the Bangladeshis, who had fled their own ecologically damaged and war-torn country, had stolen some of the region's richest soil. In an area where arable land is scarce and poverty abounds the bitterly contested elections gave the local farmers an excuse to inflict lethal punishment.

Thomas Homer-Dixon, a professor of political science and co-ordinator of peace and conflict studies at University College (University of Toronto), remembers the massacre well. He was in India at the time, a young Canadian traveling through Asia and Africa for a year before starting graduate work at the Massachusetts Institute of Technology. He recalls the jolting headlines and the widespread disbelief and anguish that followed the incident. "It was a shock to the whole nation. Every Indian newspaper in every language described it as a catastrophe." The event shook him, too, leaving him uneasy about that country's future. What frightened him, he says, is that the poverty and scarcity blamed for the massacre are a part of life in much of India. He could not help but view the event as an omen, a sign of a potential for violence in the entire region.

A decade later the bloodbath in Assam is one of several cases Homer-Dixon and two collaborators — Jeffrey Boutwell, program director for international security studies at the American Academy of Arts and Sciences in Cambridge, Massachusetts, and Professor George Rathjens of political science at the Massachusetts Institute of Technology — now cite most often to support their theory that scarcity of resources (diminished food, water and energy supplies) causes people to attack one another. As more of the world's natural resources are drained or destroyed, more people will kill each other more often, they predict. The international team of 30 researchers involved in their environmental change and acute conflict project has spent nearly two years and $500 000 examining these issues. They have concluded that there is a link between the environment and violence in the developing world. In recent articles in *Scientific American*, *The New York Times* and *The International Herald Tribune*, among others, Homer-Dixon, the study's principal author, states that the unmatched ability of human beings to raze forests, pollute and drain rivers, wipe out entire plant and animal species and erode and contaminate cropland results in poverty, hunger, unemployment, mass migrations to cities from the countryside and a lack of basic services such as housing, sanitation and transportation. The consequences as documented to date are riots, rural and urban clashes, regional disputes, student revolts, general insurgency and, as in Assam, even mass murder.

Homer-Dixon says the violence will grow and worsen in the next 50 to 100 years as the world loses resources at an unprecedented rate. The World Resources Institute of Washington, D.C., estimates that an area the size of Austria is deforested each year, that animal and plant varieties in the tropical forests are disappearing thousands of times faster than the natural rate of extinction, that moderate-to-extreme land degradation spoils millions of hectares of fertile land each year and that global fisheries are being exploited at their sustainable limit. Simultaneously the world's population is expected to reach ten billion by 2050 and global economic production to quintuple. Unless world leaders and policy-makers do something to alter this course, he warns, unprecedented civil and international strife will torment our children and grandchildren. The project's researchers have already detected signs of this impending turmoil throughout Asia, Africa and Latin America.

Mauritania and Senegal came close to war in a dispute over the Senegal River valley that lies between the two countries. After years of severe drought, increasing degradation of the area's agricultural land, food shortages and rapidly growing populations, the countries of the region dammed the river in 1988. This made it possible to irrigate previously dry territory, the value of the land soared and the Moors (Arabs) in Mauritania rewrote land ownership legislation to rescind the rights of their black compatriots in the valley where they had lived for decades. The resulting tensions, exacerbated by a history of white Moorish racism, led to an outburst of black Senegalese resentment.

In the spring of 1989 hundreds of people died in ethnic riots in both countries and more than 15 000 shops owned by Moors in Senegal were destroyed. Mauritania then enforced its new legislation and 70 000 black farmers, expelled to Senegal, launched raids from there across the river to retrieve their property.

Labourers and poor farmers in the Philippines have supported communist-led guerrilla groups since the 1970s. At the same time inequitable distribution of fertile cropland and high unemployment have sent millions of people to live in unproductive and ecologically damaged land on hillsides. There they log, produce charcoal and engage in slash-and-burn farming to subsist. The results are mass deforestation and erosion that add to the existing poverty and misery. The project's two Filipino researchers report that resource scarcity is behind the poor's backing of the revolutionaries, who routinely attack military stations and assault rich landlords and local government officials.

The South African government's apartheid policies and laws, now rescinded, have forced many blacks to live in some of the country's most environmentally vulnerable regions. When the farmers can no longer grow food

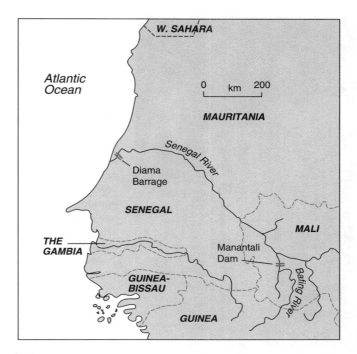

Fig. 5-27   *The Senegal-Mauritania area.*

because of erosion, thousands of them move into cities. But a lack of urban employment and shelter soon propels them into squatter settlements and illegal townships bursting with chaotic violence.

In China drought, air pollution and scarcity of fuel and land have led to rural and urban confrontations. But Homer-Dixon believes worse is ahead as that country tries

to cope with reduced crop yields caused by polluted water and deforestation-induced flooding, loss of farmland to construction and erosion and an influx of impoverished, interior-region dwellers into prospering coastal cities.

• • • • •

Suzanne Soto, *University of Toronto Magazine*, Summer 1993

A GLIMPSE INTO THE BOOMERS' RETIREMENT ABYSS

After paying into Canada's publicly administered pension system for most of their working lives, most people understandably anticipate a reasonably comfortable retirement sustained at least partly by Canada Pension Plan and Old Age Security

payments. But the demographic weight of the retiring baby-boom generation will place Canada's pension system in a cash flow crisis so severe it may buckle under the burden, warns a study released two weeks ago by Statistics Canada. Unless the system is completely restructured, the only way to guarantee the survival of social security for Canada's rapidly growing elderly population is a vast infusion of

cash, funded by massive tax increases on their children. And that, experts predict, will ignite an ugly inter-generational war between frightened pensioners and overtaxed workers.

The aging of the population is just the tip of the iceberg. Canada's pension system is perhaps the most poorly designed and self-destructive social program ever implemented by a mature industrial society. Its

Fig. 5-28 *Two of the increasing number of older people in Canada. Suggest different ways in which older people can benefit the economy of a country.*

inflexible structure was created during the baby boom of the 1950s and 1960s, when today's below-replacement birthrates seemed unimaginable. Moreover, it pays larger pensions to those least in need, discriminates against disadvantaged groups..., and is structured so that the only thing standing between poverty and each new generation of pensioners is the willingness of the next generation to pay ever-higher taxes and payroll deductions. The structural inability of the system to withstand the pressures caused by a rising population of retirees has prompted Jason Ken-

ney, executive director of the Association of Alberta Taxpayers, to describe it as "a time bomb."

The new Statscan study, *Population, Aging and the Elderly*, paints a disturbing scenario. Over the next 40 years, the number of Canadians aged 65 and over will nearly triple, to 8.6 million. The ratio of retired persons to working Canadians will increase from 19 retirees per 100 workers to 42 per 100. In 2036, the number of persons over age 80 — the group most likely to require intense and expensive medical care — will be nearly as high as today's total population of senior citizens.

· · · · ·

Neither OAS (Old Age Security) nor CPP (Canada Pension Plan) is a properly funded,... sound pension scheme, in which individuals contribute funds which are then invested to maximize eventual pension benefits. Instead, both plans are funded on a "pay-as-you-go" basis. This means that funds are distributed to current pensioners almost as soon as they are contributed by those paying into the system. As a result, the two pension plans have built no surpluses upon which they can draw when the number of retirees starts to rise. Thus the future financial burden of supporting retirees will rise in lockstep with the rising ratio of retirees to workers.

While the short-sightedness of the policy-makers who adopted the pay-as-you-go system seems extraordinary today, its attractiveness was

understandable three or four decades ago. Pay-as-you-go schemes are inexpensive to establish, since it is unnecessary for the government that sets them up to collect a large base of capital to invest. The income deductions that fund a start-up are, in practice, savings confiscated from current workers, which are paid out at once to the first generation of beneficiaries. This generation collects benefits out of all proportion to its financial contributions to the pension system. Not surprisingly a large percentage of the members of the first generation can be counted on to vote strongly in favour of the government that introduces the pay-as-you-go pension policy. The first generation of contributors goes along with the plan because it is told that it will receive similar generous treatment in the future. This initial burst of political support explains why Canada, the United States, and Britain have all adopted pay-as-you-go schemes.

· · · · ·

...the Canada Pension Plan was intended from the beginning to be a pay-as-you-go system. It was introduced in 1966 by Judy LaMarsh, then health and welfare minister in Lester Pearson's Liberal government. Because pensions fall under the constitutional jurisdiction of the provinces, LaMarsh's proposed pension plan could not be adopted without provincial support.

Nationalist pride caused Quebec to opt out and set up the parallel Quebec Pension Plan before the CPP had even been established. The other provinces consented to Ottawa's incursion onto their constitutional turf in return for access to any surpluses that CPP might run. Those surpluses, which are directed to the Canada Pension Plan's investment fund, are required by law to be used to purchase provincial government 20-year bonds at preferential rates of interest. In practice, the price of provincial support had been a vast, permanent hidden subsidy of deficit spending, at the expense of future generations of retirees.

The implications are many-fold. One is that provinces have been encouraged by the availability of cheap credit to increase their level of indebtedness. The crippling debt loads of Saskatchewan and other provinces can be partly traced to the $42.9 billion of CPP money that is "invested" in their debt.

Another result is that as the risk of provincial default increases, contributors to CPP have been saddled with the worst investment nightmare imaginable: retirement savings invested in provincial bonds that are both high risk and low yield. CPP has become, in effect, the lender of last resort to provincial governments. Section 110 (4) of the legislation governing CPP denies the federal government the right even to pick and choose among provincial government bonds, which must be purchased on a strictly proportional basis. Should any province become insolvent, Canadian pensioners will be forced to stand by helplessly and watch as billions of dollars in pension savings simply disappear.

The statutory requirement that all CPP surpluses must be turned over to the provinces makes it impossible for the federal government to adopt the measures necessary to turn CPP into a genuinely secure, self-funding plan. In any other country, the solution would be to raise CPP pay cheque deduction rates today in order to invest the surplus in high-grade securities with a respectable rate of return. Under the present legislation, however, any increase in contributions would amount to a simple tax grab, with the proceeds turned over to insolvent provincial governments.

Thus, CPP limps into the future unfunded, with pay-as-you-go premiums ticking inevitably upwards. The paycheque deductions that fund the plan were 3.6 percent of earned income as recently as 1986. Today the rate stands at five percent. By 2036, when the last baby boomer retires, it will be 13.6 percent, for a plan that promises to pay retirees only 25 percent of their previous salary. "If premiums increase at this rate, the social safety net is going to snap," warns AAT director Jason Kenney.

• • • • •

Some observers are predicting war between the generations, as taxpayers and workers try to wriggle out of subsidizing the present generation of pensioners, and pensioners fight to preserve the pension benefits that have become their main source of income. In the United States, where the old age security system is more mature than it is in Canada, systematic pension reform has been made impossible by opposition from seniors who are aware that their unfunded benefits are entirely dependent upon their political clout. Explains Dr. Stuart Butler, a senior fellow with the Heritage Foundation, a Washington D.C.-based think tank: "The fear and righteous indignation felt by older workers and retirees makes the (pension) system virtually impregnable to frontal attack. Populist politicians can pounce on any structural reform proposal, and they can inflame elderly Americans by appealing to their financial worries and their sense of justice."

"Playing on the fears of today's seniors in order to preserve a system that may leave future generations of seniors destitute is a really sleazy tactic," says Mr. Kenney. "The pension safety net was designed badly by politicians for immediate political benefit. Now that it has turned into a time bomb, the same politicians have discovered that the best way to smear a political opponent is to accuse him of tampering with the pension system. Seniors are so scared that the mere mention of the words "pension reform" can make them nervous."

• • • • •

Scott Reid, *Western Report*, 1993 5 3

THE USES OF THE FUTURE

Like most futurists, I have spent a large part of my life thinking about what the future may hold. The major differences between what I've been doing and what other futurists have been up to are, first, that I've probably been doing it a little longer than most — for about 60 years, in fact — and, second, that what I do involves a somewhat less formal methodology.

In fact, what I do is hardly formal at all; it's more like daydreaming than it is like Delphi polling or scenario writing or morphological mapping or any of the other methodologies in use in most think tanks. I'm not really trying to forecast what the future is going to be at all. What I try to do instead is to conjecture what diverse sorts of things *may* happen in the future — the things that the French futurist Bertrand de Jouvenel called *futuribles,* namely, a range of *possible* future phenomena or events. Then, when I've thought of some *futuribles* that strike me as interesting, for good or for ill, I sit down and write stories about what those things would be like to live with.

The technical term that describes that process is "writing science fiction."

In some ways, writing science fiction resembles technological forecasting, but its objectives are quite different. I would not like to give anyone the impression that every story I write is meant to be a trustworthy prediction of events that I believe are actually going to happen. More often than not, my stories are quite the opposite. They are actually intended to serve as a distant early warning of stormy weather ahead, since the futures I describe in my stories are generally the sorts of thing that I really dread and would do a lot to avoid.

· · · · ·

How Useful Is Prediction?

There is something that we can usefully do about the future, even if we can't precisely decide just what that future will be. In fact, the most useful things we can do about the future are only possible when we *don't* know exactly what it will be. There is a fundamental rule of forecasting — I call it "Pohl's Law" — which says, "The more complete and accurate a prediction is, the less use it is."

That sounds pretty counterintuitive, not to say outright stupid, so let me try to explain with a thought experiment. Let's suppose that as we all came into a room there was a Gypsy fortune-teller waiting for us at the door with a really big cup of tea, from which we all took a sip; and

Fig. 5-29 *Humanity dreamed of flying for centuries before the Wright brothers invented how to do it in 1903. The Concorde is now able to fly passengers at supersonic speeds. What will future aircraft be like?*

SOURCE: British Aircraft Corporation

let's say that, when we were all inside, she swirled the dregs around, looked at the patterns formed by the leaves, and gasped, "Oh, horrors! It is foretold here that as you leave this room you will all be run over by some giant runaway bus and instantly crushed to death."

And let's further suppose that she is a very *good* Gypsy tea-leaf reader, whose predictions are guaranteed to be accurate and complete and always come true.

The question then is, What use is that prediction to us?

It's accurate, so it's going to happen; we can't prevent it. We can't even dodge it by sneaking out the back way, for instance, because the prediction is also complete. So that sort of accurate and complete forecast turns out to have very little value to us; about the only effect it might have on our lives is to take some of the pleasure out of these last moments we share together.

In fact, the only time a forecast has any real utility is when it is

not totally reliable; that's why de Jouvenel prefers to deal in *futuribles,* so that we have a chance, here and now, to take actions in the present that will encourage the good futures and help to avert the bad ones.

Inventing the Future

Another fine futurist, physicist Dennis Gabor, once put it, in what I think of as the First Law of Futures Studies: "We can't really predict the future at all. All we can do is invent it."

That's a pretty important distinction. It's easy enough to identify *futuribles* — that is what I, and all my colleagues, do when we write science fiction. It's not at all easy to identify that particular set of futures which will at some point become our real and tangible present, because the things that do in fact happen will be only that *much*-smaller set of things that are *made* to happen — which is to say, are invented.

Space travel is an excellent illustration of how the future gets invented. Over a period of many years, thousands of science-fiction stories were written about traveling to other planets. It wasn't only science-fiction writers who thought along these lines, either, for almost every scientist who had given any serious thought to the subject was perfectly willing to predict that space travel was certainly going to be a part of some future or other.

But when the Apollo project landed two Americans on the moon a quarter of a century ago, the reason it happened then, and in that way, was that it was made to happen — was invented — by a particular human being, President John Fitzgerald Kennedy. Kennedy possessed all the immense powers of a president of the United States and was therefore in the right position to mobilize the enormous investment of money and talent and resources that made that first landing on another heavenly body happen.

Of course, it did not happen exactly as he expected. When the Apollo finally touched down on the moon, Kennedy was no longer president. By then, John Kennedy was lying in his grave at Arlington National Cemetery, because a somewhat different future had been invented by a man with a gun in Dallas.

That's a point worth remembering, too. It forces us to keep in mind that it isn't just presidents and generals who invent the future; individuals do it too, and not necessarily with a gun. In fact, we all play a part in inventing the future with every action we take.

Taking Responsibility For the Future

Recently in the United States, citizens participated in inventing a large slice of their immediate future by electing a president. If I were somehow to find myself elected president, I know one thing that I would do at once. Unlike most recent presidents, I would try to take our obligations to the future seriously. I would do my best to accept the responsibility for the ways in which things I do now would affect the future of the country, and the world, for all the long time to come.

To help make that possible, my first official act would be to add a new member to my cabinet; I would establish a Department of Consequences, with a cabinet-ranked secretary who would be charged with the task of preparing scenarios to show what the real, long-term results of measures I proposed would be before I put them into effect....

Environmental Futures

One question I would put before the new Department of Consequences and its nonpartisan think tank would be to puzzle out just what the long-term effects might be of current policies in regard to the apparent serious threats to the environment of the world we all have to live in. Does it make sense to exploit all our natural resources as fast as we can, thus providing as many jobs as possible for the current generation? Or would we be better off to conserve as many of them as possible, thus providing a sustained level of employment for our children and our children's children?

• • • • •

...What is really at issue is what we should be doing *now* to avert some truly unpleasant problems for the future. The worst things simply haven't happened yet.

It's for that reason, I think, that the dire predictions of environmentalists, though they certainly are being heard these days, have had such a tiny effect on the way most of us live our lives. We still jump into the car when we need to go to the corner drugstore, and we still turn up the thermostat when the weather gets cold instead of putting on a sweater.

But environmental predictions have had even less effect on the measures that governments are willing to take. After all, we all know perfectly well that when we wake up tomorrow morning and look out our windows we'll still see green trees, and maybe even a few birds, possibly even one or two lingering butterflies. And when we walk down the street we will not have to dodge large numbers of victims blinded by cataracts as a result of what we are doing to the ozone layer. It is our nature — and it is especially the *government's* nature — to put off taking any unpleasant medicine until we can see clearly that we have no other choice left.

But that is where futurists should be a little different from politicians and the population at large. The future is our *business.* If we don't do our best to try to understand where we are going — and how we can change our course to go in some better direction — then who will?

Futurism's Risky Business

Futurists have to run a few risks. Even our most-careful estimates of what is likely to happen at some future time may turn out to be wrong because of some factor we have neglected.

A good example of a neglected factor can be found in the predictions of global warming. It is a fact that warming has occurred. Five of the warmest years on record were in the decade of the 1980s. The year 1990 was not only a sixth, but in fact *the* warmest year ever in the century and a half that such records have been reliably kept. Then, unexpectedly, Mount Pinatubo erupted in the Philippines, and the sunshade of acid particles that it threw into the stratosphere has brought down temperatures all around the world.

This cooling is a purely temporary thing. In a few years, those little particles will be all gone, and the warming will probably return, since all the volcanic eruptions in the world will not change the fact that carbon dioxide and other heat-retaining gases are still increasing in our air. While such unexpected factors as Mount Pinatubo make it harder to convince some people that the danger is real, futurists still must risk being "wrong."

· · · · ·

So, please, let's all be unafraid to be wrong in our forecasts of what lies ahead for all of us. After all, it is only if we risk what is wrong now and then — if we look at all the consequences of present actions, even the ones we would hope to avoid and prefer to ignore — that we have any hope of learning to do what is *right*; for that is the true use of the future.

Frederik Pohl, *The Futurist*, 1993 3-4

DISCUSSION AND RESEARCH

24. Examine the list of underlying trends that you made from the readings. Check back over the topics you have covered in this course, and establish whether the underlying trends in your list make sense in terms of the evidence you have accumulated during the course. Report your findings in writing.

25. Look at the list you made of statements in the readings that did not seem to be supported by current trends. From your own current knowledge, identify any appropriate trends that might justify the statements made. Report your findings orally.

26. As an exercise in normative forecasting or planning, develop a vision of what you hope the various aspects of life in your community will be like in 20 years' time.
    (a) Set specific goals for these various aspects,
    (b) Do a gap analysis, and
    (c) List the steps that you consider necessary for reaching the goals.

STATISTICAL ANALYSIS

27. Appendix 2 contains almost 40 sets of statistics for the different countries of the world. Some of these sets of statistics, either on their own or in combination, may be used as indicators of changes that are likely to occur in the future. In groups,
    (a) Select ten sets of statistics that might be used to indicate the likelihood of changes still to come;
    (b) Justify the selection in writing;
    (c) Refer to the section on relative percentages in Appendix 3, and

for all the countries that have data in all the ten sets of statistics chosen in (a), calculate their individual data as a percentage of the data for the top country in each of the ten sets of data.

(d) Set up a table with the statistic type across the top and the name of the country down the side, so that the relative percentages for each country for all ten data sets can be entered;

(e) Add the relative percentages across, to obtain a total relative percentage for each country;

(f) Devise a method of classifying the total relative percentages into four groups;

(g) Draw a graded shading map of the world to show the four major groups classified in (f);

(h) Enter a title for your map; and

(i) Critically analyze the assumption on which this map is based.

CONCLUSION

Change has always occurred, sometimes quickly, sometimes imperceptibly. It has sometimes been beneficial, sometimes harmful. It has been often sought, and often feared. And at all times, the future has turned out to be different in some ways from what was predicted. This element of unpredictability, of chance, has created an entire *futures* apparatus. It includes a range of activities from reading crystal balls to highly sophisticated computer modelling of weather patterns or the impact of taxation changes.

Many predictions will be wrong, but the future concerns everyone. Humanity's best efforts are therefore directed toward trying to identify and understand the major trend-producing forces in the world, and — where possible — trying to ensure that the future develops in a positive manner.

The text, reinforced in this chapter, provides information about major trends, and presents arguments in favour of or opposed to those trends. There is little agreement over many of the topics, and they remain unresolved issues. Will the force of circumstances eventually cause some people to change their minds? Will, for example, shortages of land and other resources eventually force pronatalists to become antinatalist? Or will improved productivity caused by technology so reduce scarcity that antinatalists will cease to have an argument?

You should by now have established your own views about the various issues discussed in this text. As you know, others may disagree with you because they place importance on different values. You should also realize that your own opinions may change as time passes.

The issues are important and affect your future. What can you do personally to stay on top of current issues? What can you do to help bring about change in areas that are important to you?

CASE STUDY

THE FUTURE OF THE KURDISH PEOPLE

In the reading "Nationalism is not necessarily the path to a democratic world" on p. 298, the article's author questions whether nationalism is the best way to achieve world democracy. He dismisses the notions of common language and race as reasons for individuals to form a nation. This case study describes a people who would like to form a nation for just these reasons.

The Kurds are one of the largest ethnic groups in the world, but they do not have a country to call their own. They are alone in working for this cause and they are not always united. A more detailed look at their history illustrates how often they have fought for others, and how seldomly for themselves. It also points to their chances of forming a country in the near future.

The Kurdish people inhabit a great swath of territory across southeastern Turkey, northern Syria, Lebanon, Iraq, and northwestern Iran. In much of this area they form more than 80 percent of the population. Smaller populations of Kurds also live in Armenia and Azerbaijan, republics of the former U.S.S.R. The total estimated population of Kurds in this whole area is about 20 million. As well, over 500 000 live in Europe (400 000 in Germany, mostly as guest workers).

Several characteristics identify the Kurds as an ethnic group. They share a common Indo-Iranian language, albeit divided into three distinct dialects which at times inhibits communica-

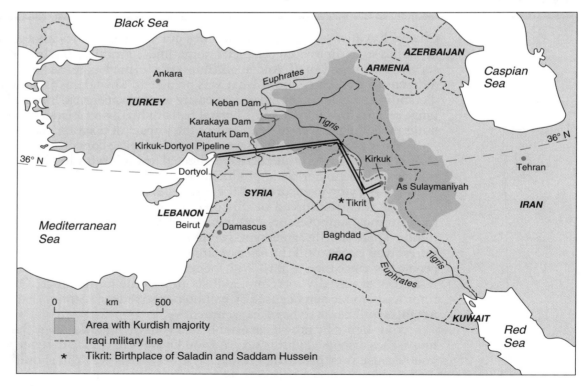

Fig. 5-30   *The chief area occupied by Kurds in southwest Asia.*

Country	Population[1]	Estimated number of Kurds[2]	Kurds as a percentage of the population
Turkey	56 704 327	10 300 000	18
Iran	55 647 001	4 600 000	8
Iraq	18 781 770	4 000 000	19
Syria	12 483 440	1 000 000	8
Lebanon	3 300 802	70 000	2
former U.S.S.R.	290 938 469	290 000	...

[1]Column 1 Appendix 2
[2]*Geographical Magazine*, June 1991

Fig. 5-31 *Numerical distribution of Kurds in southwest Asia.*

tion. They are not Turks, Arabs, or Persians, but consist of a number of tribal groups that have a common history dating back at least 4000 years. Early Sumerian inscriptions (Sumeria, the world's first urban civilization occupied the lower Tigris and Euphrates valleys) mention a country known as Karduka, and the Karduku are referred to in Greek writings of 400 BC as a warring mountain people. These people fought in battles between the Sassanids (an early Persian dynasty of about 200-600 AD) and the Romans and Byzantines. Kurd, as a collective name, was first applied to the tribal groups in the 7th century AD when the Arabs converted them to Islam. Today the Kurds are Sunni Muslims.

Three short-lived Kurdish dynasties with more than local power existed in the 10th to 12th centuries; the 12th-century Kurdish warrior, Saladin, a prominent foe of the Christian Crusaders, founded another dynasty that lasted into the 13th century. Interspersed among these dynasties, Kurdish lands were nominally included within the Seljuk (a Turkish family of the 11 and 12th centuries) and Mongol (13 and 14th centuries) Empires. Since these rulers had no interest in settling in the harsh mountains, the Kurds continued to preserve their distinct language, culture, and identity.

Throughout history, the Kurds have had such a strong affinity to their own tribal group that

unity amongst them has always been short-lived. For the most part, Kurdish leaders have concentrated on gaining local power rather than achieving a unified Kurdish country. This has exposed them to manipulation by stronger powers, with the result that different tribes have often found themselves fighting on opposing sides in a confrontation. When the Ottoman Empire gained supremacy in the area in the 15th century, this manipulation continued to occur. When needed as soldiers, Kurds were welcomed into the various armies; otherwise, they were left to live in the mountains. Among the people in power, they developed a reputation for lawlessness, and for persistently resisting central authority if attempts were made to take control of their historic homelands.

It was only at the end of World War I, with the Ottoman Empire in disarray and the victorious Allies — mainly the British, French, and Americans — set to decide how the fragments of the Empire should be treated, that the idea of Kurdish nationalism was introduced. The 1920 Treaty of Sèvres offered the Kurds local autonomy, with a right to opt for indpendence within a year, in an area east of the Euphrates to be called Kurdistan. Kurds formed a majority of the population in this area. But while the Allies were deciding this, the Turks were gaining strength under Kemal Ataturk and proceeded to assert their strong authority in the area. The result was that the Treaty of Sèvres was never ratified and a new treaty known as the 1923 Treaty of Lausanne took its place. The articles referring to Kurdistan were dropped, as the Allies by this time had changed their position with regard to the Kurds. Britain, in particular, now wanted to annex the oil-rich southern part of the Kurdish area to the new state of

Iraq, which had become a British mandate. (The former territories of the German and Ottoman Empires were administered by the victorious powers after World War I.) When Turkey signed over its rights to the oil area in northern Iraq in 1926, Britain in return agreed to end its support for the Kurds.

Nevertheless, the idea of a Kurdish state had been sown in the minds of the Kurds, and although the Turks proceeded to crush a series of Kurdish uprisings in the 1920s and 30s, the aspirations of the Kurds were raised. The abandoned Sèvres Treaty continues to be the basic documentary support for the Kurdish nationalists up to the present time. The former Soviets assisted the cause by allowing the formation of the Kurdish Republic of Mahabad in northern Iran when they occupied the area in 1945. The republic existed for one year, but was dissolved in 1946 when the former Soviets withdrew and Iran's independence was guaranteed through the support of the United Nations.

THE IRAQI KURDS

In the 1950s there were sporadic revolts in the mountains of northern Iraq led by tribal leaders but only a few educated Kurds living in the cities continued to have serious nationalistic aims during this time. Then, in the early 1960s, a serious revolt in the mountains was led by Mustafa Barzani. The revolt involved tribal groups living in the mountains as well as members of the urban-based Kurdish Democratic Party (the KDP). Barzani had exhibited sufficient charisma to entice the urban Kurds into the mountains to fight. However, although Barzani seized a corner of northeast Iraq and was able to deny access to the Iraqi government, the principal KDP members, by 1964, had had a disagreement over policy with Barzani and fled to Iran.

Although the Iraqi government was independent and a republic, it was weak, and Barzani hoped eventually to negotiate peace and some autonomy for the Kurds. In 1968, however, a new government took over in Baghdad, which

garnered support from the Soviets. Supplied with new Soviet weapons, the Iraqis began a new unsuccessful offensive in the north in 1969. A year later, the government offered the Kurds a settlement which would have given them considerable power within Iraq.

This was not to be. The Shah of Iran, then the leader of Iran, feared a peaceful end to the Kurdish problem. A leadership role for the Kurds in Iraq would inevitably create a similar desire in Iran amongst its large Kurdish population. He persuaded the Americans to support the Kurds in their quest for even more autonomy, hoping to force the Iraqis to back down from giving them so much power. The Iraqis were already nervous, because their main oil supply was in and around Kirkuk, a city populated largely by Kurds. In 1973 another Iraqi offensive against the Kurds was launched, and this time, Kurdish civilians were forced to flee from their homes. Refugees crossed the Iran-Iraq border at the rate of 30 000 a day. The Iraqi Kurds expected further help from the Americans, but none came. As well, in 1975, the Iranians closed the border to any more fleeing Iraqi Kurds in exchange for gaining disputed territory along the southern Iraqi-Iranian border. After years of battling the Iraqi government, Barzani and the Kurds had to accept defeat.

The 1980s was the time of the Gulf War between Iraq under Saddam Hussein, who became President in 1979, and Iran under the Ayatollah Khomeini. There were times during this war that Iranian Kurds fought with the Iraqis against Iraqi Kurds and Iranians. The Kurds were divided again. As soon as a ceasefire between the Iraqis and the Iranians occurred in 1988, Saddam Hussein, now with a very powerful army, punished the Iraqi Kurds for providing aid to Iran during the eight-year war. He had his army destroy over 4000 Kurdish villages, and over 100 000 people disappeared. Attacks with chemical weapons killed civilians as well as armed Kurds.

On August 2, 1990, Saddam Hussein invaded Kuwait, and until March 1991, he was occupied on that front. In March, with the defeat of Iraq at the hands of the United Nations coalition, Kurds proceeded to rebel against Baghdad. However, Hussein battered them again, sending at least a million Kurdish people over snowy mountain passes to safety in Turkey and Iran. This drew the attention of the world to the area. More than 20 000 coalition troops set up a security zone for the Kurds near the Turkish border, and the Red Cross from various countries, including Canada, responded to the world's humanitarian concerns by sending in food and supplies. The United Nations ordered Hussein's air force to stop flying helicopter gunships over the area north of the 36th parallel. This allowed the refugees to return to their homes and try to put their lives back together. However, when most of the allied security forces left in the summer of 1991, the Iraqis moved in again. This time, the Kurds launched a counteroffensive and expanded their control south of the 36th parallel, seizing the Kurdish city of As Sulaymaniyah. Since then, Hussein has set up a blockade against food and fuel entering from the south. The northwest to Turkey and the northeast to Iran have become the Kurds' lifeline to survival.

Some American, British, and French troops, using air bases in Turkey, have remained to provide an air umbrella over Kurdistan north of the 36th parallel. Because of this shield, the Kurds have been able to hold elections in order to provide some order in a territory over which the Iraqis have lost control. Kurds now have their own 105-member parliament with Massoud Barzani, son of Mustafa, as one of the leaders. They also have a police force, school boards, tax collectors, and television and radio stations. There are plans to build an international airport and a new Kurdish university. Kurdish is now taught in the schools even though there are few textbooks.

Many crippling problems remain, however. There is a desperate shortage of food and fuel. United Nations provisions, formerly trucked through Turkey, have been cut off because several of the caravans have been bombed. Heaps of stones and tents now exist where villages once stood. Attempts are being made to rebuild the villages, but parts and materials are scarce.

Although the Kurds now have some local control over their population, it is not likely that the area will become a separate country. Even the Kurds themselves are careful to call their area a part of the Iraqi federation rather than an independent country, because they know how tenuous their rule

SOURCE: Guy Tessier/CRCS

Fig. 5-32   *A woman prepares a meal in an Iraqi Kurd refugee camp on the Turkish border in the spring of 1991.*

is; they are able to maintain control because of the flyovers of the coalition forces.

An independent Kurdistan would likely mean the breakup of Iraq, as the Shiite Muslims in the south would probably also revolt. However, as the centre of the richest oil deposits in the country, as well as a source of untapped mineral wealth and immense hydroelectricity potential, Saddam Hussein would not want to lose this northern area. The Kurds certainly could not withstand an assault by the stronger and better-supplied Iraqi army.

Several political analysts state that the United Nations and the Americans probably do not want to see the breakup of Iraq. Although Saddam Hussein is not cooperative, he is considered to be a strong leader who could not be easily replaced. If Iraq broke up, it would create an even more unstable situation in southwest Asia than now exists.

Iran and Turkey are opposed to having an independent Kurdistan as their neighbour because of internal strife with their own Kurdish populations. An Iraqi Kurdistan is seen as acting as a magnet for separatists in Iran and Turkey and a potentially powerful destabilizing force.

THE TURKISH KURDS

Turkey fears the influence that a Kurdish state in Iraq may have on its own Kurdish population. The Turkish government has been suppressing Kurds for many years. The Kurds have their own nationalist party in the form of the PKK (Kurdistan Workers Party), which operates in Eastern Turkey and has a military branch with 10 000 members. It trains most of its guerrillas in the Bekaa Valley in northern Lebanon, an area which has become the world's headquarters for training guerrilla fighters. Some 3000 PKK fighters are believed to be in Turkey, with 7000 more scattered in Iraq, Syria, and Iran. Using sophisticated weapons, the Turkish Kurds have been battling the Turks for a separate state since 1984 in a war that has claimed more than 5000 lives.

To the Turks, the Kurds are an obstacle to Turkey's plan to earn international respect and serve as a go-between for the Western world and southwest Asia. Situated at the crossroads of Europe, Africa, and Asia, Turkey also occupies a pivotal position between southwest Asia and the new republics in the southern part of the former U.S.S.R.

Most of the people in the new republics of Central Asia are ethnically linked to the Turks and speak languages which are essentially dialects of Turkish. Turkey wants to be able to act as an older sibling to these predominately Muslim, former Soviet lands. But continued strife between the Turkish Kurds and Turkey, which at times is described as open guerrilla war, is not looked on favourably by those Turkey wishes to impress.

Southeast Turkey is the site of the headwaters of the Tigris and Euphrates Rivers. More than 20 years ago, Turkey embarked on its ambitious Southeast Anatolia Project. Composed of a dozen separate dam and irrigation projects on the Tigris and Euphrates, the project is aimed at boosting the country's electricity supply by 70 percent and irrigating 1.6 million hectares of land by the late 1990s. Part of this project includes a series of pipelines to provide water to various countries in southwest Asia. Since the area involved overlaps the Turkish Kurdistan area, the importance of Turkey making peace with the Kurds assumes even more significance.

In the past, Turks have stifled the use of the Kurdish language and forbidden the playing of Kurdish music. These restrictions no longer exist, and there are now Kurdish representatives in the Turkish parliament, although PKK extremists are still proving difficult for the Turks to deal with. To maintain some control of the PKK, the Turks have turned to Iraqi Kurds, as the PKK have camps within Iraqi Kurdistan. The Iraqi Kurds depend on safe passage through Turkey for their food and fuel. Hence, when the Turks approached the Iraqi Kurds for help fighting the PKK in

Fig. 5-33 *This group of Kurdish Canadians are strongly supportive of an independent Kurdish state.*

SOURCE: Marilyn MacKenzie

seized the city of Sanandaj, the capital of the Iranian province of Kurdistan, and an army barracks at Mahabad. For a while they were granted a degree of local autonomy, but it did not last and Khomeini eventually took control. Since then the Kurds in Iran have struggled under the control of the Islamic religious leaders who now control Iran. Some Iranian Kurds fought with Iraq against Iran in the Iran-Iraq Gulf War.

Even with the emergence of a larger number of Kurds advocating independence than in the past, there is no real sign that the Kurds will ever form a country. Many Kurds realize this and would be happy to be allowed to live in peace with some degree of local autonomy. They would also like to make sure they have the right to speak Kurdish freely and to have it taught in their schools. A solution that brings peace within the confines of existing natonal boundaries could become a role model to the hundreds of other separatist groups across the world today.

these camps, the Iraqi Kurds could not refuse to attempt to drive the Turkish Kurds out of their encampments. Iraqi Kurds calculate this as a necessary price for Turkish acceptance of the semi-independence they have gained. As has so often happened throughout history, Kurd is fighting Kurd.

The Turks are also having some success in cutting off the PKK guerrillas based in Syria. Turkey controls the water of the Euphrates River upstream from Syria. Syria has agreed not to offer too much support to the PKK in return for a chance to discuss its water problems with Turkey. This strategy can work two ways, however. If Turkey withholds too much water from its passage downstream, then Syria could become very interested in seeing the PKK succeed in their guerrilla attacks in Turkey. The Kurds in Turkey present a potentially volatile situation.

THE IRANIAN KURDS

In Iran, three weeks after the Khomeini revolution overcame the Shah in 1979, Iranian Kurds

FURTHER ANALYSIS

1. In recent history, various new nations have been formed. As a relatively newly created state, Israel's experience may be relevant to the formation of other new states.
   (a) Research the background surrounding the founding of Israel in 1948.
   (b) Based on this information, what steps would seem necessary if the Kurds are to create a country?

(c) What problems do you believe might exist in the future for an independent Kurdistan?

2. The issue of international interference is continuously debated as different parts of the world become embroiled in conflicts affecting civilian populations. Discuss the issue of national sovereignty with reference to another current situation.

3. Investigate examples where the international community has felt it necessary to react positively to massive television coverage of a major human problem. Evaluate the role played by television in helping to create global awareness of world issues.

APPENDIX 1
WORLD BASE MAP

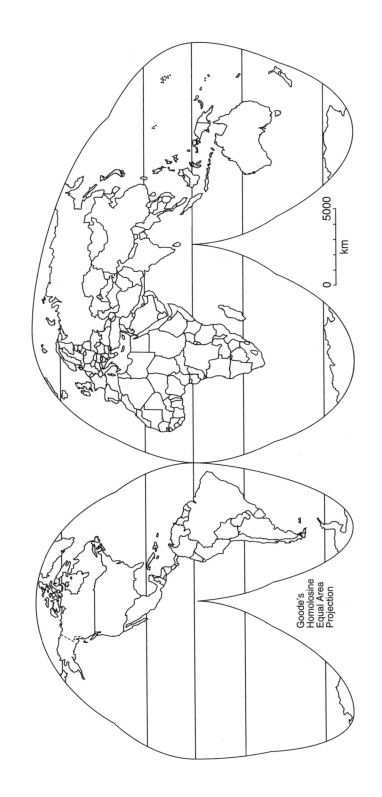

Goode's
Homolosine
Equal Area
Projection

km

0   5000

APPENDIX 2

STATISTICAL DATA

COLUMN HEADINGS

Name: Country (* = not mappable on map in Appendix 1)

1: Area, square kilometres (km^2)

2: Population [1]

3: Population density, people/km^2

4: Birth rate, births/1000 people/y [2]

5: Death rate, deaths/1000 people/y [2]

6: Natural increase rate, birth rate minus death rate/1000 people/y (Column 4 minus Column 5)

7: Projected rate of population growth, percent per year 1990-2000 [2]

8: Projected population in 2025, millions [2]

9: Percentage of population aged under 15 years [2]

10: Percentage of population aged over 64 years [2]

11: Total fertility rate, children/woman/lifetime (TFR) [2]

12: Infant mortality rate, infant deaths/1000 live births/y [2]

13: People per physician [2]

14: Kilojoules per person per day, 1990 as percentage of 1965 [2]

15: Average life expectancy at birth, years [2]

16: Literacy rate, percentage [2 and 3]

17: Male literacy rate, percentage [2]

18: Female literacy rate, percentage [2]

19: Average GNP, US$ per person per year [2 and 3]

20: Urban percentage of population in 1960 [4]

21: Urban percentage of population in 1990 [4]

22: Remaining area of wilderness, km^2 [4]

23: Percentage change in forested area, 1980-1990 [4]

24: Daily food availability per person, kJ/cap/day [4]

25: Maternal deaths per 100 000 live births [4]
26: Percentage of low-weight births (births under 2.5 kg) [4]
27: Percentage of total grain fed to livestock [4]
28: Total energy consumption, petajoules (PJ) [4]
29: Energy consumption per person per year, gigajoules (GJ) [4]
30: Traditional fuels as percentage of energy consumed [4]
31: Carbon dioxide emissions from industry per year, 000t [4]
32: Carbon dioxide emissions from land use per year, 000t [4]
33: Military spending, US$millions [5]
34: Education and Health spending, US$millions [5]
35: Percentage growth rate of GNP/cap, 1965-1990 [2]
36: Percentage of labour force in primary economic activity [6]
37: Percentage of labour force in secondary economic activity [6]
38: Percentage of labour force in tertiary economic activity [6]

Note: na = not available

Sources: [1] *The Universal Almanac 1993*
[2] *World Development Report 1992*
[3] *The 1991 Information Please Almanac*
[4] *World Resources 1992-93*
[5] *World Military and Social Expenditures 1991*
[6] *Human Development Report 1992*

Name	1	2	3	4	5	6	7	8	9	10	11	12	13	14	15	16	17
Afghanistan	652 225	15 862 293	24.32	52	21	31	na	41	na	na	6.8	na	na	na	42	29	44
Albania	28 748	3 273 131	113.86	25	6	19	1.5	5	33.5	5.3	3.1	28	na	116	72	75	na
Algeria	2 381 741	25 566 507	10.73	36	8	28	2.8	52	43.6	3.7	5.1	67	2 340	168	65	57	69
Angola	1 246 700	8 534 483	6.85	47	19	28	3.0	27	44.8	3.1	6.5	130	17 750	95	46	42	56
Argentina	2 766 889	32 290 966	11.67	20	9	11	1.0	44	29.8	9.1	2.8	29	370	98	71	95	95
Australia	7 682 300	16 293 478	2.12	15	7	8	1.4	23	22.1	10.8	1.9	8	440	105	77	99	99
Austria	83 855	7 644 275	91.16	12	11	1	0.2	8	17.5	15.1	1.5	8	390	108	76	99	99
Bahrain	691	520 186	752.80	na	na	na	na	na	na	na	na	na	na	na	69	77	85
Bangladesh	143 998	118 433 062	822.46	35	14	21	1.8	176	42.9	3.1	4.6	105	6 390	103	52	35	48
Barbados*	430	262 688	610.90	na	na	na	na	na	na	na	na	na	na	na	75	99	99
Belgium	31 519	9 909 285	314.39	13	11	2	0.1	10	17.9	15.1	1.6	8	330	na	76	99	99
Belize	22 965	219 737	9.57	na	na	na	na	na	na	na	na	na	na	na	68	93	na
Benin	112 622	4 673 964	41.50	46	15	31	2.9	10	47.6	2.7	6.3	113	15 940	114	50	23	30
Bhutan	46 500	1 565 969	33.68	39	17	22	2.4	3	39.9	3.1	5.5	122	9 730	na	49	38	51
Bolivia	1 098 581	6 706 854	6.11	36	10	26	2.5	14	42.5	3.4	4.8	92	1 530	103	60	77	83
Botswana	582 000	1 224 527	2.10	35	6	29	2.5	2	47.4	3.4	4.7	38	6 900	116	67	74	83
Brazil	8 511 965	152 505 077	17.92	27	7	20	1.7	237	35.4	4.6	3.2	57	1 080	114	66	81	82
Brunei	5 765	345 048	59.85	na	na	na	na	na	na	na	na	na	na	na	76	45	na
Bulgaria	110 912	8 933 544	80.55	13	12	1	-0.2	9	19.9	13.5	1.9	14	280	108	73	98	na
Burkina Faso	274 200	9 077 828	33.11	47	18	29	2.9	22	45.5	3.1	6.5	134	57 183	122	48	18	27
Burundi	27 834	5 645 997	202.85	49	18	31	3.1	14	45.6	3.0	6.8	107	21 020	91	47	50	60
Cambodia	181 035	6 991 107	38.62	38	15	23	1.9	14	34.8	2.9	4.5	117	na	95	50	35	48
Cameroon	475 442	11 092 470	23.33	41	12	29	2.9	28	46.3	3.8	5.8	88	na	110	57	54	65
Canada	9 976 140	26 538 229	2.66	14	7	7	0.8	32	20.9	11.3	1.7	7	510	111	77	99	99
Central African Republic	622 984	2 877 365	4.62	42	16	26	2.5	6	42.1	3.0	5.8	101	na	99	49	38	51
Chad	1 259 200	5 017 431	3.98	44	18	26	2.7	14	41.9	3.6	6.0	125	38 390	73	47	30	42
Chile	756 626	13 082 842	17.29	22	6	16	1.3	19	30.5	5.9	2.5	17	1 230	100	72	93	93
China	9 596 960	1 133 682 501	118.13	22	7	15	1.3	1597	27.0	5.8	2.5	29	1 010	137	70	73	84
Colombia	1 141 748	33 076 188	28.97	24	6	18	1.5	50	35.4	4.0	2.7	37	1 230	119	69	87	88
Congo	342 000	2 242 274	6.56	48	15	33	3.3	6	45.2	3.9	6.6	116	na	115	53	57	70
Costa Rica	51 100	3 032 795	59.35	26	4	22	1.9	5	36.1	4.2	3.1	16	960	119	75	93	93
Cuba	110 860	10 620 099	95.80	17	6	11	na	na	na	na	1.9	12	530	128	76	96	na
Cyprus	9 521	707 776	74.34	na	na	na	na	na	na	na	na	na	na	na	77	89	na
Czechoslovakia to 1993	127 905	15 682 243	122.61	14	11	3	0.3	17	23.2	11.8	2.0	12	280	107	72	99	99
Czech Republic	na	na	na	na	na	na	na	na	na	na	na	na	na	na	na	na	na
Slovakia	na	na	na	na	na	na	na	na	na	na	na	na	na	na	na	na	na
Denmark	43 092	5 131 217	119.08	11	12	-1	0.0	5	16.9	15.3	1.7	8	400	106	75	99	99
Djibouti	23 200	337 386	14.54	na	na	na	na	na	na	na	na	na	na	na	48	20	na
Dominican Republic	48 380	7 240 793	149.67	27	6	21	1.6	11	37.3	3.4	3.2	56	1 770	129	67	83	84
Ecuador	276 840	10 506 668	37.95	30	7	23	2.0	18	39.5	3.6	3.7	55	810	116	66	86	88
Egypt	997 739	54 705 746	54.83	31	10	21	1.8	86	39.2	4.2	4.0	66	770	139	60	48	62
El Salvador	21 393	5 309 865	248.21	33	8	25	1.8	9	43.7	3.6	4.2	53	2 830	125	64	73	76
Equatorial Guinea	28 051	368 935	13.15	na	na	na	na	na	na	na	na	na	na	na	47	50	63
Ethiopia	1 251 282	51 666 622	41.29	51	18	33	3.4	156	47.0	2.8	7.5	132	78 780	90	48	35	na
Eritrea	na	na	na	na	na	na	na	na	na	na	na	na	na	na	na	na	na
Fiji*	18 376	759 567	41.33	na	na	na	na	na	na	na	na	na	na	na	65	80	na
Finland	338 145	4 977 325	14.72	13	10	3	0.2	5	19.5	13.3	1.8	6	440	104	76	99	99
France	543 965	56 358 331	103.61	13	10	3	0.4	63	20.1	13.7	1.8	7	320	103	77	99	99
French Guiana	90 000	97 781	1.09	na	na	na	3.2	na	na	na	na	na	na	na	na	82	na
Gabon	267 667	1 068 240	3.99	42	15	27	2.8	3	39.1	4.9	5.7	97	2 790	122	53	61	74
Gambia, The	11 295	848 147	75.09	na	na	na	na	na	na	na	na	na	na	na	44	27	38
Germany	357 041	78 475 370	219.79	11	11	0	0.1	78	16.2	15.0	1.5	7	380	111	76	99	99
Ghana	238 537	15 167 243	63.58	44	13	31	3.0	34	46.8	2.9	6.2	85	20 390	116	55	60	69
Greece	131 957	10 028 171	76.00	11	9	2	0.2	10	19.0	14.1	1.5	11	350	127	77	93	97
Greenland	2 175 600	56 078	0.03	na	na	na	na	na	na	na	na	na	na	na	na	na	na

18	19	20	21	22	23	24	25	26	27	28	29	30	31	32	33	34	35	36	37	38
14	220	8.0	18.2	87 400	0.0	9 628	690	20	0	157	8	29	6 273	na	na	na	na	61.0	14.0	25.0
na	930	30.6	35.2	0	3.4	11 558	na	7	0	156	49	10	9 732	na	151	na	na	55.9	25.7	18.4
45	2 060	30.4	51.7	1 404 240	11.6	11 997	130	9	36	686	28	3	46 492	na	1 196	7 016	2.1	13.9	10.9	75.2
28	600	10.4	28.3	270 490	-1.7	7 564	na	17	0	78	8	55	4 965	33 000	2 040	408	na	73.8	9.5	16.7
95	2 370	73.6	86.3	149 760	-1.3	13 031	69	na	42	2 070	65	5	118 157	na	1 145	2 625	-0.3	13.1	33.8	53.1
99	17 000	80.6	85.5	2 294 310	-0.9	13 462	8	6	51	3 770	225	3	257 480	na	4 830	19 146	1.9	5.3	16.4	78.3
99	19 060	49.9	58.4	0	-2.2	14 630	7	6	72	1 153	151	1	51 699	na	1 447	13 495	2.9	7.8	27.5	64.7
69	7 550	82.7	82.9	0	0.0	na	27	na	na	228	467	1	12 161	na	207	303	na	3.0	35.0	62.0
22	210	5.1	16.4	0	-10.4	8 460	600	28	0	502	5	54	14 114	8 700	291	450	0.7	56.5	9.8	33.7
99	6 540	35.5	44.7	0	0.0	na	69	16	na	14	54	12	971	na	8	144	2.3	5.7	10.2	84.1
99	15 540	92.5	96.9	0	0.0	16 540	9	5	28	1 964	197	1	98 104	na	4 163	15 253	2.6	2.5	19.5	78.0
na	1 990	na	na	0	0.0	na	49	10	na	6	31	55	180	na	na	na	2.6	na	na	na
16	360	9.2	37.7	12 090	-12.3	9 649	na	8	0	54	12	86	667	9 500	31	100	-0.1	70.3	6.6	23.1
25	190	2.5	5.3	11 790	2.8	na	1 710	na	0	30	22	95	33	860	na	na	na	92.5	2.8	4.7
71	630	39.3	51.2	178 100	-1.1	8 020	480	12	35	105	15	16	5 064	37 000	175	123	-0.7	46.7	19.2	34.1
65	2 040	1.7	27.5	312 550	-0.9	9 942	250	8	0	na	na	na	1 700	2 600	82	178	8.4	43.2	4.8	52.0
80	2 680	44.9	74.9	2 020 610	-4.2	11 516	120	8	55	7 362	50	30	206 957	950 000	2 919	14 826	3.3	29.3	16.0	54.7
na	13 360	na	na	na	na	na	na	na	na	na	na	na	na	na	285	159	na	na	na	na
na	2 250	38.6	67.7	0	1.0	15 518	13	6	58	1 381	154	1	106 989	na	1 966	4 454	na	16.5	37.9	45.6
9	330	4.7	9.0	7 500	-8.2	9 578	810	na	2	87	10	92	520	17 000	51	67	1.3	86.6	4.3	9.1
40	210	2.0	5.5	0	8.3	8 087	na	9	0	43	8	92	176	530	32	44	3.4	92.9	1.6	5.5
22	120	10.3	11.6	0	0.0	9 067	na	na	0	58	7	89	451	11 000	na	na	na	74.4	6.7	18.9
43	960	13.9	41.2	13 200	-4.3	9 280	300	13	0	204	18	49	5 774	60 000	232	435	3.0	74.0	4.5	21.5
99	20 470	68.9	77.1	6 405 870	5.8	14 576	3	6	79	11 087	422	1	455 530	na	8 835	55 916	2.7	3.4	19.4	77.2
25	390	22.7	46.7	209 170	-0.3	8 523	600	15	0	38	13	88	264	13 000	19	66	-0.5	83.7	2.8	13.5
18	190	7.0	29.5	612 540	-5.8	7 296	960	11	0	36	7	92	202	15 000	34	18	-1.1	83.4	4.6	12.0
93	1 940	67.8	85.9	230 860	1.4	10 804	47	7	33	598	46	12	31 833	na	575	1 180	0.4	18.7	18.3	63.0
62	370	19.0	33.4	2 107 760	-7.7	11 047	44	9	20	28 805	26	6	2 388 613	na	13 418	12 504	5.8	73.7	13.6	12.7
86	1 260	48.2	70.0	151 560	-5.6	10 875	110	8	20	1 199	37	17	53 831	420 000	273	1 142	2.3	1.7	21.4	76.9
44	1 010	31.9	40.5	118 370	-0.9	10 842	900	16	0	44	20	41	1 773	12 000	92	154	3.1	62.5	11.9	25.6
93	1 900	36.6	47.1	0	-17.0	11 754	36	10	24	101	37	33	2 557	26 000	25	401	1.4	25.4	18.2	56.4
na	na	54.9	74.9	0	11.8	13 148	29	8	4	650	62	27	36 292	890	1 296	1 656	na	23.8	28.5	47.7
na	8 020	35.6	52.8	0	0.0	na	na	na	68	52	75	1	4 192	na	35	205	na	13.7	18.9	67.4
99	3 140	47.0	77.5	0	1.8	15 204	10	6	63	2 975	190	1	226 347	na	4 614	10 416	na	13.3	49.3	37.4
na	na	na	na	na	na	na	na	na	na	na	na	na	na	na	na	na	na	na	na	na
na	na	na	na	na	na	na	na	na	na	na	na	na	na	na	na	na	na	na	na	na
99	22 080	73.7	87.0	0	0.0	15 187	4	6	82	747	146	2	47 009	na	2 141	12 888	2.1	5.3	20.0	74.7
na	1 070	50.0	80.7	0	0.0	na	740	14	na	4	11	1	326	na	na	na	na	na	na	na
82	830	30.2	60.4	0	-3.1	9 875	74	16	50	115	16	23	6 745	1 300	50	147	2.3	45.7	15.5	38.8
84	980	34.4	56.0	0	-21.0	10 595	190	11	22	308	30	24	15 316	160 000	208	521	2.8	38.5	19.8	41.7
34	600	37.9	46.7	425 400	0.0	13 964	320	5	36	1 211	24	4	79 483	na	2 339	2 031	4.1	33.9	12.0	54.1
70	1 110	38.3	44.4	0	-31.6	9 699	70	15	26	87	17	46	2 352	1 600	177	140	-0.4	8.2	21.8	70.0
37	330	25.4	28.7	0	0.0	na	na	na	na	6	14	75	106	1 800	na	na	na	66.0	11.0	23.0
na	120	6.4	12.9	197 160	-3.5	6 978	na	na	0	413	8	91	2 565	30 000	472	292	-0.2	79.8	7.9	12.3
na	na	na	na	na	na	na	na	na	na	na	na	na	na	na	na	na	na	na	na	na
na	1 780	29.7	39.3	na	0.0	na	na	14	0	25	34	48	678	na	26	98	1.9	44.1	8.1	47.8
99	26 040	38.1	59.7	29 390	-0.4	13 617	6	4	62	1 164	235	3	51 300	na	1 458	10 373	3.2	8.3	21.1	70.6
99	19 490	62.4	74.3	0	1.2	14 504	14	5	62	8 815	157	1	357 163	na	34 859	105 236	2.4	6.7	19.8	73.5
na	3 230	na	na	na	na	na	na	na	na	na	na	na	na	na	na	na	na	na	na	na
48	3 330	17.5	45.6	73 330	0.0	9 975	na	na	0	71	64	35	7 826	9 300	140	262	0.9	75.5	10.8	13.7
16	260	12.5	23.2	0	-26.2	na	1 100	14	0	11	13	77	183	1 900	16	8	0.7	84.0	7.0	9.0
99	22 320	76.0	84.0	0	1.0	14 412	12	6	60	14 645	187	1	775 000	na	42 184	131 633	2.4	3.5	30.2	66.3
51	390	23.3	33.0	0	-7.9	9 410	1 000	17	5	236	16	67	3 521	31 000	45	227	-1.4	59.3	11.1	29.6
89	5 990	42.9	62.5	0	0.1	16 011	9	6	58	959	96	2	70 920	na	2 902	3 129	2.8	24.7	19.3	56.0
na	na	na	na	na	na	na	na	na	na	na	na	na	na	na	na	na	na	na	na	na

Name	1	2	3	4	5	6	7	8	9	10	11	12	13	14	15	16	17
Guatemala	108 889	9 097 636	83.55	39	8	31	2.8	20	45.2	3.0	5.4	62	2 180	110	63	55	63
Guinea	245 857	7 269 240	29.57	48	21	27	2.8	15	46.1	2.6	6.5	138	na	97	43	24	35
Guinea-Bissau	28 000	998 963	35.68	na	na	na	na	na	na	na	na	na	na	na	39	36	48
Guyana	214 969	764 649	3.56	21	5	16	na	na	na	na	2.4	na	na	na	64	96	97
Haiti	27 750	6 143 141	221.37	36	13	23	1.9	11	40.0	4.1	4.8	95	7 140	98	54	53	59
Honduras	112 088	5 259 699	46.92	38	7	31	2.9	11	44.8	3.1	5.2	64	1 510	114	65	73	75
Hong Kong*	1 069	5 759 990	5388.20	13	6	7	0.8	7	21.0	8.8	1.5	7	1 070	115	78	75	na
Hungary	93 033	10 568 686	113.60	12	13	-1	-0.4	10	19.5	13.5	1.8	15	310	116	71	99	99
Iceland	103 000	257 023	2.50	na	na	na	na	na	na	na	na	na	na	na	78	99	99
India	3 287 263	849 746 001	258.50	30	11	19	1.7	1348	36.9	4.1	4.0	92	2 520	110	59	48	62
Indonesia	1 904 569	190 136 221	99.83	26	9	17	1.6	275	35.8	3.9	3.1	61	9 410	154	62	77	86
Iran	1 648 000	55 647 001	33.77	45	9	36	3.4	166	44.4	3.0	6.2	88	2 840	154	63	54	65
Iraq	438 317	18 781 770	42.85	42	8	34	3.4	48	46.5	2.7	6.2	65	1 740	134	63	60	71
Ireland	68 895	3 550 352	51.53	16	9	7	0.1	4	26.7	11.4	2.2	7	680	105	74	99	99
Israel	21 501	4 409 218	205.07	22	6	16	3.3	8	31.2	8.9	2.8	10	350	113	76	92	na
Italy	301 277	57 664 405	191.40	10	9	1	0.1	55	16.4	14.9	1.3	9	230	113	77	97	98
Ivory Coast (Cote d'Ivoire)	318 000	12 478 024	39.24	45	12	33	3.5	31	47.4	2.5	6.7	95	na	110	55	54	68
Jamaica	10 991	2 441 396	222.13	24	6	18	0.7	3	34.2	6.5	2.8	16	2 040	117	73	99	99
Japan	377 657	123 642 641	327.39	11	7	4	0.3	128	18.4	11.9	1.6	5	660	111	79	99	99
Jordan	97 740	3 064 508	31.35	43	6	37	3.8	10	45.4	2.5	6.3	51	860	116	67	80	90
Kenya	569 250	24 639 261	43.28	45	10	35	3.5	64	49.9	2.8	6.5	67	10 050	98	59	69	80
Korea, North	120 538	21 292 649	176.65	22	5	17	na	na	na	na	2.3	26	420	138	71	95	na
Korea, South	99 173	43 045 098	434.04	16	16	0	0.9	54	25.1	5.5	1.8	17	1 160	131	71	99	99
Kuwait	17 818	2 123 711	119.19	25	3	22	2.9	4	35.6	1.4	3.4	14	640	116	74	73	79
Laos (Lao PDR)	236 800	4 023 736	16.99	47	16	31	3.2	10	44.8	1.9	6.7	103	1 360	123	49	85	na
Lebanon	10 452	3 300 802	315.81	na	na	na	na	na	na	na	na	na	na	na	65	80	87
Lesotho	30 355	1 711 072	56.37	40	12	28	2.6	4	43.4	3.5	5.6	93	18 610	112	56	65	na
Liberia	97 754	2 639 809	27.00	44	14	30	3.0	6	44.9	3.1	6.3	136	9 340	110	54	39	49
Libya	1 775 500	4 221 141	2.38	43	8	35	3.6	14	46.0	2.4	6.7	74	690	177	62	64	78
Luxembourg	2 586	383 813	148.42	na	na	na	na	na	na	na	na	na	na	na	75	99	99
Madagascar	581 540	11 800 524	20.29	45	15	30	2.8	26	45.5	3.0	6.3	116	9 780	88	51	80	87
Malawi	118 484	9 157 528	77.29	54	20	34	3.4	24	46.7	2.6	7.6	149	11 340	95	46	25	na
Malaysia	329 757	17 510 546	53.10	30	5	25	2.3	32	38.3	3.6	3.8	16	1 930	118	70	78	86
Mali	1 220 000	8 142 373	6.67	50	19	31	3.0	23	46.6	3.2	7.1	166	25 390	119	48	32	40
Mauritania	1 030 400	1 934 549	1.88	48	19	29	2.8	5	44.6	3.3	6.8	121	11 900	141	47	34	47
Mauritius*	2 040	1 070 005	524.51	17	6	11	0.9	1	29.4	5.4	1.9	20	1 900	127	70	88	na
Mexico	1 958 201	87 870 154	44.87	27	5	22	1.8	142	37.3	3.7	3.3	39	na	119	70	87	89
Mongolia	1 565 000	2 125 463	1.36	35	8	27	2.5	4	40.7	3.6	4.7	62	na	105	63	90	na
Morocco	710 850	25 648 214	36.08	35	9	26	2.4	47	40.8	3.6	4.5	67	4 730	143	62	49	60
Mozambique	784 090	14 565 656	18.58	46	18	28	3.0	42	44.1	3.2	6.4	137	na	98	47	33	45
Myanmar (Burma)	676 552	41 277 389	61.01	31	9	22	2.0	70	37.1	4.1	3.8	64	3 740	129	61	81	90
Namibia	823 290	1 452 951	1.76	42	11	31	3.0	4	45.8	3.1	5.9	100	na	102	57	30	na
Nepal	147 181	19 145 800	130.08	40	14	26	2.5	37	42.0	3.1	5.7	121	30 220	110	52	26	39
Netherlands	33 937	14 936 032	440.11	12	9	3	0.5	16	17.6	13.2	1.6	7	450	104	77	99	99
New Zealand	269 057	3 295 866	12.25	16	8	8	0.7	4	22.7	11.0	2.0	10	580	104	75	99	99
Nicaragua	120 254	3 722 683	30.96	40	7	33	3.0	9	45.9	2.6	5.3	55	1 390	98	65	87	na
Niger	1 266 700	7 969 309	6.29	51	20	31	3.3	24	47.2	2.6	7.2	128	39 670	116	45	28	39
Nigeria	910 770	118 819 377	130.46	43	14	29	2.8	255	46.4	2.6	6.0	98	6 410	106	52	51	63
Norway	323 878	4 252 806	13.13	13	10	3	0.4	5	19.0	16.4	1.8	8	450	110	77	99	99
Oman	300 000	1 457 064	4.86	44	6	38	3.9	5	46.3	2.4	7.0	33	1 700	na	66	20	na
Pakistan	803 943	114 649 406	142.61	42	12	30	2.7	240	44.2	2.8	5.8	103	2 900	125	56	35	49
Panama	77 082	2 425 400	31.47	24	5	19	1.6	4	34.9	4.7	2.9	21	1 000	113	73	88	88
Papua New Guinea	462 840	3 822 875	8.26	36	11	25	2.3	7	41.1	2.7	5.1	57	6 070	120	55	52	68
Paraguay	406 752	4 660 270	11.46	35	6	29	2.8	10	41.1	3.5	4.6	32	1 460	107	67	90	92
Peru	1 285 216	21 905 605	17.04	30	8	22	2.0	37	38.0	3.7	3.8	69	1 040	94	63	85	91

18	19	20	21	22	23	24	25	26	27	28	29	30	31	32	33	34	35	36	37	38
47	900	32.4	39.4	0	-17.0	9 356	110	14	25	156	17	57	4 071	41 000	124	239	0.7	49.8	12.3	37.9
13	440	9.9	25.6	0	-3.9	8 925	na	na	0	55	10	72	1 000	37 000	60	80	na	78.1	1.3	20.6
24	180	13.7	19.8	0	0.0	na	na	13	0	6	6	67	147	18 000	na	na	na	82.0	4.0	14.0
95	330	29.0	34.5	122 040	-2.7	na	100	11	3	14	17	33	660	1 100	29	35	-1.3	27.0	26.0	47.0
47	370	15.6	28.3	0	-30.0	8 426	230	17	9	66	10	82	725	860	28	70	0.2	50.4	5.7	43.9
71	590	22.7	43.7	11 260	-18.8	9 406	50	20	35	89	18	62	1 979	42 000	190	313	0.5	60.5	16.1	23.4
na	11 490	85.0	94.0	0	0.0	11 943	na	na	na	na	na	na	na	na	na	na	6.2	0.9	27.7	71.4
99	2 700	40.0	61.3	0	5.9	15 254	26	10	70	1 344	127	2	64 076	na	1 432	4 493	na	20.9	31.3	47.8
99	21 400	80.1	90.5	29 750	0.0	na	na	na	na	74	293	1	1 942	na	na	598	3.4	na	na	na
34	350	18.0	27.0	11 610	-0.7	9 331	340	30	2	10 693	13	25	651 936	120 000	9 815	11 073	1.9	62.6	10.8	26.6
68	570	14.6	30.5	117 610	-5.2	11 512	450	14	6	2 852	16	47	137 726	870 000	1 367	2 532	4.5	54.4	8.0	37.6
43	2 490	33.6	56.7	156 850	0.1	13 316	120	5	20	2 474	46	1	166 074	na	19 000	4 030	0.1	36.4	32.8	30.8
49	1 950	42.9	71.3	64 770	-1.6	12 085	na	9	27	572	31	1	68 898	na	9 370	1 677	na	12.5	7.8	79.7
99	9 550	45.8	57.1	0	8.4	15 815	12	4	61	400	114	1	29 352	na	435	3 803	3.0	13.0	18.4	68.6
na	10 920	77.0	91.6	0	-5.2	13 286	5	7	58	399	89	1	32 903	na	5 838	3 044	2.6	3.9	20.8	75.3
96	16 830	59.4	68.9	0	6.3	14 668	10	7	49	6 942	121	1	389 747	na	18 354	73 325	3.0	9.1	20.4	70.5
40	750	19.3	40.4	42 680	-24.1	10 787	na	14	4	169	14	59	7 595	350 000	117	725	0.5	65.2	8.3	26.5
99	1 500	33.8	52.3	0	-5.1	10 921	110	8	34	67	28	8	4 899	810	25	203	-1.3	25.3	11.5	63.2
99	25 430	62.5	77.0	0	0.4	12 374	16	5	48	16 573	135	1	1 040 554	na	24 198	239 682	4.1	7.1	23.7	69.2
70	1 240	42.7	68.0	0	12.2	11 026	na	5	31	115	29	1	9 416	na	617	352	na	10.2	25.6	64.2
58	370	7.4	23.6	112 210	-7.8	9 054	170	15	3	434	18	79	5 192	13 000	237	696	1.9	81.0	6.8	12.2
na	910	40.2	59.8	0	0.0	11 817	41	na	0	2 025	95	2	151 488	na	2 500	na	na	42.8	30.3	26.9
99	5 400	27.7	72.0	0	-1.4	11 938	26	9	39	3 165	75	1	221 104	na	6 125	5 519	7.1	17.8	26.7	55.5
67	10 410	72.3	95.6	0	0.0	13 374	6	7	77	480	234	1	31 181	na	1 335	2 095	na	na	na	na
na	200	7.9	18.6	4 370	-7.2	11 009	na	39	0	43	11	83	227	240 000	na	na	na	75.7	7.1	17.2
73	na	39.6	83.7	0	-11.1	10 465	na	10	34	122	46	4	8 720	na	na	na	na	14.3	27.3	58.4
na	530	3.4	20.2	21 330	0.0	9 624	na	11	21	na	na	na	0	na	20	41	4.9	23.3	33.1	43.6
29	410	18.7	45.9	14 200	-14.4	9 971	na	na	0	61	24	78	773	39 000	26	62	na	74.2	9.4	16.4
50	5 410	22.8	70.2	654 970	16.6	13 914	80	na	41	521	119	1	37 842	na	2 956	3 017	na	18.1	28.9	53.0
99	28 730	62.1	84.2	0	0.0	na	na	na	na	170	451	1	9 266	na	73	734	2.3	3.7	19.1	77.2
73	230	10.6	23.8	6 910	-8.7	9 033	240	10	0	87	8	82	901	120 000	37	94	-1.9	80.8	6.0	13.2
na	200	4.4	11.8	7 810	-19.3	8 954	100	20	2	146	18	90	634	58 000	21	61	0.9	81.8	3.0	15.2
70	2 320	25.2	43.0	28 440	-11.0	11 612	59	10	41	834	48	10	49 061	280 000	1 335	2 488	4.0	41.6	19.1	39.3
24	270	11.1	19.2	588 140	-4.1	9 686	na	17	2	59	7	87	425	7 700	61	76	1.7	85.5	2.0	12.5
21	500	5.8	46.8	713 700	-2.2	11 239	na	11	0	42	21	1	3 023	na	40	67	-0.6	69.4	8.9	21.7
na	2 250	33.2	40.5	0	-1.1	12 085	100	9	0	30	28	52	1 000	na	4	91	3.2	19.0	31.1	49.9
85	2 490	50.8	72.6	30 500	-12.0	12 776	82	15	31	4 720	56	5	319 702	200 000	461	5 863	2.8	22.9	20.1	57.0
na	880	35.7	52.3	241 310	-8.5	10 377	100	10	0	131	63	10	10 303	na	172	na	na	39.8	21.0	39.2
38	950	29.3	48.0	0	2.0	12 642	300	na	29	285	12	5	22 120	na	800	1 060	2.3	45.6	25.0	29.4
21	80	3.7	26.8	61 300	-7.6	7 032	300	20	0	165	11	89	1 205	30 000	102	74	na	84.5	7.4	8.1
72	230	19.3	24.8	25 470	0.7	10 214	140	16	0	268	7	69	5 009	380 000	190	271	na	63.9	9.1	27.0
na	1 060	14.9	27.8	222 390	-1.6	8 146	na	na	na	na	na	na	0	na	na	65	na	43.4	21.9	34.7
13	170	3.1	9.6	0	0.0	8 694	830	na	0	226	12	92	934	32 000	33	100	0.5	92.9	0.6	6.5
99	17 320	85.0	88.5	0	3.3	13 190	5	na	39	2 957	199	1	124 990	na	6 543	29 320	1.8	4.2	17.4	78.4
99	12 680	76.0	84.0	37 230	4.3	14 073	6	5	49	666	201	1	26 176	na	790	4 061	1.1	10.0	20.1	69.9
na	610	39.6	59.8	15 210	-23.5	9 481	47	15	0	71	19	49	2 180	59 000	592	331	-3.3	46.5	15.8	37.7
17	310	5.8	19.5	656 330	-22.1	9 661	420	15	0	55	7	73	1 008	7 400	17	82	-2.4	85.0	2.7	12.3
39	290	14.4	35.2	15 260	-19.4	9 678	800	20	1	1 589	14	62	79 263	270 000	180	400	0.1	44.6	4.2	51.2
99	23 120	49.9	75.0	56 270	0.0	13 923	2	4	65	1 638	388	1	46 009	na	2 753	11 530	3.4	6.1	16.1	77.8
na	6 110	3.6	10.6	47 690	0.0	na	na	7	20	146	98	1	10 259	na	1 518	554	na	50.0	21.6	28.4
21	380	22.1	32.0	27 370	17.3	9 289	500	25	3	1 330	12	21	60 973	4 000	2 575	791	2.5	49.6	12.4	38.0
88	1 830	41.2	53.4	0	-19.4	10 628	57	8	30	76	32	26	2 730	19 000	105	571	1.4	25.4	9.9	64.7
38	860	2.7	15.8	39 030	-0.5	10 059	900	25	0	91	24	60	2 250	12 000	42	237	0.1	76.3	10.2	13.5
88	1 110	35.6	47.5	77 260	-27.7	11 541	380	7	0	93	22	59	1 722	67 000	49	69	4.6	48.6	20.5	30.9
79	1 160	46.3	70.2	366 600	-3.5	9 151	88	9	28	484	23	20	21 174	140 000	2 184	1 848	-0.2	35.1	12.3	52.6

Name	1	2	3	4	5	6	7	8	9	10	11	12	13	14	15	16	17
Philippines	300 000	66 117 284	220.39	29	7	22	1.8	101	39.9	3.3	3.7	41	6 570	127	64	90	91
Poland	312 683	37 776 725	120.81	15	10	5	0.4	44	25.1	10.0	2.1	16	490	106	71	98	na
Portugal	92 072	10 354 497	112.46	12	9	3	0.4	11	20.7	13.0	1.6	12	140	132	75	85	89
Qatar	11 437	490 897	42.92	na	na	na	na	na	na	na	na	na	na	na	70	70	na
Romania	237 500	23 273 285	97.99	16	11	5	0.4	27	23.8	10.3	2.2	27	570	106	70	98	na
Rwanda	26 338	7 609 119	288.90	54	18	36	3.9	23	48.0	2.5	8.3	120	35 090	106	48	50	63
Saudi Arabia	2 240 000	17 115 728	7.64	43	7	36	3.7	43	45.5	2.6	7.0	65	730	155	64	62	76
Senegal	192 192	7 506 197	39.06	45	17	28	3.1	19	46.7	2.7	6.5	81	na	100	47	38	51
Sierra Leone	71 620	4 165 953	58.17	47	22	25	2.6	10	43.4	3.1	6.5	147	13 620	89	42	21	31
Singapore*	622	2 720 915	4374.46	17	5	12	1.2	4	23.6	5.5	1.9	7	1 410	140	74	86	na
Somalia	637 657	8 424 269	13.21	48	18	30	3.1	21	46.0	3.0	6.8	126	19 950	111	48	24	34
South Africa	1 221 037	39 549 941	32.39	33	9	24	2.2	65	38.2	4.0	4.3	66	na	113	62	70	na
Spain	504 782	39 268 715	77.79	11	9	2	0.2	40	19.8	13.2	1.5	8	320	129	76	95	97
Sri Lanka	64 454	17 196 436	266.80	20	6	14	1.1	24	32.3	5.0	2.4	19	5 520	105	71	88	93
Sudan	2 505 813	24 971 000	9.97	44	15	29	2.8	55	45.2	2.6	6.3	102	10 190	102	50	27	42
Suriname	163 265	396 813	2.43	na	na	na	na	na	na	na	na	na	na	na	68	95	95
Swaziland	17 363	778 525	44.84	na	na	na	na	na	na	na	na	na	na	na	57	68	na
Sweden	440 945	8 401 098	19.05	15	12	3	0.3	9	17.4	18.0	1.9	6	390	101	78	99	99
Switzerland	41 293	6 742 461	163.28	12	10	2	0.4	7	17.0	14.9	1.7	7	700	103	78	99	99
Syria	184 050	12 483 440	67.83	44	7	37	3.6	35	48.2	2.7	6.5	43	1 250	138	66	64	77
Taiwan	36 000	20 546 664	570.74	na	na	na	na	na	na	na	na	na	na	na	na	92	na
Tanzania	886 040	25 970 843	29.31	48	18	30	3.1	64	46.7	3.0	6.6	115	24 970	120	48	85	na
Thailand	513 115	55 115 683	107.41	22	7	15	1.4	84	33.9	3.0	2.5	27	6 290	108	66	93	96
Togo	56 785	3 674 355	64.71	48	14	34	3.2	9	48.1	3.1	6.6	88	8 700	90	54	43	55
Trinidad and Tobago*	5 128	1 344 639	262.22	24	6	18	1.0	2	33.9	5.5	2.8	25	940	114	71	95	na
Tunisia	163 610	8 095 492	49.48	28	7	21	1.9	14	37.8	4.1	3.6	44	2 150	141	67	65	74
Turkey	779 452	56 704 327	72.75	28	7	21	1.9	91	34.8	4.3	3.5	60	1 390	120	67	81	91
Uganda	197 058	17 960 262	91.14	51	19	32	3.3	42	48.7	2.8	7.3	117	na	91	47	48	61
United Arab Emirates	83 600	2 253 624	26.96	22	4	18	2.2	3	30.8	1.7	4.6	23	1 020	125	72	68	na
United Kingdom	244 103	57 365 665	235.01	13	11	2	0.2	61	18.9	15.7	1.8	8	na	95	76	99	99
United States	9 372 610	248 709 873	26.54	17	9	8	0.8	307	21.6	12.3	1.9	9	470	114	76	99	99
Uruguay	176 215	3 036 660	17.23	17	10	7	0.6	4	25.8	11.4	2.3	21	510	94	73	96	96
U.S.S.R. to 1991	22 272 000	290 938 469	13.06	17	10	7	na	na	na	na	2.3	24	270	106	71	99	99
Armenia	29 800	3 283 000	110.17	na	na	na	na	na	na	na	na	na	na	na	na	na	na
Azerbaijan	86 600	7 029 000	81.17	na	na	na	na	na	na	na	na	na	na	na	na	na	na
Belarus	207 600	10 200 000	49.13	na	na	na	na	na	na	na	na	na	na	na	na	na	na
Estonia	45 100	1 573 000	34.88	na	na	na	na	na	na	na	na	na	na	na	na	na	na
Georgia	69 700	5 449 000	78.18	na	na	na	na	na	na	na	na	na	na	na	na	na	na
Kazakhstan	2 717 300	16 538 000	6.09	na	na	na	na	na	na	na	na	na	na	na	na	na	na
Kyrgyzstan	198 500	4 291 000	21.62	na	na	na	na	na	na	na	na	na	na	na	na	na	na
Latvia	64 600	2 681 000	41.50	na	na	na	na	na	na	na	na	na	na	na	na	na	na
Lithuania	65 200	3 690 000	56.60	na	na	na	na	na	na	na	na	na	na	na	na	na	na
Moldova	33 700	4 341 000	128.81	na	na	na	na	na	na	na	na	na	na	na	na	na	na
Russia	17 075 400	147 386 000	8.63	na	na	na	na	na	na	na	na	na	na	na	na	na	na
Tajikistan	143 100	5 112 000	35.72	na	na	na	na	na	na	na	na	na	na	na	na	na	na
Turkmenistan	488 100	3 524 000	7.22	na	na	na	na	na	na	na	na	na	na	na	na	na	na
Ukraine	603 700	51 704 000	85.65	na	na	na	na	na	na	na	na	na	na	na	na	na	na
Uzbekistan	447 400	19 906 000	44.49	na	na	na	na	na	na	na	na	na	na	na	na	na	na
Venezuela	912 050	19 698 104	21.60	29	5	24	2.1	34	38.3	3.5	3.6	34	700	114	70	88	86
Vietnam	329 566	66 170 889	200.78	31	7	24	2.1	116	39.6	4.5	3.8	42	950	109	67	88	92
Western Sahara (Minurso)	266 000	191 707	0.72	na	na	na	na	na	na	na	na	na	na	na	na	na	na
Yemen	536 869	9 746 465	18.15	53	18	35	3.7	37	48.7	3.1	7.7	124	na	na	48	38	50
Yugoslavia to 1992	225 804	23 841 608	93.20	15	9	2	0.6	28	22.7	9.5	2.0	20	550	112	72	93	98
Bosnia-Herzegovina	51 129	4 124 256	80.66	na	na	na	na	na	na	na	na	na	na	na	na	na	na
Croatia	56 538	4 601 469	81.39	na	na	na	na	na	na	na	na	na	na	na	na	na	na

18	19	20	21	22	23	24	25	26	27	28	29	30	31	32	33	34	35	36	37	38
89	730	30.3	42.6	0	-16.4	9 942	93	18	21	983	16	38	40 960	190 000	609	915	1.3	41.5	9.5	49.0
na	1 690	47.9	61.8	0	0.9	14 672	11	8	66	5 133	136	1	440 929	na	4 801	14 679	na	27.8	28.2	44.0
81	4 900	22.1	33.6	0	0.0	14 630	12	5	42	598	58	1	40 912	na	1 131	2 997	3.0	17.5	25.2	57.3
na	15 860	73.3	89.4	0	0.0	na	na	na	71	250	593	1	13 308	na	154	na	na	3.0	28.0	69.0
na	1 640	34.2	52.7	0	0.4	13 207	150	6	67	3 228	139	1	212 193	na	1 345	3 532	na	30.5	43.5	26.0
37	310	2.4	7.7	0	-5.1	8 251	210	17	13	62	9	88	381	2 100	38	87	1.0	92.7	3.0	4.3
48	7 050	29.7	77.3	678 890	-11.8	12 031	na	6	75	2 535	176	1	173 776	na	16 500	8 228	2.6	48.4	14.4	37.2
25	710	31.9	38.4	15 860	-2.6	9 917	600	11	1	83	12	51	3 151	11 000	96	245	-0.6	80.7	6.2	13.1
11	240	13.0	32.2	0	-2.4	7 531	450	17	3	37	9	76	671	4 600	5	13	0.0	69.6	14.0	16.4
na	11 160	100.0	100.0	0	0.0	13 387	5	7	37	393	146	1	35 860	na	1 059	1 307	6.5	0.5	29.0	70.5
14	120	17.3	36.4	104 600	-1.1	7 979	1100	na	2	81	13	85	960	5 200	23	8	-0.1	75.6	8.4	16.0
na	2 530	46.6	59.5	0	8.8	13 069	83	12	41	3 272	81	6	278 468	na	3 292	4 274	1.3	13.6	24.4	62.0
93	11 020	56.6	78.4	0	1.8	14 952	11	1	69	3 399	88	1	203 227	na	6 906	21 554	2.4	11.2	21.1	67.7
83	470	17.9	21.4	0	-1.5	9 532	60	28	0	153	9	52	4 034	22 000	204	360	2.9	42.6	11.7	45.7
12	340	10.3	22.0	793 770	-6.2	8 263	660	na	0	254	10	81	3 338	98 000	800	590	na	63.4	4.3	32.3
95	3 050	47.2	47.4	110 800	-0.3	na	89	12	0	22	51	2	1 440	1 100	na	na	1.0	20.0	20.0	60.0
na	810	4.0	33.1	0	2.9	na	na	na	0	na	na	na	443	na	8	49	2.2	74.0	9.0	17.0
99	23 660	72.6	84.0	23 150	0.5	12 391	5	4	77	2 363	278	5	58 888	na	4 433	24 790	1.9	3.3	21.8	74.9
99	32 680	51.0	59.9	0	0.0	14 911	5	5	64	1 079	162	1	39 326	na	3 152	17 481	1.4	6.4	29.8	63.8
51	1 000	36.8	50.4	0	31.4	12 571	280	11	17	374	31	1	28 154	na	2 721	1 213	2.9	22.0	15.1	62.9
na	4 000	na	na	0	na	na	na	na	na	na	na	na	na	na	4 762	5 429	na	na	na	na
na	110	4.7	32.8	70 530	-2.8	9 234	340	14	3	339	14	90	2 099	21 000	171	151	-0.2	85.6	4.5	9.9
90	1 420	12.5	22.6	28 090	-15.6	9 695	50	12	26	1 631	29	34	77 680	290 000	1 657	2 251	4.4	69.8	5.9	24.3
31	410	9.8	25.7	0	-5.8	9 268	na	20	16	16	4	43	627	2 900	43	98	-0.1	64.3	6.3	29.4
na	3 610	22.5	69.1	0	4.3	11 943	54	na	33	212	168	1	18 580	330	43	383	0.0	11.8	14.9	73.3
56	1 440	36.0	54.3	19 010	17.9	13 065	310	8	27	197	25	15	13 923	na	492	695	3.2	21.6	16.3	62.1
71	1 630	29.7	61.3	0	0.2	13 546	210	7	33	1 766	32	5	126 078	na	2 890	2 053	2.6	46.8	14.6	38.6
35	220	5.1	10.4	5 300	-8.1	9 012	300	na	0	144	9	87	879	10 000	80	60	-2.4	85.9	4.4	9.7
na	19 860	40.0	77.8	19 380	50.0	13 851	na	7	0	897	581	1	50 994	na	1 580	757	na	4.6	38.0	57.4
99	16 100	85.7	89.1	0	13.8	13 182	9	7	50	9 047	158	1	568 451	na	31 489	70 107	2.0	2.1	20.1	77.8
99	21 790	70.0	75.0	440 580	-1.1	15 367	8	7	70	80 560	324	2	4 869 005	22 000	293 211	448 120	1.7	2.8	18.4	78.8
96	2 560	80.1	85.5	0	7.4	11 105	38	8	12	119	39	24	4 749	na	158	302	0.8	15.3	18.2	66.5
99	8 700	48.8	65.8	7 520 220	1.7	14 174	48	6	55	58 599	204	1	3 804 001	na	274 740	204 850	na	20.0	39.0	41.0
na	2 955	na	na	na	na	na	na	na	na	na	na	na	na	na	na	na	na	na	na	na
na	2 870	na	na	na	na	na	na	na	na	na	na	na	na	na	na	na	na	na	na	na
na	5 729	na	na	na	na	na	na	na	na	na	na	na	na	na	na	na	na	na	na	na
na	5 390	na	na	na	na	na	na	na	na	na	na	na	na	na	na	na	na	na	na	na
na	3 065	na	na	na	na	na	na	na	na	na	na	na	na	na	na	na	na	na	na	na
na	3 803	na	na	na	na	na	na	na	na	na	na	na	na	na	na	na	na	na	na	na
na	2 436	na	na	na	na	na	na	na	na	na	na	na	na	na	na	na	na	na	na	na
na	5 689	na	na	na	na	na	na	na	na	na	na	na	na	na	na	na	na	na	na	na
na	4 034	na	na	na	na	na	na	na	na	na	na	na	na	na	na	na	na	na	na	na
na	3 600	na	na	na	na	na	na	na	na	na	na	na	na	na	na	na	na	na	na	na
na	5 396	na	na	na	na	na	na	na	na	na	na	na	na	na	na	na	na	na	na	na
na	1 613	na	na	na	na	na	na	na	na	na	na	na	na	na	na	na	na	na	na	na
na	2 682	na	na	na	na	na	na	na	na	na	na	na	na	na	na	na	na	na	na	na
na	4 397	na	na	na	na	na	na	na	na	na	na	na	na	na	na	na	na	na	na	na
na	2 321	na	na	na	na	na	na	na	na	na	na	na	na	na	na	na	na	na	na	na
90	2 560	66.6	90.5	297 420	-8.6	10 808	59	9	35	1 860	97	1	95 887	59 000	1 050	3 570	-1.0	12.5	17.3	70.2
84	200	14.7	21.9	0	-28.8	9 347	140	18	0	465	7	51	18 170	150 000	na	na	na	67.5	11.8	20.7
na	na	na	na	na	na	na	na	na	na	na	na	na	na	na	na	na	na	na	na	na
26	690	12.0	29.0	117 060	-3.1	na	na	na	0	116	12	1	3 495	na	494	381	na	62.6	11.0	26.4
88	3 060	27.9	56.1	0	1.3	15 212	22	7	59	2 034	86	2	132 901	na	2 709	6 022	2.9	28.7	23.6	47.7
na	na	na	na	na	na	na	na	na	na	na	na	na	na	na	na	na	na	na	na	na
na	na	na	na	na	na	na	na	na	na	na	na	na	na	na	na	na	na	na	na	na

Name	1	2	3	4	5	6	7	8	9	10	11	12	13	14	15	16	17
Macedonia	na	na	na	na	na	na	na	na	na	na	na	na	na	na	na	na	na
Serbia/Yugoslavia	127 886	11 807 098	92.33	na	na	na	na	na	na	na	na	na	na	na	na	na	na
Slovenia	20 251	1 891 864	93.42	na	na	na	na	na	na	na	na	na	na	na	na	na	na
Zaire (Congo-Kinshasa)	2 267 600	36 589 468	16.14	45	14	31	3.0	89	46.4	2.6	6.2	94	13 540	91	52	72	83
Zambia	740 720	7 875 448	10.63	49	15	34	3.1	20	49.3	1.9	6.7	82	7 150	100	50	73	81
Zimbabwe	386 670	10 392 161	26.88	37	8	31	2.4	18	45.5	2.5	4.9	49	6 700	111	61	67	74

18	19	20	21	22	23	24	25	26	27	28	29	30	31	32	33	34	35	36	37	38
na	na	na	na	na	na	na	na	na	na	na	na	na	na	na	na	na	na	na	na	na
na	na	na	na	na	na	na	na	na	na	na	na	na	na	na	na	na	na	na	na	na
na	na	na	na	na	na	na	na	na	na	na	na	na	na	na	na	na	na	na	na	na
61	220	22.3	39.5	11 763	-1.9	8 334	na	13	7	422	12	76	3 822	130 000	82	183	-2.2	71.5	12.9	15.6
65	420	17.2	49.9	150 750	-2.4	8 694	150	14	4	201	26	58	2 612	27 000	63	94	-1.9	37.7	7.6	54.7
60	640	12.6	27.6	0	-4.0	9 624	480	15	16	295	31	25	16 059	16 000	390	684	0.7	64.7	5.6	29.7

APPENDIX 3

TECHNIQUES OF ANALYSIS

Averages (Mean, Median, Weighted)
Bar Graphs
Brainstorming
Constant Dollar Calculation
Coefficient of Correlation
Debates, Discussion
Divided Circles
Full-Log (Log-Log) Graphs
Graded Shading
Index Numbers
Inquiry Organizing
Line Graphs
Log Scales
Lorenz Curves
Population Pyramids
Proportional Circles
Questionnaires
Rates of Change (Average Annual Percentages)
Relative Percentages
Research Papers
Scales
Scattergraphs
Semi-Log Graphs
Sketch Maps
Triangular Graphs
Variation

Averages (Mean, Median, Weighted)

The most common form of average is the mean. The mean of any set of data is the sum of the values of all the items divided by the number of items. This is often written as a formula:

$$\bar{x} = \Sigma x/n$$

where $\bar{x}$ (called bar x) represents the mean,
Σ (called capital or large sigma) stands for the sum of,
x is the value of each item in the data set, and
n is the number of items.

The median is the central value in a set of data, so that half the items have values larger than the median, and half have values that are smaller.

The difference between mean and median is that the mean takes both the values and number of items into account, while the median takes only the number of items into account.

Sometimes an average (mean) is required for items that are themselves averages (means). In such cases it is essential to calculate a weighted average. Take, for example, ten people divided into two groups. Group A has eight members with an average height of 180 cm. Group B has two members with an average height of 160 cm. The average height for the two groups together is not 170 cm, which is the average of the two other averages. The number of people in each average needs to be taken into account. In other words, each original average needs to be weighted by the number of people involved. This is done by multiplying the average for each group by the number of people in each group, adding the two totals together, and dividing the grand total by the total number of people. Thus:

Group	Average height	Number of people	Average × Number (Weighted)
A	180 cm	8	1440
B	160 cm	2	320
Total		10	1760

Average height of groups A and B = 1760/10 = 176 cm.

Bar Graphs

Bar graphs are used to show comparisons of measurable attributes between different places or between related attributes (e.g., different sources of energy) in one place. The bars may be drawn vertically or horizontally, but names are often easier to write on horizontal bar graphs. In all cases the bars are either separated by a space or they are drawn so that they overlap. (Bars that just touch each other are reserved for a different kind of graph called a histogram.) The width of the bars and the spaces between them are always consistent within a single graph, although the spaces are not necessarily the same width as the bars.

In Fig. A3-1, (a) and (b) are simple bar graphs that compare a measurable characteristic between different places or different but related attributes in one place. The vertical simple bar graph is sometimes used to show the same sort of data for different times, in which case time is scaled along the horizontal axis. However, the vertical simple bar graph is generally less useful than a simple line graph for this purpose. The bars in a simple bar graph are intended for comparing quantities that differ according to place or attribute rather than time, for example, population densities in Belgium, China, and New Zealand. In all simple bar graphs, bars are arranged in either descending or ascending order.

Part (c) is a multiple or stacked bar graph used to compare the absolute values of two or three related characterisitics in each area (if more than three are compared, clarity is lost). For example, a multiple bar graph may be used to compare the annual amounts of oil, gas, and coal used in an area. Two sets of stacked bars serve to compare the quantities for two areas. If two or more stacks are drawn, the order of bars within each stack must remain the same. Any colouring or shading used to differentiate the bars in a stack must also remain constant through each stack.

A divided or compound bar graph is shown in part (d). Its purpose is similar to the multiple or stacked bar graph, but it permits the absolute

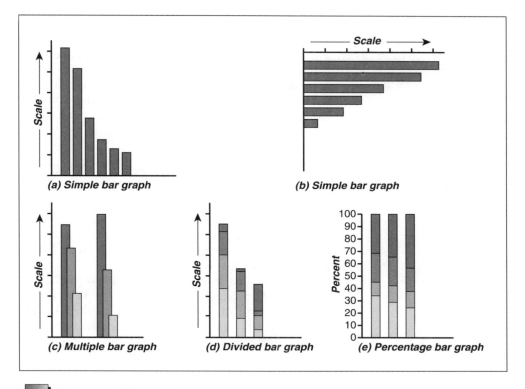

Fig. A3-1   *Bar graphs*

values for more than three related items to be shown clearly. For example, the contributions of thermal, hydro, nuclear, and alternative energy generation to total electricity production in different areas can be shown.

Part (e) shows a percentage bar graph. These bars are always divided. They show the relative contributions of several components to a whole. The whole is always standardized at 100 percent, and the components form a percentage part of the total. Percentage bars are used to compare the contributions of each component to the whole where the absolute sizes of the wholes differ from place to place, sometimes quite widely. For example, the percentages of wheat, oats, barley, and rye within the total grain harvest of different places may be compared with this method, even though totals and absolute quantities differ widely.

BRAINSTORMING

Brainstorming is one way of involving the whole class or group in generating ideas or suggestions. Normally a question is posed to the class or group, such as *What are the possible effects of an ageing population on society?* Individual members of the class or group respond, and the suggestions are recorded, usually on the board or a flip chart.

After all members of the class or group have had time to think of suggestions, the teacher or leader may add others. When the recorded list is as complete as possible, the suggestions may be grouped and analyzed. The way in which the suggestions are grouped may also be brainstormed. For example, in response to the question about an ageing population, some suggestions may possibly be grouped as economic, others as social, and so on.

Analysis of the suggestions may result in some being combined, since they may represent the same idea in different words. Other suggestions may be eliminated because — upon analysis — they are judged to be irrelevant.

CONSTANT DOLLAR CALCULATIONS

Because of inflation, money generally decreases in value as time passes. When money is the unit of measurement, it is necessary to standardize its value over a period of time in order to make meaningful comparisons between different times. Thus to say that a daily newspaper cost ten cents in 1970 and 50 cents in 1990 means little because the value of money changed during the period.

In order to standardize money values over time, the rate of inflation must be taken into account. When the money value is standardized, the results are said to be in constant dollars. The money value may be standardized to any year during the time period, but usually the starting or ending year is selected. For the period from 1970 to 1990, total inflation in Canada was 384 percent. Thus, in 1990 it cost $384 to buy what $100 bought in 1970. If nothing else had changed, a ten-cent newspaper in 1970 would have cost 38.4 cents in 1990. An actual 1990 price of 50 cents therefore represents a real price increase.

Looked at the other way round, inflation reduced the value of the dollar from $1 in 1970 to 26.04 cents in 1990 ($1/3.84 = $0.2604). Constant Canadian dollar values are therefore as follows: If values are standardized to 1970 (called constant 1970 dollars), a 1990 dollar was worth 26.04 cents; if values are standardized to 1990 (called constant 1990 dollars), a 1970 dollar was worth $3.84. If constant 1990 dollars are selected as the unit of money measurement, then all 1970 values have to be multiplied by 3.84 to make a comparison with 1990 valid. Conversely if constant 1970 dollars are selected as the measurement base, then all 1990 values must be multiplied by 0.2604 (or divided by 3.84) to make a comparison with 1970 valid.

COEFFICIENT OF CORRELATION

Calculation of the coefficient of correlation requires that the standard deviation be obtained for each of two data sets. The two data sets are known respectively as the x data and the y data.

The formula for obtaining the standard deviation of a data set is

$\sigma = \Sigma(x - \bar{x})^2$, where:

σ (called "sigma") is the standard deviation;

Σ is the symbol meaning "the sum of";

$\bar{x}$ (called bar x) is the mean of the data set;

$(x - \bar{x})$ is the deviation of each item from the mean;

$(x - \bar{x})^2$ is the square of the deviation of each item from the mean;

n is the number of items in the data set (in this case, ten).

Refer to Fig. A3-2 when calculating the following standard deviation.

Step 1. Calculate the mean of each data set, rounded to the nearest whole number. For data set x, the mean is 164 415; for data set y the mean is 22 297.

Step 2. For each item in each data set, calculate its deviation (or difference) from the mean for its particular data set. For example, the 1901 figure of 55 747 in data set x deviates from the mean for data set x by 108 668 (164 415 – 55 747 = 108 668).

Step 3. Square all the deviations from the mean that were calculated in Step 2. The squared deviation from the mean for the 1901 item in data set x is 11 808 734 224.

Step 4. For each data set separately, sum the squared deviations from the data set mean. The sum $(\Sigma(x-\bar{x})^2)$ for data set x is 49 183 203 505.

Step 5. Divide the sum of the squared deviations by the number of items in the data set, and obtain the square root of the result. This is the standard deviation of the data set. For data set x, the standard deviation is 70 131.

Once the standard deviations for data sets x and y have been obtained, the coefficient of correlation between the two data sets may be calculated.

	Immigration to Canada			Workers in strikes and lockouts		
	Data set x			Data set y		
Year	(x)	$(x-\bar{x})$	$(x-\bar{x})^2$	(y)	$(y-\bar{y})$	$(y-\bar{y})^2$
1901	55 747	–108 668	11 808 734 224	24 089	1792	3 211 264
1902	89 102	–75 313	5 672 047 969	12 709	–9 588	91 929 744
1903	138 660	–25 755	663 320 025	38 408	16 111	259 564 321
1904	131 252	–33 163	1 099 784 569	11 420	–10 877	118 309 129
1905	141 465	–22 950	526 702 500	12 513	–9784	95 726 656
1906	211 653	47 238	2 231 428 644	23 382	1085	1 177 225
1907	272 409	107 994	11 662 704 036	34 060	11 763	138 368 169
1908	143 326	–21 089	444 745 921	26 071	3774	14 243 076
1909	173 694	9279	86 099 841	18 114	–4183	17 497 489
1910	286 839	122 424	14 987 635 776	22 203	–94	8836
	$\bar{x}$ = 164 415			$\bar{y}$ = 22 297		
			$\Sigma(x-\bar{x})^2$ = 49 183 203 505			$\Sigma(y-\bar{y})^2$ = 740 035 909

Standard Deviation (σ)

$$\sigma_x = \sqrt{\Sigma(x-\bar{x})^2/n} = \sqrt{49\,183\,203\,505/10} = \sqrt{4\,918\,320\,350.5} = 70\,131$$

$$\sigma_y = \sqrt{\Sigma(y-\bar{y})^2/n} = \sqrt{740\,035\,909/10} = \sqrt{74\,003\,590.9} = 8603$$

Coefficient of Variation (V)

$$V_x = 100\sigma_x/\bar{x} = 100(70\,131)/164\,415 = 7\,013\,100/164\,415 = 42.65$$

$$V_y = 100\sigma_y/\bar{y} = 100(8603)/22\,297 = 860\,300/22\,297 = 38.58$$

SOURCE: Data from Urquhart and Buckley, *Historical Statistics of Canada*

Fig. A3-2 *Standard deviation and coefficent of variation*

The formula for the coefficient of correlation (r) is $r = \theta/\sigma_x\sigma_y$, where

r = the coefficient of correlation, between 0.00 and 1.00, with high values indicating a high degree of correlation;

$q = (\Sigma xy/n) - \bar{x}\bar{y}$ where $\bar{x}$ (called bar x) is the mean of the x data and $\bar{y}$ is the mean of the y data;

θ (called "theta") is the mean product of the x and y deviations from their respective data set means;

σ_x = standard deviation of the x data;

σ_y = standard deviation of the y data.

Application of the formula is illustrated in Fig. A3-3.

Debates, Discussion

The purposes of debating and discussing are similar in that participants attempt to persuade others to their point of view, but there are significant differences in how this end is brought about.

Year	Workers in immigration to Canada (x data)	Strikes and lockouts (y data)	xy
1901	55 747	24 089	1 342 889 483
1902	89 102	12 709	1 132 397 318
1903	138 660	38 408	5 325 653 280
1904	131 252	11 420	1 498 897 840
1905	141 465	12 513	1 770 151 545
1906	211 653	23 382	4 948 870 446
1907	272 409	34 060	9 278 250 540
1908	143 326	26 071	3 736 652 146
1909	173 694	18 114	3 146 293 116
1910	286 839	22 203	6 368 686 317

Averages: ($\bar{x}$ = 164 415) ($\bar{y}$ = 22 297) ($\Sigma xy/n$ = 3 854 874 203)

The formula for coefficient of correlation (r) is $r = \theta/\sigma_x\sigma_y$, where

θ (theta) = $(\Sigma xy/n) - \bar{x}\bar{y}$
= 3 854 874 203 – (164 415 × 22 297)
= 3 854 874 203 – 3 665 961 255
= 188 912 948

σ_x (sigma x) = $\sqrt{\Sigma(x-\bar{x})^2/n}$ (see Fig. A3-2 for details of calculations)
= 70 131

σ_y (sigma y) = $\sqrt{\Sigma(y-\bar{y})^2/n}$ (see Fig. A3-2 for details of calculations
= 8603

Insertion of calculations into the formula yields:

$r = \theta/\sigma_x\sigma_y$ = 188 912 948/(70 131 × 8603)
= 188 912 948/603 336 993
= 0.31

The coefficient of correlation lies between 0.00 and 1.00, with high values indicating a high correlation and vice versa. A correlation of 0.31 is quite low.

SOURCE: Data from Urquhart and Buckley, *Historical Statistics of Canada*

Fig. A3-3 *Coefficient of correlation*

A debate is fairly formal. The underlying principles of a debate are that all participants have the opportunity to put forward their views in an attempt to influence others, and that at the end the majority opinion will prevail. There are several styles of debate, but one commonly used in academic circles usually requires two speakers for and two speakers against the motion (such as "That developed countries should increase their annual immigration quotas"). Notice of the motion needs to be given, and the speakers need time to prepare their cases. Accordingly, a debate is not usually spontaneous.

The conduct of a debate requires that the first speaker for the motion speaks in favour of the motion, followed by the first speaker against the motion. The second speaker for the motion then speaks, followed by the second speaker against the motion. The motion is then opened for speakers from the floor. Speakers from the floor speak to the chair according to a speakers' list kept by the chair. At the end of contributions from the floor, the first speakers against and for the motion have the opportunity to summarize, highlight, rebut, and conclude. A vote is then taken. Debate procedure is summarized in Fig. A3-4.

A discussion is fairly informal, being more like a conversation among many participants. Whereas debate of an issue formally ties the arguments to only two sides (those for and against a particular motion), discussion of an issue may be much more open. Many sides may need to be moderated by a chair, who keeps a speakers' list, but it may also

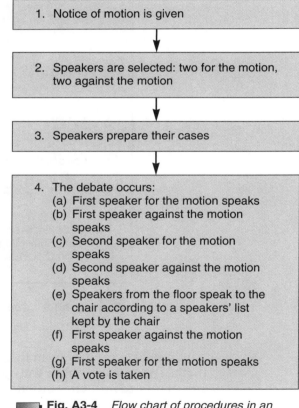

Fig. A3-4 *Flow chart of procedures in an academic debate*

operate quite informally without a chair. The aim of discussion is to achieve consensus rather than hold a vote.

DIVIDED CIRCLES

Divided circles are used to show the proportions of each of several parts of a whole. The percentages that the parts form of the whole are translated into the degrees of arc required for dividing the circle by multiplying the percentages by 3.6. The circle is then divided as shown in Fig. A3-5. Divided circles may stand alone, or, if they refer to data for points or areas for comparison purposes, they may be plotted on a map. Because circles are the most compact plane shape, therefore using less space than other shapes for any given area, they are the most suitable means of showing many types of comparative data on maps. Divided circles plotted at appropriate locations on a map are called located divided circles.

Component	Number of units	%	x 3.6	Degrees of arc
A	320	4.59	x 3.6	= 16.5
B	1600	22.94	x 3.6	= 82.6
C	756	10.84	x 3.6	= 39.0
D	3000	43.02	x 3.6	= 154.9
E	98	1.40	x 3.6	= 5.0
Others	1200	17.21	x 3.6	= 62.0
Total:	6974	100.00	x 3.6	= 360.0

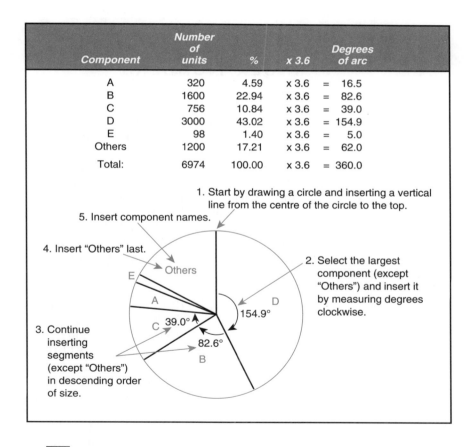

1. Start by drawing a circle and inserting a vertical line from the centre of the circle to the top.

5. Insert component names.

4. Insert "Others" last.

2. Select the largest component (except "Others") and insert it by measuring degrees clockwise.

3. Continue inserting segments (except "Others") in descending order of size.

154.9°

39.0°

82.6°

Fig. A3-5   *Divided circles*

FULL-LOG (LOG-LOG) GRAPHS

Full-log graphs are constructed with logarithmic scales on both the vertical and horizontal axes. Their main use is to accommodate data sets which have great differences between their highest and lowest values.

GRADED SHADING

The purpose of graded shading maps is to show differences in the relative values of an item from one area to another (e.g., number of items per square kilometre, or percentage change in number of items over a period of years). The values to be mapped are first grouped according to appropriately selected class intervals into size classes, so that the highest values form one class, the next highest another, and so on. There should be no more than four or five classes, or the map will become difficult to shade properly. Shading may be by line or colour, but should follow the graded shading principle that the highest value class should be the most prominent, and the lowest value class the least prominent. An example is given in Fig. A3-6.

INDEX NUMBERS

Index numbers are a device for comparing changes in different sorts of data or in different magnitudes of data over a period of time and are essentially percentages. For example, from 1970 to 1990, Algeria's population rose from 14 330 000 to 25 566 507 and China's population from 759 619 000 to 1 133 682 501. On an index number basis, 1970 (the starting year for the comparison) is called the base year, and is allocated the value of 100 (1970 = 100). The percentage-based increase to 1990 is calculated by multiplying the 1990 figure by 100, and dividing by the 1970 (base year) figure. The 1990 index figure for Algeria's population increase is thus 178.4 ([25 566 507 × 100]/14 330 000). For China, the comparable 1990 index is 149.2 ([1 133 682 501 × 100]/759 619 000), showing that China's population grew more slowly than that of Algeria.

The index figures for population growth may be compared with similarly calculated index figures for other characteristics, such as available daily food supplies. In 1970 the average consumption of food in Algeria was 7938 kilojoules per person per day; in China it was 7854 kJ/cap/d. By 1990, average food consumption in Algeria had risen to 11 997 kJ/cap/d and in China to 11 047 kJ/cap/d. Index number calculations show that the 1990 index (1970 = 100) for Algeria's average daily food consumption was 151.1 ([11 997 × 100]/7938) and for China it was 140.7 ([11 047 × 100]/7854). Comparison of all these index numbers indicates that Algeria had a faster rate of population growth than China (a 1990 index of 178.4 compared with China's 149.2) and was also able to provide its growing population with more food at a faster rate than China (a 1990 index of 151.1 compared with 140.7 for China).

Area	Population in 1970	Population in 1990	% Change 1970-1990
A	33 278	34 666	+4.2
B	41 296	57 218	+36.5
C	24 514	43 421	+77.1
D	38 629	67 306	+74.2
E	37 411	38 570	+3.1
F	28 136	31 717	+12.7
G	22 102	19 246	−12.9
H	18 955	16 817	−11.3
I	34 389	36 782	+7.0
J	35 777	43 119	+20.5

Classes are established according to personal assessment of data to be mapped (in this case, the calculated % change, 1970-1990).

e.g.

	% Change 1970-1990	% Change 1970-1990
Suggested size classes or class intervals	50.0 and over	60.0 and over
	+25.0-49.9	+ 40.0-59.9
	0.0-24.9	20.0-39.9
	−0.0-24.9	0.0-19.9
		−0.0-19.9

Suggested shading for four classes (3 positive, 1 negative):

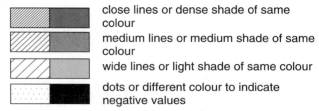

close lines or dense shade of same colour

medium lines or medium shade of same colour

wide lines or light shade of same colour

dots or different colour to indicate negative values

The legend should always read from the highest values at the top to the lowest at the bottom.

 Fig. A3-6   *Graded shading*

INQUIRY ORGANIZING

The organization of any inquiry generally follows the principles of the scientific method.

The first step is to define and focus the topic by posing a question or formulating a hypothesis. Following are two examples.

(i) Topic: Research government debt and the pace of economic activity.

Question asked in order to define the topic: What is the relationship between the level of government debt and the pace of economic activity?

(ii) Topic: Report on free trade.

A possible hypothesis used as a starting point for the inquiry: International free trade will make the world's economy more efficient.

The second step is to identify and locate appropriate information. Data may be collected through field work, interviews, and questionnaires, while published information may be obtained from commercial organizations and school, public, or government department libraries. For example, Statistics Canada libraries exist in many of the country's largest cities. Depending upon the range of the local library collections, vertical files, periodicals, yearbooks, encyclopedias, and other books may be available for use. Other sources of information include material filed in computer databases or CD-ROM.

Step three involves organizing the collected information into some sort of usable order. This usually requires that the information be sorted according to a predetermined system of classification, but the

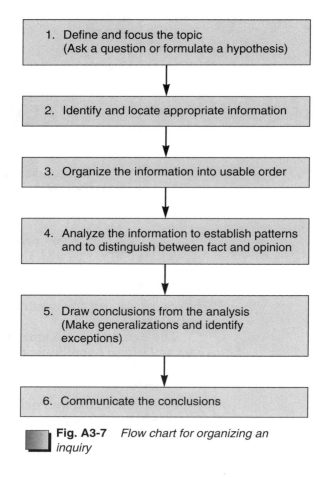

Fig. A3-7 *Flow chart for organizing an inquiry*

organization may occur according to a classification system that emerges as the information is collected. The classes within the system should accommodate all the information found. In many cases, this may mean establishing a class called "Miscellaneous" or "Other." An example of a classification system widely used in geography is: primary, secondary, and tertiary/quaternary as classes of economic activity.

The fourth step is to analyze the classified information to establish patterns of agreement and examples of disagreement. This may be done by assessing which points of information support each other, and identifying the information that does not fit the support pattern. It may also be done by evaluating the information to determine which points support a starting hypothesis and which are in opposition. An integral part of the analysis is to distinguish between fact and opinion.

Step five is to draw conclusions from the analysis made in step four. It may be possible to make a generalization, but with geographic information there is always the likelihood of exceptions which need further investigation.

The sixth and final step is to communicate the conclusions, along with supporting and exceptional information. This may be done orally or in writing. Either way, the communication should be polished; written or oral presentation may require at least two drafts. At this stage it should be possible to answer questions on the presentation, and to defend conclusions against counter-arguments.

The steps for organizing an inquiry are summarized in the flow chart in Fig. A3-7.

LINE GRAPHS

Line graphs are used for plotting continuously changing data, such as population totals or export values. A single line graph shows information for one data set only, e.g., annual numbers of immigrants to the developed world throughout a period of time, while a multiple line graph shows information for two or more data sets, which may or may not be similar. Examples of line graphs are shown in Fig. A3-8.

A graph with a number of separate lines comparing rice output for five different countries over a period of years is an example of a multiple line graph showing similar data. An example of a multiple line graph showing dissimilar — but not necessarily unrelated — data is one that compares immigration numbers with unemployment rates in the developed world.

A compound line graph shows the changing components of a total quantity, usually over a period of time. Here it is the spaces between the lines, rather than the lines themselves, that are important.

A positive-negative graph is used whenever positive and negative quantities (or gains and losses) need to be shown.

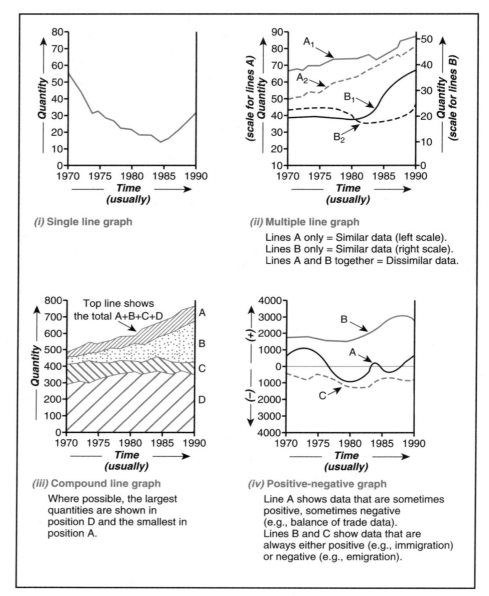

Fig. A3-8   *Line graphs*

LOG SCALES

A log scale (or logarithmic scale) is usually used on the vertical (or y) axis of a graph whenever the graph is intended to show rates of change over time in a data set. The scale is arranged so that as values increase they are represented by diminishing intervals along the scale, according to the values of the logarithms, times ten (see Fig. A3-9). The significance of this arrange-

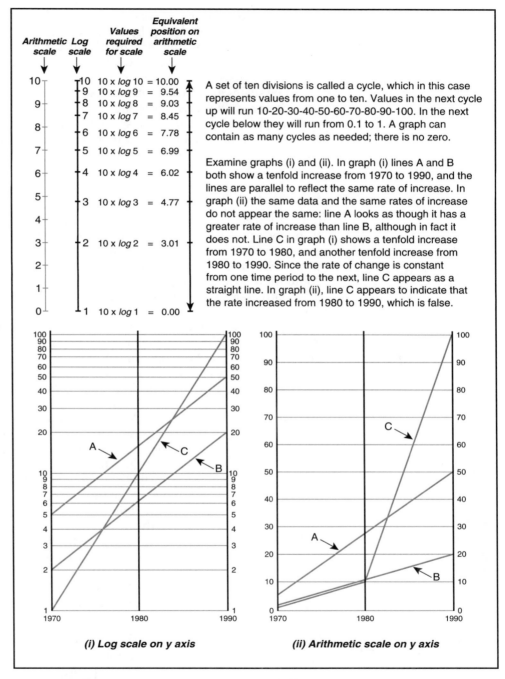

A set of ten divisions is called a cycle, which in this case represents values from one to ten. Values in the next cycle up will run 10-20-30-40-50-60-70-80-90-100. In the next cycle below they will run from 0.1 to 1. A graph can contain as many cycles as needed; there is no zero.

Examine graphs (i) and (ii). In graph (i) lines A and B both show a tenfold increase from 1970 to 1990, and the lines are parallel to reflect the same rate of increase. In graph (ii) the same data and the same rates of increase do not appear the same: line A looks as though it has a greater rate of increase than line B, although in fact it does not. Line C in graph (i) shows a tenfold increase from 1970 to 1980, and another tenfold increase from 1980 to 1990. Since the rate of change is constant from one time period to the next, line C appears as a straight line. In graph (ii), line C appears to indicate that the rate increased from 1980 to 1990, which is false.

(i) Log scale on y axis   **(ii) Arithmetic scale on y axis**

Fig. A3-9   *Log scales and arithmetic scales*

ment is that a constant rate of change over time is shown by a straight line, an increasing rate of change by a steepening line, and a decreasing rate of change by a flattening line. Arithmetically scaled graphs do not possess this quality, and should not be used to show rates of change over time; they may, however, be used to show changes in absolute quantities over time.

Log scales are also sometimes used to show data which contain large quantitative variations. Log scales compress the space taken to represent higher values and enlarge the space for lower values, making it possible to graph data that might be too varied to be graphed on an arithmetic scale. Also see Scales and Semi-Log Graphs.

LORENZ CURVES

Lorenz curves are used to show the percentage distribution of an item throughout a population, such as the distribution of income throughout a country. The graph has two axes: the vertical axis represents the item, such as income, scaled to 100 percent; the horizontal axis represents the population, also scaled to 100 percent (see Fig. A3-10).

Both ends of the Lorenz curve are fixed. The lower left is fixed at zero percent on both axes, because there is no income if there are no people. The upper right is fixed at 100 on both axes, because 100 percent of the income is gained by 100 percent of the population. If income were distributed equally, so that everyone gained an equal share, then, starting from zero, ten percent of the population would gain ten percent of the income, 20 percent of the population 20 percent of the income, and so on. The Lorenz curve would be a straight line.

More commonly, however, incomes are distributed unequally through a population. Normally, the lowest ten percent of income earners gain less than ten percent of the income, and so on, until at the other end of the scale the highest ten percent of income earners gain more than ten percent of the income. This produces a line that curves to the lower right of the graph. The more it curves to the lower right, the more unequal is the distribution of income within the country.

The *Human Development Report 1992*, published by the United Nations Development Program, gives the following data for world income distribution:

World population	World income
Richest 20%	82.7%
Second 20%	11.7%
Third 20%	2.3%
Fourth 20%	1.9%
Poorest 20%	1.4%

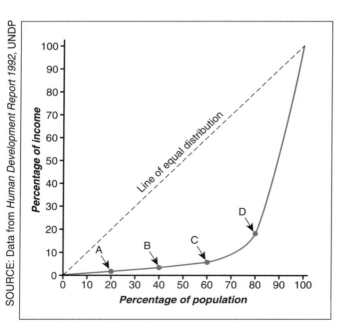

Fig. A3-10 *Lorenz curve of world income distribution*

This distribution is shown as a Lorenz curve in Fig. A3-10. It is plotted in the following way:

1. Start at the lowest point by plotting the intersect of 1.4 percent of the income and 20 percent of the population. This is point A.

2. Calculate the accumulated percentage of income gained by the lowest-earning 40 percent of the population. This is 3.3 percent (1.4 + 1.9), and is plotted at point B.

3. Calculate the accumulated percentage of income gained by the lowest-earning 60 percent of the population. This is 5.6 percent (1.4 + 1.9 + 2.3), and is plotted at point C.

4. The accumulated percentage for the lowest-earning 80 percent of the population is 17.3, plotted at point D. Draw a smooth curve through the points, with ends at zero-zero and 100-100.

POPULATION PYRAMIDS

A population pyramid is a special type of histogram showing the percentages of males and females in the population by age class (see Fig. A3-11). (A histogram is a type of frequency distribution chart. It shows the quantities of data that occur in the different classes of data. These classes are arti-

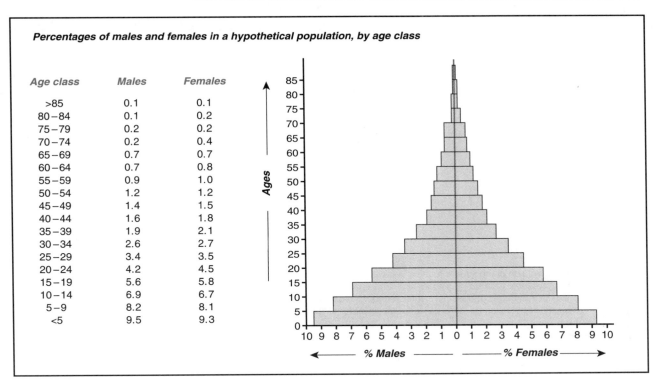

Percentages of males and females in a hypothetical population, by age class

Age class	Males	Females
>85	0.1	0.1
80–84	0.1	0.2
75–79	0.2	0.2
70–74	0.2	0.4
65–69	0.7	0.7
60–64	0.7	0.8
55–59	0.9	1.0
50–54	1.2	1.2
45–49	1.4	1.5
40–44	1.6	1.8
35–39	1.9	2.1
30–34	2.6	2.7
25–29	3.4	3.5
20–24	4.2	4.5
15–19	5.6	5.8
10–14	6.9	6.7
5–9	8.2	8.1
<5	9.5	9.3

Fig. A3-11   *A population pyramid*

ficial divisions because the data form a continuous series. The bars in a histogram therefore touch, unlike a bar graph.) Pyramids vary in shape according to the age and sex structure of the population. For example, a population with a high percentage of young people and relatively few old people appears wide at the bottom and tapers almost to a point at the top.

PROPORTIONAL CIRCLES

Proportional circles are drawn to scale, so that the areas of the circles are proportional to the quantities they represent. Large quantities are represented by large circles, and so on. If the purpose of the circle is to show only a single quantity, without comparison with any other quantity, then the size of the circle does not matter. The purpose of using proportional circles is to make visual comparisons between two or more quantities, so that there are always two or more proportional circles in a set. A circle's size is determined by its radius, which is proportional to the square root of the quantity to be shown. Fig. A3-12 shows the cal-

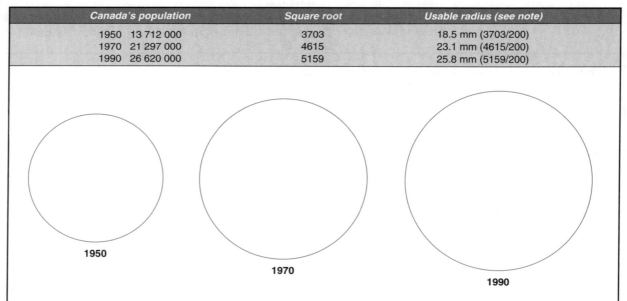

Canada's population	Square root	Usable radius (see note)
1950 13 712 000	3703	18.5 mm (3703/200)
1970 21 297 000	4615	23.1 mm (4615/200)
1990 26 620 000	5159	25.8 mm (5159/200)

1950

1970

1990

Note: The conversion of the square root into a usable radius depends upon the size of the square root and the size of the space available for drawing the circles. In this case, the three square roots are each divided by 200 to produce a usable radius in millimetres. It does not matter whether the square roots are divided or multiplied, as long as the proportions are maintained by using the same divisor or multiplier for all the square roots in a set.

SOURCE: Data from Statistics Canada

Fig. A3-12   *Proportional circles*

culations for visually comparing Canada's population in 1950, 1970, and 1990.

Proportional circles may also be divided (see "Divided Circles"), and they may be located on a map if they refer to data from point or area sources. On a map, proportional circles have the advantage of being easily centred over a point or within an area. If the points on a map are close together, it is quite possible that a number of proportional circles will overlap, which may diminish the opportunity to show divisions inside them. Individual judgment needs to be exercised in each case, either in choice of usable scale if point data are used, or in location within an area if area data are used.

QUESTIONNAIRES

The purpose of a questionnaire is to obtain a variety of opinions about a particular issue. The results should be tabulated so that it is possible to state what percentage of people surveyed responded in a certain way and what percentage responded in a different way, and so on. To obtain this objective, the questions should be set up to allow for responses that are definite and clear. Allowing respondents a choice of "Yes" or "No" provides definite answers, but greater shades of opinion may be obtained by using a four- or five-point scale with response categories such as Strongly Agree, Mildly Agree, Mildly Disagree, and Strongly Disagree. The advantage of a four-point scale is that it forces people to a decide on one side or the other; the advantage of a five-point scale is that people can select No Opinion (or Don't Know) in the centre of the scale if they wish.

In order to produce worthwhile results, a questionnaire should be administered to at least 50 people; there is no maximum number. Generally, the validity of the results goes up with the number of people asked. Commercial polls usually ask at least a thousand people, and qualify their results by stating the margin of error they are allowing for. Typically, the results for these types of polls are true nineteen times out of twenty based on statistical analysis.

If possible, the questionnaire should be administered to the respondents over the same time period. It should also target a representative sample of different types of people within the group being questioned. For example, where possible, the sample should include equal numbers of males and females, appropriate proportions of older and younger people, members of different ethnic groups, and so on.

RATES OF CHANGE (AVERAGE ANNUAL PERCENTAGES)

Given statistical information on the status of an item for two different years, it is possible to calculate the average annual percentage rate of change between the years in two ways. One way involves the use of logarithms;

the other the use of roots. It should be noted that dividing the total percentage increase by the total number of years will produce a wrong answer, because it ignores the fact that growth rates work on a compound interest basis. The statistical information chosen to demonstrate the calculation of the average annual percentage rate of change is world wheat production. In 1962 it was 258 950 t, and in 1990 it was 595 149 t.

(a) Using logarithms

The formula is r = 100 (R − 1), where

> r = average annual percentage rate of change
> R = antilog of (log A − log O)/n
> A = data at end of series (595 149 in the example)
> O = data at start of series (258 950 in the example)
> n = number of years in series (28 in the example: 1962 to 1990 = 28)

The first step is to calculate the value of R, thus:

> R = antilog of log R;
> log R = (log A − log O)/n;
>> = (5.7746 − 5.4132)/28;
>> = (0.3614)/28;
>> = 0.0129.
> R = antilog of log R, i.e., antilog of 0.0129;
>> = 1.0301.
> r = 100 (R − 1);
>> = 100 (1.0301 − 1);
>> = 100 (0.0301);
>> = 3.01%/year.

(b) Using roots

The formula is $r = 100 [(\sqrt[n]{A/O}) - 1]$

Application of the appropriate data yields:

> $r = 100 [(\sqrt[28]{595\ 149/258\ 950}) - 1]$;
>> $= 100 [(\sqrt[28]{2.2983}) - 1]$;
>> = 100 [(1.0301) − 1];
>> = 100 [0.0301];
>> = 3.01%/y.

From 1962 to 1990, therefore, world wheat production increased at an average annual rate of 3.01%/year.

In order to *calculate the number of years* required for a quantity to grow from one value to another, given an average annual rate of growth, the above formulas must be changed. For example, using logs, the formula for the number of years is:

$$n = (\log A - \log O)/\log R,$$

where n is the number of years,

log A is the log of the value at the end of the period,

log O is the log of the value at the start of the period,

log R represents the annual percentage rate of growth, log R being the log of R, which is 1 + (r/100), where r is the average annual rate of growth.

For example, to find the number of years needed for a population to increase from 20 000 000 to 30 000 000 at an average growth rate of 2%/y, apply the formula as follows:

log A (log of 30 000 000) = 7.4771

log O (log of 20 000 000) = 7.3010

R = 1 + (2/100) = 1.0200

log R (log of 1.0200) = 0.0086

Therefore, n = (7.4771 − 7.3010)/0.0086

= 0.1761/0.0086

= 20.48 years

RELATIVE PERCENTAGES

Percentages normally display the relative importance of different items within a single entity; e.g., 51 percent of Canada's population is female. Relative percentages are used to compare the relative importance of different entities with regard to a single item. For example, the world's major producers of bauxite, the raw material for aluminum, are:

Country	000 t
Australia	40 697
Guinea	16 500
Jamaica	10 921
Brazil	8 750
India	5 000

The technique of relative percentages assigns a value of 100 to production from the largest producer. Production from the other producers is then calculated as a percentage of this. For example, Guinea produces 40.54 percent as much bauxite as Australia, so that if Australia is assigned a value of 100 as the largest producer the relative percentages are Australia = 100; Guinea = 40.54 (16 500 × 100/40 697); and so on as shown below.

Australia	100.00
Guinea	40.54
Jamaica	26.83
Brazil	21.50
India	12.29

Relative percentages thus show in simple fashion how the producers stand in relation to one another. The technique is particularly useful when several items are involved and an overall ranking of countries is required. This is because the conversion of raw data to percentages eliminates difficulties caused by greatly differing quantities in the different sets of raw data.

RESEARCH PAPERS

Research papers are more formal than essays. They are longer (approximately 10 000 words) and they often include supporting documents such as photographs, maps, diagrams, graphs, tables, and newspaper or magazine clippings. They also require footnotes and a bibliography. The following procedure is usually used to write a research paper.

1. The inquiry approach (see Inquiry Organizing) may be used to develop a hypothesis and to research any necessary information. It is useful to summarize appropriate information on file cards. The cards may then be placed in an order that matches the overall order of points in the paper. It is quite possible when doing the research that additional points will emerge. These may be placed into the planned order, or the order may be amended as necessary.

2. The first draft of the paper, which consists of the introduction, body, and conclusion, may now be written. The introduction states the overall purpose of the paper and headlines the main points that will be analyzed in detail in the body of the paper. No more than approximately five percent of the length of the paper should be devoted to the introduction. The body of the paper should consist of almost 95 percent of its total length and discuss the main points arrived at in the research stage. In order to maintain a reasonable length, thoughts should be organized before they are committed to paper. The conclusion should consist of only a few lines to summarize the balance between justifying and opposing points.

3. This draft should be edited to ensure that it makes sense as a whole, and that the points are dealt with in a reasoned and clear way. It helps to read the draft aloud to ensure that the flow of the paper is smooth.

4. Write the final version of the paper. The final version should be typed or word processed.

SCALES

Scales may be arithmetic or logarithmic (see Log Scales). Arithmetic scales have equal divisions representing equal quantities. For example, if one centimetre (1 cm) represents 50 tonnes (50 t) of product, it does so everywhere along the scale. If time forms one of the axes of a graph, it will always have an arithmetic scale on the horizontal (or x) axis.

SCATTERGRAPHS

Scattergraphs (see Fig. A3-13) are used for displaying the extent and nature of the relationship between two data sets from the same time period, for example, between labour participation rates and average family incomes for a particular year. If the plotted data form a coherent linear pattern, there is a strong relationship between the data sets; if the pattern is diffuse, there is little or no relationship. Likewise, if the pattern generally slopes upward to the right, the relationship is positive, i.e., as one set of data increases, so does the other, and if the pattern generally slopes downward to the right, the relationship is negative, i.e., as one data set increases, the other decreases.

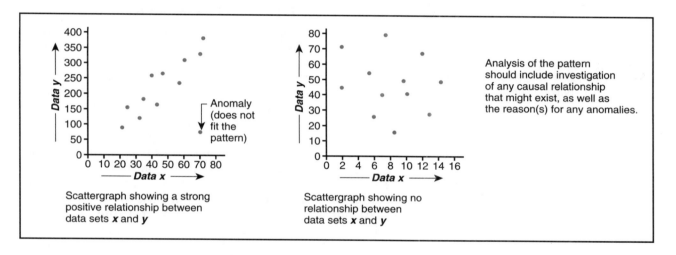

Scattergraph showing a strong positive relationship between data sets *x* and *y*

Scattergraph showing no relationship between data sets *x* and *y*

Analysis of the pattern should include investigation of any causal relationship that might exist, as well as the reason(s) for any anomalies.

Fig. A3-13   *Scattergraphs*

SEMI-LOG GRAPHS

Semi-log graphs are made by combining an arithmetic scale (see Scales) along the horizontal, or x, axis, and a log scale (see Log Scales) along the vertical, or y, axis. Semi-log graphs are usually used to show the rate of change in a data set over a period of time (e.g., population growth).

SKETCH MAPS

Sketch maps are always drawn freehand. They are drawn to show only the information that is relevant to the purpose of the map. The purpose is usually very specific, such as to show the influence of topography on trade routes. All information irrelevant to this purpose is omitted. Detail is generalized, so that, for example, a mountainous area is shown only by an approximation of its general shape. If a specific detail is relevant it is shown alone. For example, a sketch map intended to show trade routes would include a

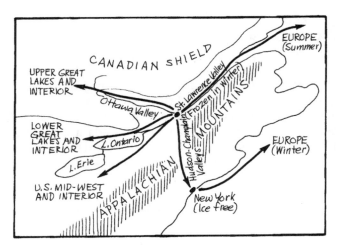

 Fig. A3-14 *Sketch map to show how topography influenced the development of Montreal as a transportation centre.*

valley that acts to channel routeways through the mountains, but would not show other, adjacent valleys.

There are many different types of sketch maps, and many different levels of detail, depending upon what is relevant. Fig. A3-14 is an example of a sketch map designed to show the influence of topography upon the development of Montreal as a transportation centre.

TRIANGULAR GRAPHS

Triangular graphs are used for showing patterns in data whenever three components of a whole are given in percentage terms. For example, the employment categories for Argentina in 1990 were: primary (13.1%); secondary (33.8%); and tertiary (53.1%). These figures may be plotted on a triangular graph in the manner shown in Fig. A3-15.

The location of plotted data on the triangular graph is important. A position close to the centre of the triangle indicates that all three components are more or less equal, whereas a position near one of the sides means that one of the components makes up only a small portion of the whole in relation to the other two components. A position close to two of the sides (i.e., near a corner) indicates that two components constitute a small part of the whole, while the remaining component makes up a larger part.

Triangular graphs are used chiefly for plotting data for several countries. The resulting groupings or clusters are then analyzed; deviations must also be accounted for.

VARIATION

There is usually a variety of values in any data set. For example, if the data set consists of the times students arrive at school, it will most likely contain a variety of different values. The differences among the values may be large or small, and it is the purpose of an index of variability to provide a measure of the extent of these differences. There are three main ways of obtaining an index of variability.

A) RANGE

The range is the simplest measure of the amount of variation within a data set. It is the difference between the highest and lowest values. For example, the highest birth rate shown in column 4 of Appendix 2 is 54 for Mali; the lowest is 10 for Italy. The range is therefore 44. Use of the range is generally limited to comparisons between data sets of roughly similar magnitude and type (e.g., annual temperature ranges).

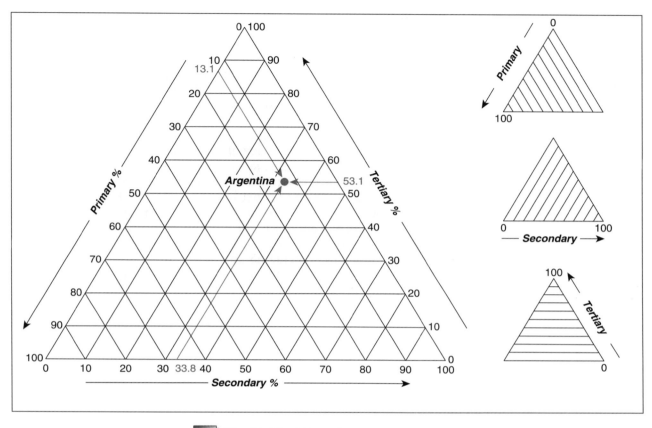

Fig. A3-15   *Triangular graphs*

B) INTER-QUARTILE RANGE

There may sometimes be extreme values in a data set which limit the usefulness of the range as a meaningful index of variability. In order to avoid false impressions created by extreme values, the inter-quartile range may be used instead. The values in a data set are first arrayed (arranged in ascending or descending order), and then divided by quantity into four equal portions. The four portions of a 20-item data set could consist of five items each: 3-8-15-22-26, 34-35-38-47-49, 50-53-56-57-59, and 61-64-72-83-91.

The dividing value between the two lower-value groups is called the lower quartile. It lies midway between 26 and 34, and thus has a value of 30. The dividing value between the two groups of higher values is called the upper quartile; it is 60. The inter-quartile range is, therefore, the difference between the values of the upper and lower quartiles, i.e., 30 (60 – 30 = 30). The mid-point of the entire array is called the median (see Averages); it lies midway between the two central values (if there is an even number of values), and in this case is 49.5. If there is an odd number of values, the median is the single central value of the array.

c) COEFFICIENT OF VARIATION

Both range and inter-quartile range have the disadvantage of being in the same units as the items in the data set, thereby making comparisons between the variability of different types or magnitudes of data difficult. This difficulty may be eliminated by calculating the coefficient of variation, which is a way of obtaining a measure of variability according to a common standard. Comparisons between different types or magnitudes of data are thus facilitated. Calculation of the coefficient of variation requires, first, that the standard deviation of the data set be obtained (see Coefficient of Correlation), and second, that the standard deviation be expressed as percentage of the mean of the data set (see Averages). For each data set in Fig. A3-2, obtain the coefficient of variation (V) by calculating the standard deviation as a percentage of the mean. The larger the coefficient of variation, the greater is the amount of internal variation within the data set. The two data sets shown may be seen to have broadly similar coefficients of variation (42.65 and 38.58), despite differences in the magnitude of the original data.

GLOSSARY

anthropocentrism   The belief that humanity matters most among all life forms. Someone with an anthropocentric view of the world looks at natural events solely in terms of their importance to humanity.

❋antinatalist   Views opposed to unrestricted births.

❋baby boom   The large rise in birth rate experienced by several countries during the 1940s and 1950s, especially in Europe and North America.

biodiversity   The number of different species of plant and animal life within any given area. It may also refer to the number of different genetic types within a given area.

biomass   The total weight of all organisms that inhabit a particular ecosystem. The earth's biomass is the total weight of all living matter on earth.

biosphere   The zone of life at and near the surface of the earth.

❋birth rate   The yearly number of live births per thousand of mid-year population. It is sometimes called the crude birth rate, because it is actual data with no allowance for the proportion of women of child-bearing age in the total population.

bonded labour   Workers who are tied to their employers through a debt which must be repaid before independence is gained. Frequently, such debts, with compound interest, cannot be repaid during the lifetime of the bonded workers. Families may thus inherit unpayable debts, and live in permanent bondage.

boycotts   Concerted action by many consumers to refrain from purchasing the goods or services of a producer whose policies and practices they wish to change.

❋capitalism   A political and economic system of production characterized by mainly private ownership of the means of production, either directly or through shareholding.

carrying capacity   The maximum number of an organism that can be supported by its natural environment, or the maximum biomass that can be supported in an ecosystem. The term is also used to indicate the maximum number of people who can use a natural or artificial resource (for example, a park) without causing degradation of the resource.

❋cash cropping   The growing of crops for sale, rather than just for feeding the growers. See also: subsistence agriculture.

❋central planning   A system of production in which all decisions are made by the central government, and handed down to local producers to implement. See also: command economy.

❋child mortality   The death of children under five years of age. The child mortality rate is the yearly number of deaths of children under five years of age per thousand of mid-year population.

climax   The ecological term for the final stage in the development of an ecosystem. A climax community is in long-term equilibrium.

❋cold war   The non-fighting struggle for world influence between the Communist bloc led by the former Soviet Union and the Western bloc led by the United States that lasted from 1945 to the collapse of the Soviet Union in 1990-91.

❋colonialism   Domination by one nation of another through control of the colony's political systems.

❋command economy   An economy in which all production decisions are made by a nation's

central authority. Producers are told what, and how much, to produce. See also: central planning.

✳**communism** A political and economic system of production characterized by mainly state ownership of the means of production.

✳**correlation** The extent to which two items are associated with each other. For example, values of one may rise as values of the other rise; or they may do the opposite; or they may be totally unrelated. High correlation does not mean that changes in one value cause changes in the other value.

✳**death rate** The yearly number of deaths per thousand of mid-year population. It is sometimes called the crude death rate, because it is actual data with no allowance for the proportion of older people in the total population. It is also sometimes called the mortality rate.

✳**debt** The sum of all previous deficits.

decomposers Small organisms that feed on dead and decaying organic matter, thereby breaking it down into smaller portions.

✳**deficit** The annual shortfall of a government's revenues from taxation compared with its expenditures. Deficits are financed by government borrowing through the sale of bonds. Payment of interest on the bonds and repayment of the bonds themselves form part of government expenditures.

✳**developed countries (developed world)** Countries that are generally characterized by relatively high average personal incomes, high average educational attainments, high average health standards, and high levels of industrialization.

✳**developing countries (developing world)** Countries that are generally characterized by relatively low average personal incomes, low average educational attainments, low average health standards, and low levels of industrialization.

diffusion The spreading out through time from one area to many other areas of such things as ideas, knowledge, cultural characteristics, and species of plants and animals.

✳**disparity** An inequality. A difference between two items that can be measured, and where one may be regarded as better than the other. Differences in life expectancy are thus disparities, whereas differences in language and religion are not.

ecological succession A sequence of plant and animal associations marking the stages of growth of an ecosystem from origins to climax.

ecology The study of the interrelationship of all life forms with their environments. The word is sometimes used to stand for the interrelationships themselves rather than just the study of the interrelationships.

✳**economy** The economy of an area is its system of production, distribution, and consumption of goods and services.

ecosystem The interaction among plants, animals, and physical environment in a given area. An ecosystem may be a very small area, or a large one such as the whole earth.

equilibrium A state of balance or stability. The term is applied widely. A pile of sand that does not collapse may be in equilibrium; so might prices that do not rise or fall significantly. Dynamic equilibrium is most common. It represents constant adjustments among different factors to maintain general stability.

✳**ethnic** Related to the ancestry, attitudes, customs, and cultural characteristics of people who regard themselves as a distinct group because of these characteristics.

ethnic group A group of people who share common ancestry, attitudes, customs, and cultural characteristics, and who perceive themselves as a distinct group.

✳**ethnocentricity** The quality of regarding one's own ethnic group as superior to others, and of judging the activities of members of other ethnic groups by the standards of one's own ethnic group.

European Community   A growing group of countries in Europe pursuing the idea of a Europe without frontiers. Member countries include Belgium, Netherlands, Luxembourg, France, Germany, Italy , Denmark, Ireland, the United Kingdom, Greece, Portugal, and Spain. By 1993, applications to join had been made by Turkey (1987), Austria (1989), Cyprus and Malta (1990), Sweden (1991), and Norway (1992), but they were still waiting for acceptance. Its name was changed to European Union at the end of 1993.

fertility   The demonstrated ability of a woman to bear children. The fertility rate is the yearly number of live births per thousand women of child-bearing age in the total population.

foreign exchange controls   Because there is no single world currency, countries need foreign money — called foreign exchange — to pay for goods and services from other countries. Normally, access to foreign exchange is uncontrolled: banks will sell what is needed. However, if a country is spending too much of its own money to buy foreign exchange, the government may limit the spending by imposing controls. For example, citizens may only be allowed to spend a certain amount on foreign travel.

fossil fuels   Fuels such as coal, petroleum, and natural gas, which are derived from the remains of once-living organisms.

free enterprise   Often called private enterprise. An economic system characterized by the right of individuals freely (or privately) to make their own production decisions, such as what to work at, what to make, how much to produce, and so on. Profits are the reward for success; bankruptcy, the penalty for failure.

freedom   The human rights group Freedom House defines freedom according to 26 criteria, divided into (a) political rights such as the ability to vote and compete for public office and to be free of military or foreign control, and (b) civil liberties such as freedom of public assembly, free media, and an impartial legal system.

GDP   see Gross Domestic Product

genocide   The killing of people because they belong to a particular ethnic or other kind of group.

geopolitics   The study of the relationships which exist between a nation, the area it occupies, and the rest of the world. The relationships include territorial extent, frontiers, economy, and political influence.

giga   The metric prefix for an amount one billion (10^9) times larger than the base unit. Its symbol is G.

GNP   See Gross National Product.

Green Revolution   The large increase in wheat and rice yields that has occurred in many tropical lands since the 1960s.

greenhouse gases   Gases released into, or occurring naturally in, the atmosphere that hinder the passage to space of the earth's radiation. Radiation from the earth returns unused solar energy back to space. Its outward passage may be blocked by greenhouse gases causing the atmosphere to retain some heat and to produce what is called the greenhouse effect.

gross domestic product (GDP)   The total market value of all finished goods and services produced by anyone resident in the nation, citizen or not, and sold within the nation during a year. Only finished goods and services are recorded because they include the prices of all components.

gross national product (GNP)   The total market value of all finished goods and services produced by the citizens of a country, operating at home or in another country, and sold anywhere in the world during a year. Only finished goods and services are recorded because the prices of all components are included.

group cultures   The beliefs, symbols, values, and behaviours of groups. Group cultures vary according to the purpose and nature of the groups.

human development index (HDI)   An international index of human development produced annually by the United Nations Development Program (UNDP) since 1990. It ranks countries according to a combination of life expectancy, educational attainment, and average income. The UNDP also produces separate HDIs to account for regional and gender variations within countries.

hybrid A plant or animal produced artificially by crossbreeding between two genetically dissimilar parents. Hybrids may be sterile, and unable to breed.

infant mortality rate The yearly number of deaths of children under one year of age per 1000 live births.

inflation A condition of rising prices, associated with the availability of increasing amounts of money in relation to the quantity of goods and services available.

infrastructure The network of systems that support the operation of an organization. For a country, these systems include — among others — transportation, communications, energy, water, banking, health, and education.

input Anything used to produce goods or services. Examples of inputs include raw materials, energy, human and animal labour, machinery, organizational skills, knowledge, and risk-taking.

kilo The metric prefix for an amount one thousand (10^3) times larger than the base unit. Its symbol is k.

kW.h a kilowatt-hour. A measure of the amount of electricity produced over a period of time. The production of one kilowatt (1kW) over one hour yields a total production of 1 kW.h.

land use controls Various government measures to control how land is used. They include banning commercial buildings in residential areas, preventing residential or commercial development of farmland, and preserving certain areas as parks or wildlife reserves.

life expectancy The average number of years a person is expected to live. Usually this is from birth, but it can be from any age.

literacy The ability to read and write. Basic literacy is the ability to read and write at least one's own name. Functional literacy is the ability to read and write well enough to function satisfactorily in the local job market. Criteria for functional literacy vary as jobs vary, but generally rise as jobs become more technologically oriented. The literacy rate is generally the percentage of the population, excluding young children, who have basic literacy.

macroeconomic A term used to describe large sectors of the economy, such as overall employment or national income.

Maoist Supporting the beliefs in the importance of a rural-based form of communism held by former Chinese leader Mao Zedong.

marginal lands Lands that are on the edge of use, regardless of geographical location. If demand for land exceeds existing supply, people will start to use marginal lands. If demand subsequently lessens, people will abandon these lands. Land may be marginal for a variety of reasons: it may be infertile, waterlogged, hilly, remote, or damaged.

market economy A system of production and consumption where decisions are largely governed by the reaction of prices to changing supply and demand conditions. For example, if shortages develop, prices tend to rise. Higher prices then tend to lessen demand and at the same time — by increasing profit margins — encourage producers to produce more, thus offsetting the shortages.

marketing boards Boards established by law to control the production, distribution, and price of certain goods and services, chiefly food products. Examples include The Canadian Egg Marketing Agency and a variety of provincial boards for milk.

mega The metric prefix for an amount one million (10^6) times larger than the base unit. Its symbol is M.

megawatt One thousand kilowatts, or one million watts, usually abbreviated to MW. It is a measure of the capacity to produce electricity.

metric prefixes World geography is concerned more with large quantities than small quantities. There are six metric prefixes that denote grades of largeness:

Metric prefix	Symbol	Scientific notation	Written form	Spoken form
Exa	E	10^{18}	1 000 000 000 000 000 000	Quintillion
Peta	P	10^{15}	1 000 000 000 000 000	Quadrillion
Tera	T	10^{12}	1 000 000 000 000	Trillion
Giga	G	10^{9}	1 000 000 000	Billion
Mega	M	10^{6}	1 000 000	Million
Kilo	k	10^{3}	1 000	Thousand

Note that symbols for values of one million and over are capital letters; all symbols for smaller values are lowercase letters.

microeconomic A term used to describe the economic behaviour of individuals or small groups, often in reference to the prices of single items.

monsoon rains Summer and fall rains brought to several tropical areas by winds blowing in from the oceans. Winters and springs in monsoon areas are generally dry because the winds reverse and blow from off the land out to sea. The heaviest monsoon rains are normally experienced throughout southeast Asia.

mortality rate See death rate.

multinational companies Very large business firms that have subsidiaries, branches, offices, and factories in several different countries. They are sometimes called transnational companies.

NAFTA North American Free Trade Agreement, signed in 1992 by representatives of Canada, Mexico, and the United States, and designed to take effect in 1994. It contains provisions for other countries to join. In late 1993 it was ratified despite some opposition within Canada and United States.

national debt The debt accumulated by a national government through borrowing from its own citizens or from other countries. The portion owed to other countries is called foreign debt.

nationalist A person who places high priority on the perceived interests of his or her own nation.

natural increase The annual difference between the number of births and the number of deaths in a country. The natural increase rate is the natural increase per thousand of mid-year population.

neocolonialism A modern form of colonialism. Control of one nation by another nation occurs through its economic systems rather than its political systems.

net reproduction rate (NRR) The average number of daughters born to a mother during her reproductive years, allowing for such factors as infertility and female mortality before and during the reproductive period. If the NRR is one, population size will be stable.

point sources Sources of various phenomena that are located at particular points, such as volcanoes and zinc smelters, rather than occurring over wide areas.

primary economic activity Any economic activity such as fishing or mining that relies directly upon the natural resources of the environment.

pronatalist Views in support of unrestricted births.

purchasing power parity (PPP) An international comparison of currency values according to the amounts needed to purchase a standard assortment of goods and services. If a standard assortment can be purchased in Canada for C$15, and in the United States for US$12, the purchasing power parity of the two currencies is achieved when C$1.25 = US$1.00 (or C$1.00 = US$0.80).

quality of life The degree of well-being felt by a person or a group of persons. It is a broader measure than standard of living, because it includes environmental and sociopolitical factors (such as access to clean water and political freedom) as well as consumption of goods and services. It is difficult to measure precisely because it includes several relatively intangible factors. There is also a psychological aspect to quality of life, because it represents how people *feel* about their lives.

quaternary economic activity See tertiary economic activity.

race A term sometimes used to classify humanity according to differences in skin colour, hair type, head shape, and facial features. It is a biological concept of limited value since all members of humanity form a single species — *Homo sapiens* — often called the human race. It is also in diminishing use as the world's people migrate and intermingle.

racism The attribution of behaviour characteristics to a person or group of persons according to the skin colour, hair type, head shape, and facial features of that person or group of persons.

real terms The value of goods and services, ignoring the effects of inflation. Over a period of time, real terms may be calculated by reducing money values at the end of the period by the inflation rate during the period. Thus a good that sells for $100 at the start of a period and $103 at the end, with an inflation rate of five percent during the period, has a cost of $98 in real terms at the end of the period.

richter scale The scale used for measuring the magnitude of earthquakes. The scale runs upward from one, and has so far not exceeded nine. The scale is logarithmic, so that an addition of one on the scale means a tenfold increase in magnitude. A value of seven represents a major earthquake.

rubles The currency of Russia, usually not abbreviated. In late 1993, US$1 = about 1200 rubles.

rupees The currency of India, usually abbreviated to Rs. In late 1993, US$1 = about Rs 30.

sanctions Official measures taken by governments in attempts to force other nations to abide by international law. Sanctions usually include placing peaceful barriers to trade and investment, but may also include more forceful measures such as boarding and searching ships.

secondary economic activity Any economic activity such as manufacturing or construction that processes natural resources into another form.

secular states Nations that operate without any religious control.

secularism A belief in the importance of worldly matters rather than spiritual or religious matters.

siltation The deposition of fine-grained soil particles which have been carried by running water from an eroded area to another area. Deposits occur when the carrying water slows, as when floods subside or a river enters a lake or harbour.

sovereignty The ability of a nation to act independently of all other nations and all international treaty constraints.

standard of living The quantity of goods and services consumed by a person or — on average — by a group of persons. Because goods and services vary greatly in type and price from one nation to another, assessment of standard of living is usually made in relation to average incomes, which may be measured on the basis of either GNP per person or GDP per person.

state control A political and economic system characterized by state direction of activities. Individual rights tend to be secondary to state needs.

subsidies Cash or other incentives provided to a producer by one or more levels of government to attract the producer to a new area or maintain the producer in an established area.

subsistence agriculture (subsistence farming) A type of farming where all produce is used to feed the household or village, and where none is intended for trade. See also: cash cropping.

tectonic plates The relatively solid parts of the earth's crust that are moved very slowly about the surface by currents in the molten rock below the surface. They form the basis of all continents, and their movements are sometimes called *continental drift*.

tertiary economic activity Any economic activity such as banking, transportation, education, entertainment, and management that assists the smooth operation of the primary and secondary sectors of an economy and helps to improve the quality of life. Some observers classify the tertiary activities dealing with information as quaternary economic activity.

Third World The name taken by a group of developing nations after the Bandung Conference in Indonesia in 1955. The name was chosen to reflect the wish of these developing nations to be accepted as a third force in the world, alongside the first world led by the United States and the second world led by the former U.S.S.R.

trade barriers Devices legislated by governments which have the effect of hindering trade, usually international trade. The most common form of trade barrier is tariffs, also called customs duties, in which a government charges a levy on imported goods. Another common trade hindrance is what are called non-tariff barriers, such as quotas, packaging regulations, odd size requirements, language restrictions, and so on.

transnational companies See multinational companies.

trickle-down A concept of economic growth and income distribution that states that economic gains go first to the socially and economically powerful people or groups within a society, with later gains going to the less powerful in a gradual progression.

urbanization The process whereby a population becomes more urban and less rural, largely through the migration of people into the cities from the countryside.

value-added A term used in production to mean the money value that is added to materials by the human knowledge, labour, and organization applied to them. It is the difference between the total price paid for all material inputs needed to make something and the money earned from selling that product.

World Bank A group of three institutions headquartered in Washington, D.C. The institutions are the International Bank for Reconstruction and Development (established in 1945), the International Finance Corporation (1956), and the International Development Association (1960). Their combined purpose is to channel funding for development assistance to the developing countries.

xenophobia Hatred of foreigners.

zoning Zoning is the practice of setting aside an area of land for a particular use or group of uses.

INDEX

CREDITS

Credit lines appear throughout the text with reproduced material. The following are specific credit lines requested by copyright holders in addition to the regular citation of the author, title, publication, and year.

ADDITIONAL TEXT CREDITS

p. 3   Lester R. Brown, et al, *State of the World 1991.* "Denial in the Decisive Decade," by Sandra Postel, Worldwatch Institute, Washington, D.C.

p. 3   "Population and Human Resources." By permission of Oxford University Press.

p. 3   Excerpted from "The West Grows Old" by Richard Evans from the April 1989 issue of *Geographical.*

p. 5   "Population: Food." Population Concern, 231 Tottenham Court Road, London W1P 9AE, England, U.K.

p. 7   "Fairer Trade." *World Watch* magazine, Jul./Aug. 1992, by Vicki Elkin, Worldwatch Institute, Washington, D.C.

p. 16   "Egypt is Thirsty." Copyright © 1988, *Der Spiegel.* Distributed by The New York Times Syndication Sales Corp.

p. 17   Excerpted from "India be Damned" by Brian Jackman from the June 1989 issue of *Geographical.*

p. 47   "Fewer Children — Fewer Burdens?" Reprinted with permission – The Toronto Star Syndicate.

p. 48   "World Population: Progress in Slowing the Increase in People on the Earth is Critical to Finding Solutions for Global Problems in the 21st Century." Reprinted by permission from *The Christian Science Monitor* © 1992 The Christian Science Publishing Society. All rights reserved.

p. 49   "Sex, Lies and Global Survival." *New Internationalist*, Sept. 92 ©.

p. 50   "Pope Decries Fall in Births." Reprinted with the permission of United Press International, Inc.

p. 51   "A Dangerous Game: The Impact of Population Growth and Increasing Carbon Combustion on the Atmosphere." Published in ECODECISION, the Environment and Policy Magazine, Edition No. 4, March 1992. 276 St-James Street, Montreal, Qc . H2Y 1N3 Canada

p. 53   "Japan Tries to Raise Birthrate. Government Targets Career Women Who Are Single, in Their 30s." Reprinted by permission from *The Christian Science Monitor* © 1992 The Christian Science Publishing Society. All rights reserved.

p. 53   "Declining Birth Rate Borne by Russias." Reprinted by permission of *Wall Street Journal* © 1992 Dow Jones & Company, Inc. All rights reserved worldwide.

p. 54   Excerpted from "Baby Power" by Charles Tyler in the Jan. 1992 issue of *Geographical.*

p. 56   "The Need for an Effective Population Policy." By permission of Oxford University Press.

p. 77   "The Price of Amazonian Gold." Reprinted with permission of the Helen Swight Reid Educational Foundation. Published by Heldref Publications, 1319 18th Street, NW, Washington, D.C. 20036-1802. Copyright 1990.

p. 79   "Women and Nature, An Alliance for Survival." Reprinted from the UNESCO Courier, March 1992.

p. 80   "Rich vs. Poor." Copyright 1992 Time Inc. Reprinted by permission.

p. 88   "Environmentalism Runs Riot." © 1992 The Economist Newspaper Group, Inc. Reprinted with permission.

p. 89   "Working with the Waste Pickers." Reprinted courtesy of *Alternatives*, Canada's environmental quarterly since 1971. Annual subscriptions $27.50 from *Alternatives*, Faculty of Environmental Studies, University of Waterloo, Ontario, Canada, N2L 3G1. The author thanks Anselm Rosario of Waste Wise for assistance with the research in Bangalore.

p. 91   "Father Sun and Mother Earth." From *Ojibway Heritage* by Basil Johnston. Used by Permission of the Canadian Publishers, McClelland & Stewart, Toronto.

p. 93   "Greenpeace Sets Sights on Fossil Fuels." Reprinted by permission of Reuters.

p. 94   "Power, Authority, and Mystery: Ecofemisim and Earth-Based Spirituality." Copyright © 1990 by Diamond & Orenstein. Reprinted with permission of Sierra Club Books.

p. 155 Excerpted from "A Geography of Well-Being" by Michael Witherick, published in the Nov. 1989 issue of *Geographical.*

p. 155 "Story by Gilbert Oskaboose, Serpent River First Nation." Copyright *Earthkeeper* Magazine, 1992.

p. 156 Margaret Brzozowicz, excerpt from "Drawing Poor and Illiterate Women into the Market Economy", *UNICEF Canada Fact Sheet, 1992.*

p. 163 "Mining the Earth." Lester R. Brown, et al, State of the World 1991, *Denial in the Decisive Decade*, by Sandra Postel, Worldwatch Institute, Washington, D.C.

ADDITIONAL VISUAL CREDITS